PENGUIN  C

PENGUIN ENGLI
GENERAL EDITOR: CHI

LORD BYRON
SELECTED POEMS

GEORGE GORDON BYRON was born on 22 January 1788 and he inherited
the barony in 1798. He went to school in Dulwich, and then in 1801 to
Harrow. In 1805 he went up to Trinity College, Cambridge, later gaining
a reputation in London for his startling good looks and extravagant behav-
iour. His first collection of poems, *Hours of Idleness* (1807), was not well
received, but with the publication of the first two cantos of *Childe Harold's
Pilgrimage* (1812) he became famous overnight and increased this fame
with a series of wildly popular 'Eastern Tales'. In 1815 he married the
heiress Annabella Milbanke, but they were separated after a year. Byron
shocked society by the rumoured relationship with his half-sister, Augusta,
and in 1816 he left England for ever. He eventually settled in Italy, where
he lived for some time with Teresa, Contessa Guiccioli. He supported
Italian revolutionary movements and in 1823 he left for Greece to fight
in its struggle for independence, but he contracted a fever and died at
Missolonghi in 1824.

Byron's contemporary popularity was based first on *Childe Harold* and
the 'Tales', and then on *Don Juan* (1819–24), his most sophisticated and
accomplished writing. He was one of the strongest exemplars of the
Romantic movement, and the Byronic hero was a prototype widely
imitated in European and American literature.

SUSAN J. WOLFSON received her PhD at the University of California,
Berkeley, where she met Peter Manning. She taught at Rutgers University
between 1978 and 1991, and is now Professor of English at Princeton
University. A noted interpreter of British Romanticism, she has published
several essays on Byron. She is the author of *The Questioning Presence:
Wordsworth, Keats, and the Interrogative Mode in Romantic Poetry* (1986)
and *Formal Charges: The Shaping of Poetry in English Romanticism* (1996).
Borderlines: The Shiftings of Gender in British Romanticism (with a chapter
on *Don Juan*) will appear in 2006.

PETER J. MANNING graduated from Harvard University and received his PhD from Yale University. He taught at the University of California from 1967 to 1975, at the University of Southern California from 1975 to 2000, and is now Professor and Chair of English at Stony Brook University. A widely recognized authority on Byron, he is the author of *Byron and His Fictions* (1978) and *Reading Romantics* (1990), which includes further essays on Byron. He has numerous other publications on various aspects of English Romanticism. His current project is *The Late Wordsworth*, a culturally situated study of Wordsworth's career.

LORD BYRON
Selected Poems

Edited with an Introduction by SUSAN J. WOLFSON
and PETER J. MANNING

PENGUIN BOOKS

PENGUIN BOOKS

Published by the Penguin Group
Penguin Books Ltd, 80 Strand, London WC2R ORL, England
Penguin Group (USA) Inc., 375 Hudson Street, New York, New York 10014, USA
Penguin Group (Canada), 90 Eglinton Avenue East, Suite 700, Toronto, Ontario, Canada M4P 2Y3
(a division of Pearson Penguin Canada Inc.)
Penguin Ireland, 25 St Stephen's Green, Dublin 2, Ireland
(a division of Penguin Books Ltd)
Penguin Group (Australia), 707 Collins Street,
Melbourne, Victoria 3008, Australia (a division of Pearson Australia Group Pty Ltd)
Penguin Books India Pvt Ltd, 11 Community Centre,
Panchsheel Park, New Delhi – 110 017, India
Penguin Group (NZ), 67 Apollo Drive,
Rosedale, Auckland 0632, New Zealand (a division of Pearson New Zealand Ltd)
Penguin Books (South Africa) (Pty) Ltd, Block D, Rosebank Office Park,
181 Jan Smuts Avenue, Parktown North, Gauteng 2193, South Africa

Penguin Books Ltd, Registered Offices: 80 Strand, London WC2R ORL, England

www.penguin.com

First published 1996
This edition with Introduction and updated Further Reading published 2005

023

Selection, Preface and Notes copyright © Susan J. Wolfson and Peter J. Manning, 1996
Introduction and updated Further Reading copyright © Susan J. Wolfson
and Peter J. Manning, 2005
All rights reserved

The moral right of the editors has been asserted

Set in 10.5/11.5 pt Monotype Ehrhardt
Typeset by RefineCatch Limited, Bungay, Suffolk

Printed and bound in Great Britain by Clays Ltd, Elcograf S.p.A.

ISBN-13: 978-0-140-42450-8

www.greenpenguin.co.uk

CONTENTS

INTRODUCTION

I

As the famous portrait by Thomas Phillips of Byron in Albanian costume makes clear, Byron himself impersonated his most famous poetic creation: the exotic, dashingly handsome, dangerous and seductive Byronic Hero. When visiting Trevesa he had been delighted by the 'very "magnifique" Albanian dresses,' as he wrote his mother, and purchased 'some' for himself: 'the only expensive articles in this country they cost 50 guineas each & have so much gold they would cost in England two hundred'.[1] It is no wonder that he commissioned Phillips to paint him in this theatrical pose, but it was not the only image in circulation: another Phillips portrait, with the open collar that Byron made the vogue, was also exhibited in 1814; a portrait by Richard Westall of the previous year showed the poet in staged profile, his chin resting in his hand; in 1817 in Rome Byron sat for a bust by Bertel Thorwaldsen, who grumbled that 'he began immediately to assume quite another countenance to what was customary to him' and commanded 'you must not make these faces'. The sculptor reported that 'everybody said, when it was finished, that I had hit the likeness', but Byron himself objected: 'It does not resemble me at all; I look more unhappy.'[2] The American William Edward West, who painted Byron in Italy in 1822, noted the same elision of the poet and his protagonist: 'I found him a bad sitter. He talked all the time . . . When he was silent, he was a better sitter than before; for he assumed a countenance that did not belong to him, as though he were thinking of a frontispiece for Childe Harold', as though, that is, he were imitating one of his own portraits.[3]

West understood Byron's self-conscious role-playing, for the portraits were engraved, widely reproduced and disseminated, as frontispieces, in annuals and as images purchasable separately. Alfred Lord Tennyson's Ulysses sighs (half boastfully, half elegiacally) that he is 'become a name';[4] by age twenty-five Byron had entered the public imagination in the language of Byromania (a term coined by his future wife on beholding his adoring female fans), Byronism, and Byronic – this adjective describing not only him and his gallery of heroes, but destined to be applied to their lineage throughout the century, the progenitor of Emily Brontë's Heathcliff and later, a figure in Bertrand Russell's *A History of Western Philosophy* (1945). He was the epitome of mysterious glamour and also a commodity opportunistically manufactured by his publisher, the celebrity machinery of the newspapers, reviews, magazines and caricaturists, and his own eye for the dramatic. The force was felt across Europe, and beyond, generating fresh inspiration not only in literature but also in the other arts: in Théodore Géricault's vivid illustrations of the Eastern tales (a watercolour of *The Giaour* led to a suite of lithographs executed in 1823 with Eugène Lami illustrating *Mazeppa, The Giaour, The Bride of Abydos* and *Lara*), in numerous paintings by Eugène Delacroix (including *The Death of Sardanapalus* (1827)), the apex of French high Romantic painting), in Hector Berlioz's *Harold in Italy* (1834), in which the composer determined to 'make [the solo viola] a kind of melancholy dreamer in the style of Byron's Childe Harold',[5] in Robert Schumann's setting of *Manfred* (1848–9) and in Peter Ilyich Tchaikovsky's symphony *Manfred* (1885). In all these figures Byron awakened, in Delacroix's phrase, 'that insatiable desire to create'.[6]

The magnetism apparent in the visual and verbal representations proceeded from, and rebounded upon, the man. Walter Scott, fellow Scot, fellow literary lion, fellow sufferer from lameness, was transfixed:

A countenance, exquisitely modeled to the expression of feeling and passion, and exhibiting the remarkable contrast of very dark hair and eye-brows, with light and expressive eyes, presented to the physiognomist the most interesting subject for the exercise of his art. The predominating expression was that of deep and habitual thought, which gave way to the most rapid play of features when he engaged in interesting discussion; so that a brother poet compared them to the sculpture of a beautiful alabaster vase, only seen to perfection when lighted up from within ... but those who had an opportunity of studying his features for a length of time, and upon various occasions,

both of rest and emotion, will agree with us that their proper language
was that of melancholy.

Scott was writing anonymously in 1816 for the most widely read
periodical of the day, the *Quarterly Review*, not coincidentally pub-
lished by Byron's publisher, John Murray: the anonymity, ex-
pressed in the inclusive editorial first person, assumed universal
agreement.[7] In a giddy suspension of disbelief, fellow poet Samuel
Taylor Coleridge had rhapsodized to a friend in April of the same
year – the month Byron left England forever amid the scandal
surrounding his separation from his wife (see Part II):

> if you had seen Lord Byron, you could scarcely disbelieve him – so
> beautiful a countenance I scarcely ever saw – his teeth so many
> stationary smiles – his eyes the open portals of the sun – things of
> light, and for light – and his forehead so ample, and yet so flexible,
> passing from marble smoothness into a hundred wreathes and lines
> and dimples correspondent to the feelings and sentiments he is
> uttering.[8]

Reading the countenance for its animating sentiments and passions,
Scott and Coleridge were part of a burning Romantic-era romance
with Byron, involving not only brother poets but also women poets,
among them Felicia Hemans and Letitia Landon, enthralled by his
dark and dazzling celebrity. Society belles who couldn't possess the
lord nonetheless felt the theatrics. Margaret Mercer Elphinstone
borrowed Byron's Albanian dress for a masquerade the same year
that he donned the costume for the Phillips portrait,[9] and Byron did
not at all mind the layered transvestite spectacle: a Regency
'Beauty' decked out as an Albanian dandy, and a female imperson-
ation of Phillips's 'Byron'. 'The more the merrier,' he said in the
last year of his life in portraits, anticipating the diverse interpreta-
tions that would multiply and prolong his fascination:

> One will represent me as a sort of sublime misanthrope, with moments
> of kind feeling. This, *par example*, is my favourite *rôle*. Another will
> portray me as a modern Don Juan; and a third ... will, it is to be
> hoped, if only for opposition sake, represent me as an *amiable*, ill-used
> gentleman 'more sinned against than sinning.' Now, if I know myself,

I should say, that I have no character at all . . . I am so changeable, being every thing by turns and nothing long.[10]

If Byron suggests a certain unease at the distance between a mercurial nature and public perception, he is here largely unthreatened by it, understanding the series of portraits as extending the grasp of Byronism.

Others were sharply critical of such Byronic performances. John Scott, the influential editor of the *London Magazine*, objected to the 'confusion' between the 'poetical sympathies' of readers and their 'recollection of some fact of the author's life, or a conviction of an analogy to the author's own character'. He continued:

> The impression left on the mind, is neither strictly that of a work of art, to be pronounced upon according to the rules applicable to art, – nor of a matter-of-fact, appealing to the principles of sound judgment in such cases; – but what is striking in poetry is made a set-off against what is objectionable in morals, – while that which would be condemned as false, theatrical, or inconsistent, according to the laws of poetical criticism, is often rendered the most taking part of the whole composition by its evident connection with real and private circumstances, that are of a nature to tickle the idle, impertinent, and most unpoetical curiosity of the public. This sort of balancing system is not fair.[11]

In underscoring Byron's play at the borders between art and life, Scott identified one of the springs of Byron's hold on his public. John Wilson teased out the paradox that nourished the fascination:

> It might, on a hasty consideration, seem to us, that such undisguised revelation of feelings and passions, which the becoming pride of human nature, jealous of its own dignity, would, in general, desire to hold in unviolated silence, could produce in the public mind only pity, sorrow, or repugnance. But, in the case of men of real genius, like Rousseau or Byron, it is otherwise. Each of us must have been aware in himself of a singular illusion, by which these disclosures, when read with that tender or high interest which attaches to poetry, seem to have something of the nature of private and confidential communications. They are not felt, while we read, as declarations published to

the world, – but almost as secrets whispered to chosen ears. Who is there that feels, for a moment, that the voice which reaches the inmost recesses of his heart is speaking to the careless multitude around him? Or, if we do so remember, the words seem to pass by others like air, and to find their way to the hearts for whom they were intended, – kindred and sympathizing spirits, who discern and own that secret language, of which the privacy is not violated, though spoken in hearing of the uninitiated, – because it is not understood. There is an unobserved beauty that smiles on us alone; and the more beautiful to us, because we feel as if chosen out from a crowd of lovers.[12]

An exotic spectacle and an erotically intimate friend: Byron had the power to enthrall.

II

Byron was born in London on 22 January 1788, the son of Captain John ('Mad Jack') Byron and his second wife, Catherine Gordon, a Scots heiress. The Captain having squandered her fortune, the family withdrew to Aberdeen in 1789, and he soon decamped to the Continent. Byron passed the next ten years in straitened circumstances; sensitive to the club-foot with which he had been born, left with a mother who displaced resentment against her absconded husband on to him, and with a Calvinist nurse whom he later said had early awakened his sexuality. In 1798 the fifth Baron Byron, 'the wicked Lord', died, and Byron unexpectedly inherited his title. Told that he was now the sixth Baron Byron of Rochdale, he asked his mother (according to his friend and memoirist Moore), 'whether she could perceive any difference in him since he had been made a lord, as he perceived none himself'.[13] Yet the difference, the more powerful for remaining elusive, helped to shape the poet.

Byron and his mother returned to England and moved into the debt-ridden Newstead Abbey, near Nottingham, the estate presented to the Byrons by Henry VIII in the sixteenth century. The profound impact made on the lonely boy by the Gothic hall and its embodiment of a tempestuous family heritage can be seen in his first poems. In 1801 Byron was sent to school at Harrow; in the same year he probably met Augusta Byron, his half-sister from his father's first marriage. Byron entered Trinity College, Cambridge, in 1805 and embarked upon dissipations that threatened his health and obligated him to moneylenders, but he also made enduring friends, such as John Cam Hobhouse, later a prominent politician, who strengthened his interest in liberal Whiggism.

Byron's first published volume appeared in 1807. The various genres he imitated – Ossianic and erotic poems, satires, poems of sensibility – show a young writer seeking his public identity, but the diffident title, *Hours of Idleness*, and aristocratic signature, 'Lord Byron, A Minor', elicited a savage notice from Henry Brougham in the *Edinburgh Review*. Byron retaliated in 1809 with a couplet satire, *English Bards and Scotch Reviewers*, excoriating the contemporary literary scene.

On reaching his majority at the age of twenty-one in 1809, Byron took his seat in the House of Lords, and then in July departed with Hobhouse on a Grand Tour of the Continent, shaped by the Napoleonic Wars that barred much of Europe to British travellers. They sailed to Lisbon, crossed Spain and proceeded by Gibraltar and Malta to Greece, venturing inland to Janina and Tepelini in Albania to visit a local overlord, Ali Pasha, through country little known to Westerners but a site in the struggle with the French for control of the eastern Mediterranean. There Byron began *Childe Harold's Pilgrimage*, which he continued in Athens where he lodged with a widow whose daughter, Theresa Macri, he celebrated in 'Maid of Athens'. In March 1810 he sailed with Hobhouse for Constantinople, visited the site of Troy and swam the Hellespont in imitation of Leander. In the East Byron found a world in which the love of an older aristocrat for a beautiful boy was accepted; he also developed a political identity: he was to become the Western hero who would liberate Greece from the Turks.

Byron arrived in London in July 1811; shortly after his return his mother fell gravely ill and died before he could reach her at Newstead. In February 1812 he made his first speech in the House of Lords, denouncing the proposed death penalty for the stocking weavers of Nottingham who had smashed the new machines they blamed for their loss of work. A potential role as opposition speaker was diverted when at the beginning of March John Murray published the first two cantos of *Childe Harold's Pilgrimage* and, in Moore's famous report, Byron 'awoke one morning and found

myself famous'.[14] The poem joined the immediacy of a travelogue
with a disillusioned speaker, who voiced the melancholy of a
generation wearied by prolonged war. Despite Byron's claim that
Harold was a fiction designed merely to connect a picaresque nar-
rative, the novelty of an author speaking passionately in his own
person overwhelmed readers. Even as Byron satirically discredited
the chivalric code on which, in *Reflections on the Revolution in
France* (1790), Edmund Burke had rested the defence of the *ancien
régime* (and which was still invoked to justify the war against
Napoleon), the magnetism of his personality offered a new
romance, offsetting the cynicism the poem displayed: the hand-
some, aristocratic poet, returned from exotic travels, himself
became a figure of force.

Only someone circumstanced as Byron was could have effected
this double operation, and the impact was tremendous. Byron fol-
lowed the success of *Childe Harold* with a series of Eastern tales that
added to his aura: *The Giaour* (1813); *The Bride of Abydos* (1813),
written in four days; *The Corsair* (1814), written in ten, and selling
10,000 copies on the day of publication; *Lara* (1814), written in a
month. *Hebrew Melodies* (1815) contains some of Byron's most
famous lyrics ('She walks in beauty' and 'The Destruction of
Sennacherib') and accorded with the vogue for nationalist themes.
This sensationally successful phase of Byron's career epitomizes the
paradoxical convergence of Murray's exploitation of the resources
of advertising, publishing and distribution to foster best-sellerdom
and star status, with a noble who gave away his copyrights because
aristocrats did not write for money. Like all myths, 'Byron' did not
resolve a contradiction but dramatically embodied it.

This literary celebrity was enhanced by Byron's lionizing in
Whig society. He was swept into a liaison with Lady Caroline
Lamb, whose summary of him as 'mad – bad – and dangerous to
know'[15] captured his notoriety. She was succeeded in his affections
by the 'autumnal' Lady Oxford, but it was his relationship with his
half-sister Augusta, now married to Colonel George Leigh, that
gave rise to most scandal; her daughter Medora, born in 1814 and
given the name of the heroine of *The Corsair*, was widely thought to
be Byron's. Seeking to escape these agitating affairs (obliquely
reflected in the Eastern tales), and to repair his debts, Byron pro-
posed (a second time) in September 1814 to the heiress Anne

Isabella ('Annabella') Milbanke, who had laid particular stress on 'the Irreligious nature of his principles' in declining his first proposal in 1812.[16] After a dilatory courting, the marriage took place in January 1815; their daughter, Augusta Ada, was born on 10 December 1815. In January 1816 Annabella unexpectedly left Byron to live with her parents, and, amid rumours charging Byron with insanity, incest and sodomy, the darker for never being explicitly articulated, she obtained a legal separation in April. Pirated editions of Byron's poems on the separation, such as 'Fare thee well!' (1816), made marital discord into public scandal. Byron's resourceful and desperate attempt to influence opinion in his favour brought forth counter-blows, pamphlets, and other defences of Lady Byron. The battle to write the public narrative intensified, though it also darkened, the poet's celebrity.

In April 1816 Byron quit England, bearing 'the pageant of his bleeding heart', in Matthew Arnold's famous phrase,[17] across Europe. He settled at Geneva, near Percy Bysshe Shelley and Mary Godwin, who had eloped, and William Godwin's step-daughter by a second marriage, Claire Clairmont, with whom Byron had begun an affair in England. Shelley, he reported, 'used to dose me with Wordsworth physic even to nausea';[18] the influence and resistance the phrase shows are evident in the third canto of *Childe Harold* (1816). The canto also memorably invokes Rousseau, Napoleon and Waterloo, the battlefield turned tourist shrine Byron visited on the way to Switzerland. He wrote *The Prisoner of Chillon* at this time, and began *Manfred* (1817), which he subtitled 'A Dramatic Poem', whose protagonist, haunted by remorse for his treatment of his beloved Astarte (the name taken from an incestuous Eastern goddess), turns the exhausted excess of Byron's Titanism to faintly comic extravagance. At the end of the summer the Shelley party left for England, where on 12 January 1817 Claire gave birth to Byron's daughter Allegra.

Byron went to Italy and described his Venetian life in brilliant letters, some of which were meant for circulation in the Murray circle. Margarita Cogni, a baker's wife, succeeded Marianna Segati, his landlord's wife, as his principal mistress, but his sexual life was hardly monogamous, and its prodigious activity was accompanied by substantial literary productivity. Byron studied Armenian, completed *Manfred* and in May joined Hobhouse in Rome, gathering materials for a fourth canto of *Childe Harold*. Published in 1818, this last canto was his longest and most sublime, and its invocation of Freedom's torn banner streaming '*against* the wind' (XCVIII, 2) fixed his revolutionary reputation. Yet Byron began to feel trapped by the poetic modes that had won him popularity; determining to 'repel the charge of monotony & mannerism',[19] he wrote *Beppo*, the tale of a Venetian *ménage á trois*, written in *ottava rima*, an eight-line stanza form derived from Italian comic poets, and published anonymously by Murray in 1818. Turning his self-exile into comic contrast between English and Italian mores, *Beppo* marks a crucial shift in tone, as would *Mazeppa* (1819), which encloses the violence of the Eastern tales in a comic, nearly self-parodic framework.

In the colloquial, digressive ease of *Beppo* Byron was testing the form of his greatest poem, *Don Juan*, at once fictional autobiography, picaresque narrative, literary burlesque and exposure of cant. The first canto, completed summer 1818, uses the name of the legendary libertine for a guileless boy through whose growth and sexual misadventures Byron slyly retells his childhood as 'An only son left with an only mother'[20] and satirizes Annabella in the guise of Juan's hypocritical mother. The first two cantos were published in 1819, in an expensive edition designed to forestall charges of blasphemously corrupting the poor and uneducated, and which bore neither the author's nor the publisher's name. The provenance was easily deduced: *Blackwood's* criticized Byron for 'a filthy and impious' attack on his wife,[21] and the second canto, which turns from the amusements of the first to shipwreck and cannibalism, redoubled charges of nihilism. Shocking the proprieties of one audience, Byron moved towards another; the poem sold well in increasingly cheap editions.

In April 1819 Byron met and fell in love with Countess Teresa Gamba Guiccioli, nineteen years old and married to a man three times her age. Byron followed her to Ravenna, and she later accompanied him to Venice. Byron returned to Ravenna at Christmas 1819 as Teresa's *cavaliere servente* (that is, a publicly acknowledged 'escort'), a role that somewhat chafed. He won the friendship of her father and brother, who initiated him into the clandestine Carbonari, a revolutionary society seeking Italy's independence from Austria. His deepening involvement with Italian patriotism may be seen in such poems as *The Prophecy of Dante* (1821). As he continued with fresh cantos of *Don Juan* Byron was also writing *Marino Faliero*, *Sardanapalus* and *The Two Foscari* (all 1821), dramas that in various historical settings explore the relationship between the powerful individual and the post-revolutionary state. Byron insisted that their neo-classicism unfitted them for stage representation and was angered when an unauthorized version of *Marino Faliero* failed at Drury Lane, but all three would be staged. To the same year belongs *Cain*, a 'mystery' drama at once declared beyond copyright for its unorthodoxy and immediately pirated by radicals, and *The Vision of Judgment*, a devastating rebuttal to poet-laureate Robert Southey's eulogy of the late George III, *A Vision of Judgement*, in the Preface to which the laureate had alluded to Byron as the head of a 'Satanic school' of literature.

When Teresa followed her father and brother into exile for their part in an abortive uprising, Byron reluctantly moved with them to Pisa, where Shelley had rented the Casa Lanfranchi for him. He arrived in November 1821, having left his daughter Allegra in a convent near Ravenna, where she died of typhus on 20 April 1822. In early summer Byron went with the Shelleys to Leghorn, where he had leased a villa near their house on the Bay of Lerici.

Shelley and Byron had jointly planned a radical journal, the *Liberal*, and Byron paid for Shelley's friend Leigh Hunt to join the collaboration. Hunt had dedicated his poem *The Story of Rimini* (1816) to Byron, but he was less famous as a poet than as the editor of the *Examiner* who had been imprisoned in 1812 for libelling the Prince Regent. Hunt and his large family arrived in July, and were installed in Byron's house in Pisa. Despite the drowning of Shelley on 8 July and increasing friction with the Hunts, the periodical went forward. The first number contained *The Vision of Judgment*, the second Byron's unfinished heterodox drama, *Heaven and Earth* (1823), the third his satire, *The Blues* (1823). At the end of September he moved to Genoa, where Teresa's family had found asylum; Mary Shelley leased another house nearby for herself and the Hunts.

Byron had begun *Don Juan* intending 'to be a little quietly facetious upon every thing',[22] but his purposes had deepened. As he narrated Juan's career from Spain to Greece and Turkey through the Siege of Ismail and the Empress Catherine's court to Regency London, he surrounded it with mordant commentary on the

Europe of restored sovereigns at the moment of writing. The darling of fame, who had stamped his name on the Byronic hero, had become a demystifier of glory and a critic of English society. Murray had published Cantos III–V of *Don Juan* in 1821, but, alarmed by Byron's politics and verbal indecencies, hesitated thereafter; undaunted, Byron transferred his works to Leigh Hunt's brother John, publisher of the *Liberal*. The shift from the prestigious Tory to a disreputable radical signaled Byron's break from the literary system that had nurtured him. Reflecting ruefully that he had formerly been reckoned 'the grand Napoleon of the realms of rhyme' (XI, 55; his inheritance, through his wife, of the Noel estates enabled Byron also to sign himself 'NB'), Byron's rupture affirmed his difference and liberated his cultural criticism. John Hunt published all Byron's later work, including *The Age of Bronze* (1823), *The Island* (1823) and Cantos VI–XVI of *Don Juan* (1823–4), which were ignored by the established reviews but avidly read.

Restive in domesticity with Teresa, Byron agreed to act as the agent of the Greek Committee in London, which had been formed to aid the Greeks in their struggle for independence. In July 1823 he left Genoa for Cephalonia. Newstead and Rochdale had been sold; clear of debt and now attentive to his literary income, Byron devoted his forture to the Greek cause. He sent £4,000 to prepare the Greek fleet and then sailed for Missolonghi on 29 December to join Prince Alexander Mavrokordatos.

The venture was no less idealistic than theatrical – Byron landed in scarlet military uniform, to welcoming crowds – and erotically tinged. Byron was accompanied by his page Loukas Chalandritsanos, an unreciprocated last passion and the subject of 'On This Day I Complete My Thirty-Sixth Year', published posthumously in the newspapers and influential in shaping the after-images that he had anticipated to Lady Blessington. Philhellenic idealism was soon confronted by the rivalrous and undisciplined Greek patriots, but Byron founded, paid and trained a brigade of Souliot soldiers. The malarial geography of Missolonghi provoked him to ominous puns: 'if we are not taken off with the sword – we are like to march off with an ague in this mud-basket – and to conclude with a very bad pun – to the ear rather than the eye – better – *mart*ially – than *marsh*-ally'.[23] A convulsion, perhaps epileptic, aggravated by tension and hypertension, in February 1824, followed by the usual remedy of bleeding, weakened him; in April he contracted the fever, treated by further bleeding, from which he died on 19 April. Deeply mourned, he became a Greek national hero, and throughout Europe his name became synonymous with Romanticism. In England the stunned reaction of the young Tennyson, who, on hearing the news, sadly wrote on a rock 'Byron is dead', spoke for many; as Arnold later recalled, in placing Byron with Wordsworth as the great English poets of the century, he had 'subjugated' his readers,[24] and his influence was immense and lasting. His body was taken to England and, denied burial in Westminster Abbey, placed in the ancestral vault near Newstead. The refusal attests the transgressive qualities in Byron, qualities that continue to resist even the canonization implied by the placement of a memorial to him in the Abbey in 1969.

NOTES

1.   *Byron's Letters and Journals*, ed. Leslie A. Marchand, 12 vols. (Cambridge, Mass./London: Harvard University Press/John Murray, 1973–82), Vol. 1, p. 231.

2.   Quoted in Ernest J. Lovell, Jr. (ed.), *His Very Self and Voice: Collected Conversations of Lord Byron* (New York and London: Macmillan, 1954), p. 212.

3.   Quoted in Thomas Moore, *Letters and Journals of Lord Byron: With Notices of His Life*, 2 vols. (London: John Murray, 1830), Vol. 2, p. 602.

4.   Alfred Lord Tennyson, 'Ulysses' (1842), l. 11.

5.   Hector Berlioz, *Memoirs of Hector Berlioz*, trans. and ed. David Cairns (New York: Knopf, 1969), p. 225.

6.   Eugène Delacroix, *The Journal of Eugène Delacroix*, tr. Walter Pach (1937; New York, Grove Press, 1961), p. 89.

7.   [Walter Scott] *Quarterly Review* 16 (issued February 1817), p. 177.

8.   James Gillman, *The Life of Samuel Taylor Coleridge* (London: William Pickering, 1838), pp. 266–7.

9.   *Byron's Letters and Journals*, ed. Marchand, Vol. 4, pp. 112–13.

10. Lady Blessington, *Conversations of Lord Byron*, ed. Ernest J. Lovell, Jr. (Princeton: Princeton University Press, 1969), p. 220.

11. John Scott, 'Living Authors, No. IV: Lord Byron', *London Magazine* 3 (January 1821), p. 51.

12. [John Wilson], review of Canto IV of *Childe Harold's Pilgrimage*, *Edinburgh Review* 30 (June 1818; issued September 1818), p. 90. Wilson, poet, essayist (chiefly under the pseudonym Christopher North for *Blackwood's Edinburgh Magazine*), and from 1820 Professor of Moral Philosophy at the University of Edinburgh.

13. Moore, *Letters and Journals of Lord Byron*, Vol. 1, p. 20.

14. Moore, *Letters and Journals of Lord Byron*, Vol. 1, p. 347.

15. Sydney Owenson, Lady Morgan, *Lady Morgan's Memoirs*, ed. W. Hepworth Dixon and Geraldine Jewsbury, 2 vols. (London: W. H. Allen, 1862), Vol. 2, p. 200.

16. Anne Isabella Milbanke to Lady Gosford, 14 October 1812, quoted in Malcolm Elwin, *Lord Byron's Wife* (New York: Harcourt, Brace, 1962), p. 152.

17. Matthew Arnold, 'Stanzas from the Grande Chartreuse' (1855), l. 116.

18. Thomas Medwin, *Conversations of Lord Byron* (1824); ed. Ernest J. Lovell, Jr. (Princeton: Princeton University Press, 1966), p. 194.

19. *Byron's Letters and Journals*, ed. Marchand, Vol, 6, p. 25.

20. *Don Juan*, ed. T. G. Steffan, E. Steffan and W. W. Pratt, with an introduction by Susan J. Wolfson and Peter J. Manning (London: Penguin, 2004), Canto 1, Stanza 37, 7.

21. *Blackwood's Edinburgh Magazine*, 5 (August 1819), p. 514.

22. *Byron's Letters and Journals*, ed. Marchand, Vol. 6, p. 67.

23. *Byron's Letters and Journals*, ed. Marchand, Vol. 12, p. 107.

24. Hallam Tennyson, *Alfred Lord Tennyson: A Memoir*, 2 vols. (London: Macmillan, 1897), Vol. 1, p. 4; Matthew Arnold, 'Byron', *Essays in Criticism, Second Series* (1888); (London: Dent, 1964), p. 315.

TABLE OF DATES

becomes member of the Drury Lane Theatre Management Committee. Financial difficulties and arrival of bailiffs; frequent visits from Augusta and beginning of alienation from Annabella.

Napoleon escapes from Elba, is defeated at Waterloo and exiled to St Helena; restoration of Louis XVIII.

Wordsworth's collected *Poems* and Charles Lloyd's translation of *The Tragedies of Alfieri* published.

1816   Publication of *The Siege of Corinth* and *Parisina* (February), *Poems* and fifth edition of *English Bards*. *The Prisoner of Chillon and Other Poems* and *Childe Harold's Pilgrimage III* published in November; at a booksellers' dinner, Murray sells 7,000 copies of each volume. Byron works on *Manfred*, 'Prometheus' and 'Darkness'.

In January, Lady Byron leaves with Ada to live with her parents; Byron writes 'Fare thee well!' in March, and, amidst dark rumours about his character, a deed of separation is drawn up in March and signed in April; he meets and begins an affair with Claire Clairmont, Mary Shelley's stepsister. Cut by London society over the separation scandal, with financial difficulties worsening, Byron auctions off his library and leaves England in April, for ever. Travels in Belgium, Waterloo, the Rhine and Switzerland. Rents Villa Diodati, on Lake Geneva, meets the Shelleys, near neighbours, and begins *Childe Harold's Pilgrimage III*. Ghost stories at Villa Diodati (the origin of *Frankenstein*), friendship with the Shelleys; the affair with Claire Clairmont cools during her pregnancy with his child. Tours the Alps and Lake Geneva with Percy Bysshe Shelley, visits Chateau de Chillon. After the Shelleys and Claire leave for England, he sets off for Italy with Hobhouse and moves to Venice later in the year; affair with Marianna Segati, his landlord's wife; studies Armenian at a monastery.

Hemans's *The Restoration of the Works of Art to Italy*, Leigh Hunt's *Story of Rimini* (with a Dedication to Byron), Shelley's *Alastor*, Wordsworth's *Thanksgiving Ode*, Austen's *Emma*, Caroline Lamb's *Glenarvon* (with a hero meant to be read as Byron, and publishing one of his letters to her) and Coleridge's *Christabel* and *Kubla Khan* published.

Elgin Marbles displayed; prosecution of William Hone for blasphemous libel (tried in 1817); Spa Field Riots (December).

1817   *Manfred* published in June; writing *Childe Harold's Pilgrimage IV*. Allegra, his and Claire Clairmont's daughter, born in England (January). Venice Carnival and dissipations. Travels to Rome with Hobhouse, returns to settle in Venice. Visits with 'Monk' Lewis; affair with Margarita Cogni. Hears the story that is the basis for *Beppo*, reads Frere's *Whistlecraft* (a poem in *ottava rima*). Sells Newstead Abbey for £94,500 in December.

Publication of Coleridge's *Biographia Literaria* and *Sibylline Leaves*, Keats's first volume of *Poems*, Moore's *Lalla Rookh*, Hemans's *Modern Greece*, Hazlitt's *Characters of Shakespear's Plays* and *The Round Table* and Southey's *Wat Tyler* (written in the 1790s), by his enemies to embarrass him. *Blackwood's Edinburgh Magazine* founded. 'Z''s articles on the 'Cockney School' appear in *Blackwood's* 1817–19, attacking Hunt, Keats and eventually Shelley.

Habeas Corpus Act suspended in England (March). Death of Princess Charlotte from complications in the delivery of a stillborn child.

1818   Writes 'My dear Mr Murray'. *Beppo* published in February, *Childe Harold's Pilgrimage IV* in April (including stanzas on the death of the Princess).

Venice Carnival, dissipations, etc. Byron leases a palazzo on the Grand Canal and begins *Don Juan* in July; spends much time with the Shelleys, encounters Contessa Teresa Guiccioli; Allegra comes to Venice with her nurse.

Keats's *Endymion*, Percy Bysshe Shelley's *The Revolt of Islam*, Scott's *Rob Roy* and Mary Shelley's *Frankenstein* published; a scathing review of *Endymion* in the *Quarterly*.

European Alliance; Habeas Corpus Act restored in England.

1819   *Mazeppa* and *Ode to Venice* published in June, *Don Juan I–II* in July, anonymously, and then pirated, to Murray's distress. Works on *Don Juan III*. All four cantos of *Childe*

Harold's Pilgrimage published together.

Venice Carnival, etc. Byron visits the Guicciolis in Ravenna and Bologna; begins affair with Teresa and at her request writes *The Prophecy of Dante*; gives his memoirs to Thomas Moore in October. Teresa's husband and her father, Count Gamba, try to end her liaison with Byron; in November, she returns to Ravenna with her husband. On Christmas Eve, Byron joins Teresa at Ravenna.

Wordsworth's *Peter Bell* and *The Waggoner*, Polidori's *The Vampyre*, Scott's *The Heart of Mid-Lothian* and Hemans's *Tales and Historical Scenes* published. Scathing review of *The Revolt of Islam* in the *Quarterly*, with a vicious attack on Shelley's character.

'Peterloo massacre' in August; Six Acts passed in December; birth of Queen Victoria. Shelley writes *The Mask of Anarchy*.

1820 Byron and Allegra live with Teresa and her husband; Byron's and Teresa's liaison continues. Byron becomes involved in the Italian Revolution against Austrian rule (the Carbonari movement) through Teresa's brother. Teresa is officially separated from her husband in July and goes to live with her father; Byron visits frequently. Sends Allegra to live in the country. Working on *Don Juan III–V*, translates 'Francesca of Rimini' from Dante's *Inferno*, Canto V.

Death of George III; the Regent becomes George IV. Dissolution of Parliament, Cato Street Conspiracy in England. Queen Caroline tried for adultery; Byron involved in seeking Italian witnesses for her.

Royalist reactions throughout Europe; revolution in Spain and Portugal.

Murray publishes an eight-volume edition of Byron's poems (1818–20). Shelley's *Swellfoot the Tyrant* published and suppressed; his *Prometheus Unbound and Other Poems*, *The Cenci*, Hemans's *The Sceptic*, Clare's *Poems Descriptive of Rural Life*, Wordsworth's *Memorials of a Tour on the Continent* and *The River Duddon*, and Keats's *Lamia* volume published. The *London Magazine* and *John Bull* founded.

1821   Byron begins his journal. *Marino Faliero* and *The Prophecy of Dante* published in April; when *Don Juan III–V* is published in August, Murray's premises are mobbed by booksellers' messengers; *Sardanapalus*, *The Two Foscari* and *Cain* are published together in December. After Southey publishes *A Vision of Judgement* with its attack on the Satanic school, Byron retaliates with *The Vision of Judgment*. Sends Murray *The Blues* in August. *Marino Faliero* flops on the London stage.

The Gambas (Teresa's family) are expelled from Romagna in July and banished to Pisa; Byron and the Gambas join the Shelleys and others of the 'Pisan circle' by November. Allegra is sent to a convent school.

Deaths of Napoleon, Queen Caroline and Keats (in Rome, February); Shelley's *Adonais* hooted at in *Blackwood's*; Baillie's *Metrical Legends* published. The 'Bowles controversy' in England: Byron writes two letters in defence of Pope and attacks the Lake poets and the Cockneys. Lockhart's unsigned pamphlet, *John Bull's Letter to the Right Hon. Lord Byron* published.

Greek War of Liberation (from the Ottoman Empire) begins.

1822   Byron publishes *A Letter to [John Murray] on the Rev. W. C. Bowles's Strictures on . . . Pope*; resumes *Don Juan*, attenuates his relationship with Murray and makes terms with the radical publisher, John Hunt. Southey attacks Byron in February in the conservative *Courier*. Leigh Hunt arrives with his large family in Pisa in July to join Byron and Shelley in publishing the *Liberal*. The first issue (15 October) includes Byron's 'Letter to the Editor of "My Grandmother's Review"' and *The Vision of Judgment*, the latter resulting in hostile reviews and John Hunt's prosecution. Murray publishes *Werner* in November. Allegra dies of typhus in April; Lady Noel, Annabella's mother, dies; Byron takes the name 'Noel Byron' and shares the estate, nearly doubling his income. Shelley leaves for Lerici in April, drowns in a boating accident in July. Byron, Mary Shelley and the Hunts move to Genoa in September. Friction with the Hunts.

Shelley's *Hellas* published in February; also published, De Quincey's *Confessions of an English Opium Eater*.

Lord Castlereagh, the Foreign Secretary, commits suicide in August.

1823 The *Liberal* publishes *Heaven and Earth* in January and *The Blues* in April. *The Age of Bronze* also published in April, *The Island* in June, *Don Juan* (now published by John Hunt) *VI–VIII* in July, *IX–XI* in August, and *XII–XIV* in December.

Byron is elected a member of the Greek Committee in London; quarrels with the Hunts and Mary Shelley; meets Countess Blessington; becomes involved in the Revolution and sails for Greece in July, arriving at Missolonghi at the end of the year; agrees to lend the Greek Government £4,000.

Mary Shelley's *Valperga* and Caroline Lamb's *Ada Reis: A Tale* published.

France and Spain at war.

1824 Byron in Greece at Missolonghi, financing the army. Writes verses on thirty-sixth birthday. *The Deformed Transformed* published in February, *Don Juan XV–XVI* in March.

The Revolution is in disarray. Byron's health deteriorates, and he dies at Missolonghi in April; his body is taken to England, where he is buried in July, with his ancestors near Newstead, having been refused interment at Westminster Abbey. His memoirs are destroyed.

Correspondence of Lord Byron with a Friend, edited by R.C. Dallas, is suppressed before it could be published; Dallas does publish *Recollections of Lord Byron* (1808–14), and Thomas Medwin publishes *Journal of the Conversations of Lord Byron at Pisa*. Also published: L.E.L.'s (Laetitia Landon) *The Improvisatrice*; Shelley's *Posthumous Poems*, including 'Julian and Maddalo', published in England by John Hunt and associates but quickly suppressed by Shelley's father.

1825 Dallas's *Correspondence* published in Paris. Murray produces an eight-volume edition of Byron's poetry, and Hazlitt's essay on 'Lord Byron' appears in *The Spirit of the Age*.

FURTHER READING

THE ROMANTIC ERA

Brown, Marshall (ed.), *The Cambridge History of Literary Criticism*, Vol. 5: *Romanticism* (Cambridge: Cambridge University Press, 2000).

Butler, Marilyn, *Romantics, Rebels, and Reactionaries: English Literature and Its Background, 1760–1830* (Oxford: Oxford University Press, 1982).

Gaull, Marilyn, *English Romanticism, The Human Context* (Norton, 1988).

Renwick, W. L., *English Literature: 1789–1815*, and Ian Jack, *English Literature: 1815–1832* (Oxford: Clarendon Press, 1963). Both in John Buxton and Norman Davis (eds.), *Oxford History of English Literature*.

Wolfson, Susan, and Peter Manning (eds.), *The Romantics and Their Contemporaries*, Vol. 2a of David Damrosch (ed.), *The Longman Anthology of British Literature*, 2nd edn (New York: Longman Publishers, 2003, 3rd edition, 2006).

BIOGRAPHIES AND MEMOIRS

Blessington, Lady, *Conversations of Lord Byron* (1834), ed. Ernest J. Lovell, Jr. (Princeton: Princeton University Press, 1969). In Genoa, Italy, in 1823, just before he left for Greece.

Eisler, Benita, *Byron: Child of Passion, Fool of Fame* (New York: Alfred A. Knopf, 1999). Sensationalizing.

Franklin, Caroline, *Byron: A Literary Life* (London: Palgrave, 2000). The forceful personality set amid readers' reactions, social and historical situations (travel, theatre culture, expatriatism, press censorship and libel trials).

Garrett, Martin, *George Gordon, Lord Byron*, in the British Library Writers' Lives series (Oxford: Oxford University Press, 2000). Short, readable narration, beautiful illustrations.

Grosskurth, Phyllis, *Byron: The Flawed Angel* (Boston, Mass.: Houghton Mifflin, 1997). Psychoanalytic.

Hunt, Leigh, *Lord Byron and Some of His Contemporaries*. (London: Henry Colburn, 1828). By one who knew him for the last ten years of his life – gossipy, biased, controversial.

Lovell, Jr., Ernest J. (ed.), *His Very Self and Voice: Collected Conversations of Lord Byron* (New York and London: Macmillan, 1954). A compendium from a range of sources.

MacCarthy, Fiona, *Byron: Life and Legend* (London: John Murray, 2002). Some new material; gorgeous plates.

Marchand, Leslie A., *Byron: A Biography*, 3 vols., (New York/London: Knopf, 1957/John Murray, 1958). Detailed chronology; abridged and revised in one volume as *Byron: A Portrait*, (Chicago: University of Chicago Press, 1970).

Medwin, Thomas, *Conversations of Lord Byron: Noted During a Residence with His Lordship at Pisa, in the Years 1821 and 1822* (1824); ed. Ernest, J. Lovell Jr. (Princeton: Princeton: University Press, 1966). The first of this genre.

Moore, Thomas, *Letters and Journals of Lord Byron With Notices of His Life*, 2 vols. (London: John Murray, 1830); the first official biography, much reprinted in the nineteenth century. Online at: http://www.worldwideschool.org/library/books/hst/european/CriticalandHistoricalEssaysVolume2/chap44.html

Page, Norman (ed.), *Byron: Interviews and Recollections* (New York: Humanities Press, 1985).

Quennell, Peter, *Byron: The Years of Fame* and *Byron in Italy* (New York: Viking Press 1935 and 1941)

Trelawny, Edward G., *Recollections of the Last Days of Shelley and Byron* (1858; new edn, 1878), ed. J. E. Morpurgo (New York: Philosophical Library, 1952). A rakish acquaintance.

EDITIONS OF POETRY, LETTERS AND PROSE

Coleridge, Ernest Hartley (ed.), *The Works of Lord Byron: Poetry*, 7 vols. (London: John Murray, 1898–1904); Prothero, Rowland E. (ed.), *The Works of Lord Byron: Letters and Journals*, 6 vols.

(London: John Murray, 1898–1904). Though the transcriptions of the latter have been superseded by Leslie Marchand's edition, the notes remain invaluable.

McGann, Jerome J. (ed.), *Lord Byron: The Complete Poetical Works*, 7 vols. (Oxford: Clarendon Press, 1980–93). Vol. VI (drama), co-edited with Barry Weller. See also his *Byron*, one-volume selection of poetry (Oxford: Oxford University Press, 1986). A standard edition.

Marchand, Leslie A. (ed.), *Byron's Letters and Journals*, 12 vols. (Cambridge, Mass./London: Harvard University Press/John Murray, 1973–82). In one volume, as *Selected Letters and Journals* (Cambridge, Mass.: Harvard University Press, 1982). The standard edition for critical and scholarly citation.

Nicholson, Andrew (ed.), *Lord Byron: The Complete Miscellaneous Prose* (Oxford: Clarendon Press, 1991). The standard edition.

Page, Frederick (ed.), *Byron: Poetical Works*, revised John Jump, (Oxford: Oxford University Press, 1970). Complete, one volume; a standard edition.

Reiman, Donald H. (gen. ed.), *Manuscripts of the Younger Romantics* (New York and London: Garland, 1985–). Photographic plates, transcriptions, notes and introductions: several volumes on Byron's works. Individual volumes ed. T. A. J. Burnett, Peter Cochran, Cheryl Guiliano, David Erdman and David Worrall, Alice Levine and Jerome McGann, and Andrew Nicholson.

Steffan, T. G., E. Steffan and W. W. Pratt (eds.), *Don Juan* (London: Penguin Classics, 1986; 2004). A standard edition.

Wordsworth, Jonathan (ed.), 'Revolution and Romanticism' series (Oxford: Woodstock). Several Byron titles in facsimile first editions, with introductions by Wordsworth.

CONTEMPORARY REVIEWS AND NINETEENTH-CENTURY VIEWS

Items relevant to specific texts are cited in the Notes; general resources include:

Arnold, Matthew, 'Byron' (preface to *Poetry of Byron* (1881)). In *Essays in Criticism: Second Series* (1888). Frequently reprinted.

Chew, Samuel C., *Byron in England: His Fame and After-Fame* (London: John Murray, 1924)

Elfenbein, Andrew, *Byron and the Victorians* (Cambridge: Cambridge University Press, 1995). The emergence and reception of 'Byronism' as literary and cultural phenomena.

Hazlitt, William, 'Lord Byron', *The Spirit of the Age* (1825), in P. P. Howe (ed.), *The Complete Works of William Hazlitt*, 21 vols. (London: J. M. Dent, 1930–34), XI, pp. 69–78

Howell, Margaret J., *Byron Tonight: A Poet's Plays on the Nineteenth Century Stage* (Windlesham: Springwood, 1982)

Meisel, Martin, 'Pictorial Engagements: Byron, Delacroix, Ford Madox Brown', *Studies in Romanticism* 27 (1988), pp. 579–603.

Redpath, Theodore (ed.), *The Young Romantics and Critical Opinion, 1807–1824: Poetry of Byron, Shelley, and Keats as Seen by Their Contemporary Critics* (New York: St Martin's Press, 1973)

Reiman, Donald H. (ed.), *The Romantics Reviewed: Contemporary Reviews of British Romantic Writers; Part B: Byron and Regency Society Poets*, 5 vols. (New York and London: Garland Publishing, 1972)

Rutherford, Andrew (ed.), *Byron: The Critical Heritage* (New York/London: Barnes and Noble/Routledge, 1970)

Soderholm, James, *Fantasy, Forgery, and the Byron Legend* (University of Kentucky Press, 1996)

GENERAL CRITICAL STUDIES

For titles relevant to specific texts, see the Notes, for those relevant to *Don Juan*, see Steffan, Steffan and Pratt, *Don Juan*.

Beaty, Frederick L., *Byron the Satirist* (De Kalb: Northern Illinois University Press, 1985)

Blackstone, Bernard, *Byron: A Survey* (London: Longman, 1975)

Bostetter, Edward E., 'Byron', *The Romantic Ventriloquists* (1963); revised edn (Seattle: University of Washington Press, 1975), pp. 241–301

Christensen, Jerome, *Lord Byron's Strength: Romantic Writing and Commercial Society* (Baltimore: Johns Hopkins University Press, 1993). How 'Byron' was constructed and marketed.

Cooke, Michael G., *The Blind Man Traces the Circle: On the Patterns and Philosophy of Byron's Poetry* (Princeton: Princeton University Press, 1969)

Crompton, Louis, *Byron and Greek Love: Homophobia in 19th-Century England* (Berkeley: University of California Press, 1985). Bisexuality, homoeroticism, cultural oppression.

Eliot, T. S., 'Byron', *On Poetry and Poets* (London: Faber and Faber, 1957)

Elledge, Paul W., *Byron and the Dynamics of Metaphor* (Nashville: Vanderbilt University Press, 1968)

Franklin, Caroline, *Byron's Heroines* (Oxford: Clarendon Press, 1992)

Garber, Frederick, *Self, Text, and Romantic Irony: The Example of Byron* (Princeton: Princeton University Press, 1988)

Gleckner, Robert F., *Byron and the Ruins of Paradise* (Baltimore: Johns Hopkins University Press, 1967)

Graham, Peter W., *Lord Byron* (New York: Twayne Publishers, 1998)

Hoagwood, Terence Allan, *Byron's Dialectic: Skepticism and the Critique of Culture* (Lewisburg: Bucknell University Press, 1993)

Hofkosh, Sonia, 'Women and the Romantic Author: The Example of Byron', in Anne K. Mellor (ed.), *Romanticism and Feminism* (Bloomington: Indiana University Press, 1988), pp. 93–114

Jones, Steven, *Satire and Romanticism* (New York: St Martin's Press, 2000)

Keach, William, "Words are Things", and "The Politics of Rhyme", both in *Arbitrary Power: Romanticism, Language, Politics* (Princeton and Oxford: Princeton University Press, 2004).

Kelsall, Malcolm, *Byron's Politics* (Sussex: Harvester Press, 1987). Political principles, political impotence.

Knight, G. Wilson, 'The Two Eternities: An Essay on Byron', *The Burning Oracle: Studies in the Poetry of Action* (London: Oxford University Press, 1939), pp. 199–288

Leavis, F. R., 'Byron's Satire', *Revaluation: Tradition and Development in English Poetry* (London: Chatto and Windus, 1956), pp. 139–44

McGann, Jerome J., 'The Book of Byron and the Book of a World', in *The Beauty of Inflections: Literary Investigations in Historical*

Method & Theory (Oxford: Clarendon Press, 1988), pp. 255–93

—, *Byron and Romanticism*, ed. James Soderholm (Cambridge: Cambridge University Press, 2002). Important essays, some revised, and some new adventures and reflections.

McGann, Jerome J., *Fiery Dust: Byron's Poetic Development* (Chicago: University of Chicago Press, 1968)

Manning, Peter J., *Byron and His Fictions* (Detroit, Mich.: Wayne State University Press, 1978)

Marchand, Leslie A., *Byron's Poetry: A Critical Introduction* (Cambridge, Mass.: Harvard University Press, 1968). Includes a bibliography.

Martin, Philip W., *Byron: A Poet before His Public* (Cambridge: Cambridge University Press, 1982). Byron's consciousness of, and ambivalence about his audiences; his rivalry with contemporaries.

Richardson, Alan, *A Mental Theater: Poetic Drama and Consciousness in the Romantic Age* (University Park: Pennsylvania University Press, 1988)

Ricks, Christopher, 'Byron', in *Allusion to Poets* (Oxford and New York: Oxford University Press, 2002), pp. 121–56. Brilliant and canny about Byron's generous, unanxious ways with literary inheritance.

Roessel, David, *In Byron's Shadow: Modern Greece in the English and American Imagination* (Oxford: Oxford University Press, 2002)

Rutherford, Andrew, *Byron: A Critical Study* (Stanford: Stanford University Press, 1961)

St Clair, William, 'The Impact of Byron's Writings', in Rutherford, *Byron: Augustan and Romantic*

Shilstone, Frederick W., *Byron and the Myth of Tradition* (Lincoln: University of Nebraska Press, 1988)

Stabler, Jane, *Byron, Poetics and History* (London: Cambridge University Press, 2002)

Storey, Mark, *Byron and the Eye of Appetite*, (New York: St Martin's Press, 1986)

Thorslev, Peter L., *The Byronic Hero: Types and Prototypes* (Minneapolis: University of Minnesota Press, 1962)

Watkins, Daniel, *Social Relations in Byron's Eastern Tales* (Rutherford, NJ: Fairleigh Dickinson University Press, 1987)

Wilkie, Brian, 'Byron and the Epic of Negation', in *Romantic Poets and Epic Tradition* (Madison: University of Wisconsin Press, 1965), pp. 188–226

Woodring, Carl, 'Byron', in *Politics in English Romantic Poetry* (Cambridge, Mass.: Harvard University Press, 1970), pp. 148–229

ANTHOLOGIES OF CRITICAL ESSAYS

Beatty, Bernard, and Vincent Newey (eds.), *Byron and the Limits of Fiction* (Liverpool: Liverpool University Press, 1988)

Bone, Drummond (ed.), *The Cambridge Companion to Lord Byron* (Cambridge: Cambridge University Press, 2004)

Gleckner, Robert F. (ed.), *Critical Essays on Lord Byron* (Boston, Mass: G. K. Hall, 1991)

Hirst, Wolf Z. (ed.), *Byron, the Bible, and Religion* (Newark: University of Delaware Press, 1991)

Levine, Alice, and Robert N. Keane (eds.), *Rereading Byron: Essays Selected from Hofstra University's Byron Bicentennial Conference* (New York and London: Garland Publishing, 1993)

Rutherford, Andrew (ed.), *Byron: Augustan and Romantic* (London: Macmillan, 1990)

Stabler, Jane (ed.), *Byron*, Longman Critical Reader (London: Longman, 1998)

Wilson, Francis (ed.), *Byromania* (London/NewYork: Macmillan/St Martin's, 1999). Cultural life and afterlife.

BIBLIOGRAPHIES

Annual bibliographies, with sections on Byron, are published by the Modern Language Association of America, Modern Humanities Research Association, the *Keats–Shelley Journal*, *The Romantic Movement* and *Year's Work in English Studies*.

Chew, Samuel C., and Ernest J. Lovell, Jr., 'Byron', in Frank Jordan (ed.), *The English Romantic Poets: A Review of Research and Criticism*, 3rd edn (New York: Modern Language Association of America, 1972)

Clubbe, John, 'George Gordon, Lord Byron', in Frank Jordan (ed.), *The English Romantic Poets: A Review of Research and Criticism*, 4th edn. (New York: Modern Language Association of America, 1985). This report includes a section on bibliographies.

Nicholson, Andrew, 'Byron', in Michael O'Neill (ed.), *Literature of the Romantic Period: A Bibliographical Guide* (Oxford: Oxford University Press, 1998)

Santucho, Oscar José, and Clement Tyson Good, Jr., *George Gordon, Lord Byron: A Comprehensive Bibliography of Secondary Materials in English, 1807–1974* (Metuchen, NJ: Scarecrow Press, 1977; 1997, updated through 1994)

CONCORDANCES AND WEBSITES

Young, Ione Dodson, *A Concordance to the Poetry of Byron*, 4 vols (Best Printing, 1975). Co-ordinated with Paul Elmer More (ed.), *Complete Poetical Works of Lord Byron* (1905), revised Robert Gleckner, (Cambridge: Cambridge University Press, 1975)

The Byron Chronology, ed. Anne R. Hawkins: http://www.rc.umd.edu/reference/byronchronology/index.html

Byronic Images: Portraits of the Poets, His Family, and Friends: http://www.englishhistory.net/byron/images.html

The International Byron Society (texts, portraits, biography, etc.): http://www.internationalbyronsociety.org/

The Life and Work of Lord Byron: http://www.englishhistory.net/byron.html

The Literature Network: Lord Byron: http://www.online-literature.com/byron/

A NOTE ON THIS EDITION

The basis of the Penguin text of *Lord Byron: Selected Poems* is the edition prepared by John Wright for the seventeen-volume *The Works of Lord Byron: With His Letters and Journals, and His Life, by Thomas Moore*, Esq., published by John Murray, 1832–4. The first six volumes presented *Letters and Journals of Lord Byron: With Notices of His Life* (first published 1830), and Volumes VII–XVII contained the poetry (emending an edition of 1831). Carefully prepared, informatively annotated, handsomely illustrated with engraved plates, and lavishly framed with numerous contemporary comments on Byron and the poems, Murray's edition virtually defined Byron for the nineteenth century; it still held a claim as 'definitive' against Ernest Hartley Coleridge's seven-volume edition of the poetry at the end of the century (based on the less reliable edition of 1831) and it served as the basis for many editions well into the twentieth century.

Unlike most editions of Byron available today, our presentation follows Murray's practice of printing Byron's numerous notes – important textual events in themselves – on the same page as the poetic texts; we also retain the spelling, punctuation, capitalization and italics of Murray's edition, adding only line numbers for convenience of reference. Our ordering of the contents diverges from Murray's (and most other editions') by presenting the works in the sequence of composition and/or initial publication. The distinct advantage is the sense afforded of how Byron's career developed not only through its productions but also in relation to current historical events, his emerging fame, and his personal circumstances. Thus *Childe Harold's Pilgrimage* – to take the salient example – appears in our edition not *in toto* as it finally did in 1819 but in the units and order of its unfolding publication across the decade. This arrangement both registers the force of Cantos I–II (written 1809–10, published 1812) in launching Byron's fame and shows how this fame flourished – not through the next two cantos but in a sensational series of Eastern tales. When Canto III appeared late in 1816, not only was it capitalizing on established celebrity (Cantos I–II had gone through over a dozen editions and the tales were best-sellers), but it also had the resonance of its historical moment, appearing after the decisive defeat in 1815 of Napoleon, Byron's self-imagined *alter ego*, and the restoration of the monarchies, and bearing the scars of the public scandal of Byron's separation from his wife and daughter and his expatriation from England in early 1816. Canto IV, published April 1818, did not follow in the train of Canto III so much as that of *Manfred* (published June 1817) and *Beppo* (February 1818), reflecting the former's suggestion of the termination, or exhaustion, of one kind of melodramatic self-fashioning and the latter's new mode of ironic self-regard.

In making our selections for this volume, we have chosen poems that defined Byron for the nineteenth century and poems less well known then but figuring in recent years in the lively discussion of Byron and the nature of Romanticism. Except for 'The Isles of Greece', which frequent anthologizing has given independent status (albeit problematically), we have not included selections from *Don Juan*, because this work is available in its entirety in the Penguin Classics Volume splendidly edited by T.G. Steffan, E. Steffan and W.W. Pratt (1986; 2004). Thus relieved from representing *Don Juan*, we have been able to provide complete texts of many works that do not appear entire in other currently available selections: all of *Childe Harold's Pilgrimage*, replete with Byron's notes, and all but one of the Eastern tales that elaborated this sensational initial success, from *The Giaour* in 1813 to *The Siege of Corinth* in 1816, again with Byron's notes. To suggest the range of Byron's remarkably productive and versatile career, we also offer one of the historical dramas that occupied him in 1820–21 (and which has a soft claim to status as a 'poem' in being written, so Byron insisted, more for the page than the stage): *Sardanapalus*. In its wry use of ancient history to highlight questions of imperialism, revolution and gender that were of concern to readers in the early 1820s, *Sardanapalus* has emerged as an important reference in the re-evaluation of Romanticism that has been taking place at the end of the twentieth century.

The double principle that has guided our selection – works of

interest to Byron's contemporaries and his nineteenth-century read-
ers as well as works of interest to readers today – has also shaped
our Notes, which collate citations from contemporary reviews with
concise pointers to modern criticism of each poem. (The list of
Works Cited in the Notes has complete references for all items
mentioned therein.) These Notes also give information about the
circumstances of composition and publication of each work and
gloss the salient literary, biographical and historical references.
Readers wanting extensive scholarly commentaries on the composi-
tional histories, manuscript states and stages, textual variants and
disputed readings, as well as more detailed annotations of historical
circumstances, references, allusions, etc., may refer to Jerome J.
McGann's major seven-volume edition of *Lord Byron: The Com-
plete Poetical Works* (1980–93).

The Introduction is supplemented by a Table of Dates that situ-
ates a detailed chronology of Byron's life and career in relation to
prominent events in England and abroad, and indicates some of the
other works of literature being published alongside his. The
chronology extends past Bryon's death to note the most important
of the posthumous presentations of his life and works that preceded
the publication of Murray's landmark edition.

November 1995

A Fragment

When, to their airy hall, my fathers' voice
Shall call my spirit, joyful in their choice;
When, pois'd upon the gale, my form shall ride,
Or, dark in mist, descend the mountain's side:
5   Oh! may my shade behold no sculptur'd urns
To mark the spot where earth to earth returns!
No lengthen'd scroll, no praise-encumber'd stone;
My epitaph shall be my name alone:
If *that* with honour fail to crown my clay,
10   Oh! may no other fame my deeds repay!
That, only *that*, shall single out the spot;
By that remember'd, or with that forgot.

1803.

To Woman

Woman! experience might have told me
That all must love thee who behold thee:
Surely experience might have taught
Thy firmest promises are nought;
5   But, placed in all thy charms before me,
All I forget, but to adore thee.
Oh memory! thou choicest blessing
When join'd with hope, when still possessing;
But how much cursed by every lover
10   When hope is fled and passion's over.
Woman, that fair and fond deceiver,
How prompt are striplings to believe her!
How throbs the pulse when first we view
The eye that rolls in glossy blue,

15 Or sparkles black, or mildly throws
 A beam from under hazel brows!
 How quick we credit every oath,
 And hear her plight the willing troth!
 Fondly we hope 'twill last for aye,
20 When, lo! she changes in a day.
 This record will for ever stand,
 'Woman, thy vows are traced in sand.'

The Cornelian

 No specious splendour of this stone
  Endears it to my memory ever;
 With lustre only once it shone,
  And blushes modest as the giver.

5 Some, who can sneer at friendship's ties,
  Have, for my weakness, oft reproved me;
 Yet still the simple gift I prize, –
  For I am sure the giver loved me.

 He offer'd it with downcast look,
10 As fearful that I might refuse it;
 I told him when the gift I took,
  My only fear should be to lose it.

 This pledge attentively I view'd,
  And sparkling as I held it near,
15 Methought one drop the stone bedew'd,
  And ever since I've loved a tear.

 Still, to adorn his humble youth,
  Nor wealth nor birth their treasures yield;
 But he who seeks the flowers of truth,
20 Must quit the garden for the field.

'Tis not the plant uprear'd in sloth,
    Which beauty shows, and sheds perfume;
The flowers which yield the most of both
    In Nature's wild luxuriance bloom.

25 Had Fortune aided Nature's care,
        For once forgetting to be blind,
    His would have been an ample share,
        If well proportion'd to his mind.

    But had the goddess clearly seen,
30   His form had fix'd her fickle breast;
    Her countless hoards would his have been,
        And none remain'd to give the rest.

To Caroline

I

You say you love, and yet your eye
    No symptom of that love conveys,
You say you love, yet know not why
    Your cheek no sign of love betrays.

II

5   Ah! did that breast with ardour glow,
    With me alone it joy could know,
    Or feel with me the listless woe,
        Which racks my heart when far from you.

III

    Whene'er we meet, my blushes rise,
10   And mantle through my purpled cheek,
    But yet no blush to mine replies,
        Nor do those eyes your love bespeak.

IV

Your voice alone declares your flame,
And though so sweet it breathes my name,
15 Our passions still are not the same,
 Though Love and Rapture still are new.

V

For e'en your lip seems steep'd in snow,
 And, though so oft it meets my kiss,
It burns with no responsive glow,
20   Nor melts, like mine, in dewy bliss.

VI

Ah! what are words to love like mine,
Though uttered by a voice divine,
I still in murmurs must repine,
 And think that love can ne'er be true,

VII

25 Which meets me with no joyous sign;
 Without a sigh which bids adieu:
How different is that love from mine,
 Which feels such grief when leaving you.

VIII

Your image fills my anxious breast,
30 Till day declines adown the West,
And when, at night, I sink to rest,
 In dreams your fancied form I view.

IX

'Tis then, your breast, no longer cold,
 With equal ardour seems to burn,
35 While close your arms around me fold,
 Your lips my kiss with warmth return.

X

Ah! would these joyous moments last!
Vain HOPE! the gay delusion's past;
That voice! – ah! no, 'tis but the blast,
40   Which echoes through the neighbouring grove!

XI

But, when *awake*, your lips I seek,
    And clasp, enraptur'd, all your charms,
So chills the pressure of your cheek,
    I fold a statue in my arms.

XII

45 If thus, when to my heart embrac'd,
No pleasure in your eyes is trac'd,
You may be prudent, fair, and chaste,
    But ah! my girl, you *do not love!*

ENGLISH BARDS AND SCOTCH REVIEWERS

A Satire

'I had rather be a kitten, and cry mew!
Than one of these same metre ballad-mongers.'   SHAKSPEARE.

'Such shameless bards we have; and yet 'tis true,
There are as mad, abandon'd critics too.'   POPE.

PREFACE[1]

All my friends, learned and unlearned, have urged me not to publish this Satire with my name. If I were to be 'turned from the career of my humour by quibbles quick, and paper bullets of the brain,' I should have complied with their counsel. But I am not to be terrified by abuse, or bullied by reviewers, with or without arms. I can safely say that I have attacked none personally, who did not commence on the offensive. An author's works are public property: he who purchases may judge, and publish his opinion if he pleases; and the authors I have endeavoured to commemorate may do by me as I have done by them. I dare say they will succeed better in condemning my scribblings, than in mending their own. But my object is not to prove that I can write well, but, if possible, to make others write better.

As the poem has met with far more success than I expected, I have endeavoured in this edition to make some additions and alterations, to render it more worthy of public perusal.

In the first edition of this satire, published anonymously, fourteen lines on the subject of Bowles's Pope were written by, and inserted at the request of, an ingenious friend of

1. ['He is, and gone again.' – B. 1816.]

mine,[1] who has now in the press a volume of poetry. In the present edition they are erased, and some of my own substituted in their stead; my only reason for this being that which I conceive would operate with any other person in the same manner, – a determination not to publish with my name any production, which was not entirely and exclusively my own composition.

With regard to the real talents of many of the poetical persons whose performances are mentioned or alluded to in the following pages, it is presumed by the author that there can be little difference of opinion in the public at large; though, like other sectaries, each has his separate tabernacle of proselytes, by whom his abilities are over-rated, his faults overlooked, and his metrical canons received without scruple and without consideration. But the unquestionable possession of considerable genius by several of the writers here censured renders their mental prostitution more to be regretted. Imbecility may be pitied, or, at worst, laughed at and forgotten; perverted powers demand the most decided reprehension. No one can wish more than the author that some known and able writer had undertaken their exposure; but Mr Gifford has devoted himself to Massinger, and, in the absence of the regular physician, a country practitioner may, in cases of absolute necessity, be allowed to prescribe his nostrum to prevent the extension of so deplorable an epidemic, provided there be no quackery in his treatment of the malady. A caustic is here offered; as it is to be feared nothing short of actual cautery can recover the numerous patients afflicted with the present prevalent and distressing *rabies* for rhyming. – As to the Edinburgh Reviewers, it would indeed require an Hercules to crush the Hydra; but if the author succeeds in merely 'bruising one of the heads of the serpent,' though his own hand should suffer in the encounter, he will be amply satisfied.

1. John Cam Hobhouse. [Editors]

Still must I hear?[1] – shall hoarse Fitzgerald[2] bawl
His creaking couplets in a tavern hall,[3]
And I not sing, lest, haply, Scotch reviews
Should dub me scribbler, and denounce my muse?
5 Prepare for rhyme – I'll publish, right or wrong:
Fools are my theme, let satire be my song.

Oh! nature's noblest gift – my grey goose-quill!
Slave of my thoughts, obedient to my will,
Torn from thy parent bird to form a pen,
10 That mighty instrument of little men!
The pen! foredoom'd to aid the mental throes
Of brains that labour, big with verse or prose,
Though nymphs forsake, and critics may deride,
The lover's solace, and the author's pride.
15 What wits! what poets dost thou daily raise!
How frequent is thy use, how small thy praise!
Condemn'd at length to be forgotten quite,
With all the pages which 'twas thine to write.
But thou, at least, mine own especial pen!
20 Once laid aside, but now assumed again,
Our task complete, like Hamlet's shall be free;
Though spurn'd by others, yet beloved by me:
Then let us soar to-day; no common theme,
No eastern vision, no distemper'd dream[4]
25 Inspires – our path, though full of thorns, is plain;
Smooth be the verse, and easy be the strain.

When Vice triumphant holds her sov'reign sway,
Obey'd by all who nought beside obey;

1. IMIT. – 'Semper ego auditor tantum? nunquamne reponam,
        Vexatus toties rauci Theeside Codri?' – *Juv*. Sat. I.
2. ['*Hoarse Fitzgerald*.' – 'Right enough; but why notice such a mountebank.'
– B. 1816.]
3. Mr Fitzgerald, facetiously termed by Cobbett the 'Small Beer Poet,'
inflicts his annual tribute of verse on the Literary Fund: not content with
writing, he spouts in person, after the company have imbibed a reasonable
quantity of bad port, to enable them to sustain the operation.
4. ['This must have been written in the spirit of prophecy.' – B. 1816.]

When Folly, frequent harbinger of crime,
30   Bedecks her cap with bells of every clime;
When knaves and fools combined o'er all prevail,
And weigh their justice in a golden scale;
E'en then the boldest start from public sneers,
Afraid of shame, unknown to other fears,
35   More darkly sin, by satire kept in awe,
And shrink from ridicule, though not from law.

    Such is the force of wit! but not belong
To me the arrows of satiric song;
The royal vices of our age demand
40   A keener weapon, and a mightier hand.
Still there are follies, e'en for me to chase,
And yield at least amusement in the race:
Laugh when I laugh, I seek no other fame;
The cry is up, and scribblers are my game.
45   Speed, Pegasus! – ye strains of great and small,
Ode, epic, elegy, have at you all!
I too can scrawl, and once upon a time
I pour'd along the town a flood of rhyme,
A schoolboy freak, unworthy praise or blame;
50   I printed – older children do the same.
'Tis pleasant, sure, to see one's name in print;
A book's a book, although there's nothing in't.
Not that a title's sounding charm can save
Or scrawl or scribbler from an equal grave:
55   This Lambe must own, since his patrician name
Fail'd to preserve the spurious farce from shame.[1]
No matter, George continues still to write,[2]
Though now the name is veil'd from public sight.
Moved by the great example, I pursue
60   The self-same road, but make my own review

1. This ingenuous youth is mentioned more particularly, with his production, in another place.
2. In the Edinburgh Review. – ['He's a very good fellow: and, except his mother and sister, the best of the set, to my mind.' – B. 1816.]

Not seek great Jeffrey's, yet, like him, will be
Self-constituted judge of poesy.

A man must serve his time to ev'ry trade
Save censure – critics all are ready made.
65 Take hackney'd jokes from Miller, got by rote
With just enough of learning to misquote;
A mind well skill'd to find or forge a fault;
A turn for punning, call it Attic salt;
To Jeffrey go, be silent and discreet,
70 His pay is just ten sterling pounds per sheet:
Fear not to lie, 'twill seem a sharper hit;
Shrink not from blasphemy, 'twill pass for wit;
Care not for feeling – pass your proper jest,
And stand a critic, hated yet caress'd.

75   And shall we own such judgment? no – as soon
Seek roses in December – ice in June;
Hope constancy in wind, or corn in chaff;
Believe a woman or an epitaph,
Or any other thing that's false, before
80 You trust in critics, who themselves are sore;
Or yield one single thought to be misled
By Jeffrey's heart, or Lambe's Bœotian head.[1]
To these young tyrants,[2] by themselves misplaced,
Combined usurpers on the throne of taste;
85 To these, when authors bend in humble awe,
And hail their voice as truth, their word as law –
While these are censors, 'twould be sin to spare;
While such are critics, why should I forbear?
But yet, so near all modern worthies run,
90 'Tis doubtful whom to seek, or whom to shun;
Nor know we when to spare, or where to strike,
Our bards and censors are so much alike.

---

1. Messrs. Jeffrey and Lambe are the alpha and omega, the first and last of
the Edinburgh Review; the others are mentioned hereafter.
2. IMIT. 'Stulta est Clementia, cum tot ubique
    — occurras perituræ parcere chartæ.' – *Juv.* Sat. I.

Then should you ask me,[1] why I venture o'er
The path which Pope and Gifford trod before;
95   If not yet sicken'd, you can still proceed:
Go on; my rhyme will tell you as you read.
'But hold!' exclaims a friend, – 'here's some neglect:
This – that – and t' other line seem incorrect.'
What then? the self-same blunder Pope has got,
100 And careless Dryden – 'Ay, but Pye has not:' –
Indeed! – 'tis granted, faith! – but what care I?
Better to err with Pope, than shine with Pye.

Time was, ere yet in these degenerate days
Ignoble themes obtain'd mistaken praise,
105 When sense and wit with poesy allied,
No fabled graces, flourish'd side by side;
From the same fount their inspiration drew,
And rear'd by taste, bloom'd fairer as they grew.
Then, in this happy isle, a Pope's pure strain
110 Sought the rapt soul to charm, nor sought in vain;
A polish'd nation's praise aspired to claim,
And raised the people's, as the poet's fame.
Like him great Dryden pour'd the tide of song,
In stream less smooth, indeed, yet doubly strong.
115 Then Congreve's scenes could cheer, or Otway's melt –
For nature then an English audience felt.
But why these names, or greater still, retrace,
When all to feebler bards resign their place?
Yet to such times our lingering looks are cast,
120 When taste and reason with those times are past.
Now look around, and turn each trifling page,
Survey the precious works that please the age;
This truth at least let satire's self allow;
No dearth of bards can be complain'd of now:
125 The loaded press beneath her labour groans,
And printers' devils shake their weary bones;

1. IMIT. 'Cur tamen hoc libeat potius decurrere campo
         Per quem magnus equos Auruncæ flexit alumnus:
         Si vacat, et placidi rationem admittitis, edam.' – *Juv.* Sat. I.

While Southey's epics cram the creaking shelves,
And Little's lyrics shine in hot-press'd twelves.
Thus saith the preacher: 'Nought beneath the sun
130 Is new;' yet still from change to change we run:
What varied wonders tempt us as they pass!
The cow-pox, tractors, galvanism, and gas,
In turns appear, to make the vulgar stare,
Till the swoln bubble bursts – and all is air!
135 Nor less new schools of Poetry arise,
Where dull pretenders grapple for the prize:
O'er taste awhile these pseudo-bards prevail;
Each country book-club bows the knee to Baal,
And, hurling lawful genius from the throne,
140 Erects a shrine and idol of its own;
Some leaden calf – but whom it matters not,
From soaring Southey down to grovelling Stott.[1]

Behold! in various throngs the scribbling crew,
For notice eager, pass in long review:
145 Each spurs his jaded Pegasus apace,
And rhyme and blank maintain an equal race;
Sonnets on sonnets crowd, and ode on ode;
And tales of terror jostle on the road;
Immeasurable measures move along;
150 For simpering folly loves a varied song,

---

1. Stott, better known in the 'Morning Post' by the name of Hafiz. This personage is at present the most profound explorer of the bathos. I remember, when the reigning family left Portugal, a special Ode of Master Stott's, beginning thus: – (*Stott loquitur quoad Hibernia.*) –

'Princely offspring of Braganza,
Erin greets thee with a stanza,' & c.

Also a Sonnet to Rats, well worthy of the subject, and a most thundering Ode, commencing as follows:-

'Oh! for a Lay! loud as the surge
That lashes Lapland's sounding shore.'

Lord have mercy on us! the 'Lay of the Last Minstrel' was nothing to this.

To strange mysterious dulness still the friend,
Admires the strain she cannot comprehend.
Thus Lays of Minstrels[1] – may they be the last! –
On half-strung harps whine mournful to the blast.
155   While mountain spirits prate to river sprites,
That dames may listen to the sound at nights;
And goblin brats, of Gilpin Horner's brood,
Decoy young border-nobles through the wood,
And skip at every step, Lord knows how high,
160   And frighten foolish babes, the Lord knows why;
While high-born ladies in their magic cell,
Forbidding knights to read who cannot spell,
Despatch a courier to a wizard's grave,
And fight with honest men to shield a knave.

165   Next view in state, proud prancing on his roan,
The golden-crested haughty Marmion,
Now forging scrolls, now foremost in the fight,
Not quite a felon, yet but half a knight,

1. See the 'Lay of the Last Minstrel,' *passim*. Never was any plan so incongruous and absurd as the groundwork of this production. The entrance of Thunder and Lightning, prologuising to Bayes' tragedy unfortunately takes away the merit of originality from the dialogue between Messieurs the Spirits of Flood and Fell in the first canto. Then we have the amiable William of Deloraine, 'a stark moss-trooper,' videlicet, a happy compound of poacher, sheep-stealer, and highwayman. The propriety of his magical lady's injunction not to read can only be equalled by his candid acknowledgment of his independence of the trammels of spelling, although, to use his own elegant phrase, "twas his neck-verse at Harribee,' i.e. the gallows. – The biography of Gilpin Horner, and the marvellous pedestrian page, who travelled twice as fast as his master's horse, without the aid of seven-leagued boots, are *chefs-d'œuvre* in the improvement of taste. For incident we have the invisible, but by no means sparing box on the ear bestowed on the page, and the entrance of a knight and charger into the castle, under the very natural disguise of a wain of hay. Marmion, the hero of the latter romance, is exactly what William of Deloraine would have been, had he been able to read and write. The poem was manufactured for Messrs Constable, Murray, and Miller, worshipful booksellers, in consideration of the receipt of a sum of money; and truly, considering the inspiration, it is a very creditable production. If Mr Scott will write for hire, let him do his best for his paymasters, but not disgrace his genius, which is undoubtedly great, by a repetition of black-letter ballad imitations.

The gibbet or the field prepared to grace;
170 A mighty mixture of the great and base.
And think'st thou, Scott! by vain conceit perchance,
On public taste to foist thy stale romance,
Though Murray with his Miller may combine
To yield thy muse just half-a-crown per line?
175 No! when the sons of song descend to trade,
Their bays are sear, their former laurels fade.
Let such forego the poet's sacred name,
Who rack their brains for lucre, not for fame:
Still for stern Mammon may they toil in vain!
180 And sadly gaze on gold they cannot gain!
Such be their meed, such still the just reward
Of prostituted muse and hireling bard!
For this we spurn Apollo's venal son,
And bid a long 'good night to Marmion.'[1]

185 These are the themes that claim our plaudits now;
These are the bards to whom the muse must bow;
While Milton, Dryden, Pope, alike forgot,
Resign their hallow'd bays to Walter Scott.

The time has been, when yet the muse was young,
190 When Homer swept the lyre, and Maro sung,
An epic scarce ten centuries could claim,
While awe-struck nations hail'd the magic name:
The work of each immortal bard appears
The single wonder of a thousand years.[2]
195 Empires have moulder'd from the face of earth,
Tongues have expired with those who gave them birth,

1. 'Good night to Marmion' – the pathetic and also prophetic exclamation
of Henry Blount, Esquire, on the death of honest Marmion.
2. As the Odyssey is so closely connected with the story of the Iliad, they
may almost be classed as one grand historical poem. In alluding to Milton
and Tasso, we consider the 'Paradise Lost,' and 'Gierusalemme Liberata,' as
their standard efforts; since neither the 'Jerusalem Conquered' of the Italian,
nor the 'Paradise Regained' of the English bard, obtained a proportionate
celebrity to their former poems. Query: Which of Mr Southey's will
survive?

Without the glory such a strain can give,
As even in ruin bids the language live.
Not so with us, though minor bards content,
On one great work a life of labour spent:
With eagle pinion soaring to the skies,
Behold the ballad-monger Southey rise!
To him let Camoëns, Milton, Tasso yield,
Whose annual strains, like armies, take the field.
First in the ranks see Joan of Arc advance,
The scourge of England and the boast of France!
Though burnt by wicked Bedford for a witch,
Behold her statue placed in glory's niche;
Her fetters burst, and just released from prison,
A virgin phœnix from her ashes risen.
Next see tremendous Thalaba come on,[1]
Arabia's monstrous, wild, and wond'rous son;
Domdaniel's dread destroyer, who o'erthrew
More mad magicians than the world e'er knew.
Immortal hero! all thy foes o'ercome,
For ever reign – the rival of Tom Thumb!
Since startled metre fled before thy face,
Well wert thou doom'd the last of all thy race!
Well might triumphant genii bear thee hence,
Illustrious conqueror of common sense!
Now, last and greatest, Madoc spreads his sails,
Cacique in Mexico, and prince in Wales;
Tells us strange tales, as other travellers do,
More old than Mandeville's, and not so true.
Oh, Southey! Southey![2] cease thy varied song!
A bard may chant too often and too long:

200
205
210
215
220
225

1. 'Thalaba,' Mr Southey's second poem, is written in open defiance of
precedent and poetry. Mr S. wished to produce something novel, and
succeeded to a miracle. 'Joan of Arc,' was marvellous enough, but 'Thalaba,'
was one of those poems 'which,' in the words of Porson, 'will be read when
Homer and Virgil are forgotten, but – *not till then.*'
2. We beg Mr Southey's pardon: 'Madoc disdains the degrading title of
epic.' See his preface. Why is epic degraded? and by whom? Certainly the
late romaunts of Masters Cottle, Laureat Pye, Ogilvy, Hole, and gentle

As thou art strong in verse, in mercy, spare!
A fourth, alas! were more than we could bear.
But if, in spite of all the world can say,
230   Thou still wilt verseward plod thy weary way;
If still in Berkley ballads most uncivil,
Thou wilt devote old women to the devil,[1]
The babe unborn thy dread intent may rue:
'God help thee,' Southey, and thy readers too.[2]

235   Next comes the dull disciple of thy school,
That mild apostate from poetic rule
The simple Wordsworth, framer of a lay
As soft as evening in his favourite May,[3]
Who warns his friend 'to shake off toil and trouble,
240   And quit his books, for fear of growing double;'[4]
Who, both by precept and example, shows
That prose is verse, and verse is merely prose;
Convincing all, by demonstration plain,
Poetic souls delight in prose insane;
245   And Christmas stories tortured into rhyme
Contain the essence of the true sublime.
Thus, when he tells the tale of Betty Foy,
The idiot mother of 'an idiot boy;'

Mistress Cowley, have not exalted the epic muse; but, as Mr Southey's poem 'disdains the appellation,' allow us to ask – has he substituted any thing better in its stead? or must he be content to rival Sir Richard Blackmore in the quantity as well as quality of his verse?

1. See 'The Old Woman of Berkley,' a ballad, by Mr Southey, wherein an aged gentlewoman is carried away by Beelzebub, on a 'high-trotting horse.'
2. The last line, 'God help thee,' is an evident plagiarism from the Anti-jacobin to Mr Southey, on his Dactylics.
3. ['*Unjust*.' – B. 1816.]
4. Lyrical Ballads, p. 4. – 'The Tables Turned.' Stanza 1.

'Up, up, my friend, and clear your looks;
    Why all this toil and trouble?
Up, up, my friend, and quit your books,
    Or surely you'll grow double.

A moon-struck, silly lad, who lost his way,
250   And, like his bard, confounded night with day;[1]
So close on each pathetic part he dwells,
And each adventure so sublimely tells,
That all who view the 'idiot in his glory'
Conceive the bard the hero of the story.

255   Shall gentle Coleridge pass unnoticed here,
To turgid ode and tumid stanza dear?
Though themes of innocence amuse him best,
Yet still obscurity's a welcome guest.
If Inspiration should her aid refuse
260   To him who takes a pixy for a muse,[2]
Yet none in lofty numbers can surpass
The bard who soars to elegise an ass.
So well the subject suits his noble mind,
He brays, the laureat of the long-ear'd kind.

265   Oh! wonder-working Lewis! monk, or bard,
Who fain wouldst make Parnassus a church-yard!
Lo! wreaths of yew, not laurel, bind thy brow,
Thy muse a sprite, Apollo's sexton thou!
Whether on ancient tombs thou takest thy stand,
270   By gibb'ring spectres hail'd, thy kindred band;
Or tracest chaste descriptions on thy page,
To please the females of our modest age;
All hail, M.P.![3] from whose infernal brain
Thin sheeted phantoms glide, a grisly train;

1. Mr W. in his preface labours hard to prove, that prose and verse are much the same; and certainly his precepts and practice are strictly conformable: –

> 'And thus to Betty's questions he
>   Made answer, like a traveller bold.
> The cock did crow, to-whoo, to-whoo,
>   And the sun did shine so cold,' &c. &c., p. 129.

2. Coleridge's Poems, p. 11, Songs of the Pixies, i.e. Devonshire Fairies; p. 42, we have, 'Lines to a young Lady:' and, p. 52, 'Lines to a young Ass.'
3. 'For every one knows little Matt's an M.P.' – See a poem to Mr Lewis, in 'The Statesman,' supposed to be written by Mr Jekyll.

275 At whose command 'grim women' throng in crowds,
And kings of fire, of water, and of clouds,
With 'small gray men,' 'wild yagers,' and what not,
To crown with honour thee and Walter Scott;
Again all hail! if tales like thine may please,
280 St Luke alone can vanquish the disease;
Even Satan's self with thee might dread to dwell,
And in thy skull discern a deeper hell.

        Who in soft guise, surrounded by a choir
Of virgins melting, not to Vesta's fire,
285 With sparkling eyes, and cheek by passion flush'd,
Strikes his wild lyre, whilst listening dames are hush'd?
'Tis Little! young Catullus of his day,
As sweet, but as immoral, in his lay!
Grieved to condemn, the muse must still be just,
290 Nor spare melodious advocates of lust.
Pure is the flame which o'er her altar burns;
From grosser incense with disgust she turns:
Yet kind to youth, this expiation o'er,
She bids thee 'mend thy line, and sin no more.'

295   For thee, translator of the tinsel song,
To whom such glittering ornaments belong,
Hibernian Strangford! with thine eyes of blue,[1]
And boasted locks of red or auburn hue,
Whose plaintive strain each love-sick miss admires,
300 And o'er harmonious fustian half expires,
Learn, if thou canst, to yield thine author's sense,
Nor vend thy sonnets on a false pretence.
Think'st thou to gain thy verse a higher place,
By dressing Camoëns[2] in a suit of lace?

1. The reader, who may wish for an explanation of this, may refer to 'Strangford's Camoëns,' p. 127, note to p. 56, or to the last page of the Edinburgh Review of Strangford's Camoëns.
2. It is also to be remarked, that the things given to the public as poems of Camoëns are no more to be found in the original Portuguese, than in the Song of Solomon.

305   Mend, Strangford! mend thy morals and thy taste;
       Be warm, but pure; be amorous, but be chaste:
       Cease to deceive; thy pilfer'd harp restore,
       Nor teach the Lusian bard to copy Moore.

       Behold! — ye tarts! one moment spare the text —
310   Hayley's last work, and worst — until his next;
       Whether he spin poor couplets into plays,
       Or damn the dead with purgatorial praise,
       His style in youth or age is still the same,
       For ever feeble and for ever tame.
315   Triumphant first see 'Temper's Triumphs' shine!
       At least I'm sure they triumph'd over mine.
       Of 'Music's Triumphs,' all who read may swear
       That luckless music never triumph'd there.[1]

       Moravians, rise! bestow some meet reward
320   On dull devotion — Lo! the Sabbath bard,
       Sepulchral Grahame,[2] pours his notes sublime
       In mangled prose, nor e'en aspires to rhyme;
       Breaks into blank the Gospel of St Luke,
       And boldly pilfers from the Pentateuch;
325   And, undisturb'd by conscientious qualms,
       Perverts the Prophets, and purloins the Psalms.

       Hail, Sympathy! thy soft idea brings
       A thousand visions of a thousand things,
       And shows, still whimpering through threescore of years,
330   The maudlin prince of mournful sonneteers.
       And art thou not their prince, harmonious Bowles!
       Thou first, great oracle of tender souls?

1. Hayley's two most notorious verse productions are 'Triumphs of Temper,' and 'The Triumph of Music.' He has also written much comedy in rhyme, epistles, &c. &c. As he is rather an elegant writer of notes and biography, let us recommend Pope's advice to Wycherley to Mr H.'s consideration, viz. 'to convert his poetry into prose,' which may be easily done by taking away the final syllable of each couplet.
2. Mr Grahame has poured forth two volumes of cant, under the name of 'Sabbath Walks,' and 'Biblical Pictures.'

Whether thou sing'st with equal ease, and grief,
The fall of empires, or a yellow leaf;
335   Whether thy muse most lamentably tells
What merry sounds proceed from Oxford bells,[1]
Or, still in bells delighting, finds a friend
In every chime that jingled from Ostend;
Ah! how much juster were thy muse's hap,
340   If to thy bells thou wouldst but add a cap!
Delightful Bowles! still blessing and still blest,
All love thy strain, but children like it best.
'Tis thine, with gentle Little's moral song,
To soothe the mania of the amorous throng!
345   With thee our nursery damsels shed their tears,
Ere miss as yet completes her infant years:
But in her teens thy whining powers are vain;
She quits poor Bowles for Little's purer strain.
Now to soft themes thou scornest to confine
350   The lofty numbers of a harp like thine;
'Awake a louder and a loftier strain,'[2]
Such as none heard before, or will again!
Where all Discoveries jumbled from the flood,
Since first the leaky ark reposed in mud,
355   By more or less, are sung in every book,
From Captain Noah down to Captain Cook.

1. See Bowles's 'Sonnet to Oxford,' and 'Stanzas on hearing the Bells of
Ostend.'
2. 'Awake a louder,' &c., is the first line in Bowles's 'Spirit of Discovery;' a
very spirited and pretty dwarf-epic. Among other exquisite lines we have
the following: –

'A kiss
Stole on the list'ning silence, never yet
Here heard; they trembled even as if the power,' &c. &c.

That is, the woods of Madeira trembled to a kiss; very much astonished, as
well they might be, at such a phenomenon. – ['Misquoted and misunder-
stood by me; but not intentionally. It was not the "woods," but the people in
them who trembled – why, Heaven only knows – unless they were overheard
making the prodigious smack.' – B. 1816.]

Nor this alone; but, pausing on the road,
The bard sighs forth a gentle episode;[1]
And gravely tells – attend, each beauteous miss! –
360   When first Madeira trembled to a kiss.
Bowles! in thy memory let this precept dwell,
Stick to thy sonnets, man! – at least they sell.
But if some new-born whim, or larger bribe,
Prompt thy crude brain, and claim thee for a scribe;
365   If chance some bard, though once by dunces fear'd,
Now, prone in dust, can only be revered;
If Pope, whose fame and genius, from the first,
Have foil'd the best of critics, needs the worst,
Do thou essay: each fault, each failing scan;
370   The first of poets was, alas! but man.
Rake from each ancient dunghill ev'ry pearl,
Consult Lord Fanny, and confide in Curll;[2]
Let all the scandals of a former age
Perch on thy pen, and flutter o'er thy page;
375   Affect a candour which thou canst not feel,
Clothe envy in the garb of honest zeal;
Write, as if St John's soul could still inspire,
And do from hate what Mallet[3] did for hire.
Oh! hadst thou lived in that congenial time,
380   To rave with Dennis, and with Ralph to rhyme;[4]

1. The episode above alluded to is the story of 'Robert a Machin' and 'Anna d'Arfet,' a pair of constant lovers, who performed the kiss above mentioned, that startled the woods of Madeira.

2. Curll is one of the heroes of the Dunciad, and was a bookseller. Lord Fanny is the poetical name of Lord Hervey, author of 'Lines to the Imitator of Horace.'

3. Lord Bolingbroke hired Mallet to traduce Pope after his decease, because the poet had retained some copies of a work by Lord Bolingbroke – the 'Patriot King,' – which that splendid, but malignant, genius had ordered to be destroyed.

4. Dennis the critic, and Ralph the rhymester. –

'Silence, ye wolves! while Ralph to Cynthia howls,
Making night hideous: answer him, ye owls!' – Dunciad.

Throng'd with the rest around his living head,
Not raised thy hoof against the lion dead;[1]
A meet reward had crown'd thy glorious gains,
And link'd thee to the Dunciad for thy pains.

385   Another epic! Who inflicts again
More books of blank upon the sons of men?
Bœotian Cottle, rich Bristowa's boast,
Imports old stories from the Cambrian coast,
And sends his goods to market – all alive!
390   Lines forty thousand, cantos twenty-five!
Fresh fish from Helicon![2] who'll buy? who'll buy?
The precious bargain's cheap – in faith, not I.
Your turtle-feeder's verse must needs be flat,
Though Bristol bloat him with the verdant fat;
395   If Commerce fills the purse, she clogs the brain,
And Amos Cottle strikes the lyre in vain.
In him an author's luckless lot behold,
Condemn'd to make the books which once he sold.
Oh, Amos Cottle! – Phœbus! what a name
400   To fill the speaking trump of future fame! –
Oh, Amos Cottle! for a moment think
What meagre profits spring from pen and ink!
When thus devoted to poetic dreams,
Who will peruse thy prostituted reams?
405   Oh pen perverted! paper misapplied!
Had Cottle[3] still adorn'd the counter's side,
Bent o'er the desk, or, born to useful toils,
Been taught to make the paper which he soils,
Plough'd, delved, or plied the oar with lusty limb,
410   He had not sung of Wales, nor I of him.

1. See Bowles's late edition of Pope's works, for which he received three hundred pounds. Thus Mr B. has experienced how much easier it is to profit by the reputation of another, than to elevate his own.
2. ['Fresh fish from Helicon!' – 'Helicon' is a mountain, and not a fish-pond. It should have been 'Hippocrene.' – B. 1816.]
3. Mr Cottle, Amos, Joseph, I don't know which, but one or both, are sellers of books they did not write, and now writers of books they do not sell, have published a pair of epics. 'Alfred,' – (poor Alfred! Pye has been at him too!) – 'Alfred,' and the 'Fall of Cambria.'

As Sisyphus against the infernal steep
Rolls the huge rock whose motions ne'er may sleep,
So up thy hill, ambrosial Richmond, heaves
Dull Maurice[1] all his granite weight of leaves:
415 Smooth, solid monuments of mental pain!
The petrifactions of a plodding brain,
That, ere they reach the top, fall lumbering back again.

With broken lyre, and cheek serenely pale,
Lo! sad Alcæus wanders down the vale;
420 Though fair they rose, and might have bloom'd at last,
His hopes have perish'd by the northern blast:
Nipp'd in the bud by Caledonian gales,
His blossoms wither as the blast prevails!
O'er his lost works let *classic* Sheffield weep;
425 May no rude hand disturb their early sleep![2]

Yet say! why should the bard at once resign
His claim to favour from the sacred nine?
For ever startled by the mingled howl
Of northern wolves, that still in darkness prowl;
430 A coward brood, which mangle as they prey,
By hellish instinct, all that cross their way;
Aged or young, the living or the dead,
No mercy find – these harpies must be fed.
Why do the injured unresisting yield
435 The calm possession of their native field?
Why tamely thus before their fangs retreat,
Nor hunt the bloodhounds back to Arthur's Seat?[3]

1. Mr Maurice hath manufactured the component parts of a ponderous
quarto, upon the beauties of 'Richmond Hill,' and the like: – it also takes in
a charming view of Turnham Green, Hammersmith, Brentford, Old and
New, and the parts adjacent.
2. Poor Montgomery, though praised by every English Review, has been
bitterly reviled by the Edinburgh. After all, the bard of Sheffield is a man of
considerable genius. His 'Wanderer of Switzerland' is worth a thousand
'Lyrical Ballads,' and at least fifty 'degraded epics.'
3. Arthur's Seat; the hill which overhangs Edinburgh.

Health to immortal Jeffrey! once, in name,
England could boast a judge almost the same;
440   In soul so like, so merciful, yet just,
Some think that Satan has resign'd his trust,
And given the spirit to the world again,
To sentence letters, as he sentenced men.
With hand less mighty, but with heart as black,
445   With voice as willing to decree the rack;
Bred in the courts betimes, though all that law
As yet hath taught him is to find a flaw;
Since well instructed in the patriot school
To rail at party, though a party tool,
450   Who knows, if chance his patrons should restore
Back to the sway they forfeited before,
His scribbling toils some recompense may meet,
And raise this Daniel to the judgment-seat?[1]
Let Jeffries' shade indulge the pious hope,
455   And greeting thus, present him with a rope:
'Heir to my virtues! man of equal mind!
Skill'd to condemn as to traduce mankind,
This cord receive, for thee reserved with care,
To wield in judgment, and at length to wear.'

460   Health to great Jeffrey! Heaven preserve his life,
To flourish on the fertile shores of Fife,
And guard it sacred in its future wars,
Since authors sometimes seek the field of Mars!
Can none remember that eventful day,[2]
465   That ever-glorious, almost fatal fray,
When Little's leadless pistol met his eye,
And Bow-street myrmidons stood laughing by?[3]
Oh, day disastrous! On her firm-set rock,
Dunedin's castle felt a secret shock;

1. ['Too ferocious – this is mere insanity.' – B. 1816.]
2. ['All this is bad, because personal.' – B. 1816.]
3. In 1806, Messrs Jeffrey and Moore met at Chalk-Farm. The duel was prevented by the interference of the magistracy; and, on examination, the balls of the pistols were found to have evaporated. This incident gave occasion to much waggery in the daily prints.

470   Dark roll'd the sympathetic waves of Forth,
      Low groan'd the startled whirlwinds of the north;
      Tweed ruffled half his waves to form a tear,
      The other half pursued its calm career;[1]
      Arthur's steep summit nodded to its base,
475   The surly Tolbooth scarcely kept her place.
      The Tolbooth felt – for marble sometimes can,
      On such occasions, feel as much as man –
      The Tolbooth felt defrauded of his charms,
      If Jeffrey died, except within her arms:[2]
480   Nay last, not least, on that portentous morn,
      The sixteenth story, where himself was born,
      His patrimonial garret, fell to ground,
      And pale Edina shudder'd at the sound:
      Strew'd were the streets around with milk-white reams,
485   Flow'd all the Canongate with inky streams;
      This of his candour seem'd the sable dew,
      That of his valour show'd the bloodless hue;
      And all with justice deem'd the two combined
      The mingled emblems of his mighty mind.
490   But Caledonia's goddess hover'd o'er
      The field, and saved him from the wrath of Moore;
      From either pistol snatch'd the vengeful lead,
      And straight restored it to her favourite's head;
      That head, with greater than magnetic pow'r,
495   Caught it, as Danaë caught the golden show'r,
      And, though the thickening dross will scarce refine,
      Augments its ore, and is itself a mine.
      'My son,' she cried, 'ne'er thirst for gore again,
      Resign the pistol and resume the pen;

1. The Tweed here behaved with proper decorum; it would have been highly reprehensible in the English half of the river to have shown the smallest symptom of apprehension.

2. This display of sympathy on the part of the Tolbooth (the principal prison in Edinburgh), which truly seems to have been most affected on this occasion, is much to be commended. It was to be apprehended, that the many unhappy criminals executed in the front might have rendered the edifice more callous. She is said to be of the softer sex, because her delicacy of feeling on this day was truly feminine, though, like most feminine impulses, perhaps a little selfish.

500 O'er politics and poesy preside,
　　Boast of thy country, and Britannia's guide!
　　For long as Albion's heedless sons submit,
　　Or Scottish taste decides on English wit,
　　So long shall last thine unmolested reign,
505 Nor any dare to take thy name in vain.
　　Behold, a chosen band shall aid thy plan,
　　And own thee chieftain of the critic clan.
　　First in the oat-fed phalanx shall be seen
　　The travell'd thane, Athenian Aberdeen.[1]
510 Herbert shall wield Thor's hammer,[2] and sometimes,
　　In gratitude, thou'lt praise his rugged rhymes,
　　Smug Sydney[3] too thy bitter page shall seek,
　　And classic Hallam,[4] much renown'd for Greek;
　　Scott may perchance his name and influence lend,
515 And paltry Pillans[5] shall traduce his friend;

1. His lordship has been much abroad, is a member of the Athenian Society, and reviewer of 'Gell's Topography of Troy.'
2. Mr Herbert is a translator of Icelandic and other poetry. One of the principal pieces is a 'Song on the Recovery of Thor's Hammer:' the translation is a pleasant chant in the vulgar tongue, and endeth thus: –

> 'Instead of money and rings, I wot,
> The hammer's bruises were her lot.
> Thus Odin's son his hammer got.'

3. The Rev. Sydney Smith, the reputed author of Peter Plymley's Letters, and sundry criticisms.
4. Mr Hallam reviewed Payne Knight's 'Taste,' and was exceedingly severe on some Greek verses therein. It was not discovered that the lines were Pindar's till the press rendered it impossible to cancel the critique, which still stands an everlasting monument of Hallam's ingenuity.
　　Note added to second edition. – The said Hallam is incensed because he is falsely accused, seeing that he never dineth at Holland House. If this be true, I am sorry – not for having said so, but on his account, as I understand his lordship's feasts are preferable to his compositions. – If he did not review Lord Holland's performance, I am glad, because it must have been painful to read, and irksome to praise it. If Mr Hallam will tell me who did review it, the real name shall find a place in the text; provided, nevertheless, the said name be of two orthodox musical syllables, and will come into the verse: till then, Hallam must stand for want of a better.
5. Pillans is a tutor at Eton.

While gay Thalia's luckless votary, Lambe,[1]
Damn'd like the devil, devil-like will damn.
Known be thy name, unbounded be thy sway!
Thy Holland's banquets shall each toil repay;
520 While grateful Britain yields the praise she owes
To Holland's hirelings and to learning's foes.
Yet mark one caution ere thy next Review
Spread its light wings of saffron and of blue,
Beware lest blundering Brougham[2] destroy the sale,
525 Turn beef to bannocks, cauliflowers to kail.'
Thus having said, the kilted goddess kist
Her son, and vanish'd in a Scottish mist.[3]

Then prosper, Jeffrey! pertest of the train
Whom Scotland pampers with her fiery grain!
530 Whatever blessing waits a genuine Scot,
In double portion swells thy glorious lot;
For thee Edina culls her evening sweets,
And showers their odours on thy candid sheets,
Whose hue and fragrance to thy work adhere –
535 This scents its pages, and that gilds its rear.[4]

1. The Hon. George Lambe reviewed 'Beresford's Miseries,' and is more-over, author of a farce enacted with much applause at the Priory, Stanmore; and damned with great expedition at the late theatre, Covent Garden. It was entitled, 'Whistle for It.'
2. Mr Brougham, in No. XXV, of the Edinburgh Review, throughout the article concerning Don Pedro de Cevallos, has displayed more politics than policy; many of the worthy burgesses of Edinburgh being so incensed at the infamous principles it evinces, as to have withdrawn their subscriptions.
3. I ought to apologise to the worthy deities for introducing a new goddess with short petticoats to their notice: but, alas! what was to be done? I could not say Caledonia's genius, it being well known there is no such genius to be found from Clackmanan to Caithness; yet, without supernatural agency, how was Jeffrey to be saved? The national 'kelpies' are too unpoetical, and the 'brownies' and 'gude neighbours' (spirits of a good disposition) refused to extricate him. A goddess, therefore, has been called for the purpose; and great ought to be the gratitude of Jeffrey, seeing it is the only communication he ever held, or is likely to hold, with any thing heavenly.
4. See the colour of the back binding of the Edinburgh Review.

Lo! blushing Itch, coy nymph, enamour'd grown,
Forsakes the rest, and cleaves to thee alone;
And, too unjust to other Pictish men,
Enjoys thy person, and inspires thy pen!

540   Illustrious Holland! hard would be his lot,
His hirelings mention'd, and himself forgot![1]
Holland, with Henry Petty at his back,
The whipper-in and huntsman of the pack.
Blest be the banquets spread at Holland House,
545   Where Scotchmen feed, and critics may carouse!
Long, long beneath that hospitable roof
Shall Grub-street dine, while duns are kept aloof.
See honest Hallam lay aside his fork,
Resume his pen, review his Lordship's work,
550   And, grateful for the dainties on his plate,
Declare his landlord can at least translate![2]
Dunedin! view thy children with delight,
They write for food – and feed because they write:
And lest, when heated with the unusual grape,
555   Some glowing thoughts should to the press escape,
And tinge with red the female reader's cheek,
My lady skims the cream of each critique;
Breathes o'er the page her purity of soul,
Reforms each error, and refines the whole.[3]

560   Now to the Drama turn – Oh! motley sight!
What precious scenes the wondering eyes invite!
Puns, and a prince within a barrel pent,[4]
And Dibdin's nonsense yield complete content.

1. ['Bad enough, and on mistaken grounds too.' – B. 1816.]
2. Lord Holland has translated some specimens of Lope de Vega, inserted in his life of the author. Both are bepraised by his *disinterested* guests. –
3. Certain it is, her ladyship is suspected of having displayed her matchless wit in the Edinburgh Review. However that may be, we know, from good authority, that the manuscripts are submitted to her perusal – no doubt, for correction.
4. In the melo-drama of Tekeli, that heroic prince is clapt into a barrel on the stage; a new asylum for distressed heroes.

Though now, thank Heaven! the Rosciomania's o'er,
565 And full-grown actors are endured once more;
Yet what avail their vain attempts to please,
While British critics suffer scenes like these;
While Reynolds vents his 'dammes!' 'poohs!' and
          'zounds!'[1]
And common-place and common sense confounds?
570 While Kenney's 'World' – ah! where is Kenney's wit? –
Tires the sad gallery, lulls the listless pit;
And Beaumont's pilfer'd Caratach affords
A tragedy complete in all but words?[2]
Who but must mourn, while these are all the rage,
575 The degradation of our vaunted stage!
Heavens! is all sense of shame and talent gone?
Have we no living bard of merit? – none!
Awake, George Colman! Cumberland, awake!
Ring the alarum bell! let folly quake!
580 Oh, Sheridan! if aught can move thy pen,
Let Comedy assume her throne again;
Abjure the mummery of the German schools;
Leave new Pizarros to translating fools;
Give, as thy last memorial to the age,
585 One classic drama, and reform the stage.
Gods! o'er those boards shall Folly rear her head,
Where Garrick trod, and Siddons lives to tread?
On those shall Farce display Buffoon'ry's mask,
And Hook conceal his heroes in a cask?
590 Shall sapient managers new scenes produce
From Cherry, Skeffington, and Mother Goose?
While Shakspeare, Otway, Massinger, forgot,
On stalls must moulder, or in closets rot?
Lo! with what pomp the daily prints proclaim
595 The rival candidates for Attic fame!

1. All these are favourite expressions of Mr Reynolds, and prominent in his
comedies, living and defunct.
2. Mr T. Sheridan, the new manager of Drury Lane theatre, stripped the
tragedy of Bonduca of the dialogue, and exhibited the scenes as the spectacle
of Caractacus. Was this worthy of his sire? or of himself? –

In grim array though Lewis' spectres rise,
Still Skeffington and Goose divide the prize.
And sure *great* Skeffington must claim our praise,
For skirtless coats and skeletons of plays
600   Renown'd alike; whose genius ne'er confines
Her flight to garnish Greenwood's gay designs;[1]
Nor sleeps with 'Sleeping Beauties,' but anon
In five facetious acts comes thundering on,[2]
While poor John Bull, bewilder'd with the scene,
605   Stares, wondering what the devil it can mean;
But as some hands applaud, a venal few!
Rather than sleep, why John applauds it too.

Such are we now. Ah! wherefore should we turn
To what our fathers were, unless to mourn?
610   Degenerate Britons! are ye dead to shame,
Or, kind to dulness, do you fear to blame?
Well may the nobles of our present race
Watch each distortion of a Naldi's face;
Well may they smile on Italy's buffoons,
615   And worship Catalani's pantaloons,[3]
Since their own drama yields no fairer trace
Of wit than puns, of humour than grimace.

Then let Ausonia, skill'd in every art
To soften manners, but corrupt the heart,
620   Pour her exotic follies o'er the town,
To sanction Vice, and hunt Decorum down:
Let wedded strumpets languish o'er Deshayes,
And bless the promise which his form displays;

1. Mr Greenwood is, we believe, scene-painter to Drury-lane theatre – as such, Mr Skeffington is much indebted to him.
2. Mr [now Sir Lumley] Skeffington is the illustrious author of the 'Sleeping Beauty;' and some comedies, particularly 'Maids and Bachelors:' Baccalaurii baculo magis quam lauro digni.
3. Naldi and Catalani require little notice; for the visage of the one and the salary of the other, will enable us long to recollect these amusing vagabonds. Besides, we are still black and blue from the squeeze on the first night of the lady's appearance in trousers.

While Gayton bounds before th' enraptured looks
625   Of hoary marquises and stripling dukes:
Let high-born lechers eye the lively Prêsle
Twirl her light limbs, that spurn the needless veil;
Let Angiolini bare her breast of snow,
Wave the white arm, and point the pliant toe;
630   Collini trill her love-inspiring song,
Strain her fair neck, and charm the listening throng!
Whet not your scythe, suppressors of our vice!
Reforming saints! too delicately nice!
By whose decrees, our sinful souls to save,
635   No Sunday tankards foam, no barbers shave;
And beer undrawn, and beards unmown, display
Your holy reverence for the Sabbath-day.

Or hail at once the patron and the pile
Of vice and folly, Greville and Argyle![1]
640   Where yon proud palace, Fashion's hallow'd fane,
Spreads wide her portals for the motley train,
Behold the new Petronius[2] of the day,
Our arbiter of pleasure and of play!
There the hired eunuch, the Hesperian choir,
645   The melting lute, the soft lascivious lyre,
The song from Italy, the step from France,
The midnight orgy, and the mazy dance,

1. To prevent any blunder, such as mistaking a street for a man, I beg leave to state, that it is the institution, and not the duke of that name, which is here alluded to. A gentleman, with whom I am slightly acquainted, lost in the Argyle Rooms several thousand pounds at backgammon. ['True. It was Billy Way who lost the money. I knew him, and was a subscriber to the Argyle at the time of the event.' – B. 1816.] It is but justice to the manager in this instance to say, that some degree of disapprobation was manifested: but why are the implements of gaming allowed in a place devoted to the society of both sexes? A pleasant thing for the wives and daughters of those who are blest or cursed with such connections, to hear the billiard-tables rattling in one room, and the dice in another! That this is the case I myself can testify, as a late unworthy member of an institution which materially affects the morals of the higher orders, while the lower may not even move to the sound of a tabor and fiddle, without a chance of indictment for riotous behaviour.

2. Petronius 'Arbiter elegantiarum' to Nero, 'and a very pretty fellow in his day,' as Mr Congreve's 'Old Bachelor' saith of Hannibal.

The smile of beauty, and the flush of wine,
For fops, fools, gamesters, knaves, and lords combine:
650 Each to his humour – Comus all allows;
Champaign, dice, music, or your neighbour's spouse.
Talk not to us, ye starving sons of trade!
Of piteous ruin, which ourselves have made;
In Plenty's sunshine Fortune's minions bask,
655 Nor think of poverty, except 'en masque,'
When for the night some lately titled ass
Appears the beggar which his grandsire was,
The curtain dropp'd, the gay burletta o'er,
The audience take their turn upon the floor;
660 Now round the room the circling dow'gers sweep,
Now in loose waltz the thin-clad daughters leap;
The first in lengthen'd line majestic swim,
The last display the free unfetter'd limb!
Those for Hibernia's lusty sons repair
665 With art the charms which nature could not spare;
These after husbands wing their eager flight,
Nor leave much mystery for the nuptial night.

Oh! blest retreats of infamy and ease,
Where, all forgotten but the power to please,
670 Each maid may give a loose to genial thought,
Each swain may teach new systems, or be taught:
There the blithe youngster, just return'd from Spain,
Cuts the light pack, or calls the rattling main;
The jovial caster's set, and seven's the nick,
675 Or – done! – a thousand on the coming trick!
If, mad with loss, existence 'gins to tire,
And all your hope or wish is to expire,
Here's Powell's pistol ready for your life,
And, kinder still, two Pagets for your wife;
680 Fit consummation of an earthly race
Begun in folly, ended in disgrace;
While none but menials o'er the bed of death,
Wash thy red wounds, or watch thy wavering breath;

Traduced by liars, and forgot by all,
685   The mangled victim of a drunken brawl,
To live like Clodius, and like Falkland fall.[1]

Truth! rouse some genuine bard, and guide his hand
To drive this pestilence from out the land.
E'en I – least thinking of a thoughtless throng,
690   Just skill'd to know the right and choose the wrong,
Freed at that age when reason's shield is lost,
To fight my course through passion's countless host,[2]
Whom every path of pleasure's flow'ry way
Has lured in turn, and all have led astray –
695   E'en I must raise my voice, e'en I must feel
Such scenes, such men, destroy the public weal;
Although some kind, censorious friend will say,
'What art thou better, meddling fool,[3] than they?'
And every brother rake will smile to see
700   That miracle, a moralist in me.
No matter – when some bard in virtue strong,
Gifford perchance, shall raise the chastening song,
Then sleep my pen for ever! and my voice
Be only heard to hail him, and rejoice;
705   Rejoice, and yield my feeble praise, though I
May feel the lash that Virtue must apply.

As for the smaller fry, who swarm in shoals
From silly Hafiz up to simple Bowles,[4]
Why should we call them from their dark abode,
710   In broad St Giles's or in Tottenham-road?

1. I knew the late Lord Falkland well. On Sunday night I beheld him presiding at his own table, in all the honest pride of hospitality; on Wednesday morning, at three o'clock, I saw stretched before me all that remained of courage, feeling, and a host of passions. He was a gallant and successful officer: his faults were the faults of a sailor – as such, Britons will forgive them. He died like a brave man in a better cause; for had he fallen in like manner on the deck of the frigate to which he was just appointed, his last moments would have been held up by his countrymen as an example to succeeding heroes.
2. ['Yes: and a precious chase they led me.' – B. 1816.]
3. ['*Fool* enough, certainly, then, and no wiser since.' – B. 1816.]
4. What would be the sentiments of the Persian Anacreon, Hafiz, could he

Or (since some men of fashion nobly dare
To scrawl in verse) from Bond-street or the Square?
If things of ton their harmless lays indite,
Most wisely doom'd to shun the public sight,
715 What harm? In spite of every critic elf,
Sir T. may read his stanzas to himself;
Miles Andrews still his strength in couplets try,
And live in prologues, though his dramas die.
Lords too are bards, such things at times befall,
720 And 'tis some praise in peers to write at all.
Yet, did or taste or reason sway the times,
Ah! who would take their titles with their rhymes?
Roscommon! Sheffield! with your spirits fled,
No future laurels deck a noble head;
725 No muse will cheer, with renovating smile,
The paralytic puling of Carlisle.
The puny schoolboy and his early lay
Men pardon, if his follies pass away;
But who forgives the senior's ceaseless verse,
730 Whose hairs grow hoary as his rhymes grow worse?
What heterogeneous honours deck the peer!
Lord, rhymester, petit-maître, pamphleteer![1]
So dull in youth, so drivelling in his age,
His scenes alone had damn'd our sinking stage;
735 But managers for once cried, 'Hold, enough!'
Nor drugg'd their audience with the tragic stuff.
Yet at their judgment let his lordship laugh,
And case his volumes in congenial calf;
Yes! doff that covering, where morocco shines,
740 And hang a calf-skin[2] on those recreant lines.[3]

------

rise from his splendid sepulchre at Sheeraz, (where he reposes with Ferdousi
and Sadi, the oriental Homer and Catullus,) and behold his name assumed
by one Stott of Dromore, the most impudent and execrable of literary
poachers for the daily prints?

1. The Earl of Carlisle has lately published an eighteen-penny pamphlet on
the state of the stage, and offers his plan for building a new theatre. It is to be
hoped his lordship will be permitted to bring forward any thing for the
stage – except his own tragedies.
2.   'Doff that lion's hide,
          And hang a calf-skin on those recreant limbs.' *Shak. King John.*

With you, ye Druids! rich in native lead,
Who daily scribble for your daily bread;
With you I war not: Gifford's heavy hand
Has crush'd, without remorse, your numerous band.
745 On 'all the talents' vent your venal spleen;
Want is your plea, let pity be your screen.
Let monodies on Fox regale your crew,
And Melville's Mantle[1] prove a blanket too!
One common Lethe waits each hapless bard,
750 And, peace be with you! 'tis your best reward.
Such damning fame as Dunciads only give
Could bid your lines beyond a morning live;
But now at once your fleeting labours close,
With names of greater note in blest repose.
755 Far be't from me unkindly to upbraid
The lovely Rosa's prose in masquerade,
Whose strains, the faithful echoes of her mind,
Leave wondering comprehension far behind.[2]
Though Crusca's bards no more our journals fill,
760 Some stragglers skirmish round the columns still;
Last of the howling host which once was Bell's,
Matilda snivels yet, and Hafiz yells;
And Merry's metaphors appear anew,
Chain'd to the signature of O.P.Q.[3]

———————

Lord Carlisle's works, most resplendently bound, form a conspicuous orna-
ment to his book-shelves: –

    'The rest is all but leather and prunella.'

3. ['Wrong also – the provocation was not sufficient to justify the acerbity.'
– B. 1816.]

1. 'Melville's Mantle,' a parody on 'Elijah's Mantle,' a poem.
2. This lovely little Jessica, the daughter of the noted Jew King, seems to be
a follower of the Della Crusca school, and has published two volumes of
very respectable absurdities in rhyme, as times go; besides sundry novels in
the style of the first edition of the Monk. – ['She since married the Morning
Post – an exceeding good match; and is now dead – which is better.' – B.
1816.]
3. These are the signatures of various worthies who figure in the poetical
departments of the newspapers.

765   When some brisk youth, the tenant of a stall,
       Employs a pen less pointed than his awl,
       Leaves his snug shop, forsakes his store of shoes,
       St Crispin quits, and cobbles for the muse,
       Heavens! how the vulgar stare! how crowds applaud!
770   How ladies read, and literati laud![1]
       If chance some wicked wag should pass his jest,
       'Tis sheer ill-nature – don't the world know best?
       Genius must guide when wits admire the rhyme,
       And Capel Lofft[2] declares 'tis quite sublime.
775   Hear, then, ye happy sons of needless trade!
       Swains! quit the plough, resign the useless spade!
       Lo! Burns and Bloomfield, nay, a greater far,
       Gifford was born beneath an adverse star,
       Forsook the labours of a servile state,
780   Stemm'd the rude storm, and triumph'd over fate:
       Then why no more? if Phœbus smiled on you,
       Bloomfield! why not on brother Nathan too?[3]
       Him too the mania, not the muse, has seized;
       Not inspiration, but a mind diseased:
785   And now no boor can seek his last abode,
       No common be enclosed without an ode.
       Oh! since increased refinement deigns to smile
       On Britain's sons, and bless our genial isle,
       Let poesy go forth, pervade the whole,
790   Alike the rustic, and mechanic soul!
       Ye tuneful cobblers! still your notes prolong,
       Compose at once a slipper and a song;
       So shall the fair your handywork peruse,
       Your sonnets sure shall please – perhaps your shoes.

1. ['This was meant for poor Blackett, who was then patronised by A. J. B.'
(Lady Byron); 'but *that* I did not know, or this would not have been
written, at least I think not.' – B. 1816.]
2. Capel Lofft, Esq., the Mæcenas of shoemakers, and preface-writer-gen-
eral to distressed versemen; a kind of gratis accoucheur to those who wish to
be delivered of rhyme, but do not know how to bring forth.
3. See Nathaniel Bloomfield's ode, elegy, or whatever he or any one else
chooses to call it, on the enclosure of 'Honington Green.'

795 May Moorland weavers[1] boast Pindaric skill,
And tailors' lays be longer than their bill!
While punctual beaux reward the grateful notes,
And pay for poems – when they pay for coats.

To the famed throng now paid the tribute due,
800 Neglected genius! let me turn to you.
Come forth, oh Campbell![2] give thy talents scope;
Who dares aspire if thou must cease to hope?
And thou, melodious Rogers![3] rise at last,
Recall the pleasing memory of the past;
805 Arise! let blest remembrance still inspire,
And strike to wonted tones thy hallow'd lyre;
Restore Apollo to his vacant throne,
Assert thy country's honour and thine own.
What! must deserted Poesy still weep
810 Where her last hopes with pious Cowper sleep?
Unless, perchance, from his cold bier she turns,
To deck the turf that wraps her minstrel, Burns!
No! though contempt hath mark'd the spurious brood,
The race who rhyme from folly, or for food,
815 Yet still some genuine sons 'tis hers to boast,
Who, least affecting, still affect the most:
Feel as they write, and write but as they feel –
Bear witness Gifford,[4] Sotheby,[5] Macneil.[6]

1. Vide 'Recollections of a Weaver in the Moorlands of Staffordshire.'
2. It would be superfluous to recall to the mind of the reader the authors of 'The Pleasures of Memory' and 'The Pleasures of Hope,' the most beautiful didactic poems in our language, if we except Pope's 'Essay on Man:' but so many poetasters have started up, that even the names of Campbell and Rogers are become strange.
3. ['Rogers has not fulfilled the promise of his first poems, but has still very great merit.' – B. 1816.]
4. Gifford, author of the Baviad and Maviad, the first satires of the day, and translator of Juvenal.
5. Sotheby, translator of Wieland's Oberon and Virgil's Georgics, and author of 'Saul,' an epic poem.
6. Macneil, whose poems are deservedly popular, particularly 'Scotland's Scaith,' and the 'Waes of War,' of which ten thousand copies were sold in one month.

'Why slumbers Gifford?' once was ask'd in vain;
820 Why slumbers Gifford? let us ask again.
Are there no follies for his pen to purge?[1]
Are there no fools whose backs demand the scourge?
Are there no sins for satire's bard to greet?
Stalks not gigantic Vice in every street?
825 Shall peers or princes tread pollution's path,
And 'scape alike the law's and muse's wrath?
Nor blaze with guilty glare through future time,
Eternal beacons of consummate crime?
Arouse thee, Gifford! be thy promise claim'd,
830 Make bad men better, or at least ashamed.

    Unhappy White![2] while life was in its spring,
And thy young muse just waved her joyous wing,
The spoiler swept that soaring lyre away,
Which else had sounded an immortal lay.
835 Oh! what a noble heart was here undone,
When Science's self destroy'd her favourite son!
Yes, she too much indulged thy fond pursuit,
She sow'd the seeds, but death has reap'd the fruit.
'Twas thine own genius gave the final blow,
840 And help'd to plant the wound that laid thee low:
So the struck eagle, stretch'd upon the plain,
No more through rolling clouds to soar again,
View'd his own feather on the fatal dart,
And wing'd the shaft that quiver'd in his heart;
845 Keen were his pangs, but keener far to feel
He nursed the pinion which impell'd the steel;
While the same plumage that had warm'd his nest
Drank the last life-drop of his bleeding breast.

1. Mr Gifford promised publicly that the Baviad and Maviad should not be his last original works: let him remember, 'Mox in reluctantes dracones.'
2. Henry Kirke White died at Cambridge, in October, 1806, in consequence of too much exertion in the pursuit of studies that would have matured a mind which disease and poverty could not impair, and which death itself destroyed rather than subdued. His poems abound in such beauties as must impress the reader with the liveliest regret that so short a period was allotted to talents which would have dignified even the sacred functions he was destined to assume.

There be, who say, in these enlighten'd days,
850   That splendid lies are all the poet's praise;
That strain'd invention, ever on the wing,
Alone impels the modern bard to sing:
'Tis true, that all who rhyme – nay, all who write,
Shrink from that fatal word to genius – trite;
855   Yet Truth sometimes will lend her noblest fires,
And decorate the verse herself inspires:
This fact in Virtue's name let Crabbe[1] attest;
Though nature's sternest painter, yet the best.

And here let Shee[2] and Genius find a place,
860   Whose pen and pencil yield an equal grace;
To guide whose hand the sister arts combine,
And trace the poet's or the painter's line;
Whose magic touch can bid the canvass glow,
Or pour the easy rhyme's harmonious flow;
865   While honours, doubly merited, attend
The poet's rival, but the painter's friend.

Blest is the man who dares approach the bower
Where dwelt the muses at their natal hour;
Whose steps have press'd, whose eye has mark'd afar,
870   The clime that nursed the sons of song and war,
The scenes which glory still must hover o'er,
Her place of birth, her own Achaian shore.
But doubly blest is he whose heart expands
With hallow'd feelings for those classic lands;
875   Who rends the veil of ages long gone by,
And views their remnants with a poet's eye!
Wright![3] 'twas thy happy lot at once to view
Those shores of glory, and to sing them too;
And sure no common muse inspired thy pen
880   To hail the land of gods and godlike men.

1. ['I consider Crabbe and Coleridge as the first of these times, in point of
power and genius.' – B. 1816.]
2. Mr Shee, author of 'Rhymes on Art,' and 'Elements of Art.'
3. Waller Rodwell Wright, late consul-general for the Seven Islands, is
author of a very beautiful poem, just published: it is entitled 'Horæ Ionicæ,'
and is descriptive of the isles and the adjacent coast of Greece.

And you, associate bards![1] who snatch'd to light
Those gems too long withheld from modern sight;
Whose mingling taste combined to cull the wreath
Where Attic flowers Aonian odours breathe,
885 And all their renovated fragrance flung,
To grace the beauties of your native tongue;
Now let those minds, that nobly could transfuse
The glorious spirit of the Grecian muse,
Though soft the echo, scorn a borrow'd tone:
890 Resign Achaia's lyre, and strike your own.

Let these, or such as these, with just applause,
Restore the muse's violated laws;
But not in flimsy Darwin's pompous chime,
That mighty master of unmeaning rhyme,
895 Whose gilded cymbals, more adorn'd than clear,
The eye delighted, but fatigued the ear;
In show the simple lyre could once surpass,
But now, worn down, appear in native brass;
While all his train of hovering sylphs around
900 Evaporate in similes and sound:
Him let them shun, with him let tinsel die:
False glare attracts, but more offends the eye.[2]

Yet let them not to vulgar Wordsworth stoop,
The meanest object of the lowly group,
905 Whose verse, of all but childish prattle void,
Seems blessed harmony to Lamb and Lloyd:[3]
Let them – but hold, my muse, nor dare to teach
A strain far, far beyond thy humble reach:
The native genius with their being given
910 Will point the path, and peal their notes to heaven.

1. The translators of the Anthology, Bland and Merivale, have since pub-
lished separate poems, which evince genius that only requires opportunity
to attain eminence.
2. The neglect of the 'Botanic Garden' is some proof of returning taste. The
scenery is its sole recommendation.
3. Messrs Lamb and Lloyd, the most ignoble followers of Southey and Co.

And thou, too, Scott![1] resign to minstrels rude
The wilder slogan of a border feud:
Let others spin their meagre lines for hire;
Enough for genius if itself inspire!
915 Let Southey sing, although his teeming muse,
Prolific every spring, be too profuse;
Let simple Wordsworth[2] chime his childish verse,
And brother Coleridge lull the babe at nurse;
Let spectre-mongering Lewis aim, at most,
920 To rouse the galleries, or to raise a ghost;
Let Moore still sigh; let Strangford steal from Moore,
And swear that Camoëns sang such notes of yore;
Let Hayley hobble on, Montgomery rave,
And godly Grahame chant a stupid stave;
925 Let sonneteering Bowles his strains refine,
And whine and whimper to the fourteenth line;
Let Stott, Carlisle,[3] Matilda, and the rest
Of Grub-street, and of Grosvenor-place the best

1. By the bye, I hope that in Mr Scott's next poem, his hero or heroine will
be less addicted to 'Gramarye,' and more to grammar, than the Lady of the
Lay and her bravo, William of Deloraine.
2. ['Unjust.' – B. 1816.]
3. It may be asked, why I have censured the Earl of Carlisle, my guardian
and relative, to whom I dedicated a volume of puerile poems a few years
ago? – The guardianship was nominal, at least as far as I have been able to
discover; the relationship I cannot help, and am very sorry for it; but as his
lordship seemed to forget it on a very essential occasion to me, I shall not
burden my memory with the recollection. I do not think that personal
differences sanction the unjust condemnation of a brother scribbler; but I
see no reason why they should act as a preventive, when the author, noble
or ignoble, has, for a series of years, beguiled a 'discerning public' (as the
advertisements have it) with divers reams of most orthodox, imperial non-
sense. Besides, I do not step aside to vituperate the earl: no – his works
come fairly in review with those of other partrician literati. If, before I
escaped from my teens, I said any thing in favour of his lordship's paper
books, it was in the way of dutiful dedication, and more from the advice of
others than my own judgment, and I seize the first opportunity of pronounc-
ing my sincere recantation. I have heard that some persons conceive me to
be under obligations to Lord Carlisle: if so, I shall be most particularly
happy to learn what they are, and when conferred, that they may be duly
appreciated and publicly acknowledged. What I have humbly advanced as
an opinion on his printed things, I am prepared to support, if necessary,

Scrawl on, 'till death release us from the strain,
930   Or Common Sense assert her rights again.
But thou, with powers that mock the aid of praise,
Shouldst leave to humbler bards ignoble lays:
Thy country's voice, the voice of all the nine,
Demand a hallow'd harp – that harp is thine.
935   Say! will not Caledonia's annals yield
The glorious record of some nobler field
Than the vile foray of a plundering clan,
Whose proudest deeds disgrace the name of man?
Or Marmion's acts of darkness, fitter food
940   For Sherwood's outlaw tales of Robin Hood?
Scotland! still proudly claim thy native bard,
And be thy praise his first, his best reward!
Yet not with thee alone his name should live,
But own the vast renown a world can give;
945   Be known, perchance, when Albion is no more,
And tell the tale of what she was before;
To future times her faded fame recall,
And save her glory, though his country fall.

Yet what avails the sanguine poet's hope,
950   To conquer ages, and with time to cope?
New eras spread their wings, new nations rise,
And other victors fill the applauding skies;
A few brief generations fleet along,
Whose sons forget the poet and his song:
955   E'en now, what once-loved minstrels scarce may claim
The transient mention of a dubious name!

---

by quotations from elegies, eulogies, odes, episodes, and certain facetious
and dainty tragedies bearing his name and mark: –

'What can ennoble knaves, or fools, or cowards?
Alas! not all the blood of all the Howards.'

So says Pope. Amen! – ['Much too savage, whatever the foundation might
be.' – B. 1816.]

When fame's loud trump hath blown its noblest blast,
Though long the sound, the echo sleeps at last;
And glory, like the phœnix[1] 'midst her fires,
960 Exhales her odours, blazes, and expires.

Shall hoary Granta call her sable sons,
Expert in science, more expert at puns?
Shall these approach the muse? ah, no! she flies,
Even from the tempting ore of Seaton's prize;
965 Though printers condescend the press to soil
With rhyme by Hoare, and epic blank by Hoyle:
Not him whose page, if still upheld by whist,
Requires no sacred theme to bid us list.[2]
Ye! who in Granta's honours would surpass,
970 Must mount her Pegasus, a full-grown ass;
A foal well worthy of her ancient dam,
Whose Helicon is duller than her Cam.

There Clarke, still striving piteously 'to please,'
Forgetting doggrel leads not to degrees,
975 A would-be satirist, a hired buffoon,
A monthly scribbler of some low lampoon,[3]
Condemn'd to drudge, the meanest of the mean,
And furbish falsehoods for a magazine,
Devotes to scandal his congenial mind;
980 Himself a living libel on mankind.[4]

---

1. ['The devil take that phœnix! How came it there?' – B. 1816.]
2. The 'Games of Hoyle,' well known to the votaries of whist, chess, &c., are not to be superseded by the vagaries of his poetical namesake, whose poem comprised, as expressly stated in the advertisement, all the 'plagues of Egypt.'
3. ['Right enough: this was well deserved, and well laid on.' – B. 1816.]
4. This person, who has lately betrayed the most rabid symptoms of confirmed authorship, is writer of a poem denominated the 'Art of Pleasing,' as 'lucus a non lucendo,' containing little pleasantry and less poetry. He also acts as monthly stipendiary and collector of calumnies for the 'Satirist.' If this unfortunate young man would exchange the magazines for the mathematics, and endeavour to take a decent degree in his university, it might eventually prove more serviceable than his present salary.

Oh! dark asylum of a Vandal race![1]
At once the boast of learning, and disgrace!
So lost to Phœbus, that nor Hodgson's[2] verse
Can make thee better, nor poor Hewson's[3] worse.
985 But where fair Isis rolls her purer wave,
The partial muse delighted loves to lave;
On her green banks a greener wreath she wove,
To crown the bards that haunt her classic grove;
Where Richards wakes a genuine poet's fires,
990 And modern Britons glory in their sires.[4]

For me, who, thus unask'd, have dared to tell
My country, what her sons should know too well,
Zeal for her honour bade me here engage
The host of idiots that infest her age;
995 No just applause her honour'd name shall lose,
As first in freedom, dearest to the muse.
Oh! would thy bards but emulate thy fame,
And rise more worthy, Albion, of thy name!
What Athens was in science, Rome in power,
1000 What Tyre appear'd in her meridian hour,
'Tis thine at once, fair Albion! to have been –
Earth's chief dictatress, ocean's lovely queen:
But Rome decay'd, and Athens strew'd the plain,
And Tyre's proud piers lie shatter'd in the main;
1005 Like these, thy strength may sink, in ruin hurl'd,
And Britain fall, the bulwark of the world.

1. 'Into Cambridgeshire the Emperor Probus transported a considerable body of Vandals.' – Gibbon's Decline and Fall, vol. ii. p. 83. There is no reason to doubt the truth of this assertion; the breed is still in high perfection.
2. This gentleman's name requires no praise: the man who in translation displays unquestionable genius may be well expected to excel in original composition, of which it is to be hoped we shall soon see a splendid specimen.
3. Hewson Clarke, *Esq.* as it is written.
4. The 'Aboriginal Britons,' an excellent poem, by Richards.

But let me cease, and dread Cassandra's fate,
With warning ever scoff'd at, till too late;
To themes less lofty still my lay confine,
1010 And urge thy bards to gain a name like thine.

Then, hapless Britain! be thy rulers blest,
The senate's oracles, the people's jest!
Still hear thy motley orators dispense
The flowers of rhetoric, though not of sense,
1015 While Canning's colleagues hate him for his wit,
And old dame Portland[1] fills the place of Pitt.

Yet once again, adieu! ere this the sail
That wafts me hence is shivering in the gale;
And Afric's coast and Calpe's adverse height,
1020 And Stamboul's minarets must greet my sight:
Thence shall I stray through beauty's native clime,[2]
Where Kaff[3] is clad in rocks, and crown'd with snows
          sublime.
But should I back return, no tempting press[4]
Shall drag my journal from the desk's recess:
1025 Let coxcombs, printing as they come from far,
Snatch his own wreath of ridicule from Carr;

1. A friend of mine being asked, why his Grace of Portland was likened to an old woman? replied, 'he supposed it was because he was past bearing.' – His Grace is now gathered to his grandmothers, where he sleeps as sound as ever; but even his sleep was better than his colleagues' waking. 1811.
2. Georgia.
3. Mount Caucasus.
4. These four lines originally stood, –

> 'But should I back return, no letter'd sage
> Shall drag my common-place book on the stage;
> Let vain Valentia* rival luckless Carr,
> And equal him whose work he sought to mar.'

* Lord Valentia (whose tremendous travels are forthcoming with due decorations, graphical, topographical, typographical) deposed, on Sir John Carr's unlucky suit, that Mr Dubois's satire prevented his purchase of the 'Stranger in Ireland.' – Oh, fie, my lord! has your lordship no more feeling for a fellow-tourist? – but 'two of a trade,' they say, &c.

Let Aberdeen and Elgin[1] still pursue
The shade of fame through regions of virtù;
Waste useless thousands on their Phidian freaks,
1030 Misshapen monuments and maim'd antiques;
And make their grand saloons a general mart
For all the mutilated blocks of art:
Of Dardan tours let dilettanti tell,
I leave topography to rapid[2] Gell;[3]
1035 And, quite content, no more shall interpose
To stun the public ear – at least with prose.

Thus far I've held my undisturb'd career,
Prepared for rancour, steel'd 'gainst selfish fear:
This thing of rhyme I ne'er disdain'd to own –
1040 Though not obtrusive, yet not quite unknown:
My voice was heard again, though not so loud,
My page, though nameless, never disavow'd;
And now at once I tear the veil away: –
Cheer on the pack! the quarry stands at bay,
1045 Unscared by all the din of Melbourne house,
By Lambe's resentment, or by Holland's spouse,
By Jeffrey's harmless pistol, Hallam's rage,
Edina's brawny sons and brimstone page.
Our men in buckram shall have blows enough,
1050 And feel they too are 'penetrable stuff:'
And though I hope not hence unscathed to go,
Who conquers me shall find a stubborn foe.
The time hath been, when no harsh sound would fall
From lips that now may seem imbued with gall;

1. Lord Elgin would fain persuade us that all the figures, with and without noses, in his stoneshop are the work of Phidias! 'Credat Judæus!'
2. The original epithet was 'classic.' Lord Byron altered it in the fifth edition, and added this note – 'Rapid,' indeed! He topographised and typographised King Priam's dominions in three days! I called him 'classic' before I saw the Troad, but since have learned better than to tack to his name what don't belong to it.' [Editors]
3. Mr Gell's Topography of Troy and Ithaca cannot fail to insure the approbation of every man possessed of classical taste, as well for the information Mr Gell conveys to the mind of the reader, as for the ability and research the respective works display. – ['Since seeing the plain of Troy, my opinions are somewhat changed as to the above note. Gell's survey was hasty and superficial.' – B. 1816.]

1055   Nor fools nor follies tempt me to despise
        The meanest thing that crawl'd beneath my eyes:
        But now, so callous grown, so changed since youth,
        I've learn'd to think, and sternly speak the truth;
        Learn'd to deride the critic's starch decree,
1060   And break him on the wheel he meant for me;
        To spurn the rod a scribbler bids me kiss,
        Nor care if courts and crowds applaud or hiss:
        Nay more, though all my rival rhymesters frown,
        I too can hunt a poetaster down;
1065   And, arm'd in proof, the gauntlet cast at once
        To Scotch marauder, and to southern dunce.
        Thus much I've dared; if my incondite lay
        Hath wrong'd these righteous times, let others say:
        This, let the world, which knows not how to spare,
1070   Yet rarely blames unjustly, now declare.[1]

POSTSCRIPT TO THE SECOND EDITION

I have been informed, since the present edition went to the press,
that my trusty and well-beloved cousins, the Edinburgh Reviewers,
are preparing a most vehement critique on my poor, gentle, *unresist-
ing*, Muse, whom they have already so be-deviled with their ungodly
ribaldry:

'Tantæne animis cœlestibus iræ!'

I suppose I must say of Jeffrey as Sir Andrew Aguecheek saith, 'an
I had known he was so cunning of fence, I had seen him damned
ere I had fought him.' What a pity it is that I shall be beyond the
Bosphorus before the next number has passed the Tweed! But I yet
hope to light my pipe with it in Persia.

My northern friends have accused me, with justice, of personality
towards their great literary anthropophagus, Jeffrey; but what else
was to be done with him and his dirty pack, who feed by 'lying and
slandering,' and slake their thirst by 'evil speaking?' I have adduced

1. ['The greater part of this satire I most sincerely wish had never been
written – not only on account of the injustice of much of the critical, and
some of the personal part of it – but the tone and temper are such as I cannot
approve.' – BYRON. July 14, 1816. *Diodati, Geneva.*]

facts already well known, and of Jeffrey's mind I have stated my free opinion, nor has he thence sustained any injury; – what scavenger was ever soiled by being pelted with mud? It may be said that I quit England because I have censured there 'persons of honour and wit about town;' but I am coming back again, and their vengeance will keep hot till my return. Those who know me can testify that my motives for leaving England are very different from fears, literary or personal: those who do not, may one day be convinced. Since the publication of this thing, my name has not been concealed; I have been mostly in London, ready to answer for my transgressions, and in daily expectation of sundry cartels; but, alas! 'the age of chivalry is over,' or, in the vulgar tongue, there is no spirit now-a-days.

There is a youth ycleped Hewson Clarke (subaudi *esquire*), a sizer of Emanuel College, and, I believe, a denizen of Berwick-upon-Tweed, whom I have introduced in these pages to much better company than he has been accustomed to meet; he is, notwithstanding, a very sad dog, and for no reason that I can discover, except a personal quarrel with a bear, kept by me at Cambridge to sit for a fellowship, and whom the jealousy of his Trinity contemporaries prevented from success, has been abusing me, and, what is worse, the defenceless innocent above mentioned, in 'The Satirist' for one year and some months. I am utterly unconscious of having given him any provocation; indeed, I am guiltless of having heard his name till coupled with 'The Satirist.' He has therefore no reason to complain, and I dare say that, like Sir Fretful Plagiary, he is rather *pleased* than otherwise. I have now mentioned all who have done me the honour to notice me and mine, that is, my bear and my book, except the editor of 'The Satirist,' who, it seems, is a gentleman – God wot! I wish he could impart a little of his gentility to his subordinate scribblers. I hear that Mr Jerningham is about to take up the cudgels for his Mæcenas, Lord Carlisle: I hope not: he was one of the few, who, in the very short intercourse I had with him, treated me with kindness when a boy; and whatever he may say or do, 'pour on, I will endure.' I have nothing further to add, save a general note of thanksgiving to readers, purchasers, and publishers, and, in the words of Scott, I wish

'To all and each a fair good night,
And rosy dreams and slumbers light.'

Lines to Mr Hodgson
WRITTEN ON BOARD THE LISBON PACKET

Huzza! Hodgson, we are going,
    Our embargo's off at last;
Favourable breezes blowing
    Bend the canvass o'er the mast.
5 From aloft the signal's streaming,
    Hark! the farewell gun is fired;
Women screeching, tars blaspheming,
    Tell us that our time's expired.
          Here's a rascal
10   Come to task all,
    Prying from the custom-house;
            Trunks unpacking,
            Cases cracking,
    Not a corner for a mouse
15 'Scapes unsearch'd amid the racket,
Ere we sail on board the Packet.

Now our boatmen quit their mooring,
    And all hands must ply the oar;
Baggage from the quay is lowering,
20   We're impatient – push from shore.
'Have a care! that case holds liquor –
    Stop the boat – I'm sick – oh Lord!'
'Sick, ma'am, damme, you'll be sicker
    Ere you've been an hour on board.'
25   Thus are screaming
           Men and women,
    Gemmen, ladies, servants, Jacks;
           Here entangling,
           All are wrangling,
30   Stuck together close as wax. –
Such the general noise and racket,
Ere we reach the Lisbon Packet.

Now we've reach'd her, lo! the captain,
    Gallant Kidd, commands the crew;
35 Passengers their berths are clapt in,
    Some to grumble, some to spew.
'Hey day! call you that a cabin?
    Why 'tis hardly three feet square;
Not enough to stow Queen Mab in –
40   Who the deuce can harbour there?'
        'Who, sir? plenty –
        Nobles twenty
    Did at once my vessel fill.' –
        'Did they? Jesus,
45   How you squeeze us!
    Would to God they did so still:
Then I'd scape the heat and racket
Of the good ship, Lisbon Packet.'

Fletcher! Murray! Bob! where are you?
50   Stretch'd along the deck like logs –
Bear a hand, you jolly tar, you!
    Here's a rope's end for the dogs.
Hobhouse muttering fearful curses,
    As the hatchway down he rolls,
55 Now his breakfast, now his verses,
    Vomits forth – and damns our souls.
        'Here's a stanza
        On Braganza –
Help!' – 'A couplet?' – 'No, a cup
60   Of warm water –'
        'What's the matter?'
    'Zounds! my liver's coming up;
I shall not survive the racket
Of this brutal Lisbon Packet.'

65 Now at length we're off for Turkey,
    Lord knows when we shall come back!
Breezes foul and tempests murky
    May unship us in a crack.

But, since life at most a jest is,
70   As philosophers allow,
Still to laugh by far the best is,
        Then laugh on – as I do now.
            Laugh at all things,
            Great and small things,
75   Sick or well, at sea or shore;
            While we're quaffing,
            Let's have laughing –
Who the devil cares for more? –
Some good wine! and who would lack it,
80   Ev'n on board the Lisbon Packet?

Falmouth Roads, June 30, 1809.

Maid of Athens, ere we part

Ζώη μοῦ, σάς ἀγαπῶ.

Maid of Athens, ere we part,
Give, oh, give me back my heart!
Or, since that has left my breast,
Keep it now, and take the rest!
5   Hear my vow before I go,
Ζώη μοῦ, σάς ἀγαπῶ.

By those tresses unconfined,
Woo'd by each Ægean wind;
By those lids whose jetty fringe
10   Kiss thy soft cheeks' blooming tinge;
By those wild eyes like the roe,
Ζώη μοῦ, σάς ἀγαπῶ.

By that lip I long to taste;
By that zone-encircled waist;
15   By all the token-flowers[1] that tell
What words can never speak so well;
By love's alternate joy and woe,
Ζώη μοῦ, σάς ἀγαπῶ.

Maid of Athens! I am gone:
20   Think of me, sweet! when alone.
Though I fly to Istambol,[2]
Athens holds my heart and soul:
Can I cease to love thee? No!
Ζώη μοῦ, σάς ἀγαπῶ.

Athens, 1810.

1. In the East (where ladies are not taught to write, lest they should scribble
assignations) flowers, cinders, pebbles, &c. convey the sentiments of the
parties by that universal deputy of Mercury – an old woman. A cinder says,
'I burn for thee;' a bunch of flowers tied with hair, 'Take me and fly;' but a
pebble declares – what nothing else can.
2. Constantinople.

Written after Swimming from Sestos to Abydos[1]

If, in the month of dark December,
    Leander, who was nightly wont
(What maid will not the tale remember?)
    To cross thy stream, broad Hellespont!

5   If, when the wintry tempest roar'd,
    He sped to Hero, nothing loth,
And thus of old thy current pour'd,
    Fair Venus! how I pity both!

For *me*, degenerate modern wretch,
10   Though in the genial month of May,
My dripping limbs I faintly stretch,
    And think I've done a feat to-day.

But since he cross'd the rapid tide,
    According to the doubtful story,
15   To woo, – and – Lord knows what beside,
    And swam for Love, as I for Glory;

1. On the 3d of May, 1810, while the Salsette (Captain Bathurst) was lying in the Dardanelles, Lieutenant Ekenhead, of that frigate and the writer of these rhymes swam from the European shore to the Asiatic – by the by, from Abydos to Sestos would have been more correct. The whole distance, from the place whence we started to our landing on the other side, including the length we were carried by the current, was computed by those on board the frigate at upwards of four English miles; though the actual breadth is barely one. The rapidity of the current is such that no boat can row directly across, and it may, in some measure, be estimated from the circumstance of the whole distance being accomplished by one of the parties in an hour and five, and by the other in an hour and ten, minutes. The water was extremely cold, from the melting of the mountain snows. About three weeks before, in April, we had made an attempt; but, having ridden all the way from the Troad the same morning, and the water being of an icy chillness, we found it necessary to postpone the completion till the frigate anchored below the castles, when we swam the straits, as just stated; entering a considerable way above the European, and landing below the Asiatic, fort. Chevalier says that a young Jew swam the same distance for his mistress; and Oliver mentions its having been done by a Neapolitan; but our consul, Tarragona, remembered neither of these circumstances, and tried to dissuade us from the attempt. A number of the Salsette's crew were known to have accomplished a greater distance; and the only thing that surprised me was, that, as

'Twere hard to say who fared the best:
    Sad mortals! thus the Gods still plague you!
He lost his labour, I my jest:
20   For he was drown'd, and I've the ague.

                         May 9, 1810.

To Thyrza

Without a stone to mark the spot,
    And say, what Truth might well have said,
By all, save one, perchance forgot,
    Ah! wherefore art thou lowly laid?

5   By many a shore and many a sea
    Divided, yet beloved in vain;
The past, the future fled to thee
    To bid us meet – no – ne'er again!

Could this have been – a word, a look
10   That softly said, 'We part in peace,'
Had taught my bosom how to brook,
    With fainter sighs, thy soul's release.

And didst thou not, since Death for thee
    Prepared a light and pangless dart,
15   Once long for him thou ne'er shalt see,
    Who held, and holds thee in his heart?

Oh! who like him had watch'd thee here?
    Or sadly mark'd thy glazing eye,
In that dread hour ere death appear,
20   When silent sorrow fears to sigh,

Till all was past? But when no more
    'Twas thine to reck of human woe,
Affection's heart-drops, gushing o'er,
    Had flow'd as fast – as now they flow.

---

doubts had been entertained of the truth of Leander's story, no traveller
had ever endeavoured to ascertain its practicability.

25 Shall they not flow, when many a day
    In these, to me, deserted towers,
  Ere call'd but for a time away,
    Affection's mingling tears were ours?

  Ours too the glance none saw beside;
30   The smile none else might understand;
  The whisper'd thought of hearts allied,
    The pressure of the thrilling hand;

  The kiss, so guiltless and refined
    That Love each warmer wish forebore;
35 Those eyes proclaim'd so pure a mind,
    Even passion blush'd to plead for more.

  The tone, that taught me to rejoice,
    When prone, unlike thee, to repine;
  The song, celestial from thy voice,
40   But sweet to me from none but thine;

  The pledge we wore – I wear it still,
    But where is thine? – Ah! where art thou?
  Oft have I borne the weight of ill,
    But never bent beneath till now!

45 Well hast thou left in life's best bloom
    The cup of woe for me to drain.
  If rest alone be in the tomb,
    I would not wish thee here again;

  But if in worlds more blest than this
50   Thy virtues seek a fitter sphere,
  Impart some portion of thy bliss,
    To wean me from mine anguish here.

  Teach me – too early taught by thee!
    To bear, forgiving and forgiven:
55 On earth thy love was such to me;
    It fain would form my hope in heaven!

                              October 11, 1811.

CHILDE HAROLD'S PILGRIMAGE
A Romaunt, Cantos I–II

L'univers est une espèce de livre, dont on n'a lu que la première page quand on n'a vu que son pays. J'en ai feuilleté un assez grand nombre, que j'ai trouvé également mauvaises. Cet examen ne m'a point été infructueux. Je haïssais ma patrie. Toutes les impertinences des peuples divers, parmi lesquels j'ai vécu, m'ont reconcilié avec elle. Quand je n'aurais tiré d'autre bénéfice de mes voyages que celui-là, je n'en regretterais ni les frais ni les fatigues.

LE COSMOPOLITE

PREFACE TO THE FIRST AND SECOND CANTOS

The following poem was written, for the most part, amidst the scenes which it attempts to describe. It was begun in Albania; and the parts relative to Spain and Portugal were composed from the author's observations in those countries. Thus much it may be necessary to state for the correctness of the descriptions. The scenes attempted to be sketched are in Spain, Portugal, Epirus, Acarnania, and Greece. There, for the present, the poem stops: its reception will determine whether the author may venture to conduct his readers to the capital of the East, through Ionia and Phrygia: these two cantos are merely experimental.

A fictitious character is introduced for the sake of giving some connection to the piece; which, however, makes no pretension to regularity. It has been suggested to me by friends, on whose opinions I set a high value, that in this fictitious character, 'Childe Harold,' I may incur the suspicion of having intended some real personage: this I beg leave, once for all, to disclaim – Harold is the child of imagination, for the purpose I have stated. In some very trivial particulars, and those merely local, there might be grounds for such a notion; but in the main points, I should hope, none whatever.

It is almost superfluous to mention that the appellation 'Childe,' as 'Childe Waters,' 'Childe Childers,' &c. is used as more consonant with the old structure of versification which I have adopted. The 'Good Night,' in the beginning of the first canto, was suggested by 'Lord Maxwell's Good Night,' in the Border Minstrelsy, edited by Mr Scott.

With the different poems which have been published on Spanish subjects, there may be found some slight coincidence in the first part, which treats of the Peninsula, but it can only be casual; as, with the exception of a few concluding stanzas, the whole of this poem was written in the Levant.

The stanza of Spenser, according to one of our most successful poets, admits of every variety. Dr Beattie makes the following observation: – 'Not long ago I began a poem in the style and stanza of Spenser, in which I propose to give full scope to my inclination, and be either droll or pathetic, descriptive or sentimental, tender or satirical, as the humour strikes me; for, if I mistake not, the measure which I have adopted admits equally of all these kinds of composition.' – Strengthened in my opinion by such authority, and by the example of some in the highest order of Italian poets, I shall make no apology for attempts at similar variations in the following composition; satisfied that, if they are unsuccessful, their failure must be in the execution, rather than in the design sanctioned by the practice of Ariosto, Thomson, and Beattie.

London, February, 1812.

ADDITION TO THE PREFACE

I have now waited till almost all our periodical journals have distributed their usual portion of criticism. To the justice of the generality of their criticisms I have nothing to object: it would ill become me to quarrel with their very slight degree of censure, when, perhaps, if they had been less kind they had been more candid. Returning, therefore, to all and each my best thanks for their liberality, on one point alone shall I venture an observation. Amongst the many objections justly urged to the very indifferent character of the 'vagrant Childe' (whom, notwithstanding many hints to the contrary, I still maintain to be a fictitious personage), it has been stated, that, besides the anachronism, he is very *unknightly*, as the times of the Knights were times of Love, Honour, and so forth. Now, it so happens that the good old times, when 'l'amour du bon vieux temps, l'amour antique' flourished, were the most profligate of all possible centuries. Those who have any doubts on this subject may consult Sainte-Palaye, *passim*, and more particularly vol. ii. p.69. The vows of chivalry were no better kept than any other vows whatsoever; and the songs of the Troubadours were not more decent, and certainly were much less refined, than those of Ovid. The 'Cours d'amour, parlemens d'amour, ou de courtésie et de gentilesse' had much more of love than of courtesy or gentleness. See Roland on the same subject with Sainte-Palaye. Whatever other objection may be urged to that most unamiable personage Childe Harold, he was so far perfectly knightly in his attributes – 'No waiter, but a knight templar.' By the by, I fear that Sir Tristrem and Sir Lancelot were no better than they should be, although very poetical personages and true knights 'sans peur,' though not 'sans reproche.' If the story of the institution of the 'Garter' be not a fable, the knights of that order have for several centuries borne the badge of a Countess of Salisbury, of indifferent memory. So much for chivalry. Burke need not have regretted that its days are over, though Marie-Antoinette was quite as chaste as most of those in whose honours lances were shivered, and knights unhorsed.

Before the days of Bayard, and down to those of Sir Joseph Banks (the most chaste and celebrated of ancient and modern times), few exceptions will be found to this statement; and I fear a little investigation will teach us not to regret these monstrous mummeries of the middle ages.

I now leave 'Childe Harold' to live his day, such as he is; it had been more agreeable, and certainly more easy, to have

drawn an amiable character. It had been easy to varnish over
his faults, to make him do more and express less, but he never
was intended as an example, further than to show, that early
perversion of mind and morals leads to satiety of past pleas-
ures and disappointment in new ones, and that even the
beauties of nature, and the stimulus of travel (except ambi-
tion, the most powerful of all excitements) are lost on a soul
so constituted, or rather misdirected. Had I proceeded with
the poem, this character would have deepened as he drew to
the close; for the outline which I once meant to fill up for
him was, with some exceptions, the sketch of a modern
Timon, perhaps a poetical Zeluco.

London, 1813.

To Ianthe

Not in those climes where I have late been straying,
  Though Beauty long hath there been matchless deem'd;
Not in those visions to the heart displaying
  Forms which it sighs but to have only dream'd,
5   Hath aught like thee in truth or fancy seem'd:
Nor, having seen thee, shall I vainly seek
  To paint those charms which varied as they beam'd –
To such as see thee not my words were weak;
To those who gaze on thee what language could they
        speak?

10   Ah! may'st thou ever be what now thou art,
  Nor unbeseem the promise of thy spring,
As fair in form, as warm yet pure in heart,
  Love's image upon earth without his wing,
  And guileless beyond Hope's imagining!
15   And surely she who now so fondly rears
  Thy youth, in thee, thus hourly brightening,
Beholds the rainbow of her future years,
Before whose heavenly hues all sorrow disappears.

Young Peri of the West! — 'tis well for me
20 My years already doubly number thine;
My loveless eye unmoved may gaze on thee,
And safely view thy ripening beauties shine;
Happy, I ne'er shall see them in decline;
Happier, that while all younger hearts shall bleed,
25 Mine shall escape the doom thine eyes assign
To those whose admiration shall succeed,
But mix'd with pangs to Love's even loveliest hours
        decreed.

Oh! let that eye, which, wild as the Gazelle's,
Now brightly bold or beautifully shy,
30 Wins as it wanders, dazzles where it dwells,
Glance o'er this page, nor to my verse deny
That smile for which my breast might vainly sigh,
Could I to thee be ever more than friend:
This much, dear maid, accord; nor question why
35 To one so young my strain I would commend,
But bid me with my wreath one matchless lily blend.

Such is thy name with this my verse entwined;
And long as kinder eyes a look shall cast
On Harold's page, Ianthe's here enshrined
40 Shall thus be first beheld, forgotten last:
My days once number'd, should this homage past
Attract thy fairy fingers near the lyre
Of him who hail'd thee, loveliest as thou wast,
Such is the most my memory may desire;
45 Though more than Hope can claim, could Friendship less
        require?

CHILDE HAROLD'S PILGRIMAGE

Canto the First

I

Oh, thou! in Hellas deem'd of heavenly birth,
Muse! form'd or fabled at the minstrel's will!
Since shamed full oft by later lyres on earth,
Mine dares not call thee from thy sacred hill:
Yet there I've wander'd by thy vaunted rill;
Yes! sigh'd o'er Delphi's long deserted shrine,[1]
Where, save that feeble fountain, all is still;
Nor mote my shell awake the weary Nine
To grace so plain a tale – this lowly lay of mine.

II

Whilome in Albion's isle there dwelt a youth,
Who ne in virtue's ways did take delight;
But spent his days in riot most uncouth,
And vex'd with mirth the drowsy ear of Night.
Ah, me! in sooth he was a shameless wight,
Sore given to revel and ungodly glee;
Few earthly things found favour in his sight
Save concubines and carnal companie,
And flaunting wassailers of high and low degree.

1. The little village of Castri stands partly on the site of Delphi. Along the path of the mountain, from Chrysso, are the remains of sepulchres hewn in and from the rock. 'One,' said the guide, 'of a king who broke his neck hunting.' His majesty had certainly chosen the fittest spot for such an achievement. A little above Castri is a cave, supposed the Pythian, of immense depth; the upper part of it is paved, and now a cowhouse. On the other side of Castri stands a Greek monastery; some way above which is the cleft in the rock, with a range of caverns difficult of ascent, and apparently leading to the interior of the mountain; probably to the Corycian Cavern mentioned by Pausanias. From this part descend the fountain and the 'Dews of Castalie.'

III

Childe Harold was he hight: – but whence his name
And lineage long, it suits me not to say;
Suffice it, that perchance they were of fame,
And had been glorious in another day:
But one sad losel soils a name for aye,
However mighty in the olden time;
Nor all that heralds rake from coffin'd clay,
Nor florid prose, nor honied lies of rhyme,
Can blazon evil deeds, or consecrate a crime.

IV

Childe Harold bask'd him in the noontide sun,
Disporting there like any other fly;
Nor deem'd before his little day was done
One blast might chill him into misery.
But long ere scarce a third of his pass'd by,
Worse than adversity the Childe befell;
He felt the fulness of satiety:
Then loathed he in his native land to dwell,
Which seem'd to him more lone than Eremite's sad cell.

V

For he through Sin's long labyrinth had run,
Nor made atonement when he did amiss,
Had sigh'd to many though he loved but one,
And that loved one, alas! could ne'er be his.
Ah, happy she! to 'scape from him whose kiss
Had been pollution unto aught so chaste;
Who soon had left her charms for vulgar bliss,
And spoil'd her goodly lands to gild his waste,
Nor calm domestic peace had ever deign'd to taste.

VI

And now Childe Harold was sore sick at heart,
And from his fellow bacchanals would flee;
'Tis said, at times the sullen tear would start,
But Pride congeal'd the drop within his ee:
Apart he stalk'd in joyless reverie,

And from his native land resolved to go,
And visit scorching climes beyond the sea;
With pleasure drugg'd, he almost long'd for woe,
And e'en for change of scene would seek the shades below.

VII

55   The Childe departed from his father's hall:
It was a vast and venerable pile;
So old, it seemed only not to fall,
Yet strength was pillar'd in each massy aisle.
Monastic dome! condemn'd to uses vile!
60   Where Superstition once had made her den
Now Paphian girls were known to sing and smile;
And monks might deem their time was come agen,
If ancient tales say true, nor wrong these holy men,

VIII

Yet oft-times in his maddest mirthful mood
65   Strange pangs would flash along Childe Harold's brow,
As if the memory of some deadly feud
Or disappointed passion lurk'd below:
But this none knew, nor haply cared to know;
For his was not that open, artless soul
70   That feels relief by bidding sorrow flow,
Nor sought he friend to counsel or condole,
Whate'er this grief mote be, which he could not control.

IX

And none did love him – though to hall and bower
He gather'd revellers from far and near,
75   He knew them flatt'rers of the festal hour;
The heartless parasites of present cheer.
Yea! none did love him – not his lemans dear –
But pomp and power alone are woman's care,
And where these are light Eros finds a feere;
80   Maidens, like moths, are ever caught by glare,
And Mammon wins his way where Seraphs might despair.

X

Childe Harold had a mother – not forgot,
Though parting from that mother he did shun;
A sister whom he loved, but saw her not
85   Before his weary pilgrimage begun:
If friends he had, he bade adieu to none.
Yet deem not thence his breast a breast of steel:
Ye, who have known what 'tis to dote upon
A few dear objects, will in sadness feel
90 Such partings break the heart they fondly hope to heal.

XI

His house, his home, his heritage, his lands,
The laughing dames in whom he did delight,
Whose large blue eyes, fair locks, and snowy hands,
Might shake the saintship of an anchorite,
95   And long had fed his youthful appetite;
His goblets brimm'd with every costly wine,
And all that mote to luxury invite,
Without a sigh he left, to cross the brine,
And traverse Paynim shores, and pass Earth's central line.

XII

100   The sails were fill'd, and fair the light winds blew,
As glad to waft him from his native home;
And fast the white rocks faded from his view,
And soon were lost in circumambient foam:
And then, it may be, of his wish to roam
105   Repented he, but in his bosom slept
The silent thought, nor from his lips did come
One word of wail, whilst others sate and wept,
And to the reckless gales unmanly moaning kept.

XIII

But when the sun was sinking in the sea
110   He seized his harp, which he at times could string,
And strike, albeit with untaught melody,
When deem'd he no strange ear was listening:

And now his fingers o'er it he did fling,
And tuned his farewell in the dim twilight.
115 While flew the vessel on her snowy wing,
And fleeting shores receded from his sight,
Thus to the elements he pour'd his last 'Good Night.'

1

   'Adieu, adieu! my native shore
     Fades o'er the waters blue;
120 The Night-winds sigh, the breakers roar,
     And shrieks the wild sea-mew.
Yon Sun that sets upon the sea
     We follow in his flight;
Farewell awhile to him and thee,
125   My native Land – Good Night!

2

   'A few short hours and He will rise
     To give the morrow birth;
And I shall hail the main and skies,
     But not my mother earth.
130 Deserted is my own good hall,
     Its hearth is desolate;
Wild weeds are gathering on the wall;
     My dog howls at the gate.

3

   'Come hither, hither, my little page!
135   Why dost thou weep and wail?
Or dost thou dread the billows' rage,
     Or tremble at the gale?
But dash the tear-drop from thine eye;
     Our ship is swift and strong:
140 Our fleetest falcon scarce can fly
     More merrily along.'

4

    'Let winds be shrill, let waves roll high,
       I fear not wave nor wind;
    Yet marvel not, Sir Childe, that I
145   Am sorrowful in mind;
    For I have from my father gone,
       A mother whom I love,
    And have no friend, save these alone,
       But thee – and one above.

5

150   'My father bless'd me fervently,
       Yet did not much complain;
    But sorely will my mother sigh
       Till I come back again.' –
    'Enough, enough, my little lad!
155   Such tears become thine eye;
    If I thy guileless bosom had,
       Mine own would not be dry.

6

    'Come hither, hither, my staunch yeoman,
       Why dost thou look so pale?
160   Or dost thou dread a French foeman?
       Or shiver at the gale?'
    'Deem'st thou I tremble for my life?
       Sir Childe, I'm not so weak;
    But thinking on an absent wife
165   Will blanch a faithful cheek.

7

    'My spouse and boys dwell near thy hall,
       Along the bordering lake,
    And when they on their father call,
       What answer shall she make?'
170   'Enough, enough, my yeoman good,
       Thy grief let none gainsay;
    But I, who am of lighter mood,
       Will laugh to flee away.

8

'For who would trust the seeming sighs
    Of wife or paramour?
175   Fresh feres will dry the bright blue eyes
    We late saw streaming o'er.
For pleasures past I do not grieve,
    Nor perils gathering near;
180   My greatest grief is that I leave
    No thing that claims a tear.

9

'And now I'm in the world alone,
    Upon the wide, wide sea:
But why should I for others groan,
185   When none will sigh for me?
Perchance my dog will whine in vain,
    Till fed by stranger hands;
But long ere I come back again,
    He'd tear me where he stands.

10

190   'With thee, my bark, I'll swiftly go
    Athwart the foaming brine;
Nor care what land thou bear'st me to,
    So not again to mine.
Welcome, welcome, ye dark-blue waves!
195   And when you fail my sight,
Welcome, ye deserts, and ye caves!
    My native Land – Good Night!'

XIV

On, on the vessel flies, the land is gone,
And winds are rude in Biscay's sleepless bay.
200   Four days are sped, but with the fifth, anon,
New shores descried make every bosom gay;
And Cintra's mountain greets them on their way,
And Tagus dashing onward to the deep,
His fabled golden tribute bent to pay;
205   And soon on board the Lusian pilots leap,
And steer 'twixt fertile shores where yet few rustics reap.

XV

Oh, Christ! it is a goodly sight to see
What Heaven hath done for this delicious land!
What fruits of fragrance blush on every tree!
210   What goodly prospects o'er the hills expand!
But man would mar them with an impious hand:
And when the Almighty lifts his fiercest scourge
'Gainst those who most transgress his high command,
With treble vengeance will his hot shafts urge
215 Gaul's locust host, and earth from fellest foemen purge.

XVI

What beauties doth Lisboa first unfold!
Her image floating on that noble tide,
Which poets vainly pave with sands of gold,
But now whereon a thousand keels did ride
220   Of mighty strength, since Albion was allied,
And to the Lusians did her aid afford:
A nation swoln with ignorance and pride,
Who lick yet loathe the hand that waves the sword
To save them from the wrath of Gaul's unsparing lord.

XVII

225 But whoso entereth within this town,
That, sheening far, celestial seems to be,
Disconsolate will wander up and down,
'Mid many things unsightly to strange ee;
For hut and palace show like filthily:
230   The dingy denizens are rear'd in dirt;
Ne personage of high or mean degree
Doth care for cleanness of surtout or shirt,
Though shent with Egypt's plague, unkempt, unwash'd;
unhurt.

XVIII

Poor, paltry slaves! yet born 'midst noblest scenes –
235   Why, Nature, waste thy wonders on such men?
Lo! Cintra's glorious Eden intervenes
In variegated maze of mount and glen.

Ah, me! what hand can pencil guide, or pen,
To follow half on which the eye dilates
240   Through views more dazzling unto mortal ken
Than those whereof such things the bard relates,
Who to the awe-struck world unlock'd Elysium's gates?

XIX

The horrid crags, by toppling convent crown'd,
The cork-trees hoar that clothe the shaggy steep,
245   The mountain-moss by scorching skies imbrown'd,
The sunken glen, whose sunless shrubs must weep,
The tender azure of the unruffled deep,
The orange tints that gild the greenest bough,
The torrents that from cliff to valley leap,
250   The vine on high, the willow branch below,
Mix'd in one mighty scene, with varied beauty glow.

XX

Then slowly climb the many-winding way,
And frequent turn to linger as you go,
From loftier rocks new loveliness survey,
255   And rest ye at 'Our Lady's house of woe;'[1]
Where frugal monks their little relics show,
And sundry legends to the stranger tell:
Here impious men have punish'd been, and lo!
Deep in yon cave Honorius long did dwell,
260   In hope to merit Heaven by making earth a Hell.

1. The convent of 'Our Lady of Punishment,' *Nossa Señora de Pena*, on the summit of the rock. Below, at some distance, is the Cork Convent, where St Honorius dug his den, over which is his epitaph. From the hills the sea adds to the beauty of the view. – [Since the publication of this poem, I have been informed of the misapprehension of the term *Nossa Señora de Pena*. It was owing to the want of the *tilde*, or mark over the *ñ* which alters the signification of the word: with it, *Peña* signifies a rock; without it, *Pena* has the sense I adopted. I do not think it necessary to alter the passage; as though the common acceptation affixed to it is 'Our Lady of the Rock,' I may well assume the other sense from the severities practised there. – *Note to 2d Edition.*]

XXI

And here and there, as up the crags you spring,
Mark many rude-carved crosses near the path:
Yet deem not these devotion's offering —
These are memorials frail of murderous wrath:
265   For wheresoe'er the shrieking victim hath
Pour'd forth his blood beneath the assassin's knife,
Some hand erects a cross of mouldering lath;
And grove and glen with thousand such are rife
Throughout this purple land, where law secures not life.[1]

XXII

270   On sloping mounds, or in the vale beneath,
Are domes where whilome kings did make repair;
But now the wild flowers round them only breathe;
Yet ruin'd splendour still is lingering there.
And yonder towers the Prince's palace fair:
275   There thou too, Vathek! England's wealthiest son,
Once form'd thy Paradise, as not aware
When wanton Wealth her mightiest deeds hath done,
Meek Peace voluptuous lures was ever wont to shun.

XXIII

Here didst thou dwell, here schemes of pleasure plan,
280   Beneath yon mountain's ever beauteous brow:
But now, as if a thing unblest by Man,
Thy fairy dwelling is as lone as thou!
Here giant weeds a passage scarce allow

1. It is a well known fact, that in the year 1809, the assassinations in the streets of Lisbon and its vicinity were not confined by the Portuguese to their countrymen; but that Englishmen were daily butchered: and so far from redress being obtained, we were requested not to interfere if we perceived any compatriot defending himself against his allies. I was once stopped in the way to the theatre at eight o'clock in the evening, when the streets were not more empty than they generally are at that hour, opposite to an open shop, and in a carriage with a friend: had we not fortunately been armed, I have not the least doubt that we should have 'adorned a tale' instead of telling one. The crime of assassination is not confined to Portugal: in Sicily and Malta we are knocked on the head at a handsome average nightly, and not a Sicilian or Maltese is ever punished!

To halls deserted, portals gaping wide;
285   Fresh lessons to the thinking bosom, how
Vain are the pleasaunces on earth supplied;
Swept into wrecks anon by Time's ungentle tide!

XXIV
Behold the hall where chiefs were late convened![1]
Oh! dome displeasing unto British eye!
290   With diadem hight foolscap, lo! a fiend,
A little fiend that scoffs incessantly,
There sits in parchment robe array'd, and by
His side is hung a seal and sable scroll,
Where blazon'd glare names known to chivalry,
295   And sundry signatures adorn the roll,
Whereat the Urchin points and laughs with all his soul.

XXV
Convention is the dwarfish demon styled
That foil'd the knights in Marialva's dome:
Of brains (if brains they had) he them beguiled,
300   And turn'd a nation's shallow joy to gloom.
Here Folly dash'd to earth the victor's plume,
And Policy regain'd what arms had lost:
For chiefs like ours in vain may laurels bloom!
Woe to the conqu'ring, not the conquer'd host,
305   Since baffled Triumph droops on Lusitania's coast!

XXVI
And ever since that martial synod met,
Britannia sickens, Cintra! at thy name;
And folks in office at the mention fret,
And fain would blush, if blush they could, for shame.
310   How will posterity the deed proclaim!
Will not our own and fellow-nations sneer,
To view these champions cheated of their fame,
By foes in fight o'erthrown, yet victors here,
Where Scorn her finger points through many a coming
                    year?

1. The Convention of Cintra was signed in the palace of the Marchese
Marialva.

XXVII

315   So deem'd the Childe, as o'er the mountains he
          Did take his way in solitary guise:
          Sweet was the scene, yet soon he thought to flee,
          More restless than the swallow in the skies:
          Though here awhile he learn'd to moralize,
320   For Meditation fix'd at times on him;
          And conscious Reason whisper'd to despise
          His early youth, misspent in maddest whim;
But as he gazed on truth his aching eyes grew dim.

XXVIII

          To horse! to horse! he quits, for ever quits
325   A scene of peace, though soothing to his soul:
          Again he rouses from his moping fits,
          But seeks not now the harlot and the bowl.
          Onward he flies, nor fix'd as yet the goal
          Where he shall rest him on his pilgrimage;
330   And o'er him many changing scenes must roll
          Ere toil his thirst for travel can assuage,
Or he shall calm his breast, or learn experience sage.

XXIX

          Yet Mafra shall one moment claim delay,
          Where dwelt of yore the Lusians' luckless queen;
335   And church and court did mingle their array,
          And mass and revel were alternate seen;
          Lordlings and freres – ill-sorted fry I ween!
          But here the Babylonian whore hath built
          A dome, where flaunts she in such glorious sheen,
340   That men forget the blood which she hath spilt,
And bow the knee to Pomp that loves to varnish guilt.[1]

---

1. The extent of Mafra is prodigious: it contains a palace, convent, and most superb church. The six organs are the most beautiful I ever beheld, in point of decoration: we did not hear them, but were told that their tones were correspondent to their splendour. Mafra is termed the Escurial of Portugal.

XXX

O'er vales that teem with fruits, romantic hills,
(Oh, that such hills upheld a freeborn race!)
Whereon to gaze the eye with joyaunce fills,
345   Childe Harold wends through many a pleasant place.
Though sluggards deem it but a foolish chase,
And marvel men should quit their easy chair,
The toilsome way, and long, long league to trace,
Oh! there is sweetness in the mountain air,
350 And life, that bloated Ease can never hope to share.

XXXI

More bleak to view the hills at length recede,
And, less luxuriant, smoother vales extend;
Immense horizon-bounded plains succeed!
Far as the eye discerns, withouten end,
355   Spain's realms appear whereon her shepherds tend
Flocks, whose rich fleece right well the trader knows —
Now must the pastor's arm his lambs defend:
For Spain is compass'd by unyielding foes,
And all must shield their all, or share Subjection's woes.

XXXII

360   Where Lusitania and her Sister meet,
Deem ye what bounds the rival realms divide?
Or ere the jealous queens of nations greet,
Doth Tayo interpose his mighty tide?
Or dark Sierras rise in craggy pride?
365   Or fence of art, like China's vasty wall? —
Ne barrier wall, ne river deep and wide,
Ne horrid crags, nor mountains dark and tall,
Rise like the rocks that part Hispania's land from Gaul:

XXXIII

But these between a silver streamlet glides,
370   And scarce a name distinguisheth the brook,
Though rival kingdoms press its verdant sides.
Here leans the idle shepherd on his crook,
And vacant on the rippling waves doth look,

That peaceful still 'twixt bitterest foemen flow;
375   For proud each peasant as the noblest duke:
Well doth the Spanish hind the difference know
'Twixt him and Lusian slave, the lowest of the low.[1]

XXXIV

But ere the mingling bounds have far been pass'd
Dark Guadiana rolls his power along
380   In sullen billows, murmuring and vast,
So noted ancient roundelays among.
Whilome upon his banks did legions throng
Of Moor and Knight, in mailed splendour drest:
Here ceased the swift their race, here sunk the strong;
385   The Paynim turban and the Christian crest
Mix'd on the bleeding stream, by floating hosts oppress'd.

XXXV

Oh, lovely Spain! renown'd, romantic land!
Where is that standard which Pelagio bore,
When Cava's traitor-sire first call'd the band
390   That dyed thy mountain streams with Gothic gore?[2]
Where are those bloody banners which of yore
Waved o'er thy sons, victorious to the gale,
And drove at last the spoilers to their shore?
Red gleam'd the cross, and waned the crescent pale,
395   While Afric's echoes thrill'd with Moorish matrons' wail.

1. As I found the Portuguese, so have I characterised them. That they are since improved, at least in courage, is evident. The late exploits of Lord Wellington have effaced the follies of Cintra. He has, indeed, done wonders: he has, perhaps, changed the character of a nation, reconciled rival superstitions, and baffled an enemy who never retreated before his predecessors. – 1812.

2. Count Julian's daughter, the Helen of Spain. Pelagius preserved his independence in the fastnesses of the Asturias, and the descendants of his followers, after some centuries, completed their struggle by the conquest of Grenada.

XXXVI

Teems not each ditty with the glorious tale?
Ah! such, alas! the hero's amplest fate!
When granite moulders and when records fail,
A peasant's plaint prolongs his dubious date.
400 Pride! bend thine eye from heaven to thine estate,
See how the Mighty shrink into a song!
Can Volume, Pillar, Pile, preserve thee great?
Or must thou trust Tradition's simple tongue,
When Flattery sleeps with thee, and History does thee
wrong?

XXXVII

405 Awake, ye sons of Spain! awake! advance!
Lo! Chivalry, your ancient goddess, cries;
But wields not, as of old, her thirsty lance,
Nor shakes her crimson plumage in the skies:
Now on the smoke of blazing bolts she flies,
410 And speaks in thunder through yon engine's roar:
In every peal she calls – 'Awake! arise!'
Say, is her voice more feeble than of yore,
When her war-song was heard on Andalusia's shore?

XXXVIII

Hark! heard you not those hoofs of dreadful note?
415 Sounds not the clang of conflict on the heath?
Saw ye not whom the reeking sabre smote;
Nor saved your brethren ere they sank beneath
Tyrants and tyrants' slaves? – the fires of death,
The bale-fires flash on high: – from rock to rock
420 Each volley tells that thousands cease to breathe;
Death rides upon the sulphury Siroc,
Red Battle stamps his foot, and nations feel the shock.

XXXIX

Lo! where the Giant on the mountain stands,
His blood-red tresses deep'ning in the sun,
425 With death-shot glowing in his fiery hands,
And eye that scorcheth all it glares upon;

Restless it rolls, now fix'd, and now anon
Flashing afar, – and at his iron feet
Destruction cowers, to mark what deeds are done;
430   For on this morn three potent nations meet,
To shed before his shrine the blood he deems most sweet.

XL

By Heaven! it is a splendid sight to see
(For one who hath no friend, no brother there)
Their rival scarfs of mix'd embroidery,
435   Their various arms that glitter in the air!
What gallant war-hounds rouse them from their lair,
And gnash their fangs, loud yelling for the prey!
All join the chase, but few the triumph share;
The Grave shall bear the chiefest prize away,
440   And Havoc scarce for joy can number their array.

XLI

Three hosts combine to offer sacrifice;
Three tongues prefer strange orisons on high;
Three gaudy standards flout the pale blue skies;
The shouts are France, Spain, Albion, Victory!
445   The foe, the victim, and the fond ally
That fights for all, but ever fights in vain,
Are met – as if at home they could not die –
To feed the crow on Talavera's plain,
And fertilize the field that each pretends to gain.

XLII

450   There shall they rot – Ambition's honour'd fools!
Yes, Honour decks the turf that wraps their clay!
Vain Sophistry! in these behold the tools,
The broken tools, that tyrants cast away
By myriads, when they dare to pave their way
455   With human hearts – to what? – a dream alone.
Can despots compass aught that hails their sway?
Or call with truth one span of earth their own,
Save that wherein at last they crumble bone by bone?

XLIII

Oh, Albuera, glorious field of grief!
460   As o'er thy plain the Pilgrim prick'd his steed,
Who could foresee thee, in a space so brief,
A scene where mingling foes should boast and bleed!
Peace to the perish'd! may the warrior's meed
And tears of triumph their reward prolong!
465   Till others fall where other chieftains lead,
Thy name shall circle round the gaping throng,
And shine in worthless lays, the theme of transient song.

XLIV

Enough of Battle's minions! let them play
Their game of lives, and barter breath for fame:
470   Fame that will scarce re-animate their clay,
Though thousands fall to deck some single name.
In sooth 'twere sad to thwart their noble aim
Who strike, blest hirelings! for their country's good,
And die, that living might have proved her shame;
475   Perish'd, perchance, in some domestic feud,
Or in a narrower sphere wild Rapine's path pursued.

XLV

Full swiftly Harold wends his lonely way
Where proud Sevilla triumphs unsubdued:
Yet is she free – the spoiler's wish'd-for prey!
480   Soon, soon shall Conquest's fiery foot intrude,
Blackening her lovely domes with traces rude.
Inevitable hour! 'Gainst fate to strive
Where Desolation plants her famish'd brood
Is vain, or Ilion, Tyre might yet survive,
485   And Virtue vanquish all, and Murder cease to thrive.

XLVI

But all unconscious of the coming doom,
The feast, the song, the revel here abounds;
Strange modes of merriment the hours consume,
Nor bleed these patriots with their country's wounds:
490   Nor here War's clarion, but Love's rebeck sounds;

Here Folly still his votaries inthralls;
And young-eyed Lewdness walks her midnight rounds:
Girt with the silent crimes of Capitals,
Still to the last kind Vice clings to the tott'ring walls.

XLVII

495   Not so the rustic – with his trembling mate
He lurks, nor casts his heavy eye afar,
Lest he should view his vineyard desolate,
Blasted below the dun hot breath of war.
No more beneath soft Eve's consenting star
500   Fandango twirls his jocund castanet:
Ah, monarchs! could ye taste the mirth ye mar,
Not in the toils of Glory would ye fret;
The hoarse dull drum would sleep, and Man be happy yet!

XLVIII

How carols now the lusty muleteer?
505   Of love, romance, devotion is his lay,
As whilome he was wont the leagues to cheer,
His quick bells wildly jingling on the way?
No! as he speeds, he chants 'Vivã el Rey!'[1]
And checks his song to execrate Godoy,
510   The royal wittol Charles, and curse the day
When first Spain's queen beheld the black-eyed boy,
And gore-faced Treason sprung from her adulterate joy.

XLIX

On yon long, level plain, at distance crown'd
With crags, whereon those Moorish turrets rest,
515   Wide scatter'd hoof-marks dint the wounded ground;
And, scathed by fire, the greensward's darken'd vest

---

1. 'Vivã el Rey Fernando!' Long live King Ferdinand! is the chorus of most of the Spanish patriotic songs. They are chiefly in dispraise of the old King Charles, the Queen, and the Prince of Peace. I have heard many of them: some of the airs are beautiful. Don Manuel Godoy, the *Principe de la Paz*, of an ancient but decayed family, was born at Badajoz, on the frontiers of Portugal, and was originally in the ranks of the Spanish guards; till his person attracted the queen's eyes, and raised him to the dukedom of Alcudia, &c. &c. It is to this man that the Spaniards universally impute the ruin of their country.

Tells that the foe was Andalusia's guest:
Here was the camp, the watch-flame, and the host,
Here the bold peasant storm'd the dragon's nest;
520   Still does he mark it with triumphant boast,
And points to yonder cliffs, which oft were won and lost.

L

And whomsoe'er along the path you meet
Bears in his cap the badge of crimson hue,
Which tells you whom to shun and whom to greet:[1]
525   Woe to the man that walks in public view
Without of loyalty this token true:
Sharp is the knife, and sudden is the stroke;
And sorely would the Gallic foeman rue,
If subtle poniards, wrapt beneath the cloke,
530 Could blunt the sabre's edge, or clear the cannon's smoke.

LI

At every turn Morena's dusky height
Sustains aloft the battery's iron load;
And, far as mortal eye can compass sight,
The mountain-howitzer, the broken road,
535   The bristling palisade, the fosse o'erflow'd,
The station'd bands, the never-vacant watch,
The magazine in rocky durance stow'd,
The holster'd steed beneath the shed of thatch,
The ball-piled pyramid,[2] the ever-blazing match,

LII

540   Portend the deeds to come: – but he whose nod
Has tumbled feebler despots from their sway,
A moment pauseth ere he lifts the rod;
A little moment deigneth to delay:
Soon will his legions sweep through these their way;

1. The red cockade, with 'Fernando VII,' in the centre.
2. All who have seen a battery will recollect the pyramidal form in which
shot and shells are piled. The Sierra Morena was fortified in every defile
through which I passed in my way to Seville.

545   The West must own the Scourger of the world.
    Ah! Spain! how sad will be thy reckoning-day,
    When soars Gaul's Vulture, with his wings unfurl'd,
  And thou shalt view thy sons in crowds to Hades hurl'd.

  LIII
    And must they fall? the young, the proud, the brave,
550   To swell one bloated Chief's unwholesome reign?
    No step between submission and a grave?
    The rise of rapine and the fall of Spain?
    And doth the Power that man adores ordain
    Their doom, nor heed the suppliant's appeal?
555   Is all that desperate Valour acts in vain?
    And Counsel sage, and patriotic Zeal,
  The Veteran's skill, Youth's fire, and Manhood's heart of
     steel?

  LIV
    Is it for this the Spanish maid, aroused,
    Hangs on the willow her unstrung guitar,
560   And, all unsex'd, the anlace hath espoused,
    Sung the loud song, and dared the deed of war?
    And she, whom once the semblance of a scar
    Appall'd, an owlet's larum chill'd with dread,
    Now views the column-scattering bay'net jar,
565   The falchion flash, and o'er the yet warm dead
  Stalks with Minerva's step where Mars might quake to
     tread.

  LV
    Ye who shall marvel when you hear her tale,
    Oh! had you known her in her softer hour,
    Mark'd her black eye that mocks her coal-black veil,
570   Heard her light, lively tones in Lady's bower,
    Seen her long locks that foil the painter's power,
    Her fairy form, with more than female grace,
    Scarce would you deem that Saragoza's tower
    Beheld her smile in Danger's Gorgon face,
575 Thin the closed ranks, and lead in Glory's fearful chase.

LVI

    Her lover sinks – she sheds no ill-timed tear;
    Her chief is slain – she fills his fatal post;
    Her fellows flee – she checks their base career;
    The foe retires – she heads the sallying host:
580   Who can appease like her a lover's ghost?
    Who can avenge so well a leader's fall?
    What maid retrieve when man's flush'd hope is lost?
    Who hang so fiercely on the flying Gaul,
Foil'd by a woman's hand, before a batter'd wall?[1]

LVII

585   Yet are Spain's maids no race of Amazons,
    But form'd for all the witching arts of love:
    Though thus in arms they emulate her sons,
    And in the horrid phalanx dare to move,
    'Tis but the tender fierceness of the dove,
590   Pecking the hand that hovers o'er her mate:
    In softness as in firmness far above
    Remoter females, famed for sickening prate;
Her mind is nobler sure, her charms perchance as great.

LVIII

    The seal Love's dimpling finger hath impress'd
595   Denotes how soft that chin which bears his touch:[2]
    Her lips, whose kisses pout to leave their nest,
    Bid man be valiant ere he merit such:
    Her glance how wildly beautiful! how much
    Hath Phœbus woo'd in vain to spoil her cheek,
600   Which glows yet smoother from his amorous clutch!
    Who round the North for paler dames would seek?
How poor their forms appear! how languid, wan, and weak!

1. Such were the exploits of the Maid of Saragoza, who by her valour elevated herself to the highest rank of heroines. When the author was at Seville she walked daily on the Prado, decorated with medals and orders, by command of the Junta.
2.

       'Sigilla in mento impressa Amoris digitulo
       Vestigio demonstrant mollitudinem.'
                                  AUL. GEL.

LIX

Match me, ye climes! which poets love to laud;
Match me, ye harams of the land! where now[1]
605   I strike my strain, far distant, to applaud
Beauties that ev'n a cynic must avow;
Match me those Houries, whom ye scarce allow
To taste the gale lest Love should ride the wind,
With Spain's dark-glancing daughters – deign to know,
610   There your wise Prophet's paradise we find,
His black-eyed maids of Heaven, angelically kind.

LX

Oh, thou Parnassus![2] whom I now survey,
Not in the phrensy of a dreamer's eye,
Not in the fabled landscape of a lay,
615   But soaring snow-clad through thy native sky,
In the wild pomp of mountain majesty!
What marvel if I thus essay to sing?
The humblest of thy pilgrims passing by
Would gladly woo thine Echoes with his string,
620   Though from thy heights no more one Muse will wave her
              wing.

LXI

Oft have I dream'd of Thee! whose glorious name
Who knows not, knows not man's divinest lore:
And now I view thee, 'tis, alas! with shame
That I in feeblest accents must adore.
625   When I recount thy worshippers of yore
I tremble, and can only bend the knee;
Nor raise my voice, nor vainly dare to soar,
But gaze beneath thy cloudy canopy
In silent joy to think at last I look on Thee!

1. This stanza was written in Turkey.
2. These stanzas were written in Castri (Delphos), at the foot of Parnassus, now called Λιακυρά (Liakura), Dec. 1809.

LXII

630   Happier in this than mightiest bards have been,
       Whose fate to distant homes confined their lot,
       Shall I unmoved behold the hallow'd scene,
       Which others rave of, though they know it not?
       Though here no more Apollo haunts his grot,
635   And thou, the Muses' seat, art now their grave,
       Some gentle spirit still pervades the spot,
       Sighs in the gale, keeps silence in the cave,
And glides with glassy foot o'er yon melodious wave.

LXIII

       Of thee hereafter. – Ev'n amidst my strain
640   I turn'd aside to pay my homage here;
       Forgot the land, the sons, the maids of Spain;
       Her fate, to every freeborn bosom dear;
       And hail'd thee, not perchance without a tear.
       Now to my theme – but from thy holy haunt
645   Let me some remnant, some memorial bear;
       Yield me one leaf of Daphne's deathless plant,
Nor let thy votary's hope be deem'd an idle vaunt.

LXIV

       But ne'er didst thou, fair Mount! when Greece was
              young,
       See round thy giant base a brighter choir,
650   Nor e'er did Delphi, when her priestess sung
       The Pythian hymn with more than mortal fire,
       Behold a train more fitting to inspire
       The song of love than Andalusia's maids,
       Nurst in the glowing lap of soft desire:
655   Ah! that to these were given such peaceful shades
As Greece can still bestow, though Glory fly her glades.

LXV

       Fair is proud Seville; let her country boast
       Her strength, her wealth, her site of ancient days;[1]
       But Cadiz, rising on the distant coast,
660   Calls forth a sweeter, though ignoble praise.

1. Seville was the Hispalis of the Romans.

Ah, Vice! how soft are thy voluptuous ways!
While boyish blood is mantling, who can 'scape
The fascination of thy magic gaze?
A Cherub-hydra round us dost thou gape,
665   And mould to every taste thy dear delusive shape.

LXVI

When Paphos fell by time – accursed Time!
The Queen who conquers all must yield to thee –
The Pleasures fled, but sought as warm a clime;
And Venus, constant to her native sea,
670   To nought else constant, hither deign'd to flee;
And fix'd her shrine within these walls of white;
Though not to one dome circumscribeth she
Her worship, but, devoted to her rite,
A thousand altars rise, for ever blazing bright.

LXVII

675   From morn till night, from night till startled Morn
Peeps blushing on the revel's laughing crew,
The song is heard, the rosy garland worn;
Devices quaint, and frolics ever new,
Tread on each other's kibes. A long adieu
680   He bids to sober joy that here sojourns:
Nought interrupts the riot, though in lieu
Of true devotion monkish incense burns,
And love and prayer unite, or rule the hour by turns.

LXVIII

The Sabbath comes, a day of blessed rest;
685   What hallows it upon this Christian shore?
Lo! it is sacred to a solemn feast;
Hark! heard you not the forest-monarch's roar?
Crashing the lance, he snuffs the spouting gore
Of man and steed, o'erthrown beneath his horn;
690   The throng'd arena shakes with shouts for more;
Yells the mad crowd o'er entrails freshly torn,
Nor shrinks the female eye, nor ev'n affects to mourn.

LXIX

  The seventh day this; the jubilee of man.
  London! right well thou know'st the day of prayer:
695 Then thy spruce citizen, wash'd artisan,
  And smug apprentice gulp their weekly air:
  Thy coach of hackney, whiskey, one-horse chair,
  And humblest gig through sundry suburbs whirl;
  To Hampstead, Brentford, Harrow make repair;
700 Till the tired jade the wheel forgets to hurl,
Provoking envious gibe from each pedestrian churl.

LXX

  Some o'er thy Thamis row the ribbon'd fair,
  Others along the safer turnpike fly;
  Some Richmond-hill ascend, some scud to Ware,
705 And many to the steep of Highgate hie.
  Ask ye, Bœotian shades! the reason why?[1]
  'Tis to the worship of the solemn Horn,
  Grasp'd in the holy hand of Mystery,
  In whose dread name both men and maids are sworn,
710 And consecrate the oath with draught, and dance till morn.

LXXI

  All have their fooleries – not alike are thine,
  Fair Cadiz, rising o'er the dark blue sea!
  Soon as the matin bell proclaimeth nine,
  Thy saint adorers count the rosary:
715 Much is the VIRGIN teased to shrive them free
  (Well do I ween the only virgin there)
  From crimes as numerous as her beadsmen be;
  Then to the crowded circus forth they fare:
Young, old, high, low, at once the same diversion share.

1. This was written at Thebes and consequently in the best situation for asking and answering such a question; not as the birthplace of Pindar, but as the capital of Bœotia, where the first riddle was propounded and solved.

LXXII

720   The lists are oped, the spacious area clear'd,
       Thousands on thousands piled are seated round;
       Long ere the first loud trumpet's note is heard,
       Ne vacant space for lated wight is found:
       Here dons, grandees, but chiefly dames abound,
725   Skill'd in the ogle of a roguish eye,
       Yet ever well inclined to heal the wound;
       None through their cold disdain are doom'd to die,
As moon-struck bards complain, by Love's sad archery.

LXXIII

       Hush'd is the din of tongues – on gallant steeds,
730   With milk-white crest, gold spur, and light-pois'd lance
       Four cavaliers prepare for venturous deeds,
       And lowly bending to the lists advance;
       Rich are their scarfs, their charges featly prance:
       If in the dangerous game they shine to-day,
735   The crowd's loud shout and ladies' lovely glance,
       Best prize of better acts, they bear away,
And all that kings or chiefs e'er gain their toils repay.

LXXIV

       In costly sheen and gaudy cloak array'd,
       But all afoot, the light-limb'd Matadore
740   Stands in the centre, eager to invade
       The lord of lowing herds; but not before
       The ground, with cautious tread, is traversed o'er,
       Lest aught unseen should lurk to thwart his speed:
       His arms a dart, he fights aloof, nor more
745   Can man achieve without the friendly steed –
Alas! too oft condemn'd for him to bear and bleed.

LXXV

       Thrice sounds the clarion; lo! the signal falls,
       The den expands, and Expectation mute
       Gapes round the silent circle's peopled walls.
750   Bounds with one lashing spring the mighty brute,
       And, wildly staring, spurns, with sounding foot,

The sand, nor blindly rushes on his foe:
Here, there, he points his threatening front, to suit
His first attack, wide waving to and fro
755   His angry tail; red rolls his eye's dilated glow.

LXXVI

Sudden he stops; his eye is fix'd: away,
Away, thou heedless boy! prepare the spear:
Now is thy time, to perish, or display
The skill that yet may check his mad career.
760   With well-timed croupe the nimble coursers veer;
On foams the bull, but not unscathed he goes;
Streams from his flank the crimson torrent clear:
He flies, he wheels, distracted with his throes;
Dart follows dart; lance, lance; loud bellowings speak his
    woes.

LXXVII

765   Again he comes; nor dart nor lance avail,
Nor the wild plunging of the tortured horse;
Though man and man's avenging arms assail,
Vain are his weapons, vainer is his force.
One gallant steed is stretch'd a mangled corse;
770   Another, hideous sight! unseam'd appears,
His gory chest unveils life's panting source;
Though death-struck, still his feeble frame he rears;
Staggering, but stemming all, his lord unharm'd he bears.

LXXVIII

Foil'd, bleeding, breathless, furious to the last,
775   Full in the centre stands the bull at bay,
Mid wounds, and clinging darts, and lances brast,
And foes disabled in the brutal fray:
And now the Matadores around him play,
Shake the red cloak, and poise the ready brand:
780   Once more through all he bursts his thundering way –
Vain rage! the mantle quits the conynge hand,
Wraps his fierce eye – 'tis past – he sinks upon the sand!

LXXIX

Where his vast neck just mingles with the spine,
Sheathed in his form the deadly weapon lies.
785   He stops – he starts – disdaining to decline:
Slowly he falls, amidst triumphant cries,
Without a groan, without a struggle dies.
The decorated car appears – on high
The corse is piled – sweet sight for vulgar eyes –
790   Four steeds that spurn the rein, as swift as shy,
Hurl the dark bulk along, scarce seen in dashing by.

LXXX

Such the ungentle sport that oft invites
The Spanish maid, and cheers the Spanish swain.
Nurtured in blood betimes, his heart delights
795   In vengeance, gloating on another's pain.
What private feuds the troubled village stain!
Though now one phalanx'd host should meet the foe,
Enough, alas! in humble homes remain,
To meditate 'gainst friends the secret blow,
800   For some slight cause of wrath, whence life's warm stream
must flow.

LXXXI

But Jealousy has fled: his bars, his bolts,
His wither'd centinel, Duenna sage!
And all whereat the generous soul revolts,
Which the stern dotard deem'd he could encage,
805   Have pass'd to darkness with the vanish'd age.
Who late so free as Spanish girls were seen,
(Ere War uprose in his volcanic rage,)
With braided tresses bounding o'er the green,
While on the gay dance shone Night's lover-loving Queen?

LXXXII

810   Oh! many a time, and oft, had Harold loved,
Or dream'd he loved, since Rapture is a dream;
But now his wayward bosom was unmoved,
For not yet had he drunk of Lethe's stream;
And lately had he learn'd with truth to deem

815   Love has no gift so grateful as his wings:
           How fair, how young, how soft soe'er he seem,
           Full from the fount of Joy's delicious springs
        Some bitter o'er the flowers its bubbling venom flings.[1]

        LXXXIII
           Yet to the beauteous form he was not blind,
820   Though now it moved him as it moves the wise;
           Not that Philosophy on such a mind
           E'er deign'd to bend her chastely-awful eyes:
           But Passion raves itself to rest, or flies;
           And Vice, that digs her own voluptuous tomb,
825   Had buried long his hopes, no more to rise:
           Pleasure's pall'd victim! life-abhorring gloom
        Wrote on his faded brow curst Cain's unresting doom.

        LXXXIV
           Still he beheld, nor mingled with the throng;
           But view'd them not with misanthropic hate:
830   Fain would be now have join'd the dance, the song;
           But who may smile that sinks beneath his fate?
           Nought that he saw his sadness could abate:
           Yet once he struggled 'gainst the demon's sway,
           And as in Beauty's bower he pensive sate,
835   Pour'd forth this unpremeditated lay,
        To charms as fair as those that soothed his happier day.

1. 'Medio de fonte leporum,' &c. – Luc.

To Inez

1

    Nay, smile not at my sullen brow;
        Alas! I cannot smile again:
    Yet Heaven avert that ever thou
840   Shouldst weep, and haply weep in vain.

2

    And dost thou ask, what secret woe
        I bear, corroding joy and youth?
    And wilt thou vainly seek to know
        A pang, ev'n thou must fail to soothe?

3

845 It is not love, it is not hate,
        Nor low Ambition's honours lost,
    That bids me loathe my present state,
        And fly from all I prized the most:

4

    It is that weariness which springs
850   From all I meet, or hear, or see:
    To me no pleasure Beauty brings;
        Thine eyes have scarce a charm for me.

5

    It is that settled, ceaseless gloom
        The fabled Hebrew wanderer bore;
855 That will not look beyond the tomb,
        But cannot hope for rest before.

6

    What Exile from himself can flee?
        To zones, though more and more remote,
    Still, still pursues, where-e'er I be,
860   The blight of life – the demon Thought.

7

Yet others rapt in pleasure seem,
    And taste of all that I forsake;
Oh! may they still of transport dream,
    And ne'er, at least like me, awake!

8

865   Through many a clime 'tis mine to go,
    With many a retrospection curst;
And all my solace is to know,
    Whate'er betides, I've known the worst.

9

What is that worst? Nay do not ask —
870   In pity from the search forbear:
Smile on — nor venture to unmask
    Man's heart, and view the Hell that's there.

LXXXV

Adieu, fair Cadiz! yea, a long adieu!
Who may forget how well thy walls have stood?
875   When all were changing thou alone wert true,
First to be free and last to be subdued:
And if amidst a scene, a shock so rude,
Some native blood was seen thy streets to die;
A traitor only fell beneath the feud;[1]
880   Here all were noble, save Nobility;
None hugg'd a conqueror's chain, save fallen Chivalry!

LXXXVI

Such be the sons of Spain, and strange her fate!
They fight for freedom who were never free,
A Kingless people for a nerveless state,
885   Her vassals combat when their chieftains flee,
True to the veriest slaves of Treachery:

1. Alluding to the conduct and death of Solano, the governor of Cadiz, in
May, 1809.

Fond of a land which gave them nought but life,
Pride points the path that leads to Liberty;
Back to the struggle, baffled in the strife,
890   War, war is still the cry, 'War even to the knife!'[1]

LXXXVII

Ye, who would more of Spain and Spaniards know,
Go, read whate'er is writ of bloodiest strife:
Whate'er keen Vengeance urged on foreign foe
Can act, is acting there against man's life:
895   From flashing scimitar to secret knife,
War mouldeth there each weapon to his need –
So may he guard the sister and the wife,
So may he make each curst oppressor bleed,
So may such foes deserve the most remorseless deed!

LXXXVIII

900   Flows there a tear of pity for the dead?
Look o'er the ravage of the reeking plain;
Look on the hands with female slaughter red;
Then to the dogs resign the unburied slain,
Then to the vulture let each corse remain;
905   Albeit unworthy of the prey-bird's maw,
Let their bleach'd bones, and blood's unbleaching stain,
Long mark the battle-field with hideous awe:
Thus only may our sons conceive the scenes we saw!

LXXXIX

Nor yet, alas! the dreadful work is done;
910   Fresh legions pour adown the Pyrenees:
It deepens still, the work is scarce begun,
Nor mortal eye the distant end foresees.
Fall'n nations gaze on Spain; if freed, she frees
More than her fell Pizarros once enchain'd:
915   Strange retribution! now Columbia's ease
Repairs the wrongs that Quito's sons sustain'd,
While o'er the parent clime prowls Murder unrestrain'd.

1. 'War to the knife.' Palafox's answer to the French general at the siege of Saragoza.

XC

Not all the blood at Talavera shed,
Not all the marvels of Barossa's fight,
920   Not Albuera lavish of the dead,
Have won for Spain her well asserted right.
When shall her Olive-Branch be free from blight?
When shall she breathe her from the blushing toil?
How many a doubtful day shall sink in night,
925   Ere the Frank robber turn him from his spoil,
And Freedom's stranger-tree grow native of the soil!

XCI

And thou, my friend![1] – since unavailing woe
Bursts from my heart, and mingles with the strain –
Had the sword laid thee with the mighty low,
930   Pride might forbid e'en Friendship to complain:
But thus unlaurel'd to descend in vain,
By all forgotten, save the lonely breast,
And mix unbleeding with the boasted slain,
While Glory crowns so many a meaner crest!
935   What hadst thou done to sink so peacefully to rest?

1. The Honourable John Wingfield, of the Guards, who died of a fever at Coimbra. I had known him ten years, the better half of his life, and the happiest part of mine. In the short space of one month, I have lost *her* who gave me being, and most of those who had made that being tolerable. To me the lines of Young are no fiction: –

'Insatiate archer: could not one suffice?
Thy shaft flew thrice, and thrice my peace was slain,
And thrice ere thrice yon moon had fill'd her horn.'

I should have ventured a verse to the memory of the late Charles Skinner Matthews, Fellow of Downing College, Cambridge, were he not too much above all praise of mine. His powers of mind, shown in the attainment of greater honours, against the ablest candidates, than those of any graduate on record at Cambridge, have sufficiently established his fame on the spot where it was acquired; while his softer qualities live in the recollection of friends who loved him too well to envy his superiority.

XCII

Oh, known the earliest, and esteem'd the most!
Dear to a heart where nought was left so dear!
Though to my hopeless days for ever lost,
In dreams deny me not to see thee here!
940   And Morn in secret shall renew the tear
Of Consciousness awaking to her woes,
And Fancy hover o'er thy bloodless bier,
Till my frail frame return to whence it rose,
And mourn'd and mourner lie united in repose.

XCIII

945   Here is one fytte of Harold's pilgrimage:
Ye who of him may further seek to know,
Shall find some tidings in a future page,
If he that rhymeth now may scribble moe.
Is this too much? stern Critic! say not so:
950   Patience! and ye shall hear what he beheld
In other lands, where he was doom'd to go:
Lands that contain the monuments of Eld,
Ere Greece and Grecian arts by barbarous hands were
quell'd.

Canto the Second

I

Come, blue-eyed maid of heaven! – but thou, alas!
Didst never yet one mortal song inspire –
Goddess of Wisdom! here thy temple was,
And is, despite of war and wasting fire,[1]
5   And years, that bade thy worship to expire:
But worse than steel, and flame, and ages slow,
Is the dread sceptre and dominion dire
Of men who never felt the sacred glow
That thoughts of thee and thine on polish'd breasts bestow.

1. Part of the Acropolis was destroyed by the explosion of a magazine during the Venetian siege.

II

10   Ancient of days! august Athena![1] where,
        Where are thy men of might? thy grand in soul?
        Gone – glimmering through the dream of things that
            were:
        First in the race that led to Glory's goal,
        They won, and pass'd away – is this the whole?
15   A schoolboy's tale, the wonder of an hour!
        The warrior's weapon and the sophist's stole
        Are sought in vain, and o'er each mouldering tower,
    Dim with the mist of years, gray flits the shade of power.

III

        Sun of the morning, rise! approach you here!
20   Come – but molest not yon defenceless urn:
        Look on this spot – a nation's sepulchre!
        Abode of gods, whose shrines no longer burn.

1. We can all feel, or imagine, the regret with which the ruins of cities once the capitals of empires, are beheld: the reflections suggested by such objects are too trite to require recapitulation. But never did the littleness of man, and the vanity of his very best virtues, of patriotism to exalt, and of valour to defend his country, appear more conspicuous than in the record of what Athens was, and the certainty of what she now is. This theatre of contention between mighty factions, of the struggles of orators, the exaltation and deposition of tyrants, the triumph and punishment of generals, is now become a scene of petty intrigue and perpetual disturbance, between the bickering agents of certain British nobility and gentry. 'The wild foxes, the owls and serpents in the ruins of Babylon,' were surely less degrading than such inhabitants. The Turks have the plea of conquest for their tyranny, and the Greeks have only suffered the fortune of war, incidental to the bravest; but how are the mighty fallen, when two painters contest the privilege of plundering the Parthenon, and triumph in turn, according to the tenor of each succeeding firman! Sylla could but punish, Philip subdue, and Xerxes burn Athens; but it remained for the paltry antiquarian, and his despicable agents, to render her contemptible as himself and his pursuits. The Parthenon, before its destruction in part, by fire during the Venetian siege, had been a temple, a church, and a mosque. In each point of view it is an object of regard: it changed its worshippers; but still it was a place of worship thrice sacred to devotion: its violation is a triple sacrilege. But –

            'Man, proud man,
        Drest in a little brief authority,
        Plays such fantastic tricks before high heaven
        As make the angels weep.'

Even gods must yield – religions take their turn:
'Twas Jove's – 'tis Mahomet's – and other creeds
25   Will rise with other years, till man shall learn
Vainly his incense soars, his victim bleeds;
Poor child of Doubt and Death, whose hope is built on reeds.

IV

Bound to the earth, he lifts his eye to heaven –
Is't not enough, unhappy thing! to know
30   Thou art? Is this a boon so kindly given,
That being, thou woulds't be again, and go,
Thou know'st not, reck'st not to what region, so
On earth no more, but mingled with the skies?
Still wilt thou dream on future joy and woe?
35   Regard and weigh yon dust before it flies:
That little urn saith more than thousand homilies.

V

Or burst the vanish'd Hero's lofty mound;
Far on the solitary shore he sleeps:[1]
He fell, and falling nations mourn'd around;
40   But now not one of saddening thousands weeps,
Nor warlike-worshipper his vigil keeps
Where demi-gods appear'd, as records tell.
Remove yon skull from out the scatter'd heaps:
Is that a temple where a God may dwell?
45   Why ev'n the worm at last disdains her shatter'd cell!

VI

Look on its broken arch, its ruin'd wall,
Its chambers desolate, and portals foul:
Yes, this was once Ambition's airy hall,
The dome of Thought, the palace of the Soul:

1. It was not always the custom of the Greeks to burn their dead; the greater
Ajax, in particular, was interred entire. Almost all the chiefs became gods
after their decease; and he was indeed neglected, who had not annual games
near his tomb, or festivals in honour of his memory by his countrymen, as
Achilles, Brasidas, &c. and at last even Antinous, whose death was as heroic
as his life was infamous.

50   Behold through each lack-lustre, eyeless hole,
       The gay recess of Wisdom and of Wit
       And Passion's host, that never brook'd control:
       Can all saint, sage, or sophist ever writ,
People this lonely tower, this tenement refit?

VII

55   Well didst thou speak, Athena's wisest son!
       'All that we know is, nothing can be known.'
       Why should we shrink from what we cannot shun?
       Each hath his pang, but feeble sufferers groan
       With brain-born dreams of evil all their own.
60   Pursue what Chance or Fate proclaimeth best;
       Peace waits us on the shores of Acheron:
       There no forced banquet claims the sated guest,
But Silence spreads the couch of ever welcome rest.

VIII

       Yet if, as holiest men have deem'd, there be
65   A land of souls beyond that sable shore,
       To shame the doctrine of the Sadducee
       And sophists, madly vain of dubious lore;
       How sweet it were in concert to adore
       With those who made our mortal labours light!
70   To hear each voice we fear'd to hear no more!
       Behold each mighty shade reveal'd to sight,
The Bactrian, Samian sage, and all who taught the right!

IX

       There, thou! – whose love and life together fled,
       Have left me here to love and live in vain –
75   Twined with my heart, and can I deem thee dead
       When busy Memory flashes on my brain?
       Well – I will dream that we may meet again,
       And woo the vision to my vacant breast:
       If aught of young Remembrance then remain,
80   Be as it may Futurity's behest,
For me 'twere bliss enough to know thy spirit blest!

X

Here let me sit upon this massy stone,
The marble column's yet unshaken base;
Here, son of Saturn! was thy fav'rite throne:[1]
85   Mightiest of many such! Hence let me trace
The latent grandeur of thy dwelling-place.
It may not be: nor ev'n can Fancy's eye
Restore what Time hath labour'd to deface.
Yet these proud pillars claim no passing sigh;
90 Unmoved the Moslem sits, the light Greek carols by.

XI

But who, of all the plunderers of yon fane
On high, where Pallas linger'd, loth to flee
The latest relic of her ancient reign;
The last, the worst, dull spoiler, who was he?
95   Blush, Caledonia! such thy son could be!
England! I joy no child he was of thine:
Thy free-born men should spare what once was free;
Yet they could violate each saddening shrine,
And bear these altars o'er the long-reluctant brine.[2]

XII

100 But most the modern Pict's ignoble boast,
To rive what Goth, and Turk, and Time hath spared:[3]
Cold as the crags upon his native coast,
His mind as barren and his heart as hard,
Is he whose head conceived, whose hand prepared,
105   Aught to displace Athena's poor remains:
Her sons too weak the sacred shrine to guard,
Yet felt some portion of their mother's pains,[4]
And never knew, till then, the weight of Despot's chains.

1. The temple of Jupiter Olympius, of which sixteen columns, entirely of marble, yet survive: originally there were one hundred and fifty. These columns, however, are by many supposed to have belonged to the Parthenon.
2. The ship was wrecked in the Archipelago.
3. See Appendix to this Canto [A], for a note too long to be placed here.
4. I cannot resist availing myself of the permission of my friend Dr Clarke, whose name requires no comment with the public, but whose sanction will

XIII

What! shall it e'er be said by British tongue,
Albion was happy in Athena's tears?
Though in thy name the slaves her bosom wrung,
Tell not the deed to blushing Europe's ears;
The ocean queen, the free Britannia, bears
The last poor plunder from a bleeding land:
Yes, she, whose gen'rous aid her name endears,
Tore down those remnants with a harpy's hand,
Which envious Eld forbore, and tyrants left to stand.

XIV

Where was thine Ægis, Pallas! that appall'd
Stern Alaric and Havoc on their way?[1]
Where Peleus' son? whom Hell in vain enthrall'd
His shade from Hades upon that dread day
Bursting to light in terrible array!
What! could not Pluto spare the chief once more,
To scare a second robber from his prey?
Idly he wander'd on the Stygian shore,
Nor now preserved the walls he loved to shield before.

XV

Cold is the heart, fair Greece! that looks on thee,
Nor feels as lovers o'er the dust they loved;
Dull is the eye that will not weep to see
Thy walls defaced, thy mouldering shrines removed
By British hands, which it had best behoved

---

add tenfold weight to my testimony, to insert the following extract from a
very obliging letter of his to me, as a note to the above lines: – 'When the
last of the Metopes was taken from the Parthenon, and, in moving of it,
a great part of the superstructure with one of the triglyphs was thrown down
by the workmen whom Lord Elgin employed, the Disdar who beheld the
mischief done to the building, took his pipe from his mouth, dropped a tear,
and, in a supplicating tone of voice, said to Lusieri, Τέλος! –I was present.'
The Disdar alluded to was the father of the present Disdar.

1. According to Zosimus, Minerva and Achilles frightened Alaric from the
Acropolis; but others relate that the Gothic king was nearly as mischievous
as the Scottish peer. – See CHANDLER.

Line numbers: 110, 115, 120, 125, 130

To guard those relics ne'er to be restored.
Curst be the hour when from their isle they roved,
And once again thy hapless bosom gored,
135   And snatch'd thy shrinking Gods to northern climes
abhorr'd!

XVI

But where is Harold? shall I then forget
To urge the gloomy wanderer o'er the wave?
Little reck'd he of all that men regret;
No loved-one now in feign'd lament could rave;
140   No friend the parting hand extended gave,
Ere the cold stranger pass'd to other climes:
Hard is his heart whom charms may not enslave;
But Harold felt not as in other times,
And left without a sigh the land of war and crimes.

XVII

145   He that has sail'd upon the dark blue sea
Has view'd at times, I ween, a full fair sight;
When the fresh breeze is fair as breeze may be,
The white sail set, the gallant frigate tight;
Masts, spires, and strand retiring to the right,
150   The glorious main expanding o'er the bow,
The convoy spread like wild swans in their flight,
The dullest sailer wearing bravely now,
So gaily curl the waves before each dashing prow.

XVIII

And oh, the little warlike world within!
155   The well-reeved guns, the netted canopy,[1]
The hoarse command, the busy humming din,
When, at a word, the tops are mann'd on high:
Hark, to the Boatswain's call, the cheering cry!
While through the seaman's hand the tackle glides;
160   Or schoolboy Midshipman that, standing by,
Strains his shrill pipe as good or ill betides,
And well the docile crew that skilful urchin guides.

1. To prevent blocks or splinters from falling on deck during action.

XIX

    White is the glassy deck, without a stain,
    Where on the watch the staid Lieutenant walks:
165   Look on that part which sacred doth remain
    For the lone chieftain, who majestic stalks,
    Silent and fear'd by all – not oft he talks
    With aught beneath him, if he would preserve
    That strict restraint, which broken, ever balks
170   Conquest and Fame: but Britons rarely swerve
From law, however stern, which tends their strength to
        nerve.

XX

    Blow! swiftly blow, thou keel-compelling gale!
    Till the broad sun withdraws his lessening ray;
    Then must the pennant-bearer slacken sail,
175   That lagging barks may make their lazy way.
    Ah! grievance sore, and listless dull delay,
    To waste on sluggish hulks the sweetest breeze!
    What leagues are lost, before the dawn of day,
    Thus loitering pensive on the willing seas,
180 The flapping sail haul'd down to halt for logs like these!

XXI

    The moon is up; by Heaven, a lovely eve!
    Long streams of light o'er dancing waves expand;
    Now lads on shore may sigh, and maids believe:
    Such be our fate when we return to land!
185   Meantime some rude Arion's restless hand
    Wakes the brisk harmony that sailors love;
    A circle there of merry listeners stand,
    Or to some well-known measure featly move,
Thoughtless, as if on shore they still were free to rove.

XXII

190   Through Calpe's straits survey the steepy shore;
    Europe and Afric on each other gaze!
    Lands of the dark-eyed Maid and dusky Moor
    Alike beheld beneath pale Hecate's blaze:

How softly on the Spanish shore she plays,
195   Disclosing rock, and slope, and forest brown,
Distinct, though darkening with her waning phase;
But Mauritania's giant-shadows frown,
From mountain-cliff to coast descending sombre down.

XXIII
'Tis night, when Meditation bids us feel
200   We once have loved, though love is at an end:
The heart, lone mourner of its baffled zeal,
Though friendless now, will dream it had a friend.
Who with the weight of years would wish to bend,
When Youth itself survives young Love and Joy?
205   Alas! when mingling souls forget to blend,
Death hath but little left him to destroy?
Ah! happy years! once more who would not be a boy?

XXIV
Thus bending o'er the vessel's laving side,
To gaze on Dian's wave-reflected sphere,
210   The soul forgets her schemes of Hope and Pride,
And flies unconscious o'er each backward year.
None are so desolate but something dear,
Dearer than self, possesses or possess'd
A thought, and claims the homage of a tear;
215   A flashing pang! of which the weary breast
Would still, albeit in vain, the heavy heart divest.

XXV
To sit on rocks, to muse o'er flood and fell,
To slowly trace the forest's shady scene,
Where things that own not man's dominion dwell,
220   And mortal foot hath ne'er or rarely been;
To climb the trackless mountain all unseen,
With the wild flock that never needs a fold;
Alone o'er steeps and foaming falls to lean;
This is not solitude; 'tis but to hold
225   Converse with Nature's charms, and view her stores
unroll'd.

XXVI

But midst the crowd, the hum, the shock of men,
To hear, to see, to feel, and to possess,
And roam along, the world's tired denizen,
With none who bless us, none whom we can bless;
230   Minions of splendour shrinking from distress!
None that, with kindred consciousness endued,
If we were not, would seem to smile the less
Of all that flatter'd, follow'd, sought, and sued;
This is to be alone; this, this is solitude!

XXVII

235   More blest the life of godly eremite,
Such as on lonely Athos may be seen,
Watching at eve upon the giant height,
Which looks o'er waves so blue, skies so serene,
That he who there at such an hour hath been
240   Will wistful linger on that hallow'd spot;
Then slowly tear him from the witching scene,
Sigh forth one wish that such had been his lot,
Then turn to hate a world he had almost forgot.

XXVIII

Pass we the long, unvarying course, the track
245   Oft trod, that never leaves a trace behind;
Pass we the calm, the gale, the change, the tack,
And each well known caprice of wave and wind;
Pass we the joys and sorrows sailors find,
Coop'd in their winged sea-girt citadel;
250   The foul, the fair, the contrary, the kind,
As breezes rise and fall and billows swell,
Till on some jocund morn – lo, land! and all is well.

XXIX

But not in silence pass Calypso's isles,[1]
The sister tenants of the middle deep;
255   There for the weary still a haven smiles,
Though the fair goddess long hath ceased to weep,

1. Goza is said to have been the island of Calypso.

And o'er her cliffs a fruitless watch to keep
For him who dared prefer a mortal bride:
Here, too, his boy essay'd the dreadful leap
260   Stern Mentor urged from high to yonder tide;
While thus of both bereft, the nymph-queen doubly
        sighed.

XXX

Her reign is past, her gentle glories gone:
But trust not this; too easy youth, beware!
A mortal sovereign holds her dangerous throne,
265   And thou may'st find a new Calypso there.
Sweet Florence! could another ever share
This wayward, loveless heart, it would be thine:
But check'd by every tie, I may not dare
To cast a worthless offering at thy shrine,
270   Nor ask so dear a breast to feel one pang for mine.

XXXI

Thus Harold deem'd, as on that lady's eye
He look'd, and met its beam without a thought,
Save Admiration glancing harmless by:
Love kept aloof, albeit not far remote,
275   Who knew his votary often lost and caught,
But knew him as his worshipper no more,
And ne'er again the boy his bosom sought:
Since now he vainly urged him to adore,
Well deem'd the little God his ancient sway was o'er.

XXXII

280   Fair Florence found, in sooth with some amaze,
One who, 'twas said, still sigh'd to all he saw,
Withstand, unmoved, the lustre of her gaze,
Which others hail'd with real or mimic awe,
Their hope, their doom, their punishment, their law;
285   All that gay Beauty from her bondsmen claims:
And much she marvell'd that a youth so raw
Nor felt, nor feign'd at least, the oft-told flames,
Which, though sometimes they frown, yet rarely anger
        dames.

XXXIII
    Little knew she that seeming marble heart,
290   Now mask'd in silence or withheld by pride,
    Was not unskilful in the spoiler's art,
    And spread its snares licentious far and wide;
    Nor from the base pursuit had turn'd aside,
    As long as aught was worthy to pursue:
295   But Harold on such arts no more relied;
    And had he doted on those eyes so blue,
Yet never would he join the lover's whining crew.

XXXIV
    Not much he kens, I ween, of woman's breast,
    Who thinks that wanton thing is won by sighs;
300   What careth she for hearts when once possess'd?
    Do proper homage to thine idol's eyes;
    But not too humbly, or she will despise
    Thee and thy suit, though told in moving tropes:
    Disguise ev'n tenderness, if thou art wise;
305   Brisk Confidence still best with woman copes;
Pique her and soothe in turn, soon Passion crowns thy
        hopes.

XXXV
    'Tis an old lesson; Time approves it true,
    And those who know it best, deplore it most;
    When all is won that all desire to woo,
310   The paltry prize is hardly worth the cost:
    Youth wasted, minds degraded, honour lost,
    These are thy fruits, successful Passion! these!
    If, kindly cruel, early Hope is crost,
    Still to the last it rankles, a disease,
315 Not to be cured when Love itself forgets to please.

XXXVI
    Away! nor let me loiter in my song,
    For we have many a mountain-path to tread,
    And many a varied shore to sail along,
    By pensive Sadness, not by Fiction, led –

320   Climes, fair withal as ever mortal head
    Imagined in its little schemes of thought;
    Or e'er in new Utopias were ared,
    To teach man what he might be, or he ought;
  If that corrupted thing could ever such be taught.

   XXXVII

325   Dear Nature is the kindest mother still,
    Though alway changing, in her aspect mild;
    From her bare bosom let me take my fill,
    Her never-wean'd, though not her favour'd child.
    Oh! she is fairest in her features wild,

330   Where nothing polish'd dares pollute her path:
    To me by day or night she ever smiled,
    Though I have mark'd her when none other hath,
  And sought her more and more, and loved her best in
      wrath.

   XXXVIII

   Land of Albania! where Iskander rose,

335   Theme of the young, and beacon of the wise,
    And he his namesake, whose oft-baffled foes
    Shrunk from his deeds of chivalrous emprize:
    Land of Albania![1] let me bend mine eyes
    On thee, thou rugged nurse of savage men!

340   The cross descends, thy minarets arise,
    And the pale crescent sparkles in the glen,
  Through many a cypress grove within each city's ken.

   XXXIX

   Childe Harold sail'd, and pass'd the barren spot,
    Where sad Penelope o'erlook'd the wave;[2]

345   And onward view'd the mount, not yet forgot,
    The lover's refuge, and the Lesbian's grave.
    Dark Sappho! could not verse immortal save

   1. See Appendix to this Canto, Note [B].
   2. Ithaca.

That breast imbued with such immortal fire?
Could she not live who life eternal gave?
350   If life eternal may await the lyre,
That only heaven to which Earth's children may aspire.

XL

'Twas on a Grecian autumn's gentle eve
Childe Harold hail'd Leucadia's cape afar;[1]
A spot he longed to see, nor cared to leave:
355   Oft did he mark the scenes of vanish'd war,
Actium, Lepanto, fatal Trafalgar;[2]
Mark them unmoved, for he would not delight
(Born beneath some remote inglorious star)
In themes of bloody fray, or gallant fight,
360   But loathed the bravo's trade, and laughed at martial
          wight.

XLI

But when he saw the evening star above
Leucadia's far-projecting rock of woe,
And hail'd the last resort of fruitless love,
He felt, or deem'd he felt, no common glow:
365   And as the stately vessel glided slow
Beneath the shadow of that ancient mount,
He watch'd the billows' melancholy flow,
And, sunk albeit in thought as he was wont,
More placid seem'd his eye, and smooth his pallid front.

XLII

370   Morn dawns; and with it stern Albania's hills,
Dark Suli's rocks, and Pindus' inland peak,
Robed half in mist, bedew'd with snowy rills,
Array'd in many a dun and purple streak,
Arise; and, as the clouds along them break,

1. Leucadia, now Santa Maura. From the promontory (the Lover's Leap)
Sappho is said to have thrown herself.
2. Actium and Trafalgar need no further mention. The battle of Lepanto,
equally bloody and considerable, but less known, was fought in the Gulf of
Patras. Here the author of Don Quixote lost his left hand.

375   Disclose the dwelling of the mountaineer:
        Here roams the wolf, the eagle whets his beak,
        Birds, beasts of prey, and wilder men appear,
And gathering storms around convulse the closing year.

XLIII

        Now Harold felt himself at length alone,
380   And bade to Christian tongues a long adieu;
        Now he adventured on a shore unknown,
        Which all admire, but many dread to view:
        His breast was arm'd 'gainst fate, his wants were few;
        Peril he sought not, but ne'er shrank to meet:
385   The scene was savage, but the scene was new;
        This made the ceaseless toil of travel sweet,
Beat back keen winter's blast, and welcomed summer's
                heat.

XLIV

        Here the red cross, for still the cross is here,
        Though sadly scoff'd at by the circumcised,
390   Forgets that pride to pamper'd priesthood dear;
        Churchman and votary alike despised.
        Foul Superstition! howsoe'er disguised,
        Idol, saint, virgin, prophet, crescent, cross,
        For whatsoever symbol thou art prized,
395   Thou sacerdotal gain, but general loss!
Who from true worship's gold can separate thy dross?

XLV

        Ambracia's gulf behold, where once was lost
        A world for woman, lovely, harmless thing!
        In yonder rippling bay, their naval host
400   Did many a Roman chief and Asian king[1]

1. It is said, that, on the day previous to the battle of Actium, Antony had thirteen kings at his levee.

To doubtful conflict, certain slaughter bring:
Look where the second Cæsar's trophies rose:[1]
Now, like the hands that rear'd them, withering:
Imperial anarchs, doubling human woes!
405   GOD! was thy globe ordain'd for such to win and lose?

XLVI

From the dark barriers of that rugged clime,
Ev'n to the centre of Illyria's vales,
Childe Harold pass'd o'er many a mount sublime,
Through lands scarce noticed in historic tales;
410   Yet in famed Attica such lovely dales
Are rarely seen; nor can fair Tempe boast
A charm they know not; loved Parnassus fails,
Though classic ground and consecrated most,
To match some spots that lurk within this lowering coast.

XLVII

415   He pass'd bleak Pindus, Acherusia's lake,[2]
And left the primal city of the land,
And onwards did his further journey take
To greet Albania's chief,[3] whose dread command
Is lawless law; for with a bloody hand
420   He sways a nation, turbulent and bold,
Yet here and there some daring mountain-band
Disdain his power, and from their rocky hold
Hurl their defiance far, nor yield, unless to gold.[4]

---

1. Nicopolis, whose ruins are most extensive, is at some distance from Actium, where the wall of the Hippodrome survives in a few fragments. These ruins are large masses of brickwork, the bricks of which are joined by interstices of mortar, as large as the bricks themselves, and equally durable.
2. According to Pouqueville, the lake of Yanina: but Pouqueville is always out.
3. The celebrated Ali Pacha. Of this extraordinary man there is an incorrect account in Pouqueville's Travels.
4. Five thousand Suliotes, among the rocks and in the castle of Suli, withstood thirty thousand Albanians for eighteen years; the castle at last was taken by bribery. In this contest there were several acts performed not unworthy of the better days of Greece.

XLVIII
Monastic Zitza![1] from thy shady brow,
425   Thou small, but favour'd spot of holy ground!
Where'er we gaze, around, above, below,
What rainbow tints, what magic charms are found!
Rock, river, forest, mountain, all abound,
And bluest skies that harmonise the whole:
430   Beneath, the distant torrent's rushing sound
Tells where the volumed cataract doth roll
Between those hanging rocks, that shock yet please the
        soul.

XLIX
Amidst the grove that crowns yon tufted hill,
Which, were it not for many a mountain nigh
435   Rising in lofty ranks, and loftier still,
Might well itself be deem'd of dignity,
The convent's white walls glisten fair on high:
Here dwells the caloyer,[2] nor rude is he,
Nor niggard of his cheer; the passer by
440   Is welcome still; nor heedless will he flee
From hence, if he delight kind Nature's sheen to see.

L
Here in the sultriest season let him rest,
Fresh is the green beneath those aged trees;
Here winds of gentlest wing will fan his breast,
445   From heaven itself he may inhale the breeze:
The plain is far beneath – oh! let him seize

1. The convent and village of Zitza are four hours' journey from Joannina or Yanina, the capital of the Pachalick. In the valley the river Kalamas (once the Acheron) flows, and, not far from Zitza, forms a fine cataract. The situation is perhaps the finest in Greece, though the approach to Delvinachi and parts of Acarnania and Ætolia may contest the palm. Delphi, Parnassus, and, in Attica, even Cape Colonna and Port Raphti, are very inferior; as also every scene in Ionia, or the Troad: I am almost inclined to add the approach to Constantinople; but, from the different features of the last, a comparison can hardly be made.
2. The Greek monks are so called.

Pure pleasure while he can; the scorching ray
Here pierceth not, impregnate with disease:
Then let his length the loitering pilgrim lay,
450   And gaze, untired, the morn, the noon, the eve away.

LI

Dusky and huge, enlarging on the sight,
Nature's volcanic amphitheatre,[1]
Chimæra's alps extend from left to right:
Beneath, a living valley seems to stir;
455   Flocks play, trees wave, streams flow, the mountain-fir
Nodding above; behold black Acheron![2]
Once consecrated to the sepulchre.
Pluto! if this be hell I look upon,
Close shamed Elysium's gates, my shade shall seek for
none.

LII

460   Ne city's towers pollute the lovely view;
Unseen is Yanina, though not remote,
Veil'd by the screen of hills: here men are few,
Scanty the hamlet, rare the lonely cot:
But peering down each precipice, the goat
465   Browseth; and, pensive o'er his scatter'd flock,
The little shepherd in his white capote[3]
Doth lean his boyish form along the rock,
Or in his cave awaits the tempest's short-lived shock.

LIII

Oh! where, Dodona! is thine aged grove,
470   Prophetic fount, and oracle divine?
What valley echo'd the response of Jove?
What trace remaineth of the Thunderer's shrine?
All, all forgotten – and shall man repine

1. The Chimariot mountains appear to have been volcanic.
2. Now called Kalamas.
3. Albanese cloak.

That his frail bonds to fleeting life are broke?
475   Cease, fool! the fate of gods may well be thine:
Wouldst thou survive the marble or the oak?
When nations, tongues, and worlds must sink beneath the
stroke!

LIV

Epirus' bounds recede, and mountains fail;
Tired of up-gazing still, the wearied eye
480   Reposes gladly on as smooth a vale
As ever Spring yclad in grassy die:
Ev'n on a plain no humble beauties lie,
Where some bold river breaks the long expanse,
And woods along the banks are waving high,
485   Whose shadows in the glassy waters dance,
Or with the moonbeam sleep in midnight's solemn trance.

LV

The sun had sunk behind vast Tomerit,[1]
And Laos wide and fierce came roaring by;[2]
The shades of wonted night were gathering yet,
490   When, down the steep banks winding warily,
Childe Harold saw, like meteors in the sky,
The glittering minarets of Tepalen,
Whose walls o'erlook the stream; and drawing nigh,
He heard the busy hum of warrior-men
495   Swelling the breeze that sigh'd along the lengthening glen.

LVI

He pass'd the sacred Haram's silent tower,
And underneath the wide o'erarching gate
Survey'd the dwelling of this chief of power,
Where all around proclaim'd his high estate.

1. Anciently Mount Tomarus.
2. The river Laos was full at the time the author passed it; and, immediately
above Tepaleen, was to the eye as wide as the Thames at Westminster; at
least in the opinion of the author and his fellow traveller. In the summer it
must be much narrower. It certainly is the finest river in the Levant; neither
Achelous, Alpheus, Acheron, Scamander, nor Cayster, approached it in
breadth or beauty.

500   Amidst no common pomp the despot sate,
       While busy preparation shook the court,
       Slaves, eunuchs, soldiers, guests, and santons wait;
       Within, a palace, and without, a fort:
Here men of every clime appear to make resort.

LVII

505   Richly caparison'd, a ready row
       Of armed horse, and many a warlike store,
       Circled the wide extending court below;
       Above, strange groups adorn'd the corridore:
       And oft-times through the area's echoing door,
510   Some high-capp'd Tartar spurr'd his steed away:
       The Turk, the Greek, the Albanian, and the Moor,
       Here mingled in their many-hued array,
While the deep war-drum's sound announced the close of
              day.

LVIII

       The wild Albanian kirtled to his knee,
515   With shawl-girt head and ornamented gun,
       And gold-embroider'd garments, fair to see:
       The crimson-scarfed men of Macedon;
       The Delhi with his cap of terror on,
       And crooked glaive; the lively, supple Greek;
520   And swarthy Nubia's mutilated son;
       The bearded Turk, that rarely deigns to speak,
Master of all around, too potent to be meek,

LIX

       Are mix'd conspicuous: some recline in groups,
       Scanning the motley scene that varies round;
525   There some grave Moslem to devotion stoops,
       And some that smoke, and some that play, are found;
       Here the Albanian proudly treads the ground;
       Half whispering there the Greek is heard to prate;
       Hark! from the mosque the nightly solemn sound,
530   The Muezzin's call doth shake the minaret,
'There is no god but God! – to prayer – lo! God is great!'

LX

    Just at this season Ramazani's fast
    Through the long day its penance did maintain:
    But when the lingering twilight hour was past,
535   Revel and feast assumed the rule again:
    Now all was bustle, and the menial train
    Prepared and spread the plenteous board within;
    The vacant gallery now seem'd made in vain,
    But from the chambers came the mingling din,
540 As page and slave anon were passing out and in.

LXI

    Here woman's voice is never heard: apart,
    And scarce permitted, guarded, veil'd, to move,
    She yields to one her person and her heart,
    Tamed to her cage, nor feels a wish to rove:
545   For, not unhappy in her master's love,
    And joyful in a mother's gentlest cares,
    Blest cares! all other feelings far above!
    Herself more sweetly rears the babe she bears,
Who never quits the breast, no meaner passion shares.

LXII

550   In marble-paved pavilion, where a spring
    Of living water from the centre rose,
    Whose bubbling did a genial freshness fling,
    And soft voluptuous couches breathed repose,
    ALI reclined, a man of war and woes:
555   Yet in his lineaments ye cannot trace,
    While Gentleness her milder radiance throws
    Along that aged venerable face,
The deeds that lurk beneath, and stain him with disgrace.

LXIII

    It is not that yon hoary lengthening beard
560   Ill suits the passions which belong to youth;
    Love conquers age – so Hafiz hath averr'd,
    So sings the Teian, and he sings in sooth –
    But crimes that scorn the tender voice of Ruth,

Beseeming all men ill, but most the man
565   In years, have mark'd him with a tiger's tooth;
Blood follows blood, and, through their mortal span,
In bloodier acts conclude those who with blood began.

LXIV

'Mid many things most new to ear and eye
The pilgrim rested here his weary feet,
570   And gazed around on Moslem luxury,
Till quickly wearied with that spacious seat
Of Wealth and Wantonness, the choice retreat
Of sated Grandeur from the city's noise:
And were it humbler it in sooth were sweet;
575   But Peace abhorreth artificial joys,
And Pleasure, leagued with Pomp, the zest of both
           destroys.

LXV

Fierce are Albania's children, yet they lack
Not virtues, were those virtues more mature.
Where is the foe that ever saw their back?
580   Who can so well the toil of war endure?
Their native fastnesses not more secure
Than they in doubtful time of troublous need:
Their wrath how deadly! but their friendship sure,
When Gratitude or Valour bids them bleed,
585 Unshaken rushing on where'er their chief may lead.

LXVI

Childe Harold saw them in their chieftain's tower
Thronging to war in splendour and success;
And after view'd them, when, within their power,
Himself awhile the victim of distress;
590   That saddening hour when bad men hotlier press:
But these did shelter him beneath their roof,
When less barbarians would have cheer'd him less,
And fellow-countrymen have stood aloof –[1]
In aught that tries the heart how few withstand the proof!

1. Alluding to the wreckers of Cornwall.

LXVII

595   It chanced that adverse winds once drove his bark
Full on the coast of Suli's shaggy shore,
When all around was desolate and dark;
To land was perilous, to sojourn more;
Yet for a while the mariners forbore,
600   Dubious to trust where treachery might lurk:
At length they ventured forth, though doubting sore
That those who loathe alike the Frank and Turk
Might once again renew their ancient butcher-work.

LXVIII

Vain fear! the Suliotes stretch'd the welcome hand,
605   Led them o'er rocks and past the dangerous swamp,
Kinder than polish'd slaves though not so bland,
And piled the hearth, and wrung their garments damp,
And fill'd the bowl, and trimm'd the cheerful lamp,
And spread their fare; though homely, all they had:
610   Such conduct bears Philanthropy's rare stamp –
To rest the weary and to soothe the sad,
Doth lesson happier men, and shames at least the bad.

LXIX

It came to pass, that when he did address
Himself to quit at length this mountain-land,
615   Combined marauders half-way barr'd egress,
And wasted far and near with glaive and brand;
And therefore did he take a trusty band
To traverse Acarnania's forest wide.
In war well season'd, and with labours tann'd,
620   Till he did greet white Achelous' tide,
And from his further bank Ætolia's wolds espied.

LXX

Where lone Utraikey forms its circling cove,
And weary waves retire to gleam at rest,
How brown the foliage of the green hill's grove,
625   Nodding at midnight o'er the calm bay's breast,

As winds come lightly whispering from the west,
Kissing, not ruffling, the blue deep's serene: –
Here Harold was received a welcome guest;
Nor did he pass unmoved the gentle scene,
630   For many a joy could he from Night's soft presence glean.

LXXI

On the smooth shore the night-fires brightly blazed,
The feast was done, the red wine circling fast,[1]
And he that unawares had there ygazed
With gaping wonderment had stared aghast;
635   For ere night's midmost, stillest hour was past,
The native revels of the troop began;
Each Palikar[2] his sabre from him cast,
And bounding hand in hand, man link'd to man,
Yelling their uncouth dirge, long daunced the kirtled clan.

LXXII

640   Childe Harold at a little distance stood
And view'd, but not displeased, the revelrie,
Nor hated harmless mirth, however rude:
In sooth, it was no vulgar sight to see
Their barbarous, yet their not indecent, glee;
645   And, as the flames along their faces gleam'd,
Their gestures nimble, dark eyes flashing free,
The long wild locks that to their girdles stream'd,
While thus in concert they this lay half sang, half
scream'd: –[3]

1. The Albanian Mussulmans do not abstain from wine, and, indeed, very
few of the others.
2. Palikar, shortened when addressed to a single person, from Παλικαρί, a
general name for a soldier amongst the Greeks and Albanese who speak
Romaic: it means, properly, 'a lad.'
3. [For a specimen of the Albanian or Arnaout dialect of the Illyric, see
Appendix to this Canto, Note [C].]

1

Tambourgi! Tambourgi![1] thy 'larum afar
650   Gives hope to the valiant, and promise of war;
All the sons of the mountains arise at the note,
Chimariot, Illyrian, and dark Suliote![2]

2

Oh! who is more brave than a dark Suliote,
In his snowy camese and his shaggy capote?
655   To the wolf and the vulture he leaves his wild flock,
And descends to the plain like the stream from the rock.

3

Shall the sons of Chimari, who never forgive
The fault of a friend, bid an enemy live?
Let those guns so unerring such vengeance forego?
660   What mark is so fair as the breast of a foe?

4

Macedonia sends forth her invincible race;
For a time they abandon the cave and the chase;
But those scarfs of blood-red shall be redder, before
The sabre is sheathed and the battle is o'er.

5

665   Then the pirates of Parga that dwell by the waves
And teach the pale Franks what it is to be slaves,
Shall leave on the beach the long galley and oar,
And track to his covert the captive on shore.

6

I ask not the pleasures that riches supply,
670   My sabre shall win what the feeble must buy;
Shall win the young bride with her long flowing hair,
And many a maid from her mother shall tear.

1. Drummer.
2. These stanzas are partly taken from different Albanese songs, as far as I
was able to make them out by the exposition of the Albanese in Romaic and
Italian.

7

I love the fair face of the maid in her youth,
Her caresses shall lull me, her music shall soothe;
675   Let her bring from the chamber her many-toned lyre,
And sing us a song on the fall of her sire.

8

Remember the moment when Previsa fell,[1]
The shrieks of the conquer'd, the conquerors' yell;
The roofs that we fired, and the plunder we shared,
680   The wealthy we slaughter'd, the lovely we spared.

9

I talk not of mercy, I talk not of fear;
He neither must know who would serve the Vizier:
Since the days of our prophet the Crescent ne'er saw
A chief ever glorious like Ali Pashaw.

10

685   Dark Muchtar his son to the Danube is sped,
Let the yellow-hair'd[2] Giaours[3] view his horse-tail[4] with
dread;
When his Delhis[5] come dashing in blood o'er the banks,
How few shall escape from the Muscovite ranks!

11

Selictar![6] unsheathe then our chief's scimitar:
690   Tambourgi! thy 'larum gives promise of war.
Ye mountains, that see us descend to the shore,
Shall view us as victors, or view us no more!

1. It was taken by storm from the French.
2. Yellow is the epithet given to the Russians.
3. Infidel.
4. The insignia of a Pacha.
5. Horsemen, answering to our forlorn hope.
6. Sword-bearer.

LXXIII

Fair Greece! sad relic of departed worth![1]
Immortal, though no more; though fallen, great!
695   Who now shall lead thy scatter'd children forth,
And long accustom'd bondage uncreate?
Not such thy sons who whilome did await,
The hopeless warriors of a willing doom,
In bleak Thermopylae's sepulchral strait –
700   Oh! who that gallant spirit shall resume,
Leap from Eurotas' banks, and call thee from the tomb?

LXXIV

Spirit of freedom! when on Phyle's brow[2]
Thou sat'st with Thrasybulus and his train,
Couldst thou forebode the dismal hour which now
705   Dims the green beauties of thine Attic plain?
Not thirty tyrants now enforce the chain,
But every carle can lord it o'er thy land;
Nor rise thy sons, but idly rail in vain,
Trembling beneath the scourge of Turkish hand,
710   From birth till death enslaved; in word, in deed, unmann'd.

LXXV

In all save form alone, how changed! and who
That marks the fire still sparkling in each eye,
Who but would deem their bosoms burn'd anew
With thy unquenched beam, lost Liberty!
715   And many dream withal the hour is nigh
That gives them back their fathers' heritage:
For foreign arms and aid they fondly sigh,
Nor solely dare encounter hostile rage,
Or tear their name defiled from Slavery's mournful page.

1. Some thoughts on the present state of Greece will be found in the
Appendix to this Canto, Note [D].
2. Phyle, which commands a beautiful view of Athens, has still considerable
remains: it was seized by Thrasybulus, previous to the expulsion of the
Thirty.

LXXVI

720   Hereditary bondsmen! know ye not
      Who would be free themselves must strike the blow?
      By their right arms the conquest must be wrought?
      Will Gaul or Muscovite redress ye? no!
      True, they may lay your proud despoilers low,
725   But not for you will Freedom's altars flame.
      Shades of the Helots! triumph o'er your foe!
      Greece! change thy lords, thy state is still the same;
Thy glorious day is o'er, but not thine years of shame.

LXXVII

      The city won for Allah from the Giaour,
730   The Giaour from Othman's race again may wrest;
      And the Serai's impenetrable tower
      Receive the fiery Frank, her former guest;[1]
      Or Wahab's rebel brood who dared divest
      The prophet's[2] tomb of all its pious spoil,
735   May wind their path of blood along the West;
      But ne'er will freedom seek this fated soil,
But slave succeed to slave through years of endless toil.

LXXVIII

      Yet mark their mirth – ere lenten days begin,
      That penance which their holy rites prepare
740   To shrive from man his weight of mortal sin,
      By daily abstinence and nightly prayer;
      But ere his sackcloth garb Repentance wear,
      Some days of joyaunce are decreed to all,
      To take of pleasaunce each his secret share,
745   In motley robe to dance at masking ball,
And join the mimic train of merry Carnival.

1. When taken by the Latins, and retained for several years.
2. Mecca and Medina were taken some time ago by the Wahabees, a sect
yearly increasing.

LXXIX

And whose more rife with merriment than thine,
Oh Stamboul! once the empress of their reign?
Though turbans now pollute Sophia's shrine,
750   And Greece her very altars eyes in vain:
(Alas! her woes will still pervade my strain!)
Gay were her minstrels once, for free her throng,
All felt the common joy they now must feign,
Nor oft I've seen such sight, nor heard such song,
755 As woo'd the eye, and thrill'd the Bosphorus along.

LXXX

Loud was the lightsome tumult on the shore,
Oft Music changed, but never ceased her tone,
And timely echo'd back the measured oar,
And rippling waters made a pleasant moan:
760   The Queen of tides on high consenting shone,
And when a transient breeze swept o'er the wave,
'Twas, as if darting from her heavenly throne,
A brighter glance her form reflected gave,
Till sparkling billows seem'd to light the banks they lave.

LXXXI

765   Glanced many a light caique along the foam,
Danced on the shore the daughters of the land,
Ne thought had man or maid of rest or home,
While many a languid eye and thrilling hand
Exchanged the look few bosoms may withstand,
770   Or gently prest, return'd the pressure still:
Oh Love! young Love! bound in thy rosy band,
Let sage or cynic prattle as he will,
These hours, and only these, redeem Life's years of ill!

LXXXII

But, midst the throng in merry masquerade,
775   Lurk there no hearts that throb with secret pain,
Even through the closest searment half betray'd?
To such the gentle murmurs of the main
Seem to re-echo all they mourn in vain;

To such the gladness of the gamesome crowd
780   Is source of wayward thought and stern disdain:
How do they loathe the laughter idly loud,
And long to change the robe of revel for the shroud!

LXXXIII

This must he feel, the true-born son of Greece,
If Greece one true-born patriot still can boast:
785   Not such as prate of war, but skulk in peace,
The bondsman's peace, who sighs for all he lost,
Yet with smooth smile his tyrant can accost,
And wield the slavish sickle, not the sword:
Ah! Greece! they love thee least who owe thee most;
790   Their birth, their blood, and that sublime record
Of hero sires, who shame thy now degenerate horde!

LXXXIV

When riseth Lacedemon's hardihood,
When Thebes Epaminondas rears again,
When Athens' children are with hearts endued,
795   When Grecian mothers shall give birth to men,
Then may'st thou be restored; but not till then.
A thousand years scarce serve to form a state;
An hour may lay it in the dust: and when
Can man its shatter'd splendour renovate,
800   Recall its virtues back, and vanquish Time and Fate?

LXXXV

And yet how lovely in thine age of woe,
Land of lost gods and godlike men! art thou!
Thy vales of evergreen, thy hills of snow,[1]
Proclaim thee Nature's varied favourite now;
805   Thy fanes, thy temples to thy surface bow,
Commingling slowly with heroic earth,
Broke by the share of every rustic plough:
So perish monuments of mortal birth,
So perish all in turn, save well-recorded Worth;

1. On many of the mountains, particularly Liakura, the snow never is en-
tirely melted, notwithstanding the intense heat of the summer; but I never
saw it lie on the plains, even in winter.

LXXXVI

810   Save where some solitary column mourns
         Above its prostrate brethren of the cave[1]
         Save where Tritonia's airy shrine adorns
         Colonna's cliff,[2] and gleams along the wave;
         Save o'er some warrior's half-forgotten grave,
815   Where the gray stones and unmolested grass
         Ages, but not oblivion, feebly brave,
         While strangers only not regardless pass,
Lingering like me, perchance, to gaze, and sigh 'Alas!'

1. Of Mount Pentelicus, from whence the marble was dug that constructed the public edifices of Athens. The modern name is Mount Mendeli. An immense cave, formed by the quarries, still remains, and will till the end of time.
2. In all Attica, if we except Athens itself and Marathon, there is no scene more interesting than Cape Colonna. To the antiquary and artist, sixteen columns are an inexhaustible source of observation and design; to the philosopher, the supposed scene of some of Plato's conversations will not be unwelcome; and the traveller will be struck with the beauty of the prospect over 'Isles that crown the Ægean deep:' but, for an Englishman, Colonna has yet an additional interest, as the actual spot of Falconer's Shipwreck. Pallas and Plato are forgotten, in the recollection of Falconer and Campbell:–

> 'Here in the dead of night by Lonna's steep,
> The seaman's cry was heard along the deep.'

This temple of Minerva may be seen at sea from a great distance. In two journeys which I made, and one voyage to Cape Colonna, the view from either side, by land, was less striking than the approach from the isles. In our second land excursion, we had a narrow escape from a party of Mainotes, concealed in the caverns beneath. We were told afterwards, by one of their prisoners, subsequently ransomed, that they were deterred from attacking us by the appearance of my two Albanians: conjecturing very sagaciously, but falsely, that we had a complete guard of these Arnaouts at hand, they remained stationary, and thus saved our party, which was too small to have opposed any effectual resistance. Colonna is no less a resort of painters than of pirates; there

> 'The hireling artist plants his paltry desk,
> And makes degraded nature picturesque.'
>   (See Hodgson's Lady Jane Grey, &c)

But there Nature, with the aid of Art, has done that for herself. I was fortunate enough to engage a very superior German artist; and hope to renew my acquaintance with this and many other Levantine scenes, by the arrival of his performances.

LXXXVII

Yet are thy skies as blue, thy crags as wild;
Sweet are thy groves, and verdant are thy fields,
Thine olive ripe as when Minerva smiled,
And still his honied wealth Hymettus yields;
There the blithe bee his fragrant fortress builds,
The freeborn wanderer of thy mountain-air;
Apollo still thy long, long summer gilds,
Still in his beam Mendeli's marbles glare;
Art, Glory, Freedom fail, but Nature still is fair.

LXXXVIII

Where'er we tread 'tis haunted, holy ground;
No earth of thine is lost in vulgar mould,
But one vast realm of wonder spreads around,
And all the Muse's tales seem truly told,
Till the sense aches with gazing to behold
The scenes our earliest dreams have dwelt upon;
Each hill and dale, each deepening glen and wold
Defies the power which crush'd thy temples gone:
Age shakes Athena's tower, but spares gray Marathon.

LXXXIX

The sun, the soil, but not the slave, the same;
Unchanged in all except its foreign lord –
Preserves alike its bounds and boundless fame
The Battle-field, where Persia's victim horde
First bow'd beneath the brunt of Hellas' sword,
As on the morn to distant Glory dear,
When Marathon became a magic word;[1]
Which utter'd, to the hearer's eye appear
The camp, the host, the fight, the conqueror's career,

---

1. 'Siste Viator – heroa calcas!' was the epitaph on the famous Count Merci;
– what then must be our feelings when standing on the tumulus of the two
hundred (Greeks) who fell on Marathon? The principal barrow has recently
been opened by Fauvel: few or no relics, as vases, &c. were found by the
excavator. The plain of Marathon was offered to me for sale at the sum of
sixteen thousand piastres, about nine hundred pounds! Alas! – 'Expende –
quot *libras* in duce summo – invenies!' – was the dust of Miltiades worth no
more? It could scarcely have fetched less if sold by *weight*.

XC

The flying Mede, his shaftless broken bow;
The fiery Greek, his red pursuing spear;
Mountains above, Earth's, Ocean's plain below;
Death in the front, Destruction in the rear!
850   Such was the scene – what now remaineth here?
What sacred trophy marks the hallow'd ground,
Recording Freedom's smile and Asia's tear?
The rifled urn, the violated mound,
The dust thy courser's hoof, rude stranger! spurns around.

XCI

855   Yet to the remnants of thy splendour past
Shall pilgrims, pensive, but unwearied, throng;
Long shall the voyager, with th' Ionian blast,
Hail the bright clime of battle and of song;
Long shall thine annals and immortal tongue
860   Fill with thy fame the youth of many a shore;
Boast of the aged! lesson of the young!
Which sages venerate and bards adore,
As Pallas and the Muse unveil their awful lore.

XCII

The parted bosom clings to wonted home,
865   If aught that's kindred cheer the welcome hearth;
He that is lonely, hither let him roam,
And gaze complacent on congenial earth.
Greece is no lightsome land of social mirth:
But he whom Sadness sootheth may abide,
870   And scarce regret the region of his birth,
When wandering slow by Delphi's sacred side,
Or gazing o'er the plains where Greek and Persian died.

XCIII

Let such approach this consecrated land,
And pass in peace along the magic waste;
875   But spare its relics – let no busy hand
Deface the scenes, already how defaced!
Not for such purpose were these altars placed:

Revere the remnants nations once revered:
So may our country's name be undisgraced,
So may'st thou prosper where thy youth was rear'd,
By every honest joy of love and life endear'd!

880

XCIV

For thee, who thus in too protracted song
Hast soothed thine idlesse with inglorious lays,
Soon shall thy voice be lost amid the throng
Of louder minstrels in these later days:
To such resign the strife for fading bays –
Ill may such contest now the spirit move
Which heeds nor keen reproach nor partial praise;
Since cold each kinder heart that might approve,
And none are left to please when none are left to love.

885

890

XCV

Thou too art gone, thou loved and lovely one!
Whom youth and youth's affections bound to me;
Who did for me what none beside have done,
Nor shrank from one albeit unworthy thee.
What is my being? thou hast ceased to be!
Nor staid to welcome here thy wanderer home,
Who mourns o'er hours which we no more shall see –
Would they had never been, or were to come!
Would he had ne'er return'd to find fresh cause to roam!

895

XCVI

Oh! ever loving, lovely, and beloved!
How selfish Sorrow ponders on the past,
And clings to thoughts now better far removed!
But Time shall tear thy shadow from me last.
All thou couldst have of mine, stern Death! thou hast;
The parent, friend, and now the more than friend:
Ne'er yet for one thine arrows flew so fast,
And grief with grief continuing still to blend,
Hath snatch'd the little joy that life had yet to lend.

900

905

XCVII

Then must I plunge again into the crowd,
And follow all that Peace disdains to seek?
Where Revel calls, and Laughter, vainly loud,
False to the heart, distorts the hollow cheek,
To leave the flagging spirit doubly weak;
Still o'er the features, which perforce they cheer,
To feign the pleasure or conceal the pique;
Smiles form the channel of a future tear,
Or raise the writhing lip with ill-dissembled sneer.

XCVIII

What is the worst of woes that wait on age?
What stamps the wrinkle deeper on the brow?
To view each loved one blotted from life's page,
And be alone on earth, as I am now.
Before the Chastener humbly let me bow,
O'er hearts divided and o'er hopes destroy'd:
Roll on, vain days! full reckless may ye flow,
Since Time hath reft whate'er my soul enjoy'd,
And with the ills of Eld mine earlier years alloy'd.

APPENDIX TO CANTO THE SECOND

Note [A]

'To rive what Goth, and Turk, and Time hath spared.'

STANZA xii. LINE 2.

At this moment (January 3, 1810), besides what has been already deposited in London, an Hydriot vessel is in the Pyræus to receive every portable relic. Thus, as I heard a young Greek observe, in common with many of his countrymen – for, lost as they are, they yet feel on this occasion – thus may Lord Elgin boast of having ruined Athens. An Italian painter of the first eminence, named Lusieri, is the agent of devastation; and like the Greek *finder* of Verres in Sicily, who followed the same profession, he has proved the able instrument of plunder. Between this artist and the French Consul Fauvel, who wishes to rescue the remains for his own government, there is now a violent dispute concerning a car employed in their conveyance, the wheel of which – I wish they were both broken upon it – has been locked up by the Consul, and Lusieri has laid his complaint before the Waywode. Lord Elgin has been extremely happy in his choice of Signor Lusieri. During a residence of ten years in Athens, he never had the curiosity to proceed as far as Sunium (now Caplonna), till he accompanied us in our second excursion. However, his works, as far as they go, are most beautiful: but they are almost all unfinished. While he and his patrons confine themselves to tasting medals, appreciating cameos, sketching columns, and cheapening gems, their little absurdities are as harmless as insect or fox-hunting, maiden speechifying, barouche-driving, or any such pastime; but when they carry away three or four shiploads of the most valuable and massy relics that time and barbarism have left to the most injured and most celebrated of cities; when they destroy, in a vain attempt to tear down, those works which have been the admiration of ages, I know no motive which can excuse, no name which can designate, the perpetrators of this dastardly devastation. It was not the least of the crimes laid to the charge of Verres, that he had plundered Sicily, in the manner since imitated at Athens. The most unblushing impudence could hardly go farther than to affix the name of its plunderer to the walls of the Acropolis; while the wanton and useless defacement of the whole range of the basso-relievos, in one compartment of the temple, will never permit that name to be pronounced by an observer without execration.

On this occasion I speak impartially: I am not a collector or admirer of collections, consequently no rival; but I have some early prepossession in favour of Greece, and do not think the honour of England advanced by plunder, whether of India or Attica.

Another noble Lord has done better, because he has done less: but some others, more or less noble, yet 'all honourable men,' have done *best*, because, after a deal of excavation and execration, bribery to the Waywode, mining and countermining, they have done nothing at all. We had such ink-shed, and wine-shed, which almost ended in bloodshed! Lord E.'s 'prig' – see Jonathan Wild for the definition of 'priggism' – quarrelled with another, *Gropius** by

* This Sr Gropius was employed by a noble Lord for the sole purpose of sketching, in which he excels; but I am sorry to say, that he has, through the

name (a very good name too for his business), and muttered something about satisfaction, in a verbal answer to a note of the poor Prussian: this was stated at table to Gropius, who laughed, but could eat no dinner afterwards. The rivals were not reconciled when I left Greece. I have reason to remember their squabble, for they wanted to make me their arbitrator.

Note [B]

'Land of Albania! let me bend mine eyes
On thee, thou rugged nurse of savage men!'

STANZA XXXVII. LINES 5. AND 6.

Albania comprises part of Macedonia, Illyria, Chaonia, and Epirus. Iskander is the Turkish word for Alexander; and the celebrated Scanderbeg (Lord Alexander) is alluded to in the third and fourth lines of the thirty-eighth stanza. I do not know whether I am correct in making Scanderbeg the countryman of Alexander, who was born at Pella in Macedon, but Mr Gibbon terms him so, and adds Pyrrhus to the list, in speaking of his exploits.

Of Albania Gibbon remarks, that a country 'within sight of Italy is less known than the interior of America.' Circumstances, of little consequence to mention, led Mr Hobhouse and myself into that country before we visited any other part of the Ottoman dominions; and with the exception of Major Leake, then officially resident at Joannina, no other Englishmen have ever advanced beyond the capital into the interior, as that gentleman very lately assured me. Ali Pacha was at that time (October, 1809) carrying on war against

---

abused sanction of that most respectable name, been treading at humble distance in the steps of Sr Lusieri. – A shipful of his trophies was detained, and I believe confiscated, at Constantinople, in 1810. I am most happy to be now enabled to state, that 'this was not in his bond;' that he was employed solely as a painter, and that his noble patron disavows all connection with him, except as an artist. If the error in the first and second edition of this poem has given the noble Lord a moment's pain, I am very sorry for it: Sr Gropius has assumed for years the name of his agent; and though I cannot much condemn myself for sharing in the mistake of so many, I am happy in being one of the first to be undeceived. Indeed, I have as much pleasure in contradicting this as I felt regret in stating it. – *Note to third edition.*

Ibrahim Pacha, whom he had driven to Berat, a strong fortress which he was then besieging: on our arrival at Joannina we were invited to Tepaleni, his highness's birthplace, and favourite Serai, only one day's distance from Berat; at this juncture the Vizier had made it his headquarters. After some stay in the capital, we accordingly followed; but though furnished with every accommodation, and escorted by one of the Vizier's secretaries, we were nine days (on account of the rains) in accomplishing a journey which, on our return, barely occupied four. On our route we passed two cities, Argyrocastro and Libochabo, apparently little inferior to Yanina in size; and no pencil or pen can ever do justice to the scenery in the vicinity of Zitza and Delvinachi, the frontier village of Epirus and Albania Proper.

On Albania and its inhabitants I am unwilling to descant, because this will be done so much better by my fellow-traveller, in a work which may probably precede this in publication, that I as little wish to follow as I would to anticipate him. But some few observations are necessary to the text. The Arnaouts, or Albanese, struck me forcibly by their resemblance to the Highlanders of Scotland, in dress, figure, and manner of living. Their very mountains seemed Caledonian, with a kinder climate. The kilt, though white; the spare, active form; their dialect, Celtic in its sound, and their hardy habits, all carried me back to Morven. No nation are so detested and dreaded by their neighbours as the Albanese; the Greeks hardly regard them as Christians, or the Turks as Moslems; and in fact they are a mixture of both, and sometimes neither. Their habits are predatory – all are armed; and the red-shawled Arnaouts, the Montenegrins, Chimariots, and Gegdes, are treacherous; the others differ somewhat in garb, and essentially in character. As far as my own experience goes, I can speak favourably. I was attended by two, an Infidel and a Mussulman, to Constantinople and every other part of Turkey which came within my observation; and more faithful in peril, or indefatigable in service, are rarely to be found. The Infidel was named Basilius, the Moslem, Dervish Tahiri; the former a man of middle age, and the latter about my own. Basili was strictly charged by Ali Pacha in person to attend us; and Dervish was one of fifty who accompanied us through the forests of Acarnania to the banks of Achelous, and onward to Messalonghi in Ætolia. There I took him into my own service, and never had occasion to repent it till the moment of my departure.

When in 1810, after the departure of my friend Mr Hobhouse for England, I was seized with a severe fever in the Morea, these men saved my life by frightening away my physician, whose throat they threatened to cut if I was not cured within a given time. To this consolatory assurance of posthumous retribution, and a resolute refusal of Dr Romanelli's prescriptions, I attributed my recovery. I had left my last remaining English servant at Athens; my dragoman was as ill as myself, and my poor Arnaouts nursed me with an attention which would have done honour to civilisation. They had a variety of adventures; for the Moslem, Dervish, being a remarkably handsome man, was always squabbling with the husbands of Athens; insomuch that four of the principal Turks paid me a visit of remonstrance at the Convent, on the subject of his having taken a woman from the bath – whom he had lawfully bought however – a thing quite contrary to etiquette. Basili also was extremely gallant amongst his own persuasion, and had the greatest veneration for the church, mixed with the highest contempt of churchmen, whom he cuffed upon occasion in a most heterodox manner. Yet he never passed a church without crossing himself; and I remember the risk he ran in entering St Sophia, in Stambol, because it had once been a place of his worship. On remonstrating with him on his inconsistent proceedings, he invariably answered, 'Our church is holy, our priests are thieves;' and then he crossed himself as usual, and boxed the ears of the first 'papas' who refused to assist in any required operation, as was always found to be necessary where a priest had any influence with the Cogia Bashi of his village. Indeed, a more abandoned race of miscreants cannot exist than the lower orders of the Greek clergy.

When preparations were made for my return, my Albanians were summoned to receive their pay. Basili took his with an awkward show of regret at my intended departure, and marched away to his quarters with his bag of piastres. I sent for Dervish, but for some time he was not to be found; at last he entered, just as Signor Logotheti, father to the ci-devant Anglo consul of Athens, and some other of my Greek acquaintances, paid me a visit. Dervish took the money, but on a sudden dashed it to the ground; and clasping his hands, which he raised to his forehead, rushed out of the room weeping bitterly. From that moment to the hour of my embarkation, he continued his lamentations, and all our efforts to console him only produced this answer, 'Μά φεινει,' ' He leaves me.' Signor Logotheti, who never wept before for any thing less than the loss of a para (about the fourth of a farthing), melted; the padre of the convent, my attendants, my visiters – and I verily believe that even Sterne's 'foolish fat scullion' would have left her 'fish-kettle,' to sympathise with the unaffected and unexpected sorrow of this barbarian.

For my own part, when I remembered that, a short time before my departure from England, a noble and most intimate associate had excused himself from taking leave of me because he had to attend a relation 'to a milliner's,' I felt no less surprised than humiliated by the present occurrence and the past recollection. That Dervish would leave me with some regret was to be expected: when master and man have been scrambling over the mountains of a dozen provinces together, they are unwilling to separate; but his present feelings, contrasted with his native ferocity, improved my opinion of the human heart. I believe this almost feudal fidelity is frequent amongst them. One day, on our journey over Parnassus, an Englishman in my service gave him a push in some dispute about the baggage, which he unluckily mistook for a blow; he spoke not, but sat down leaning his head upon his hands. Foreseeing the consequences, we endeavoured to explain away the affront, which produced the following answer: – 'I *have been* a robber; I *am* a soldier; no captain ever struck me; *you* are my master, I have eaten your bread, but by *that* bread! (an usual oath) had it been otherwise, I would have stabbed the dog your servant, and gone to the mountains.' So the affair ended, but from that day forward, he never thoroughly forgave the thoughtless fellow who insulted him. Dervish excelled in the dance of his country, conjectured to be a remnant of the ancient Pyrrhic: be that as it may, it is manly, and requires wonderful agility. It is very distinct from the stupid Romaika, the dull round-about of the Greeks, of which our Athenian party had so many specimens.

The Albanians in general (I do not mean the cultivators of the earth in the provinces, who have also that appellation, but the mountaineers) have a fine cast of countenance; and the most beautiful women I ever beheld, in stature and in features, we saw *levelling* the *road* broken down by the torrents between Delvinachi and Libo-chabo. Their manner of walking is truly theatrical; but this strut is probably the effect of the capote, or cloak, depending from one shoulder. Their long hair reminds you of the Spartans, and their courage in desultory warfare is unquestionable. Though they have some cavalry amongst the Gegdes, I never saw a good Arnaout horse-man; my own preferred the English saddles, which, however, they could never keep. But on foot they are not to be subdued by fatigue.

Note [C]

'*While thus in concert,*' &c.

STANZA lxxii. LINE LAST.

As a specimen of the Albanian or Arnaout dialect of the Illyric, I here insert two of their most popular choral songs, which are gener-ally chanted in dancing by men or women indiscriminately. The first words are merely a kind of chorus without meaning, like some in our own and all other languages.

1

Bo, Bo, Bo, Bo, Bo, Bo, Naciarura, popuso.

1

Lo, Lo, I come, I come; be thou silent.

2

Naciarura na civin Ha peh derini ti hin.

2

I come I run; open the door that I may enter.

3

Ha pe uderi escrotini Ti vin ti mar servetini.

3

Open the door by halves, that I may take my turban.

4

Caliriote me surme Ea ha pe pse dua tive.

4

Caliriotes* with the dark eyes, open the gate, that I may enter.

* The Albanese, particularly the women, are frequently termed 'Caliriotes;' for what reason I enquired in vain.

5
Buo, Bo, Bo, Bo, Bo,
Gi egem spirta esimiro.

5
Lo, Lo, I hear thee, my soul.

6
Caliriote vu le funde
Ede vete tunde tunde.

6
An Arnaout girl, in costly garb,
    walks with graceful pride.

7
Caliriote me surme
Ti mi put e poi mi le.

7
Caliriot maid of the dark eyes,
    give me a kiss.

8
Se ti puta citi mora
Si mi ri ni veti udo gia.

8
If I have kissed thee, what hast
    thou gained? My soul is
    consumed with fire.

9
Va le ni il che cadale
Celo more, more celo.

9
Dance lightly, more gently, and
    gently still.

10
Plu hari ti tirete
Plu huron cia pra seti.

10
Make not so much dust to
    destroy your embroidered
    hose.

The last stanza would puzzle a commentator: the men have certainly buskins of the most beautiful texture, but the ladies (to whom the above is supposed to be addressed) have nothing under their little yellow boots and slippers but a well-turned and sometimes very white ankle. The Arnaout girls are much handsomer than the Greeks, and their dress is far more picturesque. They preserve their shape much longer also, from being always in the open air. It is to be observed, that the Arnaout is not a *written* language: the words of this song, therefore, as well as the one which follows, are spelt according to their pronunciation. They are copied by one who speaks and understands the dialect perfectly, and who is a native of Athens.

1

Ndi sefda tinde ulavossa
Vettimi upri vi lofsa.

1

I am wounded by thy love, and
have loved but to scorch
myself.

2

Ah vaisisso mi privi lofse
Si mi rini mi la vosse.

2

Thou hast consumed me! Ah,
maid! thou hast struck me
to the heart.

3

Uti tasa roba stua
Sitti eve tulati dua.

3

I have said I wish no dowry,
but thine eyes and eye
lashes.

4

Roba stinori ssidua
Qu mi sini vetti dua.

4

The accursed dowry I want
not, but thee only.

5

Qurmini dua civileni
Roba ti siarmi tildi eni.

5

Give me thy charms, and let the
portion feed the flames.

6

Utara pisa vaisisso me simi rin
ti hapti
Eti mi bire a piste si gui
dendroi, tiltati.

6

I have loved thee, maid, with a
sincere soul, but thou hast
left me like a withered tree.

7

Udi vura udorini udiri cicova
cilti mora
Udorini talti hollna u ede
caimoni mora.

7

If I have placed my hand on
thy bosom, what have I
gained? my hand is with-
drawn, but retains the
flame.

I believe the two last stanzas, as they are in a different measure,
ought to belong to another ballad. An idea something similar to the
thought in the last lines was expressed by Socrates, whose arm

having come in contact with one of his '*ὑποκολπιοι*,'Critobulus or Cleobulus, the philosopher complained of a shooting pain as far as his shoulder for some days after, and therefore very properly resolved to teach his disciples in future without touching them.

Note [D]

'Fair Greece! sad relic of departed worth!
Immortal, though no more; though fallen, great!'

STANZA lxxiii. LINES 1. AND 2.

I

Before I say any thing about a city of which every body, traveller or not, has thought it necessary to say something, I will request Miss Owenson, when she next borrows an Athenian heroine for her four volumes, to have the goodness to marry her to somebody more of a gentleman than a 'Disdar Aga' (who by the by is not an Aga), the most impolite of petty officers, the greatest patron of larceny Athens ever saw (except Lord E.) and the unworthy occupant of the Acropolis, on a handsome annual stipend of 150 piastres (eight pounds sterling), out of which he has only to pay his garrison, the most ill-regulated corps in the ill-regulated Ottoman Empire. I speak it tenderly, seeing I was once the cause of the husband of 'Ida of Athens' nearly suffering the bastinado; and because the said 'Disdar' is a turbulent husband, and beats his wife; so that I exhort and beseech Miss Owenson to sue for a separate maintenance in behalf of 'Ida.' Having premised thus much, on a matter of such import to the readers of romances, I may now leave Ida, to mention her birthplace.

Setting aside the magic of the name, and all those associations which it would be pedantic and superfluous to recapitulate, the very situation of Athens would render it the favourite of all who have eyes for art or nature. The climate, to me at least, appeared a perpetual spring; during eight months I never passed a day without being as many hours on horseback: rain is extremely rare, snow never lies in the plains, and a cloudy day is an agreeable rarity. In Spain, Portugal, and every part of the East which I visited, except Ionia and Attica, I perceived no such superiority of climate to our own; and at Constantinople, where I passed May, June, and part of

July (1810), you might 'damn the climate, and complain of spleen,' five days out of seven.

The air of the Morea is heavy and unwholesome, but the moment you pass the isthmus in the direction of Megara the change is strikingly perceptible. But I fear Hesiod will still be found correct in his description of a Bœotian winter.

We found at Livadia an 'esprit fort' in a Greek bishop, of all freethinkers! This worthy hypocrite rallied his own religion with great intrepidity (but not before his flock), and talked of a mass as a 'coglioneria.' It was impossible to think better of him for this; but, for a Bœotian, he was brisk with all his absurdity. This phenomenon (with the exception indeed of Thebes, the remains of Chæronea, the plain of Platea, Orchomenus, Livadia, and its nominal cave of Trophonius) was the only remarkable thing we saw before we passed Mount Cithæron.

The fountain of Dirce turns a mill: at least my companion (who, resolving to be at once cleanly and classical, bathed in it) pronounced it to be the fountain of Dirce, and any body who thinks it worth while may contradict him. At Castri we drank of half a dozen streamlets, some not of the purest, before we decided to our satisfaction which was the true Castalian, and even that had a villanous twang, probably from the snow, though it did not throw us into an epic fever, like poor Dr Chandler.

From Fort Phyle, of which large remains still exist, the Plain of Athens, Pentelicus, Hymettus, the Ægean, and the Acropolis, burst upon the eye at once; in my opinion, a more glorious prospect than even Cintra or Istambol. Not the view from the Troad, with Ida, the Hellespont, and the more distant Mount Athos, can equal it, though so superior in extent.

I heard much of the beauty of Arcadia, but excepting the view from the monastery of Megaspelion (which is inferior to Zitza in a command of country) and the descent from the mountains on the way from Tripolitza to Argos, Arcadia has little to recommend it beyond the name.

'Sternitur, et *dulces* moriens reminiscitur Argos.'

Virgil could have put this into the mouth of none but an Argive, and (with reverence be it spoken) it does not deserve the epithet.

And if the polynices of Statius, 'In mediis audit duo litora campis,' did actually hear both shores in crossing the isthmus of Corinth, he had better ears than have ever been worn in such a journey since.

'Athens,' says a celebrated topographer, 'is still the most polished city of Greece.' Perhaps it may of *Greece*, but not of the *Greeks*; for Joannina in Epirus is universally allowed, amongst themselves, to be superior in the wealth, refinement, learning, and dialect of its inhabitants. The Athenians are remarkable for their cunning; and the lower orders are not improperly characterised in that proverb, which classes them with 'the Jews of Salonica, and the Turks of the Negropont.'

Among the various foreigners resident in Athens, French, Italians, Germans, Ragusans, &c., there was never a difference of opinion in their estimate of the Greek character, though on all other topics they disputed with great acrimony.

M Fauvel, the French consul, who has passed thirty years principally at Athens, and to whose talents as an artist, and manners as a gentleman, none who have known him can refuse their testimony, has frequently declared in my hearing, that the Greeks do not deserve to be emancipated; reasoning on the grounds of their 'national and individual depravity!' while he forgot that such depravity is to be attributed to causes which can only be removed by the measure he reprobates.

M Roque, a French merchant of respectability long settled in Athens, asserted with the most amusing gravity, 'Sir, they are the same *canaille* that existed *in the days of Themistocles*!' an alarming remark to the 'Laudator temporis acti.' The ancients banished Themistocles; the moderns cheat Monsieur Roque: thus great men have ever been treated!

In short, all the Franks who are fixtures, and most of the Englishmen, Germans, Danes, &c. of passage, came over by degrees to their opinion, on much the same grounds that a Turk in England would condemn the nation by wholesale, because he was wronged by his lacquey, and overcharged by his washerwoman.

Certainly it was not a little staggering when the Sieurs Fauvel and Lusieri, the two greatest demagogues of the day, who divide between them the power of Pericles and the popularity of Cleon, and puzzle the poor Waywode with perpetual differences, agreed in the utter condemnation, 'nulla virtute redemptum,' of the Greeks in general, and of the Athenians in particular.

For my own humble opinion, I am loth to hazard it, knowing as I do, that there be now in MS. no less than five tours of the first magnitude and of the most threatening aspect, all in typographical array, by persons of wit, and honour, and regular common-place books: but, if I may say this without offence, it seems to me rather hard to declare so positively and pertinaciously, as almost every body has declared, that the Greeks, because they are very bad, will never be better.

Eton and Sonnini have led us astray by their panegyrics and projects; but, on the other hand, De Pauw and Thornton have debased the Greeks beyond their demerits.

The Greeks will never be independent; they will never be sovereigns as heretofore, and God forbid they ever should! but they may be subjects without being slaves. Our colonies are not independent, but they are free and industrious, and such may Greece be hereafter.

At present, like the Catholics of Ireland and the Jews throughout the world, and such other cudgelled and heterodox people, they suffer all the moral and physical ills that can afflict humanity. Their life is a struggle against truth; they are vicious in their own defence. They are so unused to kindness, that when they occasionally meet with it they look upon it with suspicion, as a dog often beaten snaps at your fingers if you attempt to caress him. 'They are ungrateful, notoriously, abominably ungrateful!' – this is the general cry. Now, in the name of Nemesis! for what are they to be grateful? Where is the human being that ever conferred a benefit on Greek or Greeks? They are to be grateful to the Turks for their fetters, and to the Franks for their broken promises and lying counsels. They are to be grateful to the artist who engraves their ruins, and to the antiquary who carries them away; to the traveller whose janissary flogs them, and to the scribbler whose journal abuses them! This is the amount of their obligations to foreigners.

II

Franciscan Convent, Athens, January 23, 1811.

Amongst the remnants of the barbarous policy of the earlier ages, are the traces of bondage which yet exist in different countries;

whose inhabitants, however divided in religion and manners, almost all agree in oppression.

The English have at last compassionated their negroes, and under a less bigoted government, may probably one day release their Catholic brethren: but the interposition of foreigners alone can emancipate the Greeks, who, otherwise, appear to have as small a chance of redemption from the Turks, as the Jews have from mankind in general.

Of the ancient Greeks we know more than enough; at least the younger men of Europe devote much of their time to the study of the Greek writers and history, which would be more usefully spent in mastering their own. Of the moderns, we are perhaps more neglectful than they deserve; and while every man of any pretensions to learning is tiring out his youth, and often his age, in the study of the language and of the harangues of the Athenian demagogues in favour of freedom, the real or supposed descendants of these sturdy republicans are left to the actual tyranny of their masters, although a very slight effort is required to strike off their chains.

To talk, as the Greeks themselves do, of their rising again to their pristine superiority, would be ridiculous; as the rest of the world must resume its barbarism, after reasserting the sovereignty of Greece: but there seems to be no very great obstacle, except in the apathy of the Franks, to their becoming an useful dependency, or even a free state with a proper guarantee; – under correction, however, be it spoken, for many and well-informed men doubt the practicability even of this.

The Greeks have never lost their hope, though they are now more divided in opinion on the subject of their probable deliverers. Religion recommends the Russians; but they have twice been deceived and abandoned by that power, and the dreadful lesson they received after the Muscovite desertion in the Morea has never been forgotten. The French they dislike; although the subjugation of the rest of Europe will, probably, be attended by the deliverance of continental Greece. The islanders look to the English for succour, as they have very lately possessed themselves of the Ionian republic, Corfu excepted. But whoever appear with arms in their hands will be welcome; and when that day arrives, Heaven have mercy on the Ottomans, they cannot expect it from the Giaours.

But instead of considering what they have been, and speculating on what they may be, let us look at them as they are.

And here it is impossible to reconcile the contrariety of opinions: some, particularly the merchants, decrying the Greeks in the strongest language; others, generally travellers, turning periods in their eulogy, and publishing very curious speculations grafted on their former state, which can have no more effect on their present lot, than the existence of the Incas on the future fortunes of Peru.

One very ingenious person terms them the 'natural allies of Englishmen;' another no less ingenious, will not allow them to be the allies of anybody, and denies their very descent from the ancients; a third, more ingenious than either, builds a Greek empire on a Russian foundation, and realises (on paper) all the chimeras of Catherine II. As to the question of their descent, what can it import whether the Mainotes are the lineal Laconians or not? or the present Athenians as indigenous as the bees of Hymettus, or as the grasshoppers, to which they once likened themselves? What Englishman cares if he be of a Danish, Saxon, Norman, or Trojan blood? or who, except a Welshman, is afflicted with a desire of being descended from Caractacus?

The poor Greeks do not so much abound in the good things of this world, as to render even their claims to antiquity an object of envy; it is very cruel, then, in Mr Thornton to disturb them in the possession of all that time has left them; viz. their pedigree, of which they are the more tenacious, as it is all they can call their own. It would be worth while to publish together, and compare, the works of Messrs. Thornton and De Pauw, Eton and Sonnini; paradox on one side, and prejudice on the other. Mr Thornton conceives himself to have claims to public confidence from a fourteen years' residence at Pera; perhaps he may on the subject of the Turks, but this can give him no more insight into the real state of Greece and her inhabitants, than as many years spent in Wapping into that of the Western Highlands.

The Greeks of Constantinople live in Fanal; and if Mr Thornton did not oftener cross the Golden Horn than his brother merchants are accustomed to do, I should place no great reliance on his information. I actually heard one of these gentlemen boast of their little general intercourse with the city, and assert of himself, with an air of triumph, that he had been but four times at Constantinople in as many years.

As to Mr Thornton's voyages in the Black Sea with Greek vessels, they gave him the same idea of Greece as a cruise to Berwick in a Scotch smack would of Johnny Grot's house. Upon what grounds then does he arrogate the right of condemning by wholesale a body of men, of whom he can know little? It is rather a curious circumstance that Mr Thornton, who so lavishly dispraises Pouqueville on every occasion of mentioning the Turks, has yet recourse to him as authority on the Greeks, and terms him an impartial observer. Now, Dr Pouqueville is as little entitled to that appellation, as Mr Thornton to confer it on him.

The fact is, we are deplorably in want of information on the subject of the Greeks, and in particular their literature; nor is there any probability of our being better acquainted, till our intercourse becomes more intimate, or their independence confirmed: the relations of passing travellers are as little to be depended on as the invectives of angry factors; but till something more can be attained, we must be content with the little to be acquired from similar sources.*

---

* A word, *en passant*, with Mr Thornton and Dr Pouqueville, who have been guilty between them of sadly clipping the Sultan's Turkish.

Dr Pouqueville tells a long story of a Moslem who swallowed corrosive sublimate in such quantities that he acquired the name of '*Suleyman Yeyen*,' i.e. quoth the Doctor, '*Suleyman, the eater of corrosive sublimate*.' 'Aha,' thinks Mr Thornton, (angry with the Doctor for the fiftieth time), 'have I caught you?' – Then, in a note twice the thickness of the Doctor's anecdote, he questions the Doctor's proficiency in the Turkish tongue, and his veracity in his own. – 'For,' observes Mr Thornton (after inflicting on us the tough participle of a Turkish verb), 'it means nothing more than *Suleyman the eater*,' and quite cashiers the supplementary '*sublimate*.' Now both are right, and both are wrong. If Mr Thornton, when he next resides, 'fourteen years in the factory,' will consult his Turkish dictionary, or ask any of his Stambo-line acquaintance, he will discover that '*Suleyma'n yeyen*,' put together discreetly, means the '*Swallower of sublimate*,' without any '*Suleyman*' in the case: '*Suleyma*' signifying '*corrosive sublimate*,' and not being a proper name on this occasion, although it be an orthodox name enough with the addition of *n*. After Mr Thornton's frequent hints of profound Orientalism, he might have found this out before he sang such pæans over Dr Pouqueville.

After this, I think 'Travellers *versus* Factors' shall be our motto, though the above Mr Thornton has condemned 'hoc genus omne,' for mistake and misrepresentation. 'Ne Sutor ultra crepidam,' 'No merchant beyond his bales.' N. B. For the benefit of Mr Thornton, 'Sutor' is not a proper name.

However defective these may be, they are preferable to the para-
doxes of men who have read superficially of the ancients, and seen
nothing of the moderns, such as De Pauw; who, when he asserts
that the British breed of horses is ruined by Newmarket, and that
the Spartans were cowards in the field, betrays an equal knowledge
of English horses and Spartan men. His 'philosophical observations'
have a much better claim to the title of 'poetical.' It could not be
expected that he who so liberally condemns some of the most
celebrated institutions of the ancient, should have mercy on the
modern Greeks; and it fortunately happens, that the absurdity of
his hypothesis on their forefathers refutes his sentence on
themselves.

Let us trust, then, that, in spite of the prophecies of De Pauw,
and the doubts of Mr Thornton, there is a reasonable hope of the
redemption of a race of men, who, whatever may be the errors of
their religion and policy, have been amply punished by three centu-
ries and a half of captivity.

III

Athens, Franciscan Convent, March 17, 1811.

'I must have some talk with this learned Theban.'

Some time after my return from Contantinople to this city I received
the thirty-first number of the Edinburgh Review as a great favour,
and certainly at this distance an acceptable one, from the captain of
an English frigate off Salamis. In that number, Art. 3. containing
the review of a French translation of Strabo, there are introduced
some remarks on the modern Greeks and their literature, with a
short account of Coray, a co-translator in the French version. On
those remarks I mean to ground a few observations; and the spot
where I now write will, I hope, be sufficient excuse for introducing
them in a work in some degree connected with the subject. Coray,
the most celebrated of living Greeks, at least among the Franks,
was born at Scio (in the Review, Smyrna is stated, I have reason to
think, incorrectly), and besides the translation of Beccaria and other
works mentioned by the Reviewer, has published a lexicon in
Romaic and French, if I may trust the assurance of some Danish
travellers lately arrived from Paris; but the latest we have seen here

in French and Greek is that of Gregory Zolikogloou.* Coray has recently been involved in an unpleasant controversy with M. Gail,† a Parisian commentator and editor of some translations from the Greek poets, in consequence of the Institute having awarded him the prize for his version of Hippocrates 'Περὶ ὑδάτων,'& to the disparagement, and consequently displeasure, of the said Gail. To his exertions, literary and patriotic, great praise is undoubtedly due, but a part of that praise ought not to be withheld from the two brothers Zosimado (merchants settled in Leghorn), who sent him to Paris, and maintained him, for the express purpose of elucidating the ancient, and adding to the modern, researches of his country-men. Coray, however, is not considered by his countrymen equal to some who lived in the two last centuries; more particularly Dor-otheus of Mitylene, whose Hellenic writings are so much esteemed by the Greeks, that Meletius terms him ' Μετὰ τὸν Θουκυδίδην καὶ Ξενοφῶντα ἄριστος Ἑλλήνων.'Ρ. 224, Ecclesiastical History, vol. iv.)

Panagiotes Kodrikas, the translator of Fontenelle, and Kamar-ases, who translated Ocellus Lucanus on the Universe into French, Christodoulus, and more particularly Psalida, whom I have con-versed with in Joannina, are also in high repute among their literati. The last mentioned has published in Romaic and Latin a work on 'True Happiness,' dedicated to Catherine II. But Polyzois, who is stated by the Reviewer to be the only modern except Coray who has distinguished himself by a knowledge of Hellenic, if he be the Poly-zois Lampanitziotes of Yanina, who has published a number of edi-tions in Romaic, was neither more nor less than an itinerant vender of books; with the contents of which he had no concern beyond his name on the title page, placed there to secure his property in the publication; and he was, moreover, a man utterly destitute of scholastic acquirements. As the name, however, is not uncommon,

* I have in my possession an excellent lexicon 'τρίγλωσσον,'which I received in exchange from S. G—, Esq. for a small gem: my antiquarian friends have never forgotten it, or forgiven me.

† In Gail's pamphlet against Coray, he talks of 'throwing the insolent Hellen-ist out of the windows.' On this a French critic exclaims, 'Ah, my God! throw an Hellenist out of the window! what sacrilege!' It certainly would be a serious business for those authors who dwell in the attics: but I have quoted the passage merely to prove the similarity of style among the contro-versialists of all polished countries; London or Edinburgh could hardly parallel this Parisian ebullition.

some other Polyzois may have edited the Epistles of Aristænetus.

It is to be regretted that the system of continental blockade has closed the few channels through which the Greeks received their publications, particularly Venice and Trieste. Even the common grammars for children are become too dear for the lower orders. Amongst their original works the Geography of Meletius, Archbishop of Athens, and a multitude of theological quartos and poetical pamphlets, are to be met with; their grammars and lexicons of two, three, and four languages are numerous and excellent. Their poetry is in rhyme. The most singular piece I have lately seen is a satire in dialogue between a Russian, English, and French traveller, and the Waywode of Wallachia (or Blackbey, as they term him), an archbishop, a merchant, and Cogia Bachi (or primate), in succession; to all of whom under the Turks the writer attributes their present degeneracy. Their songs are sometimes pretty and pathetic, but their tunes generally unpleasing to the ear of a Frank; the best is the famous '$\Delta\varepsilon\hat{v}\tau\varepsilon$ $\pi\alpha\hat{i}\delta\varepsilon\varsigma$ $\tau\hat{\omega}v$ $\dot{E}\lambda\lambda\acute{\eta}\nu\omega v$,' by the unfortunate Riga. But from a catalogue of more than sixty authors, now before me, only fifteen can be found who have touched on any theme except theology.

I am intrusted with a commission by a Greek of Athens named Marmarotouri to make arrangements, if possible, for printing in London a translation of Barthelemi's Anacharsis in Romaic, as he has no other opportunity, unless he despatches the MS to Vienna by the Black Sea and Danube.

The Reviewer mentions a school established at Hecatonesi, and suppressed at the instigation of Sebastiani: he means Cidonies, or, in Turkish, Haivali; a town on the continent, where that institution for a hundred students and three professors still exists. It is true that this establishment was disturbed by the Porte, under the ridiculous pretext that the Greeks were constructing a fortress instead of a college: but on investigation, and the payment of some purses to the Divan, it has been permitted to continue. The principal professor, named Ueniamin (i.e. Benjamin), is stated to be a man of talent, but a freethinker. He was born in Lesbos, studied in Italy, and is master of Hellenic, Latin, and some Frank languages; besides a smattering of the sciences.

Though it is not my intention to enter farther on this topic than may allude to the article in question, I cannot but observe that the

Reviewer's lamentation over the fall of the Greeks appears singular, when he closes it with these words: *'The change is to be attributed to their misfortunes rather than to any "physical degradation."'* It may be true that the Greeks are not physically degenerated, and that Constantinople contained on the day when it changed masters as many men of six feet and upwards as in the hour of prosperity; but ancient history and modern politics instruct us that something more than physical perfection is necessary to preserve a state in vigour and independence; and the Greeks, in particular, are a melancholy example of the near connection between moral degradation and national decay.

The Reviewer mentions a plan *'we believe'* by Potemkin for the purification of the Romaic; and I have endeavoured in vain to procure any tidings or traces of its existence. There was an academy in St Petersburg for the Greeks; but it was suppressed by Paul, and has not been revived by his successor.

There is a slip of the pen, and it can only be a slip of the pen, in p. 58, No. 31 of the Edinburgh Review, where these words occur: – 'We are told that when the capital of the East yielded to *Solyman*' – It may be presumed that this last word will, in a future edition, be altered to Mahomet II.* The 'ladies of Constantinople,' it seems, at that period spoke a dialect, 'which would not have disgraced the lips of an Athenian.' I do not know how that might be, but am

---

* In a former number of the Edinburgh Review, 1808, it is observed: 'Lord Byron passed some of his early years in Scotland, where he might have learned that *pibroch* does not mean a *bagpipe*, any more than *duet* means a *fiddle*.' Query, – Was it in Scotland that the young gentlemen of the Edinburgh Review *learned* that *Solyman* means *Mahomet II*, any more than *criticism* means *infallibility?* – but thus it is,

'Cædimus inque vicem præbemus crura sagittis.'

The mistake seemed so completely a lapse of the pen (from the great *similarity* of the two words, and the *total absence of error* from the former pages of the literary leviathan) that I should have passed it over as in the text, had I not perceived in the Edinburgh Review much facetious exultation on all such detections, particularly a recent one, where words and syllables are subjects of disquisition and transposition; and the above-mentioned parallel passage in my own case irresistibly propelled me to hint how much easier it is to be critical than correct. The *gentlemen*, having enjoyed many a *triumph* on such victories, will hardly begrudge me a slight *ovation* for the present.

sorry to say the ladies in general, and the Athenians in particular, are much altered; being far from choice either in their dialect or expressions, as the whole Attic race are barbarous to a proverb: –

> '῀Ω Ἀθήνα, πρότη χώρα,
> Τί γαιδάρους τρέφεις τώρα.'

In Gibbon, vol. x. p. 161 is the following sentence: – 'The vulgar dialect of the city was gross and barbarous, though the compositions of the church and palace sometimes affected to copy the purity of the Attic models.' Whatever may be asserted on the subject, it is difficult to conceive that the 'ladies of Constantinople,' in the reign of the last Cæsar, spoke a purer dialect than Anna Comnena wrote three centuries before: and those royal pages are not esteemed the best models of composition, although the princess γλωτταν ειχεν ΑΚΡΙΒΩΣ Αττιχιζουσαν. In the Fanal, and in Yanina, the best Greek is spoken: in the latter there is a flourishing school under the direction of Psalida.

There is now in Athens a pupil of Psalida's, who is making a tour of observation through Greece: he is intelligent, and better educated than a fellow-commoner of most colleges. I mention this as a proof that the spirit of inquiry is not dormant among the Greeks.

The Reviewer mentions Mr Wright, the author of the beautiful poem 'Horæ Ionicæ,' as qualified to give details of these nominal Romans and degenerate Greeks; and also of their language: but Mr Wright, though a good poet and an able man, has made a mistake where he states the Albanian dialect of the Romaic to approximate nearest to the Hellenic: for the Albanians speak a Romaic as notoriously corrupt as the Scotch of Aberdeenshire, or the Italian of Naples. Yanina, (where, next to the Fanal, the Greek is purest,) although the capital of Ali Pacha's dominions, is not in Albania but Epirus; and beyond Delvinachi in Albania Proper up to Argyro-castro and Tepaleen (beyond which I did not advance) they speak worse Greek than even the Athenians. I was attended for a year and a half by two of these singular mountaineers, whose mother tongue is Illyric, and I never heard them or their countrymen (whom I have seen, not only at home, but to the amount of twenty thousand in the army of Vely Pacha) praised for their Greek, but often laughed at for their provincial barbarisms.

I have in my possession about twenty-five letters, amongst which some from the Bey of Corinth, written to me by Notaras, the Cogia Bachi, and others by the dragoman of the Caimacam of the Morea (which last governs in Vely Pacha's absence) are said to be favourable specimens of their epistolary style. I also received some at Constantinople from private persons, written in a most hyperbolical style, but in the true antique character.

The Reviewer proceeds, after some remarks on the tongue in its past and present state, to a paradox (page 59.) on the great mischief the knowledge of his own language has done to Coray, who, it seems, is less likely to understand the ancient Greek, because he is perfect master of the modern! This observation follows a paragraph, recommending, in explicit terms, the study of the Romaic, as 'a powerful auxiliary,' not only to the traveller and foreign merchant, but also to the classical scholar; in short, to every body except the only person who can be thoroughly acquainted with its uses; and by a parity of reasoning, our old language is conjectured to be probably more attainable by 'foreigners' than by ourselves! Now, I am inclined to think, that a Dutch Tyro in our tongue (albeit himself of Saxon blood) would be sadly perplexed with 'Sir Tristrem,' or any other given 'Auchinleck MS,' with or without a grammar or glossary; and to most apprehensions it seems evident, that none but a native can acquire a competent, far less complete, knowledge of our obsolete idioms. We may give the critic credit for his ingenuity, but no more believe him than we do Smollett's Lismahago, who maintains that the purest English is spoken in Edinburgh. That Coray may err is very possible; but if he does, the fault is in the man rather than in his mother tongue, which is, as it ought to be, of the greatest aid to the native student. – Here the Reviewer proceeds to business on Strabo's translators, and here I close my remarks.

Sir W. Drummond, Mr Hamilton, Lord Aberdeen, Dr Clarke, Captain Leake, Mr Gell, Mr Walpole, and many others now in England, have all the requisites to furnish details of this fallen people. The few observations I have offered I should have left where I made them, had not the article in question, and above all the spot where I read it, induced me to advert to those pages, which the advantage of my present situation enabled me to clear, or at least to make the attempt.

I have endeavoured to waive the personal feelings, which rise in despite of me in touching upon any part of the Edinburgh Review; not from a wish to conciliate the favour of its writers, or to cancel the remembrance of a syllable I have formerly published, but simply from a sense of the impropriety of mixing up private resentments with a disquisition of the present kind, and more particularly at this distance of time and place.

ADDITIONAL NOTE, ON THE TURKS

The difficulties of travelling in Turkey have been much exaggerated, or rather have considerably diminished of late years. The Mussulmans have been beaten into a kind of sullen civility, very comfortable to voyagers.

It is hazardous to say much on the subject of Turks and Turkey; since it is possible to live amongst them twenty years without acquiring information, at least from themselves. As far as my own slight experience carried me, I have no complaint to make; but am indebted for many civilities (I might almost say for friendship), and much hospitality, to Ali Pacha, his son Veli Pacha of the Morea, and several others of high rank in the provinces. Suleyman Aga, late Governor of Athens, and now of Thebes, was a *bon vivant*, and as social a being as ever sat cross-legged at a tray or a table. During the carnival, when our English party were masquerading, both himself and his successor were more happy to 'receive masks' than any dowager in Grosvenor-square.

On one occasion of his supping at the convent, his friend and visiter, the Cadi of Thebes, was carried from table perfectly qualified for any club in Christendom; while the worthy Waywode himself triumphed in his fall.

In all money transactions with the Moslems, I ever found the strictest honour, the highest disinterestedness. In transacting business with them, there are none of those dirty peculations, under the name of interest, difference of exchange, commission, &c. &c. uniformly found in applying to a Greek consul to cash bills, even on the first houses in Pera.

With regard to presents, an established custom in the East, you will rarely find yourself a loser; as one worth acceptance is generally returned by another of similar value – a horse, or a shawl.

In the capital and at court the citizens and courtiers are formed in the same school with those of Christianity; but there does not exist a more honourable, friendly, and high-spirited character than the true Turkish provincial Aga, or Moslem country gentleman. It is not meant here to designate the governors of towns, but those Agas who, by a kind of feudal tenure, possess lands and houses, of more or less extent, in Greece and Asia Minor.

The lower orders are in as tolerable discipline as the rabble in countries with greater pretensions to civilisation. A Moslem, in walking the streets of our country-towns, would be more incommoded in England than a Frank in a similar situation in Turkey. Regimentals are the best travelling dress.

The best accounts of the religion and different sects of Islamism, may be found in D'Ohsson's French; of their manners, &c. perhaps in Thornton's English. The Ottomans, with all their defects, are not a people to be despised. Equal, at least, to the Spaniards, they are superior to the Portuguese. If it be difficult to pronounce what they are, we can at least say what they are *not:* they are *not* treacherous, they are *not* cowardly, they do *not* burn heretics, they are *not* assassins, nor has an enemy advanced to *their* capital. They are faithful to their sultan till he becomes unfit to govern, and devout to their God without an inquisition. Were they driven from St Sophia to-morrow, and the French or Russians enthroned in their stead, it would become a question whether Europe would gain by the exchange? England would certainly be the loser.

With regard to that ignorance of which they are so generally, and sometimes justly accused, it may be doubted, always excepting France and England, in what useful points of knowledge they are excelled by other nations. Is it in the common arts of life? In their manufactures? Is a Turkish sabre inferior to a Toledo? or is a Turk worse clothed or lodged, or fed and taught, than a Spaniard? Are their Pachas worse educated than a Grandee? or an Effendi than a Knight of St Jago? I think not.

I remember Mahmout, the grandson of Ali Pacha, asking whether my fellow-traveller and myself were in the upper or lower House of Parliament. Now, this question from a boy of ten years old proved that his education had not been neglected. It may be doubted if an English boy at that age knows the difference of the Divan from a College of Dervises; but I am very sure a Spaniard does not. How little Mahmout, surrounded, as he had been, entirely by his Turkish tutors, had learned that there was such a thing as a Parliament, it were useless to conjecture, unless we suppose that his instructors did not confine his studies to the Koran.

In all the mosques there are schools established, which are very regularly attended; and the poor are taught without the church of Turkey being put into peril. I believe the system is not yet printed (though there is such a thing as a Turkish press, and books printed on the late military institution of the Nizam Gedidd); nor have I heard whether the Mufti and the Mollas have subscribed, or the Caimacam and the Tefterdar taken the alarm, for fear the ingenuous youth of the turban should be taught not to 'pray to God their way.' The Greeks also – a kind of Eastern Irish papists – have a college of their own at Maynooth – no, at Haivali; where the hetero-dox receive much the same kind of countenance from the Ottoman as the Catholic college from the English legislature. Who shall then affirm, that the Turks are ignorant bigots, when they thus evince the exact proportion of Christian charity which is tolerated in the most prosperous and orthodox of all possible kingdoms? But though they allow all this, they will not suffer the Greeks to participate in their privileges: no, let them fight their battles, and pay their haratch (taxes), be drubbed in this world, and damned in the next. And shall we then emancipate our Irish Helots? Mahomet forbid! We should then be bad Mussulmans, and worse Christians: at present we unite the best of both – jesuitical faith, and something not much inferior to Turkish toleration.

An Ode to the Framers of the Frame Bill

Oh well done Lord E[ldo]n! and better Lord R[yde]r!
Britannia must prosper with councils like yours;
HAWKESBURY, HARROWBY, help you to guide her,
Whose remedy only must *kill* ere it cures:
5   Those villains, the Weavers, are all grown refractory,
Asking some succour for Charity's sake –
So hang them in clusters round each Manufactory,
That will at once put an end to *mistake*.

The rascals, perhaps, may betake them to robbing,
10   The dogs to be sure have got nothing to eat –
So if we can hang them for breaking a bobbin,
'Twill save all the Government's money and meat:
Men are more easily made than machinery –
Stockings fetch better prices than lives –
15   Gibbets on Sherwood will *heighten* the scenery,
Showing how Commerce, *how* Liberty thrives!

Justice is now in pursuit of the wretches,
Grenadiers, Volunteers, Bow-street Police,
Twenty-two Regiments, a score of Jack Ketches,
20   Three of the Quorum and two of the Peace;
Some Lords, to be sure, would have summoned the Judges,
To take their opinion, but that they ne'er shall,
For LIVERPOOL such a concession begrudges,
So now they're condemned by *no Judges* at all.

25   Some folks for certain have thought it was shocking,
When Famine appeals, and when Poverty groans,
That life should be valued at less than a stocking,
And breaking of frames lead to breaking of bones.

If it should prove so, I trust, by this token,
30 (And who will refuse to partake in the hope?)
That the frames of the fools may be first to be *broken*,
Who, when asked for a *remedy*, sent down a *rope*.

Lines to a Lady Weeping

Weep, daughter of a royal line,
    A Sire's disgrace, a realm's decay;
Ah! happy if each tear of thine
    Could wash a father's fault away!

5   Weep – for thy tears are Virtue's tears –
    Auspicious to these suffering isles;
And be each drop in future years
    Repaid thee by thy people's smiles!

March, 1812.

THE WALTZ

An Apostrophic Hymn

'Qualis in Eurotæ ripis, aut per juga Cynthi,
Exercet Diana choros.'   VIRGIL.

'Such on Eurota's banks, or Cynthia's height,
Diana seems: and so she charms the sight,
When in the dance the graceful goddess leads
The quire of nymphs, and overtops their heads.'

DRYDEN'S VIRGIL.

TO THE PUBLISHER

SIR,

I am a country gentleman of a midland county. I might
have been a parliament-man for a certain borough; having
had the offer of as many votes as General T. at the general
election in 1812. But I was all for domestic happiness; as,
fifteen years ago, on a visit to London, I married a middle-
aged maid of honour. We lived happily at Hornem Hall till
last season, when my wife and I were invited by the Countess
of Waltzaway (a distant relation of my spouse) to pass the
winter in town. Thinking no harm, and our girls being come
to a marriageable (or, as they call it, *marketable*) age, and
having besides a Chancery suit inveterately entailed upon the
family estate, we came up in our old chariot, – of which, by
the bye, my wife grew so much ashamed in less than a
week, that I was obliged to buy a second-hand barouche, of
which I might mount the box, Mrs H. says, if I could drive,
but never see the inside – that place being reserved for the
Honourable Augustus Tiptoe, her partner-general and
opera-knight. Hearing great praises of Mrs H.'s dancing (she
was famous for birthnight minuets in the latter end of the
last century), I unbooted, and went to a ball at the Countess's,

expecting to see a country dance, or, at most, cotillions, reels, and all the old paces to the newest tunes. But, judge of my surprise, on arriving, to see poor dear Mrs Hornem with her arms half round the loins of a huge hussar-looking gentleman I never set eyes on before; and his, to say truth, rather more than half round her waist, turning round, and round, and round, to a d——d see-saw up-and-down sort of tune, that reminded me of the 'Black joke,' only more '*affettuoso*,' till it made me quite giddy with wondering they were not so. By-and-by they stopped a bit, and I thought they would sit or fall down: – but no; with Mrs H.'s hand on his shoulder, '*quam familiariter*'[1] (as Terence said, when I was at school), they walked about a minute, and then at it again, like two cockchafers spitted on the same bodkin. I asked what all this meant, when, with a loud laugh, a child no older than our Wilhelmina (a name I never heard but in the Vicar of Wakefield, though her mother would call her after the Princess of Swappenbach,) said, 'Lord! Mr Hornem, can't you see they are valtzing?' or waltzing (I forget which); and then up she got, and her mother and sister, and away they went, and round-abouted it till supper-time. Now, that I know what it is, I like it of all things, and so does Mrs H. (though I have broken my shins, and four times overturned Mrs Hornem's maid, in practising the preliminary steps in a morning). Indeed, so much do I like it, that having a turn for rhyme, tastily displayed in some election ballads, and songs in honour of all the victories (but till lately I have had little practice in that way), I sat down, and with the aid of William Fitzgerald, Esq., and a few hints from Dr Busby, (whose recitations I attend, and am monstrous fond of Master Busby's manner of delivering his father's late successful 'Drury Lane Address,') I composed the following hymn,

1. My Latin is all forgotten, if a man can be said to have forgotten what he never remembered; but I bought my title-page motto of a Catholic priest for a three-shilling bank token, after much haggling for the *even* sixpence. I grudged the money to a papist, being all for the memory of Perceval and 'No popery,' and quite regretting the downfall of the pope, because we can't burn him any more.

wherewithal to make my sentiments known to the public; whom, nevertheless, I heartily despise, as well as the critics.

I am, Sir, yours, &c. &c.,

HORACE HORNEM.

Muse of the many-twinkling feet![1] whose charms
Are now extended up from legs to arms;
Terpsichore! – too long misdeem'd a maid –
Reproachful term – bestow'd but to upbraid –
5   Henceforth in all the bronze of brightness shine,
The least a vestal of the virgin Nine.
Far be from thee and thine the name of prude;
Mock'd, yet triumphant; sneer'd at, unsubdued;
Thy legs must move to conquer as they fly,
10   If but thy coats are reasonably high;
Thy breast – if bare enough – requires no shield;
Dance forth – *sans armour* thou shalt take the field,
And own – impregnable to *most* assaults,
Thy not too lawfully begotten 'Waltz.'

15   Hail, nimble nymph! to whom the young hussar,
The whisker'd votary of waltz and war,
His night devotes, despite of spur and boots;
A sight unmatch'd since Orpheus and his brutes:
Hail, spirit-stirring Waltz! – beneath whose banners
20   A modern hero fought for modish manners;
On Hounslow's heath to rival Wellesley's[2] fame,
Cock'd – fired – and miss'd his man – but gain'd his aim;
Hail, moving Muse! to whom the fair one's breast
Gives all it can, and bids us take the rest.

1. 'Glance their many-twinkling feet.' – GRAY.
2. To rival Lord Wellesley's, or his nephew's, as the reader pleases: – the one gained a pretty woman, whom he deserved, by fighting for; and the other has been fighting in the Peninsula many a long day, 'by Shrewsbury clock,' without gaining any thing in *that* country but the title of 'the Great

25   Oh! for the flow of Busby, or of Fitz,
      The latter's loyalty, the former's wits,
      To 'energise the object I pursue,'
      And give both Belial and his dance their due!

      Imperial Waltz! imported from the Rhine
30   (Famed for the growth of pedigrees and wine),
      Long be thine import from all duty free,
      And hock itself be less esteem'd than thee;
      In some few qualities alike – for hock
      Improves our cellar – *thou* our living stock.
35   The head to hock belongs – thy subtler art
      Intoxicates alone the heedless heart:
      Through the full veins thy gentler poison swims,
      And wakes to wantonness the willing limbs.

Lord,' and 'the Lord;' which savours of profanation, having been hitherto
applied only to that Being to whom '*Te Deums*' for carnage are the rankest
blasphemy. – It is to be presumed the general will one day return to his
Sabine farm; there

> 'To tame the genius of the stubborn plain,
> *Almost as quickly* as he conquer'd Spain!'

The Lord Peterborough conquered continents in a summer; we do more –
we contrive both to conquer and lose them in a shorter season. If the 'great
Lord's' *Cincinnatian* progress in agriculture be no speedier than the propor-
tional average of time in Pope's couplet, it will, according to the farmers'
proverb, be 'ploughing with dogs.'
      By the bye – one of this illustrious person's new titles is forgotten – it is,
however, worth remembering – '*Salvador del mundo!*' *credite, posteri!* If this
be the appellation annexed by the inhabitants of the Peninsula to the name
of a *man* who has not yet saved them – query – are they worth saving, even
in this world? for, according to the mildest modifications of any Christian
creed, those three words make the odds much against them in the next. –
'Saviour of the world,' quotha! – it were to be wished that he, or any one
else, could save a corner of it – his country. Yet this stupid misnomer,
although it shows the near connection between superstition and impiety, so
far has its use, that it proves there can be little to dread from those Catholics
(inquisitorial Catholics too) who can confer such an appellation on a *Protes-
tant.* I suppose next year he will be entitled the 'Virgin Mary:' if so, Lord
George Gordon himself would have nothing to object to such liberal bastards
of our Lady of Babylon.

Oh, Germany! how much to thee we owe,
40   As heaven-born Pitt can testify below,
Ere cursed confederation made thee France's,
And only left us thy d——d debts and dances!
Of subsidies and Hanover bereft,
We bless thee still – for George the Third is left!
45   Of kings the best – and last, not least in worth,
For graciously begetting George the Fourth.
To Germany, and highnesses serene,
Who owe us millions – don't we owe the queen?
To Germany, what owe we not besides?
50   So oft bestowing Brunswickers and brides;
Who paid for vulgar, with her royal blood,
Drawn from the stem of each Teutonic stud:
Who sent us – so be pardon'd all her faults –
A dozen dukes, some kings, a queen – and Waltz.

55   But peace to her – her emperor and diet,
Though now transferr'd to Buonaparte's 'fiat!'
Back to my theme – O Muse of motion! say,
How first to Albion found thy Waltz her way?

Borne on the breath of hyperborean gales,
60   From Hamburg's port (while Hamburg yet had *mails*),
Ere yet unlucky Fame – compell'd to creep
To snowy Gottenburg – was chill'd to sleep;
Or, starting from her slumbers, deign'd arise,
Heligoland! to stock thy mart with lies;
65   While unburnt Moscow[1] yet had news to send,
Nor owed her fiery exit to a friend,
She came – Waltz came – and with her certain sets
Of true despatches, and as true gazettes;

1. The patriotic arson of our amiable allies cannot be sufficiently com-
mended – nor subscribed for. Amongst other details omitted in the various
despatches of our eloquent ambassador, he did not state (being too much
occupied with the exploits of Colonel C——, in swimming rivers frozen, and
galloping over roads impassable,) that one entire province perished by
famine in the most melancholy manner, as follows: – In General Rostop-
chin's consummate conflagration, the consumption of tallow and train oil

Then flamed of Austerlitz the blest despatch,
70 Which Moniteur nor Morning Post can match;
And – almost crush'd beneath the glorious news –
Ten plays, and forty tales of Kotzebue's;
One envoy's letters, six composers' airs,
And loads from Frankfort and from Leipsic fairs;
75 Meiner's four volumes upon womankind,
Like Lapland witches to ensure a wind;
Brunck's heaviest tome for ballast, and, to back it,
Of Heyné, such as should not sink the packet.

Fraught with this cargo – and her fairest freight,
80 Delightful Waltz, on tiptoe for a mate,
The welcome vessel reach'd the genial strand,
And round her flock'd the daughters of the land.
Not decent David, when, before the ark,
His grand pas-seul excited some remark;
85 Not love-lorn Quixote, when his Sancho thought
The knight's fandango friskier than it ought;
Not soft Herodias, when, with winning tread,
Her nimble feet danced off another's head;
Not Cleopatra on her galley's deck,
90 Display'd so much of *leg*, or more of *neck*,
Than thou, ambrosial Waltz, when first the moon
Beheld thee twirling to a Saxon tune!

To you, ye husbands of ten years! whose brows
Ache with the annual tributes of a spouse;
95 To you of nine years less, who only bear
The budding sprouts of those that you *shall* wear,

---

was so great, that the market was inadequate to the demand: and thus one
hundred and thirty-three thousand persons were starved to death, by being
reduced to wholesome diet! The lamplighters of London have since sub-
scribed a pint (of oil) a piece, and the tallow-chandlers have unanimously
voted a quantity of best moulds (four to the pound), to the relief of the sur-
viving Scythians; – the scarcity will soon, by such exertions, and a proper
attention to the *quality* rather than the quantity of provision, be totally
alleviated. It is said, in return, that the untouched Ukraine has subscribed
sixty thousand beeves for a day's meal to our suffering manufacturers.

With added ornaments around them roll'd
Of native brass, or law-awarded gold;
To you, ye matrons, ever on the watch
100 To mar a son's, or make a daughter's, match;
To you, ye children of – whom chance accords –
Always the ladies, and *sometimes* their lords;
To you, ye single gentlemen, who seek
Torments for life, or pleasures for a week;
105 As Love or Hymen your endeavours guide,
To gain your own, or snatch another's bride; –
To one and all the lovely stranger came,
And every ball-room echoes with her name.

Endearing Waltz! – to thy more melting tune
110 Bow Irish jig, and ancient rigadoon.
Scotch reels, avaunt! and country-dance, forego
Your future claims to each fantastic toe!
Waltz – Waltz alone – both legs and arms demands,
Liberal of feet, and lavish of her hands;
115 Hands which may freely range in public sight
Where ne'er before – but – pray 'put out the light.'
Methinks the glare of yonder chandelier
Shines much too far – or I am much too near;
And true, though strange – Waltz whispers this remark,
120 'My slippery steps are safest in the dark!'
But here the Muse with due decorum halts,
And lends her longest petticoat to Waltz.

Observant travellers of every time!
Ye quartos publish'd upon every clime!
125 O say, shall dull Romaika's heavy round,
Fandango's wriggle, or Bolero's bound;
Can Egypt's Almas[1] – tantalising group –
Columbia's caperers to the warlike whoop –
Can aught from cold Kamschatka to Cape Horn
130 With Waltz compare, or after Waltz be borne?
Ah, no! from Morier's pages down to Galt's,
Each tourist pens a paragraph for 'Waltz.'

1. Dancing girls – who do for hire what Waltz doth gratis.

Shades of those belles whose reign began of yore,
With George the Third's – and ended long before! –
135   Though in your daughters' daughters yet you thrive,
Burst from your lead, and be yourselves alive!
Back to the ball-room speed your spectred host:
Fool's Paradise is dull to that you lost.
No treacherous powder bids conjecture quake;
140   No stiff-starch'd stays make meddling fingers ache;
(Transferr'd to those ambiguous things that ape
Goats in their visage,[1] women in their shape;)
No damsel faints when rather closely press'd,
But more caressing seems when most caress'd;
145   Superfluous hartshorn, and reviving salts,
Both banish'd by the sovereign cordial 'Waltz.'

Seductive Waltz! – though on thy native shore
Even Werter's self proclaim'd thee half a whore;
Werter – to decent vice though much inclined,
150   Yet warm, not wanton; dazzled, but not blind –
Though gentle Genlis, in her strife with Stael,
Would even proscribe thee from a Paris ball;

---

1. It cannot be complained now, as in the Lady Baussière's time, of the 'Sieur de la Croix,' that there be 'no whiskers;' but how far these are indications of valour in the field, or elsewhere, may *still* be questionable. Much may be, and hath been, avouched on both sides. In the olden time philosophers had whiskers, and soldiers none – Scipio himself was shaven – Hannibal thought his one eye handsome enough without a beard; but Adrian, the emperor, wore a beard (having warts on his chin, which neither the Empress Sabina nor even the courtiers could abide) – Turenne had whiskers, Marlborough none – Buonaparte is unwhiskered, the Regent whiskered; '*argal*' greatness of mind and whiskers may or may not go together: but certainly the different occurrences, since the growth of the last mentioned, go further in behalf of whiskers than the anathema of Anselm did *against* long hair in the reign of Henry I. – Formerly, *red* was a favourite colour. See Lodowick Barrey's comedy of Ram Alley, 1661; Act 1. Scene 1.

'TAFFETA: Now for a wager – What coloured beard comes next by the window?

'ADRIANA: A black man's, I think.

'TAFFETA: I think not so: I think a *red*, for that is most in fashion.'

There is 'nothing new under the sun;' but *red*, then a *favourite*, has now subsided into a *favourite*'s colour.

The fashion hails – from countesses to queens,
And maids and valets waltz behind the scenes;
155 Wide and more wide thy witching circle spreads,
And turns – if nothing else – at least our *heads*;
With thee even clumsy cits attempt to bounce,
And cockneys practise what they can't pronounce.
Gods! how the glorious theme my strain exalts,
160 And rhyme finds partner rhyme in praise of 'Waltz!'

Blest was the time Waltz chose for her *début*;
The court, the Regent, like herself were new;[1]
New face for friends, for foes some new rewards;
New ornaments for black and royal guards;
165 New laws to hang the rogues that roar'd for bread:
New coins (most new)[2] to follow those that fled;
New victories – nor can we prize them less,
Though Jenky wonders at his own success;
New wars, because the old succeed so well,
170 That most survivors envy those who fell;
New mistresses – no, old – and yet 'tis true,
Though they be *old*, the *thing* is something new;
Each new, quite new – (except some ancient tricks),[3]
New white-sticks, gold-sticks, broom-sticks, all new sticks!

1. An anachronism – Waltz and the battle of Austerlitz are before said to
have opened the ball together: the bard means (if he means any thing),
Waltz was not so much in vogue till the Regent attained the acmé of his
popularity. Waltz, the comet, whiskers, and the new government, il-
luminated heaven and earth, in all their glory, much about the same time: of
these the comet only has disappeared; the other three continue to astonish
us still. – *Printer's Devil.*
2. Amongst others a new ninepence – a creditable coin now forthcoming,
worth a pound, in paper, at the fairest calculation.
3. 'Oh that *right* should thus overcome *might*!' Who does not remember the
'delicate investigation' in the 'Merry Wives of Windsor?' –
 'FORD: Pray you, come near: if I suspect without cause, why then make
   sport at me; then let me be your jest; I deserve it. How now? whither
   bear you this?
 'MRS FORD: What have you to do whither they bear it? – you were best
   meddle with buck-washing.'

175 With vests or ribands – deck'd alike in hue,
New troopers strut, new turncoats blush in blue:
So saith the muse: my — —,[1] what say you?
Such was the time when Waltz might best maintain
Her new preferments in this novel reign;
180 Such was the time, nor ever yet was such;
Hoops are *no more*, and petticoats *not much;*
Morals and minuets, virtue and her stays,
And tell-tale powder – all have had their days.
The ball begins – the honours of the house
185 First duly done by daughter or by spouse,
Some potentate – or royal or serene –
With Kent's gay grace, or sapient Gloster's mien,
Leads forth the ready dame, whose rising flush
Might once have been mistaken for a blush.
190 From where the garb just leaves the bosom free,
That spot where hearts[2] were once supposed to be;
Round all the confines of the yielded waist,
The strangest hand may wander undisplaced;
The lady's in return may grasp as much
195 As princely paunches offer to her touch.
Pleased round the chalky floor how well they trip,
One hand reposing on the royal hip;
The other to the shoulder no less royal
Ascending with affection truly loyal!

1. The gentle, or ferocious, reader may fill up the blank as he pleases – there are several dissyllabic names at *his* service (being already in the Regent's): it would not be fair to back any peculiar initial against the alphabet, as every month will add to the list now entered for the sweepstakes: – a distinguished consonant is said to be the favourite, much against the wishes of the *knowing ones.*

2. 'We have changed all that,' says the Mock Doctor – 'tis all gone – Asmodeus knows where. After all, it is of no great importance how women's hearts are disposed of; they have nature's privilege to distribute them as absurdly as possible. But there are also some men with hearts so thoroughly bad, as to remind us of those phenomena often mentioned in natural history; viz. a mass of solid stone – only to be opened by force – and when divided, you discover a *toad* in the centre, lively, and with the reputation of being venomous.

200 Thus front to front the partners move or stand,
     The foot may rest, but none withdraw the hand;
     And all in turn may follow in their rank,
     The Earl of – Asterisk – and Lady – Blank;
     Sir – Such-a-one – with those of fashion's host,
205 For whose blest surnames – vide 'Morning Post'
     (Or if for that impartial print too late,
     Search Doctors' Commons six months from my date) –
     Thus all and each, in movement swift or slow,
     The genial contact gently undergo;
210 Till some might marvel, with the modest Turk,
     If 'nothing follows all this palming work?'[1]
     True, honest Mirza! – you may trust my rhyme –
     Something does follow at a fitter time;
     The breast thus publicly resign'd to man,
215 In private may resist him — if it can.

     O ye who loved our grandmothers of yore,
     Fitzpatrick, Sheridan, and many more!
     And thou, my prince! whose sovereign taste and will
     It is to love the lovely beldames still!
220 Thou ghost of Queensbury! whose judging sprite
     Satan may spare to peep a single night,
     Pronounce – if ever in your days of bliss
     Asmodeus struck so bright a stroke as this;
     To teach the young ideas how to rise,
225 Flush in the cheek, and languish in the eyes;
     Rush to the heart, and lighten through the frame,
     With half-told wish and ill-dissembled flame
     For prurient nature still will storm the breast –
     Who, tempted thus, can answer for the rest?

230   But ye – who never felt a single thought
     For what our morals are to be, or ought;
     Who wisely wish the charms you view to reap,
     Say – would you make those beauties quite so cheap?

1. In Turkey a pertinent, here an impertinent and superfluous, question –
literally put, as in the text, by a Persian to Morier, on seeing a waltz in Pera
– *Vide Morier's Travels.*

Hot from the hands promiscuously applied,
235   Round the slight waist, or down the glowing side,
Where were the rapture then to clasp the form
From this lewd grasp and lawless contact warm?
At once love's most endearing thought resign,
To press the hand so press'd by none but thine;
240   To gaze upon that eye which never met
Another's ardent look without regret;
Approach the lip which all, without restraint,
Come near enough – if not to touch – to taint;
If such thou lovest – love her then no more,
245   Or give – like her – caresses to a score;
Her mind with these is gone, and with it go
The little left behind it to bestow.

Voluptuous Waltz! and dare I thus blaspheme?
Thy bard forgot thy praises were his theme.
250   Terpsichore, forgive! – at every ball
My wife *now* waltzes – and my daughters *shall*;
My son – (or stop – 'tis needless to enquire –
These little accidents should ne'er transpire;
Some ages hence our genealogic tree
255   Will wear as green a bough for him as me) –
Waltzing shall rear, to make our name amends,
Grandsons for me – in heirs to all his friends.

Remember Thee! Remember Thee!

Remember thee! remember thee!
    Till Lethe quench life's burning stream,
Remorse and shame shall cling to thee,
    And haunt thee like a feverish dream!

5   Remember thee! Ay, doubt it not;
    Thy husband too shall think of thee!
By neither shalt thou be forgot,
    Thou *false* to him, thou *fiend* to me!

THE GIAOUR

A Fragment of a Turkish Tale

'One fatal remembrance – one sorrow that throws
Its bleak shade alike o'er our joys and our woes –
To which Life nothing darker nor brighter can bring,
For which joy hath no balm – and affliction no sting.'

[THOMAS] MOORE. [*Irish Melodies*]

TO SAMUEL ROGERS, ESQ.
AS A SLIGHT BUT MOST SINCERE TOKEN OF ADMIRATION OF
HIS GENIUS, RESPECT FOR HIS CHARACTER, AND GRATITUDE
FOR HIS FRIENDSHIP, THIS PRODUCTION IS INSCRIBED BY HIS
OBLIGED AND AFFECTIONATE SERVANT,

BYRON.

London, May, 1813.

ADVERTISEMENT

The tale which these disjointed fragments present is founded upon circumstances now less common in the East than formerly; either because the ladies are more circumspect than in the 'olden time,' or because the Christians have better fortune, or less enterprise. The story, when entire, contained the adventures of a female slave, who was thrown, in the Mussulman manner, into the sea for infidelity, and avenged by a young Venetian, her lover, at the time the Seven Islands were possessed by the Republic of Venice, and soon after the Arnauts were beaten back from the Morea, which they had ravaged for some time subsequent to the Russian invasion. The desertion of the Mainotes, on being refused the plunder of Misitra, led to the abandonment of that enterprise, and to the desolation of the Morea, during which the cruelty exercised on all sides was unparalleled even in the annals of the faithful.

No breath of air to break the wave
That rolls below the Athenian's grave,
That tomb[1] which, gleaming o'er the cliff,
First greets the homeward-veering skiff,
5   High o'er the land he saved in vain:
When shall such hero live again?

*   *   *   *   *

Fair clime! where every season smiles
Benignant o'er those blessed isles,
Which, seen from far Colonna's height,
10   Make glad the heart that hails the sight,
And lend to loneliness delight.
There mildly dimpling, Ocean's cheek
Reflects the tints of many a peak
Caught by the laughing tides that lave
15   These Edens of the eastern wave:
And if at times a transient breeze
Break the blue crystal of the seas,
Or sweep one blossom from the trees,
How welcome is each gentle air
20   That wakes and wafts the odours there!
For there – the Rose o'er crag or vale,
Sultana of the Nightingale,[2]
      The maid for whom his melody,
      His thousand songs are heard on high,
25   Blooms blushing to her lover's tale:
His queen, the garden queen, his Rose,
Unbent by winds, unchill'd by snows,
Far from the winters of the west,
By every breeze and season blest,
30   Returns the sweets by nature given
In softest incense back to heaven;
And grateful yields that smiling sky
Her fairest hue and fragrant sigh.

1. A tomb above the rocks on the promontory, by some supposed the
sepulchre of Themistocles.
2. The attachment of the nightingale to the rose is a well-known Persian
fable. If I mistake not, the 'Bulbul of a thousand tales' is one of his
appellations.

And many a summer flower is there,
35   And many a shade that love might share,
And many a grotto, meant for rest,
That holds the pirate for a guest;
Whose bark in sheltering cove below
Lurks for the passing peaceful prow,
40   Till the gay mariner's guitar[1]
Is heard, and seen the evening star;
Then stealing with the muffled oar
Far shaded by the rocky shore,
Rush the night-prowlers on the prey,
45   And turn to groans his roundelay.
Strange – that where Nature loved to trace,
As if for Gods, a dwelling place,
And every charm and grace hath mix'd
Within the paradise she fix'd,
50   There man, enamour'd of distress,
Should mar it into wilderness,
And trample, brute-like, o'er each flower
That tasks not one laborious hour;
Nor claims the culture of his hand
55   To bloom along the fairy land,
But springs as to preclude his care,
And sweetly woos him – but to spare!
Strange – that where all is peace beside,
There passion riots in her pride,
60   And lust and rapine wildly reign
To darken o'er the fair domain.
It is as though the fiends prevail'd
Against the seraphs they assail'd,
And, fix'd on heavenly thrones, should dwell
65   The freed inheritors of hell;
So soft the scene, so form'd for joy,
So curst the tyrants that destroy!

1. The guitar is the constant amusement of the Greek sailor by night: with a steady fair wind, and during a calm, it is accompanied always by the voice, and often by dancing.

He who hath bent him o'er the dead
Ere the first day of death is fled,
70   The first dark day of nothingness,
The last of danger and distress,
(Before Decay's effacing fingers
Have swept the lines where beauty lingers,)
And mark'd the mild angelic air,
75   The rapture of repose that's there,
The fix'd yet tender traits that streak
The languor of the placid cheek,
And – but for that sad shrouded eye,
    That fires not, wins not, weeps not, now,
80   And but for that chill, changeless brow,
Where cold Obstruction's apathy[1]
Appals the gazing mourner's heart,
As if to him it could impart
The doom he dreads, yet dwells upon;
85   Yes, but for these and these alone,
Some moments, ay, one treacherous hour,
He still might doubt the tyrant's power;
So fair, so calm, so softly seal'd,
The first, last look by death reveal'd![2]
90   Such is the aspect of this shore;
'Tis Greece, but living Greece no more!
So coldly sweet, so deadly fair,
We start, for soul is wanting there.
Hers is the loveliness in death,
95   That parts not quite with parting breath;

1. 'Ay, but to die and go we know not where,
    To lye in cold obstruction?'
                        Measure for Measure. [III.i.118–19]
2. I trust that few of my readers have ever had an opportunity of witnessing what is here attempted in description, but those who have will probably retain a painful remembrance of that singular beauty which pervades, with few exceptions, the features of the dead, a few hours, and but for a few hours, after 'the spirit is not there.' It is to be remarked in cases of violent death by gun-shot wounds, the expression is always that of languor, whatever the natural energy of the sufferer's character: but in death from a stab the countenance preserves its traits of feeling or ferocity, and the mind its bias, to the last.

But beauty with that fearful bloom,
That hue which haunts it to the tomb,
Expression's last receding ray,
A gilded halo hovering round decay,
100   The farewell beam of Feeling past away!
Spark of that flame, perchance of heavenly birth,
Which gleams, but warms no more its cherish'd earth!

Clime of the unforgotten brave!
Whose land from plain to mountain-cave
105   Was Freedom's home or Glory's grave!
Shrine of the mighty! can it be,
That this is all remains of thee?
Approach, thou craven crouching slave:
Say, is not this Thermopylæ?
110   These waters blue that round you lave,
Oh servile offspring of the free –
Pronounce what sea, what shore is this?
The gulf, the rock of Salamis!
These scenes, their story not unknown,
115   Arise, and make again your own;
Snatch from the ashes of your sires
The embers of their former fires;
And he who in the strife expires
Will add to theirs a name of fear
120   That Tyranny shall quake to hear,
And leave his sons a hope, a fame,
They too will rather die than shame:
For Freedom's battle once begun,
Bequeath'd by bleeding Sire to Son,
125   Though baffled oft is ever won.
Bear witness, Greece, thy living page,
Attest it many a deathless age!
While kings, in dusty darkness hid,
Have left a nameless pyramid,
130   Thy heroes, though the general doom
Hath swept the column from their tomb,
A mightier monument command,
The mountains of their native land!

There points thy Muse to stranger's eye
135   The graves of those that cannot die!
'Twere long to tell, and sad to trace,
Each step from splendour to disgrace;
Enough – no foreign foe could quell
Thy soul, till from itself it fell;
140   Yes! Self-abasement paved the way
To villain-bonds and despot sway.

What can he tell who treads thy shore?
    No legend of thine olden time,
No theme on which the muse might soar
145   High as thine own in days of yore,
    When man was worthy of thy clime.
The hearts within thy valleys bred,
The fiery souls that might have led
    Thy sons to deeds sublime,
150   Now crawl from cradle to the grave,
Slaves – nay, the bondsmen of a slave,[1]
    And callous, save to crime;
Stain'd with each evil that pollutes
Mankind, where least above the brutes;
155   Without even savage virtue blest,
Without one free or valiant breast,
Still to the neighbouring ports they waft
Proverbial wiles, and ancient craft;
In this the subtle Greek is found,
160   For this, and this alone, renown'd.
In vain might Liberty invoke
The spirit to its bondage broke,
Or raise the neck that courts the yoke:
No more her sorrows I bewail,
165   Yet this will be a mournful tale,
And they who listen may believe,
Who heard it first had cause to grieve.

1. Athens is the property of the Kislar Aga (the slave of the seraglio and guardian of the women), who appoints the Way-wode. A pander and eunuch – these are not polite, yet true appellations – now *governs* the *governor* of Athens!

*   *   *   *   *

     Far, dark, along the blue sea glancing,
The shadows of the rocks advancing
170   Start on the fisher's eye like boat
Of island-pirate or Mainote;
And fearful for his light caique,
He shuns the near but doubtful creek:
Though worn and weary with his toil,
175   And cumber'd with his scaly spoil,
Slowly, yet strongly, plies the oar,
Till Port Leone's safer shore
Receives him by the lovely light
That best becomes an Eastern night.

*   *   *   *   *

180   Who thundering comes on blackest steed,
With slacken'd bit and hoof of speed?
Beneath the clattering iron's sound
The cavern'd echoes wake around
In lash for lash, and bound for bound;
185   The foam that streaks the courser's side
Seems gather'd from the ocean-tide:
Though weary waves are sunk to rest,
There's none within his rider's breast;
And though to-morrow's tempest lower,
190   'Tis calmer than thy heart, young Giaour!
I know thee not, I loathe thy race,
But in thy lineaments I trace
What time shall strengthen, not efface:
Though young and pale, that sallow front
195   Is scathed by fiery passion's brunt;
Though bent on earth thine evil eye,
As meteor-like thou glidest by,
Right well I view and deem thee one
Whom Othman's sons should slay or shun.

200   On – on he hasten'd, and he drew
      My gaze of wonder as he flew:
      Though like a demon of the night
      He pass'd, and vanish'd from my sight,
      His aspect and his air impress'd
205   A troubled memory on my breast,
      And long upon my startled ear
      Rung his dark courser's hoofs of fear.
      He spurs his steed; he nears the steep,
      That, jutting, shadows o'er the deep;
210   He winds around; he hurries by;
      The rock relieves him from mine eye;
      For well I ween unwelcome he
      Whose glance is fix'd on those that flee;
      And not a star but shines too bright
215   On him who takes such timeless flight.
      He wound along; but ere he pass'd
      One glance he snatch'd, as if his last,
      A moment check'd his wheeling steed,
      A moment breathed him from his speed,
220   A moment on his stirrup stood –
      Why looks he o'er the olive wood?
      The crescent glimmers on the hill,
      The Mosque's high lamps are quivering still:
      Though too remote for sound to wake
225   In echoes of the far tophaike,[1]
      The flashes of each joyous peal
      Are seen to prove the Moslem's zeal,
      To-night, set Rhamazani's sun;
      To-night, the Bairam feast's begun;
230   To-night – but who and what art thou
      Of foreign garb and fearful brow?
      And what are these to thine or thee,
      That thou should'st either pause or flee?

---

1. 'Tophaike,' musket. – The Bairam is announced by the cannon at sunset; the illumination of the Mosques, and the firing of all kinds of small arms, loaded with *ball*, proclaim it during the night.

He stood – some dread was on his face,
235   Soon Hatred settled in its place:
It rose not with the reddening flush
Of transient Anger's hasty blush,
But pale as marble o'er the tomb,
Whose ghastly whiteness aids its gloom.
240   His brow was bent, his eye was glazed;
He raised his arm, and fiercely raised,
And sternly shook his hand on high,
As doubting to return or fly:
Impatient of his flight delay'd,
245   Here loud his raven charger neigh'd –
Down glanced that hand, and grasp'd his blade;
That sound had burst his waking dream,
As Slumber starts at owlet's scream.
The spur hath lanced his courser's sides;
250   Away, away, for life he rides:
Swift as the hurl'd on high jerreed[1]
Springs to the touch his startled steed;
The rock is doubled, and the shore
Shakes with the clattering tramp no more;
255   The crag is won, no more is seen
His Christian crest and haughty mien.
'Twas but an instant he restrain'd
That fiery barb so sternly rein'd;
'Twas but a moment that he stood,
260   Then sped as if by death pursued:
But in that instant o'er his soul
Winters of Memory seem'd to roll,
And gather in that drop of time
A life of pain, an age of crime.
265   O'er him who loves, or hates, or fears,
Such moment pours the grief of years:

1. Jerreed, or Djerrid, a blunted Turkish javelin, which is darted from
horseback with great force and precision. It is a favourite exercise of the
Mussulmans; but I know not if it can be called a *manly* one, since the most
expert in the art are the Black Eunuchs of Constantinople. I think, next to
these, a Mamlouk at Smyrna was the most skilful that came within my
observation.

What felt *he* then, at once opprest
By all that most distracts the breast?
That pause, which ponder'd o'er his fate,
270   Oh, who its dreary length shall date!
Though in Time's record nearly nought,
It was Eternity to Thought!
For infinite as boundless space
The thought that Conscience must embrace,
275   Which in itself can comprehend
Woe without name, or hope, or end.

The hour is past, the Giaour is gone;
And did he fly or fall alone?
Woe to that hour he came or went!
280   The curse for Hassan's sin was sent
To turn a palace to a tomb;
He came, he went, like the Simoom,[1]
That harbinger of fate and gloom,
Beneath whose widely-wasting breath
285   The very cypress droops to death –
Dark tree, still sad when others' grief is fled,
The only constant mourner o'er the dead!

The steed is vanish'd from the stall;
No serf is seen in Hassan's hall;
290   The lonely Spider's thin gray pall
Waves slowly widening o'er the wall;
The Bat builds in his Haram bower
And in the fortress of his power
The Owl usurps the beacon-tower;
295   The wild-dog howls o'er the fountain's brim,
With baffled thirst, and famine, grim;
For the stream has shrunk from its marble bed,
Where the weeds and the desolate dust are spread.
'Twas sweet of yore to see it play
300   And chase the sultriness of day,

1. The blast of the desert, fatal to every thing living, and often alluded to in eastern poetry.

As springing high the silver dew
In whirls fantastically flew,
And flung luxurious coolness round
The air, and verdure o'er the ground.
305 'Twas sweet, when cloudless stars were bright,
To view the wave of watery light,
And hear its melody by night.
And oft had Hassan's Childhood play'd
Around the verge of that cascade;
310 And oft upon his mother's breast
That sound had harmonized his rest;
And oft had Hassan's Youth along
Its bank been soothed by Beauty's song;
And softer seem'd each melting tone
315 Of Music mingled with its own.
But ne'er shall Hassan's Age repose
Along the brink at Twilight's close:
The stream that fill'd that font is fled —
The blood that warm'd his heart is shed!
320 And here no more shall human voice
Be heard to rage, regret, rejoice.
The last sad note that swell'd the gale
Was woman's wildest funeral wail:
That quench'd in silence, all is still,
325 But the lattice that flaps when the wind is shrill:
Though raves the gust, and floods the rain,
No hand shall close its clasp again.
On desert sands 'twere joy to scan
The rudest steps of fellow man,
330 So here the very voice of Grief
Might wake an Echo like relief —
At least 't would say, 'All are not gone;
There lingers Life, though but in one' —
For many a gilded chamber's there,
335 Which Solitude might well forbear;
Within that dome as yet Decay
Hath slowly work'd her cankering way —
But gloom is gather'd o'er the gate,
Nor there the Fakir's self will wait;

340 Nor there will wandering Dervise stay,
 For bounty cheers not his delay;
 Nor there will weary stranger halt
 To bless the sacred 'bread and salt.'[1]
 Alike must Wealth and Poverty
345 Pass heedless and unheeded by,
 For Courtesy and Pity died
 With Hassan on the mountain side.
 His roof, that refuge unto men,
 Is Desolation's hungry den.
350 The guest flies the hall, and the vassal from labour,
 Since his turban was cleft by the infidel's sabre![2]

  *   *   *   *   *

 I hear the sound of coming feet,
 But not a voice mine ear to greet;
 More near — each turban I can scan,
355 And silver-sheathed ataghan;[3]
 The foremost of the band is seen
 An Emir by his garb of green:[4]
 'Ho! who art thou?' — 'This low salam[5]
 Replies of Moslem faith I am.' —
360 'The burthen ye so gently bear
 Seems one that claims your utmost care,
 And, doubtless, holds some precious freight,
 My humble bark would gladly wait.'

1. To partake of food, to break bread and salt with your host, ensures the safety of the guest: even though an enemy, his person from that moment is sacred.

2. I need hardly observe, that Charity and Hospitality are the first duties enjoined by Mahomet; and to say truth, very generally practised by his disciples. The first praise that can be bestowed on a chief, is a panegyric on his bounty; the next, on his valour.

3. The ataghan, a long dagger worn with pistols in the belt, in a metal scabbard, generally of silver; and, among the wealthier, gilt, or of gold.

4. Green is the privileged colour of the prophet's numerous pretended descendants; with them, as here, faith (the family inheritance) is supposed to supersede the necessity of good works: they are the worst of a very indifferent brood.

5. 'Salam aleikoum! aleikoum salam!' peace be with you; be with you peace – the salutation reserved for the faithful: – to a Christian, 'Urlarula,' a good journey; or 'saban hiresem, saban serula;' good morn, good even; and sometimes, 'may your end be happy;' are the usual salutes.

'Thou speakest sooth: thy skiff unmoor,
365 And waft us from the silent shore;
Nay, leave the sail still furl'd, and ply
The nearest oar that's scatter'd by,
And midway to those rocks where sleep
The channel'd waters dark and deep.
370 Rest from your task — so — bravely done,
Our course has been right swiftly run;
Yet 'tis the longest voyage, I trow,
That one of —   *   *   *
*   *   *   *   *'

Sullen it plunged, and slowly sank,
375 The calm wave rippled to the bank;
I watch'd it as it sank, methought
Some motion from the current caught
Bestirr'd it more, — 'twas but the beam
That checker'd o'er the living stream:
380 I gazed, till vanishing from view,
Like lessening pebble it withdrew;
Still less and less, a speck of white
That gemm'd the tide, then mock'd the sight;
And all its hidden secrets sleep,
385 Known but to Genii of the deep,
Which, trembling in their coral caves,
They dare not whisper to the waves.

*   *   *   *   *

As rising on its purple wing
The insect-queen[1] of eastern spring,
390 O'er emerald meadows of Kashmeer
Invites the young pursuer near,
And leads him on from flower to flower
A weary chase and wasted hour,
Then leaves him, as it soars on high,
395 With panting heart and tearful eye:
So Beauty lures the full-grown child,
With hue as bright, and wing as wild;

1. The blue-winged butterfly of Kashmeer, the most rare and beautiful of
the species.

A chase of idle hopes and fears,
Begun in folly, closed in tears.
400   If won, to equal ills betray'd,
Woe waits the insect and the maid;
A life of pain, the loss of peace,
From infant's play, and man's caprice:
The lovely toy so fiercely sought
405   Hath lost its charm by being caught,
For every touch that woo'd its stay
Hath brush'd its brightest hues away,
Till charm, and hue, and beauty gone,
'Tis left to fly or fall alone.
410   With wounded wing, or bleeding breast,
Ah! where shall either victim rest?
Can this with faded pinion soar
From rose to tulip as before?
Or Beauty, blighted in an hour,
415   Find joy within her broken bower?
No: gayer insects fluttering by
Ne'er droop the wing o'er those that die,
And lovelier things have mercy shown
To every failing but their own,
420   And every woe a tear can claim
Except an erring sister's shame.

*   *   *   *   *

The Mind, that broods o'er guilty woes,
      Is like the Scorpion girt by fire,
In circle narrowing as it glows,
425   The flames around their captive close,
Till inly search'd by thousand throes,
      And maddening in her ire,
One sad and sole relief she knows,
The sting she nourish'd for her foes,
430   Whose venom never yet was vain,
Gives but one pang, and cures all pain,
And darts into her desperate brain;

So do the dark in soul expire,
Or live like Scorpion girt by fire;[1]
435   So writhes the mind Remorse hath riven,
Unfit for earth, undoom'd for heaven,
Darkness above, despair beneath,
Around it flame, within it death!

*   *   *   *   *

Black Hassan from the Haram flies,
440   Nor bends on woman's form his eyes;
The unwonted chase each hour employs,
Yet shares he not the hunter's joys.
Not thus was Hassan wont to fly
When Leila dwelt in his Serai.
445   Doth Leila there no longer dwell?
That tale can only Hassan tell:
Strange rumours in our city say
Upon that eve she fled away
When Rhamazan's[2] last sun was set,
450   And flashing from each minaret
Millions of lamps proclaim'd the feast
Of Bairam through the boundless East.
'Twas then she went as to the bath,
Which Hassan vainly search'd in wrath;
455   For she was flown her master's rage
In likeness of a Georgian page,
And far beyond the Moslem's power
Had wrong'd him with the faithless Giaour.
Somewhat of this had Hassan deem'd;
460   But still so fond, so fair she seem'd,
Too well he trusted to the slave
Whose treachery deserved a grave:

1. Alluding to the dubious suicide of the scorpion, so placed for experiment
by gentle philosophers. Some maintain that the position of the sting, when
turned towards the head, is merely a convulsive movement; but others have
actually brought in the verdict 'Felo de se.' The scorpions are surely inter-
ested in a speedy decision of the question; as, if once fairly established as
insect Catos, they will probably be allowed to live as long as they think
proper, without being martyred for the sake of an hypothesis.
2. The cannon at sunset close the Rhamazan.

And on that eve had gone to mosque,
And thence to feast in his kiosk.
465   Such is the tale his Nubians tell,
Who did not watch their charge too well;
But others say, that on that night,
By pale Phingari's[1] trembling light,
The Giaour upon his jet black steed
470   Was seen, but seen alone to speed
With bloody spur along the shore,
Nor maid nor page behind him bore.

*   *   *   *   *

Her eye's dark charm 't were vain to tell,
But gaze on that of the Gazelle,
475   It will assist thy fancy well;
As large, as languishingly dark,
But Soul beam'd forth in every spark
That darted from beneath the lid,
Bright as the jewel of Giamschid.[2]
480   Yea, *Soul*, and should our prophet say
That form was nought but breathing clay,
By Alla! I would answer nay;
Though on Al-Sirat's[3] arch I stood,
Which totters o'er the fiery flood,
485   With Paradise within my view,
And all his Houris beckoning through.
Oh! who young Leila's glance could read
And keep that portion of his creed,

1. Phingari, the moon.
2. The celebrated fabulous ruby of Sultan Giamschid, the embellisher of Istakhar; from its splendour, named Schebgerag, 'the torch of night;' also 'the cup of the sun,' &c. In the first edition, 'Giamschid' was written as a word of three syllables, so D'Herbelot has it; but I am told Richardson reduces it to a dissyllable, and writes 'Jamshid.' I have left in the text the orthography of the one with the pronunciation of the other.
3. Al-Sirat, the bridge of breadth, narrower than the thread of a famished spider, and sharper than the edge of a sword, over which the Mussulmans must *skate* into Paradise, to which it is the only entrance; but this is not the worst, the river beneath being hell itself, into which, as may be expected, the unskilful and tender of foot contrive to tumble with a 'facilis descensus Averni,' not very pleasing in prospect to the next passenger. There is a shorter cut downwards for the Jews and Christians.

Which saith that woman is but dust,
490   A soulless toy for tyrant's lust?[1]
On her might Muftis gaze, and own
That through her eye the Immortal shone;
On her fair cheek's unfading hue
The young pomegranate's[2] blossoms strew
495   Their bloom in blushes ever new;
Her hair in hyacynthine[3] flow,
When left to roll its folds below,
As midst her handmaids in the hall
She stood superior to them all,
500   Hath swept the marble where her feet
Gleam'd whiter than the mountain sleet
Ere from the cloud that gave it birth
It fell, and caught one stain of earth.
The cygnet nobly walks the water;
505   So moved on earth Circassia's daughter,
The loveliest bird of Franguestan![4]
As rears her crest the ruffled Swan,
    And spurns the wave with wings of pride,
When pass the steps of stranger man
510   Along the banks that bound her tide;
Thus rose fair Leila's whiter neck:–
Thus arm'd with beauty would she check
Intrusion's glance, till Folly's gaze
Shrunk from the charms it meant to praise.
515   Thus high and graceful was her gait;
Her heart as tender to her mate;
Her mate – stern Hassan, who was he?
Alas! that name was not for thee!

*   *   *   *   *

1. A vulgar error: the Koran allots at least a third of Paradise to well-behaved women; but by far the greater number of Mussulmans interpret the text their own way, and exclude their moieties from heaven. Being enemies to Platonics, they cannot discern 'any fitness of things' in the souls of the other sex, conceiving them to be superseded by the Houris.
2. An oriental simile, which may, perhaps, though fairly stolen, be deemed 'plus Arabe qu'en Arabie.'
3. Hyacinthine, in Arabic 'Sunbul;' as common a thought in the eastern poets as it was among the Greeks.
4. 'Franguestan,' Circassia.

Stern Hassan hath a journey ta'en
520 With twenty vassals in his train,
Each arm'd, as best becomes a man,
With arquebuss and ataghan;
The chief before, as deck'd for war,
Bears in his belt the scimitar
525 Stain'd with the best of Arnaut blood,
When in the pass the rebels stood,
And few return'd to tell the tale
Of what befell in Parne's vale.
The pistols which his girdle bore
530 Were those that once a pasha wore,
Which still, though gemm'd and boss'd with gold,
Even robbers tremble to behold.
'Tis said he goes to woo a bride
More true than her who left his side;
535 The faithless slave that broke her bower,
And, worse than faithless, for a Giaour!

*   *   *   *   *

The sun's last rays are on the hill,
And sparkle in the fountain rill,
Whose welcome waters, cool and clear,
540 Draw blessings from the mountaineer:
Here may the loitering merchant Greek
Find that repose 't were vain to seek
In cities lodged too near his lord,
And trembling for his secret hoard –
545 Here may he rest where none can see,
In crowds a slave, in deserts free;
And with forbidden wine may stain
The bowl a Moslem must not drain.

*   *   *   *   *

The foremost Tartar's in the gap,
550 Conspicuous by his yellow cap;
The rest in lengthening line the while
Wind slowly through the long defile:

Above, the mountain rears a peak,
Where vultures whet the thirsty beak,
555   And theirs may be a feast to-night,
Shall tempt them down ere morrow's light;
Beneath, a river's wintry stream
Has shrunk before the summer beam,
And left a channel bleak and bare,
560   Save shrubs that spring to perish there:
Each side the midway path there lay
Small broken crags of granite gray,
By time, or mountain lightning, riven
From summits clad in mists of heaven;
565   For where is he that hath beheld
The peak of Liakura unveil'd?

*   *   *   *   *

They reach the grove of pine at last:
'Bismillah!¹ now the peril's past;
For yonder view the opening plain,
570   And there we'll prick our steeds amain:'
The Chiaus spake, and as he said,
A bullet whistled o'er his head;
The foremost Tartar bites the ground!
    Scarce had they time to check the rein,
575   Swift from their steeds the riders bound;
    But three shall never mount again:
Unseen the foes that gave the wound,
    The dying ask revenge in vain.
With steel unsheath'd, and carbine bent,
580   Some o'er their courser's harness leant,
    Half shelter'd by the steed;
Some fly behind the nearest rock,
And there await the coming shock,
    Nor tamely stand to bleed
585   Beneath the shaft of foes unseen,
Who dare not quit their craggy screen.

1. Bismillah – 'In the name of God;' the commencement of all the chapters
of the Koran but one, and of prayer and thanksgiving.

Stern Hassan only from his horse
Disdains to light, and keeps his course,
Till fiery flashes in the van
590　Proclaim too sure the robber-clan
Have well secured the only way
Could now avail the promised prey;
Then curl'd his very beard[1] with ire,
And glared his eye with fiercer fire:
595　'Though far and near the bullets hiss,
I've scaped a bloodier hour than this.'
And now the foe their covert quit,
And call his vassals to submit;
But Hassan's frown and furious word
600　Are dreaded more than hostile sword,
Nor of his little band a man
Resign'd carbine or ataghan,
Nor raised the craven cry, Amaun![2]
In fuller sight, more near and near,
605　The lately ambush'd foes appear,
And, issuing from the grove, advance
Some who on battle-charger prance.
Who leads them on with foreign brand,
Far flashing in his red right hand?
610　''Tis he! 'tis he! I know him now;
I know him by his pallid brow;
I know him by the evil eye[3]
That aids his envious treachery;
I know him by his jet-black barb:
615　Though now array'd in Arnaut garb,

1. A phenomenon not uncommon with an angry Mussulman. In 1809, the
Capitan Pacha's whiskers at a diplomatic audience were no less lively with
indignation than a tiger cat's, to the horror of all the dragomans; the porten-
tous mustachios twisted, they stood erect of their own accord, and were
expected every moment to change their colour, but at last condescended to
subside, which, probably, saved more heads than they contained hairs.
2. 'Amaun,' quarter, pardon.
3. The 'evil eye,' a common superstition in the Levant, and of which the
imaginary effects are yet very singular on those who conceive themselves
affected.

Apostate from his own vile faith,
It shall not save him from the death:
'Tis he! well met in any hour,
Lost Leila's love, accursed Giaour!'
620 As rolls the river into ocean,
In sable torrent wildly streaming;
  As the sea-tide's opposing motion,
In azure column proudly gleaming,
Beats back the current many a rood,
625 In curling foam and mingling flood,
While eddying whirl, and breaking wave,
Roused by the blast of winter, rave;
Through sparkling spray, in thundering clash,
The lightnings of the waters flash
630 In awful whiteness o'er the shore,
That shines and shakes beneath the roar;
Thus – as the stream and ocean greet,
With waves that madden as they meet –
Thus join the bands, whom mutual wrong,
635 And fate, and fury, drive along.
The bickering sabres' shivering jar;
  And pealing wide or ringing near
  Its echoes on the throbbing ear,
The deathshot hissing from afar;
640 The shock, the shout, the groan of war,
  Reverberate along that vale,
  More suited to the shepherd's tale:
Though few the numbers – theirs the strife,
That neither spares nor speaks for life!
645 Ah! fondly youthful hearts can press,
To seize and share the dear caress:
But Love itself could never pant
For all that Beauty sighs to grant
With half the fervour Hate bestows
650 Upon the last embrace of foes,
When grappling in the fight they fold
Those arms that ne'er shall lose their hold:
Friends meet to part; Love laughs at faith;
True foes, once met, are join'd till death!

  * * * * *

655 With sabre shiver'd to the hilt,
 Yet dripping with the blood he spilt;
 Yet strain'd within the sever'd hand
 Which quivers round that faithless brand;
 His turban far behind him roll'd,
660 And cleft in twain its firmest fold;
 His flowing robe by falchion torn,
 And crimson as those clouds of morn
 That, streak'd with dusky red, portend
 The day shall have a stormy end;
665 A stain on every bush that bore
 A fragment of his palampore,[1]
 His breast with wounds unnumber'd riven,
 His back to earth, his face to heaven,
 Fall'n Hassan lies – his unclosed eye
670 Yet lowering on his enemy,
 As if the hour that seal'd his fate
 Surviving left his quenchless hate;
 And o'er him bends that foe with brow
 As dark as his that bled below. –

  * * * * *

675 'Yes, Leila sleeps beneath the wave,
 But his shall be a redder grave;
 Her spirit pointed well the steel
 Which taught that felon heart to feel.

 He call'd the Prophet, but his power
680 Was vain against the vengeful Giaour:
 He call'd on Alla – but the word
 Arose unheeded or unheard.
 Thou Paynim fool! could Leila's prayer
 Be pass'd, and thine accorded there?
685 I watch'd my time, I leagued with these,
 The traitor in his turn to seize;
 My wrath is wreak'd, the deed is done,
 And now I go – but go alone.'
  * * * * *
  * * * * *

1. The flowered shawls generally worn by persons of rank.

The browsing camels' bells are tinkling:
690   His Mother look'd from her lattice high,
     She saw the dews of eve besprinkling
The pasture green beneath her eye,
     She saw the planets faintly twinkling:
     ' 'Tis twilight – sure his train is nigh.'
695 She could not rest in the garden-bower,
But gazed through the grate of his steepest tower:
'Why comes he not? his steeds are fleet,
Nor shrink they from the summer heat;
Why sends not the Bridegroom his promised gift:
700 Is his heart more cold, or his barb less swift?
Oh, false reproach! yon Tartar now
Has gain'd our nearest mountain's brow,
And warily the steep descends,
And now within the valley bends;
705 And he bears the gift at his saddle bow –
How could I deem his courser slow?
Right well my largess shall repay
His welcome speed, and weary way.'

The Tartar lighted at the gate,
710 But scarce upheld his fainting weight:
His swarthy visage spake distress,
But this might be from weariness;
His garb with sanguine spots was dyed,
But these might be from his courser's side;
715 He drew the token from his vest –
Angel of Death! 'tis Hassan's cloven crest!
His calpac[1] rent – his caftan red –
'Lady, a fearful bride thy Son hath wed:
Me, not from mercy, did they spare,
720 But this empurpled pledge to bear.
Peace to the brave! whose blood is spilt;
Woe to the Giaour! for his the guilt.'

*   *   *   *   *

1. The 'Calpac' is the solid cap or centre part of the head-dress; the shawl is wound round it, and forms the turban.

A turban[1] carved in coarsest stone,
A pillar with rank weeds o'ergrown,

725   Whereon can now be scarcely read
The Koran verse that mourns the dead,
Point out the spot where Hassan fell
A victim in that lonely dell.
There sleeps as true an Osmanlie

730   As e'er at Mecca bent the knee;
As ever scorn'd forbidden wine,
Or pray'd with face towards the shrine,
In orisons resumed anew
At solemn sound of 'Alla Hu!'[2]

735   Yet died he by a stranger's hand,
And stranger in his native land;
Yet died he as in arms he stood,
And unavenged, at least in blood.
But him the maids of Paradise

740   Impatient to their halls invite,
And the dark Heaven of Houris' eyes
      On him shall glance for ever bright;
They come – their kerchiefs green they wave,[3]
And welcome with a kiss the brave!

745   Who falls in battle 'gainst a Giaour
Is worthiest an immortal bower.

*   *   *   *   *

But thou, false Infidel! shalt writhe
Beneath avenging Monkir's[4] scythe;

1. The turban, pillar, and inscriptive verse, decorate the tombs of the Osman-
lies, whether in the cemetery or the wilderness. In the mountains you fre-
quently pass similar mementos: and on enquiry you are informed that they
record some victim of rebellion, plunder, or revenge.
2. 'Alla Hu!' the concluding words of the Muezzin's call to prayer from the
highest gallery on the exterior of the Minaret. On a still evening, when the
Muezzin has a fine voice, which is frequently the case, the effect is solemn
and beautiful beyond all the bells in Christendom.
3. The following is part of a battle song of the Turks: – 'I see – I see a dark-
eyed girl of Paradise, and she waves a handkerchief, a kerchief of green; and
cries aloud, "Come, kiss me, for I love thee,"' &c.
4. Monkir and Nekir are the inquisitors of the dead, before whom the corpse
undergoes a slight noviciate and preparatory training for damnation. If

And from its torment 'scape alone
750 To wander round lost Eblis'[1] throne;
And fire unquench'd, unquenchable,
Around, within, thy heart shall dwell;
No ear can hear nor tongue can tell
The tortures of that inward hell!

755 But first, on earth as vampire[2] sent,
Thy corse shall from its tomb be rent:
Then ghastly haunt thy native place,
And suck the blood of all thy race;
There from thy daughter, sister, wife,
760 At midnight drain the stream of life;
Yet loathe the banquet which perforce
Must feed thy livid living corse:
Thy victims ere they yet expire
Shall know the demon for their sire,
765 As cursing thee, thou cursing them,
Thy flowers are wither'd on the stem.
But one that for thy crime must fall,
The youngest, most beloved of all,
Shall bless thee with a *father*'s name –
770 That word shall wrap thy heart in flame!
Yet must thou end thy task, and mark
Her cheek's last tinge, her eye's last spark,

---

the answers are none of the clearest, he is hauled up with a scythe and
thumped down with a red hot mace till properly seasoned, with a variety of
subsidiary probations. The office of these angels is no sinecure; there are
but two, and the number of orthodox deceased being in a small proportion
to the remainder, their hands are always full. See *Relig. Ceremon.* and Sale's
Koran.

1. Eblis, the Oriental Prince of Darkness.
2. The Vampire superstition is still general in the Levant. Honest
Tournefort tells a long story, which Mr Southey, in the notes on Thalaba,
quotes, about these 'Vroucolochas,' as he calls them. The Romaic term is
'Vardoulacha.' I recollect a whole family being terrified by the scream of a
child, which they imagined must proceed from such a visitation. The Greeks
never mention the word without horror. I find that 'Broucolokas' is an old
legitimate Hellenic appellation – at least is so applied to Arsenius, who,
according to the Greeks, was after his death animated by the Devil. – The
moderns, however, use the word I mention.

And the last glassy glance must view
Which freezes o'er its lifeless blue;
775   Then with unhallow'd hand shall tear
The tresses of her yellow hair,
Of which in life a lock when shorn
Affection's fondest pledge was worn;
But now is borne away by thee,
780   Memorial of thine agony!
Wet with thine own best blood shall drip[1]
Thy gnashing tooth and haggard lip;
Then stalking to thy sullen grave,
Go – and with Gouls and Afrits rave;
785   Till these in horror shrink away
From spectre more accursed than they!

*   *   *   *   *

'How name ye yon lone Caloyer?
    His features I have scann'd before
In mine own land: 'tis many a year,
790   Since, dashing by the lonely shore,
I saw him urge as fleet a steed
As ever served a horseman's need.
But once I saw that face, yet then
It was so mark'd with inward pain,
795   I could not pass it by again;
It breathes the same dark spirit now,
As death were stamp'd upon his brow.

"'Tis twice three years at summer tide
    Since first among our freres he came;
800   And here it soothes him to abide
    For some dark deed he will not name.
But never at our vesper prayer,
Nor e'er before confession chair
Kneels he, nor recks he when arise
805   Incense or anthem to the skies,

1. The freshness of the face, and the wetness of the lip with blood, are the never-failing signs of a Vampire. The stories told in Hungary and Greece of these foul feeders are singular, and some of them most *incredibly* attested.

But broods within his cell alone,
His faith and race alike unknown.
The sea from Paynim land he crost,
And here ascended from the coast;
810　Yet seems he not of Othman race,
But only Christian in his face:
I'd judge him some stray renegade,
Repentant of the change he made,
Save that he shuns our holy shrine,
815　Nor tastes the sacred bread and wine.
Great largess to these walls he brought,
And thus our abbot's favour bought;
But were I Prior, not a day
Should brook such stranger's further stay,
820　Or pent within our penance cell
Should doom him there for aye to dwell.
Much in his visions mutters he
Of maiden whelm'd beneath the sea;
Of sabres clashing, foemen flying,
825　Wrong avenged, and Moslem dying.
On cliff he hath been known to stand,
And rave as to some bloody hand
Fresh sever'd from its parent limb,
Invisible to all but him,
830　Which beckons onward to his grave,
And lures to leap into the wave.'
　　*　　　*　　　*　　　*　　　*
　　*　　　*　　　*　　　*　　　*

Dark and unearthly is the scowl
That glares beneath his dusky cowl:
The flash of that dilating eye
835　Reveals too much of times gone by;
Though varying, indistinct its hue,
Oft will his glance the gazer rue,
For in it lurks that nameless spell,
Which speaks, itself unspeakable,
840　A spirit yet unquell'd and high,
That claims and keeps ascendency;
And like the bird whose pinions quake,
But cannot fly the gazing snake,

Will others quail beneath his look,
845   Nor 'scape the glance they scarce can brook.
From him the half-affrighted Friar
When met alone would fain retire,
As if that eye and bitter smile
Transferr'd to others fear and guile:
850   Not oft to smile descendeth he,
And when he doth 'tis sad to see
That he but mocks at Misery.
How that pale lip will curl and quiver!
Then fix once more as if for ever;
855   As if his sorrow or disdain
Forbade him e'er to smile again.
Well were it so – such ghastly mirth
From joyaunce ne'er derived its birth.
But sadder still it were to trace
860   What once were feelings in that face:
Time hath not yet the features fix'd,
But brighter traits with evil mix'd;
And there are hues not always faded,
Which speak a mind not all degraded
865   Even by the crimes through which it waded:
The common crowd but see the gloom
Of wayward deeds, and fitting doom;
The close observer can espy
A noble soul, and lineage high:
870   Alas! though both bestow'd in vain,
Which Grief could change, and Guilt could stain,
It was no vulgar tenement
To which such lofty gifts were lent,
And still with little less than dread
875   On such the sight is riveted.
The roofless cot, decay'd and rent,
    Will scarce delay the passer by;
The tower by war or tempest bent,
While yet may frown one battlement,
880   Demands and daunts the stranger's eye;
Each ivied arch, and pillar lone,
Pleads haughtily for glories gone!

'His floating robe around him folding,
   Slow sweeps he through the column'd aisle;
885   With dread beheld, with gloom beholding
     The rites that sanctify the pile.
But when the anthem shakes the choir,
And kneel the monks, his steps retire;
By yonder lone and wavering torch
890   His aspect glares within the porch;
There will be pause till all is done —
And hear the prayer, but utter none.
See — by the half-illumined wall
His hood fly back, his dark hair fall,
895   That pale brow wildly wreathing round,
As if the Gorgon there had bound
The sablest of the serpent-braid
That o'er her fearful forehead stray'd:
For he declines the convent oath,
900   And leaves those locks unhallow'd growth,
But wears our garb in all beside;
And, not from piety but pride,
Gives wealth to walls that never heard
Of his one holy vow nor word.
905   Lo! — mark ye, as the harmony
Peals louder praises to the sky,
That livid cheek, that stony air
Of mix'd defiance and despair!
Saint Francis, keep him from the shrine!
910   Else may we dread the wrath divine
Made manifest by awful sign.
If ever evil angel bore
The form of mortal, such he wore:
By all my hope of sins forgiven,
915   Such looks are not of earth nor heaven!'

To love the softest hearts are prone,
But such can ne'er be all his own;
Too timid in his woes to share,
Too meek to meet, or brave despair;
920   And sterner hearts alone may feel
The wound that time can never heal.

The rugged metal of the mine
Must burn before its surface shine,
But plunged within the furnace-flame,
925   It bends and melts – though still the same;
Then temper'd to thy want, or will,
'Twill serve thee to defend or kill;
A breast-plate for thine hour of need,
Or blade to bid thy foeman bleed;
930   But if a dagger's form it bear,
Let those who shape its edge, beware!
Thus passion's fire, and woman's art,
Can turn and tame the sterner heart;
From these its form and tone are ta'en,
935   And what they make it, must remain,
But break – before it bend again.

*   *   *   *   *
*   *   *   *   *

If solitude succeed to grief,
Release from pain is slight relief;
The vacant bosom's wilderness
940   Might thank the pang that made it less.
We loathe what none are left to share:
Even bliss – 't were woe alone to bear;
The heart once left thus desolate
Must fly at last for ease – to hate.
945   It is as if the dead could feel
The icy worm around them steal,
And shudder, as the reptiles creep
To revel o'er their rotting sleep,
Without the power to scare away
950   The cold consumers of their clay!
It is as if the desert-bird,[1]
        Whose beak unlocks her bosom's stream
        To still her famish'd nestlings' scream,
Nor mourns a life to them transferr'd,
955   Should rend her rash devoted breast,
And find them flown her empty nest.

1. The pelican is, I believe, the bird so libelled, by the imputation of feeding her chickens with her blood.

The keenest pangs the wretched find
   Are rapture to the dreary void,
The leafless desert of the mind,
960   The waste of feelings unemploy'd.
Who would be doom'd to gaze upon
A sky without a cloud or sun?
Less hideous far the tempest's roar
Than ne'er to brave the billows more –
965   Thrown, when the war of winds is o'er,
A lonely wreck on fortune's shore,
'Mid sullen calm, and silent bay,
Unseen to drop by dull decay; –
Better to sink beneath the shock
970   Than moulder piecemeal on the rock!

    *   *   *   *   *

'Father! thy days have pass'd in peace,
   'Mid counted beads, and countless prayer;
To bid the sins of others cease,
   Thyself without a crime or care,
975   Save transient ills that all must bear,
Has been thy lot from youth to age;
And thou wilt bless thee from the rage
Of passions fierce and uncontroll'd,
Such as thy penitents unfold,
980   Whose secret sins and sorrows rest
Within thy pure and pitying breast.
My days, though few, have pass'd below
In much of joy, but more of woe;
Yet still in hours of love or strife,
985   I've 'scaped the weariness of life:
Now leagued with friends, now girt by foes,
I loathed the languor of repose.
Now nothing left to love or hate,
No more with hope or pride elate,
990   I'd rather be the thing that crawls
Most noxious o'er a dungeon's walls,
Than pass my dull, unvarying days,
Condemn'd to meditate and gaze.

Yet, lurks a wish within my breast
995   For rest – but not to feel 't is rest.
Soon shall my fate that wish fulfil;
 And I shall sleep without the dream
Of what I was, and would be still,
 Dark as to thee my deeds may seem:
1000   My memory now is but the tomb
Of joys long dead; my hope, their doom:
Though better to have died with those
Than bear a life of lingering woes.
My spirit shrunk not to sustain
1005   The searching throes of ceaseless pain;
Nor sought the self-accorded grave
Of ancient fool and modern knave:
Yet death I have not fear'd to meet;
And in the field it had been sweet,
1010   Had danger woo'd me on to move
The slave of glory, not of love.
I've braved it – not for honour's boast;
I smile at laurels won or lost;
To such let others carve their way,
1015   For high renown, or hireling pay:
But place again before my eyes
Aught that I deem a worthy prize,
The maid I love, the man I hate;
And I will hunt the steps of fate,
1020   To save or slay, as these require,
Through rending steel, and rolling fire:
Nor needst thou doubt this speech from one
Who would but do – what he *hath* done.
Death is but what the haughty brave,
1025   The weak must bear, the wretch must crave;
Then let Life go to him who gave:
I have not quail'd to danger's brow
When high and happy – need I *now*?

  * * * * *

'I loved her, Friar! nay, adored –
1030   But these are words that all can use –
I proved it more in deed than word;
There's blood upon that dinted sword,
    A stain its steel can never lose:
'Twas shed for her, who died for me,
1035   It warm'd the heart of one abhorr'd:
Nay, start not – no – nor bend thy knee,
    Nor midst my sins such act record;
Thou wilt absolve me from the deed,
For he was hostile to thy creed!
1040 The very name of Nazarene
Was wormwood to his Paynim spleen.
Ungrateful fool! since but for brands
Well wielded in some hardy hands,
And wounds by Galileans given,
1045 The surest pass to Turkish heaven,
For him his Houris still might wait
Impatient at the Prophet's gate.
I loved her – love will find its way
Through paths where wolves would fear to prey;
1050 And if it dares enough, 't were hard
If passion met not some reward –
No matter how, or where, or why,
I did not vainly seek, nor sigh:
Yet sometimes, with remorse, in vain
1055 I wish she had not loved again.
She died – I dare not tell thee how;
But look – 't is written on my brow!
There read of Cain the curse and crime,
In characters unworn by time:
1060 Still, ere thou dost condemn me, pause;
Not mine the act, though I the cause.
Yet did he but what I had done
Had she been false to more than one.
Faithless to him, he gave the blow;
1065 But true to me, I laid him low:
Howe'er deserved her doom might be,
Her treachery was truth to me;

To me she gave her heart, that all
Which tyranny can ne'er enthrall;
1070   And I, alas! too late to save!
Yet all I then could give, I gave,
'Twas some relief, our foe a grave.
His death sits lightly; but her fate
Has made me – what thou well may'st hate.
1075   His doom was seal'd – he knew it well
Warn'd by the voice of stern Taheer,
Deep in whose darkly boding ear[1]
The deathshot peal'd of murder near,

1. This superstition of a second hearing (for I never met with downright second-sight in the East) fell once under my own observation. On my third journey to Cape Colonna, early in 1811, as we passed through the defile that leads from the hamlet between Keratia and Colonna, I observed Dervish Tahiri riding rather out of the path, and leaning his head upon his hand, as if in pain. I rode up and enquired. 'We are in peril,' he answered. 'What peril? we are not now in Albania, nor in the passes to Ephesus, Messalunghi, or Lepanto; there are plenty of us, well armed, and the Choriates have not courage to be thieves.' – 'True, Affendi, but nevertheless the shot is ringing in my ears.' – 'The shot! not a tophaike has been fired this morning.' – 'I hear it notwithstanding – Bom – Bom – as plainly as I hear your voice.' – 'Psha!' – 'As you please, Affendi; if it is written, so will it be.' – I left this quick-eared predestinarian, and rode up to Basili, his Christian compatriot, whose ears, though not at all prophetic, by no means relished the intelligence. We all arrived at Colonna, remained some hours, and returned leisurely, saying a variety of brilliant things, in more languages than spoiled the building of Babel, upon the mistaken seer. Romaic, Arnaout, Turkish, Italian, and English were all exercised, in various conceits, upon the unfortunate Mussulman. While we were contemplating the beautiful prospect, Dervish was occupied about the columns. I thought he was deranged into an antiquarian, and asked him if he had become a '*Palao-castro*' man? 'No,' said he, 'but these pillars will be useful in making a stand;' and added other remarks, which at least evinced his own belief in his troublesome faculty of *forehearing*. On our return to Athens we heard from Leoné (a prisoner set ashore some days after) of the intended attack of the Mainotes, mentioned, with the cause of its not taking place, in the notes to Childe Harold, Canto 2d. I was at some pains to question the man, and he described the dresses, arms, and marks of the horses of our party so accurately, that, with other circumstances, we could not doubt of *his* having been in 'villanous company,' and ourselves in a bad neighbourhood. Dervish became a soothsayer for life, and I dare say is now hearing more musketry than ever will be fired, to the great refreshment of the Arnaouts of Berat, and his native mountains. – I shall mention one trait more of this singular race. In March, 1811, a remarkably stout and active Arnaout came (I believe the fiftieth on the same errand) to offer himself as an attendant, which was declined: 'Well, Affendi,'

As filed the troop to where they fell!
1080   He died too in the battle broil,
A time that heeds nor pain nor toil;
One cry to Mahomet for aid,
One prayer to Alla all he made:
He knew and cross'd me in the fray –
1085   I gazed upon him where he lay,
And watch'd his spirit ebb away:
Though pierced like pard by hunters' steel,
He felt not half that now I feel.
I search'd, but vainly search'd, to find
1090   The workings of a wounded mind;
Each feature of that sullen corse
Betray'd his rage, but no remorse.
Oh, what had Vengeance given to trace
Despair upon his dying face!
1095   The late repentance of that hour,
When Penitence hath lost her power
To tear one terror from the grave,
And will not soothe, and cannot save.

*   *   *   *   *

'The cold in clime are cold in blood,
1100   Their love can scarce deserve the name;
But mine was like the lava flood
       That boils in Ætna's breast of flame.
I cannot prate in puling strain
Of ladye-love, and beauty's chain:
1105   If changing cheek, and scorching vein,
Lips taught to writhe, but not complain,
If bursting heart, and madd'ning brain,
And daring deed, and vengeful steel,
And all that I have felt, and feel,

---

quoth he, 'may you live! – you would have found me useful. I shall leave the town for the hills to-morrow, in the winter I return, perhaps you will then receive me.' – Dervish, who was present, remarked as a thing of course, and of no consequence, 'in the mean time he will join the Klephtes' (robbers), which was true to the letter. If not cut off, they come down in the winter, and pass it unmolested in some town, where they are often as well known as their exploits.

1110 Betoken love – that love was mine,
And shown by many a bitter sign.
'Tis true, I could not whine nor sigh,
I knew but to obtain or die.
I die – but first I have possess'd,
1115 And come what may, I *have been* blest.
Shall I the doom I sought upbraid?
No – reft of all, yet undismay'd
But for the thought of Leila slain,
Give me the pleasure with the pain,
1120 So would I live and love again.
I grieve, but not, my holy guide!
For him who dies, but her who died:
She sleeps beneath the wandering wave –
Ah! had she but an earthly grave,
1125 This breaking heart and throbbing head
Should seek and share her narrow bed.
She was a form of life and light,
That, seen, became a part of sight;
And rose, where'er I turn'd mine eye,
1130 The Morning-star of Memory!

'Yes, Love indeed is light from heaven;
      A spark of that immortal fire
With angels shared, by Alla given,
      To lift from earth our low desire.
1135 Devotion wafts the mind above,
But Heaven itself descends in love;
A feeling from the Godhead caught,
To wean from self each sordid thought;
A Ray of him who form'd the whole;
1140 A Glory circling round the soul!
I grant *my* love imperfect, all
That mortals by the name miscall;
Then deem it evil, what thou wilt;
But say, oh say, *hers* was not guilt!
1145 She was my life's unerring light:
That quench'd, what beam shall break my night?
Oh! would it shone to lead me still,
Although to death or deadliest ill!

Why marvel ye, if they who lose
1150   This present joy, this future hope,
        No more with sorrow meekly cope;
In phrensy then their fate accuse:
In madness do those fearful deeds
        That seem to add but guilt to woe?
1155   Alas! the breast that inly bleeds
        Hath nought to dread from outward blow:
Who falls from all he knows of bliss,
Cares little into what abyss.
Fierce as the gloomy vulture's now
1160   To thee, old man, my deeds appear:
I read abhorrence on thy brow,
        And this too was I born to bear!
'Tis true, that, like that bird of prey,
With havock have I mark'd my way:
1165   But this was taught me by the dove,
To die — and know no second love.
This lesson yet hath man to learn,
Taught by the thing he dares to spurn:
The bird that sings within the brake,
1170   The swan that swims upon the lake,
One mate, and one alone, will take.
And let the fool still prone to range,
And sneer on all who cannot change,
Partake his jest with boasting boys;
1175   I envy not his varied joys,
But deem such feeble, heartless man,
Less than yon solitary swan;
Far, far beneath the shallow maid
He left believing and betray'd.
1180   Such shame at least was never mine —
Leila! each thought was only thine!
My good, my guilt, my weal, my woe,
My hope on high — my all below.
Earth holds no other like to thee,
1185   Or, if it doth, in vain for me:
For worlds I dare not view the dame
Resembling thee, yet not the same.

The very crimes that mar my youth,
This bed of death – attest my truth!
1190   'Tis all too late – thou wert, thou art
The cherish'd madness of my heart!

'And she was lost – and yet I breathed,
But not the breath of human life:
A serpent round my heart was wreathed,
1195   And stung my every thought to strife.
Alike all time, abhorred all place,
Shuddering I shrunk from Nature's face,
Where every hue that charm'd before
The blackness of my bosom wore.
1200   The rest thou dost already know,
And all my sins, and half my woe.
But talk no more of penitence;
Thou see'st I soon shall part from hence:
And if thy holy tale were true,
1205   The deed that's done canst *thou* undo?
Think me not thankless – but this grief
Looks not to priesthood for relief.[1]
My soul's estate in secret guess:
But wouldst thou pity more, say less.
1210   When thou canst bid my Leila live,
Then will I sue thee to forgive;
Then plead my cause in that high place
Where purchased masses proffer grace.
Go, when the hunter's hand hath wrung
1215   From forest-cave her shrieking young,
And calm the lonely lioness:
But soothe not – mock not *my* distress!

---

1. The monk's sermon is omitted. It seems to have had so little effect upon the patient, that it could have no hopes from the reader. It may be sufficient to say, that it was of a customary length (as may be perceived from the interruptions and uneasiness of the patient), and was delivered in the usual tone of all orthodox preachers.

'In earlier days, and calmer hours,
    When heart with heart delights to blend,
1220 Where bloom my native valley's bowers
    I had – Ah! have I now? – a friend!
To him this pledge I charge thee send,
    Memorial of a youthful vow;
I would remind him of my end:
1225   Though souls absorb'd like mine allow
Brief thought to distant friendship's claim,
Yet dear to him my blighted name.
'Tis strange – he prophesied my doom,
    And I have smiled – I then could smile –
1230 When Prudence would his voice assume,
    And warn – I reck'd not what – the while:
But now remembrance whispers o'er
Those accents scarcely mark'd before.
Say – that his bodings came to pass,
1235   And he will start to hear their truth,
    And wish his words had not been sooth:
Tell him, unheeding as I was,
    Through many a busy bitter scene
    Of all our golden youth had been,
1240 In pain, my faltering tongue had tried
To bless his memory ere I died;
But Heaven in wrath would turn away,
If Guilt should for the guiltless pray.
I do not ask him not to blame,
1245 Too gentle he to wound my name;
And what have I to do with fame?
I do not ask him not to mourn,
Such cold request might sound like scorn;
And what than friendship's manly tear
1250 May better grace a brother's bier?
But bear this ring, his own of old,
And tell him – what thou dost behold!
The wither'd frame, the ruin'd mind,
The wrack by passion left behind,
1255 A shrivelled scroll, a scatter'd leaf,
Sear'd by the autumn blast of grief!

*   *   *   *   *

'Tell me no more of fancy's gleam,
No, father, no, 'twas not a dream;
Alas! the dreamer first must sleep,
1260   I only watch'd, and wish'd to weep;
But could not, for my burning brow
Throbb'd to the very brain as now:
I wish'd but for a single tear,
As something welcome, new, and dear:
1265   I wish'd it then, I wish it still;
Despair is stronger than my will.
Waste not thine orison, despair
Is mightier than thy pious prayer:
I would not, if I might, be blest;
1270   I want no paradise, but rest.
'Twas then, I tell thee, father! then
I saw her; yes, she lived again;
And shining in her white symar,[1]
As through yon pale gray cloud the star
1275   Which now I gaze on, as on her,
Who look'd and looks far lovelier;
Dimly I view its trembling spark;
To-morrow's night shall be more dark;
And I, before its rays appear,
1280   That lifeless thing the living fear.
I wander, father! for my soul
Is fleeting towards the final goal.
I saw her, friar! and I rose
Forgetful of our former woes;
1285   And rushing from my couch, I dart,
And clasp her to my desperate heart;
I clasp – what is it that I clasp?
No breathing form within my grasp,
No heart that beats reply to mine,
1290   Yet, Leila! yet the form is thine!
And art thou, dearest, changed so much,
As meet my eye, yet mock my touch?
Ah! were thy beauties e'er so cold,
I care not; so my arms enfold
1295   The all they ever wish'd to hold.

1. 'Symar,' a shroud.

Alas! around a shadow prest
They shrink upon my lonely breast;
Yet still 'tis there! In silence stands,
And beckons with beseeching hands!
1300 With braided hair, and bright-black eye –
I knew 'twas false – she could not die!
But he is dead! within the dell
I saw him buried where he fell;
He comes not, for he cannot break
1305 From earth; why then art thou awake?
They told me wild waves roll'd above
The face I view, the form I love;
They told me – 'twas a hideous tale!
I'd tell it, but my tongue would fail:
1310 If true, and from thine ocean-cave
Thou com'st to claim a calmer grave,
Oh! pass thy dewy fingers o'er
This brow that then will burn no more;
Or place them on my hopeless heart:
1315 But, shape or shade! whate'er thou art,
In mercy ne'er again depart!
Or farther with thee bear my soul
Than winds can waft or waters roll!

*　　*　　*　　*　　*

'Such is my name, and such my tale.
1320 Confessor! to thy secret ear
I breathe the sorrows I bewail,
And thank thee for the generous tear
This glazing eye could never shed.
Then lay me with the humblest dead,
1325 And, save the cross above my head,
Be neither name nor emblem spread,
By prying stranger to be read,
Or stay the passing pilgrim's tread.'[1]

1. The circumstance to which the above story relates was not very un-
common in Turkey. A few years ago the wife of Muchtar Pacha complained
to his father of his son's supposed infidelity; he asked with whom, and she
had the barbarity to give in a list of the twelve handsomest women in

He pass'd – nor of his name and race
1330   Hath left a token or a trace,
Save what the father must not say
Who shrived him on his dying day:
This broken tale was all we knew
Of her he loved, or him he slew.

Yanina. They were seized, fastened up in sacks, and drowned in the lake the same night! One of the guards who was present informed me, that not one of the victims uttered a cry, or showed a symptom of terror at so sudden a 'wrench from all we know, from all we love.' The fate of Phrosine, the fairest of this sacrifice, is the subject of many a Romaic and Arnaout ditty. The story in the text is one told of a young Venetian many years ago, and now nearly forgotten. I heard it by accident recited by one of the coffee-house story-tellers who abound in the Levant, and sing or recite their narratives. The additions and interpolations by the translator will be easily distinguished from the rest, by the want of Eastern imagery; and I regret that my memory has retained so few fragments of the original. For the contents of some of the notes I am indebted partly to D'Herbelot, and partly to that most Eastern, and, as Mr Weber justly entitles it, 'sublime tale,' the 'Caliph Vathek.' I do not know from what source the author of that singular volume may have drawn his materials; some of his incidents are to be found in the 'Bibliothèque Orientale;' but for correctness of costume, beauty of description, and power of imagination, it far surpasses all European imitations; and bears such marks of originality, that those who have visited the East will find some difficulty in believing it to be more than a translation. As an Eastern tale, even Rasselas must bow before it; his 'Happy Valley' will not bear a comparison with the 'Hall of Eblis.'

THE BRIDE OF ABYDOS
A Turkish Tale

'Had we never loved so kindly,
Had we never loved so blindly,
Never met or never parted,
We had ne'er been broken-hearted.'

[ROBERT] BURNS. ['Ae fond kiss', ll. 13–16]

TO THE RIGHT HONOURABLE LORD HOLLAND,
THIS TALE IS INSCRIBED, WITH EVERY SENTIMENT OF REGARD
AND RESPECT, BY HIS GRATEFULLY OBLIGED AND SINCERE
FRIEND,

BYRON.

Canto the First

I

Know ye the land where the cypress and myrtle
   Are emblems of deeds that are done in their clime,
Where the rage of the vulture, the love of the turtle,
   Now melt into sorrow, now madden to crime?
5 Know ye the land of the cedar and vine,
Where the flowers ever blossom, the beams ever shine;
Where the light wings of Zephyr oppressed with perfume,
Wax faint o'er the gardens of Gúl¹ in her bloom;
Where the citron and olive are fairest of fruit,
10 And the voice of the nightingale never is mute:

1. 'Gúl,' the rose.

Where the tints of the earth, and the hues of the sky,
In colour though varied, in beauty may vie,
And the purple of Ocean is deepest in dye;
Where the virgins are soft as the roses they twine,
15 And all, save the spirit of man, is divine?
'Tis the clime of the East; 'tis the land of the Sun –
Can he smile on such deeds as his children have done?[1]
Oh! wild as the accents of lovers' farewell
Are the hearts which they bear, and the tales which they
            tell.

            II
20   Begirt with many a gallant slave,
        Apparell'd as becomes the brave,
        Awaiting each his lord's behest
        To guide his steps, or guard his rest,
        Old Giaffir sate in his Divan:
25   Deep thought was in his aged eye;
        And though the face of Mussulman
            Not oft betrays to standers by
        The mind within, well skill'd to hide
        All but unconquerable pride,
30   His pensive cheek and pondering brow
        Did more than he was wont avow.

            III
'Let the chamber be clear'd.' – The train disappear'd –
'Now call me the chief of the Haram guard.'
With Giaffir is none but his only son,
35   And the Nubian awaiting the sire's award.
        'Haroun – when all the crowd that wait
        Are pass'd beyond the outer gate,
        (Woe to the head whose eye beheld
        My child Zuleika's face unveil'd!)
40   Hence, lead my daughter from her tower;
        Her fate is fix'd this very hour:

1.   'Souls made of fire, and children of the Sun,
        With whom revenge is virtue.'

                                YOUNG'S *Revenge*.

Yet not to her repeat my thought;
By me alone be duty taught!'
'Pacha! to hear is to obey.'
45   No more must slave to despot say —
Then to the tower had ta'en his way,
But here young Selim silence brake,
First lowly rendering reverence meet;
And downcast look'd, and gently spake,
50   Still standing at the Pacha's feet:
For son of Moslem must expire,
Ere dare to sit before his sire!

'Father! for fear that thou shouldst chide
My sister, or her sable guide,
55   Know — for the fault, if fault there be,
Was mine, then fall thy frowns on me —
So lovelily the morning shone,
      That — let the old and weary sleep —
I could not; and to view alone
60   The fairest scenes of land and deep,
With none to listen and reply
To thoughts with which my heart beat high
Were irksome — for whate'er my mood,
In sooth I love not solitude;
65   I on Zuleika's slumber broke,
      And, as thou knowest that for me
      Soon turns the Haram's grating key,
Before the guardian slaves awoke
We to the cypress groves had flown,
70   And made earth, main, and heaven our own!
There linger'd we, beguiled too long
With Mejnoun's tale, or Sadi's song;[1]
Till I, who heard the deep tambour[2]
Beat thy Divan's approaching hour,
75   To thee, and to my duty true,
Warn'd by the sound, to greet thee flew:

1. Mejnoun and Leila, the Romeo and Juliet of the East. Sadi, the moral poet of Persia.
2. Tambour, Turkish drum, which sounds at sunrise, noon, and twilight.

But there Zuleika wanders yet –
Nay, Father, rage not – nor forget
That none can pierce that secret bower
80   But those who watch the women's tower.'

IV

'Son of a slave' – the Pacha said –
'From unbelieving mother bred,
Vain were a father's hope to see
Aught that beseems a man in thee.
85   Thou, when thine arm should bend the bow,
           And hurl the dart, and curb the steed,
             Thou, Greek in soul if not in creed,
         Must pore where babbling waters flow,
         And watch unfolding roses blow.
90   Would that yon orb, whose matin glow
         Thy listless eyes so much admire,
         Would lend thee something of his fire!
         Thou, who would'st see this battlement
         By Christian cannon piecemeal rent;
95   Nay, tamely view old Stambol's wall
         Before the dogs of Moscow fall,
         Nor strike one stroke for life and death
         Against the curs of Nazareth!
         Go – let thy less than woman's hand
100   Assume the distaff – not the brand.
         But, Haroun! – to my daughter speed:
         And hark – of thine own head take heed –
         If thus Zuleika oft takes wing –
         Thou see'st yon bow – it hath a string!'

V

105   No sound from Selim's lip was heard,
           At least that met old Giaffir's ear,
         But every frown and every word
         Pierced keener than a Christian's sword.
           'Son of a slave! – reproach'd with fear!
110   Those gibes had cost another dear.
         Son of a slave! – and *who* my sire?'
           Thus held his thoughts their dark career;

And glances ev'n of more than ire
        Flash forth, then faintly disappear.
115   Old Giaffir gazed upon his son
        And started; for within his eye
He read how much his wrath had done;
He saw rebellion there begun:
        'Come hither, boy – what, no reply?
120   I mark thee – and I know thee too;
But there be deeds thou dar'st not do:
But if thy beard had manlier length,
And if thy hand had skill and strength,
I'd joy to see thee break a lance,
125   Albeit against my own perchance.'

As sneeringly these accents fell,
On Selim's eye he fiercely gazed:
        That eye return'd him glance for glance,
        And proudly to his sire's was raised,
130   Till Giaffir's quail'd and shrunk askance –
And why – he felt, but durst not tell.
'Much I misdoubt this wayward boy
Will one day work me more annoy:
I never loved him from his birth,
135   And – but his arm is little worth,
And scarcely in the chase could cope
With timid fawn or antelope,
Far less would venture into strife
Where man contends for fame and life –
140   I would not trust that look or tone:
No – nor the blood so near my own.
That blood – he hath not heard – no more –
I'll watch him closer than before.
He is an Arab[1] to my sight,
145   Or Christian crouching in the fight –
But hark! – I hear Zuleika's voice;
        Like Houris' hymn it meets mine ear:
She is the offspring of my choice;
        Oh! more than ev'n her mother dear,

---

1. The Turks abhor the Arabs (who return the compliment a hundred fold)
even more than they hate the Christians.

150   With all to hope, and nought to fear –
       My Peri! ever welcome here!
       Sweet as the desert fountain's wave
       To lips just cool'd in time to save –
           Such to my longing sight art thou;
155   Nor can they waft to Mecca's shrine
       More thanks for life, than I for thine,
           Who blest thy birth, and bless thee now.'

       VI
       Fair, as the first that fell of womankind,
           When on that dread yet lovely serpent smiling,
160   Whose image then was stamp'd upon her mind –
           But once beguiled – and ever more beguiling;
       Dazzling, as that, oh! too transcendent vision
           To Sorrow's phantom-peopled slumber given,
       When heart meets heart again in dreams Elysian,
165   And paints the lost on Earth revived in Heaven;
       Soft, as the memory of buried love;
       Pure, as the prayer which Childhood wafts above;
       Was she – the daughter of that rude old Chief,
       Who met the maid with tears – but not of grief.

170   Who hath not proved how feebly words essay
       To fix one spark of Beauty's heavenly ray?
       Who doth not feel, until his failing sight
       Faints into dimness with its own delight,
       His changing cheek, his sinking heart confess
175   The might – the majesty of Loveliness?
       Such was Zuleika – such around her shone
       The nameless charms unmark'd by her alone;
       The light of love, the purity of grace,
       The mind, the Music[1] breathing from her face,

       1. This expression has met with objections. I will not refer to 'Him who
       hath not Music in his soul,' but merely request the reader to recollect, for
       ten seconds, the features of the woman whom he believes to be the most
       beautiful; and, if he then does not comprehend fully what is feebly expressed
       in the above line, I shall be sorry for us both. For an eloquent passage in the
       latest work of the first female writer of this, perhaps of any, age, on the

180   The heart whose softness harmonized the whole –
       And, oh! that eye was in itself a Soul!

            Her graceful arms in meekness bending
               Across her gently-budding breast;
            At one kind word those arms extending
185   To clasp the neck of him who blest
               His child caressing and carest
               Zuleika came – and Giaffir felt
               His purpose half within him melt:
               Not that against her fancied weal
190   His heart though stern could ever feel;
               Affection chain'd her to that heart;
               Ambition tore the links apart.

       VII
       'Zuleika! child of gentleness!
          How dear this very day must tell,
195   When I forget my own distress,
          In losing what I love so well,
          To bid thee with another dwell:
          Another! and a braver man
          Was never seen in battle's van.
200   We Moslem reck not much of blood;
          But yet the line of Carasman[1]
       Unchanged, unchangeable hath stood

_____

analogy (and the immediate comparison excited by that analogy) between
'painting and music,' see vol. iii. cap. 10. DE L'ALLEMAGNE. And is not
this connection still stronger with the original than the copy? With the
colouring of Nature than of Art? After all, this is rather to be felt than
described; still I think there are some who will understand it, at least they
would have done had they beheld the countenance whose speaking harmony
suggested the idea; for this passage is not drawn from imagination but
memory, that mirror which Affliction dashes to the earth, and looking down
upon the fragments, only beholds the reflection multiplied!

1. Carasman Oglou, or Kara Osman Oglou, is the principal landholder in
Turkey; he governs Magnesia: those who, by a kind of feudal tenure,
possess land on condition of service, are called Timariots: they serve as
Spahis, according to the extent of territory, and bring a certain number into
the field, generally cavalry.

First of the bold Timariot bands
That won and well can keep their lands.
205 Enough that he who comes to woo
Is kinsman of the Bey Oglou:
His years need scarce a thought employ;
I would not have thee wed a boy.
And thou shalt have a noble dower:
210 And his and my united power
Will laugh to scorn the death-firman,
Which others tremble but to scan,
And teach the messenger[1] what fate
The bearer of such boon may wait.
215 And now thou know'st thy father's will;
All that thy sex hath need to know:
'Twas mine to teach obedience still –
The way to love, thy lord may show.'

VIII

In silence bow'd the virgin's head;
220 And if her eye was fill'd with tears
That stifled feeling dare not shed,
And changed her cheek from pale to red,
And red to pale, as through her ears
Those winged words like arrows sped,
225 What could such be but maiden fears?
So bright the tear in Beauty's eye,
Love half regrets to kiss it dry;
So sweet the blush of Bashfulness,
Even Pity scarce can wish it less!

1. When a Pacha is sufficiently strong to resist, the single messenger, who is always the first bearer of the order for his death, is strangled instead, and sometimes five or six, one after the other on the same errand, by command of the refractory patient; if, on the contrary, he is weak or loyal, he bows, kisses the Sultan's respectable signature, and is bowstrung with great complacency. In 1810, several of these presents were exhibited in the niche of the Seraglio gate; among others, the head of the Pacha of Bagdat, a brave young man, cut off by treachery, after a desperate resistance.

230   What'er it was the sire forgot;
       Or if remember'd, mark'd it not;
       Thrice clapp'd his hands, and call'd his steed,[1]
         Resign'd his gem-adorn'd chibouque,[2]
       And mounting featly for the mead,
235   With Maugrabee[3] and Mamaluke,
         His way amid his Delis took,[4]
       To witness many an active deed
       With sabre keen, or blunt jerreed.
       The Kislar only and his Moors
240   Watch well the Haram's massy doors.

         IX

       His head was leant upon his hand,
         His eye look'd o'er the dark blue water
       That swiftly glides and gently swells
       Between the winding Dardanelles;
245   But yet he saw nor sea nor strand,
       Nor even his Pacha's turban'd band
         Mix in the game of mimic slaughter,
       Careering cleave the folded felt[5]
       With sabre stroke right sharply dealt;
250   Nor mark'd the javelin-darting crowd,
       Nor heard their Ollahs[6] wild and loud –
         He thought but of old Giaffir's daughter!

1. Clapping of the hands calls the servants. The Turks hate a superfluous expenditure of voice, and they have no bells.
2. 'Chibouque,' the Turkish pipe, of which the amber mouth-piece, and sometimes the ball which contains the leaf, is adorned with precious stones, if in possession of the wealthier orders.
3. 'Maugrabee,' Moorish mercenaries.
4. 'Delis,' bravos who form the forlorn hope of the cavalry, and always begin the action.
5. A twisted fold of *felt* is used for scimitar practice by the Turks, and few but Mussulman arms can cut through it at a single stroke: sometimes a tough turban is used for the same purpose. The jerreed is a game of blunt javelins, animated and graceful.
6. 'Ollahs,' Alla il Allah, the 'Leilies,' as the Spanish poets call them, the sound is Ollah; a cry of which the Turks, for a silent people, are somewhat profuse, particularly during the jerreed, or in the chase, but mostly in battle. Their animation in the field, and gravity in the chamber, with their pipes and comboloios, form an amusing contrast.

X

No word from Selim's bosom broke;
One sigh Zuleika's thought bespoke:
255 Still gazed he through the lattice grate,
Pale, mute, and mournfully sedate.
To him Zuleika's eye was turn'd,
But little from his aspect learn'd:
Equal her grief, yet not the same;
260 Her heart confess'd a gentler flame:
But yet that heart alarm'd or weak,
She knew not why, forbade to speak.
Yet speak she must – but when essay?
'How strange he thus should turn away!
265 Not thus we e'er before have met;
Not thus shall be our parting yet.'
Thrice pac'd she slowly through the room,
And watch'd his eye – it still was fix'd:
She snatch'd the urn wherein was mix'd
270 The Persian Atar-gul's[1] perfume,
And sprinkled all its odours o'er
The pictured roof[2] and marble floor:
The drops, that through his glittering vest
The playful girl's appeal address'd,
275 Unheeded o'er his bosom flew,
As if that breast were marble too.
'What, sullen yet? it must not be –
Oh! gentle Selim, this from thee!'
She saw in curious order set
280 The fairest flowers of eastern land –
'He lov'd them once; may touch them yet,
If offer'd by Zuleika's hand.'
The childish thought was hardly breathed
Before the Rose was pluck'd and wreathed;

1. 'Atar-gul,' ottar of roses. The Persian is the finest.
2. The ceiling and wainscots, or rather walls, of the Mussulman apartments are generally painted, in great houses, with one eternal and highly coloured view of Constantinople, wherein the principal feature is a noble contempt of perspective; below, arms, scimitars, &c. are in general fancifully and not inelegantly disposed.

285 The next fond moment saw her seat
   Her fairy form at Selim's feet:
   'This rose to calm my brother's cares
   A message from the Bulbul[1] bears;
   It says to-night he will prolong
290 For Selim's ear his sweetest song;
   And though his note is somewhat sad,
   He'll try for once a strain more glad,
   With some faint hope his alter'd lay
   May sing these gloomy thoughts away.

   XI

295 'What! not receive my foolish flower?
    Nay then I am indeed unblest:
   On me can thus thy forehead lower?
    And know'st thou not who loves thee best?
   Oh, Selim dear! oh, more than dearest!
300 Say, is it me thou hat'st or fearest?
   Come, lay thy head upon my breast,
   And I will kiss thee into rest,
   Since words of mine, and songs must fail,
   Ev'n from my fabled nightingale.
305 I knew our sire at times was stern,
   But this from thee had yet to learn:
   Too well I know he loves thee not;
   But is Zuleika's love forgot?
   Ah! deem I right? the Pacha's plan –
310 This kinsman Bey of Carasman
   Perhaps may prove some foe of thine.
   If so, I swear by Mecca's shrine,
   If shrines that ne'er approach allow
   To woman's step admit her vow,
315 Without thy free consent, command,
   The Sultan should not have my hand!

1. It has been much doubted whether the notes of this 'Lover of the rose' are sad or merry; and Mr Fox's remarks on the subject have provoked some learned controversy as to the opinions of the ancients on the subject. I dare not venture a conjecture on the point, though a little inclined to the 'errare mallem,' &c. *if* Mr Fox *was* mistaken.

Think'st thou that I could bear to part
With thee, and learn to halve my heart?
Ah! were I sever'd from thy side,
320   Where were thy friend – and who my guide?
Years have not seen, Time shall not see
The hour that tears my soul from thee:
Ev'n Azrael[1] from his deadly quiver
    When flies that shaft, and fly it must,
325   That parts all else, shall doom for ever
    Our hearts to undivided dust!'

XII

He lived – he breathed – he moved – he felt;
He raised the maid from where she knelt;
His trance was gone – his keen eye shone
330   With thoughts that long in darkness dwelt;
With thoughts that burn – in rays that melt.
As the stream late conceal'd
    By the fringe of its willows,
When it rushes reveal'd
335   In the light of its billows;
As the bolt bursts on high
    From the black cloud that bound it,
Flash'd the soul of that eye
    Through the long lashes round it.
340   A war-horse at the trumpet's sound,
A lion roused by heedless hound,
A tyrant waked to sudden strife
By graze of ill-directed knife,
Starts not to more convulsive life
345   Than he, who heard that vow, display'd,
And all, before repress'd, betray'd:
'Now thou art mine, for ever mine,
With life to keep, and scarce with life resign;
Now thou art mine, that sacred oath,
350   Though sworn by one, hath bound us both.

1. 'Azrael,' the angel of death.

Yes, fondly, wisely hast thou done;
That vow hath saved more heads than one;
But blench not thou – thy simplest tress
Claims more from me than tenderness;
355   I would not wrong the slenderest hair
That clusters round thy forehead fair,
For all the treasures buried far
Within the caves of Istakar.[1]
This morning clouds upon me lower'd,
360   Reproaches on my head were shower'd,
And Giaffir almost call'd me coward!
Now I have motive to be brave;
The son of his neglected slave,
Nay, start not, 'twas the term he gave,
365   May show, though little apt to vaunt,
A heart his words nor deeds can daunt.
His son, indeed! – yet, thanks to thee,
Perchance I am, at least shall be;
But let our plighted secret vow
370   Be only known to us as now.
I know the wretch who dares demand
From Giaffir thy reluctant hand;
More ill-got wealth, a meaner soul
Holds not a Musselim's[2] control:
375   Was he not bred in Egripo?[3]
A viler race let Israel show;
But let that pass – to none be told
Our oath; the rest shall time unfold.
To me and mine leave Osman Bey;
380   I've partisans for peril's day:
Think not I am what I appear;
I've arms, and friends, and vengeance near.'

1. The treasures of the Pre-adamite Sultans. See D'Herbelot, article *Istakar*.
2. 'Musselim,' a governor, the next in rank after a Pacha; a Waywode is the third; and then come the Agas.
3. 'Egripo,' the Negropont. According to the proverb, the Turks of Egripo, the Jews of Salonica, and the Greeks of Athens, are the worst of their respective races.

XIII

    'Think not thou art what thou appearest!
      My Selim, thou art sadly changed:
385   This morn I saw thee gentlest, dearest;
      But now thou'rt from thyself estranged.
    My love thou surely knew'st before,
    It ne'er was less, nor can be more.
    To see thee, hear thee, near thee stay,
390   And hate the night I know not why,
    Save that we meet not but by day;
      With thee to live, with thee to die,
      I dare not to my hope deny:
    Thy cheek, thine eyes, thy lips to kiss,
395   Like this – and this – no more then this:
    For, Alla! sure thy lips are flame:
      What fever in thy veins is flushing?
    My own have nearly caught the same,
      At least I feel my cheek too blushing.
400   To soothe thy sickness, watch thy health,
    Partake, but never waste thy wealth,
    Or stand with smiles unmurmuring by,
    And lighten half thy poverty;
    Do all but close thy dying eye,
405   For that I could not live to try;
    To these alone my thoughts aspire:
    More can I do? or thou require?
    But, Selim, thou must answer why
    We need so much of mystery?
410   The cause I cannot dream nor tell,
    But be it, since thou say'st 't is well;
    Yet what thou mean'st by 'arms' and 'friends,'
    Beyond my weaker sense extends.
    I meant that Giaffir should have heard
415   The very vow I plighted thee;
    His wrath would not revoke my word:
      But surely he would leave me free.
      Can this fond wish seem strange in me,
    To be what I have ever been?
420   What other hath Zuleika seen

From simple childhood's earliest hour?
　　What other can she seek to see
Than thee, companion of her bower,
　　The partner of her infancy?
These cherish'd thoughts with life begun,
　　Say, why must I no more avow?
What change is wrought to make me shun
　　The truth; my pride, and thine till now?
To meet the gaze of stranger's eyes
Our law, our creed, our God denies;
Nor shall one wandering thought of mine
At such, our Prophet's will, repine:
No! happier made by that decree,
He left me all in leaving thee.
Deep were my anguish, thus compell'd
To wed with one I ne'er beheld:
This wherefore should I not reveal?
Why wilt thou urge me to conceal?
I know the Pacha's haughty mood
To thee hath never boded good;
And he so often storms at nought,
Allah! forbid that e'er he ought!
And why, I know not, but within
My heart concealment weighs like sin.
If then such secrecy be crime,
　　And such it feels while lurking here;
Oh, Selim! tell me yet in time,
　　Nor leave me thus to thoughts of fear.
Ah! yonder see the Tchocadar,[1]
My father leaves the mimic war;
I tremble now to meet his eye –
Say, Selim, canst thou tell me why?'

XIV

'Zuleika – to thy tower's retreat
Betake thee – Giaffir I can greet:
And now with him I fain must prate
Of firmans, impost, levies, state.

1. 'Tchocadar' – one of the attendants who precedes a man of authority.

There's fearful news from Danube's banks,
Our Vizier nobly thins his ranks,
For which the Giaour may give him thanks!
460   Our Sultan hath a shorter way
Such costly triumph to repay.
But, mark me, when the twilight drum
      Hath warn'd the troops to food and sleep,
Unto thy cell will Selim come:
465   Then softly from the Haram creep
      Where we may wander by the deep:
      Our garden-battlements are steep;
Nor these will rash intruder climb
To list our words, or stint our time;
470   And if he doth, I want not steel
Which some have felt, and more may feel.
Then shalt thou learn of Selim more
Than thou hast heard or thought before:
Trust me, Zuleika – fear not me!
475   Thou know'st I hold a Haram key.'

'Fear thee, my Selim! ne'er till now
Did word like this –'
                        'Delay not thou;
I keep the key – and Haroun's guard
Have *some*, and hope of *more* reward.
480   To-night, Zuleika, thou shalt hear
My tale, my purpose, and my fear:
I am not, love! what I appear.'

Canto the Second

I

The winds are high on Helle's wave,
    As on that night of stormy water
When Love, who sent, forgot to save
The young, the beautiful, the brave,
5   The lonely hope of Sestos' daughter.
Oh! when alone along the sky
Her turret-torch was blazing high,
Though rising gale, and breaking foam,
And shrieking sea-birds warn'd him home;
10   And clouds aloft and tides below,
With signs and sounds, forbade to go,
He could not see, he would not hear,
Or sound or sign foreboding fear;
His eye but saw that light of love,
15   The only star it hail'd above;
His ear but rang with Hero's song,
'Ye waves, divide not lovers long!' –
That tale is old, but love anew
May nerve young hearts to prove as true.

II

20   The winds are high, and Helle's tide
        Rolls darkly heaving to the main;
And Night's descending shadows hide
        That field with blood bedew'd in vain,
    The desert of old Priam's pride;
25   The tombs, sole relics of his reign,
All – save immortal dreams that could beguile
The blind old man of Scio's rocky isle!

III

Oh! yet – for there my steps have been;
        These feet have press'd the sacred shore,
30   These limbs that buoyant wave hath borne –
    Minstrel! with thee to muse, to mourn,

To trace again those fields of yore,
　　Believing every hillock green
　　　Contains no fabled hero's ashes,
35　And that around the undoubted scene
　　　Thine own 'broad Hellespont'[1] still dashes,
　Be long my lot! and cold were he
　Who there could gaze denying thee!

IV

　The night hath closed on Helle's stream,
40　　Nor yet hath risen on Ida's hill
　That moon, which shone on his high theme:
　No warrior chides her peaceful beam,
　　But conscious shepherds bless it still.
　Their flocks are grazing on the mound
45　　Of him who felt the Dardan's arrow:
　That mighty heap of gather'd ground
　Which Ammon's son ran proudly round,[2]
　　Is now a lone and nameless barrow!
50　　Within – thy dwelling-place how narrow!
　Without – can only strangers breathe
　The name of him that *was* beneath:
　Dust long outlasts the storied stone;
　But Thou – thy very dust is gone!

1. The wrangling about this epithet, 'the broad Hellespont' or the 'boundless Hellespont,' whether it means one or the other, or what it means at all, has been beyond all possibility of detail. I have even heard it disputed on the spot; and not foreseeing a speedy conclusion to the controversy, amused myself with swimming across it in the mean time; and probably may again, before the point is settled. Indeed, the question as to the truth of 'the tale of Troy divine' still continues, much of it resting upon the talismanic word 'απειρος:'probably Homer had the same notion of distance that a coquette has of time; and when he talks of boundless, means half a mile; as the latter, by a like figure, when she says *eternal* attachment, simply specifies three weeks.

2. Before his Persian invasion, and crowned the altar with laurel, &c. He was afterwards imitated by Caracalla in his race. It is believed that the last also poisoned a friend, named Festus, for the sake of new Patroclan games. I have seen the sheep feeding on the tombs of Æsietes and Antilochus: the first is in the centre of the plain.

V

55   Late, late to-night will Dian cheer
      The swain, and chase the boatman's fear:
      Till then – no beacon on the cliff
      May shape the course of struggling skiff;
      The scatter'd lights that skirt the bay,
60   All, one by one, have died away;
      The only lamp of this lone hour
      Is glimmering in Zuleika's tower.
      Yes! there is light in that lone chamber,
          And o'er her silken Ottoman
65   Are thrown the fragrant beads of amber,
          O'er which her fairy fingers ran;[1]
      Near these, with emerald rays beset,
      (How could she thus that gem forget?)
      Her mother's sainted amulet,[2]
70   Whereon engraved the Koorsee text,
      Could smooth this life, and win the next;
      And by her comboloio[3] lies
      A Koran of illumined dyes;
      And many a bright emblazon'd rhyme
75   By Persian scribes redeem'd from time;
      And o'er those scrolls, not oft so mute,
      Reclines her now neglected lute;
      And round her lamp of fretted gold
      Bloom flowers in urns of China's mould;
80   The richest work of Iran's loom,
      And Sheeraz' tribute of perfume;

1. When rubbed, the amber is susceptible of a perfume, which is slight but *not* disagreeable.
2. The belief in amulets engraved on gems, or enclosed in gold boxes, containing scraps from the Koran, worn round the neck, wrist, or arm, is still universal in the East. The Koorsee (throne) verse in the second chap. of the Koran describes the attributes of the Most High, and is engraved in this manner, and worn by the pious, as the most esteemed and sublime of all sentences.
3. 'Comboloio' – a Turkish rosary. The MSS., particularly those of the Persians, are richly adorned and illuminated. The Greek females are kept in utter ignorance; but many of the Turkish girls are highly accomplished, though not actually qualified for a Christian coterie. Perhaps some of our own '*blues*' might not be the worse for *bleaching*.

All that can eye or sense delight
    Are gather'd in that gorgeous room:
    But yet it hath an air of gloom.
85   She, of this Peri cell the sprite,
    What doth she hence, and on so rude a night?

VI

Wrapt in the darkest sable vest,
    Which none save noblest Moslem wear,
To guard from winds of heaven the breast
90   As heaven itself to Selim dear,
With cautious steps the thicket threading,
    And starting oft, as through the glade
    The gust its hollow moanings made,
Till on the smoother pathway treading,
95   More free her timid bosom beat,
    The maid pursued her silent guide;
And though her terror urged retreat,
    How could she quit her Selim's side?
    How teach her tender lips to chide?

VII

100   They reach'd at length a grotto, hewn
    By nature, but enlarged by art,
Where oft her lute she wont to tune,
    And oft her Koran conn'd apart;
And oft in youthful reverie
105   She dream'd what Paradise might be:
Where woman's parted soul shall go
Her Prophet had disdain'd to show;
But Selim's mansion was secure,
Nor deem'd she, could he long endure
110   His bower in other worlds of bliss,
Without *her*, most beloved in this!
Oh! who so dear with him could dwell?
What Houri soothe him half so well?

VIII

Since last she visited the spot
115   Some change seem'd wrought within the grot
It might be only that the night
Disguised things seen by better light:
That brazen lamp but dimly threw
A ray of no celestial hue;
120   But in a nook within the cell
Her eye on stranger objects fell.
There arms were piled, not such as wield
The turban'd Delis in the field;
But brands of foreign blade and hilt,
125   And one was red – perchance with guilt!
Ah! how without can blood be spilt?
A cup too on the board was set
That did not seem to hold sherbet.
What may this mean? she turn'd to see
130   Her Selim – 'Oh! can this be he?'

IX

His robe of pride was thrown aside,
His brow no high-crown'd turban bore,
But in its stead a shawl of red,
Wreathed lightly round, his temples wore:
135   That dagger, on whose hilt the gem
Where worthy of a diadem,
No longer glitter'd at his waist,
Where pistols unadorn'd were braced;
And from his belt a sabre swung,
140   And from his shoulder loosely hung
The cloak of white, the thin capote
That decks the wandering Candiote;
Beneath – his golden plated vest
Clung like a cuirass to his breast;
145   The greaves below his knee that wound
With silvery scales were sheathed and bound.

But were it not that high command
Spake in his eye, and tone, and hand,
All that a careless eye could see
150   In him was some young Galiongée.[1]

X

'I said I was not what I seem'd;
    And now thou see'st my words were true:
I have a tale thou hast not dream'd,
    If sooth – its truth must others rue.
155   My story now 'twere vain to hide,
I must not see thee Osman's bride:
But had not thine own lips declared
How much of that young heart I shared,
I could not, must not, yet have shown
160   The darker secret of my own.
In this I speak not now of love;
That, let time, truth, and peril prove:
But first – Oh! never wed another –
Zuleika! I am not thy brother!'

XI

165   'Oh! not my brother! – yet unsay –
    God! am I left alone on earth
To mourn – I dare not curse – the day
    That saw my solitary birth?
Oh! thou wilt love me now no more!
170   My sinking heart foreboded ill;
But know *me* all I was before,
    Thy sister – friend – Zuleika still.
Thou led'st me here perchance to kill;

---

1. 'Galiongée' – or Galiongi, a sailor, that is, a Turkish sailor; the Greeks
navigate, the Turks work the guns. Their dress is picturesque; and I have
seen the Capitan Pacha more than once wearing it as a kind of *incog*. Their
legs, however, are generally naked. The buskins described in the text as
sheathed behind with silver are those of an Arnaut robber, who was my host
(he had quitted the profession) at his Pyrgo, near Gastouni in the Morea;
they were plated in scales one over the other, like the back of an armadillo.

If thou hast cause for vengeance, see!
175   My breast is offer'd – take thy fill!
               Far better with the dead to be
               Than live thus nothing now to thee:
           Perhaps far worse, for now I know
           Why Giaffir always seem'd thy foe;
180   And I, alas! am Giaffir's child,
           For whom thou wert contemn'd, reviled.
           If not thy sister – would'st thou save
           My life, oh! bid me be thy slave!'

XII

           'My slave, Zuleika! – nay, I'm thine:
185   But, gentle love, this transport calm,
           Thy lot shall yet be link'd with mine;
           I swear it by our Prophet's shrine,
               And be that thought thy sorrow's balm.
           So may the Koran[1] verse display'd
190   Upon its steel direct my blade,
           In danger's hour to guard us both,
           As I preserve that awful oath!
           The name in which thy heart hath prided
               Must change; but, my Zuleika, know,
195   That tie is widen'd, not divided,
               Although thy Sire's my deadliest foe.
           My father was to Giaffir all
               That Selim late was deem'd to thee;
           That brother wrought a brother's fall,
200   But spared, at least, my infancy;
           And lull'd me with a vain deceit
           That yet a like return may meet.

1. The characters on all Turkish scimitars contain sometimes the name of
the place of their manufacture, but more generally a text from the Koran, in
letters of gold. Amongst those in my possession is one with a blade of
singular construction; it is very broad, and the edge notched into serpentine
curves like the ripple of water, or the wavering of flame. I asked the
Arminian who sold it, what possible use such a figure could add: he said, in
Italian, that he did not know; but the Mussulmans had an idea that those of
this form gave a severer wound; and liked it because it was 'piu feroce.' I did
not much admire the reason, but bought it for its peculiarity.

He rear'd me, not with tender help,
   But like the nephew of a Cain;[1]
205 He watch'd me like a lion's whelp,
   That gnaws and yet may break his chain.
   My father's blood in every vein
   Is boiling; but for thy dear sake
   No present vengeance will I take;
210   Though here I must no more remain.
   But first, beloved Zuleika! hear
   How Giaffir wrought this deed of fear.

XIII

'How first their strife to rancour grew,
   If love or envy made them foes,
215 It matters little if I knew;
   In fiery spirits, slights, though few
      And thoughtless, will disturb repose.
   In war Abdallah's arm was strong,
   Remember'd yet in Bosniac song,
220 And Paswan's[2] rebel hordes attest
   How little love they bore such guest:
   His death is all I need relate,
   The stern effect of Giaffir's hate;
   And how my birth disclosed to me,
225 Whate'er beside it makes, hath made me free.

1. It is to be observed, that every allusion to any thing or personage in the Old Testament, such as the Ark, or Cain, is equally the privilege of Mussulman and Jew: indeed, the former profess to be much better acquainted with the lives, true and fabulous, of the patriarchs, than is warranted by our own sacred writ; and not content with Adam, they have a biography of Pre-Adamites. Solomon is the monarch of all necromancy, and Moses a prophet inferior only to Christ and Mahomet. Zuleika is the Persian name of Potiphar's wife; and her amour with Joseph constitutes one of the finest poems in their language. It is, therefore, no violation of costume to put the names of Cain, or Noah, into the mouth of a Moslem.
2. Paswan Oglou, the rebel of Widin; who, for the last years of his life, set the whole power of the Porte at defiance.

XIV

'When Paswan, after years of strife,
At last for power, but first for life,
In Widin's walls too proudly sate,
Our Pachas rallied round the state;
230   Nor last nor least in high command,
Each brother led a separate band;
They gave their horsetails[1] to the wind,
    And mustering in Sophia's plain
Their tents were pitch'd, their post assign'd;
235   To one, alas! assign'd in vain!
What need of words? the deadly bowl,
    By Giaffir's order drugg'd and given.
With venom subtle as his soul,
    Dismiss'd Abdallah's hence to heaven.
240   Reclined and feverish in the bath,
    He, when the hunter's sport was up,
But little deem'd a brother's wrath
    To quench his thirst had such a cup:
The bowl a bribed attendant bore;
245   He drank one draught[2] nor needed more!
If thou my tale, Zuleika, doubt,
Call Haroun – he can tell it out.

XV

'The deed once done, and Paswan's feud
In part suppress'd, though ne'er subdued,
250   Abdallah's Pachalick was gain'd: –
Thou know'st not what in our Divan
Can wealth procure for worse than man –
    Abdallah's honours were obtain'd
By him a brother's murder stain'd;

---

1. 'Horse-tail,' the standard of a Pacha.
2. Giaffir, Pacha of Argyro Castro, or Scutari, I am not sure which, was actually taken off by the Albanian Ali, in the manner described in the text. Ali Pacha, while I was in the country, married the daughter of his victim, some years after the event had taken place at a bath in Sophia, or Adrianople. The poison was mixed in the cup of coffee, which is presented before the sherbet by the bath-keeper, after dressing.

255   'Tis true, the purchase nearly drain'd
        His ill got treasure, soon replaced.
        Would'st question whence? Survey the waste,
        And ask the squalid peasant how
        His gains repay his broiling brow! –
260   Why me the stern usurper spared,
        Why thus with me his palace shared,
        I know not. Shame, regret, remorse,
        And little fear from infant's force;
        Besides, adoption as a son
265   By him whom Heaven accorded none,
        Or some unknown cabal, caprice,
        Preserved me thus; – but not in peace:
        He cannot curb his haughty mood,
        Nor I forgive a father's blood.

                    XVI

270   'Within thy father's house are foes;
            Not all who break his bread are true:
        To these should I my birth disclose,
            His days, his very hours were few:
        They only want a heart to lead,
275   A hand to point them to the deed.
        But Haroun only knows or knew
            This tale, whose close is almost nigh:
        He in Abdallah's palace grew,
            And held that post in his Serai
280   Which holds he here – he saw him die:
        But what could single slavery do?
        Avenge his lord? alas! too late;
        Or save his son from such a fate?
        He chose the last, and when elate
285   With foes subdued, or friends betray'd,
        Proud Giaffir in high triumph sate,
        He led me helpless to his gate,
            And not in vain it seems essay'd
            To save the life for which he pray'd.
290   The knowledge of my birth secured
            From all and each, but most from me;
        Thus Giaffir's safety was ensured.

Removed he too from Roumelie
To this our Asiatic side,
295   Far from our seats by Danube's tide,
With none but Haroun, who retains
Such knowledge – and that Nubian feels
A tyrant's secrets are but chains,
From which the captive gladly steals,
300   And this and more to me reveals:
Such still to guilt just Alla sends –
Slaves, tools, accomplices – no friends!

XVII
'All this, Zuleika, harshly sounds;
But harsher still my tale must be:
305   Howe'er my tongue thy softness wounds,
Yet I must prove all truth to thee.
I saw thee start this garb to see,
Yet is it one I oft have worn,
And long must wear: this Galiongée,
310   To whom thy plighted vow is sworn,
Is leader of those pirate hordes,
Whose laws and lives are on their swords;
To hear whose desolating tale
Would make thy waning cheek more pale:
315   Those arms thou see'st my band have brought,
The hands that wield are not remote;
This cup too for the rugged knaves
Is fill'd – once quaff'd, they ne'er repine:
Our prophet might forgive the slaves;
320   They're only infidels in wine.

XVIII
'What could I be? Proscribed at home,
And taunted to a wish to roam;
And listless left – for Giaffir's fear
Denied the courser and the spear –
325   Though oft – Oh, Mahomet! how oft! –
In full Divan the despot scoff'd,
As if *my* weak unwilling hand
Refused the bridle or the brand:

He ever went to war alone,
330 And pent me here untried – unknown;
To Haroun's care with women left,
By hope unblest, of fame bereft,
While thou – whose softness long endear'd,
Though it unmann'd me, still had cheer'd –
335 To Brusa's walls for safety sent,
Awaited'st there the field's event.
Haroun, who saw my spirit pining
   Beneath inaction's sluggish yoke,
His captive, though with dread resigning,
340   My thraldom for a season broke,
On promise to return before
The day when Giaffir's charge was o'er.
'Tis vain – my tongue can not impart
My almost drunkenness of heart,
345 When first this liberated eye
Survey'd Earth, Ocean, Sun, and Sky,
As if my spirit pierced them through,
And all their inmost wonders knew!
One word alone can paint to thee
350 That more than feeling – I was Free!
E'en for thy presence ceased to pine;
The World – nay, Heaven itself was mine!

                    XIX

'The shallop of a trusty Moor
Convey'd me from this idle shore;
355 I long'd to see the isles that gem
Old Ocean's purple diadem:
I sought by turns, and saw them all;[1]
   But when and where I join'd the crew,
With whom I'm pledged to rise or fall,
360   When all that we design to do
Is done, 't will then be time more meet
To tell thee, when the tale's complete.

---

1. The Turkish notions of almost all islands are confined to the Archipelago, the sea alluded to.

XX

'Tis true, they are a lawless brood,
But rough in form, nor mild in mood;
365 And every creed, and every race,
With them hath found – may find a place:
But open speech, and ready hand,
Obedience to their chief's command;
A soul for every enterprise,
370 That never sees with Terror's eyes;
Friendship for each, and faith to all,
And vengeance vow'd for those who fall,
Have made them fitting instruments
For more than ev'n my own intents.
375 And some – and I have studied all
  Distinguish'd from the vulgar rank,
But chiefly to my council call
  The wisdom of the cautious Frank –
And some to higher thoughts aspire,
380 The last of Lambro's[1] patriots there
  Anticipated freedom share;
And oft around the cavern fire
On visionary schemes debate,
To snatch the Rayahs[2] from their fate.
385 So let them ease their hearts with prate
Of equal rights, which man ne'er knew;
I have a love for freedom too.
Ay! let me like the ocean-Patriarch[3] roam,
Or only know on land the Tartar's home![4]

1. Lambro Canzani, a Greek, famous for his efforts, in 1789–90, for the independence of his country. Abandoned by the Russians, he became a pirate, and the Archipelago was the scene of his enterprises. He is said to be still alive at Petersburg. He and Riga are the two most celebrated of the Greek revolutionists.
2. 'Rayahs,' – all who pay the capitation tax, called the 'Haratch.'
3. The first of voyages is one of the few with which the Mussulmans profess much acquaintance.
4. The wandering life of the Arabs, Tartars, and Turkomans, will be found well detailed in any book of Eastern travels. That it possesses a charm peculiar to itself, cannot be denied. A young French renegado confessed to Chateaubriand, that he never found himself alone, galloping in the desert, without a sensation approaching to rapture which was indescribable.

390   My tent on shore, my galley on the sea,
Are more than cities and Serais to me:
Borne by my steed, or wafted by my sail,
Across the desert, or before the gale,
Bound where thou wilt, my barb! or glide, my prow!
395   But be the star that guides the wanderer, Thou!
Thou, my Zuleika, share and bless my bark;
The Dove of peace and promise to mine ark!
Or, since that hope denied in worlds of strife,
Be thou the rainbow to the storms of life!
400   The evening beam that smiles the clouds away,
And tints to-morrow with prophetic ray!
Blest — as the Muezzin's strain from Mecca's wall
To pilgrims pure and prostrate at his call;
Soft — as the melody of youthful days,
405   That steals the trembling tear of speechless praise;
Dear — as his native song to Exile's ears,
Shall sound each tone thy long-loved voice endears.
For thee in those bright isles is built a bower
Blooming as Aden[1] in its earliest hour.
410   A thousand swords, with Selim's heart and hand,
Wait — wave — defend — destroy — at thy command!
Girt by my band, Zuleika at my side,
The spoil of nations shall bedeck my bride.
The Haram's languid years of listless ease
415   Are well resign'd for cares — for joys like these:
Not blind to fate, I see, where'er I rove,
Unnumbered perils, — but one only love!
Yet well my toils shall that fond breast repay,
Though fortune frown, or falser friends betray.
420   How dear the dream in darkest hours of ill,
Should all be changed, to find thee faithful still!
Be but thy soul, like Selim's, firmly shown;
To thee be Selim's tender as thine own;
To soothe each sorrow, share in each delight,
425   Blend every thought, do all — but disunite!
Once free, 'tis mine our horde again to guide;
Friends to each other, foes to aught beside:

---

1. 'Jannat al Aden,' the perpetual abode, the Mussulman paradise.

Yet there we follow but the bent assign'd
By fatal Nature to man's warring kind:
430 Mark! where his carnage and his conquests cease!
He makes a solitude, and calls it – peace!
I like the rest must use my skill or strength,
But ask no land beyond my sabre's length:
Power sways but by division – her resource
435 The blest alternative of fraud or force!
Ours be the last; in time deceit may come
When cities cage us in a social home:
There ev'n thy soul might err – how oft the heart
Corruption shakes which peril could not part!
440 And woman, more than man, when death or woe,
Or even Disgrace, would lay her lover low,
Sunk in the lap of Luxury will shame –
Away suspicion! – *not* Zuleika's name!
But life is hazard at the best; and here
445 No more remains to win, and much to fear:
Yes, fear! – the doubt, the dread of losing thee,
By Osman's power, and Giaffir's stern decree.
That dread shall vanish with the favouring gale,
Which love to-night hath promised to my sail:
450 No danger daunts the pair his smile hath blest,
Their steps still roving, but their hearts at rest.
With thee all toils are sweet, each clime hath charms;
Earth – sea alike – our world within our arms!
Ay – let the loud winds whistle o'er the deck,
455 So that those arms cling closer round my neck:
The deepest murmur of this lip shall be
No sigh for safety, but a prayer for thee!
The war of elements no fears impart
To Love, whose deadliest bane is human Art:
460 *There* lie the only rocks our course can check;
Here moments menace – *there* are years of wreck!
But hence ye thoughts that rise in Horror's shape!
This hour bestows, or ever bars escape.
Few words remain of mine my tale to close:
465 Of thine but *one* to waft us from our foes;
Yea – foes – to me will Giaffir's hate decline?
And is not Osman, who would part us, thine?

XXI

      'His head and faith from doubt and death
        Return'd in time my guard to save;
470   Few heard, none told, that o'er the wave
      From isle to isle I roved the while:
      And since, though parted from my band,
      Too seldom now I leave the land,
      No deed they've done, nor deed shall do,
475   Ere I have heard and doom'd it too:
      I form the plan, decree the spoil,
      'Tis fit I oftener share the toil.
      But now too long I've held thine ear;
      Time presses, floats my bark, and here
480   We leave behind but hate and fear.
      To-morrow Osman with his train
      Arrives – to-night must break thy chain:
      And would'st thou save that haughty Bey,
        Perchance, *his* life who gave thee thine,
485   With me, this hour away – away!
        But yet, though thou art plighted mine,
      Would'st thou recall thy willing vow,
      Appall'd by truths imparted now,
      Here rest I – not to see thee wed:
490   But be that peril on *my* head!'

XXII

      Zuleika, mute and motionless,
      Stood like that statue of distress,
      When, her last hope for ever gone,
      The mother harden'd into stone;
495   All in the maid that eye could see
      Was but a younger Niobé.
      But ere her lip, or even her eye,
      Essay'd to speak, or look reply,
      Beneath the garden's wicket porch
500   Far flash'd on high a blazing torch!
      Another – and another – and another –
      'Oh! fly – no more – yet now my more than brother!'

Far, wide, through every thicket spread,
The fearful lights are gleaming red;
505   Nor these alone — for each right hand
Is ready with a sheathless brand.
They part, pursue, return, and wheel
With searching flambeau, shining steel;
And last of all, his sabre waving,
510   Stern Giaffir in his fury raving:
And now almost they touch the cave —
Oh! must that grot be Selim's grave?

XXIII

Dauntless he stood — "'T is come — soon past —
One kiss, Zuleika — 'tis my last:
515   But yet my band not far from shore
May hear this signal, see the flash;
Yet now too few — the attempt were rash:
        No matter — yet one effort more.'
Forth to the cavern mouth he stept;
520   His pistol's echo rang on high,
Zuleika started not, nor wept,
        Despair benumb'd her breast and eye! —
'They hear me not, or if they ply
Their oars, 't is but to see me die;
525   That sound hath drawn my foes more nigh.
Then forth my father's scimitar,
Thou ne'er hast seen less equal war!
Farewell, Zuleika! — Sweet! retire:
        Yet stay within — here linger safe,
530   At thee his rage will only chafe.
Stir not — lest even to thee perchance
Some erring blade or ball should glance.
Fear'st thou for him? — may I expire
If in this strife I seek thy sire!
535   No — though by him that poison pour'd:
No — though again he call me coward!
But tamely shall I meet their steel?
No — as each crest save *his* may feel!'

XXIV

One bound he made, and gain'd the sand:
540 Already at his feet hath sunk
The foremost of the prying band,
A gasping head, a quivering trunk:
Another falls — but round him close
A swarming circle of his foes;
545 From right to left his path he cleft,
And almost met the meeting wave:
His boat appears — not five oars' length —
His comrades strain with desperate strength —
Oh! are they yet in time to save?
550 His feet the foremost breakers lave;
His band are plunging in the bay,
Their sabres glitter through the spray;
Wet — wild — unwearied to the strand
They struggle — now they touch the land!
555 They come — 'tis but to add to slaughter —
His heart's best blood is on the water.

XXV

Escaped from shot, unharm'd by steel,
Or scarcely grazed its force to feel,
Had Selim won, betray'd, beset,
560 To where the strand and billows met;
There as his last step left the land,
And the last death-blow dealt his hand —
Ah! wherefore did he turn to look
For her his eye but sought in vain?
565 That pause, that fatal gaze he took,
Hath doom'd his death, or fix'd his chain.
Sad proof, in peril and in pain,
How late will Lover's hope remain!
His back was to the dashing spray;
570 Behind, but close, his comrades lay,
When, at the instant, hiss'd the ball —
'So may the foes of Giaffir fall!'
Whose voice is heard? whose carbine rang?
Whose bullet through the night-air sang,

575   Too nearly, deadly aim'd to err?
        'Tis thine – Abdallah's Murderer!
        The father slowly rued thy hate,
        The son hath found a quicker fate:
        Fast from his breast the blood is bubbling,
580   The whiteness of the sea-foam troubling –
        If aught his lips essay'd to groan,
        The rushing billows choked the tone!

XXVI
        Morn slowly rolls the clouds away;
          Few trophies of the fight are there:
585   The shouts that shook the midnight-bay
        Are silent; but some signs of fray
          That strand of strife may bear,
        And fragments of each shiver'd brand;
        Steps stamp'd; and dash'd into the sand
590   The print of many a struggling hand
          May there be mark'd; nor far remote
          A broken torch, an oarless boat;
        And tangled on the weeds that heap
        The beach where shelving to the deep
595   There lies a white capote!
        'Tis rent in twain – one dark-red stain
        The wave yet ripples o'er in vain:
          But where is he who wore?
        Ye! who would o'er his relics weep,
600   Go, seek them where the surges sweep
        Their burthen round, Sigaeum's steep
          And cast on Lemnos' shore:
        The sea-birds shriek above the prey,
        O'er which their hungry beaks delay,
605   As shaken on his restless pillow,
        His head heaves with the heaving billow;
        That hand, whose motion is not life,
        Yet feebly seems to menace strife,
        Flung by the tossing tide on high,
610   Then levell'd with the wave –
        What recks it, though that corse shall lie
          Within a living grave?

The bird that tears that prostrate form
Hath only robb'd the meaner worm;
615   The only heart, the only eye
Had bled or wept to see him die,
Had seen those scatter'd limbs composed,
        And mourn'd above his turban-stone,[1]
That heart hath burst – that eye was closed –
620   Yea – closed before his own!

XXVII
By Helle's stream there is a voice of wail!
And woman's eye is wet – man's cheek is pale:
Zuleika! last of Giaffir's race,
        Thy destined lord is come too late:
625   He sees not – ne'er shall see thy face!
        Can he not hear
The loud Wul-wulleh[2] warn his distant ear?
        Thy handmaids weeping at the gate,
        The Koran-chanters of the hymn of fate,
630   The silent slaves with folded arms that wait,
Sighs in the hall, and shrieks upon the gale,
        Tell him thy tale!
Thou didst not view thy Selim fall!
        That fearful moment when he left the cave
635   Thy heart grew chill:
He was thy hope – thy joy – thy love – thine all –
And that last thought on him thou could'st not save
        Sufficed to kill;
Burst forth in one wild cry – and all was still.
640   Peace to thy broken heart, and virgin grave!
Ah! happy! but of life to lose the worst!
That grief – though deep – though fatal – was thy first!
Thrice happy! ne'er to feel nor fear the force
Of absence, shame, pride, hate, revenge, remorse!
645   And, oh! that pang where more than Madness lies!
The worm that will not sleep – and never dies;

1. A turban is carved in stone above the graves of *men* only.
2. The death-song of the Turkish women. The 'silent slaves' are the men, whose notions of decorum forbid complaint in *public*.

Thought of the gloomy day and ghastly night,
That dreads the darkness, and yet loathes the light,
That winds around and tears the quivering heart!
650   Ah! wherefore not consume it – and depart!
Woe to thee, rash and unrelenting chief!
    Vainly thou heap'st the dust upon thy head,
    Vainly the sackcloth o'er thy limbs dost spread:
    By that same hand Abdallah – Selim bled.
655   Now let it tear thy beard in idle grief:
Thy pride of heart, thy bride for Osman's bed,
She, whom thy sultan had but seen to wed,
            Thy Daughter's dead!
    Hope of thine age, thy twilight's lonely beam,
660   The Star hath set that shone on Helle's stream.
What quench'd its ray? – the blood that thou hast shed!
Hark! to the hurried question of Despair:
'Where is my child?' – an Echo answers – 'Where?'[1]

XXVIII
    Within the place of thousand tombs
665   That shine beneath, while dark above
    The sad but living cypress glooms,
        And withers not, though branch and leaf
    Are stamp'd with an eternal grief,
        Like early unrequited Love,
670   One spot exists, which ever blooms,
        Ev'n in that deadly grove –
    A single rose is shedding there
        Its lonely lustre, meek and pale:
    It looks as planted by Despair –

1. 'I came to the place of my birth, and cried, "The friends of my youth,
where are they?" and an Echo answered, "Where are they?"' – *From an
Arabic MS.* The above quotation (from which the idea in the text is taken)
must be already familiar to every reader: it is given in the first annotation, p.
67., of 'The Pleasures of Memory,' a poem so well known as to render a
reference almost superfluous; but to whose pages all will be delighted to
recur.

675   So white – so faint – the slightest gale
      Might whirl the leaves on high;
         And yet, though storms and blight assail,
      And hands more rude than wintry sky
         May wring it from the stem – in vain –
680   To-morrow sees it bloom again!
      The stalk some spirit gently rears,
      And waters with celestial tears;
         For well may maids of Helle deem
      That this can be no earthly flower,
685   Which mocks the tempest's withering hour,
      And buds unshelter'd by a bower;
      Nor droops, though spring refuse her shower,
         Nor woos the summer beam:
      To it the livelong night there sings
690   A bird unseen – but not remote:
      Invisible his airy wings,
      But soft as harp that Houri strings
         His long entrancing note!
      It were the Bulbul; but his throat,
695   Though mournful, pours not such a strain;
      For they who listen cannot leave
      The spot, but linger there and grieve,
         As if they loved in vain!
      And yet so sweet the tears they shed,
700   'Tis sorrow so unmix'd with dread,
      They scarce can bear the morn to break
         That melancholy spell,
      And longer yet would weep and wake,
         He sings so wild and well!
705 But when the day-blush bursts from high
      Expires that magic melody.
      And some have been who could believe,
      (So fondly youthful dreams deceive,

Yet harsh be they that blame,)
710 That note so piercing and profound
Will shape and syllable[1] its sound
   Into Zuleika's name.
'Tis from her cypress summit heard,
That melts in air the liquid word:
715 'Tis from her lowly virgin earth
That white rose takes its tender birth.
There late was laid a marble stone;
Eve saw it placed – the Morrow gone!
It was no mortal arm that bore
720 That deep fixed pillar to the shore;
For there, as Helle's legends tell,
Next morn 'twas found where Selim fell;
Lash'd by the tumbling tide, whose wave
Denied his bones a holier grave:
725 And there by night, reclined, 'tis said,
Is seen a ghastly turban'd head:
   And hence extended by the billow,
   'Tis named the 'Pirate-phantom's pillow!'
Where first it lay that mourning flower
730 Hath flourished; flourisheth this hour,
Alone and dewy, coldly pure and pale;
As weeping Beauty's cheek at Sorrow's tale!

1.   'And airy tongues that *syllable* men's names.' – MILTON.
For a belief that the souls of the dead inhabit the form of birds, we need not travel to the East. Lord Lyttleton's ghost story, the belief of the Duchess of Kendal, that George I flew into her window in the shape of a raven (see Orford's Reminiscences), and many other instances, bring this superstition nearer home. The most singular was the whim of a Worcester lady, who, believing her daughter to exist in the shape of a singing bird, literally furnished her pew in the cathedral with cages full of the kind; and as she was rich, and a benefactress in beautifying the church, no objection was made to her harmless folly. For this anecdote, see Orford's Letters.

THE CORSAIR
A Tale

'— I suoi pensieri in lui dormir non ponno.'

TASSO, *Gerusalemme Liberata*, canto x.

TO THOMAS MOORE, ESQ.

My Dear Moore,

I dedicate to you the last production with which I shall trespass on public patience, and your indulgence, for some years; and I own that I feel anxious to avail myself of this latest and only opportunity of adorning my pages with a name, consecrated by unshaken public principle, and the most undoubted and various talents. While Ireland ranks you among the firmest of her patriots; while you stand alone the first of her bards in her estimation, and Britain repeats and ratifies the decree, permit one, whose only regret, since our first acquaintance, has been the years he had lost before it commenced, to add the humble but sincere suffrage of friendship, to the voice of more than one nation. It will at least prove to you, that I have neither forgotten the gratification derived from your society, nor abandoned the prospect of its renewal, whenever your leisure or inclination allows you to atone to your friends for too long an absence. It is said among those friends, I trust truly, that you are engaged in the composition of a poem whose scene will be laid in the East; none can do those scenes so much justice. The wrongs of your own country, the magnificent and fiery spirit of her sons, the beauty and feeling of her daughters, may there be found; and Collins, when he denominated his Oriental his Irish Eclogues, was not aware how true, at least, was a part of his parallel. Your imagination will create a warmer sun, and less clouded sky; but wildness, tenderness, and originality, are part of your national claim of oriental descent, to which you have already thus far proved your title more clearly than the most zealous of your country's antiquarians.

May I add a few words on a subject on which all men are supposed to be fluent, and none agreeable, – Self? I have written much, and published more than enough to demand a longer silence than I now meditate; but, for some years to come, it is my intention to tempt no further the award of 'Gods, men, nor columns.' In the present composition I have attempted not the most difficult, but, perhaps, the best adapted measure to our language, the good old and now neglected heroic couplet. The stanza of Spenser is perhaps too slow and dignified for narrative; though, I confess, it is the measure most after my own heart: Scott alone, of the present generation, has hitherto completely triumphed over the fatal facility of the octo-syllabic verse; and this is not the least victory of his fertile and mighty genius: in blank verse, Milton, Thomson, and our dramatists, are the beacons that shine along the deep, but warn us from the rough and barren rock on which they are kindled. The heroic couplet is not the most popular measure certainly; but as I did not deviate into the other from a wish to flatter what is called public opinion, I shall quit it without further apology, and take my chance once more with that versification, in which I have hitherto published nothing but compositions whose former circulation is part of my present, and will be of my future regret.

With regard to my story, and stories in general, I should have been glad to have rendered my personages more perfect and amiable, if possible, inasmuch as I have been sometimes criticised, and considered no less responsible for their deeds and qualities than if all had been personal. Be it so – if I have deviated into the gloomy vanity of 'drawing from self,' the pictures are probably like, since they are unfavourable; and if not, those who know me are undeceived, and those who do not, I have little interest in undeceiving. I have no particular desire that any but my acquaintance should think the author better than the beings of his imagining; but I cannot help a little surprise, and perhaps amusement, at some odd critical exceptions in the present instance, when I see several bards (far more deserving, I allow) in very reputable plight, and quite exempted from all participation in the faults of those heroes, who, nevertheless, might be found with little more morality than 'The Giaour,' and perhaps – but no – I must admit Childe Harold to be a very repulsive personage; and as to his identity, those who like it must give him whatever 'alias' they please.

If, however, it were worth while to remove the impression, it might be of some service to me, that the man who is alike the delight of his readers and his friends, the poet of all circles, and the idol of his own, permits me here and elsewhere to subscribe myself,

Most truly,

And affectionately,

His obedient servant,

January 2, 1814.   BYRON.

Canto the First[1]

'————nessun maggior dolore,
Che ricordarsi del tempo felice
Nella miseria,————'

DANTE.

I

'O'er the glad waters of the dark blue sea,
Our thoughts as boundless, and our souls as free,
Far as the breeze can bear, the billows foam,
Survey our empire, and behold our home!
5   These are our realms, no limits to their sway –
Our flag the sceptre all who meet obey.

---

1. The time in this poem may seem too short for the occurrences, but the whole of the Ægean isles are within a few hours' sail of the continent, and the reader must be kind enough to take the *wind* as I have often found it.

Ours the wild life in tumult still to range
From toil to rest, and joy in every change.
Oh, who can tell? not thou, luxurious slave!
10   Whose soul would sicken o'er the heaving wave;
Not thou, vain lord of wantonness and ease!
Whom slumber soothes not – pleasure cannot please –
Oh, who can tell, save he whose heart hath tried,
And danced in triumph o'er the waters wide,
15   The exulting sense – the pulse's maddening play,
That thrills the wanderer of that trackless way?
That for itself can woo the approaching fight,
And turn what some deem danger to delight;
That seeks what cravens shun with more than zeal,
20   And where the feebler faint – can only feel –
Feel – to the rising bosom's inmost core,
Its hope awaken and its spirit soar?
No dread of death – if with us die our foes –
Save that it seems even duller than repose:
25   Come when it will – we snatch the life of life –
When lost – what recks it – by disease or strife?
Let him who crawls enamour'd of decay
Cling to his couch, and sicken years away;
Heave his thick breath, and shake his palsied head;
30   Ours – the fresh turf, and not the feverish bed.
While gasp by gasp he falters forth his soul,
Ours with one pang – one bound – escapes control.
His corse may boast its urn and narrow cave,
And they who loath'd his life may gild his grave:
35   Ours are the tears, though few, sincerely shed,
When Ocean shrouds and sepulchres our dead.
For us, even banquets fond regret supply
In the red cup that crowns our memory;
And the brief epitaph in danger's day,
40   When those who win at length divide the prey,
And cry, Remembrance saddening o'er each brow,
How had the brave who fell exulted *now*!'

II

Such were the notes that from the Pirate's isle
Around the kindling watch-fire rang the while:
45   Such were the sounds that thrill'd the rocks along,
And unto ears as rugged seem'd a song!
In scatter'd groups upon the golden sand,
They game – carouse – converse – or whet the brand;
Select the arms – to each his blade assign,
50   And careless eye the blood that dims its shine;
Repair the boat, replace the helm or oar,
While others straggling muse along the shore;
For the wild bird the busy springes set,
Or spread beneath the sun the dripping net;
55   Gaze where some distant sail a speck supplies,
With all the thirsting eye of Enterprise;
Tell o'er the tales of many a night of toil,
And marvel where they next shall seize a spoil:
No matter where – their chief's allotment this;
60   Theirs, to believe no prey nor plan amiss.
But who that CHIEF? his name on every shore
Is famed and fear'd – they ask and know no more.
With these he mingles not but to command;
Few are his words, but keen his eye and hand.
65   Ne'er seasons he with mirth their jovial mess,
But they forgive his silence for success.
Ne'er for his lip the purpling cup they fill,
That goblet passes him untasted still –
And for his fare – the rudest of his crew
70   Would that, in turn, have pass'd untasted too;
Earth's coarsest bread, the garden's homeliest roots,
And scarce the summer luxury of fruits,
His short repast in humbleness supply
With all a hermit's board would scarce deny.
75   But while he shuns the grosser joys of sense,
His mind seems nourished by that abstinence.
'Steer to that shore!' – they sail. 'Do this!' 'tis done:
'Now form and follow me!' – the spoil is won.
Thus prompt his accents and his actions still,
80   And all obey and few enquire his will;

To such, brief answer and contemptuous eye
Convey reproof, nor further deign reply.

III
'A sail! – a sail!' – a promised prize to Hope!
Her nation – flag – how speaks the telescope?
85   No prize, alas! – but yet a welcome sail:
The blood-red signal glitters in the gale.
Yes – she is ours – a home returning bark –
Blow fair, thou breeze! – she anchors ere the dark.
Already doubled is the cape – our bay
90   Receives that prow which proudly spurns the spray.
How gloriously her gallant course she goes!
Her white wings flying – never from her foes –
She walks the waters like a thing of life,
And seems to dare the elements to strife.
95   Who would not brave the battle-fire – the wreck –
To move the monarch of her peopled deck?

IV
Hoarse o'er her side the rustling cable rings;
The sails are furl'd; and anchoring round she swings:
And gathering loiterers on the land discern
100   Her boat descending from the latticed stern.
'Tis mann'd – the oars keep concert to the strand,
Till grates her keel upon the shallow sand.
Hail to the welcome shout! – the friendly speech!
When hand grasps hand uniting on the beach;
105   The smile, the question, and the quick reply,
And the heart's promise of festivity!

V
The tidings spread, and gathering grows the crowd:
The hum of voices, and the laughter loud,
And woman's gentler anxious tone is heard –
110   Friends' – husbands' – lovers' names in each dear word:
'Oh! are they safe? we ask not of success –
But shall we see them? will their accents bless?

From where the battle roars – the billows chafe –
They doubtless boldly did – but who are safe?
115   Here let them haste to gladden and surprise,
And kiss the doubt from these delighted eyes!'

VI

'Where is our chief? for him we bear report –
And doubt that joy – which hails our coming – short;
Yet thus sincere – 'tis cheering, though so brief;
120   But, Juan! instant guide us to our chief:
Our greeting paid, we'll feast on our return,
And all shall hear what each may wish to learn.'
Ascending slowly by the rock-hewn way,
To where his watch-tower beetles o'er the bay,
125   By bushy brake, and wild flowers blossoming,
And freshness breathing from each silver spring,
Whose scatter'd streams from granite basins burst,
Leap into life, and sparkling woo your thirst;
From crag to cliff they mount – Near yonder cave,
130   What lonely straggler looks along the wave?
In pensive posture leaning on the brand,
Not oft a resting-staff to that red hand?
''Tis he – 'tis Conrad – here – as wont – alone;
On – Juan! – on – and make our purpose known
135   The bark he views – and tell him we would greet
His ear with tidings he must quickly meet:
We dare not yet approach – thou know'st his mood,
When strange or uninvited steps intrude.'

VII

Him Juan sought, and told of their intent; –
140   He spake not – but a sign expressed assent.
These Juan calls – they come – to their salute
He bends him slightly, but his lips are mute.
'These letters, Chief, are from the Greek – the spy,
Who still proclaims our spoil or peril nigh:
145   Whate'er his tidings, we can well report,
Much that' – 'Peace, peace!' – he cuts their prating short.

Wondering they turn, abash'd, while each to each
Conjecture whispers in his muttering speech:
They watch his glance with many a stealing look,
150 To gather how that eye the tidings took;
But, this as if guess'd, with head aside,
Perchance from some emotion, doubt, or pride,
He read the scroll – 'My tablets, Juan, hark –
Where is Gonsalvo?
             'In the anchor'd bark.'
155 'There let him stay – to him this order bear –
Back to your duty – for my course prepare:
Myself this entreprise to-night will share.'
'To-night, Lord Conrad?'
             'Ay! at set of sun:
The breeze will freshen when the day is done.
160 My corslet – cloak – one hour – and we are gone.
Sling on thy bugle – see that free from rust
My carbine-lock springs worthy of my trust;
Be the edge sharpen'd of my boarding-brand,
And give its guard more room to fit my hand.
165 This let the Armourer with speed dispose;
Last time, it more fatigued my arm than foes:
Mark that the signal-gun be duly fired,
To tell us when the hour of stay's expired.'

VIII

They make obeisance, and retire in haste,
170 Too soon to seek again the watery waste:
Yet they repine not – so that Conrad guides;
And who dare question aught that he decides?
That man of loneliness and mystery,
Scarce seen to smile, and seldom heard to sigh;
175 Whose name appals the fiercest of his crew,
And tints each swarthy cheek with sallower hue;
Still sways their souls with that commanding art
That dazzles, leads, yet chills the vulgar heart.
What is that spell, that thus his lawless train
180 Confess and envy, yet oppose in vain?

What should it be, that thus their faith can bind?
The power of Thought – the magic of the Mind!
Link'd with success, assumed and kept with skill,
That moulds another's weakness to its will;
185 Wields with their hands, but, still to these unknown,
Makes even their mightiest deeds appear his own.
Such hath it been – shall be – beneath the sun
The many still must labour for the one!
'Tis Nature's doom – but let the wretch who toils,
190 Accuse not, hate not *him* who wears the spoils.
Oh! if he knew the weight of splendid chains,
How light the balance of his humbler pains!

IX

Unlike the heroes of each ancient race,
Demons in act, but Gods at least in face,
195 In Conrad's form seems little to admire
Though his dark eyebrow shades a glance of fire:
Robust but not Herculean – to the sight
No giant frame sets forth his common height;
Yet, in the whole, who paused to look again,
200 Saw more than marks the crowd of vulgar men;
They gaze and marvel how – and still confess
That thus it is, but why they cannot guess.
Sun-burnt his cheek, his forehead high and pale
The sable curls in wild profusion veil;
205 And oft perforce his rising lip reveals
The haughtier thought it curbs, but scarce conceals.
Though smooth his voice, and calm his general mien,
Still seems there something he would not have seen:
His features' deepening lines and varying hue
210 At times attracted, yet perplex'd the view,
As if within that murkiness of mind
Work'd feelings fearful, and yet undefined;
Such might it be – that none could truly tell –
Too close enquiry his stern glance would quell.
215 There breathe but few whose aspect might defy
The full encounter of his searching eye:

He had the skill, when Cunning's gaze would seek
To probe his heart and watch his changing cheek,
At once the observer's purpose to espy,
220 And on himself roll back his scrutiny,
Lest he to Conrad rather should betray
Some secret thought, than drag that chief's to day.
There was a laughing Devil in his sneer,
That raised emotions both of rage and fear;
225 And where his frown of hatred darkly fell,
Hope withering fled – and Mercy sigh'd farewell!

X

Slight are the outward signs of evil thought,
Within – within – 'twas there the spirit wrought!
Love shows all changes – Hate, Ambition, Guile,
230 Betray no further than the bitter smile;
The lip's least curl, the lightest paleness thrown
Along the govern'd aspect, speak alone
Of deeper passions; and to judge their mien,
He, who would see, must be himself unseen.
235 Then – with the hurried tread, the upward eye,
The clenched hand, the pause of agony,
That listens, starting, lest the step too near
Approach intrusive on that mood of fear:
Then – with each feature working from the heart,
240 With feelings loosed to strengthen – not depart:
That rise – convulse – contend – that freeze or glow,
Flush in the cheek, or damp upon the brow;
Then – Stranger! if thou canst, and tremblest not,
Behold his soul – the rest that soothes his lot!
245 Mark – how that lone and blighted bosom sears
The scathing thought of execrated years!
Behold – but who hath seen, or e'er shall see,
Man as himself – the secret spirit free?

XI

Yet was not Conrad thus by Nature sent
250 To lead the guilty – guilt's worst instrument –
His soul was changed, before his deeds had driven
Him forth to war with man and forfeit heaven.
Warp'd by the world in Disappointment's school,
In words too wise, in conduct *there* a fool;
255 Too firm to yield, and far too proud to stoop,
Doom'd by his very virtues for a dupe,
He cursed those virtues as the cause of ill,
And not the traitors who betray'd him still;
Nor deem'd that gifts bestow'd on better men
260 Had left him joy, and means to give again.
Fear'd – shunn'd – belied – ere youth had lost her force,
He hated man too much to feel remorse,
And thought the voice of wrath a sacred call,
To pay the injuries of some on all.
265 He knew himself a villain – but he deem'd
The rest no better than the thing he seem'd;
And scorn'd the best as hypocrites who hid
Those deeds the bolder spirit plainly did.
He knew himself detested, but he knew
270 The hearts that loath'd him, crouch'd and dreaded too.
Lone, wild, and strange, he stood alike exempt
From all affection and from all contempt:
His name could sadden, and his acts surprise;
But they that fear'd him dared not to despise:
275 Man spurns the worm, but pauses ere he wake
The slumbering venom of the folded snake;
The first may turn – but not avenge the blow;
The last expires – but leaves no living foe;
Fast to the doom'd offender's form it clings,
280 And he may crush – not conquer – still it stings!

XII

None are all evil – quickening round his heart,
One softer feeling would not yet depart;
Oft could he sneer at others as beguiled
By passions worthy of a fool or child;

285   Yet 'gainst that passion vainly still he strove,
     And even in him it asks the name of Love!
     Yes, it was love – unchangeable – unchanged,
     Felt but for one from whom he never ranged;
     Though fairest captives daily met his eye,
290   He shunn'd, nor sought, but coldly pass'd them by;
     Though many a beauty droop'd in prison'd bower,
     None ever sooth'd his most unguarded hour.
     Yes – it was Love – if thoughts of tenderness,
     Tried in temptation, strengthen'd by distress,
295   Unmoved by absence, firm in every clime,
     And yet – Oh more than all! – untired by time;
     Which nor defeated hope, nor baffled wile,
     Could render sullen were she ne'er to smile,
     Nor rage could fire, nor sickness fret to vent
300   On her one murmur of his discontent;
     Which still would meet with joy, with calmness part,
     Lest that his look of grief should reach her heart;
     Which nought removed, nor menaced to remove –
     If there be love in mortals – this was love!
305   He was a villain – ay – reproaches shower
     On him – but not the passion, nor its power,
     Which only proved, all other virtues gone,
     Not guilt itself could quench this loveliest one!

     XIII
     He paused a moment – till his hastening men
310   Pass'd the first winding downward to the glen.
     'Strange tidings! – many a peril have I past,
     Nor know I why this next appears the last!
     Yet so my heart forebodes, but must not fear,
     Nor shall my followers find me falter here.
315   'Tis rash to meet, but surer death to wait
     Till here they hunt us to undoubted fate;
     And, if my plan but hold, and Fortune smile,
     We'll furnish mourners for our funeral pile.
     Ay – let them slumber – peaceful be their dreams!
320   Morn ne'er awoke them with such brilliant beams

As kindle high to-night (but blow, thou breeze!)
To warm these slow avengers of the seas.
Now to Medora – Oh! my sinking heart,
Long may her own be lighter than thou art!
325 Yet was I brave – mean boast where all are brave!
Ev'n insects sting for aught they seek to save.
This common courage which with brutes we share,
That owes its deadliest efforts to despair,
Small merit claims – but 'twas my nobler hope
330 To teach my few with numbers still to cope;
Long have I led them – not to vainly bleed;
No medium now – we perish or succeed!
So let it be – it irks not me to die;
But thus to urge them whence they cannot fly.
335 My lot hath long had little of my care,
But chafes my pride thus baffled in the snare:
'Is this my skill? my craft? to set at last
Hope, power, and life upon a single cast?
Oh, Fate! – accuse thy folly, not thy fate –
340 She may redeem thee still – nor yet too late.'

XIV

Thus with himself communion held he, till
He reach'd the summit of his tower-crown'd hill:
There at the portal paused – for wild and soft
He heard those accents never heard too oft;
345 Through the high lattice far yet sweet they rung,
And these the notes the bird of beauty sung:

I

'Deep in my soul that tender secret dwells,
    Lonely and lost to light for evermore,
Save when to thine my heart responsive swells,
350   Then trembles into silence as before.

2
'There, in its centre, a sepulchral lamp
    Burns the slow flame, eternal – but unseen;
Which not the darkness of despair can damp,
    Though vain its ray as it had never been.

3
355 'Remember me – Oh! pass not thou my grave
    Without one thought whose relics there recline:
The only pang my bosom dare not brave
    Must be to find forgetfulness in thine.

4
'My fondest – faintest – latest accents hear –
360   Grief for the dead not Virtue can reprove;
Then give me all I ever ask'd – a tear,
    The first – last – sole reward of so much love!'

He pass'd the portal – cross'd the corridore,
And reach'd the chamber as the strain gave o'er:
365 'My own Medora! sure thy song is sad –'

'In Conrad's absence wouldst thou have it glad?
Without thine ear to listen to my lay,
Still must my song my thoughts, my soul betray:
Still must each accent to my bosom suit,
370 My heart unhush'd – although my lips were mute!
Oh! many a night on this lone couch reclined,
My dreaming fear with storms hath wing'd the wind,
And deem'd the breath that faintly fann'd thy sail
The murmuring prelude of the ruder gale;
375 Though soft, it seem'd the low prophetic dirge,
That mourn'd thee floating on the savage surge:
Still would I rise to rouse the beacon fire,
Lest spies less true should let the blaze expire;
And many a restless hour outwatch'd each star,
380 And morning came – and still thou wert afar.
Oh! how the chill blast on my bosom blew,
And day broke dreary on my troubled view,

And still I gazed and gazed – and not a prow
Was granted to my tears – my truth – my vow!
385 At length – 'twas noon – I hail'd and blest the mast
That met my sight – it near'd – Alas! it past!
Another came – Oh God! 'twas thine at last!
Would that those days were over! wilt thou ne'er,
My Conrad! learn the joys of peace to share?
390 Sure thou hast more than wealth, and many a home
As bright as this invites us not to roam:
Thou know'st it is not peril that I fear:
I only tremble when thou art not here;
Then not for mine, but that far dearer life,
395 Which flies from love and languishes for strife –
How strange that heart, to me so tender still,
Should war with nature and its better will!'

'Yea, strange indeed – that heart hath long been changed;
Worm-like 'twas trampled – adder-like avenged,
400 Without one hope on earth beyond thy love,
And scarce a glimpse of mercy from above.
Yet the same feeling which thou dost condemn,
My very love to thee is hate to them,
So closely mingling here, that disentwined,
405 I cease to love thee when I love mankind:
Yet dread not this – the proof of all the past
Assures the future that my love will last;
But – Oh, Medora! nerve thy gentler heart,
This hour again – but not for long – we part.'

410 'This hour we part! – my heart foreboded this:
Thus ever fade my fairy dreams of bliss.
This hour – it cannot be – this hour away!
Yon bark hath hardly anchor'd in the bay;
Her consort still is absent, and her crew
415 Have need of rest before they toil anew:
My love! thou mock'st my weakness; and wouldst steel
My breast before the time when it must feel;
But trifle now no more with my distress,
Such mirth hath less of play than bitterness.

420   Be silent, Conrad! – dearest! come and share
       The feast these hands delighted to prepare;
       Light toil! to cull and dress thy frugal fare!
       See, I have pluck'd the fruit that promised best,
       And where not sure, perplex'd, but pleased, I guess'd
425   At such as seem'd the fairest; thrice the hill
       My steps have wound to try the coolest rill;
       Yes! thy sherbet to-night will sweetly flow,
       See how it sparkles in its vase of snow!
       The grapes' gay juice thy bosom never cheers;
430   Thou more than Moslem when the cup appears:
       Think not I mean to chide – for I rejoice
       What others deem a penance is thy choice.
       But come, the board is spread; our silver lamp
       Is trimm'd, and heeds not the sirocco's damp:
435   Then shall my handmaids while the time along,
       And join with me the dance, or wake the song;
       Or my guitar, which still thou lov'st to hear,
       Shall soothe or lull – or, should it vex thine ear,
       We'll turn the tale, by Ariosto told,
440   Of fair Olympia loved and left of old.[1]
       Why – thou wert worse than he who broke his vow
       To that lost damsel, shouldst thou leave me now;
       Or even that traitor chief – I've seen thee smile,
       When the clear sky show'd Ariadne's Isle,
445   Which I have pointed from these cliffs the while:
       And thus half sportive, half in fear, I said,
       Lest Time, should raise that doubt to more than dread,
       Thus Conrad, too will quit me for the main:
       And he deceived me – for – he came again!'

450   'Again – again – and oft again – my love!
       If there be life below, and hope above,
       He will return – but now, the moments bring
       The time of parting with redoubled wing:
       The why – the where – what boots it now to tell

       1. Orlando Furioso, Canto x.

455   Since all must end in that wild word – farewell!
       Yet would I fain – did time allow – disclose –
       Fear not – these are no formidable foes;
       And here shall watch a more than wonted guard,
       For sudden siege and long defence prepared:
460   Nor be thou lonely – though thy lord's away,
       Our matrons and thy handmaids with thee stay;
       And this thy comfort – that, when next we meet,
       Security shall make repose more sweet.
       List! – 'tis the bugle – Juan shrilly blew –
465   One kiss – one more – another – Oh! Adieu!'

       She rose – she sprung – she clung to his embrace,
       Till his heart heaved beneath her hidden face.
       He dared not raise to his that deep-blue eye,
       Which downcast droop'd in tearless agony.
470   Her long fair hair lay floating o'er his arms,
       In all the wildness of dishevell'd charms;
       Scarce beat that bosom where his image dwelt
       So full – *that* feeling seem'd almost unfelt!
       Hark – peals the thunder of the signal-gun!
475   It told 'twas sunset – and he cursed that sun.
       Again – again – that form he madly press'd,
       Which mutely clasp'd, imploring caress'd!
       And tottering to the couch his bride he bore,
       One moment gazed – as if to gaze no more;
480   Felt – that for him earth held but her alone,
       Kiss'd her cold forehead – turn'd – is Conrad gone?

       XV
       'And is he gone?' – on sudden solitude
       How oft that fearful question will intrude!
       ''Twas but an instant past – and here he stood!
485   And now' – without the portal's porch she rush'd,
       And then at length her tears in freedom gush'd;
       Big – bright – and fast, unknown to her they fell;
       But still her lips refused to send – 'Farewell!'
       For in that word – that fatal word – howe'er
490   We promise – hope – believe – there breathes despair.

O'er every feature of that still, pale face,
Had sorrow fix'd what time can ne'er erase:
The tender blue of that large loving eye
Grew frozen with its gaze on vacancy,
495 Till – Oh, how far! – it caught a glimpse of him,
And then it flow'd – and phrensied seem'd to swim
Through those long, dark, and glistening lashes dew'd
With drops of sadness oft to be renew'd.
'He's gone!' – against her heart that hand is driven,
500 Convulsed and quick – then gently raised to heaven;
She look'd and saw the heaving of the main;
The white sail set – she dared not look again;
But turn'd with sickening soul within the gate –
'It is no dream – and I am desolate!'

XVI

505 From crag to crag descending – swiftly sped
Stern Conrad down, nor once he turn'd his head;
But shrunk whene'er the windings of his way
Forced on his eye what he would not survey,
His lone, but lovely dwelling on the steep,
510 That hail'd him first when homeward from the deep:
And she – the dim and melancholy star,
Whose ray of beauty reach'd him from afar,
On her he must not gaze, he must not think,
There he might rest – but on Destruction's brink:
515 Yet once almost he stopp'd – and nearly gave
His fate to chance, his projects to the wave:
But no – it must not be – a worthy chief
May melt, but not betray to woman's grief.
He sees his bark, he notes how fair the wind,
520 And sternly gathers all his might of mind.
Again he hurries on – and as he hears
The clang of tumult vibrate on his ears,
The busy sounds, the bustle of the shore,
The shout, the signal, and the dashing oar;
525 As marks his eye the seaboy on the mast,
The anchors rise, the sails unfurling fast,

The waving kerchiefs of the crowd that urge
That mute adieu to those who stem the surge;
And more than all, his blood-red flag aloft,
530   He marvell'd how his heart could seem so soft.
Fire in his glance, and wildness in his breast,
He feels of all his former self possest;
He bounds – he flies – until his footsteps reach
The verge where ends the cliff, begins the beach,
535   There checks his speed; but pauses less to breathe
The breezy freshness of the deep beneath,
Than there his wonted statelier step renew;
Nor rush, disturb'd by haste, to vulgar view:
For well had Conrad learn'd to curb the crowd,
540   By arts that veil, and oft preserve the proud;
His was the lofty port, the distant mien,
That seems to shun the sight – and awes if seen:
The solemn aspect, and the high-born eye,
That checks low mirth, but lacks not courtesy;
545   All these he wielded to command assent:
But where he wished to win, so well unbent,
That kindness cancell'd fear in those who heard,
And others' gifts show'd mean beside his word,
When echo'd to the heart as from his own
550   His deep yet tender melody of tone:
But such was foreign to his wonted mood,
He cared not what he soften'd, but subdued;
The evil passions of his youth had made
Him value less who loved – than what obey'd.

XVII
555   Around him mustering ranged his ready guard.
Before him Juan stands – 'Are all prepared?'
'They are – nay more – embark'd: the latest boat
Waits but my chief —'
                   'My sword, and my capote.'
Soon firmly girded on, and lightly slung,
560   His belt and cloak were o'er his shoulders flung:
'Call Pedro here!' He comes – and Conrad bends,
With all the courtesy he deign'd his friends;

'Receive these tablets, and peruse with care,
Words of high trust and truth are graven there;
565 Double the guard, and when Anselmo's bark
Arrives, let him alike these orders mark:
In three days (serve the breeze) the sun shall shine
On our return – till then all peace be thine!'
This said, his brother Pirate's hand he wrung,
570 Then to his boat with haughty gesture sprung.
Flash'd the dipt oars, and sparkling with the stroke,
Around the waves' phosphoric[1] brightness broke;
They gain the vessel – on the deck he stands, –
Shrieks the shrill whistle – ply the busy hands –
575 He marks how well the ship her helm obeys,
How gallant all her crew – and deigns to praise.
His eyes of pride to young Gonsalvo turn –
Why doth he start, and inly seem to mourn?
Alas! those eyes beheld his rocky tower,
580 And live a moment o'er the parting hour;
She – his Medora – did she mark the prow?
Ah! never loved he half so much as now!
But much must yet be done ere dawn of day –
Again he mans himself and turns away;
585 Down to the cabin with Gonsalvo bends,
And there unfolds his plan – his means – and ends;
Before them burns the lamp, and spreads the chart,
And all that speaks and aids the naval art;
They to the midnight watch protract debate;
590 To anxious eyes what hour is ever late?
Meantime, the steady breeze serenely blew,
And fast and falcon-like the vessel flew;
Pass'd the high headlands of each clustering isle
To gain their port – long – long ere morning smile:
595 And soon the night-glass through the narrow bay
Discovers where the Pacha's galleys lay.
Count they each sail – and mark how there supine
The lights in vain o'er heedless Moslem shine.

1. By night, particularly in a warm latitude, every stroke of the oar, every
motion of the boat or ship, is followed by a slight flash like sheet lightning
from the water.

Secure, unnoted, Conrad's prow pass'd by,
600   And anchor'd where his ambush meant to lie;
Screen'd from espial by the jutting cape,
That rears on high its rude fantastic shape.
Then rose his band to duty – not from sleep –
Equipp'd for deeds alike on land or deep;
605   While lean'd their leader o'er the fretting flood,
And calmly talk'd – and yet he talk'd of blood!

Canto the Second

'Conosceste i dubiosi desiri?'   DANTE.

I

In Coron's bay floats many a galley light,
Through Coron's lattices the lamps are bright,
For Seyd, the Pacha, makes a feast to-night:
A feast for promised triumph yet to come,
5   When he shall drag the fetter'd Rovers home;
This hath he sworn by Alla and his sword,
And faithful to his firman and his word,
His summon'd prows collect along the coast,
And great the gathering crews, and loud the boast;
10   Already shared the captives and the prize,
Though far the distant foe they thus despise;
'Tis but to sail – no doubt to-morrow's Sun
Will see the Pirates bound – their haven won!
Meantime the watch may slumber, if they will,
15   Nor only wake to war, but dreaming kill.
Though all, who can, disperse on shore and seek
To flesh their glowing valour on the Greek;
How well such deed becomes the turban'd brave –
To bare the sabre's edge before a slave!

20   Infest his dwelling – but forbear to slay,
        Their arms are strong, yet merciful to-day,
        And do not deign to smite because they may!
        Unless some gay caprice suggests the blow,
        To keep in practice for the coming foe.
25   Revel and rout the evening hours beguile,
        And they who wish to wear a head must smile;
        For Moslem mouths produce their choicest cheer,
        And hoard their curses, till the coast is clear.

        II
        High in his hall reclines the turban'd Seyd;
30   Around – the bearded chiefs he came to lead.
        Removed the banquet, and the last pilaff –
        Forbidden draughts, 'tis said, he dared to quaff,
        Though to the rest the sober berry's juice[1]
        The slaves bear round for rigid Moslems' use;
35   The long chibouque's[2] dissolving cloud supply,
        While dance the Almas[3] to wild minstrelsy.
        The rising morn will view the chiefs embark;
        But waves are somewhat treacherous in the dark:
        And revellers may more securely sleep
40   On silken couch than o'er the rugged deep;
        Feast there who can – nor combat till they must,
        And less to conquest than to Korans trust;
        And yet the numbers crowded in his host
        Might warrant more than even the Pacha's boast.

        III
45   With cautious reverence from the outer gate
        Slow stalks the slave, whose office there to wait,
        Bows his bent head – his hand salutes the floor,
        Ere yet his tongue the trusted tidings bore:

        1. Coffee.
        2. 'Chibouque,' pipe.
        3. Dancing girls.

'A captive Dervise, from the pirate's nest
50   Escaped, is here – himself would tell the rest.'[1]
He took the sign from Seyd's assenting eye,
And led the holy man in silence nigh.
His arms were folded on his dark-green vest,
His step was feeble, and his look deprest;
55   Yet worn he seem'd of hardship more than years,
And pale his cheek with penance, not from fears.
Vow'd to his God – his sable locks he wore,
And these his lofty cap rose proudly o'er:
Around his form his loose long robe was thrown,
60   And wrapt a breast bestow'd on heaven alone;
Submissive, yet with self-possession mann'd,
He calmly met the curious eyes that scann'd;
And question of his coming fain would seek,
Before the Pacha's will allow'd to speak.

1. It has been observed, that Conrad's entering disguised as a spy is out of nature. Perhaps so. I find something not unlike it in history. – 'Anxious to explore with his own eyes the state of the Vandals, Majorian ventured, after disguising the colour of his hair, to visit Carthage in the character of his own ambassador; and Genseric was afterwards mortified by the discovery, that he had entertained and dismissed the Emperor of the Romans. Such an anecdote may be rejected as an improbable fiction; but it is a fiction which would not have been imagined unless in the life of a hero.' – See GIBBON's Decline and Fall, vol. vi. p. 180.

That Conrad is a character not altogether out of nature, I shall attempt to prove by some historical coincidences which I have met with since writing 'The Corsair.'

'Eccelin prisonnier,' dit Rolandini, 's'enfermoit dans un silence menaçant, il fixoit sur la terre son visage féroce, et ne donnoit point d'essor à sa profonde indignation. De toutes partes cependant les soldats et les peuples accouroient; ils vouloient voir cet homme, jadis si puissant, et la joie universelle éclatoit de toutes partes. * * * 'Eccelin étoit d'une petite taille; mais tout l'aspect de sa personne, tous ses mouvemens, indiquoient un soldat. – Son langage étoit amer, son déportement superbe – et par son seul regard, il faisoit trembler les plus hardis.' – Sismondi, tome iii. p. 219.

Again, 'Gizericus (Genseric, king of the Vandals, the conqueror of both Carthage and Rome), staturá mediocrís, et equi casu claudicans, animo profundus, sermone rarus, luxuria contemptor, ira turbidus, habendi cupidus, ad solicitandas gentes providentissimus,' & c. & c. Jornandes de Rebus Getieis, c. 33.

I beg leave to quote these gloomy realities to keep in countenance my Giaour and Corsair.

IV

65 'Whence com'st thou, Dervise?'

                           'From the outlaw's den,
A fugitive –'

              'Thy capture where and when?'

'From Scalanovo's port to Scio's isle,
The Saick was bound; but Alla did not smile
Upon our course – the Moslem merchant's gains
70 The Rovers won: our limbs have worn their chains.
I had no death to fear, nor wealth to boast,
Beyond the wandering freedom which I lost;
At length a fisher's humble boat by night
Afforded hope, and offer'd chance of flight;
75 I seized the hour, and find my safety here –
With thee – most mighty Pacha! who can fear?'

'How speed the outlaws? stand they well prepared,
Their plunder'd wealth, and robber's rock, to guard?
Dream they of this our preparation, doom'd
80 To view with fire their scorpion nest consumed?'

'Pacha! the fetter'd captive's mourning eye,
That weeps for flight, but ill can play the spy;
I only heard the reckless waters roar,
Those waves that would not bear me from the shore;
85 I only mark'd the glorious sun and sky,
Too bright – too blue – for my captivity;
And felt – that all which Freedom's bosom cheers,
Must break my chain before it dried my tears.
This may'st thou judge, at least, from my escape,
90 They little deem of aught in peril's shape;
Else vainly had I pray'd or sought the chance
That leads me here – if eyed with vigilance:
The careless guard that did not see me fly,
May watch as idly when thy power is nigh:
95 Pacha! – my limbs are faint – and nature craves
Food for my hunger, rest from tossing waves:
Permit my absence – peace be with thee! Peace
With all around! – now grant repose – release.'

'Stay, Dervise! I have more to question – stay,
100   I do command thee – sit – dost hear? – obey!
More I must ask, and food the slaves shall bring;
Thou shalt not pine where all are banqueting:
The supper done – prepare thee to reply,
Clearly and full – I love not mystery.'
105   'Twere vain to guess what shook the pious man,
Who look'd not lovingly on that Divan;
Nor show'd high relish for the banquet prest,
And less respect for every fellow guest.
'Twas but a moment's peevish hectic past
110   Along his cheek, and tranquillised as fast:
He sate him down in silence, and his look
Resumed the calmness which before forsook:
The feast was usher'd in – but sumptuous fare
He shunn'd as if some poison mingled there.
115   For one so long condemn'd to toil and fast,
Methinks he strangely spares the rich repast.
'What ails thee, Dervise? eat – dost thou suppose
This feast a Christian's? or my friends thy foes?
Why dost thou shun the salt? that sacred pledge,
120   Which, once partaken, blunts the sabre's edge,
Makes even contending tribes in peace unite,
And hated hosts seem brethren to the sight!'

'Salt seasons dainties – and my food is still
The humblest root, my drink the simplest rill;
125   And my stern vow and order's[1] laws oppose
To break or mingle bread with friends or foes;
It may seem strange – if there be aught to dread,
That peril rests upon my single head;
But for thy sway – nay more – thy Sultan's throne,
130   I taste nor bread nor banquet – save alone;
Infringed our order's rule, the Prophet's rage
To Mecca's dome might bar my pilgrimage.'
'Well – as thou wilt – ascetic as thou art –
One question answer; then in peace depart.

1. The Dervises are in colleges, and of different orders, as the monks.

135   How many? – Ha! it cannot sure be day?
      'What star – what sun is bursting on the bay?
      It shines a lake of fire! – away – away!
      Ho! treachery! my guards! my scimitar!
      The galleys feed the flames – and I afar!
140   Accursed Dervise! – these thy tidings – thou
      Some villain spy – seize – cleave him – slay him now!'

      Up rose the Dervise with that burst of light,
      Nor less his change of form appall'd the sight:
      Up rose that Dervise – not in saintly garb,
145   But like a warrior bounding on his barb,
      Dash'd his high cap, and tore his robe away –
      Shone his mail'd breast, and flash'd his sabre's ray!
      His close but glittering casque, and sable plume,
      More glittering eye, and black brow's sabler gloom,
150   Glared on the Moslems' eyes some Afrit sprite,
      Whose demon death-blow left no hope for fight.
      The wild confusion, and the swarthy glow
      Of flames on high, and torches from below;
      The shriek of terror, and the mingling yell –
155   For swords began to clash, and shouts to swell –
      Flung o'er that spot of earth the air of hell!
      Distracted, to and fro, the flying slaves
      Behold but bloody shore and fiery waves;
      Nought heeded they the Pacha's angry cry,
160   *They* seize that Dervise! – seize on Zatanai![1]
      He saw their terror – check'd the first despair
      That urged him but to stand and perish there,
      Since far too early and too well obey'd,
      The flame was kindled ere the signal made;
165   He saw their terror – from his baldric drew
      His bugle – brief the blast – but shrilly blew;
      'Tis answer'd – 'Well ye speed, my gallant crew!
      Why did I doubt their quickness of career?
      And deem design had left me single here?'

---

1. 'Zatanai,' Satan.

170   Sweeps his long arm – that sabre's whirling sway
      Sheds fast atonement for its first delay;
      Completes his fury, what their fear begun,
      And makes the many basely quail to one.
      The cloven turbans o'er the chamber spread,
175   And scarce an arm dare rise to guard its head:
      Even Seyd, convulsed, o'erwhelm'd, with rage, surprise,
      Retreats before him, though he still defies.
      No craven he – and yet he dreads the blow,
      So much Confusion magnifies his foe!
180   His blazing galleys still distract his sight,
      He tore his beard, and foaming fled the fight;[1]
      For now the pirates pass'd the Haram gate,
      And burst within – and it were death to wait;
      Where wild Amazement shrieking – kneeling – throws
185   The sword aside – in vain – the blood o'erflows!
      The Corsairs pouring, haste to where within,
      Invited Conrad's bugle, and the din
      Of groaning victims, and wild cries for life,
      Proclaim'd how well he did the work of strife.
190   A glutted tiger mangling in his lair!
      They shout to find him grim and lonely there,
      But short their greeting – shorter his reply –
      "Tis well – but Seyd escapes – and he must die –
      Much hath been done – but more remains to do –
195   Their galleys blaze – why not their city too?'

      V
      Quick at the word – they seized him each a torch,
      And fire the dome from minaret to porch.
      A stern delight was fix'd in Conrad's eye,
      But sudden sunk – for on his ear the cry
200   Of women struck, and like a deadly knell
      Knock'd at that heart unmoved by battle's yell.

---

1. A common and not very novel effect of Mussulman anger. See Prince
Eugene's Memoirs, page 24. 'The Seraskier received a wound in the thigh;
he plucked up his beard by the roots, because he was obliged to quit the
field.'

'Oh! burst the Haram – wrong not on your lives
One female form – remember – *we* have wives.
On them such outrage Vengeance will repay;
205   Man is our foe, and such 'tis ours to slay:
But still we spared – must spare the weaker prey.
Oh! I forgot – but Heaven will not forgive
If at my word the helpless cease to live:
Follow who will – I go – we yet have time
210   Our souls to lighten of at least a crime.'
He climbs the crackling stair – he bursts the door,
Nor feels his feet glow scorching with the floor;
His breath choked gasping with the volumed smoke,
But still from room to room his way he broke.
215   They search – they find – they save: with lusty arms
Each bears a prize of unregarded charms;
Calm their loud fears; sustain their sinking frames
With all the care defenceless beauty claims:
So well could Conrad tame their fiercest mood,
220   And check the very hands with gore imbrued.
But who is she? whom Conrad's arms convey
From reeking pile and combat's wreck – away –
Who but the love of him he dooms to bleed?
The Haram queen – but still the slave of Seyd!

VI

225   Brief time had Conrad now to greet Gulnare,[1]
Few words to re-assure the trembling fair;
For in that pause compassion snatch'd from war,
The foe before retiring, fast and far,
With wonder saw their footsteps unpursued,
230   First slowlier fled – then rallied – then withstood.
This Seyd perceives, then first perceives how few,
Compared with his, the Corsair's roving crew,
And blushes o'er his error, as he eyes
The ruin wrought by panic and surprise.
235   Alla il Alla! Vengeance swells the cry –
Shame mounts to rage that must atone or die!

1. Gulnare, a female name; it means, literally, the flower of the pomegranate.

And flame for flame and blood for blood must tell,
The tide of triumph ebbs that flow'd too well –
When wrath returns to renovated strife,
240   And those who fought for conquest strike for life.
Conrad beheld the danger – he beheld
His followers faint by freshening foes repell'd:
'One effort – one – to break the circling host!'
They form – unite – charge – waver – all is lost!
245   Within a narrower ring compress'd, beset,
Hopeless, not heartless, strive and struggle yet –
Ah! now they fight in firmest file no more,
Hemm'd in – cut off – cleft down – and trampled o'er;
But each strikes singly, silently, and home,
250   And sinks outwearied rather than o'ercome,
His last faint quittance rendering with his breath,
Till the blade glimmers in the grasp of death!

VII
But first, ere came the rallying host to blows,
And rank to rank, and hand to hand oppose,
255   Gulnare and all her Haram handmaids freed,
Safe in the dome of one who held their creed,
By Conrad's mandate safely were bestow'd,
And dried those tears for life and fame that flow'd:
And when that dark-eyed lady, young Gulnare,
260   Recall'd those thoughts late wandering in despair,
Much did she marvel o'er the courtesy
That smooth'd his accents; soften'd in his eye:
'Twas strange – *that* robber thus with gore bedew'd,
Seem'd gentler then than Seyd in fondest mood.
265   The Pacha woo'd as if he deem'd the slave
Must seem delighted with the heart he gave;
The Corsair vow'd protection, soothed affright,
As if his homage were a woman's right.
'The wish is wrong – nay, worse for female – vain:
270   Yet much I long to view that chief again;
If but to thank for, what my fear forgot,
The life – my loving lord remember'd not!'

VIII

And him she saw, where thickest carnage spread,
But gather'd breathing from the happier dead;
275 Far from his band, and battling with a host
That deem right dearly won the field he lost,
Fell'd – bleeding – baffled of the death he sought,
And snatch'd to expiate all the ills he wrought;
Preserved to linger and to live in vain,
280 While Vengeance ponder'd o'er new plans of pain,
And stanch'd the blood she saves to shed again –
But drop for drop, for Seyd's unglutted eye
Would doom him ever dying – ne'er to die!
Can this be he? triumphant late she saw,
285 When his red hand's wild gesture waved, a law!
'Tis he indeed – disarm'd but undeprest,
His sole regret the life he still possest;
His wounds too slight, though taken with that will,
Which would have kiss'd the hand that then could kill.
290 Oh were there none, of all the many given,
To send his soul – he scarcely ask'd to heaven?
Must he alone of all retain his breath,
Who more than all had striven and struck for death?
He deeply felt – what mortal hearts must feel,
295 When thus reversed on faithless fortune's wheel,
For crimes committed, and the victor's threat
Of lingering tortures to repay the debt –
He deeply, darkly felt; but evil pride
That led to perpetrate – now serves to hide.
300 Still in his stern and self-collected mien
A conqueror's more than captive's air is seen,
Though faint with wasting toil and stiffening wound,
But few that saw – so calmly gazed around:
Though the far shouting of the distant crowd,
305 Their tremors o'er, rose insolently loud,
The better warriors who beheld him near,
Insulted not the foe who taught them fear;
And the grim guards that to his durance led,
In silence eyed him with a secret dread.

IX

310   The Leech was sent – but not in mercy – there,
       To note how much the life yet left could bear;
       He found enough to load with heaviest chain,
       And promise feeling for the wrench of pain:
       To-morrow – yea – to-morrow's evening sun
315   Will sinking see impalement's pangs begun,
       And rising with the wonted blush of morn
       Behold how well or ill those pangs are borne.
       Of torments this the longest and the worst,
       Which adds all other agony to thirst,
320   That day by day death still forbears to slake,
       While famish'd vultures flit around the stake.
       'Oh! water – water!' – smiling Hate denies
       The victim's prayer – for if he drinks – he dies.
       This was his doom; – the Leech, the guard, were gone,
325   And left proud Conrad fetter'd and alone.

X

       'Twere vain to paint to what his feelings grew –
       It even were doubtful if their victim knew.
       There is a war, a chaos of the mind,
       When all its elements convulsed – combined –
330   Lie dark and jarring with perturbed force,
       And gnashing with impenitent Remorse;
       That juggling fiend – who never spake before –
       But cries 'I warn'd thee!' when the deed is o'er.
       Vain voice! the spirit burning but unbent,
335   May writhe – rebel – the weak alone repent!
       Even in that lonely hour when most it feels,
       And, to itself, all – all that self reveals,
       No single passion, and no ruling thought
       That leaves the rest as once unseen, unsought;
340   But the wild prospect when the soul reviews –
       All rushing through their thousand avenues,
       Ambition's dreams expiring, love's regret,
       Endangered glory, life itself beset;
       The joy untasted, the contempt or hate
345   'Gainst those who fain would triumph in our fate;

The hopeless past, the hasting future driven
Too quickly on to guess if hell or heaven;
Deeds, thoughts, and words, perhaps remember'd not
So keenly till that hour, but ne'er forgot;
350 Things light or lovely in their acted time,
But now to stern reflection each a crime;
The withering sense of evil unreveal'd,
Not cankering less because the more conceal'd –
All, in a word, from which all eyes must start,
355 That opening sepulchre – the naked heart
Bares with its buried woes, till Pride awake,
To snatch the mirror from the soul – and break.
Ay – Pride can veil, and Courage brave it all,
All – all – before – beyond – the deadliest fall.
360 Each has some fear, and he who least betrays,
The only hypocrite deserving praise:
Not the loud recreant wretch who boasts and flies;
But he who looks on death – and silent dies.
So steel'd by pondering o'er his far career,
365 He half-way meets him should he menace near!

XI

In the high chamber of his highest tower
Sate Conrad, fetter'd in the Pacha's power.
His palace perish'd in the flame – this fort
Contain'd at once his captive and his court.
370 Not much could Conrad of his sentence blame,
His foe, if vanquish'd, had but shared the same:–
Alone he sate – in solitude had scann'd
His guilty bosom, but that breast he mann'd:
One thought alone he could not – dared not meet –
375 'Oh, how these tidings will Medora greet?'
Then – only then – his clanking hands he raised,
And strain'd with rage the chain on which he gazed:
But soon he found – or feign'd – or dream'd relief,
And smiled in self-derision of his grief,
380 'And now come torture when it will – or may
More need of rest to nerve me for the day!'

This said, with languor to his mat he crept,
And, whatsoe'er his visions, quickly slept.
'Twas hardly midnight when that fray begun,
For Conrad's plans matured, at once were done:
And Havoc loathes so much the waste of time,
She scarce had left an uncommitted crime.
One hour beheld him since the tide he stemm'd –
Disguised – discover'd – conquering – ta'en – condemn'd –
A chief on land – an outlaw on the deep –
Destroying – saving – prison'd – and asleep!

XII

He slept in calmest seeming – for his breath
Was hush'd so deep – Ah! happy if in death!
He slept – Who o'er his placid slumber bends?
His foes are gone – and here he hath no friends;
Is it some seraph sent to grant him grace?
No, 'tis an earthly form with heavenly face!
Its white arm raised a lamp – yet gently hid,
Lest the ray flash abruptly on the lid
Of that closed eye, which opens but to pain,
And once unclosed – but once may close again.
That form, with eye so dark, and cheek so fair,
And auburn waves of gemm'd and braided hair;
With shape of fairy lightness – naked foot,
That shines like snow, and falls on earth as mute –
Through guards and dunnest night how came it there?
Ah! rather ask what will not woman dare?
Whom youth and pity lead like thee, Gulnare!
She could not sleep – and while the Pacha's rest
In muttering dreams yet saw his pirate-guest,
She left his side – his signet-ring she bore,
Which oft in sport adorn'd her hand before –
And with it, scarcely question'd, won her way
Through drowsy guards that must that sign obey.
Worn out with toil, and tired with changing blows,
Their eyes had envied Conrad his repose;

And chill and nodding at the turret door,
They stretch their listless limbs, and watch no more:
Just raised their heads to hail the signet-ring,
420 Nor ask or what or who the sign may bring.

XIII
She gazed in wonder, 'Can he calmly sleep,
While other eyes his fall or ravage weep?
And mine in restlessness are wandering here –
What sudden spell hath made this man so dear?
425 True – 'tis to him my life, and more, I owe,
And me and mine he spared from worse than woe:
'Tis late to think – but soft – his slumber breaks –
How heavily he sighs! – he starts – awakes!'

He raised his head – and dazzled with the light,
430 His eye seem'd dubious if it saw aright:
He moved his hand – the grating of his chain
Too harshly told him that he lived again.
'What is that form? if not a shape of air,
Methinks, my jailor's face shows wond'rous fair!'

435 'Pirate! thou know'st me not – but I am one,
Grateful for deeds thou hast too rarely done;
Look on me – and remember her, thy hand
Snatch'd from the flames, and thy more fearful band.
I come through darkness – and I scarce know why –
440 Yet not to hurt – I would not see thee die.'

'If so, kind lady! thine the only eye
That would not here in that gay hope delight:
Theirs is the chance – and let them use their right.
But still I thank their courtesy or thine,
445 That would confess me at so fair a shrine!'
Strange though it seem – yet with extremest grief
Is link'd a mirth – it doth not bring relief –
That playfulness of Sorrow ne'er beguiles,
And smiles in bitterness – but still it smiles;

450 And sometimes with the wisest and the best,
Till even the scaffold[1] echoes with their jest!
Yet not the joy to which it seems akin –
It may deceive all hearts, save that within.
Whate'er it was that flash'd on Conrad, now
455 A laughing wildness half unbent his brow:
And these his accents had a sound of mirth,
As if the last he could enjoy on earth;
Yet 'gainst his nature – for through that short life,
Few thoughts had he to spare from gloom and strife.

XIV
460 'Corsair! thy doom is named – but I have power
To soothe the Pacha in his weaker hour.
Thee would I spare – nay more – would save thee now,
But this – time – hope – nor even thy strength allow;
But all I can, I will: at least delay
465 The sentence that remits thee scarce a day.
More now were ruin – even thyself were loth
The vain attempt should bring but doom to both.'

'Yes! – loth indeed: – my soul is nerved to all,
Or fall'n too low to fear a further fall:
470 Tempt not thyself with peril; me with hope
Of flight from foes with whom I could not cope:
Unfit to vanquish – shall I meanly fly,
The one of all my band that would not die?
Yet there is one – to whom my memory clings,
475 Till to these eyes her own wild softness springs.
My sole resources in the path I trod
Were these – my bark – my sword – my love – my God!
The last I left in youth – he leaves me now –
And Man but works his will to lay me low.

1. In Sir Thomas More, for instance, on the scaffold, and Anne Boleyn, in the Tower, when grasping her neck, she remarked, that it 'was too slender to trouble the headsman much.' During one part of the French Revolution, it became a fashion to leave some 'mot' as a legacy; and the quantity of facetious last words spoken during that period would form a melancholy jest-book of a considerable size.

480　I have no thought to mock his throne with prayer
　　Wrung from the coward crouching of despair;
　　It is enough – I breathe – and I can bear.
　　My sword is shaken from the worthless hand
　　That might have better kept so true a brand;
485　My bark is sunk or captive – but my love –
　　For her in sooth my voice would mount above:
　　Oh! she is all that still to earth can bind –
　　And this will break a heart so more than kind,
　　And blight a form – till thine appear'd, Gulnare!
490　Mine eye ne'er ask'd if others were as fair.'

　　'Thou lov'st another then? – but what to me
　　Is this – 'tis nothing – nothing e'er can be:
　　But yet – thou lov'st – and – Oh! I envy those
　　Whose hearts on hearts as faithful can repose,
495　Who never feel the void – the wandering thought
　　That sighs o'er visions – such as mine hath wrought.'

　　'Lady – methought thy love was his, for whom
　　This arm redeem'd thee from a fiery tomb.'
　　'My love stern Seyd's! Oh – No – No – not my love –
500　Yet much this heart, that strives no more, once strove
　　To meet his passion – but it would not be.
　　I felt – I feel – love dwells with – with the free.
　　I am a slave, a favour'd slave at best,
　　To share his splendour, and seem very blest!
505　Oft must my soul the question undergo,
　　Of – 'Dost thou love?' and burn to answer, 'No!'
　　Oh! hard it is that fondness to sustain,
　　And struggle not to feel averse in vain;
　　But harder still the heart's recoil to bear,
510　And hide from one – perhaps another there.
　　He takes the hand I give not – nor withhold –
　　Its pulse nor check'd – nor quicken'd – calmly cold:
　　And when resign'd, it drops a lifeless weight
　　From one I never loved enough to hate.
515　No warmth these lips return by his imprest,
　　And chill'd remembrance shudders o'er the rest.

Yes – had I ever proved that passion's zeal,
The change to hatred were at least to feel:
But still – he goes unmourn'd – returns unsought –
520   And oft when present – absent from my thought.
Or when reflection comes – and come it must –
I fear that henceforth 'twill but bring disgust;
I am his slave – but, in despite of pride,
'Twere worse than bondage to become his bride.
525   Oh! that this dotage of his breast would cease!
Or seek another and give mine release,
But yesterday – I could have said, to peace!
Yes – if unwonted fondness now I feign,
Remember – captive! 'tis to break thy chain;
530   Repay the life that to thy hand I owe;
To give thee back to all endear'd below,
Who share such love as I can never know.
Farewell – morn breaks – and I must now away:
'Twill cost me dear – but dread no death to-day!'

XV

535   She press'd his fetter'd fingers to her heart,
And bow'd her head, and turn'd her to depart,
And noiseless as a lovely dream is gone.
And was she here? and is he now alone?
What gem hath dropp'd and sparkles o'er his chain?
540   The tear most sacred, shed for others' pain,
That starts at once – bright – pure – from Pity's mine,
Already polish'd by the hand divine!

Oh! too convincing – dangerously dear –
In woman's eye the unanswerable tear!
545   That weapon of her weakness she can wield,
To save, subdue – at once her spear and shield:
Avoid it – Virtue ebbs and Wisdom errs,
Too fondly gazing on that grief of hers!
What lost a world, and bade a hero fly?
550   The timid tear in Cleopatra's eye.
Yet be the soft triumvir's fault forgiven,
By this – how many lose not earth – but heaven!

Consign their souls to man's eternal foe,
And seal their own to spare some wanton's woe.

XVI

555 'Tis morn – and o'er his alter'd features play
The beams – without the hope of yesterday.
What shall he be ere night? perchance a thing
O'er which the raven flaps her funeral wing:
By his closed eye unheeded and unfelt,
560 While sets that sun, and dews of evening melt,
Chill – wet – and misty round each stiffen'd limb,
Refreshing earth – reviving all but him! –

Canto the Third

'Come vedi – ancor non m'abbandona.'

DANTE.

I

Slow sinks, more lovely ere his race be run,
Along Morea's hills the setting sun;
Not, as in Northern climes, obscurely bright,
But one unclouded blaze of living light!
5 O'er the hush'd deep the yellow beam he throws,
Gilds the green wave, that trembles as it glows.
On old Ægina's rock, and Idra's isle,
The god of gladness sheds his parting smile;
O'er his own regions lingering, loves to shine,
10 Though there his altars are no more divine.
Descending fast the mountain shadows kiss
Thy glorious gulf, unconquer'd Salamis!
Their azure arches through the long expanse
More deeply purpled meet his mellowing glance,
15 And tenderest tints, along their summits driven,
Mark his gay course, and own the hues of heaven;
Till, darkly shaded from the land and deep,
Behind his Delphian cliff he sinks to sleep.

On such an eve, his palest beam he cast,
20   When – Athens! here thy Wisest look'd his last.
How watch'd thy better sons his farewell ray,
That closed their murder'd sage's[1] latest day!
Not yet – not yet – Sol pauses on the hill –
The precious hour of parting lingers still;
25   But sad his light to agonising eyes,
And dark the mountain's once delightful dyes:
Gloom o'er the lovely land he seem'd to pour,
The land, where Phœbus never frown'd before;
But ere he sank below Cithæron's head,
30   The cup of woe was quaff'd – the spirit fled;
The soul of him who scorn'd to fear or fly –
Who lived and died, as none can live or die!

But lo! from high Hymettus to the plain,
The queen of night asserts her silent reign.[2]
35   No murky vapour, herald of the storm,
Hides her fair face, nor girds her glowing form;
With cornice glimmering as the moon-beams play,
There the white column greets her grateful ray,
And, bright around with quivering beams beset,
40   Her emblem sparkles o'er the minaret:
The groves of olive scatter'd dark and wide
Where meek Cephisus pours his scanty tide,
The cypress saddening by the sacred mosque,
The gleaming turret of the gay kiosk,[3]
45   And, dun and sombre 'mid the holy calm,
Near Theseus' fane yon solitary palm,

1. Socrates drank the hemlock a short time before sunset (the hour of execution), notwithstanding the entreaties of his disciples to wait till the sun went down.
2. The twilight in Greece is much shorter than in our own country: the days in winter are longer, but in summer of shorter duration.
3. The Kiosk is a Turkish summer-house: the palm is without the present walls of Athens, not far from the temple of Theseus, between which and the tree the wall intervenes. – Cephisus' stream is indeed scanty, and Ilissus has no stream at all.

All tinged with varied hues arrest the eye —
And dull were his that pass'd them heedless by.
Again the Ægean, heard no more afar,
50   Lulls his chafed breast from elemental war;
Again his waves in milder tints unfold
Their long array of sapphire and of gold,
Mix'd with the shades of many a distant isle,
That frown — where gentler ocean seems to smile.[1]

II

55   Not now my theme — why turn my thoughts to thee?
Oh! who can look along thy native sea,
Nor dwell upon thy name, whate'er the tale,
So much its magic must o'er all prevail?
Who that beheld that Sun upon thee set,
60   Fair Athens! could thine evening face forget?
Not he — whose heart nor time nor distance frees,
Spell-bound within the clustering Cyclades!
Nor seems this homage foreign to his strain,
His Corsair's isle was once thine own domain —
65   Would that with freedom it were thine again!

III

The Sun hath sunk — and, darker than the night,
Sinks with its beam upon the beacon height
Medora's heart — the third day's come and gone —
With it he comes not — sends not — faithless one!
70   The wind was fair though light; and storms were none.
Last eve Anselmo's bark return'd, and yet
His only tidings that they had not met!
Though wild, as now, far different were the tale
Had Conrad waited for that single sail.
75   The night-breeze freshens — she that day had pass'd
In watching all that Hope proclaim'd a mast;

1. The opening lines as far as section II have, perhaps, little business here, and were annexed to an unpublished (though printed) poem; but they were written on the spot in the Spring of 1811, and — I scarce know why — the reader must excuse their appearance here if he can.

Sadly she sate – on high – Impatience bore
At last her footsteps to the midnight shore,
And there she wander'd, heedless of the spray
80   That dash'd her garments oft, and warn'd away:
She saw not – felt not this – nor dared depart,
Nor deem'd it cold – her chill was at her heart;
Till grew such certainty from that suspense –
His very Sight had shock'd from life or sense!

85   It came at last – a sad and shatter'd boat,
Whose inmates first beheld whom first they sought;
Some bleeding – all most wretched – these the few –
Scarce knew they how escaped – *this* all they knew.
In silence, darkling, each appear'd to wait
90   His fellow's mournful guess at Conrad's fate:
Something they would have said; but seem'd to fear
To trust their accents to Medora's ear.
She saw at once, yet sunk not – trembled not –
Beneath that grief, that loneliness of lot,
95   Within that meek fair form, were feelings high,
That deem'd not till they found their energy.
While yet was Hope – they soften'd – flutter'd – wept –
All lost – that softness died not – but it slept;
And o'er its slumber rose that Strength which said,
100   'With nothing left to love – there's nought to dread.'
'Tis more than nature's; like the burning might
Delirium gathers from the fever's height.

'Silent you stand – nor would I hear you tell
What – speak not – breathe not – for I know it well –
105   Yet would I ask – almost my lip denies
The – quick your answer – tell me where he lies.'

'Lady! we know not – scarce with life we fled;
But here is one denies that he is dead:
He saw him bound; and bleeding – but alive.'

110   She heard no further – 'twas in vain to strive –
     So throbb'd each vein – each thought – till then withstood;
     Her own dark soul – these words at once subdued:
     She totters – falls – and senseless had the wave
     Perchance but snatch'd her from another grave;
115   But that with hands though rude, yet weeping eyes,
     They yield such aid as Pity's haste supplies:
     Dash o'er her deathlike cheek the ocean dew,
     Raise – fan – sustain – till life returns anew;
     Awake her handmaids, with the matrons leave
120   That fainting form o'er which they gaze and grieve;
     Then seek Anselmo's cavern, to report
     The tale too tedious – when the triumph short.

     IV

     In that wild council words wax'd warm and strange
     With thoughts of ransom, rescue, and revenge;
125   All, save repose or flight: still lingering there
     Breathed Conrad's spirit, and forbade despair;
     Whate'er his fate – the breasts he form'd and led
     Will save him living, or appease him dead.
     Woe to his foes! there yet survive a few,
130   Whose deeds are daring, as their hearts are true.

     V

     Within the Haram's secret chamber sate
     Stern Seyd, still pondering o'er his Captive's fate;
     His thoughts on love and hate alternate dwell,
     Now with Gulnare, and now in Conrad's cell;
135   Here at his feet the lovely slave reclined
     Surveys his brow – would soothe his gloom of mind:
     While many an anxious glance her large dark eye
     Sends in its idle search for sympathy,
     His only bends in seeming o'er his beads,[1]
140   But inly views his victim as he bleeds.

1. The comboloio, or Mahometan rosary; the beads are in number ninety-nine.

'Pacha! the day is thine; and on thy crest
Sits Triumph – Conrad taken – fall'n the rest!
His doom is fix'd – he dies: and well his fate
Was earn'd – yet much too worthless for thy hate:
145 Methinks, a short release, for ransom told
With all his treasure, not unwisely sold;
Report speaks largely of his pirate-hoard –
Would that of this my Pacha were the lord!
While baffled, weaken'd by this fatal fray –
150 Watch'd – follow'd – he were then an easier prey;
But once cut off – the remnant of his band
Embark their wealth, and seek a safer strand.'

'Gulnare! – if for each drop of blood a gem
Were offer'd rich as Stamboul's diadem;
155 If for each hair of his a massy mine
Of virgin ore should supplicating shine;
If all our Arab tales divulge or dream
Of wealth were here – that gold should not redeem!
It had not now redeem'd a single hour;
160 But that I know him fetter'd, in my power;
And, thirsting for revenge, I ponder still
On pangs that longest rack, and latest kill.'

'Nay, Seyd! – I seek not to restrain thy rage,
Too justly moved for mercy to assuage;
165 My thoughts were only to secure for thee
His riches – thus released, he were not free:
Disabled, shorn of half his might and band,
His capture could but wait thy first command.'

'His capture *could!* – and shall I then resign
170 One day to him – the wretch already mine?
Release my foe! – at whose remonstrance? – thine!
Fair suitor! – to thy virtuous gratitude,
That thus repays this Giaour's relenting mood,
Which thee and thine alone of all could spare,
175 No doubt – regardless if the prize were fair,

My thanks and praise alike are due – now hear,
I have a counsel for thy gentler ear:
I do mistrust thee, woman! and each word
Of thine stamps truth on all Suspicion heard.
180 Borne in his arms through fire from yon Serai –
Say, wert thou lingering there with him to fly?
Thou need'st not answer – thy confession speaks,
Already reddening on thy guilty cheeks;
Then, lovely dame, bethink thee! and beware:
185 'Tis not *his* life alone may claim such care!
Another word and – nay – I need no more.
Accursed was the moment when he bore
Thee from the flames, which better far – but – no –
I then had mourn'd thee with a lover's woe –
190 Now 'tis thy lord that warns – deceitful thing!
Know'st thou that I can clip thy wanton wing?
In words alone I am not wont to chafe:
Look to thyself – nor deem thy falsehood safe!'

He rose – and slowly, sternly thence withdrew,
195 Rage in his eye and threats in his adieu:
Ah! little reck'd that chief of womanhood –
Which frowns ne'er quell'd, nor menaces subdued;
And little deem'd he what thy heart, Gulnare!
When soft could feel, and when incensed could dare.
200 His doubts appear'd to wrong – nor yet she knew
How deep the root from whence compassion grew –
She was a slave – from such may captives claim
A fellow-feeling, differing but in name;
Still half unconscious – heedless of his wrath,
205 Again she ventured on the dangerous path,
Again his rage repell'd – until arose
That strife of thought, the source of woman's woes!

VI
Meanwhile – long anxious – weary – still – the same
Roll'd day and night – his soul could never tame –
210 This fearful interval of doubt and dread,
When every hour might doom him worse than dead,

When every step that echo'd by the gate
Might entering lead where axe and stake await;
When every voice that grated on his ear
215   Might be the last that he could ever hear;
Could terror tame – that spirit stern and high
Had proved unwilling as unfit to die;
'Twas worn – perhaps decay'd – yet silent bore
That conflict, deadlier far than all before:
220   The heat of fight, the hurry of the gale,
Leave scarce one thought inert enough to quail;
But bound and fix'd in fetter'd solitude,
To pine, the prey of every changing mood;
To gaze on thine own heart; and meditate
225   Irrevocable faults, and coming fate –
Too late the last to shun – the first to mend –
To count the hours that struggle to thine end,
With not a friend to animate, and tell
To other ears that death became thee well:
230   Around thee foes to forge the ready lie,
And blot life's latest scene with calumny;
Before thee tortures, which the soul can dare,
Yet doubts how well the shrinking flesh may bear;
But deeply feels a single cry would shame,
235   To valour's praise thy last and dearest claim;
The life thou leav'st below, denied above
By kind monopolists of heavenly love;
And more than doubtful paradise – thy heaven
Of earthly hope – thy loved one from thee riven.
240   Such were the thoughts that outlaw must sustain,
And govern pangs surpassing mortal pain:
And those sustain'd he – boots it well or ill?
Since not to sink beneath, is something still!

VII
The first day pass'd – he saw not her – Gulnare –
245   The second – third – and still she came not there;
But what her words avouch'd, her charms had done,
Or else he had not seen another sun.

The fourth day roll'd along, and with the night
Came storm and darkness in their mingling might:
250 Oh! how he listen'd to the rushing deep,
That ne'er till now so broke upon his sleep:
And his wild spirit wilder wishes sent,
Roused by the roar of his own element!
Oft had he ridden on that winged wave,
255 And loved its roughness for the speed it gave;
And now its dashing echo'd on his ear,
A long known voice – alas! too vainly near!
Loud sung the wind above; and, doubly loud,
Shook o'er his turret cell the thunder-cloud;
260 And flash'd the lightning by the latticed bar,
To him more genial than the midnight star:
Close to the glimmering grate he dragg'd his chain,
And hoped *that* peril might not prove in vain.
He raised his iron hand to Heaven, and pray'd
265 One pitying flash to mar the form it made:
His steel and impious prayer attract alike –
The storm roll'd onward, and disdain'd to strike;
Its peal wax'd fainter – ceased – he felt alone,
As if some faithless friend had spurn'd his groan!

VIII
270 The midnight pass'd – and to the massy door
A light step came – it paused – it moved once more;
Slow turns the grating bolt and sullen key:
'Tis as his heart foreboded – that fair she!
Whate'er her sins, to him a guardian saint,
275 And beauteous still as hermit's hope can paint;
Yet changed since last within that cell she came,
More pale her cheek, more tremulous her frame:
On him she cast her dark and hurried eye,
Which spoke before her accents – 'Thou must die!
280 Yes, thou must die – there is but one resource,
The last – the worst – if torture were not worse.'

'Lady! I look to none – my lips proclaim
What last proclaim'd they – Conrad still the same:

Why should'st thou seek an outlaw's life to spare,
285   And change the sentence I deserve to bear?
Well have I earn'd – nor here alone – the meed
Of Seyd's revenge, by many a lawless deed.'

'Why should I seek? because – Oh! didst thou not
Redeem my life from worse than slavery's lot?
290   Why should I seek? – hath misery made thee blind
To the fond workings of a woman's mind!
And must I say? albeit my heart rebel
With all that woman feels, but should not tell –
Because – despite thy crimes – that heart is moved:
295   It fear'd thee – thank'd thee – pitied – madden'd – loved.
Reply not, tell not now thy tale again,
Thou lov'st another – and I love in vain;
Though fond as mine her bosom, form more fair,
I rush through peril which she would not dare.
300   If that thy heart to hers were truly dear,
Were I thine own – thou wert not lonely here:
An outlaw's spouse – and leave her lord to roam!
What hath such gentle dame to do with home?
But speak not now – o'er thine and o'er my head
305   Hangs the keen sabre by a single thread;
If thou hast courage still, and wouldst be free,
Receive this poniard – rise – and follow me!'

'Ay – in my chains! my steps will gently tread,
With these adornments, o'er each slumbering head!
310   Thou hast forgot – is this a garb for flight?
Or is that instrument more fit for fight?'

'Misdoubting Corsair! I have gain'd the guard,
Ripe for revolt, and greedy for reward.
A single word of mine removes that chain:
315   Without some aid how here could I remain?

Well, since we met, hath sped my busy time,
If in aught evil, for thy sake the crime:
The crime – 'tis none to punish those of Seyd.
That hated tyrant, Conrad – he must bleed!
320 I see thee shudder – but my soul is changed –
Wrong'd, spurn'd, reviled – and it shall be avenged –
Accused of what till now my heart disdain'd.
Too faithful, though to bitter bondage chain'd.
Yes, smile! – but he had little cause to sneer,
325 I was not treacherous then – nor thou too dear.
But he has said it – and the jealous well,
Those tyrants, teasing, tempting to rebel,
Deserve the fate their fretting lips foretell.
I never loved – he bought me – somewhat high –
330 Since with me came a heart he could not buy.
I was a slave unmurmuring: he hath said,
But for his rescue I with thee had fled.
'Twas false thou know'st – but let such augurs rue,
Their words are omens Insult renders true.
335 Nor was thy respite granted to my prayer;
This fleeting grace was only to prepare
New torments for thy life, and my despair.
Mine too he threatens; but his dotage still
Would fain reserve me for his lordly will:
340 When wearier of these fleeting charms and me,
There yawns the sack – and yonder rolls the sea!
What, am I then a toy for dotard's play,
To wear but till the gilding frets away?
I saw thee – loved thee – owe thee all – would save,
345 If but to show how grateful is a slave.
But had he not thus menaced fame and life,
(And well he keeps his oaths pronounced in strife,)
I still had saved thee – but the Pacha spared.
Now I am all thine own – for all prepared:
350 Thou lov'st me not – nor know'st – or but the worst.
Alas! this love – that hatred are the first –
Oh! couldst thou prove my truth, thou would'st not start,
Nor fear the fire that lights an Eastern heart;

'Tis now the beacon of thy safety – now
355   It points within the port a Mainote prow:
But in one chamber, where our path must lead,
There sleeps – he must not wake – the oppressor Seyd!'

'Gulnare – Gulnare – I never felt till now
My abject fortune, wither'd fame so low:
360   Seyd is mine enemy: had swept my band
From earth with ruthless but with open hand,
And therefore came I, in my bark of war,
To smite the smiter with the scimitar;
Such is my weapon – not the secret knife –
365   Who spares a woman's seeks not slumber's life.
Thine saved gladly, Lady, not for this –
Let me not deem that mercy shown amiss.
Now fare thee well – more peace be with thy breast!
Night wears apace – my last of earthly rest!'

370   'Rest! rest! by sunrise must thy sinews shake,
And thy limbs writhe around the ready stake.
I heard the order – saw – I will not see –
If thou wilt perish, I will fall with thee.
My life – my love – my hatred – all below
375   Are on this cast – Corsair! 'tis but a blow!
Without it flight were idle – how evade
His sure pursuit? my wrongs too unrepaid,
My youth disgraced – the long, long wasted years,
One blow shall cancel with our future fears;
380   But since the dagger suits thee less than brand,
I'll try the firmness of a female hand.
The guards are gain'd – one moment all were o'er –
Corsair! we meet in safety or no more;
If errs my feeble hand, the morning cloud
385   Will hover o'er thy scaffold, and my shroud.'

IX
She turn'd, and vanish'd ere he could reply,
But his glance followed far with eager eye;
And gathering, as he could, the links that bound
His form, to curl their length, and curb their sound,

390   Since bar and bolt no more his steps preclude,
       He, fast as fetter'd limbs allow, pursued.
       'Twas dark and winding, and he knew not where
       That passage led; nor lamp nor guard were there:
       He sees a dusky glimmering – shall he seek
395   Or shun that ray so indistinct and weak?
       Chance guides his steps – a freshness seems to bear
       Full on his brow, as if from morning air –
       He reach'd an open gallery – on his eye
       Gleam'd the last star of night, the clearing sky:
400   Yet scarcely heeded these – another light
       From a lone chamber struck upon his sight.
       Towards it he moved; a scarcely closing door
       Reveal'd the ray within, but nothing more.
       With hasty step a figure outward past,
405   Then paused – and turn'd – and paused – 'tis She at last!
       No poniard in that hand – nor sign of ill –
       'Thanks to that softening heart – she could not kill!'
       Again he look'd, the wildness of her eye
       Starts from the day abrupt and fearfully.
410   She stopp'd – threw back her dark far-floating hair,
       That nearly veil'd her face and bosom fair:
       As if she late had bent her leaning head
       Above some object of her doubt or dread.
       They meet – upon her brow – unknown – forgot –
415   Her hurrying hand had left – 'twas but a spot –
       Its hue was all he saw, and scarce withstood –
       Oh! slight but certain pledge of crime – 'tis blood!

       X
       He had seen battle – he had brooded lone
       O'er promised pangs to sentenced guilt foreshown;
420   He had been tempted – chasten'd – and the chain
       Yet on his arms might ever there remain:
       But ne'er from strife – captivity – remorse –
       From all his feelings in their inmost force –
       So thrill'd – so shudder'd every creeping vein,
425   As now they froze before that purple stain.
       That spot of blood, that light but guilty streak,
       Had banish'd all the beauty from her cheek!

Blood he had view'd – could view unmoved – but then
It flow'd in combat, or was shed by men!

XI

430 ''Tis done – he nearly waked – but it is done.
Corsair! he perish'd – thou art dearly won.
All words would now be vain – away – away!
Our bark is tossing – 'tis already day.
The few gain'd over, now are wholly mine,
435 And these thy yet surviving band shall join:
Anon my voice shall vindicate my hand,
When once our sail forsakes this hated strand.'

XII

She clapp'd her hands – and through the gallery pour,
Equipp'd for flight, her vassals – Greek and Moor:
440 Silent but quick they stoop, his chains unbind;
Once more his limbs are free as mountain wind!
But on his heavy heart such sadness sate,
As if they there transferr'd that iron weight.
No words are utter'd – at her sign, a door
445 Reveals the secret passage to the shore;
The city lies behind – they speed, they reach
The glad waves dancing on the yellow beach;
And Conrad following, at her beck, obey'd,
Nor cared he now if rescued or betray'd;
450 Resistance were as useless as if Seyd
Yet lived to view the doom his ire decreed.

XIII

Embark'd, the sail unfurl'd, the light breeze blew –
How much had Conrad's memory to review!
Sunk he in Contemplation, till the cape
455 Where last he anchor'd rear'd its giant shape.
Ah! – since that fatal night, though brief the time,
Had swept an age of terror, grief, and crime.
As its far shadow frown'd above the mast,
He veil'd his face, and sorrow'd as he pass'd;

460   He thought of all – Gonsalvo and his band,
      His fleeting triumph and his failing hand;
      He thought on her afar, his lonely bride:
      He turn'd and saw – Gulnare, the homicide!

      XIV
      She watch'd his features till she could not bear
465   Their freezing aspect and averted air,
      And that strange fierceness foreign to her eye,
      Fell quench'd in tears, too late to shed or dry.
      She knelt beside him and his hand she press'd,
      'Thou may'st forgive though Allah's self detest;
470   But for that deed of darkness what wert thou?
      Reproach me – but not yet – Oh! spare me *now!*
      I am not what I seem – this fearful night
      My brain bewilder'd – do not madden quite!
      If I had never loved – though less my guilt,
475   Thou hadst not lived to – hate me – if thou wilt.'

      XV
      She wrongs his thoughts, they more himself upbraid
      Than her, though undesign'd, the wretch he made;
      But speechless all, deep, dark, and unexprest,
      They bleed within that silent cell – his breast.
480   Still onward, fair the breeze, nor rough the surge,
      The blue waves sport around the stern they urge;
      Far on the horizon's verge appears a speck,
      A spot – a mast – a sail – an armed deck!
      Their little bark her men of watch descry,
485   And ampler canvass woos the wind from high;
      She bears her down majestically near,
      Speed on her prow, and terror in her tier;
      A flash is seen – the ball beyond her bow
      Booms harmless, hissing to the deep below.
490   Up rose keen Conrad from his silent trance,
      A long, long absent gladness in his glance;
      ''Tis mine – my blood-red flag! again – again –
      I am not all deserted on the main!'

They own the signal, answer to the hail,
495   Hoist out the boat at once, and slacken sail.
''Tis Conrad! Conrad!' shouting from the deck,
Command nor duty could their transport check!
With light alacrity and gaze of pride,
They view him mount once more his vessel's side;
500   A smile relaxing in each rugged face,
Their arms can scarce forbear a rough embrace.
He, half forgetting danger and defeat,
Returns their greeting as a chief may greet,
Wrings with a cordial grasp Anselmo's hand,
505   And feels he yet can conquer and command!

XVI

These greetings o'er, the feelings that o'erflow,
Yet grieve to win him back without a blow;
They sail'd prepared for vengeance — had they known
A woman's hand secured that deed her own,
510   She were their queen — less scrupulous are they
Than haughty Conrad how they win their way.
With many an asking smile, and wondering stare,
They whisper round, and gaze upon Gulnare;
And her, at once above — beneath her sex,
515   Whom blood appall'd not, their regards perplex.
To Conrad turns her faint imploring eye,
She drops her veil, and stands in silence by;
Her arms are meekly folded on that breast,
Which — Conrad safe — to fate resign'd the rest.
520   Though worse than frenzy could that bosom fill,
Extreme in love or hate, in good or ill,
The worst of crimes had left her woman still!

XVII

This Conrad mark'd, and felt — ah! could he less? —
Hate of that deed — but grief for her distress;
525   What she has done no tears can wash away,
And Heaven must punish on its angry day:
But — it was done: he knew, whate'er her guilt,
For him that poniard smote, that blood was spilt;

And he was free! – and she for him had given
530   Her all on earth, and more than all in heaven!
And now he turn'd him to that dark'd-eyed slave
Whose brow was bow'd beneath the glance he gave,
Who now seem'd changed and humbled: – faint and meek,
But varying oft the colour of her cheek
535   To deeper shades of paleness – all its red
That fearful spot which stain'd it from the dead!
He took that hand – it trembled – now too late –
So soft in love – so wildly nerved in hate;
He clasp'd that hand – it trembled – and his own
540   Had lost its firmness, and his voice its tone.
'Gulnare!' – but she replied not – 'dear Gulnare!'
She raised her eye – her only answer there –
At once she sought and sunk in his embrace:
If he had driven her from that resting-place,
545   His had been more or less than mortal heart,
But – good or ill – it bade her not depart.
Perchance, but for the bodings of his breast,
His latest virtue then had join'd the rest.
Yet even Medora might forgive the kiss
550   That ask'd from form so fair no more than this,
The first, the last that Frailty stole from Faith –
To lips where Love had lavish'd all his breath,
To lips – whose broken sighs such fragrance fling,
As he had fann'd them freshly with his wing!

XVIII

555   They gain by twilight's hour their lonely isle.
To them the very rocks appear to smile;
The haven hums with many a cheering sound,
The beacons blaze their wonted stations round,
The boats are darting o'er the curly bay,
560   And sportive dolphins bend them through the spray;
Even the hoarse sea-bird's shrill, discordant shriek,
Greets like the welcome of his tuneless beak!
Beneath each lamp that through its lattice gleams,
Their fancy paints the friends that trim the beams.
565   Oh! what can sanctify the joys of home,
Like Hope's gay glance from Ocean's troubled foam?

XIX

The lights are high on beacon and from bower,
And 'midst them Conrad seeks Medora's tower:
He looks in vain – 'tis strange – and all remark,
570   Amid so many, hers alone is dark.
'Tis strange – of yore its welcome never fail'd,
Nor now, perchance, extinguish'd, only veil'd.
With the first boat descends he for the shore,
And looks impatient on the lingering oar.
575   Oh! for a wing beyond the falcon's flight,
To bear him like an arrow to that height!
With the first pause the resting rowers gave,
He waits not – looks not – leaps into the wave,
Strives through the surge, bestrides the beach, and high
580   Ascends the path familiar to his eye.

He reach'd his turret door – he paused – no sound
Broke from within; and all was night around.
He knock'd, and loudly – footstep nor reply
Announced that any heard or deem'd him nigh;
585   He knock'd – but faintly – for his trembling hand
Refused to aid his heavy heart's demand.
The portal opens – 'tis a well known face –
But not the form he panted to embrace.
Its lips are silent – twice his own essay'd,
590   And fail'd to frame the question they delay'd;
He snatch'd the lamp – its light will answer all –
It quits his grasp, expiring in the fall.
He would not wait for that reviving ray –
As soon could he have linger'd there for day;
595   But, glimmering through the dusky corridore,
Another chequers o'er the shadow'd floor;
His steps the chamber gain – his eyes behold
All that his heart believed not – yet foretold!

XX

He turn'd not – spoke not – sunk not – fix'd his look,
600   And set the anxious frame that lately shook:

He gazed – how long we gaze despite of pain,
And know, but dare not own, we gaze in vain!
In life itself she was so still and fair,
That death with gentler aspect wither'd there;
605   And the cold flowers[1] her colder hand contain'd,
In that last grasp as tenderly were strain'd
As if she scarcely felt, but feign'd a sleep,
And made it almost mockery yet to weep:
The long dark lashes fringed her lids of snow,
610   And veil'd – thought shrinks from all that lurk'd below –
Oh! o'er the eye Death most exerts his might,
And hurls the spirit from her throne of light!
Sinks those blue orbs in that long last eclipse,
But spares, as yet, the charm around her lips –
615   Yet, yet they seem as they forbore to smile,
And wish'd repose – but only for a while;
But the white shroud, and each extended tress,
Long – fair – but spread in utter lifelessness,
Which, late the sport of every summer wind,
620   Escaped the baffled wreath that strove to bind;
These – and the pale pure cheek, became the bier –
But she is nothing – wherefore is he here?

XXI
He ask'd no question – all were answer'd now
By the first glance on that still – marble brow.
625   It was enough – she died – what reck'd it how?
The love of youth, the hope of better years,
The source of softest wishes, tenderest fears,
The only living thing he could not hate,
Was reft at once – and he deserved his fate,
630   But did not feel it less; – the good explore,
For peace, those realms where guilt can never soar:
The proud – the wayward – who have fix'd below
Their joy, and find this earth enough for woe,

1. In the Levant it is the custom to strew flowers on the bodies of the dead, and in the hands of young persons to place a nosegay.

Lose in that one their all – perchance a mite –
635 But who in patience parts with all delight?
Full many a stoic eye and aspect stern
Mask hearts where grief hath little left to learn;
And many a withering thought lies hid, not lost,
In smiles that least befit who wear them most.

XXII

640 By those, that deepest feel, is ill exprest
The indistinctness of the suffering breast;
Where thousand thoughts begin to end in one,
Which seeks from all the refuge found in none;
No words suffice the secret soul to show,
645 For Truth denies all eloquence to Woe.
On Conrad's stricken soul exhaustion prest,
And stupor almost lull'd it into rest;
So feeble now – his mother's softness crept
To those wild eyes, which like an infant's wept:
650 It was the very weakness of his brain,
Which thus confess'd without relieving pain
None saw his trickling tears – perchance, if seen,
That useless flood of grief had never been:
Nor long they flow'd – he dried them to depart,
655 In helpless – hopeless – brokenness of heart:
The sun goes forth – but Conrad's day is dim;
And the night cometh – ne'er to pass from him.
There is no darkness like the cloud of mind,
On Grief's vain eye – the blindest of the blind!
660 Which may not – dare not see – but turns aside
To blackest shade – nor will endure a guide!

XXIII

His heart was form'd for softness – warp'd to wrong;
Betray'd too early, and beguiled too long;
Each feeling pure – as falls the dropping dew
665 Within the grot; like that had harden'd too;
Less clear, perchance, its earthly trials pass'd,
But sunk, and chill'd, and petrified at last.

Yet tempests wear, and lightning cleaves the rock,
If such his heart, so shatter'd it the shock.
670 There grew one flower beneath its rugged brow,
Though dark the shade – it shelter'd – saved till now.
The thunder came – that bolt hath blasted both,
The Granite's firmness, and the Lily's growth:
The gentle plant hath left no leaf to tell
675 Its tale, but shrunk and wither'd where it fell;
And of its cold protector, blacken round
But shiver'd fragments on the barren ground!

XXIV
'Tis morn – to venture on his lonely hour
Few dare; though now Anselmo sought his tower.
680 He was not there – nor seen along the shore;
Ere night, alarm'd, their isle is traversed o'er:
Another morn – another bids them seek,
And shout his name till echo waxeth weak;
Mount – grotto – cavern – valley search'd in vain,
685 They find on shore a sea-boat's broken chain:
Their hope revives – they follow o'er the main.
'Tis idle all – moons roll on moons away,
And Conrad comes not – came not since that day:
Nor trace, nor tidings of his doom declare
690 Where lives his grief, or perished his despair!
Long mourn'd his band whom none could mourn beside;
And fair the monument they gave his bride:
For him they raise not the recording stone –
His death yet dubious, deeds too widely known;
695 He left a Corsair's name to other times,
Link'd with one virtue, and a thousand crimes.[1]

1. That the point of honour which is represented in one instance of Conrad's
character has not been carried beyond the bounds of probability, may
perhaps be in some degree confirmed by the following anecdote of a brother
buccaneer in the year 1814: – 'Our readers have all seen the account of the
enterprise against the pirates of Barrataria; but few, we believe, were in-
formed of the situation, history, or nature of that establishment. For the
information of such as were unacquainted with it, we have procured from a
friend the following interesting narrative of the main facts, of which he has

personal knowledge, and which cannot fail to interest some of our readers: –
Barrataria is a bay, or a narrow arm, of the Gulf of Mexico; it runs through
a rich but very flat country, until it reaches within a mile of the Mississippi
river, fifteen miles below the city of New Orleans. The bay has branches
almost innumerable, in which persons can lie concealed from the severest
scrutiny. It communicates with three lakes which lie on the south-west side,
and these, with the lake of the same name, and which lies contiguous to the
sea, where there is an island formed by the two arms of this lake and the sea.
The east and west points of this island were fortified, in the year 1811, by a
band of pirates, under the command of one Monsieur La Fitte. A large
majority of these outlaws are of that class of the population of the state of
Louisiana who fled from the island of St Domingo during the troubles
there, and took refuge in the island of Cuba; and when the last war between
France and Spain commenced, they were compelled to leave that island
with the short notice of a few days. Without ceremony they entered the
United States, the most of them the state of Louisiana, with all the negroes
they had possessed in Cuba. They were notified by the Governor of that
State of the clause in the constitution which forbade the importation of
slaves; but, at the same time, received the assurance of the Governor that he
would obtain, if possible, the approbation of the General Government for
their retaining this property. – The island of Barrataria is situated about lat.
29 deg. 15 min., lon. 92.30.; and is as remarkable for its health as for the
superior scale and shell fish with which its waters abound. The chief of this
horde, like Charles de Moor, had, mixed with his many vices, some virtues.
In the year 1813, this party had, from its turpitude and boldness, claimed
the attention of the Governor of Louisiana; and to break up the establish-
ment he thought proper to strike at the head. He therefore offered a reward
of 500 dollars for the head of Monsieur La Fitte, who was well known to the
inhabitants of the city of New Orleans, from his immediate connexion, and
his once having been a fencing-master in that city of great reputation, which
art he learnt in Buonaparte's army, where he was a captain. The reward
which was offered by the Governor for the head of La Fitte was answered
by the offer of a reward from the latter of 15,000 for the head of the
Governor. The Governor ordered out a company to march from the city to
La Fitte's island, and to burn and destroy all the property, and to bring to
the city of New Orleans all his banditti. This company, under the command
of a man who had been the intimate associate of this bold Captain, ap-
proached very near to the fortified island, before he saw a man, or heard a
sound, until he heard a whistle, not unlike a boatswain's call. Then it was he
found himself surrounded by armed men who had emerged from the secret
avenues which led into Bayou. Here it was that the modern Charles de
Moor developed his few noble traits; for to this man, who had come to
destroy his life and all that was dear to him, he not only spared his life, but
offered him that which would have made the honest soldier easy for the
remainder of his days; which was indignantly refused. He then, with the
approbation of his captor, returned to the city. This circumstance, and
some concomitant events, proved that this band of pirates was not to be
taken by land. Our naval force having always been small in that quarter,

exertions for the destruction of this illicit establishment could not be expected from them until augmented; for an officer of the navy, with most of the gun-boats on that station, had to retreat from an overwhelming force of La Fitte's. So soon as the augmentation of the navy authorized an attack, one was made; the overthrow of this banditti has been the result; and now this almost invulnerable point and key to New Orleans is clear of an enemy, it is to be hoped the government will hold it by a strong military force.' – *American Newspaper*.

In Noble's continuation of 'Granger's Biographical History' there is a singular passage in his account of Archbishop Blackbourne; and as in some measure connected with the profession of the hero of the foregoing poem, I cannot resist the temptation of extracting it. – 'There is something mysterious in the history and character of Dr Blackbourne. The former is but imperfectly known; and report has even asserted he was a buccaneer; and that one of his brethren in that profession having asked, on his arrival in England, what had become of his old chum, Blackbourne, was answered, he is Archbishop of York. We are informed that Blackbourne was installed sub-dean of Exeter in 1694, which office he resigned in 1702; but after his successor Lewis Barnet's death, in 1704, he regained it. In the following year he became dean; and in 1714 held with it the archdeaconry of Cornwall. He was consecrated bishop of Exeter, February 24, 1716; and translated to York, November 28, 1724, as a reward, according to court scandal, for uniting George I. to the Duchess of Munster. This, however, appears to have been an unfounded calumny. As archbishop he behaved with great prudence, and was equally respectable as the guardian of the revenues of the see. Rumour whispered he retained the vices of his youth, and that a passion for the fair sex formed an item in the list of his weaknesses; but so far from being convicted by seventy witnesses, he does not appear to have been directly criminated by one. In short, I look upon these aspersions as the effects of mere malice. How is it possible a buccaneer should have been so good a scholar as Blackbourne certainly was? He who had so perfect a knowledge of the classics (particularly of the Greek tragedians), as to be able to read them with the same ease as he could Shakespeare, must have taken great pains to acquire the learned languages; and have had both leisure and good masters. But he was undoubtedly educated at Christ-church College, Oxford. He is allowed to have been a pleasant man; this, however, was turned against him, by its being said, "he gained more hearts than souls."'

Ode to Napoleon Buonaparte

'Expende Annibalem: – quot libras in duce summo Invenles!'

JUVENAL, *Sat.* X.

'The Emperor Nepos was acknowledged by the Senate, by the Italians, and by the Provincials of Gaul; his moral virtues, and military talents, were loudly celebrated; and those who derived any private benefit from his government announced in prophetic strains the restoration of public felicity.

*　　*　　*　　*　　*　　*　　*

*　　*　　*　　*　　*　　*　　*

By this shameful abdication, he protracted his life a few years, in a very ambiguous state, between an Emperor and an Exile, till —'

GIBBON's *Decline and Fall*, vol. vi. p. 220.

I

'Tis done – but yesterday a King!
　　And arm'd with Kings to strive –
And now thou art a nameless thing:
　　So abject – yet alive!
5　Is this the man of thousand thrones,
Who strew'd our earth with hostile bones,
　　And can he thus survive?
Since he, miscall'd the Morning Star,
Nor man nor fiend hath fallen so far.

II

10　Ill-minded man! why scourge thy kind
　　Who bow'd so low the knee?
By gazing on thyself grown blind,
　　Thou taught'st the rest to see.
With might unquestion'd, – power to save, –
15　Thine only gift hath been the grave
　　To those that worshipp'd thee;

Nor till thy fall could mortals guess
Ambition's less than littleness!

III

Thanks for that lesson – it will teach
20   To after-warriors more
Than high Philosophy can preach,
         And vainly preach'd before.
That spell upon the minds of men
Breaks never to unite again,
25   That led them to adore
Those Pagod things of sabre sway,
With fronts of brass, and feet of clay.

IV

The triumph, and the vanity,
         The rapture of the strife[1] –
30 The earthquake voice of Victory,
         To thee the breath of life;
The sword, the sceptre, and that sway
Which man seem'd made but to obey,
         Wherewith renown was rife –
35 All quell'd! – Dark Spirit! what must be
The madness of thy memory!

V

The Desolator desolate!
         The Victor overthrown!
The Arbiter of others' fate
40   A Suppliant for his own!
Is it some yet imperial hope
That with such change can calmly cope?
         Or dread of death alone?
To die a prince – or live a slave –
45 Thy choice is most ignobly brave!

1. 'Certaminis *gaudia*' – the expression of Attila in his harangue to his army, previous to the battle of Chalons, given in Cassiodorus.

VI

He who of old would rend the oak,
   Dream'd not of the rebound;
Chain'd by the trunk he vainly broke –
   Alone – how look'd he round?
50 Thou in the sternness of thy strength
An equal deed hast done at length,
   And darker fate hast found:
He fell, the forest prowlers' prey;
But thou must eat thy heart away!

VII

55 The Roman,[1] when his burning heart
   Was slaked with blood of Rome,
Threw down the dagger – dared depart,
   In savage grandeur, home. –
He dared depart in utter scorn
60 Of men that such a yoke had borne,
   Yet left him such a doom!
His only glory was that hour
Of self-upheld abandon'd power.

VIII

The Spaniard, when the lust of sway
65   Had lost its quickening spell,
Cast crowns for rosaries away,
   An empire for a cell;
A strict accountant of his beads,
A subtle disputant on creeds,
70   His dotage trifled well:
Yet better had he neither known
A bigot's shrine, nor despot's throne.

IX

But thou – from thy reluctant hand
   The thunderbolt is wrung –
75 Too late thou leav'st the high command
   To which thy weakness clung;

1. Sylla.

All Evil Spirit as thou art,
It is enough to grieve the heart
    To see thine own unstrung;
80 To think that God's fair world hath been
The footstool of a thing so mean;

X

And Earth hath spilt her blood for him,
    Who thus can hoard his own!
And Monarchs bow'd the trembling limb,
85   And thank'd him for a throne!
Fair Freedom! we may hold thee dear,
When thus thy mightiest foes their fear
    In humblest guise have shown.
Oh! ne'er may tyrant leave behind
90 A brighter name to lure mankind!

XI

Thine evil deeds are writ in gore,
    Nor written thus in vain —
Thy triumphs tell of fame no more,
    Or deepen every stain:
95 If thou hadst died as honour dies,
Some new Napoleon might arise,
    To shame the world again —
But who would soar the solar height,
To set in such a starless night?

XII

100 Weigh'd in the balance, here dust
    Is vile as vulgar clay;
Thy scales, Mortality! are just
    To all that pass away:
But yet methought the living great
105 Some higher sparks should animate,
    To dazzle and dismay:
Nor deem'd Contempt could thus make mirth
Of these, the Conquerors of the earth.

XIII

And she, proud Austria's mournful flower,
110   Thy still imperial bride;
How bears her breast the torturing hour?
     Still clings she to thy side?
Must she too bend, must she too share
Thy late repentance, long despair,
115   Thou throneless Homicide?
If still she loves thee, hoard that gem,
'Tis worth thy vanish'd diadem!

XIV

Then haste thee to thy sullen Isle,
     And gaze upon the sea;
120 That element may meet thy smile –
     It ne'er was ruled by thee!
Or trace with thine all idle hand
In loitering mood upon the sand
     That Earth is now as free!
125 That Corinth's pedagogue hath now
Transferr'd his by-word to thy brow.

XV

Thou Timour! in his captive's cage[1]
     What thoughts will there be thine,
While brooding in thy prison'd rage?
130   But one – 'The world *was* mine!'
Unless, like he of Babylon,
All sense is with thy sceptre gone,
     Life will not long confine
That spirit pour'd so widely forth –
135 So long obey'd – so little worth!

XVI

Or, like the thief of fire from heaven,[2]
     Wilt thou withstand the shock?
And share with him, the unforgiven,
     His vulture and his rock!

1. The cage of Bajazet, by order of Tamerlane.
2. Prometheus.

140 Foredoom'd by God – by man accurst,
    And that last act, though not thy worst,
        The very Fiend's arch mock;[1]
    He in his fall preserved his pride,
    And, if a mortal, had as proudly died!

    XVII
145 There was a day – there was an hour,
        While earth was Gaul's – Gaul thine –
    When that immeasurable power
        Unsated to resign
    Had been an act of purer fame
150 Than gathers round Marengo's name
        And gilded thy decline,
    Through the long twilight of all time,
    Despite some passing clouds of crime.

    XVIII
    But thou forsooth must be a king,
155   And don the purple vest, –
    As if that foolish robe could wring
        Remembrance from thy breast.
    Where is that faded garment? where
    The gewgaws thou wert fond to wear,
160   The star – the string – the crest?
    Vain froward child of empire! say,
    Are all thy playthings snatch'd away?

    XIX
    Where may the wearied eye repose
        When gazing on the Great;
165 Where neither guilty glory glows,
        Nor despicable state?

1.   —'The very fiend's arch mock –
      To lip a wanton, and suppose her chaste.' – SHAKSPEARE.

Yes – one – the first – the last – the best –
The Cincinnatus of the West,
   Whom envy dared not hate,
170   Bequeath'd the name of Washington,
To make man blush there was but one!

Stanzas for Music

I speak not, I trace not, I breathe not thy name,
There is grief in the sound, there is guilt in the fame:
But the tear which now burns on my cheek may impart
The deep thoughts that dwell in that silence of heart.

5   Too brief for our passion, too long for our peace
Were those hours – can their joy or their bitterness cease?
We repent – we abjure – we will break from our chain, –
We will part, – we will fly to – unite it again!

Oh! thine be the gladness, and mine be the guilt!
10   Forgive me, adored one! – forsake, if thou wilt; –
But the heart which is thine shall expire undebased,
And *man* shall not break it – whatever *thou* mayst.

And stern to the haughty, but humble to thee,
This soul, in its bitterest blackness, shall be;
15   And our days seem as swift, and our moments more sweet,
With thee by my side, than with worlds at our feet.

One sigh of thy sorrow, one look of thy love,
Shall turn me or fix, shall reward or reprove;
And the heartless may wonder at all I resign –
20   Thy lip shall reply, not to them, but to *mine*.

                      May, 1814.

She walks in beauty

I
She walks in beauty, like the night
 Of cloudless climes and starry skies;
And all that's best of dark and bright
 Meet in her aspect and her eyes:
5 Thus mellow'd to that tender light
 Which heaven to gaudy day denies.

II
One shade the more, one ray the less,
 Had half impair'd the nameless grace
Which waves in every raven tress,
10 Or softly lightens o'er her face;
Where thoughts serenely sweet express
 How pure, how dear their dwelling-place.

III
And on that cheek, and o'er that brow,
 So soft, so calm, yet eloquent,
15 The smiles that win, the tints that glow,
 But tell of days in goodness spent,
A mind at peace with all below,
 A heart whose love is innocent!

LARA

A Tale

Canto the First

I

The Serfs[1] are glad through Lara's wide domain,
And Slavery half forgets her feudal chain;
He, their unhoped, but unforgotten lord,
The long self-exiled chieftain, is restored:
5   There be bright faces in the busy hall,
Bowls on the board, and banners on the wall;
Far checkering o'er the pictured window, plays
The unwonted faggots' hospitable blaze;
And gay retainers gather round the hearth,
10   With tongues all loudness, and with eyes all mirth.

II

The chief of Lara is return'd again:
And why had Lara cross'd the bounding main?
Left by his sire, too young such loss to know,
Lord of himself; – that heritage of woe,
15   That fearful empire which the human breast
But holds to rob the heart within of rest! –
With none to check, and few to point in time
The thousand paths that slope the way to crime;
Then, when he most required commandment, then
20   Had Lara's daring boyhood govern'd men.
It skills not, boots not step by step to trace
His youth through all the mazes of its race;

1. The reader is apprised, that the name of Lara being Spanish, and no
circumstance of local and natural description fixing the scene or hero of the
poem to any country or age, the word 'Serf,' which could not be correctly
applied to the lower classes in Spain, who were never vassals of the soil, has
nevertheless been employed to designate the followers of our fictitious
chieftain.

Short was the course his restlessness had run,
But long enough to leave him half undone.

III

25   And Lara left in youth his father-land;
But from the hour he waved his parting hand
Each trace wax'd fainter of his course, till all
Had nearly ceased his memory to recall.
His sire was dust, his vassals could declare,
30   'Twas all they knew, that Lara was not there;
Nor sent, nor came he, till conjecture grew
Cold in the many, anxious in the few.
His hall scarce echoes with his wonted name,
His portrait darkens in its fading frame,
35   Another chief consoled his destined bride,
The young forgot him, and the old had died;
'Yet doth he live!' exclaims the impatient heir,
And sighs for sables which he must not wear.
A hundred scutcheons deck with gloomy grace
40   The Laras' last and longest dwelling-place;
But one is absent from the mouldering file,
That now were welcome in that Gothic pile.

IV

He comes at last in sudden loneliness,
And whence they know not, why they need not guess;
45   They more might marvel, when the greeting's o'er,
Not that he came, but came not long before:
No train is his beyond a single page,
Of foreign aspect, and of tender age.
Years had roll'd on, and fast they speed away
50   To those that wander as to those that stay;
But lack of tidings from another clime
Had lent a flagging wing to weary Time.
They see, they recognise, yet almost deem
The present dubious, or the past a dream.

55   He lives, nor yet is past his manhood's prime,
       Though sear'd by toil, and something touch'd by time;
       His faults, whate'er they were, if scarce forgot,
       Might be untaught him by his varied lot;
       Nor good nor ill of late were known, his name
60   Might yet uphold his patrimonial fame:
       His soul in youth was haughty, but his sins
       No more than pleasure from the stripling wins;
       And such, if not yet harden'd in their course,
       Might be redeem'd, nor ask a long remorse.

       V

65   And they indeed were changed – 'tis quickly seen,
       Whate'er he be, 'twas not what he had been:
       That brow in furrow'd lines had fix'd at last,
       And spake of passions, but of passion past:
       The pride, but not the fire, of early days,
70   Coldness of mien, and carelessness of praise;
       A high demeanour, and a glance that took
       Their thoughts from others by a single look;
       And that sarcastic levity of tongue,
       The stinging of a heart the world hath stung,
75   That darts in seeming playfulness around,
       And makes those feel that will not own the wound;
       All these seem'd his, and something more beneath
       Than glance could well reveal, or accent breathe.
       Ambition, glory, love, the common aim,
80   That some can conquer, and that all would claim,
       Within his breast appear'd no more to strive,
       Yet seem'd as lately they had been alive;
       And some deep feeling it were vain to trace
       At moments lighten'd o'er his livid face.

       VI

85   Not much he loved long question of the past,
       Nor told of wondrous wilds, and deserts vast,
       In those far lands where he had wander'd lone,
       And – as himself would have it seem – unknown:

Yet these in vain his eye could scarcely scan,
90 Nor glean experience from his fellow man;
But what he had beheld he shunn'd to show,
As hardly worth a stranger's care to know;
If still more prying such enquiry grew,
His brow fell darker, and his words more few.

VII

95 Not unrejoiced to see him once again,
Warm was his welcome to the haunts of men;
Born of high lineage, link'd in high command,
He mingled with the Magnates of his land;
Join'd the carousals of the great and gay,
100 And saw them smile or sigh their hours away;
But still he only saw, and did not share,
The common pleasure or the general care;
He did not follow what they all pursued
With hope still baffled still to be renew'd;
105 Nor shadowy honour, nor substantial gain,
Nor beauty's preference, and the rival's pain:
Around him some mysterious circle thrown
Repell'd approach, and show'd him still alone;
Upon his eye sat something of reproof
110 That kept at least frivolity aloof;
And things more timid that beheld him near,
In silence gazed, or whisper'd mutual fear;
And they the wiser, friendlier few confess'd
They deem'd him better than his air express'd.

VIII

115 'Twas strange – in youth all action and all life,
Burning for pleasure, not averse from strife;
Woman – the field – the ocean – all that gave
Promise of gladness, peril of a grave,
In turn he tried – he ransack'd all below,
120 And found his recompense in joy or woe,
No tame, trite medium; for his feelings sought
In that intenseness an escape from thought:

The tempest of his heart in scorn had gazed
On that the feebler elements hath raised;
125   The rapture of his heart had look'd on high,
And ask'd if greater dwelt beyond the sky:
Chain'd to excess, the slave of each extreme,
How woke he from the wildness of that dream?
Alas! he told not – but he did awake
130   To curse the wither'd heart that would not break.

IX

Books, for his volume heretofore was Man,
With eye more curious he appear'd to scan,
And oft, in sudden mood, for many a day,
From all communion he would start away:
135   And then, his rarely call'd attendants said,
Through night's long hours would sound his hurried tread
O'er the dark gallery, where his fathers frown'd
In rude but antique portraiture around:
They heard, but whisper'd – 'that must not be known –
140   The sound of words less earthly than his own.
Yes, they who chose might smile, but some had seen
They scarce knew what, but more than should have been
Why gazed he so upon the ghastly head
Which hands profane had gather'd from the dead,
145   That still beside his open'd volume lay,
As if to startle all save him away?
Why slept he not when others were at rest?
Why heard no music, and received no guest?
All was not well, they deem'd – but where the wrong?
150   Some knew perchance – but 'twere a tale too long;
And such besides were too discreetly wise,
To more than hint their knowledge in surmise;
But if they would – they could' – around the board,
Thus Lara's vassals prattled of their lord.

X

155 It was the night – and Lara's glassy stream
The stars are studding, each with imaged beam;
So calm, the waters scarcely seem to stray,
And yet they glide like happiness away;
Reflecting far and fairy-like from high
160 The immortal lights that live along the sky:
Its banks are fringed with many a goodly tree,
And flowers the fairest that may feast the bee;
Such in her chaplet infant Dian wove,
And Innocence would offer to her love.
165 These deck the shore; the waves their channel make
In windings bright and mazy like the snake.
All was so still, so soft in earth and air,
You scarce would start to meet a spirit there;
Secure that nought of evil could delight
170 To walk in such a scene, on such a night!
It was a moment only for the good:
So Lara deem'd, nor longer there he stood,
But turn'd in silence to his castle-gate;
Such scene his soul no more could contemplate:
175 Such scene reminded him of other days,
Of skies more cloudless, moons of purer blaze,
Of nights more soft and frequent, hearts that now –
No – no – the storm may beat upon his brow,
Unfelt – unsparing – but a night like this,
180 A night of beauty, mock'd such breast as his.

XI

He turn'd within his solitary hall,
And his high shadow shot along the wall:
There were the painted forms of other times,
'Twas all they left of virtues or of crimes,
185 Save vague tradition; and the gloomy vaults
That hid their dust, their foibles, and their faults;
And half a column of the pompous page,
That speeds the specious tale from age to age;
Where history's pen its praise or blame supplies,
190 And lies like truth, and still most truly lies.

He wandering mused, and as the moonbeam shone
Through the dim lattice o'er the floor of stone,
And the high fretted roof, and saints, that there
O'er Gothic windows knelt in pictured prayer,
195 Reflected in fantastic figures grew,
Like life, but not like mortal life, to view;
His bristling locks of sable, brow of gloom,
And the wide waving of his shaken plume,
Glanced like a spectre's attributes, and gave
200 His aspect all that terror gives the grave.

XII

'Twas midnight – all was slumber; the lone light
Dimm'd in the lamp, as loth to break the night.
Hark! there be murmurs heard in Lara's hall –
A sound – a voice – a shriek – a fearful call!
205 A long, loud shriek – and silence – did they hear
That frantic echo burst the sleeping ear?
They heard and rose, and, tremulously brave,
Rush where the sound invoked their aid to save;
They come with half-lit tapers in their hands,
210 And snatch'd in startled haste unbelted brands.

XIII

Cold as the marble where his length was laid,
Pale as the beam that o'er his features play'd,
Was Lara stretch'd; his half drawn sabre near,
Dropp'd it should seem in more than nature's fear;
215 Yet he was firm, or had been firm till now,
And still defiance knit his gather'd brow;
Though mix'd with terror, senseless as he lay,
There lived upon his lip the wish to slay;
Some half form'd threat in utterance there had died,
220 Some imprecation of despairing pride;
His eye was almost seal'd, but not forsook
Even in its trance the gladiator's look,
That oft awake his aspect could disclose,
And now was fix'd in horrible repose.

225　They raise him – bear him; – hush! he breathes, he speaks,
　　　The swarthy blush recolours in his cheeks,
　　　His lip resumes its red, his eye, though dim,
　　　Rolls wide and wild, each slowly quivering limb
　　　Recalls its function, but his words are strung
230　In terms that seem not of his native tongue;
　　　Distinct but strange, enough they understand
　　　To deem them accents of another land;
　　　And such they were, and meant to meet an ear
　　　That hears him not – alas! that cannot hear!

XIV

235　His page approach'd, and he alone appear'd
　　　To know the import of the words they heard;
　　　And, by the changes of his cheek and brow,
　　　They were not such as Lara should avow,
　　　Nor he interpret, – yet with less surprise
240　Than those around their chieftain's state he eyes,
　　　But Lara's prostrate form he bent beside,
　　　And in that tongue which seem'd his own replied,
　　　And Lara heeds those tones that gently seem
　　　To soothe away the horrors of his dream –
245　If dream it were, that thus could overthrow
　　　A breast that needed not ideal woe.

XV

　　　Whate'er his frenzy dream'd or eye beheld,
　　　If yet remember'd ne'er to be reveal'd,
　　　Rests at his heart: the custom'd morning came,
250　And breathed new vigour in his shaken frame;
　　　And solace sought he none from priest nor leech,
　　　And soon the same in movement and in speech
　　　As heretofore he fill'd the passing hours, –
　　　Nor less he smiles, nor more his forehead lowers,
255　Than these were wont; and if the coming night
　　　Appear'd less welcome now to Lara's sight,
　　　He to his marvelling vassals show'd it not,
　　　Whose shuddering proved *their* fear was less forgot.

In trembling pairs (alone they dared not) crawl
260   The astonish'd slaves, and shun the fated hall;
The waving banner, and the clapping door,
The rustling tapestry, and the echoing floor;
The long dim shadows of surrounding trees,
The flapping bat, the night song of the breeze;
265   Aught they behold or hear their thought appals,
As evening saddens o'er the dark grey walls.

XVI

Vain thought! that hour of ne'er unravell'd gloom
Came not again, or Lara could assume
A seeming of forgetfulness, that made
270   His vassals more amazed nor less afraid –
Had memory vanish'd then with sense restored?
Since word, nor look, nor gesture of their lord
Betray'd a feeling that recall'd to these
That fever'd moment of his mind's disease.
275   Was it a dream? was his the voice that spoke
Those strange wild accents; his the cry that broke
Their slumber? his the oppress'd, o'erlabour'd heart
That ceased to beat, the look that made them start?
Could he who thus had suffer'd so forget,
280   When such as saw that suffering shudder yet?
Or did that silence prove his memory fix'd
Too deep for words, indelible, unmix'd
In that corroding secrecy which gnaws
The heart to show the effect, but not the cause?
285   Not so in him; his breast had buried both,
Nor common gazers could discern the growth
Of thoughts that mortal lips must leave half told;
They choke the feeble words that would unfold.

XVII

In him inexplicably mix'd appear'd
290   Much to be loved and hated, sought and fear'd;
Opinion varying o'er his hidden lot,
In praise or railing ne'er his name forgot:

His silence form'd a theme for others' prate –
They guess'd – they gazed – they fain would know his fate.
295 What had he been? what was he, thus unknown,
Who walk'd their world, his lineage only known?
A hater of his kind? yet some would say,
With them he could seem gay amidst the gay;
But own'd that smile, if oft observed and near,
300 Waned in its mirth, and wither'd to a sneer;
That smile might reach his lip, but pass'd not by,
None e'er could trace its laughter to his eye:
Yet there was softness too in his regard,
At times, a heart as not by nature hard,
305 But once perceived, his spirit seem'd to chide
Such weakness, as unworthy of its pride,
And steel'd itself, as scorning to redeem
One doubt from others' half withheld esteem;
In self-inflicted penance of a breast
310 Which tenderness might once have wrung from rest;
In vigilance of grief that would compel
The soul to hate for having loved too well.

XVIII

There was in him a vital scorn of all:
As if the worst had fall'n which could befall,
315 He stood a stranger in this breathing world,
An erring spirit from another hurl'd;
A thing of dark imaginings, that shaped
By choice the perils he by chance escaped;
But 'scaped in vain, for in their memory yet
320 His mind would half exult and half regret:
With more capacity for love than earth
Bestows on most of mortal mould and birth,
His early dreams of good outstripp'd the truth,
And troubled manhood follow'd baffled youth;
325 With thought of years in phantom chase misspent,
And wasted powers for better purpose lent;
And fiery passions that had pour'd their wrath
In hurried desolation o'er his path,

And left the better feelings all at strife
330   In wild reflection o'er his stormy life;
But haughty still, and loth himself to blame,
He call'd on Nature's self to share the shame,
And charged all faults upon the fleshly form
She gave to clog the soul, and feast the worm;
335   Till he at last confounded good and ill,
And half mistook for fate the acts of will:
Too high for common selfishness, he could
At times resign his own for others' good,
But not in pity, not because he ought,
340   But in some strange perversity of thought,
That sway'd him onward with a secret pride
To do what few or none would do beside;
And this same impulse would, in tempting time,
Mislead his spirit equally to crime;
345   So much he soar'd beyond, or sunk beneath,
The men with whom he felt condemn'd to breathe,
And long'd by good or ill to separate
Himself from all who shared his mortal state;
His mind abhorring this had fix'd her throne
350   Far from the world, in regions of her own:
Thus coldly passing all that pass'd below,
His blood in temperate seeming now would flow:
Ah! happier if it ne'er with guilt had glow'd,
But ever in that icy smoothness flow'd!
355   'Tis true, with other men their path he walk'd,
And like the rest in seeming did and talk'd,
Nor outraged Reason's rules by flaw nor start,
His madness was not of the head, but heart;
And rarely wander'd in his speech, or drew
360   His thoughts so forth as to offend the view.

XIX

With all that chilling mystery of mien,
And seeming gladness to remain unseen,
He had (if 'twere not nature's boon) an art
Of fixing memory on another's heart:
365   It was not love perchance—nor hate—nor aught

That words can image to express the thought;
But they who saw him did not see in vain,
And once beheld, would ask of him again:
And those to whom he spake remembered well,
370 And on the words, however light, would dwell:
None knew, nor how, nor why, but he entwined
Himself perforce around the hearer's mind;
There he was stamp'd, in liking, or in hate,
If greeted once; however brief the date
375 That friendship, pity, or aversion knew,
Still there within the inmost thought he grew.
You could not penetrate his soul, but found,
Despite your wonder, to your own he wound;
His presence haunted still; and from the breast
380 He forced an all unwilling interest:
Vain was the struggle in that mental net,
His spirit seem'd to dare you to forget!

XX

There is a festival, where knights and dames,
And aught that wealth or lofty lineage claims,
385 Appear—a highborn and a welcome guest
To Otho's hall came Lara with the rest.
The long carousal shakes the illumined hall,
Well speeds alike the banquet and the ball;
And the gay dance of bounding Beauty's train
390 Links grace and harmony in happiest chain:
Blest are the early hearts and gentle hands
That mingle there in well according bands;
It is a sight the careful brow might smoothe,
And make Age smile, and dream itself to youth,
395 And Youth forget such hour was past on earth,
So springs the exulting bosom to that mirth!

XXI

And Lara gazed on these, sedately glad,
His brow belied him if his soul was sad;
And his glance follow'd fast each fluttering fair,
400 Whose steps of lightness woke no echo there:

He lean'd against the lofty pillar nigh,
With folded arms and long attentive eye,
Nor mark'd a glance so sternly fix'd on his—
Ill brook'd high Lara scrutiny like this:
405   At length he caught it, 'tis a face unknown,
But seems as searching his, and his alone;
Prying and dark, a stranger's by his mien,
Who still till now had gazed on him unseen:
At length encountering meets the mutual gaze
410   Of keen enquiry, and of mute amaze;
On Lara's glance emotion gathering grew,
As if distrusting that the stranger threw;
Along the stranger's aspect, fix'd and stern,
Flash'd more than thence the vulgar eye could learn.

XXII

415   ''Tis he!' the stranger cried, and those that heard
Re-echoed fast and far the whisper'd word.
''Tis he!'— ''Tis who?' they question far and near,
Till louder accents rung on Lara's ear;
So widely spread, few bosoms well could brook
420   The general marvel, or that single look:
But Lara stirr'd not, changed not, the surprise
That sprung at first to his arrested eyes
Seem'd now subsided, neither sunk nor raised
Glanced his eye round, though still the stranger gazed;
425   And drawing nigh, exclaim'd, with haughty sneer,
''Tis he!—how came he thence?—What doth he here?'

XXIII

It were too much for Lara to pass by
Such questions, so repeated fierce and high;
With look collected, but with accent cold,
430   More mildly firm than petulantly bold,
He turn'd, and met the inquisitorial tone—
'My name is Lara!—when thine own is known,
Doubt not my fitting answer to requite
The unlook'd for courtesy of such a knight.

435   'Tis Lara!—further wouldst thou mark or ask?
       I shun no question, and I wear no mask.'

       'Thou shunn'st no question! Ponder—is there none
       Thy heart must answer, though thine ear would shun?
       And deem'st thou me unknown too? Gaze again!
440   At least thy memory was not given in vain.
       Oh! never canst thou cancel half her debt,
       Eternity forbids thee to forget.'
       With slow and searching glance upon his face
       Grew Lara's eyes, but nothing there could trace
445   They knew, or chose to know—with dubious look
       He deign'd no answer, but his head he shook,
       And half contemptuous turn'd to pass away;
       But the stern stranger motion'd him to stay.
       'A word!—I charge thee stay, and answer here
450   To one, who, wert thou noble, were thy peer,
       But as thou wast and art—nay, frown not, lord,
       If false, 'tis easy to disprove the word—
       But as thou wast and art, on thee looks down,
       Distrusts thy smiles, but shakes not at thy frown.
455   Art thou not he? whose deeds—'
                          'Whate'er I be,
       Words wild as these, accusers like to thee
       I list no further; those with whom they weigh
       May hear the rest, nor venture to gainsay
       The wondrous tale no doubt thy tongue can tell,
460   Which thus begins so courteously and well.
       Let Otho cherish here his polish'd guest,
       To him my thanks and thoughts shall be express'd.'
       And here their wondering host hath interposed—
       'Whate'er there be between you undisclosed,
465   This is no time nor fitting place to mar
       The mirthful meeting with a wordy war.
       If thou, Sir Ezzelin, hast aught to show
       Which it befits Count Lara's ear to know,
       To-morrow, here, or elsewhere, as may best
470   Beseem your mutual judgment, speak the rest;

I pledge myself for thee, as not unknown,
Though, like Count Lara, now return'd alone
From other lands, almost a stranger grown;
And if from Lara's blood and gentle birth
475 I augur right of courage and of worth,
He will not that untainted line belie,
Nor aught that knighthood may accord, deny.'

'To-morrow be it,' Ezzelin replied,
'And here our several worth and truth be tried;
480 I gage my life, my falchion to attest
My words, so may I mingle with the blest!'
What answers Lara? to its centre shrunk
His soul, in deep abstraction sudden sunk;
The words of many, and the eyes of all
485 That there were gather'd, seem'd on him to fall;
But his were silent, his appear'd to stray
In far forgetfulness away – away –
Alas! that heedlessness of all around
Bespoke remembrance only too profound.

XXIV
490 'To-morrow! – ay, to-morrow!' further word
Than those repeated none from Lara heard;
Upon his brow no outward passion spoke;
From his large eye no flashing anger broke;
Yet there was something fix'd in that low tone,
495 Which show'd resolve, determined, though unknown.
He seized his cloak – his head he slightly bow'd,
And passing Ezzelin, he left the crowd;
And, as he pass'd him, smiling met the frown
With which that chieftain's brow would bear him down:
500 It was nor smile of mirth, nor struggling pride
That curbs to scorn the wrath it cannot hide;
But that of one in his own heart secure
Of all that he would do, or could endure.
Could this mean peace? the calmness of the good?
505 Or guilt grown old in desperate hardihood?

Alas! too like in confidence are each,
For man to trust to mortal look or speech;
From deeds, and deeds alone, may he discern
Truths which it wrings the unpractised heart to learn.

XXV

510 And Lara call'd his page, and went his way —
Well could that stripling word or sign obey:
His only follower from those climes afar,
Where the soul glows beneath a brighter star;
For Lara left the shore from whence he sprung,
515 In duty patient, and sedate though young;
Silent as him he served, his faith appears
Above his station, and beyond his years.
Though not unknown the tongue of Lara's land,
In such from him he rarely heard command;
520 But fleet his step, and clear his tones would come,
When Lara's lip breathed forth the words of home:
Those accents, as his native mountains dear,
Awake their absent echoes in his ear,
Friends', kindreds', parents', wonted voice recall,
525 Now lost, abjured, for one — his friend, his all:
For him earth now disclosed no other guide;
What marvel then he rarely left his side?

XXVI

Light was his form, and darkly delicate
That brow whereon his native sun had sate,
530 But had not marr'd, though in his beams he grew,
The cheek where oft the unbidden blush shone through;
Yet not such blush as mounts when health would show
All the heart's hue in that delighted glow;
But 'twas a hectic tint of secret care
535 That for a burning moment fever'd there;
And the wild sparkle of his eye seem'd caught
From high, and lighten'd with electric thought,
Though its black orb those long low lashes' fringe
Had temper'd with a melancholy tinge;

540 Yet less of sorrow than of pride was there,
Or, if 'twere grief, a grief that none should share:
And pleased not him the sports that please his age,
The tricks of youth, the frolics of the page;
For hours on Lara he would fix his glance,
545 As all-forgotten in that watchful trance;
And from his chief withdrawn, he wander'd lone,
Brief were his answers, and his questions none;
His walk the wood, his sport some foreign book;
His resting-place the bank that curbs the brook:
550 He seem'd, like him he served, to live apart
From all that lures the eye, and fills the heart;
To know no brotherhood, and take from earth
No gift beyond that bitter boon – our birth.

XXVII

If aught he loved, 'twas Lara; but was shown
555 His faith in reverence and in deeds alone;
In mute attention; and his care, which guess'd
Each wish, fulfill'd it ere the tongue express'd.
Still there was haughtiness in all he did,
A spirit deep that brook'd not to be chid;
560 His zeal, though more than that of servile hands,
In act alone obeys, his air commands;
As if 'twas Lara's less than *his* desire
That thus he served, but surely not for hire.
Slight were the tasks enjoin'd him by his lord,
565 To hold the stirrup, or to bear the sword;
To tune his lute, or, if he will'd it more,
On tomes of other times and tongues to pore;
But ne'er to mingle with the menial train,
To whom he show'd nor deference nor disdain,
570 But that well-worn reserve which proved he knew
No sympathy with that familiar crew:
His soul, whate'er his station or his stem,
Could bow to Lara, not descend to them.
Of higher birth he seem'd, and better days,
575 Nor mark of vulgar toil that hand betrays,

So femininely white it might bespeak
Another sex, when match'd with that smooth cheek,
But for his garb, and something in his gaze,
More wild and high than woman's eye betrays;
580   A latent fierceness that far more became
His fiery climate than his tender frame:
True, in his words it broke not from his breast,
But from his aspect might be more than guess'd.
Kaled his name, though rumour said he bore
585   Another ere he left his mountain-shore;
For sometimes he would hear, however nigh,
That name repeated loud without reply,
As unfamiliar, or, if roused again,
Start to the sound, as but remember'd then;
590   Unless 'twas Lara's wonted voice that spake,
For then, ear, eyes, and heart would all awake.

XXVIII
He had look'd down upon the festive hall,
And mark'd that sudden strife so mark'd of all;
And when the crowd around and near him told
595   Their wonder at the calmness of the bold,
Their marvel how the high-born Lara bore
Such insult from a stranger, doubly sore,
The colour of young Kaled went and came,
The lip of ashes, and the cheek of flame;
600   And o'er his brow the dampening heart-drops threw
The sickening iciness of that cold dew,
That rises as the busy bosom sinks
With heavy thoughts from which reflection shrinks.
Yes – there be things which we must dream and dare,
605   And execute ere thought be half aware:
Whate'er might Kaled's be, it was enow
To seal his lip, but agonise his brow.
He gazed on Ezzelin till Lara cast
That sidelong smile upon the knight he past;
610   When Kaled saw that smile his visage fell,
As if on something recognised right well;

His memory read in such a meaning more
Than Lara's aspect unto others wore:
Forward he sprung – a moment, both were gone,
615   And all within that hall seem'd left alone;
Each had so fix'd his eye on Lara's mien,
All had so mix'd their feelings with that scene,
That when his long dark shadow through the porch
No more relieves the glare of yon high torch,
620   Each pulse beats quicker, and all bosoms seem
To bound as doubting from too black a dream,
Such as we know is false, yet dread in sooth,
Because the worst is ever nearest truth.
And they are gone – but Ezzelin is there,
625   With thoughtful visage and imperious air;
But long remain'd not; ere an hour expired
He waved his hand to Otho, and retired.

XXIX
The crowd are gone, the revellers at rest;
The courteous host, and all-approving guest,
630   Again to that accustom'd couch must creep
Where joy subsides, and sorrow sighs to sleep,
And man, o'erlabour'd with his being's strife,
Shrinks to that sweet forgetfulness of life:
There lie love's feverish hope, and cunning's guile,
635   Hate's working brain, and lull'd ambition's wile;
O'er each vain eye oblivion's pinions wave,
And quench'd existence crouches in a grave.
What better name may slumber's bed become?
Night's sepulchre, the universal home,
640   Where weakness, strength, vice, virtue, sunk supine,
Alike in naked helplessness recline;
Glad for awhile to heave unconscious breath,
Yet wake to wrestle with the dread of death,
And shun, though day but dawn on ills increased,
645   That sleep, the loveliest, since it dreams the least.

Canto the Second

I

Night wanes – the vapours round the mountains curl'd
Melt into morn, and Light awakes the world.
Man has another day to swell the past,
And lead him near to little, but his last;
5   But mighty Nature bounds as from her birth,
The sun is in the heavens, and life on earth;
Flowers in the valley, splendour in the beam,
Health on the gale, and freshness in the stream.
Immortal man! behold her glories shine,
10 And cry, exulting inly, 'They are thine!'
Gaze on, while yet thy gladden'd eye may see;
A morrow comes when they are not for thee:
And grieve what may above thy senseless bier,
Nor earth nor sky will yield a single tear;
15 Nor cloud shall gather more, nor leaf shall fall,
Nor gale breathe forth one sigh for thee, for all;
But creeping things shall revel in their spoil,
And fit thy clay to fertilise the soil.

II

'Tis morn – 'tis noon – assembled in the hall,
20 The gather'd chieftains come to Otho's call;
'Tis now the promised hour, that must proclaim
The life or death of Lara's future fame;
When Ezzelin his charge may here unfold,
And whatsoe'er the tale, it must be told.
25 His faith was pledged, and Lara's promise given,
To meet it in the eye of man and heaven.
Why comes he not? Such truths to be divulged,
Methinks the accuser's rest is long indulged.

III

The hour is past, and Lara too is there,
30 With self-confiding, coldly patient air;
Why comes not Ezzelin? The hour is past,
And murmurs rise, and Otho's brow's o'ercast.
'I know my friend! his faith I cannot fear,
If yet he be on earth, expect him here;
35 The roof that held him in the valley stands
Between my own and noble Lara's lands;
My halls from such a guest had honour gain'd,
Nor had Sir Ezzelin his host disdain'd,
But that some previous proof forbade his stay,
40 And urged him to prepare against to-day;
The word I pledged for his I pledge again,
Or will myself redeem his knighthood's stain.'

He ceased – and Lara answer'd, 'I am here
To lend at thy demand a listening ear
45 To tales of evil from a stranger's tongue,
Whose words already might my heart have wrung,
But that I deem'd him scarcely less than mad,
Or, at the worst, a foe ignobly bad.
I know him not – but me it seems he knew
50 In lands where – but I must not trifle too:
Produce this babbler – or redeem the pledge;
Here in thy hold, and with thy falchion's edge.'

Proud Otho on the instant, reddening, threw
His glove on earth, and forth his sabre flew.
55 'The last alternative befits me best,
And thus I answer for mine absent guest.'

With cheek unchanging from its sallow gloom,
However near his own or other's tomb;
With hand, whose almost careless coolness spoke
60 Its grasp well-used to deal the sabre-stroke;
With eye, though calm, determined not to spare,
Did Lara too his willing weapon bare.

In vain the circling chieftains round them closed,
For Otho's frenzy would not be opposed;
65 And from his lip those words of insult fell –
His sword is good who can maintain them well.

IV

Short was the conflict; furious, blindly rash,
Vain Otho gave his bosom to the gash:
He bled, and fell; but not with deadly wound,
70 Stretch'd by a dextrous sleight along the ground.
'Demand thy life!' He answer'd not: and then
From that red floor he ne'er had risen again,
For Lara's brow upon the moment grew
Almost to blackness in its demon hue;
75 And fiercer shook his angry falchion now
Than when his foe's was levell'd at his brow;
Then all was stern collectedness and art,
Now rose the unleaven'd hatred of his heart;
So little sparing to the foe he fell'd,
80 That when the approaching crowd his arm withheld,
He almost turn'd the thirsty point on those
Who thus for mercy dared to interpose;
But to a moment's thought that purpose bent;
Yet look'd he on him still with eye intent,
85 As if he loathed the ineffectual strife
That left a foe, howe'er o'erthrown, with life;
As if to search how far the wound he gave
Had sent its victim onward to his grave.

V

They raised the bleeding Otho, and the Leech
90 Forbade all present question, sign, and speech;
The others met within a neighbouring hall,
And he, incensed and heedless of them all,
The cause and conqueror in this sudden fray,
In haughty silence slowly strode away;
95 He back'd his steed, his homeward path he took,
Nor cast on Otho's towers a single look.

VI

But where was he? that meteor of a night,
Who menaced but to disappear with light.
Where was this Ezzelin? who came and went
100   To leave no other trace of his intent.
He left the dome of Otho long ere morn,
In darkness, yet so well the path was worn
He could not miss it: near his dwelling lay;
But there he was not, and with coming day
105   Came fast enquiry, which unfolded nought
Except the absence of the chief it sought.
A chamber tenantless, a steed at rest,
His host alarm'd, his murmuring squires distress'd:
Their search extends along, around the path,
110   In dread to meet the marks of prowlers' wrath:
But none are there, and not a brake hath borne
Nor gout of blood, nor shred of mantle torn;
Nor fall nor struggle hath defaced the grass,
Which still retains a mark where murder was;
115   Nor dabbling fingers left to tell the tale,
The bitter print of each convulsive nail,
When agonised hands that cease to guard,
Wound in that pang the smoothness of the sward.
Some such had been, if here a life was reft,
120   But these were not; and doubting hope is left;
And strange suspicion, whispering Lara's name,
Now daily mutters o'er his blacken'd fame;
Then sudden silent when his form appear'd,
Awaits the absence of the thing it fear'd
125   Again its wonted wondering to renew,
And dye conjecture with a darker hue.

VII

Days roll along, and Otho's wounds are heal'd,
But not his pride; and hate no more conceal'd:
He was a man of power, and Lara's foe,
130   The friend of all who sought to work him woe,
And from his country's justice now demands
Account of Ezzelin at Lara's hands.

Who else than Lara could have cause to fear
His presence? who had made him disappear,
135 If not the man on whom his menaced charge
Had sate too deeply were he left at large?
The general rumour ignorantly loud,
The mystery dearest to the curious crowd;
The seeming friendlessness of him who strove
140 To win no confidence, and wake no love;
The sweeping fierceness which his soul betray'd,
The skill with which he wielded his keen blade;
Where had his arm unwarlike caught that art?
Where had that fierceness grown upon his heart?
145 For it was not the blind capricious rage
A word can kindle and a word assuage;
But the deep working of a soul unmix'd
With aught of pity where its wrath had fix'd;
Such as long power and overgorged success
150 Concentrates into all that's merciless:
These, link'd with that desire which ever sways
Mankind, the rather to condemn than praise,
'Gainst Lara gathering raised at length a storm,
Such as himself might fear, and foes would form,
155 And he must answer for the absent head
Of one that haunts him still, alive or dead.

VIII

Within that land was many a malcontent,
Who cursed the tyranny to which he bent;
That soil full many a wringing despot saw,
160 Who work'd his wantonness in form of law;
Long war without and frequent broil within
Had made a path for blood and giant sin,
That waited but a signal to begin
New havoc, such as civil discord blends,
165 Which knows no neuter, owns but foes or friends;
Fix'd in his feudal fortress each was lord,
In word and deed obey'd, in soul abhorr'd.
Thus Lara had inherited his lands,
And with them pining hearts and sluggish hands;

170 But that long absence from his native clime
     Had left him stainless of oppression's crime,
     And now, diverted by his milder sway,
     All dread by slow degrees had worn away.
     The menials felt their usual awe alone,
175 But more for him than them that fear was grown;
     They deem'd him now unhappy, though at first
     Their evil judgment augur'd of the worst,
     And each long restless night, and silent mood,
     Was traced to sickness, fed by solitude:
180 And though his lonely habits threw of late
     Gloom o'er his chamber, cheerful was his gate;
     For thence the wretched ne'er unsoothed withdrew,
     For them, at least, his soul compassion knew.
     Cold to the great, contemptuous to the high,
185 The humble pass'd not his unheeding eye;
     Much he would speak not, but beneath his roof
     They found asylum oft, and ne'er reproof.
     And they who watch'd might mark that, day by day,
     Some new retainers gather'd to his sway;
190 But most of late, since Ezzelin was lost,
     He play'd the courteous lord and bounteous host:
     Perchance his strife with Otho made him dread
     Some snare prepared for his obnoxious head;
     Whate'er his view, his favour more obtains
195 With these, the people, than his fellow thanes.
     If this were policy, so far 'twas sound,
     The million judged but of him as they found;
     From him by sterner chiefs to exile driven
     They but required a shelter, and 'twas given.
200 By him no peasant mourn'd his rifled cot,
     And scarce the Serf could murmur o'er his lot;
     With him old avarice found its hoard secure,
     With him contempt forbore to mock the poor;
     Youth present cheer and promised recompense
205 Detain'd, till all too late to part from thence:
     To hate he offer'd, with the coming change,
     The deep reversion of delay'd revenge;

To love, long baffled by the unequal match,
The well-won charms success was sure to snatch.
210   All now was ripe, he waits but to proclaim
That slavery nothing which was still a name.
The moment came, the hour when Otho thought
Secure at last the vengeance which he sought:
His summons found the destined criminal
215   Begirt by thousands in his swarming hall,
Fresh from their feudal fetters newly riven,
Defying earth, and confident of heaven.
That morning he had freed the soil-bound slaves
Who dig no land for tyrants but their graves!
220   Such is their cry – some watchword for the fight
Must vindicate the wrong, and warp the right;
Religion – freedom – vengeance – what you will,
A word's enough to raise mankind to kill;
Some factious phrase by cunning caught and spread,
225   That guilt may reign, and wolves and worms be fed!

IX
Throughout that clime the feudal chiefs had gain'd
Such sway, their infant monarch hardly reign'd;
Now was the hour for faction's rebel growth,
The Serfs contemn'd the one, and hated both:
230   They waited but a leader, and they found
One to their cause inseparably bound;
By circumstance compell'd to plunge again,
In self-defence, amidst the strife of men.
Cut off by some mysterious fate from those
235   Whom birth and nature meant not for his foes,
Had Lara from that night, to him accurst,
Prepared to meet, but not alone, the worst:
Some reason urged, whate'er it was, to shun
Enquiry into deeds at distance done;
240   By mingling with his own the cause of all,
E'en if he fail'd, he still delay'd his fall.
The sullen calm that long his bosom kept,
The storm that once had spent itself and slept,

Roused by events that seem'd foredoom'd to urge
245　His gloomy fortunes to their utmost verge,
Burst forth, and made him all he once had been,
And is again; he only changed the scene.
Light care had he for life, and less for fame,
But not less fitted for the desperate game:
250　He deem'd himself mark'd out for others' hate,
And mock'd at ruin so they shared his fate.
What cared he for the freedom of the crowd?
He raised the humble but to bend the proud.
He had hoped quiet in his sullen lair,
255　But man and destiny beset him there:
Inured to hunters, he was found at bay;
And they must kill, they cannot snare the prey.
Stern, unambitious, silent, he had been
Henceforth a calm spectator of life's scene;
260　But dragg'd again upon the arena, stood
A leader not unequal to the feud;
In voice – mien – gesture – savage nature spoke,
And from his eye the gladiator broke.

X

What boots the oft-repeated tale of strife,
265　The feast of vultures, and the waste of life?
The varying fortune of each separate field,
The fierce that vanquish, and the faint that yield?
The smoking ruin, and the crumbled wall?
In this the struggle was the same with all;
270　Save that distemper'd passions lent their force
In bitterness that banish'd all remorse.
None sued, for Mercy knew her cry was vain,
The captive died upon the battle-slain:
In either cause, one rage alone possess'd
275　The empire of the alternate victor's breast;
And they that smote for freedom or for sway,
Deem'd few were slain, while more remain'd to slay.

It was too late to check the wasting brand,
And Desolation reap'd the famish'd land;
280   The torch was lighted, and the flame was spread,
And Carnage smiled upon her daily dead.

XI
Fresh with the nerve the new-born impulse strung,
The first success to Lara's numbers clung:
But that vain victory hath ruin'd all;
285   They form no longer to their leader's call:
In blind confusion on the foe they press,
And think to snatch is to secure success.
The lust of booty, and the thirst of hate,
Lure on the broken brigands to their fate:
290   In vain he doth whate'er a chief may do,
To check the headlong fury of that crew;
In vain their stubborn ardour he would tame,
The hand that kindles cannot quench the flame;
The wary foe alone hath turn'd their mood,
295   And shown their rashness to that erring brood:
The feign'd retreat, the nightly ambuscade,
The daily harass, and the fight delay'd,
The long privation of the hoped supply,
The tentless rest beneath the humid sky,
300   The stubborn wall that mocks the leaguer's art,
And palls the patience of his baffled heart,
Of these they had not deem'd: the battle-day
They could encounter as a veteran may;
But more preferr'd the fury of the strife,
305   And present death, to hourly suffering life:
And famine wrings, and fever sweeps away
His numbers melting fast from their array;
Intemperate triumph fades to discontent,
And Lara's soul alone seems still unbent:
310   But few remain to aid his voice and hand,
And thousands dwindled to a scanty band:

Desperate, though few, the last and best remain'd
To mourn the discipline they late disdain'd.
One hope survives, the frontier is not far,
315 And thence they may escape from native war;
And bear within them to the neighbouring state
An exile's sorrows, or an outlaw's hate:
Hard is the task their father-land to quit,
But harder still to perish or submit.

XII

320 It is resolved – they march – consenting Night
Guides with her star their dim and torchless flight;
Already they perceive its tranquil beam
Sleep on the surface of the barrier stream;
Already they descry – Is yon the bank?
325 Away! 'tis lined with many a hostile rank.
Return or fly! – What glitters in the rear?
'Tis Otho's banner – the pursuer's spear!
Are those the shepherds' fires upon the height?
Alas! they blaze too widely for the flight:
330 Cut off from hope, and compass'd in the toil,
Less blood perchance hath bought a richer spoil!

XIII

A moment's pause – 'tis but to breathe their band,
Or shall they onward press, or here withstand?
It matters little – if they charge the foes
335 Who by their border-stream their march oppose,
Some few, perchance, may break and pass the line,
However link'd to baffle such design.
'The charge be ours! to wait for their assault
Were fate well worthy of a coward's halt.'
340 Forth flies each sabre, rein'd is every steed,
And the next word shall scarce outstrip the deed:
In the next tone of Lara's gathering breath
How many shall but hear the voice of death!

XIV

His blade is bared, – in him there is an air
345   As deep, but far too tranquil for despair;
A something of indifference more than then
Becomes the bravest, if they feel for men.
He turn'd his eye on Kaled, ever near,
And still too faithful to betray one fear;
350   Perchance 'twas but the moon's dim twilight threw
Along his aspect an unwonted hue
Of mournful paleness, whose deep tint express'd
The truth, and not the terror of his breast.
This Lara mark'd, and laid his hand on his:
355   It trembled not in such an hour as this;
His lip was silent, scarcely beat his heart,
His eye alone proclaim'd, 'We will not part!
Thy band may perish, or thy friends may flee,
Farewell to life, but not adieu to thee!'

360   The word hath pass'd his lips, and onward driven,
Pours the link'd band through ranks asunder riven;
Well has each steed obey'd the armed heel,
And flash the scimitars, and rings the steel;
Outnumber'd, not outbraved, they still oppose
365   Despair to daring, and a front to foes;
And blood is mingled with the dashing stream,
Which runs all redly till the morning beam.

XV

Commanding, aiding, animating all,
Where foe appear'd to press, or friend to fall,
370   Cheers Lara's voice, and waves or strikes his steel,
Inspiring hope himself had ceased to feel.
None fled, for well they knew that flight were vain;
But those that waver turn to smite again,
While yet they find the firmest of the foe
375   Recoil before their leader's look and blow:
Now girt with numbers, now almost alone,
He foils their ranks, or re-unites his own;

Himself he spared not – once they seem'd to fly –
Now was the time, he waved his hand on high,
380 And shook – Why sudden droops that plumed crest?
The shaft is sped – the arrow's in his breast!
That fatal gesture left the unguarded side,
And Death hath stricken down yon arm of pride.
The word of triumph fainted from his tongue;
385 That hand, so raised, how droopingly it hung!
But yet the sword instinctively retains,
Though from its fellow shrink the falling reins;
These Kaled snatches: dizzy with the blow,
And senseless bending o'er his saddle-bow,
390 Perceives not Lara that his anxious page
Beguiles his charger from the combat's rage:
Meantime his followers charge, and charge again;
Too mix'd the slayers now to heed the slain!

XVI

Day glimmers on the dying and the dead,
395 The cloven cuirass, and the helmless head;
The war-horse masterless is on the earth,
And that last gasp hath burst his bloody girth;
And near, yet quivering with what life remain'd,
The heel that urged him and the hand that rein'd;
400 And some too near that rolling torrent lie,
Whose waters mock the lip of those that die;
That panting thirst which scorches in the breath
Of those that die the soldier's fiery death,
In vain impels the burning mouth to crave
405 One drop – the last – to cool it for the grave;
With feeble and convulsive effort swept,
Their limbs along the crimson'd turf have crept;
The faint remains of life such struggles waste,
But yet they reach the stream, and bend to taste:
410 They feel its freshness, and almost partake –
Why pause? No further thirst have they to slake –
It is unquench'd, and yet they feel it not;
It was an agony – but now forgot!

XVII

Beneath a lime, remoter from the scene,
415 Where but for him that strife had never been,
A breathing but devoted warrior lay:
'Twas Lara bleeding fast from life away.
His follower once, and now his only guide,
Kneels Kaled watchful o'er his welling side,
420 And with his scarf would stanch the tides that rush,
With each convulsion, in a blacker gush;
And then, as his faint breathing waxes low,
In feebler, not less fatal tricklings flow:
He scarce can speak, but motions him 'tis vain,
425 And merely adds another throb to pain.
He clasps the hand that pang which would assuage,
And sadly smiles his thanks to that dark page,
Who nothing fears, nor feels, nor heeds, nor sees,
Save that damp brow which rests upon his knees;
430 Save that pale aspect, where the eye, though dim,
Held all the light that shone on earth for him.

XVIII

The foe arrives, who long had search'd the field,
Their triumph nought till Lara too should yield;
They would remove him, but they see 'twere vain,
435 And he regards them with a calm disdain,
That rose to reconcile him with his fate,
And that escape to death from living hate:
And Otho comes, and leaping from his steed,
Looks on the bleeding foe that made him bleed,
440 And questions of his state; he answers not,
Scarce glances on him as on one forgot,
And turns to Kaled: – each remaining word
They understood not, if distinctly heard;
His dying tones are in that other tongue,
445 To which some strange remembrance wildly clung.
They spake of other scenes, but what – is known
To Kaled, whom their meaning reach'd alone;
And he replied, though faintly, to their sound,
While gazed the rest in dumb amazement round:

450   They seem'd even then – that twain – unto the last
   To half forget the present in the past;
   To share between themselves some separate fate,
   Whose darkness none beside should penetrate.

XIX
   Their words though faint were many – from the tone
455   Their import those who heard could judge alone;
   From this, you might have deem'd young Kaled's death
   More near than Lara's by his voice and breath,
   So sad, so deep, and hesitating broke
   The accents his scarce-moving pale lips spoke;
460   But Lara's voice, though low, at first was clear
   And calm, till murmuring death gasp'd hoarsely near:
   But from his visage little could we guess,
   So unrepentant, dark, and passionless,
   Save that when struggling nearer to his last,
465   Upon that page his eye was kindly cast;
   And once, as Kaled's answering accents ceased,
   Rose Lara's hand, and pointed to the East:
   Whether (as then the breaking sun from high
   Roll'd back the clouds) the morrow caught his eye,
470   Or that 'twas chance, or some remember'd scene,
   That raised his arm to point where such had been,
   Scarce Kaled seem'd to know, but turn'd away,
   As if his heart abhorr'd that coming day,
   And shrunk his glance before that morning light,
475   To look on Lara's brow – where all grew night.
   Yet sense seem'd left, though better were its loss;
   For when one near display'd the absolving cross,
   And proffer'd to his touch the holy bead,
   Of which his parting soul might own the need,
480   He look'd upon it with an eye profane,
   And smiled – Heaven pardon! if 'twere with disdain:
   And Kaled, though he spoke not, nor withdrew
   From Lara's face his fix'd despairing view,
   With brow repulsive, and with gesture swift,
485   Flung back the hand which held the sacred gift,

As if such but disturb'd the expiring man,
Nor seem'd to know his life but *then* began,
That life of Immortality, secure
To none, save them whose faith in Christ is sure.

XX

490   But gasping heaved the breath that Lara drew,
And dull the film along his dim eye grew;
His limbs stretch'd fluttering, and his head droop'd o'er
The weak yet still untiring knee that bore;
He press'd the hand he held upon his heart —
495   It beats no more, but Kaled will not part
With the cold grasp, but feels, and feels in vain,
For that faint throb which answers not again.
'It beats!' — Away, thou dreamer! he is gone —
It once was Lara which thou look'st upon.

XXI

500   He gazed, as if not yet had pass'd away
The haughty spirit of that humble clay;
And those around have roused him from his trance,
But cannot tear from thence his fixed glance;
And when, in raising him from where he bore
505   Within his arms the form that felt no more,
He saw the head his breast would still sustain,
Roll down like earth to earth upon the plain;
He did not dash himself thereby, nor tear
The glossy tendrils of his raven hair,
510   But strove to stand and gaze, but reel'd and fell,
Scarce breathing more than that he loved so well.
Than that *he* loved! Oh! never yet beneath
The breast of man such trusty love may breathe!
That trying moment hath at once reveal'd
515   The secret long and yet but half conceal'd;
In baring to revive that lifeless breast,
Its grief seem'd ended, but the sex confess'd;
And life return'd, and Kaled felt no shame —
What now to her was Womanhood or Fame?

XXII

520 And Lara sleeps not where his fathers sleep,
But where he died his grave was dug as deep;
Nor is his mortal slumber less profound,
Though priest nor bless'd nor marble deck'd the mound,
And he was mourn'd by one whose quiet grief,
525 Less loud, outlasts a people's for their chief.
Vain was all question ask'd her of the past,
And vain e'en menace – silent to the last;
She told nor whence, nor why she left behind
Her all for one who seem'd but little kind.
530 Why did she love him? Curious fool! – be still –
Is human love the growth of human will?
To her he might be gentleness; the stern
Have deeper thoughts than your dull eyes discern,
And when they love, your smilers guess not how
535 Beats the strong heart, though less the lips avow.
They were not common links, that form'd the chain
That bound to Lara Kaled's heart and brain;
But that wild tale she brook'd not to unfold,
And seal'd is now each lip that could have told.

XXIII

540 They laid him in the earth, and on his breast,
Besides the wound that sent his soul to rest,
They found the scatter'd dints of many a scar,
Which were not planted there in recent war;
Where'er had pass'd his summer years of life,
545 It seems they vanish'd in a land of strife;
But all unknown his glory or his guilt,
These only told that somewhere blood was spilt,
And Ezzelin, who might have spoke the past,
Return'd no more – that night appear'd his last.

XXIV

550 Upon that night (a peasant's is the tale)
A Serf that cross'd the intervening vale,[1]
When Cynthia's light almost gave way to morn,
And nearly veil'd in mist her waning horn;

1. The event in this section was suggested by the description of the death, or rather burial, of the Duke of Gandia. The most interesting and particular account of it is given by Burchard, and is in substance as follows: – 'On the eighth day of June, the Cardinal of Valenza and the Duke of Gandia, sons of the Pope, supped with their mother, Vanozza, near the church of *S. Pietro ad vincula*; several other persons being present at the entertainment. A late hour approaching, and the cardinal having reminded his brother, that it was time to return to the apostolic palace, they mounted their horses or mules, with only a few attendants, and proceeded together as far as the palace of Cardinal Ascanio Sforza, when the duke informed the cardinal that, before he returned home, he had to pay a visit of pleasure. Dismissing therefore all his attendants, excepting his *staffiero*, or footman, and a person in a mask, who had paid him a visit whilst at supper, and who, during the space of a month or thereabouts, previous to this time, had called upon him almost daily, at the apostolic palace, he took this person behind him on his mule, and proceeded to the street of the Jews, where he quitted his servant, directing him to remain there until a certain hour; when, if he did not return, he might repair to the palace. The duke then seated the person in the mask behind him, and rode, I know not whither; but in that night he was assassinated, and thrown into the river. The servant, after having been dismissed, was also assaulted and mortally wounded; and although he was attended with great care, yet such was his situation, that he could give no intelligible account of what had befallen his master. In the morning, the duke not having returned to the palace, his servants began to be alarmed; and one of them informed the pontiff of the evening excursion of his sons, and that the duke had not yet made his appearance. This gave the pope no small anxiety; but he conjectured that the duke had been attracted by some courtesan to pass the night with her, and, not choosing to quit the house in open day, had waited till the following evening to return home. When, however, the evening arrived, and he found himself disappointed in his expectations, he became deeply afflicted, and began to make enquiries from different persons, whom he ordered to attend him for that purpose. Amongst these was a man named Giorgio Schiavoni, who, having discharged some timber from a bark in the river, had remained on board the vessel to watch it; and being interrogated whether he had seen any one thrown into the river on the night preceding, he replied, that he saw two men on foot, who came down the street, and looked diligently about, to observe whether any person was passing. That seeing no one, they returned, and a short time afterwards two others came, and looked around in the same manner as the former: no person still appearing, they gave a sign to their companions, when a man came, mounted on a white horse, having behind him a dead

A Serf, that rose betimes to thread the wood,
555 And hew the bough that bought his children's food,
Pass'd by the river that divides the plain
Of Otho's lands and Lara's broad domain:
He heard a tramp – a horse and horseman broke
From out the wood – before him was a cloak
560 Wrapt round some burthen at his saddle-bow,
Bent was his head, and hidden was his brow.
Roused by the sudden sight at such a time,
And some foreboding that it might be crime,
Himself unheeded watch'd the stranger's course,
565 Who reach'd the river, bounded from his horse,
And lifting thence the burthen which he bore,
Heaved up the bank, and dash'd it from the shore,

---

body, the head and arms of which, hung on one side, and the feet on the
other side of the horse; the two persons on foot supporting the body, to
prevent its falling. They thus proceeded towards that part, where the filth
of the city is usually discharged into the river, and turning the horse, with
his tail towards the water, the two persons took the dead body by the arms
and feet, and with all their strength flung it into the river. The person on
horseback then asked if they had thrown it in; to which they replied, *Signor,
sì* (yes, Sir). He then looked towards the river, and seeing a mantle floating
on the stream, he enquired what it was that appeared black, to which they
answered, it was a mantle; and one of them threw stones upon it, in conse-
quence of which it sunk. The attendants of the pontiff then enquired from
Giorgio, why he had not revealed this to the governor of the city; to which
he replied, that he had seen in his time a hundred dead bodies thrown into
the river at the same place, without any enquiry being made respecting
them; and that he had not, therefore, considered it as a matter of any
importance. The fishermen and seamen were then collected, and ordered to
search the river, where, on the following evening, they found the body of
the duke, with his habit entire, and thirty ducats in his purse. He was
pierced with nine wounds, one of which was in his throat, the others in his
head, body, and limbs. No sooner was the pontiff informed of the death of
his son, and that he had been thrown, like filth, into the river, than, giving
way to his grief, he shut himself up in a chamber, and wept bitterly. The
Cardinal of Segovia, and other attendants on the pope, went to the door,
and after many hours spent in persuasions and exhortations, prevailed upon
him to admit them. From the evening of Wednesday till the following
Saturday the pope took no food; nor did he sleep from Thursday morning
till the same hour on the ensuing day. At length, however, giving way to the
entreaties of his attendants, he began to restrain his sorrow, and to consider
the injury which his own health might sustain, by the further indulgence of
his grief.' – ROSCOE's *Leo Tenth*, vol. I. p. 265.

Then paused, and look'd, and turn'd, and seem'd to watch,
And still another hurried glance would snatch,
570 And follow with his step the stream that flow'd,
As if even yet too much its surface show'd:
At once he started, stoop'd, around him strown
The winter floods had scatter'd heaps of stone;
Of these the heaviest thence he gather'd there,
575 And slung them with a more than common care.
Meantime the Serf had crept to where unseen
Himself might safely mark what this might mean;
He caught a glimpse, as of a floating breast,
And something glitter'd starlike on the vest;
580 But ere he well could mark the buoyant trunk,
A massy fragment smote it, and it sunk:
It rose again, but indistinct to view,
And left the waters of a purple hue,
Then deeply disappear'd: the horseman gazed
585 Till ebb'd the latest eddy it had raised;
Then turning, vaulted on his pawing steed,
And instant spurr'd him into panting speed.
His face was mask'd – the features of the dead,
If dead it were, escaped the observer's dread;
590 But if in sooth a star its bosom bore,
Such is the badge that knighthood ever wore,
And such 'tis known Sir Ezzelin had worn
Upon the night that led to such a morn.
If thus he perish'd, Heaven receive his soul!
595 His undiscover'd limbs to ocean roll;
And charity upon the hope would dwell
It was not Lara's hand by which he fell.

XXV
And Kaled – Lara – Ezzelin, are gone,
Alike without their monumental stone!
600 The first, all efforts vainly strove to wean
From lingering where her chieftain's blood had been;
Grief had so tamed a spirit once too proud,
Her tears were few, her wailing never loud;

But furious would you tear her from the spot
605   Where yet she scarce believed that he was not,
Her eye shot forth with all the living fire
That haunts the tigress in her whelpless ire;
But left to waste her weary moments there,
She talk'd all idly unto shapes of air,
610   Such as the busy brain of Sorrow paints,
And woos to listen to her fond complaints:
And she would sit beneath the very tree
Where lay his drooping head upon her knee;
And in that posture where she saw him fall,
615   His words, his looks, his dying grasp recall;
And she had shorn, but saved her raven hair,
And oft would snatch it from her bosom there,
And fold, and press it gently to the ground,
As if she stanch'd anew some phantom's wound.
620   Herself would question, and for him reply;
Then rising, start, and beckon him to fly
From some imagined spectre in pursuit;
Then seat her down upon some linden's root,
And hide her visage with her meagre hand,
625   Or trace strange characters along the sand –
This could not last – she lies by him she loved;
Her tale untold – her truth too dearly proved.

The Destruction of Sennacherib

I

The Assyrian came down like the wolf on the fold,
And his cohorts were gleaming in purple and gold;
And the sheen of their spears was like stars on the sea,
When the blue wave rolls nightly on deep Galilee.

II

5   Like the leaves of the forest when Summer is green,
That host with their banners at sunset were seen:
Like the leaves of the forest when Autumn hath blown,
That host on the morrow lay wither'd and strown.

III

For the Angel of Death spread his wings on the blast,
10   And breathed in the face of the foe as he pass'd;
And the eyes of the sleepers wax'd deadly and chill,
And their hearts but once heaved, and for ever grew still!

IV

And there lay the steed with his nostril all wide,
But through it there roll'd not the breath of his pride:
15   And the foam of his gasping lay white on the turf,
And cold as the spray of the rock-beating surf.

V

And there lay the rider distorted and pale,
With the dew on his brow, and the rust on his mail;
And the tents were all silent, the banners alone,
20   The lances unlifted, the trumpet unblown.

VI

And the widows of Ashur are loud in their wail,
And the idols are broke in the temple of Baal;
And the might of the Gentile, unsmote by the sword,
Hath melted like snow in the glance of the Lord!

Napoleon's Farewell (From the French)

I

Farewell to the Land, where the gloom of my Glory
Arose and o'ershadow'd the earth with her name –
She abandons me now – but the page of her story,
The brightest or blackest, is fill'd with my fame.
5   I have warr'd with a world which vanquish'd me only
When the meteor of conquest allured me too far;
I have coped with the nations which dread me thus lonely,
The last single Captive to millions in war.

II

Farewell to thee, France! when thy diadem crown'd me,
10   I made thee the gem and the wonder of earth, –
But thy weakness decrees I should leave as I found thee,
Decay'd in thy glory, and sunk in thy worth.
Oh! for the veteran hearts that were wasted
In strife with the storm, when their battles were won –
15   Then the Eagle, whose gaze in that moment was blasted,
Had still soar'd with eyes fix'd on victory's sun!

III

Farewell to thee, France! – but when Liberty rallies
Once more in thy regions, remember me then, –
The violet still grows in the depth of thy valleys;
20   Though wither'd, thy tear will unfold it again –
Yet, yet, I may baffle the hosts that surround us,
And yet may thy heart leap awake to my voice –
There are links which must break in the chain that has
        bound us,
Then turn thee and call on the Chief of thy choice!

From the French ('Must thou go, my glorious Chief')[1]

I

Must thou go, my glorious Chief,
    Sever'd from thy faithful few?
Who can tell thy warrior's grief,
    Maddening o'er that long adieu?
5 Woman's love, and friendship's zeal,
    Dear as both have been to me –
What are they to all I feel,
    With a soldier's faith for thee?

II

Idol of the soldier's soul!
10   First in fight, but mightiest now:
Many could a world control;
    Thee alone no doom can bow.
By thy side for years I dared
    Death; and envied those who fell,
15 When their dying shout was heard,
    Blessing him they served so well.[2]

III

Would that I were cold with those,
    Since this hour I live to see;
When the doubts of coward foes
20   Scarce dare trust a man with thee,

1. 'All wept, but particularly Savary, and a Polish officer who had been exalted from the ranks by Buonaparte. He clung to his master's knees; wrote a letter to Lord Keith, entreating permission to accompany him, even in the most menial capacity, which could not be admitted.'
2. 'At Waterloo, one man was seen, whose left arm was shattered by a cannon ball, to wrench it off with the other, and throwing it up in the air, exclaimed to his comrades, "Vive l'Empereur, jusqu'à la mort!" There were many other instances of the like: this you may, however, depend on as true.' – *Private Letter from Brussels.*

Dreading each should set thee free!
    Oh! although in dungeons pent,
All their chains were light to me,
    Gazing on thy soul unbent.

IV

25 Would the sycophants of him
        Now so deaf to duty's prayer,
    Were his borrow'd glories dim,
        In his native darkness share?
    Were that world this hour his own,
30   All thou calmly dost resign,
    Could he purchase with that throne
        Hearts like those which still are thine?

V

    My chief, my king, my friend, adieu!
        Never did I droop before;
35 Never to my sovereign sue,
        As his foes I now implore:
    All I ask is to divide
        Every peril he must brave;
    Sharing by the hero's side
40   His fall, his exile, and his grave.

THE SIEGE OF CORINTH

TO JOHN HOBHOUSE, ESQ.
THIS POEM IS INSCRIBED BY HIS FRIEND.

January 22, 1816.

ADVERTISEMENT

'The grand army of the Turks (in 1715), under the Prime
Vizier, to open to themselves a way into the heart of the
Morea, and to form the siege of Napoli di Romania, the most
considerable place in all that country,[1] thought it best in the
first place to attack Corinth, upon which they made several
storms. The garrison being weakened, and the governor
seeing it was impossible to hold out against so mighty a
force, thought it fit to beat a parley: but while they were
treating about the articles, one of the magazines in the Turk-
ish camp, wherein they had six hundred barrels of powder,
blew up by accident, whereby six or seven hundred men
were killed; which so enraged the infidels, that they would
not grant any capitulation, but stormed the place with so
much fury, that they took it, and put most of the garrison,
with Signior Minotti, the governor, to the sword. The rest,
with Antonio Bembo, proveditor extraordinary, were made
prisoners of war.' – *History of the Turks*, vol. iii. p. 151.

1. Napoli di Romania is not now the most considerable place in the
Morea, but Tripolitza, where the Pacha resides, and maintains his
government. Napoli is near Argos. I visited all three in 1810–11; and in the
course of journeying through the country from my first arrival in 1809,
I crossed the Isthmus eight times in my way from Attica to the Morea,
over the mountains, or in the other direction, when passing from the Gulf
of Athens to that of Lepanto. Both the routes are picturesque and
beautiful, though very different: that by sea has more sameness; but
the voyage being always within sight of land, and often very near it,
presents many attractive views of the islands Salamis, Ægina, Poro, &c, and
the coast of the Continent.

In the year since Jesus died for men,
Eighteen hundred years and ten,
We were a gallant company,
Riding o'er land, and sailing o'er sea.
5   Oh! but we went merrily!
We forded the river, and clomb the high hill,
Never our steeds for a day stood still;
Whether we lay in the cave or the shed,
Our sleep fell soft on the hardest bed;
10   Whether we couch'd in our rough capote,
On the rougher plank of our gliding boat,
Or stretch'd on the beach, or our saddles spread
As a pillow beneath the resting head,
Fresh we woke upon the morrow:
15   All our thoughts and words had scope,
        We had health, and we had hope,
Toil and travel, but no sorrow.
We were of all tongues and creeds; –
Some were those who counted beads,
20   Some of mosque, and some of church,
        And some, or I mis-say, of neither;
Yet through the wide world might ye search,
        Nor find a motlier crew nor blither.

But some are dead, and some are gone,
25   And some are scatter'd and alone,
And some are rebels on the hills[1]
        That look along Epirus' valleys,
        Where freedom still at moments rallies,
And pays in blood oppression's ills;
30   And some are in a far countree,
And some all restlessly at home;
        But never more, oh! never, we
Shall meet to revel and to roam.
But those hardy days flew cheerily,
35   And when they now fall drearily,

1. The last tidings recently heard of Dervish (one of the Arnaouts who followed me) state him to be in revolt upon the mountains, at the head of some of the bands common in that country in times of trouble.

My thoughts, like swallows, skim the main,
And bear my spirit back again
Over the earth, and through the air,
A wild bird and a wanderer.
40 'Tis this that ever wakes my strain,
And oft, too oft, implores again
The few who may endure my lay,
To follow me so far away.
Stranger – wilt thou follow now,
45 And sit with me on Acro-Corinth's brow?

I
Many a vanish'd year and age,
And tempest's breath, and battle's rage,
Have swept o'er Corinth; yet she stands,
A fortress form'd to Freedom's hands.
5 The whirlwind's wrath, the earthquake's shock,
Have left untouch'd her hoary rock,
The keystone of a land, which still,
Though fall'n, looks proudly on that hill,
The landmark to the double tide
10 That purpling rolls on either side,
As if their waters chafed to meet,
Yet pause and crouch beneath her feet.
But could the blood before her shed
Since first Timoleon's brother bled,
15 Or baffled Persia's despot fled,
Arise from out the earth which drank
The stream of slaughter as it sank,
That sanguine ocean would o'erflow
Her isthmus idly spread below:
20 Or could the bones of all the slain,
Who perish'd there, be piled again,
That rival pyramid would rise
More mountain-like, through those clear skies,
Than yon tower-capp'd Acropolis,
25 Which seems the very clouds to kiss.

II

On dun Cithæron's ridge appears
The gleam of twice ten thousand spears;
And downward to the Isthmian plain,
From shore to shore of either main,
The tent is pitch'd, the crescent shines
Along the Moslem's leaguering lines;
And the dusk Spahi's bands advance
Beneath each bearded pacha's glance;
And far and wide as eye can reach
The turban'd cohorts throng the beach;
And there the Arab's camel kneels,
And there his steed the Tartar wheels;
The Turcoman hath left his herd,[1]
The sabre round his loins to gird;
And there the volleying thunders pour
Till waves grow smoother to the roar.
The trench is dug, the cannon's breath
Wings the far hissing globe of death;
Fast whirl the fragments from the wall,
Which crumbles with the ponderous ball;
And from that wall the foe replies,
O'er dusty plain and smoky skies,
With fires that answer fast and well
The summons of the Infidel.

III

But near and nearest to the wall
Of those who wish and work its fall,
With deeper skill in war's black art,
Than Othman's sons, and high of heart
As any chief that ever stood
Triumphant in the fields of blood;
From post to post, and deed to deed,
Fast spurring on his reeking steed,
Where sallying ranks the trench assail,
And make the foremost Moslem quail;

1. The life of the Turcomans is wandering and patriarchal: they dwell in tents.

60   Or where the battery, guarded well,
      Remains as yet impregnable,
      Alighting cheerly to inspire
      The soldier slackening in his fire;
      The first and freshest of the host
65   Which Stamboul's sultan there can boast,
      To guide the follower o'er the field,
      To point the tube, the lance to wield,
      Or whirl around the bickering blade; –
      Was Alp, the Adrian renegade!

      IV
70   From Venice – once a race of worth
      His gentle sires – he drew his birth;
      But late an exile from her shore,
      Against his countrymen he bore
      The arms they taught to bear; and now
75   The turban girt his shaven brow.
      Through many a change had Corinth pass'd
      With Greece to Venice' rule at last;
      And here, before her walls, with those
      To Greece and Venice equal foes,
80   He stood a foe, with all the zeal
      Which young and fiery converts feel,
      Within whose heated bosom throngs
      The memory of a thousand wrongs.
      To him had Venice ceased to be
85   Her ancient civic boast – 'the Free;'
      And in the palace of St Mark
      Unnamed accusers in the dark
      Within the 'Lion's mouth' had placed
      A charge against him uneffaced:
90   He fled in time, and saved his life,
      To waste his future years in strife,
      That taught his land how great her loss
      In him who triumph'd o'er the Cross,
      'Gainst which he rear'd the Crescent high,
95   And battled to avenge or die.

V

Coumourgi[1] – he whose closing scene
Adorn'd the triumph of Eugene,
When on Carlowitz' bloody plain,
The last and mightiest of the slain,
100 He sank, regretting not to die,
But cursed the Christian's victory –
Coumourgi – can his glory cease,
That latest conqueror of Greece,
Till Christian hands to Greece restore
105 The freedom Venice gave of yore?
A hundred years have roll'd away
Since he refix'd the Moslem's sway,
And now he led the Mussulman,
And gave the guidance of the van
110 To Alp, who well repaid the trust
By cities levell'd with the dust;
And proved, by many a deed of death,
How firm his heart in novel faith.

VI

The walls grew weak; and fast and hot
115 Against them pour'd the ceaseless shot,
With unabating fury sent
From battery to battlement;
And thunder-like the pealing din
Rose from each heated culverin;
120 And here and there some crackling dome
Was fired before the exploding bomb:

1. Ali Coumourgi, the favourite of three sultans, and Grand Vizier to Achmet III., after recovering Peloponnesus from the Venetians in one campaign, was mortally wounded in the next, against the Germans, at the battle of Peterwaradin (in the plain of Carlowitz), in Hungary, endeavouring to rally his guards. He died of his wounds next day. His last order was the decapitation of General Breuner, and some other German prisoners; and his last words, 'Oh that I could thus serve all the Christian dogs!' a speech and act not unlike one of Caligula. He was a young man of great ambition and unbounded presumption: on being told that Prince Eugene, then opposed to him, 'was a great general,' he said, 'I shall become a greater, and at his expense.'

And as the fabric sank beneath
The shattering shell's volcanic breath,
In red and wreathing columns flash'd
125 The flame, as loud the ruin crash'd,
Or into countless meteors driven,
Its earth-stars melted into heaven;
Whose clouds that day grew doubly dun,
Impervious to the hidden sun,
130 With volumed smoke that slowly grew
To one wide sky of sulphurous hue.

VII

But not for vengeance, long delay'd,
Alone, did Alp, the renegade,
The Moslem warriors sternly teach
135 His skill to pierce the promised breach:
Within these walls a maid was pent
His hope would win without consent
Of that inexorable sire,
Whose heart refused him in its ire,
140 When Alp, beneath his Christian name,
Her virgin hand aspired to claim.
In happier mood, and earlier time,
While unimpeach'd for traitorous crime,
Gayest in gondola or hall,
145 He glitter'd through the Carnival;
And tuned the softest serenade
That e'er on Adria's waters play'd
At midnight to Italian maid.

VIII

And many deem'd her heart was won;
150 For sought by numbers, given to none,
Had young Francesca's hand remain'd
Still by the church's bonds unchain'd:
And when the Adriatic bore
Lanciotto to the Paynim shore,
155 Her wonted smiles were seen to fail,
And pensive wax'd the maid and pale;

More constant at confessional,
More rare at masque and festival;
Or seen at such, with downcast eyes,
160   Which conquer'd hearts they ceased to prize:
With listless look she seems to gaze:
With humbler care her form arrays;
Her voice less lively in the song;
Her step, though light, less fleet among
165   The pairs, on whom the Morning's glance
Breaks, yet unsated with the dance.

IX

Sent by the state to guard the land,
(Which, wrested from the Moslem's hand,
While Sobieski tamed his pride
170   By Buda's wall and Danube's side,
The chiefs of Venice wrung away
From Patra to Euboea's bay,)
Minotti held in Corinth's towers
The Doge's delegated powers,
175   While yet the pitying eye of Peace
Smiled o'er her long forgotten Greece:
And ere that faithless truce was broke
Which freed her from the unchristian yoke,
With him his gentle daughter came;
180   Nor there, since Menelaus' dame
Forsook her lord and land, to prove
What woes await on lawless love,
Had fairer form adorn'd the shore
Than she, the matchless stranger, bore.

X

185   The wall is rent, the ruins yawn;
And, with to-morrow's earliest dawn,
O'er the disjointed mass shall vault
The foremost of the fierce assault.
The bands are rank'd; the chosen van
190   Of Tartar and of Mussulman,
The full of hope, misnamed 'forlorn,'
Who hold the thought of death in scorn,

And win their way with falchion's force,
Or pave the path with many a corse,
195   O'er which the following brave may rise,
Their stepping-stone – the last who dies!

XI
'Tis midnight: on the mountains brown
The cold, round moon shines deeply down;
Blue roll the waters, blue the sky
200   Spreads like an ocean hung on high,
Bespangled with those isles of light,
So wildly, spiritually bright;
Who ever gazed upon them shining
And turn'd to earth without repining,
205   Nor wish'd for wings to flee away,
And mix with their eternal ray?
The waves on either shore lay there
Calm, clear, and azure as the air;
And scarce their foam the pebbles shook,
210   But murmur'd meekly as the brook.
The winds were pillow'd on the waves;
The banners droop'd along their staves,
And, as they fell around them furling,
Above them shone the crescent curling;
215   And that deep silence was unbroke,
Save where the watch his signal spoke,
Save where the steed neigh'd oft and shrill,
And echo answer'd from the hill,
And the wide hum of that wild host
220   Rustled like leaves from coast to coast,
As rose the Muezzin's voice in air
In midnight call to wonted prayer;
It rose, that chanted mournful strain,
Like some lone spirit's o'er the plain:
225   'Twas musical, but sadly sweet,
Such as when winds and harp-strings meet,
And take a long unmeasured tone,
To mortal minstrelsy unknown.
It seem'd to those within the wall
230   A cry prophetic of their fall:

It struck even the besieger's ear
With something ominous and drear,
An undefined and sudden thrill,
Which makes the heart a moment still,
235   Then beat with quicker pulse, ashamed
Of that strange sense its silence framed;
Such as a sudden passing-bell
Wakes, though but for a stranger's knell.

XII

The tent of Alp was on the shore;
240   The sound was hush'd, the prayer was o'er;
The watch was set, the night-round made,
All mandates issued and obey'd:
'Tis but another anxious night,
His pains the morrow may require
245   With all revenge and love can pay,
In guerdon for their long delay.
Few hours remain, and he hath need
Of rest, to nerve for many a deed
Of slaughter; but within his soul
250   The thoughts like troubled waters roll.
He stood alone among the host;
Not his the loud fanatic boast
To plant the crescent o'er the cross,
Or risk a life with little loss,
255   Secure in paradise to be
By Houris loved immortally:
Nor his, what burning patriots feel,
The stern exaltedness of zeal,
Profuse of blood, untired in toil,
260   When battling on the parent soil.
He stood alone – a renegade
Against the country he betray'd;
He stood alone amidst his band,
Without a trusted heart or hand:
265   They follow'd him, for he was brave,
And great the spoil he got and gave;
They crouch'd to him, for he had skill
To warp and wield the vulgar will:

But still his Christian origin
270   With them was little less than sin.
They envied even the faithless fame
He earn'd beneath a Moslem name;
Since he, their mightiest chief, had been
In youth a bitter Nazarene.
275   They did not know how pride can stoop,
When baffled feelings withering droop;
They did not know how hate can burn
In hearts once changed from soft to stern;
Nor all the false and fatal zeal
280   The convert of revenge can feel.
He ruled them – man may rule the worst,
By ever daring to be first;
So lions o'er the jackal sway;
The jackal points, he fells the prey,
285   Then on the vulgar yelling press,
To gorge the relics of success.

XIII

His head grows fever'd, and his pulse
The quick successive throbs convulse;
In vain from side to side he throws
290   His form, in courtship of repose;
Or if he dozed, a sound, a start
Awoke him with a sunken heart.
The turban on his hot brow press'd,
The mail weigh'd lead-like on his breast,
295   Though oft and long beneath its weight
Upon his eyes had slumber sate,
Without or couch or canopy,
Except a rougher field and sky
Than now might yield a warrior's bed,
300   Than now along the heaven was spread.
He could not rest, he could not stay
Within his tent to wait for day,
But walk'd him forth along the sand,
Where thousand sleepers strew'd the strand.
305   What pillow'd them? and why should he
More wakeful than the humblest be,

Since more their peril, worse their toil?
And yet they fearless dream of spoil;
While he alone, where thousands pass'd
310 A night of sleep, perchance their last,
In sickly vigil wander'd on,
And envied all he gazed upon.

XIV

He felt his soul become more light
Beneath the freshness of the night.
315 Cool was the silent sky, though calm,
And bathed his brow with airy balm:
Behind, the camp – before him lay,
In many a winding creek and bay,
Lepanto's gulf; and, on the brow
320 Of Delphi's hill, unshaken snow,
High and eternal, such as shone
Through thousand summers brightly gone,
Along the gulf, the mount, the clime;
It will not melt, like man, to time:
325 Tyrant and slave are swept away,
Less form'd to wear before the ray;
But that white veil, the lightest, frailest,
Which on the mighty mount thou hailest,
While tower and tree are torn and rent,
330 Shines o'er its craggy battlement;
In form a peak, in height a cloud,
In texture like a hovering shroud,
Thus high by parting Freedom spread,
As from her fond abode she fled,
335 And linger'd on the spot, where long
Her prophet spirit spake in song.
Oh! still her step at moments falters
O'er wither'd fields, and ruin'd altars,
And fain would wake, in souls too broken,
340 By pointing to each glorious token:
But vain her voice, till better days
Dawn in those yet remember'd rays
Which shone upon the Persian flying,
And saw the Spartan smile in dying.

XV

345   Not mindless of these mighty times
         Was Alp, despite his flight and crimes;
         And through this night, as on he wander'd,
         And o'er the past and present ponder'd,
         And thought upon the glorious dead
350   Who there in better cause had bled,
         He felt how faint and feebly dim
         The fame that could accrue to him,
         Who cheer'd the band, and waved the sword,
         A traitor in a turban'd horde;
355   And led them to the lawless siege,
         Whose best success were sacrilege.
         Not so had those his fancy number'd,
         The chiefs whose dust around him slumber'd;
         Their phalanx marshall'd on the plain,
360   Whose bulwarks were not then in vain.
         They fell devoted, but undying;
         The very gale their names seem'd sighing:
         The waters murmur'd of their name;
         The woods were peopled with their fame;
365   The silent pillar, lone and grey,
         Claim'd kindred with their sacred clay;
         Their spirits wrapp'd the dusky mountain,
         Their memory sparkled o'er the fountain;
         The meanest rill, the mightiest river
370   Roll'd mingling with their fame for ever.
         Despite of every yoke she bears,
         That land is glory's still and theirs!
         'Tis still a watch-word to the earth:
         When man would do a deed of worth
375   He points to Greece, and turns to tread,
         So sanction'd, on the tyrant's head:
         He looks to her, and rushes on
         Where life is lost, or freedom won.

XVI

Still by the shore Alp mutely mused,
380   And woo'd the freshness Night diffused.
There shrinks no ebb in that tideless sea,[1]
Which changeless rolls eternally;
So that wildest of waves, in their angriest mood,
Scarce break on the bounds of the land for a rood;
385   And the powerless moon beholds them flow,
Heedless if she come or go:
Calm or high, in main or bay,
On their course she hath no sway.
The rock unworn its base doth bare,
390   And looks o'er the surf, but it comes not there;
And the fringe of the foam may be seen below,
On the line that it left long ages ago:
A smooth short space of yellow sand
Between it and the greener land.

395   He wander'd on, along the beach,
Till within the range of a carbine's reach
Of the leaguer'd wall; but they saw him not,
Or how could he 'scape from the hostile shot?
Did traitors lurk in the Christians' hold?
400   Were their hands grown stiff, or their hearts wax'd cold?
I know not, in sooth; but from yonder wall
There flash'd no fire, and there hiss'd no ball,
Though he stood beneath the bastion's frown,
That flank'd the sea-ward gate of the town;
405   Though he heard the sound, and could almost tell
The sullen words of the sentinel,
As his measured step on the stone below
Clank'd, as he paced it to and fro;
And he saw the lean dogs beneath the wall
410   Hold o'er the dead their carnival,
Gorging and growling o'er carcass and limb;
They were too busy to bark at him!

---

1. The reader need hardly be reminded that there are no perceptible tides in the Mediterranean.

From a Tartar's skull they had stripp'd the flesh,
As ye peel the fig when its fruit is fresh;
415   And their white tusks crunch'd o'er the whiter skull,[1]
As it slipp'd through their jaws, when their edge grew dull,
As they lazily mumbled the bones of the dead,
When they scarce could rise from the spot where they fed;
So well had they broken a lingering fast
420   With those who had fallen for that night's repast.
And Alp knew, by the turbans that roll'd on the sand,
The foremost of these were the best of his band:
Crimson and green were the shawls of their wear,
And each scalp had a single long tuft of hair,[2]
425   All the rest was shaven and bare.
The scalps were in the wild dog's maw,
The hair was tangled round his jaw.
But close by the shore, on the edge of the gulf,
There sat a vulture flapping a wolf,
430   Who had stolen from the hills, but kept away,
Scared by the dogs, from the human prey;
But he seized on his share of a steed that lay,
Pick'd by the birds, on the sands of the bay.

XVII

Alp turn'd him from the sickening sight:
435   Never had shaken his nerves in fight;
But he better could brook to behold the dying,
Deep in the tide of their warm blood lying,
Scorch'd with the death-thirst, and writhing in vain,
Than the perishing dead who are past all pain.
440   There is something of pride in the perilous hour,
Whate'er be the shape in which death may lower;

1. The spectacle I have seen, such as described, beneath the wall of the
Seraglio at Constantinople, in the little cavities worn by the Bosphorus in
the rock, a narrow terrace of which projects between the wall and the water.
I think the fact is also mentioned in Hobhouse's Travels. The bodies were
probably those of some refractory Janizaries.
2. This tuft, or long lock, is left from a superstition that Mahomet will draw
them into Paradise by it.

For Fame is there to say who bleeds,
And Honour's eye on daring deeds!
But when all is past, it is humbling to tread
445   O'er the weltering field of the tombless dead,
And see worms of the earth, and fowls of the air,
Beasts of the forest, all gathering there;
All regarding man as their prey,
All rejoicing in his decay.

XVIII

450   There is a temple in ruin stands,
Fashion'd by long forgotten hands;
Two or three columns, and many a stone,
Marble and granite, with grass o'ergrown!
Out upon Time! it will leave no more
455   Of the things to come than the things before!
Out upon Time! who for ever will leave
But enough of the past for the future to grieve
O'er that which hath been, and o'er that which must be:
What we have seen, our sons shall see;
460   Remnants of things that have pass'd away,
Fragments of stone, rear'd by creatures of clay!

XIX

He sate him down at a pillar's base,
And pass'd his hand athwart his face;
Like one in dreary musing mood,
465   Declining was his attitude;
His head was drooping on his breast,
Fever'd, throbbing, and oppress'd;
And o'er his brow, so downward bent,
Oft his beating fingers went,
470   Hurriedly, as you may see
Your own run over the ivory key,
Ere the measured tone is taken
By the chords you would awaken.
There he sate all heavily,
475   As he heard the night-wind sigh.

Was it the wind, through some hollow stone,
Sent that soft and tender moan?[1]
He lifted his head, and he look'd on the sea,
But it was unrippled as glass may be;
480   He look'd on the long grass – it waved not a blade;
How was that gentle sound convey'd?
He look'd to the banners – each flag lay still,
So did the leaves on Cithæron's hill,
And he felt not a breath come over his cheek;
485   What did that sudden sound bespeak?
He turn'd to the left – is he sure of sight?
There sate a lady, youthful and bright!

XX
He started up with more of fear
Than if an armed foe were near.
490   'God of my fathers! what is here?
Who art thou, and wherefore sent
So near a hostile armament?'
His trembling hands refused to sign
The cross he deem'd no more divine:
495   He had resumed it in that hour,
But conscience wrung away the power.
He gazed, he saw: he knew the face
Of beauty, and the form of grace;
It was Francesca by his side,
500   The maid who might have been his bride!

The rose was yet upon her cheek,
But mellow'd with a tenderer streak:

1. I must here acknowledge a close, though unintentional, resemblance in these twelve lines to a passage in an unpublished poem of Mr Coleridge, called 'Christabel.' It was not till after these lines were written that I heard that wild and singularly original and beautiful poem recited; and the MS. of that production I never saw till very recently, by the kindness of Mr Coleridge himself, who, I hope, is convinced that I have not been a wilful plagiarist. The original idea undoubtedly pertains to Mr Coleridge, whose poem has been composed above fourteen years. Let me conclude by a hope that he will not longer delay the publication of a production, of which I can only add my mite of approbation to the applause of far more competent judges.

Where was the play of her soft lips fled?
Gone was the smile that enliven'd their red.
505   The ocean's calm within their view,
Beside her eye had less of blue;
But like that cold wave it stood still,
And its glance, though clear, was chill.
Around her form a thin robe twining,
510   Nought conceal'd her bosom shining;
Through the parting of her hair,
Floating darkly downward there,
Her rounded arm show'd white and bare:
And ere yet she made reply,
515   Once she raised her hand on high;
It was so wan, and transparent of hue,
You might have seen the moon shine through.

XXI

'I come from my rest to him I love best,
That I may be happy, and he may be bless'd.
520   I have pass'd the guards, the gate, the wall;
Sought thee in safety through foes and all.
'Tis said the lion will turn and flee
From a maid in the pride of her purity;
And the Power on high, that can shield the good
525   Thus from the tyrant of the wood,
Hath extended its mercy to guard me as well
From the hands of the leaguering infidel.
I come – and if I come in vain,
Never, oh never, we meet again!
530   Thou hast done a fearful deed
In falling away from thy father's creed:
But dash that turban to earth, and sign
The sign of the cross, and for ever be mine;
Wring the black drop from thy heart,
535   And to-morrow unites us no more to part.'

'And where should our bridal couch be spread?
In the midst of the dying and the dead?
For to-morrow we give to the slaughter and flame
The sons and the shrines of the Christian name.

540 None, save thou and thine, I've sworn,
Shall be left upon the morn:
But thee will I bear to a lovely spot,
Where our hands shall be join'd, and our sorrow forgot.
There thou yet shalt be my bride,
545 When once again I've quell'd the pride
Of Venice; and her hated race
Have felt the arm they would debase
Scourge, with a whip of scorpions, those
Whom vice and envy made my foes.'

550 Upon his hand she laid her own —
Light was the touch, but it thrill'd to the bone,
And shot a chillness to his heart,
Which fix'd him beyond the power to start.
Though slight was that grasp so mortal cold,
555 He could not loose him from its hold;
But never did clasp of one so dear
Strike on the pulse with such feeling of fear,
As those thin fingers, long and white,
Froze through his blood by their touch that night.
560 The feverish glow of his brow was gone,
And his heart sank so still that it felt like stone,
As he look'd on the face, and beheld its hue,
So deeply changed from what he knew:
Fair but faint — without the ray
565 Of mind, that made each feature play
Like sparkling waves on a sunny day;
And her motionless lips lay still as death,
And her words came forth without her breath,
And there rose not a heave o'er her bosom's swell,
570 And there seem'd not a pulse in her veins to dwell.
Though her eye shone out, yet the lids were fix'd,
And the glance that it gave was wild and unmix'd
With aught of change, as the eyes may seem
Of the restless who walk in a troubled dream;
575 Like the figures on arras, that gloomily glare,
Stirr'd by the breath of the wintry air,
So seen by the dying lamp's fitful light,
Lifeless, but life-like, and awful to sight;

As they seem, through the dimness, about to come down
580 From the shadowy wall where their images frown;
Fearfully flitting to and fro,
As the gusts on the tapestry come and go.
'If not for love of me be given
Thus much, then, for the love of heaven, –
585 Again I say – that turban tear
From off thy faithless brow, and swear
Thine injured country's sons to spare,
Or thou art lost; and never shalt see –
Not earth – that's past – but heaven or me.
590 If this thou dost accord, albeit
A heavy doom 'tis thine to meet,
That doom shall half absolve thy sin,
And mercy's gate may receive thee within:
But pause one moment more, and take
595 The curse of Him thou didst forsake;
And look once more to heaven, and see
Its love for ever shut from thee.
There is a light cloud by the moon –[1]
'Tis passing, and will pass full soon –
600 If, by the time its vapoury sail
Hath ceased her shaded orb to veil,
Thy heart within thee is not changed,
Then God and man are both avenged;
Dark will thy doom be, darker still
605 Thine immortality of ill.'

Alp look'd to heaven, and saw on high
The sign she spake of in the sky;
But his heart was swollen, and turn'd aside
By deep interminable pride.

1. I have been told that the idea expressed in this and the five following
lines has been admired by those whose approbation is valuable. I am glad of
it: but it is not original – at least not mine; it may be found much better
expressed in pages 182–3–4 of the English version of 'Vathek' (I forget the
precise page of the French), a work to which I have before referred; and
never recur to, or read, without a renewal of gratification.

610   This first false passion of his breast
    Roll'd like a torrent o'er the rest.
    He sue for mercy! *He* dismay'd
    By wild words of a timid maid!
    He, wrong'd by Venice, vow to save
615   Her sons, devoted to the grave!
    No – though that cloud were thunder's worst,
    And charged to crush him – let it burst!
    He look'd upon it earnestly,
    Without an accent of reply;
620   He watch'd it passing; it is flown:
    Full on his eye the clear moon shone,
    And thus he spake – 'Whate'er my fate,
    I am no changeling – 'tis too late:
    The reed in storms may bow and quiver,
625   Then rise again; the tree must shiver.
    What Venice made me, I must be,
    Her foe in all, save love to thee:
    But thou art safe: oh, fly with me!'
    He turn'd, but she is gone!
630   Nothing is there but the column stone.
    Hath she sunk in the earth, or melted in air?
    He saw not – he knew not – but nothing is there.

    XXII
    The night is past, and shines the sun
    As if that morn were a jocund one.
635   Lightly and brightly breaks away
    The Morning from her mantle grey,
    And the Noon will look on a sultry day.
    Hark to the trump, and the drum,
    And the mournful sound of the barbarous horn,
640   And the flap of the banners, that flit as they're borne,
    And the neigh of the steed, and the multitude's hum,
    And the clash, and the shout, 'They come! they come!'
    The horsetails[1] are pluck'd from the ground, and the sword
    From its sheath: and they form, and but wait for the word.

1. The horsetails, fixed upon a lance, a pacha's standard.

645   Tartar, and Spahi, and Turcoman,
        Strike your tents, and throng to the van;
        Mount ye, spur ye, skirr the plain,
        That the fugitive may flee in vain,
        When he breaks from the town; and none escape,
650   Aged or young, in the Christian shape;
        While your fellows on foot, in a fiery mass,
        Bloodstain the breach through which they pass.
        The steeds are all bridled, and snort to the rein;
        Curved is each neck, and flowing each mane;
655   White is the foam of their champ on the bit;
        The spears are uplifted; the matches are lit;
        The cannon are pointed, and ready to roar,
        And crush the wall they have crumbled before:
        Forms in his phalanx each Janizar;
660   Alp at their head; his right arm is bare,
        So is the blade of his scimitar;
        The khan and the pachas are all at their post;
        The vizier himself at the head of the host.
        When the culverin's signal is fired, then on;
665   Leave not in Corinth a living one –
        A priest at her altars, a chief in her halls,
        A hearth in her mansions, a stone on her walls.
        God and the prophet – Alla Hu!
        Up to the skies with that wild halloo!
670   'There the breach lies for passage, the ladder to scale;
        And your hands on your sabres, and how should ye fail?
        He who first downs with the red cross may crave
        His heart's dearest wish; let him ask it, and have!'
        Thus utter'd Coumourgi, the dauntless vizier;
675   The reply was the brandish of sabre and spear,
        And the shout of fierce thousands in joyous ire: –
        Silence – hark to the signal – fire!

        XXIII
        As the wolves, that headlong go
        On the stately buffalo,
680   Though with fiery eyes, and angry roar,
        And hoofs that stamp, and horns that gore,

He tramples on earth, or tosses on high
The foremost, who rush on his strength but to die:
Thus against the wall they went,
685   Thus the first were backward bent;
Many a bosom, sheathed in brass,
Strew'd the earth like broken glass,
Shiver'd by the shot, that tore
The ground whereon they moved no more:
690   Even as they fell, in files they lay,
Like the mower's grass at the close of day,
When his work is done on the levell'd plain;
Such was the fall of the foremost slain.

XXIV

As the spring-tides, with heavy plash,
695   From the cliffs invading dash
Huge fragments, sapp'd by the ceaseless flow,
Till white and thundering down they go,
Like the avalanche's snow
On the Alpine vales below;
700   Thus at length, outbreathed and worn,
Corinth's sons were downward borne
By the long and oft renew'd
Charge of the Moslem multitude.
In firmness they stood, and in masses they fell,
705   Heap'd by the host of the infidel,
Hand to hand, and foot to foot:
Nothing there, save death, was mute;
Stroke, and thrust, and flash, and cry
For quarter, or for victory,
710   Mingle there with the volleying thunder,
Which makes the distant cities wonder
How the sounding battle goes,
If with them, or for their foes;
If they must mourn, or may rejoice
715   In that annihilating voice,
Which pierces the deep hills through and through
With an echo dread and new:

You might have heard it, on that day,
O'er Salamis and Megara;
720   (We have heard the hearers say,)
Even unto Piræus' bay.

XXV

From the point of encountering blades to the hilt,
Sabres and swords with blood were gilt;
But the rampart is won, and the spoil begun,
725   And all but the after carnage done.
Shriller shrieks now mingling come
From within the plunder'd dome:
Hark to the haste of flying feet,
That splash in the blood of the slippery street;
730   But here and there, where 'vantage ground
Against the foe may still be found,
Desperate groups, of twelve or ten,
Make a pause, and turn again –
With banded backs against the wall,
735   Fiercely stand, or fighting fall.

There stood an old man – his hairs were white,
But his veteran arm was full of might:
So gallantly bore he the brunt of the fray,
The dead before him, on that day,
740   In a semicircle lay;
Still he combated unwounded,
Though retreating, unsurrounded.
Many a scar of former fight
Lurk'd beneath his corslet bright;
745   But of every wound his body bore,
Each and all had been ta'en before:
Though aged, he was so iron of limb,
Few of our youth could cope with him;
And the foes, whom he singly kept at bay,
750   Outnumber'd his thin hairs of silver grey.
From right to left his sabre swept;
Many an Othman mother wept
Sons that were unborn, when dipp'd

His weapon first in Moslem gore,
755   Ere his years could count a score.
Of all he might have been the sire
Who fell that day beneath his ire:
For, sonless left long years ago,
His wrath made many a childless foe;
760   And since the day, when in the strait[1]
His only boy had met his fate,
His parent's iron hand did doom
More than a human hecatomb.
If shades by carnage be appeased,
765   Patroclus' spirit less was pleased
Than his, Minotti's son, who died
Where Asia's bounds and ours divide.
Buried he lay, where thousands before
For thousands of years were inhumed on the shore;
770   What of them is left, to tell
Where they lie, and how they fell?
Not a stone on their turf, nor a bone in their graves;
But they live in the verse that immortally saves.

XXVI
Hark to the Allah shout! a band
775   Of the Mussulman bravest and best is at hand:
Their leader's nervous arm is bare,
Swifter to smite, and never to spare –
Unclothed to the shoulder it waves them on;
Thus in the fight is he ever known:
780   Others a gaudier garb may show,
To tempt the spoil of the greedy foe;
Many a hand's on a richer hilt,
But none on a steel more ruddily gilt;
Many a loftier turban may wear, –
785   Alp is but known by the white arm bare;
Look through the thick of the fight, 'tis there!

1. In the naval battle at the mouth of the Dardanelles, between the Venetians
and Turks.

There is not a standard on that shore
So well advanced the ranks before;
There is not a banner in Moslem war
790   Will lure the Delhis half so far;
It glances like a falling star!
Where'er that mighty arm is seen,
The bravest be, or late have been;
There the craven cries for quarter
795   Vainly to the vengeful Tartar;
Or the hero, silent lying,
Scorns to yield a groan in dying;
Mustering his last feeble blow
'Gainst the nearest levell'd foe,
800   Though faint beneath the mutual wound,
Grappling on the gory ground.

XXVII

Still the old man stood erect,
And Alp's career a moment check'd.
'Yield thee, Minotti; quarter take,
805   For thine own, thy daughter's sake.'
'Never, renegado, never!
Though the life of thy gift would last for ever.'

'Francesca! – Oh, my promised bride!
Must she too perish by thy pride?'
810   'She is safe.' – 'Where? where?' – 'In heaven;
From whence thy traitor soul is driven –
Far from thee, and undefiled.'
Grimly then Minotti smiled,
As he saw Alp staggering bow
815   Before his words, as with a blow.

'Oh God! when died she?' – 'Yesternight –
Nor weep I for her spirit's flight:
None of my pure race shall be
Slaves to Mahomet and thee –
820   Come on!' – That challenge is in vain –
Alp's already with the slain!

While Minotti's words were wreaking
More revenge in bitter speaking
Than his falchion's point had found,
825   Had the time allow'd to wound,
From within the neighbouring porch
Of a long defended church,
Where the last and desperate few
Would the failing fight renew,
830   The sharp shot dash'd Alp to the ground;
Ere an eye could view the wound
That crash'd through the brain of the infidel,
Round he spun, and down he fell;
A flash like fire within his eyes
835   Blazed, as he bent no more to rise,
And then eternal darkness sunk
Through all the palpitating trunk;
Nought of life left, save a quivering
Where his limbs were slightly shivering:
840   They turn'd him on his back; his breast
And brow were stain'd with gore and dust,
And through his lips the life-blood oozed,
From its deep veins lately loosed;
But in his pulse there was no throb,
845   Nor on his lips one dying sob;
Sigh, nor word, nor struggling breath
Heralded his way to death:
Ere his very thought could pray,
Unaneled he pass'd away,
850   Without a hope from mercy's aid, –
To the last – a Renegade.

XXVIII
Fearfully the yell arose
Of his followers, and his foes;
These in joy, in fury those:
855   Then again in conflict mixing,
Clashing swords, and spears transfixing,
Interchanged the blow and thrust,
Hurling warriors in the dust.

Street by street, and foot by foot,
860 Still Minotti dares dispute
The latest portion of the land
Left beneath his high command;
With him, aiding heart and hand,
The remnant of his gallant band.
865 Still the church is tenable,
   Whence issued late the fated ball
   That half avenged the city's fall,
When Alp, her fierce assailant, fell:
Thither bending sternly back,
870 They leave before a bloody track;
And, with their faces to the foe,
Dealing wounds with every blow,
The chief, and his retreating train,
Join to those within the fane;
875 There they yet may breathe awhile,
Shelter'd by the massy pile.

XXIX

Brief breathing-time! the turban'd host,
With adding ranks and raging boast,
Press onwards with such strength and heat,
880 Their numbers balk their own retreat;
For narrow the way that led to the spot
Where still the Christians yielded not;
And the foremost, if fearful, may vainly try
Through the massy column to turn and fly;
885 They perforce must do or die.
They die; but ere their eyes could close,
Avengers o'er their bodies rose;
Fresh and furious, fast they fill
The ranks unthinn'd, though slaughter'd still;
890 And faint the weary Christians wax
Before the still renew'd attacks:
And now the Othmans gain the gate;
Still resists its iron weight,
And still, all deadly aim'd and hot,
895 From every crevice comes the shot;

From every shatter'd window pour
The volleys of the sulphurous shower:
But the portal wavering grows and weak –
The iron yields, the hinges creak –
900 It bends – it falls – and all is o'er;
Lost Corinth may resist no more!

XXX

Darkly, sternly, and all alone,
Minotti stood o'er the altar stone:
Madonna's face upon him shone,
905 Painted in heavenly hues above,
With eyes of light and looks of love;
And placed upon that holy shrine
To fix our thoughts on things divine,
When pictured there, we kneeling see
910 Her, and the boy-God on her knee,
Smiling sweetly on each prayer
To heaven, as if to waft it there,
Still she smiled; even now she smiles,
Though slaughter streams along her aisles:
915 Minotti lifted his aged eye,
And made the sign of a cross with a sigh,
Then seized a torch which blazed thereby;
And still he stood, while, with steel and flame,
Inward and onward the Mussulman came.

XXXI

920 The vaults beneath the mosaic stone
Contain'd the dead of ages gone;
Their names were on the graven floor,
But now illegible with gore;
The carved crests, and curious hues
925 The varied marble's veins diffuse,
Were smear'd, and slippery – stain'd, and strown
With broken swords, and helms o'erthrown:
There were dead above, and the dead below
Lay cold in many a coffin'd row;

930 You might see them piled in sable state,
     By a pale light through a gloomy grate;
     But War had enter'd their dark caves,
     And stored along the vaulted graves
     Her sulphurous treasures, thickly spread
935 In masses by the fleshless dead:
     Here, throughout the siege, had been
     The Christian's chiefest magazine;
     To these a late form'd train now led,
     Minotti's last and stern resource
940 Against the foe's o'erwhelming force.

     XXXII
     The foe came on, and few remain
     To strive, and those must strive in vain:
     For lack of further lives, to slake
     The thirst of vengeance now awake,
945 With barbarous blows they gash the dead,
     And lop the already lifeless head,
     And fell the statues from their niche,
     And spoil the shrines of offering rich,
     And from each other's rude hands wrest
950 The silver vessels saints had bless'd.
     To the high altar on they go;
     Oh, but it made a glorious show!
     On its table still behold
     The cup of consecrated gold;
955 Massy and deep, a glittering prize,
     Brightly it sparkles to plunderers' eyes:
     That morn it held the holy wine,
     Converted by Christ to his blood so divine,
     Which his worshippers drank at the break of day,
960 To shrive their souls ere they join'd in the fray.
     Still a few drops within it lay;
     And round the sacred table glow
     Twelve lofty lamps, in splendid row,
     From the purest metal cast;
965 A spoil – the richest, and the last.

XXXIII

So near they came, the nearest stretch'd
To grasp the spoil he almost reach'd,
        When old Minotti's hand
Touch'd with the torch the train —
970   'Tis fired!
Spire, vaults, the shrine, the spoil, the slain,
        The turban'd victors, the Christian band,
All that of living or dead remain,
Hurl'd on high with the shiver'd fane,
975   In one wild roar expired!
The shatter'd town — the walls thrown down —
The waves a moment backward bent —
The hills that shake, although unrent,
        As if an earthquake pass'd —
980 The thousand shapeless things all driven
In cloud and flame athwart the heaven,
        By that tremendous blast —
Proclaim'd the desperate conflict o'er
On that too long afflicted shore:
985 Up to the sky like rockets go
All that mingled there below:
Many a tall and goodly man,
Scorch'd and shrivell'd to a span,
When he fell to earth again
990 Like a cinder strew'd the plain:
Down the ashes shower like rain;
Some fell in the gulf, which received the sprinkles
With a thousand circling wrinkles;
Some fell on the shore, but, far away,
995 Scatter'd o'er the isthmus lay;
Christian or Moslem, which be they?
Let their mothers see and say!
When in cradled rest they lay,
And each nursing mother smiled
1000 On the sweet sleep of her child,
Little deem'd she such a day
Would rend those tender limbs away.

Not the matrons that them bore
Could discern their offspring more;
1005   That one moment left no trace
More of human form or face
Save a scatter'd scalp or bone:
And down came blazing rafters, strown
Around, and many a falling stone,
1010   Deeply dinted in the clay,
All blacken'd there and reeking lay.
All the living things that heard
That deadly earth-shock disappear'd:
The wild birds flew; the wild dogs fled,
1015   And howling left the unburied dead;
The camels from their keepers broke;
The distant steer forsook the yoke –
The nearer steed plunged o'er the plain,
And burst his girth, and tore his rein;
1020   The bull-frog's note, from out the marsh,
Deep-mouth'd arose, and doubly harsh;
The wolves yell'd on the cavern'd hill
Where echo roll'd in thunder still;
The jackal's troop, in gather'd cry,[1]
1025   Bay'd from afar complainingly,
With a mix'd and mournful sound,
Like crying babe, and beaten hound:
With sudden wing, and ruffled breast,
The eagle left his rocky nest,
1030   And mounted nearer to the sun,
The clouds beneath him seem'd so dun;
Their smoke assail'd his startled beak,
And made him higher soar and shriek –
        Thus was Corinth lost and won!

---

1. I believe I have taken a poetical licence to transplant the jackal from Asia.
In Greece, I never saw nor heard these animals; but among the ruins of
Ephesus I have heard them by hundreds. They haunt ruins, and follow
armies.

When we two parted

When we two parted
   In silence and tears,
Half broken-hearted
   To sever for years,
5 Pale grew thy cheek and cold,
   Colder thy kiss;
Truly that hour foretold
   Sorrow to this.

The dew of the morning
10   Sunk chill on my brow –
It felt like the warning
   Of what I feel now.
Thy vows are all broken,
   And light is thy fame;
15 I hear thy name spoken,
   And share in its shame.

They name thee before me,
   A knell to mine ear;
A shudder comes o'er me –
20   Why wert thou so dear?
They know not I knew thee,
   Who knew thee too well: –
Long, long shall I rue thee,
   Too deeply to tell.

25 In secret we met –
   In silence I grieve,
That thy heart could forget,
   Thy spirit deceive.
If I should meet thee
30   After long years,
How should I greet thee? –
   With silence and tears.

1808.

Fare thee well!

'Alas! they had been friends in Youth;
But whispering tongues can poison truth;
And constancy lives in realms above;
And Life is thorny; and youth is vain:
And to be wroth with one we love,
Doth work like madness in the brain;

*   *   *   *   *

But never either found another
To free the hollow heart from paining –
They stood aloof, the scars remaining,
Like cliffs, which had been rent asunder;
A dreary sea now flows between,
But neither heat, nor frost, nor thunder
Shall wholly do away, I ween,
The marks of that which once hath been.'

COLERIDGE's *Christabel.*

Fare thee well! and if for ever,
    Still for ever, fare *thee well:*
Even though unforgiving, never
    'Gainst thee shall my heart rebel.

5   Would that breast were bared before thee
        Where thy head so oft hath lain,
    While that placid sleep came o'er thee
        Which thou ne'er canst know again:

    Would that breast, by thee glanced over,
10   Every inmost thought could show!
    Then thou would'st at last discover
        'Twas not well to spurn it so.

Though the world for this commend thee –
　　Though it smile upon the blow,
15 Even its praises must offend thee,
　　Founded on another's woe:

Though my many faults defaced me,
　　Could no other arm be found,
Than the one which once embraced me,
20 　　To inflict a cureless wound?

Yet, oh yet, thyself deceive not;
　　Love may sink by slow decay,
But by sudden wrench, believe not
　　Hearts can thus be torn away:

25 Still thine own its life retaineth –
　　Still must mine, though bleeding, beat;
And the undying thought which paineth
　　Is – that we no more may meet.

These are words of deeper sorrow
30 　　Than the wail above the dead;
Both shall live, but every morrow
　　Wake us from a widow'd bed.

And when thou would solace gather,
　　When our child's first accents flow,
35 Wilt thou teach her to say 'Father!'
　　Though his care she must forego?

When her little hands shall press thee,
　　When her lip to thine is press'd,
Think of him whose prayer shall bless thee,
40 　　Think of him thy love had bless'd!

Should her lineaments resemble
　　Those thou never more may'st see,
Then thy heart will softly tremble
　　With a pulse yet true to me.

45   All my faults perchance thou knowest,
          All my madness none can know;
      All my hopes, where'er thou goest,
          Wither, yet with *thee* they go.

      Every feeling hath been shaken;
50   Pride, which not a world could bow,
      Bows to thee — by thee forsaken,
          Even my soul forsakes me now:

      But 'tis done — all words are idle —
          Words from me are vainer still;
55   But the thoughts we cannot bridle
          Force their way without the will. —

      Fare thee well! — thus disunited,
          Torn from every nearer tie,
      Sear'd in heart, and lone, and blighted,
60   More than this I scarce can die.

                                    March 17, 1816.

Prometheus

I

      Titan! to whose immortal eyes
          The sufferings of mortality,
          Seen in their sad reality,
      Were not as things that gods despise;
5   What was thy pity's recompense?
      A silent suffering, and intense;
      The rock, the vulture, and the chain,
      All that the proud can feel of pain,
      The agony they do not show,
10   The suffocating sense of woe,
          Which speaks but in its loneliness,
      And then is jealous lest the sky
      Should have a listener, nor will sigh
          Until its voice is echoless.

II

15 Titan! to thee the strife was given
        Between the suffering and the will,
        Which torture where they cannot kill;
    And the inexorable Heaven,
    And the deaf tyranny of Fate,
20 The ruling principle of Hate,
    Which for its pleasure doth create
    The things it may annihilate,
    Refused thee even the boon to die:
    The wretched gift eternity
25 Was thine – and thou hast borne it well.
    All that the Thunderer wrung from thee
    Was but the menace which flung back
    On him the torments of thy rack;
    The fate thou didst so well foresee,
30 But would not to appease him tell;
    And in thy Silence was his Sentence,
    And in his Soul a vain repentance,
    And evil dread so ill dissembled
    That in his hand the lightnings trembled.

III

35 Thy Godlike crime was to be kind,
        To render with thy precepts less
        The sum of human wretchedness,
    And strengthen Man with his own mind;
    But baffled as thou wert from high,
40 Still in thy patient energy,
    In the endurance, and repulse
        Of thine impenetrable Spirit,
    Which Earth and Heaven could not convulse,
        A mighty lesson we inherit:
45 Thou art a symbol and a sign
        To Mortals of their fate and force;
    Like thee, Man is in part divine,
        A troubled stream from a pure source;
    And Man in portions can foresee
50 His own funereal destiny;

His wretchedness, and his resistance,
And his sad unallied existence:
To which his Spirit may oppose
Itself – and equal to all woes,
55   And a firm will, and a deep sense,
Which even in torture can descry
      Its own concenter'd recompense,
Triumphant where it dares defy,
And making Death a Victory.

Diodati, July, 1816.

THE PRISONER OF CHILLON
A Fable

Sonnet on Chillon

Eternal Spirit of the chainless Mind!
    Brightest in dungeons, Liberty! thou art,
    For there thy habitation is the heart –
The heart which love of thee alone can bind;
5 And when thy sons to fetters are consign'd –
    To fetters, and the damp vault's dayless gloom,
    Their country conquers with their martyrdom,
And Freedom's fame finds wings on every wind.
Chillon! thy prison is a holy place,
10 And thy sad floor an altar – for 'twas trod,
Until his very steps have left a trace
    Worn, as if thy cold pavement were a sod,
By Bonnivard! – May none those marks efface!
    For they appeal from tyranny to God.

When this poem was composed, I was not sufficiently aware of the history of Bonnivard, or I should have endeavoured to dignify the subject by an attempt to celebrate his courage and his virtues. With some account of his life I have been furnished, by the kindness of a citizen of that republic, which is still proud of the memory of a man worthy of the best age of ancient freedom: –

'François de Bonnivard, fils de Louis de Bonnivard, originaire de Seyssel et Seigneur de Lunes, naquit en 1496. Il fit ses études à Turin: en 1510 Jean Aimé de Bonnivard, son oncle, lui résigna le Prieuré de St Victor, qui aboutissoit aux murs de Genève, et qui formoit un bénéfice considérable.

'Ce grand homme – (Bonnivard mérite ce titre par la force de son âme, la droiture de son cœur, la noblesse de ses intentions, la sagesse de ses conseils, le courage de ses démarches, l'étendue de ses connaissances et la vivacité de son esprit), – ce grand homme, qui excitera l'admiration de tous ceux qu'une vertu héroïque peut encore émouvoir, inspirera encore la plus vive reconnaissance dans les cœurs des Génévois qui aiment Genève. Bonnivard en fut toujours un des plus fermes appuis: pour assurer la liberté de notre République, il ne craignit pas de perdre souvent la sienne; il oublia son repos; il méprisa ses richesses; il ne négligea rien pour affermir le bonheur d'une patrie qu'il honora de son choix: dès ce moment il la chérit comme le plus zélé de ses citoyens; il la servit avec l'intrépidité d'un héros, et il écrivit son Histoire avec la naïveté d'un philosophe et la chaleur d'un patriote.

'Il dit dans le commencement de son Histoire de Genève, que, *dès qu'il eut commencé de lire l'histoire des nations, il se sentit entraîné par son goût pour les Républiques, dont il épousa toujours les intérêts*: c'est ce goût pour la liberté qui lui fit sans doute adopter Genève pour sa patrie.

'Bonnivard, encore jeune, s'annonça hautement comme le défenseur de Genève contre le Duc de Savoye et l'Evêque.

'En 1519, Bonnivard devient le martyr de sa patrie. Le Duc de Savoye étant entré dans Genève avec cinq cent hommes, Bonnivard craint le ressentiment du Duc; il voulut se retirer à Fribourg pour en éviter les suites; mais il fut trahi par deux hommes qui l'accompagnoient, et conduit par ordre du Prince à Grolée, où il resta prisonnier pendant deux ans. Bonnivard etoit malheureux dans ses voyages: comme ses malheurs n'avoient point ralenti son zèle pour Genève, il etoit toujours un ennemi redoutable pour ceux qui la menaçoient, et par conséquent il devait être exposé à leurs coups. Il fut rencontré en 1530 sur le Jura par des voleurs, qui le dépouillèrent et qui le mirent encore entre les mains du Duc de Savoye: ce Prince le fit enfermer dans le Château de Chillon, où il resta sans être interrogé jusques en 1536; il fut alors delivré par les Bernois, qui s'emparèrent du Pays de Vaud.

'Bonnivard, en sortant de sa captivité, eut le plaisir de trouver Genève libre et réformée: la République s'empressa de lui témoigner sa reconnaissance, et de le dédommager des maux qu'il avoit soufferts; elle le reçut Bourgeois de la ville au mois de Juin, 1536; elle lui donna la maison habitée autrefois par le Vicaire-Général, et elle lui assigna une pension de deux cent écus d'or tant qu'il séjourneroit à Genève. Il fut admis dans le Conseil de Deux-Cent en 1537.

'Bonnivard n'a pas fini d'être utile: après avoir travaillé à rendre Genève libre, il réussit à la rendre tolérante. Bonnivard engagea le Conseil à accorder aux Ecclésiastiques et aux paysans un tems suffisant pour examiner les propositions qu'on leur faisoit; il réussit par sa douceur: on prêche toujours le Christianisme avec succès quand on le prêche avec charité.

'Bonnivard fut savant: ses manuscrits, qui sont dans la Bibliothèque publique, prouvent qu'il avoit bien lu les auteurs classiques Latins, et qu'il avoit approfondi la théologie et l'histoire. Ce grand homme aimoit les sciences, et il croyoit qu'elles pouvoient faire la gloire de Genève; aussi il ne négligea rien pour les fixer dans cette ville naissante; en 1551 il donna sa bibliothèque au public; elle fut le commencement de notre biblothèque publique; et ces livres sont en partie les rares et belles éditions du quinzième siècle qu'on voit dans notre collection. Enfin, pendant la même année, ce bon patriote institua la République son héritière, à condition qu'elle employeroit ses biens à entretenir le collège dont on projettoit la fondation.

'Il paroit que Bonnivard mourut en 1570; mais on ne peut l'assurer, parcequ'il y a une lacune dans le Nécrologe depuis le mois de Juillet, 1570, jusques en 1571.'

THE PRISONER OF CHILLON

I

My hair is grey, but not with years,
    Nor grew it white
    In a single night,[1]
As men's have grown from sudden fears:
5   My limbs are bow'd, though not with toil,
    But rusted with a vile repose,
For they have been a dungeon's spoil,
    And mine has been the fate of those
To whom the goodly earth and air
10   Are bann'd, and barr'd – forbidden fare;
But this was for my father's faith
I suffer'd chains and courted death;
That father perish'd at the stake
For tenets he would not forsake;
15 And for the same his lineal race
In darkness found a dwelling-place;
We were seven – who now are one,
    Six in youth and one in age,
Finish'd as they had begun,
20   Proud of Persecution's rage;
One in fire, and two in field,
Their belief with blood have seal'd:
Dying as their father died,
For the God their foes denied; –
25 Three were in a dungeon cast,
Of whom this wreck is left the last.

II

There are seven pillars of Gothic mould,
In Chillon's dungeons deep and old,
There are seven columns massy and grey,
30 Dim with a dull imprison'd ray,

1. Ludovico Sforza, and others. – The same is asserted of Marie Antoinette's, the wife of Louis the Sixteenth, though not in quite so short a period. Grief is said to have the same effect: to such, and not to fear, this change in *hers* was to be attributed.

A sunbeam which hath lost its way,
And through the crevice and the cleft
Of the thick wall is fallen and left:
Creeping o'er the floor so damp,
35   Like a marsh's meteor lamp:
And in each pillar there is a ring,
        And in each ring there is a chain;
That iron is a cankering thing,
        For in these limbs its teeth remain,
40   With marks that will not wear away,
Till I have done with this new day,
Which now is painful to these eyes,
Which have not seen the sun so rise
For years – I cannot count them o'er,
45   I lost their long and heavy score
When my last brother droop'd and died,
And I lay living by his side.

III
They chain'd us each to a column stone,
And we were three – yet, each alone;
50   We could not move a single pace,
We could not see each other's face,
But with that pale and livid light
That made us strangers in our sight:
And thus together – yet apart,
55   Fetter'd in hand, but pined in heart;
'Twas still some solace, in the dearth
Of the pure elements of earth,
To hearken to each other's speech,
And each turn comforter to each
60   With some new hope or legend old,
Or song heroically bold;
But even these at length grew cold.
Our voices took a dreary tone,
An echo of the dungeon stone,
65   A grating sound – not full and free
        As they of yore were wont to be;
        It might be fancy – but to me
They never sounded like our own.

IV

I was the eldest of the three,
    And to uphold and cheer the rest
    I ought to do – and did my best –
And each did well in his degree.
    The youngest, whom my father loved,
Because our mother's brow was given
To him – with eyes as blue as heaven,
    For him my soul was sorely moved:
And truly might it be distress'd
To see such bird in such a nest;
For he was beautiful as day –
    (When day was beautiful to me
    As to young eagles being free) –
    A polar day, which will not see
A sunset till its summer's gone
    Its sleepless summer of long light,
The snow-clad offspring of the sun:
    And thus he was as pure and bright,
And in his natural spirit gay,
With tears for nought but others' ills,
And then they flow'd like mountain rills,
Unless he could assuage the woe
Which he abhorr'd to view below.

V

The other was as pure of mind,
But form'd to combat with his kind;
Strong in his frame, and of a mood
    Which 'gainst the world in war had stood,
And perish'd in the foremost rank
    With joy: – but not in chains to pine:
His spirit wither'd with their clank,
    I saw it silently decline –
    And so perchance in sooth did mine:
But yet I forced it on to cheer
Those relics of a home so dear.

70

75

80

85

90

95

100

He was a hunter of the hills,
    Had follow'd there the deer and wolf;
105   To him this dungeon was a gulf,
And fetter'd feet the worst of ills.

VI

    Lake Leman lies by Chillon's walls:
A thousand feet in depth below
Its massy waters meet and flow;
110 Thus much the fathom-line was sent
From Chillon's snow-white battlement,[1]
    Which round about the wave inthrals:
A double dungeon wall and wave
Have made – and like a living grave.
115 Below the surface of the lake
The dark vault lies wherein we lay,
We heard it ripple night and day;
    Sounding o'er our heads it knock'd;
And I have felt the winter's spray
120 Wash through the bars when winds were high
And wanton in the happy sky;
    And then the very rock hath rock'd,
    And I have felt it shake, unshock'd,
Because I could have smiled to see
125 The death that would have set me free.

1. The Château de Chillon is situated between Clarens and Villeneuve, which last is at one extremity of the Lake of Geneva. On its left are the entrances of the Rhone, and opposite are the heights of Meillerie and the range of Alps above Boveret and St Gingo. Near it, on a hill behind, is a torrent: below it, washing its walls, the lake has been fathomed to the depth of 800 feet, French measure: within it are a range of dungeons, in which the early reformers, and subsequently prisoners of state, were confined. Across one of the vaults is a beam black with age, on which we were informed that the condemned were formerly executed. In the cells are seven pillars, or, rather, eight, one being half merged in the wall; in some of these are rings for the fetters and the fettered: in the pavement the steps of Bonnivard have left their traces. He was confined here several years. It is by this castle that Rousseau has fixed the catastrophe of his Héloïse, in the rescue of one of her children by Julie from the water; the shock of which, and the illness produced by the immersion, is the cause of her death. The château is large, and seen along the lake for a great distance. The walls are white.

VII

I said my nearer brother pined,
I said his mighty heart declined,
He loathed and put away his food;
It was not that 'twas coarse and rude,
130   For we were used to hunter's fare,
And for the like had little care:
The milk drawn from the mountain goat
Was changed for water from the moat,
Our bread was such as captive's tears
135   Have moisten'd many a thousand years,
Since man first pent his fellow men
Like brutes within an iron den;
But what were these to us or him?
These wasted not his heart or limb;
140   My brother's soul was of that mould
Which in a palace had grown cold,
Had his free breathing been denied
The range of the steep mountain's side;
But why delay the truth? – he died.
145   I saw, and could not hold his head,
Nor reach his dying hand – nor dead, –
Though hard I strove, but strove in vain,
To rend and gnash my bonds in twain.
He died – and they unlock'd his chain,
150   And scoop'd for him a shallow grave
Even from the cold earth of our cave.
I begg'd them, as a boon, to lay
His corse in dust whereon the day
Might shine – it was a foolish thought,
155   But then within my brain it wrought,
That even in death his freeborn breast
In such a dungeon could not rest.
I might have spared my idle prayer –
They coldly laugh'd – and laid him there:
160   The flat and turfless earth above
The being we so much did love;
His empty chain above it leant,
Such murder's fitting monument!

VIII

But he, the favourite and the flower,
165 Most cherish'd since his natal hour,
His mother's image in fair face,
The infant love of all his race,
His martyr'd father's dearest thought,
My latest care, for whom I sought
170 To hoard my life, that his might be
Less wretched now, and one day free;
He, too, who yet had held untired
A spirit natural or inspired –
He, too, was struck, and day by day
175 Was wither'd on the stalk away.
Oh, God! it is a fearful thing
To see the human soul take wing
In any shape, in any mood: –
I've seen it rushing forth in blood,
180 I've seen it on the breaking ocean
Strive with a swoln convulsive motion,
I've seen the sick and ghastly bed
Of Sin delirious with its dread:
But these were horrors – this was woe
185 Unmix'd with such – but sure and slow:
He faded, and so calm and meek,
So softly worn, so sweetly weak,
So tearless, yet so tender – kind,
And grieved for those he left behind;
190 With all the while a cheek whose bloom
Was as a mockery of the tomb,
Whose tints as gently sunk away
As a departing rainbow's ray –
An eye of most transparent light,
195 That almost made the dungeon bright,
And not a word of murmur – not
A groan o'er his untimely lot, –
A little talk of better days,
A little hope my own to raise,
200 For I was sunk in silence – lost
In this last loss, of all the most;

And then the sighs he would suppress
Of fainting nature's feebleness,
More slowly drawn, grew less and less:
205 I listen'd, but I could not hear –
I call'd, for I was wild with fear;
I knew 'twas hopeless, but my dread
Would not be thus admonished;
I call'd, and thought I heard a sound –
210 I burst my chain with one strong bound,
And rush'd to him: – I found him not,
I only stirr'd in this black spot,
I only lived – *I* only drew
The accursed breath of dungeon-dew;
215 The last – the sole – the dearest link
Between me and the eternal brink,
Which bound me to my failing race,
Was broken in this fatal place.
One on the earth, and one beneath –
220 My brothers – both had ceased to breathe :
I took that hand which lay so still,
Alas! my own was full as chill;
I had not strength to stir, or strive,
But felt that I was still alive –
225 A frantic feeling, when we know
That what we love shall ne'er be so.
I know not why
I could not die,
I had no earthly hope – but faith,
230 And that forbade a selfish death.

IX
What next befell me then and there
I know not well – I never knew –
First came the loss of light, and air,
And then of darkness too:
235 I had no thought, no feeling – none –
Among the stones I stood a stone,
And was, scarce conscious what I wist,
As shrubless crags within the mist;

For all was blank, and bleak, and grey,
240 It was not night – it was not day,
It was not even the dungeon-light,
So hateful to my heavy sight,
But vacancy absorbing space,
And fixedness – without a place;
245 There were no stars – no earth – no time –
No check – no change – no good – no crime
But silence, and a stirless breath
Which neither was of life nor death;
A sea of stagnant idleness,
250 Blind, boundless, mute, and motionless!

X

A light broke in upon my brain, –
   It was the carol of a bird;
It ceased, and then it came again,
   The sweetest song ear ever heard,
255 And mine was thankful till my eyes
Ran over with the glad surprise,
And they that moment could not see
I was the mate of misery;
But then by dull degrees came back
260 My senses to their wonted track,
I saw the dungeon walls and floor
Close slowly round me as before,
I saw the glimmer of the sun
Creeping as it before had done,
265 But through the crevice where it came
That bird was perch'd, as fond and tame,
   And tamer than upon the tree;
A lovely bird, with azure wings,
And song that said a thousand things,
270   And seem'd to say them all for me!
I never saw its like before,
I ne'er shall see its likeness more:
It seem'd like me to want a mate,
But was not half so desolate,
275 And it was come to love me when
None lived to love me so again,

And cheering from my dungeon's brink,
Had brought me back to feel and think.
I know not if it late were free,
280 Or broke its cage to perch on mine,
But knowing well captivity,
  Sweet bird! I could not wish for thine!
Or if it were, in winged guise,
A visitant from Paradise;
285 For – Heaven forgive that thought! the while
Which made me both to weep and smile;
I sometimes deem'd that it might be
My brother's soul come down to me;
But then at last away it flew,
290 And then 'twas mortal – well I knew,
For he would never thus have flown,
And left me twice so doubly lone, –
Lone – as the corse within its shroud,
Lone – as a solitary cloud,
295 A single cloud on a sunny day,
While all the rest of heaven is clear,
A frown upon the atmosphere,
That hath no business to appear
  When skies are blue, and earth is gay.

XI

300 A kind of change came in my fate,
My keepers grew compassionate;
I know not what had made them so,
They were inured to sights of woe,
But so it was: – my broken chain
305 With links unfasten'd did remain,
And it was liberty to stride
Along my cell from side to side,
And up and down, and then athwart,
And tread it over every part;
310 And round the pillars one by one,
Returning where my walk begun,
Avoiding only, as I trod,
My brothers' graves without a sod;

For if I thought with heedless tread
315   My step profaned their lowly bed,
My breath came gaspingly and thick,
And my crush'd heart fell blind and sick.

XII

I made a footing in the wall,
    It was not therefrom to escape,
320 For I had buried one and all
    Who loved me in a human shape;
And the whole earth would henceforth be
A wider prison unto me:
No child – no sire – no kin had I,
325 No partner in my misery;
I thought of this, and I was glad,
For thought of them had made me mad;
But I was curious to ascend
To my barr'd windows, and to bend
330 Once more, upon the mountains high,
The quiet of a loving eye.

XIII

I saw them – and they were the same,
They were not changed like me in frame;
I saw their thousand years of snow
335 On high – their wide long lake below,
And the blue Rhone in fullest flow;
I heard the torrents leap and gush
O'er channell'd rock and broken bush;
I saw the white-wall'd distant town,
340 And whiter sails go skimming down;
And then there was a little isle,[1]
Which in my very face did smile,
      The only one in view;

1. Between the entrances of the Rhone and Villeneuve, not far from Chillon,
is a very small island; the only one I could perceive, in my voyage round and
over the lake, within its circumference. It contains a few trees (I think not
above three), and from its singleness and diminutive size has a peculiar effect
upon the view.

A small green isle, it seem'd no more,
345 Scarce broader than my dungeon floor,
But in it there were three tall trees,
And o'er it blew the mountain breeze,
And by it there were waters flowing,
And on it there were young flowers growing,
350   Of gentle breath and hue.
The fish swam by the castle wall,
And they seem'd joyous each and all;
The eagle rode the rising blast,
Methought he never flew so fast
355 As then to me he seem'd to fly,
And then new tears came in my eye,
And I felt troubled – and would fain
I had not left my recent chain;
And when I did descend again,
360 The darkness of my dim abode
Fell on me as a heavy load;
It was as is a new-dug grave,
Closing o'er one we sought to save, –
And yet my glance, too much oppress'd,
365 Had almost need of such a rest.

XIV
It might be months, or years, or days,
    I kept no count – I took no note,
I had no hope my eyes to raise,
    And clear them of their dreary mote;
370 At last men came to set me free,
    I ask'd not why, and reck'd not where,
It was at length the same to me,
Fetter'd or fetterless to be,
    I learn'd to love despair.
375 And thus when they appear'd at last,
And all my bonds aside were cast,
These heavy walls to me had grown
A hermitage – and all my own!
And half I felt as they were come
380 To tear me from a second home:

With spiders I had friendship made,
And watch'd them in their sullen trade,
Had seen the mice by moonlight play,
And why should I feel less than they?
385 We were all inmates of one place,
And I, the monarch of each race,
Had power to kill – yet, strange to tell!
In quiet we had learn'd to dwell –[1]
My very chains and I grew friends,
390 So much a long communion tends
To make us what we are: – even I
Regain'd my freedom with a sigh.

1. McGann's edition restores a couplet between lines 388 and 389 that Murray's had removed without Byron's authorization (*CPW*, Vol. 4, p. 449):

> Nor slew I of my subjects one,
> What Sovereign hath so little done?

[Editors]

Darkness

I had a dream, which was not all a dream.
The bright sun was extinguish'd, and the stars
Did wander darkling in the eternal space,
Rayless, and pathless, and the icy earth
5   Swung blind and blackening in the moonless air;
Morn came and went – and came, and brought no day,
And men forgot their passions in the dread
Of this their desolation; and all hearts
Were chill'd into a selfish prayer for light:
10   And they did live by watchfires – and the thrones,
The palaces of crowned kings – the huts,
The habitations of all things which dwell,
Were burnt for beacons; cities were consumed,
And men were gather'd round their blazing homes
15   To look once more into each other's face;
Happy were those who dwelt within the eye
Of the volcanos, and their mountain-torch:
A fearful hope was all the world contain'd;
Forests were set on fire – but hour by hour
20   They fell and faded – and the crackling trunks
Extinguish'd with a crash – and all was black.
The brows of men by the despairing light
Wore an unearthly aspect, as by fits
The flashes fell upon them; some lay down
25   And hid their eyes and wept; and some did rest
Their chins upon their clenched hands, and smiled;
And others hurried to and fro, and fed
Their funeral piles with fuel, and look'd up
With mad disquietude on the dull sky,
30   The pall of a past world; and then again
With curses cast them down upon the dust,
And gnash'd their teeth and howl'd: the wild birds
        shriek'd,
And, terrified, did flutter on the ground,
And flap their useless wings; the wildest brutes
35   Came tame and tremulous; and vipers crawl'd

And twined themselves among the multitude,
Hissing, but stingless – they were slain for food:
And War, which for a moment was no more,
Did glut himself again; – a meal was bought
40   With blood, and each sate sullenly apart
Gorging himself in gloom: no love was left;
All earth was but one thought – and that was death,
Immediate and inglorious; and the pang
Of famine fed upon all entrails – men
45   Died, and their bones were tombless as their flesh;
The meagre by the meagre were devour'd,
Even dogs assail'd their masters, all save one,
And he was faithful to a corse, and kept
The birds and beasts and famish'd men at bay,
50   Till hunger clung them, or the dropping dead
Lured their lank jaws; himself sought out no food,
But with a piteous and perpetual moan,
And a quick desolate cry, licking the hand
Which answer'd not with a caress – he died.
55   The crowd was famish'd by degrees; but two
Of an enormous city did survive,
And they were enemies: they met beside
The dying embers of an altar-place
Where had been heap'd a mass of holy things
60   For an unholy usage; they raked up,
And shivering scraped with their cold skeleton hands
The feeble ashes, and their feeble breath
Blew for a little life, and made a flame
Which was a mockery; then they lifted up
65   Their eyes as it grew lighter, and beheld
Each other's aspects – saw, and shriek'd, and died –
Even of their mutual hideousness they died,
Unknowing who he was upon whose brow
Famine had written Fiend. The world was void,
70   The populous and the powerful was a lump,
Seasonless, herbless, treeless, manless, lifeless –
A lump of death – a chaos of hard clay.
The rivers, lakes, and ocean all stood still,
And nothing stirr'd within their silent depths;

75   Ships sailorless lay rotting on the sea,
        And their masts fell down piecemeal; as they dropp'd
        They slept on the abyss without a surge –
        The waves were dead; the tides were in their grave,
        The Moon, their mistress, had expired before;
80   The winds were wither'd in the stagnant air,
        And the clouds perish'd; Darkness had no need
        Of aid from them – She was the Universe.

                                    Diodati, July, 1816.

CHILDE HAROLD'S PILGRIMAGE

Canto the Third

'A fin que cette application vous forçât de penser à autre chose; il
n'y a en vérité de remède que celui-là et le temps.' – *Lettre du Roi
de Prusse à D'Alembert, Sept.* 7, 1776.

I

Is thy face like thy mother's, my fair child!
ADA! sole daughter of my house and heart?
When last I saw thy young blue eyes they smiled,
And when we parted, – not as now we part,
5   But with a hope. –
              Awaking with a start,
The waters heave around me; and on high
The winds lift up their voices: I depart,
Whither I know not; but the hour's gone by,
When Albion's lessening shores could grieve or glad mine
      eye.

II

10   Once more upon the waters! yet once more!
And the waves bound beneath me as a steed
That knows his rider. Welcome, to their roar!
Swift be their guidance, wheresoe'er it lead!
Though the strain'd mast should quiver as a reed,
15   And the rent canvass fluttering strew the gale,
Still must I on; for I am as a weed,
Flung from the rock, on Ocean's foam, to sail
Where'er the surge may sweep, the tempest's breath
      prevail.

III

    In my youth's summer I did sing of One,
20   The wandering outlaw of his own dark mind;
    Again I seize the theme, then but begun,
    And bear it with me, as the rushing wind
    Bears the cloud onwards: in that Tale I find
    The furrows of long thought, and dried-up tears,
25   Which, ebbing, leave a sterile track behind,
    O'er which all heavily the journeying years
Plod the last sands of life, – where not a flower appears.

IV

    Since my young days of passion – joy, or pain,
    Perchance my heart and harp have lost a string,
30   And both may jar: it may be, that in vain
    I would essay as I have sung to sing.
    Yet, though a dreary strain, to this I cling
    So that it wean me from the weary dream
    Of selfish grief or gladness – so it fling
35   Forgetfulness around me – it shall seem
To me, though to none else, a not ungrateful theme.

V

    He, who grown aged in this world of woe,
    In deeds, not years, piercing the depths of life,
    So that no wonder waits him; nor below
40   Can love, or sorrow, fame, ambition, strife,
    Cut to his heart again with the keen knife
    Of silent, sharp endurance: he can tell
    Why thought seeks refuge in lone caves, yet rife
    With airy images, and shapes which dwell
45   Still unimpair'd, though old, in the soul's haunted cell.

VI

    'Tis to create, and in creating live
    A being more intense, that we endow
    With form our fancy, gaining as we give
    The life we image, even as I do now.

50   What am I? Nothing: but not so art thou,
          Soul of my thought! with whom I traverse earth,
          Invisible but gazing, as I glow
          Mix'd with thy spirit, blended with thy birth,
     And feeling still with thee in my crush'd feelings' dearth.

     VII

55   Yet must I think less wildly: — I *have* thought
          Too long and darkly, till my brain became,
          In its own eddy boiling and o'erwrought,
          A whirling gulf of phantasy and flame:
          And thus, untaught in youth my heart to tame,
60   My springs of life were poison'd. 'Tis too late!
          Yet am I changed; though still enough the same
          In strength to bear what time can not abate,
     And feed on bitter fruits without accusing Fate.

     VIII

          Something too much of this: — but now 'tis past,
65   And the spell closes with its silent seal.
          Long absent HAROLD re-appears at last;
          He of the breast which fain no more would feel,
          Wrung with the wounds which kill not, but ne'er heal;
          Yet Time, who changes all, had alter'd him
70   In soul and aspect as in age: years steal
          Fire from the mind as vigour from the limb;
     And life's enchanted cup but sparkles near the brim.

     IX

          His had been quaff'd too quickly, and he found
          The dregs were wormwood; but he fill'd again,
75   And from a purer fount, on holier ground,
          And deem'd its spring perpetual; but in vain!
          Still round him clung invisibly a chain
          Which gall'd for ever, fettering though unseen,
          And heavy though it clank'd not; worn with pain,
80   Which pined although it spoke not, and grew keen,
     Entering with every step he took through many a scene.

X

Secure in guarded coldness, he had mix'd
Again in fancied safety with his kind,
And deem'd his spirit now so firmly fix'd
85   And sheath'd with an invulnerable mind,
That, if no joy, no sorrow lurk'd behind;
And he, as one, might 'midst the many stand
Unheeded, searching through the crowd to find
Fit speculation; such as in strange land
90 He found in wonder-works of God and Nature's hand.

XI

But who can view the ripen'd rose, nor seek
To wear it? who can curiously behold
The smoothness and the sheen of beauty's cheek,
Nor feel the heart can never all grow old?
95   Who can contemplate Fame through clouds unfold
The star which rises o'er her steep, nor climb?
Harold, once more within the vortex, roll'd
On with the giddy circle, chasing Time,
Yet with a nobler aim than in his youth's fond prime.

XII

100   But soon he knew himself the most unfit
Of men to herd with Man; with whom he held
Little in common; untaught to submit
His thoughts to others, though his soul was quell'd
In youth by his own thoughts; still uncompell'd
105   He would not yield dominion of his mind
To spirits against whom his own rebell'd;
Proud though in desolation; which could find
A life within itself, to breathe without mankind.

XIII

Where rose the mountains, there to him were friends;
110   Where roll'd the ocean, thereon was his home;
Where a blue sky, and glowing clime, extends,
He had the passion and the power to roam;
The desert, forest, cavern, breaker's foam,

Were unto him companionship; they spake
115   A mutual language, clearer than the tome
Of his land's tongue, which he would oft forsake,
For Nature's pages glass'd by sunbeams on the lake.

XIV

Like the Chaldean, he could watch the stars,
Till he had peopled them with beings bright
120   As their own beams; and earth, and earth-born jars,
And human frailties, were forgotten quite:
Could he have kept his spirit to that flight
He had been happy; but this clay will sink
Its spark immortal, envying it the light
125   To which it mounts, as if to break the link
That keeps us from yon heaven which woos us to its brink.

XV

But in Man's dwellings he became a thing
Restless and worn, and stern and wearisome,
Droop'd as a wild-born falcon with clipt wing,
130   To whom the boundless air alone were home:
Then came his fit again, which to o'ercome,
As eagerly the barr'd-up bird will beat
His breast and beak against his wiry dome
Till the blood tinge his plumage, so the heat
135   Of his impeded soul would through his bosom eat.

XVI

Self-exiled Harold wanders forth again,
With nought of hope left, but with less of gloom;
The very knowledge that he lived in vain,
140   That all was over on this side the tomb,
Had made Despair a smilingness assume,
Which, though 'twere wild, – as on the plunder'd wreck
When mariners would madly meet their doom
With draughts intemperate on the sinking deck, –
Did yet inspire a cheer, which he forebore to check.

XVII

145   Stop! – for thy tread is on an Empire's dust!
        An Earthquake's spoil is sepulchred below!
        Is the spot mark'd with no colossal bust?
        Nor column trophied for triumphal show?
        None; but the moral's truth tells simpler so,
150   As the ground was before, thus let it be; –
        How that red rain hath made the harvest grow!
        And is this all the world has gain'd by thee,
    Thou first and last of fields! king-making Victory?

XVIII

        And Harold stands upon this place of skulls,
155   The grave of France, the deadly Waterloo;
        How in an hour the power which gave annuls
        Its gifts, transferring fame as fleeting too!
        In 'pride of place'[1] here last the eagle flew,
        Then tore with bloody talon the rent plain,
160   Pierced by the shaft of banded nations through;
        Ambition's life and labours all were vain;
    He wears the shatter'd links of the world's broken chain.

XIX

        Fit retribution! Gaul may champ the bit
        And foam in fetters; – but is Earth more free?
165   Did nations combat to make *One* submit;
        Or league to teach all kings true sovereignty?
        What! shall reviving Thraldom again be
        The patch'd-up idol of enlighten'd days?
        Shall we, who struck the Lion down, shall we
170   Pay the Wolf homage? proffering lowly gaze
    And servile knees to thrones? No; *prove* before ye praise!

1. 'Pride of place' is a term of falconry, and means the highest pitch of
flight. See Macbeth, &c.
        'An eagle towering in his pride of place,' &c.

XX

If not, o'er one fallen despot boast no more!
In vain fair cheeks were furrow'd with hot tears
For Europe's flowers long rooted up before
175   The trampler of her vineyards; in vain years
Of death, depopulation, bondage, fears,
Have all been borne, and broken by the accord
Of roused-up millions: all that most endears
Glory, is when the myrtle wreathes a sword
180 Such as Harmodius[1] drew on Athens' tyrant lord.

XXI

There was a sound of revelry by night,
And Belgium's capital had gather'd then
Her Beauty and her Chivalry, and bright
The lamps shone o'er fair women and brave men;
185   A thousand hearts beat happily; and when
Music arose with its voluptuous swell,
Soft eyes look'd love to eyes which spake again,
And all went merry as a marriage-bell;[2]
But hush! hark! a deep sound strikes like a rising knell!

XXII

190   Did ye not hear it? – No; 'twas but the wind,
Or the car rattling o'er the stony street;
On with the dance! let joy be unconfined;
No sleep till morn, when Youth and Pleasure meet
To chase the glowing Hours with flying feet –
195   But, hark! – that heavy sound breaks in once more,
As if the clouds its echo would repeat;
And nearer, clearer, deadlier than before!
Arm! Arm! it is – it is – the cannon's opening roar!

---

1. See the famous song on Harmodius and Aristogiton. The best English translation is in Bland's Anthology, by Mr (Now Sir Thomas) Denman, –
    'With myrtle my sword will I wreathe,' &c.
2. On the night previous to the action, it is said that a ball was given at Brussels.

XXIII

Within a window'd niche of that high hall
200   Sate Brunswick's fated chieftain; he did hear
That sound the first amidst the festival,
And caught its tone with Death's prophetic ear;
And when they smiled because he deem'd it near,
His heart more truly knew that peal too well
205   Which stretch'd his father on a bloody bier,
And roused the vengeance blood alone could quell:
He rush'd into the field, and, foremost fighting, fell.

XXIV

Ah! then and there was hurrying to and fro,
And gathering tears, and tremblings of distress,
210   And cheeks all pale, which but an hour ago
Blush'd at the praise of their own loveliness;
And there were sudden partings, such as press
The life from out young hearts, and choking sighs
Which ne'er might be repeated; who could guess
215   If ever more should meet those mutual eyes,
Since upon night so sweet such awful morn could rise!

XXV

And there was mounting in hot haste: the steed,
The mustering squadron, and the clattering car,
Went pouring forward with impetuous speed,
220   And swiftly forming in the ranks of war;
And the deep thunder peal on peal afar;
And near, the beat of the alarming drum
Roused up the soldier ere the morning star;
While throng'd the citizens with terror dumb,
225   Or whispering, with white lips – 'The foe! they come! they
            come!'

XXVI

And wild and high the 'Cameron's gathering' rose!
The war-note of Lochiel, which Albyn's hills
Have heard, and heard, too, have her Saxon foes: –
How in the noon of night that pibroch thrills,

230   Savage and shrill! But with the breath which fills
        Their mountain-pipe, so fill the mountaineers
        With the fierce native daring which instils
        The stirring memory of a thousand years,
And Evan's, Donald's[1] fame rings in each clansman's ears!

XXVII

235   And Ardennes[2] waves above them her green leaves,
        Dewy with nature's tear-drops, as they pass,
        Grieving, if aught inanimate e'er grieves,
        Over the unreturning brave, – alas!
        Ere evening to be trodden like the grass
240   Which now beneath them, but above shall grow
        In its next verdure, when this fiery mass
        Of living valour, rolling on the foe
And burning with high hope, shall moulder cold and low.

XXVIII

        Last noon beheld them full of lusty life,
245   Last eve in Beauty's circle proudly gay,
        The midnight brought the signal-sound of strife,
        The morn the marshalling in arms, – the day
        Battle's magnificently-stern array!
        The thunder-clouds close o'er it, which when rent
250   The earth is cover'd thick with other clay,
        Which her own clay shall cover, heap'd and pent,
Rider and horse, – friend, foe, – in one red burial blent!

---

1. Sir Evan Cameron, and his descendant Donald, the 'gentle Lochiel' of
the 'forty-five.'

2. The wood of Soignies is supposed to be a remnant of the forest of
Ardennes, famous in Boiardo's Orlando, and immortal in Shakspeare's 'As
You Like It.' It is also celebrated in Tacitus as being the spot of successful
defence by the Germans against the Roman encroachments. I have ventured
to adopt the name connected with nobler associations than those of mere
slaughter.

XXIX

Their praise is hymn'd by loftier harps than mine;
Yet one I would select from that proud throng,
255   Partly because they blend me with his line,
And partly that I did his sire some wrong,
And partly that bright names will hallow song;
And his was of the bravest, and when shower'd
The death-bolts deadliest the thinn'd files along,
260   Even where the thickest of war's tempest lower'd,
They reach'd no nobler breast than thine, young, gallant
        Howard!

XXX

There have been tears and breaking hearts for thee,
And mine were nothing, had I such to give;
But when I stood beneath the fresh green tree,
265   Which living waves where thou didst cease to live,
And saw around me the wide field revive
With fruits and fertile promise, and the Spring
Come forth her work of gladness to contrive,
With all her reckless birds upon the wing,
270   I turn'd from all she brought to those she could not bring.[1]

1. My guide from Mont St Jean over the field seemed intelligent and accurate. The place where Major Howard fell was not far from two tall and solitary trees (there was a third cut down, or shivered in the battle), which stand a few yards from each other at a pathway's side. Beneath these he died and was buried. The body has since been removed to England. A small hollow for the present marks where it lay, but will probably soon be effaced; the plough has been upon it, and the grain is. – After pointing out the different spots where Picton and other gallant men had perished; the guide said, 'Here Major Howard lay: I was near him when wounded.' I told him my relationship, and he seemed then still more anxious to point out the particular spot and circumstances. The place is one of the most marked in the field, from the peculiarity of the two trees above mentioned. I went on horseback twice over the field, comparing it with my recollection of similar scenes. As a plain, Waterloo seems marked out for the scene of some great action, though this may be mere imagination: I have viewed with attention those of Platea, Troy, Mantinea, Leuctra, Chæronea, and Marathon; and the field around Mont St Jean and Hougoumont appears to want little but a better cause, and that undefinable but impressive halo which the lapse of ages throws around a celebrated spot, to vie in interest with any or all of these, except, perhaps, the last mentioned.

XXXI

  I turn'd to thee, to thousands, of whom each
  And one as all a ghastly gap did make
  In his own kind and kindred, whom to teach
  Forgetfulness were mercy for their sake;
275 The Archangel's trump, not Glory's, must awake
  Those whom they thirst for; though the sound of Fame
  May for a moment soothe, it cannot slake
  The fever of vain longing, and the name
So honour'd but assumes a stronger, bitterer claim.

XXXII

280 They mourn, but smile at length; and, smiling, mourn:
  The tree will wither long before it fall;
  The hull drives on, though mast and sail be torn;
  The roof-tree sinks, but moulders on the hall
  In massy hoariness; the ruin'd wall
285 Stands when its wind-worn battlements are gone;
  The bars survive the captive they enthral;
  The day drags through though storms keep out the sun;
And thus the heart will break, yet brokenly live on:

XXXIII

  Even as a broken mirror, which the glass
290 In every fragment multiplies; and makes
  A thousand images of one that was,
  The same, and still the more, the more it breaks;
  And thus the heart will do which not forsakes,
  Living in shatter'd guise, and still, and cold,
295 And bloodless, with its sleepless sorrow aches,
  Yet withers on till all without is old,
Showing no visible sign, for such things are untold.

XXXIV

  There is a very life in our despair,
  Vitality of poison, – a quick root
300 Which feeds these deadly branches; for it were
  As nothing did we die; but Life will suit
  Itself to Sorrow's most detested fruit,

Like to the apples[1] on the Dead Sea's shore,
All ashes to the taste: Did man compute
305   Existence by enjoyment, and count o'er
Such hours 'gainst years of life, – say, would he name
    threescore?

XXXV

The Psalmist number'd out the years of man:
They are enough; and if thy tale be *true*,
Thou, who didst grudge him even that fleeting span,
310   More than enough, thou fatal Waterloo!
Millions of tongues record thee, and anew
Their children's lips shall echo them, and say –
'Here, where the sword united nations drew,
Our countrymen were warring on that day!'
315   And this is much, and all which will not pass away.

XXXVI

There sunk the greatest, nor the worst of men,
Whose spirit antithetically mixt
One moment of the mightiest, and again
On little objects with like firmness fixt,
320   Extreme in all things! hadst thou been betwixt,
Thy throne had still been thine, or never been;
For daring made thy rise as fall: thou seek'st
Even now to re-assume the imperial mien,
And shake again the world, the Thunderer of the scene!

XXXVII

325   Conqueror and captive of the earth art thou!
She trembles at thee still, and thy wild name
Was ne'er more bruited in men's minds than now
That thou art nothing, save the jest of Fame,

1. The (fabled) apples on the brink of the lake Asphaltes were said to be air without, and, within, ashes. Vide Tacitus, Histor. lib. v. 7.

Who woo'd thee once, thy vassal, and became
330   The flatterer of thy fierceness, till thou wert
A god unto thyself; nor less the same
To the astounded kingdoms all inert,
Who deem'd thee for a time whate'er thou didst assert.

XXXVIII

Oh, more or less than man – in high or low,
335   Battling with nations, flying from the field;
Now making monarchs' necks thy footstool, now
More than thy meanest soldier taught to yield;
An empire thou couldst crush, command, rebuild,
But govern not thy pettiest passion, nor,
340   However deeply in men's spirits skill'd,
Look through thine own, nor curb the lust of war,
Nor learn that tempted Fate will leave the loftiest star.

XXXIX

Yet well thy soul hath brook'd the turning tide
With that untaught innate philosophy,
345   Which, be it wisdom, coldness, or deep pride,
Is gall and wormwood to an enemy.
When the whole host of hatred stood hard by,
To watch and mock thee shrinking, thou hast smiled
With a sedate and all-enduring eye; –
350   When Fortune fled her spoil'd and favourite child,
He stood unbow'd beneath the ills upon him piled.

XL

Sager than in thy fortunes; for in them
Ambition steel'd thee on too far to show
That just habitual scorn, which could contemn
355   Men and their thoughts; 'twas wise to feel, not so
To wear it ever on thy lip and brow,
And spurn the instruments thou wert to use
Till they were turn'd unto thine overthrow;
'Tis but a worthless world to win or lose;
360   So hath it proved to thee, and all such lot who choose.

XLI

If, like a tower upon a headlong rock,
Thou hadst been made to stand or fall alone,
Such scorn of man had help'd to brave the shock;
But men's thoughts were the steps which paved thy
    throne,
365   *Their* admiration thy best weapon shone;
The part of Philip's son was thine, not then
(Unless aside thy purple had been thrown)
Like stern Diogenes to mock at men;
For sceptred cynics earth were far too wide a den.[1]

XLII

370   But quiet to quick bosoms is a hell,
And *there* hath been thy bane; there is a fire
And motion of the soul which will not dwell
In its own narrow being, but aspire
Beyond the fitting medium of desire;
375   And, but once kindled, quenchless evermore,
Preys upon high adventure, nor can tire
Of aught but rest; a fever at the core,
Fatal to him who bears, to all who ever bore.

XLIII

This makes the madmen who have made men mad
380   By their contagion; Conquerors and Kings,
Founders of sects and systems, to whom add
Sophists, Bards, Statesmen, all unquiet things

---

1. The great error of Napoleon, 'if we have writ our annals true,' was a
continued obtrusion on mankind of his want of all community of feeling for,
or with them; perhaps more offensive to human vanity than the active cruelty
of more trembling and suspicious tyranny. Such were his speeches to public
assemblies as well as individuals; and the single expression which he is said to have
used on returning to Paris after the Russian winter had destroyed his army,
rubbing his hands over a fire, 'This is pleasanter than Moscow,' would probably
alienate more favour from his cause than the destruction and reverses which led
to the remark.

Which stir too strongly the soul's secret springs,
And are themselves the fools to those they fool;
385   Envied, yet how unenviable! what stings
Are theirs! One breast laid open were a school
Which would unteach mankind the lust to shine or rule:

XLIV

Their breath is agitation, and their life
A storm whereon they ride, to sink at last,
390   And yet so nursed and bigoted to strife,
That should their days, surviving perils past,
Melt to calm twilight, they feel overcast
With sorrow and supineness, and so die;
Even as a flame unfed, which runs to waste
395   With its own flickering, or a sword laid by,
Which eats into itself, and rusts ingloriously.

XLV

He who ascends to mountain-tops, shall find
The loftiest peaks most wrapt in clouds and snow;
He who surpasses or subdues mankind,
400   Must look down on the hate of those below.
Though high *above* the sun of glory glow,
And far *beneath* the earth and ocean spread,
Round him are icy rocks, and loudly blow
Contending tempests on his naked head,
405   And thus reward the toils which to those summits led.

XLVI

Away with these! true Wisdom's world will be
Within its own creation, or in thine,
Maternal Nature! for who teems like thee,
Thus on the banks of thy majestic Rhine?
410   There Harold gazes on a work divine,
A blending of all beauties; streams and dells,
Fruit, foliage, crag, wood, cornfield, mountain vine,
And chiefless castles breathing stern farewells
From gray but leafy walls, where Ruin greenly dwells.

XLVII

415
And there they stand, as stands a lofty mind,
Worn, but unstooping to the baser crowd,
All tenantless, save to the crannying wind,
Or holding dark communion with the cloud.
There was a day when they were young and proud,
420
Banners on high, and battles pass'd below;
But they who fought are in a bloody shroud,
And those which waved are shredless dust ere now,
And the bleak battlements shall bear no future blow.

XLVIII

Beneath these battlements, within those walls,
425
Power dwelt amidst her passions; in proud state
Each robber chief upheld his armed halls,
Doing his evil will, nor less elate
Than mightier heroes of a longer date.
What want these outlaws[1] conquerors should have?
430
But History's purchased page to call them great?
A wider space, an ornamented grave?
Their hopes were not less warm, their souls were full as
            brave.

XLIX

In their baronial feuds and single fields,
What deeds of prowess unrecorded died!
435
And Love, which lent a blazon to their shields,
With emblems well devised by amorous pride,
Through all the mail of iron hearts would glide;
But still their flame was fierceness, and drew on
Keen contest and destruction near allied,
440
And many a tower for some fair mischief won,
Saw the discolour'd Rhine beneath its ruin run.

1. 'What wants that knave that a king should have?' was King James's
question on meeting Johnny Armstrong and his followers in full accoutre-
ments. – See the Ballad.

L

But Thou, exulting and abounding river!
Making their waves a blessing as they flow
Through banks whose beauty would endure for ever
445 Could man but leave thy bright creation so,
Nor its fair promise from the surface mow
With the sharp scythe of conflict, – then to see
Thy valley of sweet waters, were to know
Earth paved like Heaven; and to seem such to me,
450 Even now what wants thy stream? – that it should Lethe
be.

LI

A thousand battles have assail'd thy banks,
But these and half their fame have pass'd away,
And Slaughter heap'd on high his weltering ranks;
Their very graves are gone, and what are they?
455 Thy tide wash'd down the blood of yesterday,
And all was stainless, and on thy clear stream
Glass'd with its dancing light the sunny ray;
But o'er the blacken'd memory's blighting dream
Thy waves would vainly roll, all sweeping as they seem.

LII

460 Thus Harold inly said, and pass'd along,
Yet not insensibly to all which here
Awoke the jocund birds to early song
In glens which might have made even exile dear:
Though on his brow were graven lines austere,
465 And tranquil sternness which had ta'en the place
Of feelings fierier far but less severe,
Joy was not always absent from his face,
But o'er it in such scenes would steal with transient trace.

LIII

Nor was all love shut from him, though his days
470 Of passion had consumed themselves to dust.
It is in vain that we would coldly gaze
On such as smile upon us; the heart must

Leap kindly back to kindness, though disgust
Hath wean'd it from all worldlings: thus he felt,
475   For there was soft remembrance, and sweet trust
In one fond breast, to which his own would melt,
And in its tenderer hour on that his bosom dwelt.

LIV

And he had learn'd to love, – I know not why,
For this in such as him seems strange of mood, –
480   The helpless looks of blooming infancy,
Even in its earliest nurture; what subdued,
To change like this, a mind so far imbued
With scorn of man, it little boots to know;
But thus it was; and though in solitude
485   Small power the nipp'd affections have to grow,
In him this glow'd when all beside had ceased to glow.

LV

And there was one soft breast, as hath been said,
Which unto his was bound by stronger ties
Than the church links withal; and, though unwed,
490   *That* love was pure, and, far above disguise,
Had stood the test of mortal enmities
Still undivided, and cemented more
By peril, dreaded most in female eyes;
But this was firm, and from a foreign shore
495   Well to that heart might his these absent greetings pour!

I

The castled crag of Drachenfels[1]
Frowns o'er the wide and winding Rhine,
Whose breast of waters broadly swells
Between the banks which bear the vine,

1. The castle of Drachenfels stands on the highest summit of 'the Seven Mountains,' over the Rhine banks: it is in ruins, and connected with some singular traditions: it is the first in view on the road from Bonn, but on the opposite side of the river; on this bank, nearly facing it, are the remains of another, called the Jew's Castle, and a large cross commemorative of the murder of a chief by his brother. The number of castles and cities along the course of the Rhine on both sides is very great, and their situations remarkably beautiful.

500 And hills all rich with blossom'd trees,
And fields which promise corn and wine,
And scatter'd cities crowning these,
Whose far white walls along them shine,
Have strew'd a scene, which I should see
505 With double joy wert *thou* with me.

2

And peasant girls, with deep blue eyes,
And hands which offer early flowers,
Walk smiling o'er this paradise;
Above, the frequent feudal towers
510 Through green leaves lift their walls of gray;
And many a rock which steeply lowers,
And noble arch in proud decay,
Look o'er this vale of vintage-bowers;
But one thing want these banks of Rhine, –
515 Thy gentle hand to clasp in mine!

3

I send the lilies given to me;
Though long before thy hand they touch,
I know that they must wither'd be,
But yet reject them not as such;
520 For I have cherish'd them as dear,
Because they yet may meet thine eye,
And guide thy soul to mine even here,
When thou behold'st them drooping nigh,
And know'st them gather'd by the Rhine,
525 And offer'd from my heart to thine!

4

The river nobly foams and flows,
The charm of this enchanted ground,
And all its thousand turns disclose
Some fresher beauty varying round:
530 The haughtiest breast its wish might bound
Through life to dwell delighted here;
Nor could on earth a spot be found
To nature and to me so dear,

Could thy dear eyes in following mine
535   Still sweeten more these banks of Rhine!

LVI

By Coblentz, on a rise of gentle ground,
There is a small and simple pyramid,
Crowning the summit of the verdant mound;
Beneath its base are heroes' ashes hid,
540   Our enemy's – but let not that forbid
Honour to Marceau! o'er whose early tomb
Tears, big tears, gush'd from the rough soldier's lid,
Lamenting and yet envying such a doom,
Falling for France, whose rights he battled to resume.

LVII

545   Brief, brave, and glorious was his young career, –
His mourners were two hosts, his friends and foes;
And fitly may the stranger lingering here
Pray for his gallant spirit's bright repose;
For he was Freedom's champion, one of those,
550   The few in number, who had not o'erstept
The charter to chastise which she bestows
On such as wield her weapons; he had kept
The whiteness of his soul, and thus men o'er him wept.[1]

1. The monument of the young and lamented General Marceau (killed by a rifle-ball at Alterkirchen, on the last day of the fourth year of the French republic) still remains as described. The inscriptions on his monument are rather too long, and not required: his name was enough; France adored, and her enemies admired; both wept over him. His funeral was attended by the generals and detachments from both armies. In the same grave General Hoche is interred, a gallant man also in every sense of the word; but though he distinguished himself greatly in battle, *he* had not the good fortune to die there: his death was attended by suspicions of poison. A separate monument (not over his body, which is buried by Marceau's) is raised for him near Andernach, opposite to which one of his most memorable exploits was performed, in throwing a bridge to an island on the Rhine. The shape and style are different from that of Marceau's, and the inscription more simple and pleasing: – 'The Army of the Sambre and Meuse to its Commander-in-Chief Hoche.' This is all, and as it should be. Hoche was esteemed among the first of France's earlier generals, before Buonaparte monopolised her triumphs. He was the destined commander of the invading army of Ireland.

LVIII

Here Ehrenbreitstein,[1] with her shatter'd wall
555   Black with the miner's blast, upon her height
Yet shows of what she was, when shell and ball
Rebounding idly on her strength did light:
A tower of victory! from whence the flight
Of baffled foes was watch'd along the plain:
560   But Peace destroy'd what War could never blight,
And laid those proud roofs bare to Summer's rain —
On which the iron shower for years had pour'd in vain.

LIX

Adieu to thee, fair Rhine! How long delighted
The stranger fain would linger on his way!
565   Thine is a scene alike where souls united
Or lonely Contemplation thus might stray;
And could the ceaseless vultures cease to prey
On self-condemning bosoms, it were here,
Where Nature, nor too sombre nor too gay,
570   Wild but not rude, awful yet not austere,
Is to the mellow Earth as Autumn to the year.

LX

Adieu to thee again! a vain adieu!
There can be no farewell to scene like thine;
The mind is colour'd by thy every hue;
575   And if reluctantly the eyes resign
Their cherish'd gaze upon thee, lovely Rhine!
'Tis with the thankful glance of parting praise;
More mighty spots may rise — more glaring shine,
But none unite in one attaching maze
580   The brilliant, fair, and soft, — the glories of old days,

1. Ehrenbreitstein, *i.e.* 'the broad stone of honour,' one of the strongest
fortresses in Europe, was dismantled and blown up by the French at the
truce of Leoben. It had been, and could only be, reduced by famine or
treachery. It yielded to the former, aided by surprise. After having seen the
fortifications of Gibraltar and Malta, it did not much strike by comparison;
but the situation is commanding. General Marceau besieged it in vain for
some time, and I slept in a room where I was shown a window at which he
is said to have been standing observing the progress of the siege by moon-
light, when a ball struck immediately below it.

LXI

The negligently grand, the fruitful bloom
Of coming ripeness, the white city's sheen,
The rolling stream, the precipice's gloom,
The forest's growth, and Gothic walls between,
585   The wild rocks shaped as they had turrets been
In mockery of man's art; and these withal
A race of faces happy as the scene,
Whose fertile bounties here extend to all,
Still springing o'er thy banks, though Empires near them
        fall.

LXII

590   But these recede. Above me are the Alps,
The palaces of Nature, whose vast walls
Have pinnacled in clouds their snowy scalps,
And throned Eternity in icy halls
Of cold sublimity, where forms and falls
595   The avalanche – the thunderbolt of snow!
All that expands the spirit, yet appals,
Gather around these summits, as to show
How Earth may pierce to Heaven, yet leave vain man
        below.

LXIII

But ere these matchless heights I dare to scan,
600   There is a spot should not be pass'd in vain, –
Morat! the proud, the patriot field! where man
May gaze on ghastly trophies of the slain,
Nor blush for those who conquer'd on that plain;
Here Burgundy bequeath'd his tombless host,
605   A bony heap, through ages to remain,
Themselves their monument; – the Stygian coast
Unsepulchred they roam'd, and shriek'd each wandering
        ghost.[1]

1. The chapel is destroyed, and the pyramid of bones diminished to a small
number by the Burgundian legion in the service of France; who anxiously
effaced this record of their ancestors' less successful invasions. A few still

LXIV

    While Waterloo with Cannæ's carnage vies,
    Morat and Marathon twin names shall stand;
610   They were true Glory's stainless victories,
    Won by the unambitious heart and hand
    Of a proud, brotherly, and civic band,
    All unbought champions in no princely cause
    Of vice-entail'd Corruption; they no land
615   Doom'd to bewail the blasphemy of laws
Making kings' rights divine, by some Draconic clause.

LXV

    By a lone wall a lonelier column rears
    A gray and grief-worn aspect of old days;
    'Tis the last remnant of the wreck of years,
620   And looks as with the wild-bewilder'd gaze
    Of one to stone converted by amaze,
    Yet still with consciousness; and there it stands
    Making a marvel that it not decays,
    When the coeval pride of human hands,
625   Levell'd Aventicum,[1] hath strew'd her subject lands.

LXVI

    And there – oh! sweet and sacred be the name! –
    Julia – the daughter, the devoted – gave
    Her youth to Heaven; her heart, beneath a claim
    Nearest to Heaven's, broke o'er a father's grave.

---

remain, notwithstanding the pains taken by the Burgundians for ages (all who passed that way removing a bone to their own country), and the less justifiable larcenies of the Swiss postilions, who carried them off to sell for knife-handles; a purpose for which the whiteness imbibed by the bleaching of years had rendered them in great request. Of these relics I ventured to bring away as much as may have made a quarter of a hero, for which the sole excuse is, that if I had not, the next passer by might have perverted them to worse uses than the careful preservation which I intend for them.

1. Aventicum, near Morat, was the Roman capital of Helvetia, where Avenches now stands.

630   Justice is sworn 'gainst tears, and hers would crave
         The life she lived in; but the judge was just,
         And then she died on him she could not save.
         Their tomb was simple, and without a bust,
         And held within their urn one mind, one heart, one dust.[1]

LXVII

635   But these are deeds which should not pass away,
         And names that must not wither, though the earth
         Forgets her empires with a just decay,
         The enslavers and the enslaved, their death and birth;
         The high, the mountain-majesty of worth
640   Should be, and shall, survivor of its woe,
         And from its immortality look forth
         In the sun's face, like yonder Alpine snow,[2]
         Imperishably pure beyond all things below.

LXVIII

         Lake Leman woos me with its crystal face,
645   The mirror where the stars and mountains view
         The stillness of their aspect in each trace
         Its clear depth yields of their far height and hue:
         There is too much of man here, to look through
         With a fit mind the might which I behold;
650   But soon in me shall Loneliness renew

1. Julia Alpinula, a young Aventian priestess, died soon after a vain endeav-
our to save her father, condemned to death as a traitor by Aulus Cæcina. Her
epitaph was discovered many years ago; – it is thus: – 'Julia Alpinula: Hic
jaceo. Infelicis patris infelix proles. Deæ Aventiæ Sacerdos. Exorare patris
necem non potui: Male mori in fatis ille erat. Vixi annos XXIII.' – I know
of no human composition so affecting as this, nor a history of deeper
interest. These are the names and actions which ought not to perish, and to
which we turn with a true and healthy tenderness, from the wretched and
glittering detail of a confused mass of conquests and battles, with which the
mind is roused for a time to a false and feverish sympathy, from whence it
recurs at length with all the nausea consequent on such intoxication.
2. This is written in the eye of Mont Blanc (June 3d, 1816), which even at
this distance dazzles mine. – (July 20th.) I this day observed for some time
the distinct reflection of Mont Blanc and Mont Argentière in the calm of
the lake, which I was crossing in my boat; the distance of these mountains
from their mirror is sixty miles.

Thoughts hid, but not less cherish'd than of old,
Ere mingling with the herd had penn'd me in their fold.

LXIX

To fly from, need not be to hate, mankind:
All are not fit with them to stir and toil,
655   Nor is it discontent to keep the mind
Deep in its fountain, lest it overboil
In the hot throng, where we become the spoil
Of our infection, till too late and long
We may deplore and struggle with the coil,
660   In wretched interchange of wrong for wrong
Midst a contentious world, striving where none are strong.

LXX

There, in a moment, we may plunge our years
In fatal penitence, and in the blight
Of our own soul turn all our blood to tears,
665   And colour things to come with hues of Night;
The race of life becomes a hopeless flight
To those that walk in darkness: on the sea,
The boldest steer but where their ports invite,
But there are wanderers o'er Eternity
670   Whose bark drives on and on, and anchor'd ne'er shall be.

LXXI

It is not better, then, to be alone,
And love Earth only for its earthly sake?
By the blue rushing of the arrowy Rhone,[1]
Or the pure bosom of its nursing lake,
675   Which feeds it as a mother who doth make
A fair but froward infant her own care,
Kissing its cries away as these awake; –
Is it not better thus our lives to wear,
Than join the crushing crowd, doom'd to inflict or bear?

1. The colour of the Rhone at Geneva is blue, to a depth of tint which I have never seen equalled in water, salt or fresh, except in the Mediterranean and Archipelago.

LXXII

680　　I live not in myself, but I become
　　　　Portion of that around me; and to me
　　　　High mountains are a feeling, but the hum
　　　　Of human cities torture: I can see
　　　　Nothing to loathe in nature, save to be
685　　A link reluctant in a fleshly chain,
　　　　Class'd among creatures, when the soul can flee,
　　　　And with the sky, the peak, the heaving plain
Of ocean, or the stars, mingle, and not in vain.

LXXIII

　　　　And thus I am absorb'd, and this is life;
690　　I look upon the peopled desert past,
　　　　As on a place of agony and strife,
　　　　Where, for some sin, to sorrow I was cast,
　　　　To act and suffer, but remount at last
　　　　With a fresh pinion; which I feel to spring,
695　　Though young, yet waxing vigorous, as the blast
　　　　Which it would cope with, on delighted wing,
Spurning the clay-cold bonds which round our being cling.

LXXIV

　　　　And when, at length, the mind shall be all free
　　　　From what it hates in this degraded form,
700　　Reft of its carnal life, save what shall be
　　　　Existent happier in the fly and worm, –
　　　　When elements to elements conform,
　　　　And dust is as it should be, shall I not
　　　　Feel all I see, less dazzling, but more warm?
705　　The bodiless thought? the Spirit of each spot?
Of which, even now, I share at times the immortal lot?

LXXV

　　　　Are not the mountains, waves, and skies, a part
　　　　Of me and of my soul, as I of them?
　　　　Is not the love of these deep in my heart
710　　With a pure passion? should I not contemn
　　　　All objects, if compared with these? and stem

A tide of suffering, rather than forego
Such feelings for the hard and worldly phlegm
Of those whose eyes are only turn'd below,
715   Gazing upon the ground, with thoughts which dare not
            glow?

LXXVI

But this is not my theme; and I return
To that which is immediate, and require
Those who find contemplation in the urn,
To look on One, whose dust was once all fire,
720   A native of the land where I respire
The clear air for a while – a passing guest,
Where he became a being, – whose desire
Was to be glorious; 'twas a foolish quest,
The which to gain and keep, he sacrificed all rest.

LXXVII

725   Here the self-torturing sophist, wild Rousseau,
The apostle of affliction, he who threw
Enchantment over passion, and from woe
Wrung overwhelming eloquence, first drew
The breath which made him wretched; yet he knew
730   How to make madness beautiful, and cast
O'er erring deeds and thoughts a heavenly hue
Of words, like sunbeams, dazzling as they past
The eyes, which o'er them shed tears feelingly and fast.

LXXVIII

His love was passion's essence – as a tree
735   On fire by lightning; with ethereal flame
Kindled he was, and blasted; for to be
Thus, and enamour'd, were in him the same.
But his was not the love of living dame,
Nor of the dead who rise upon our dreams,
740   But of ideal beauty, which became
In him existence, and o'erflowing teems
Along his burning page, distemper'd though it seems.

LXXIX

This breathed itself to life in Julie, *this*
Invested her with all that's wild and sweet;
745   This hallow'd, too, the memorable kiss[1]
Which every morn his fever'd lip would greet,
From hers, who but with friendship his would meet;
But to that gentle touch, through brain and breast
Flash'd the thrill'd spirit's love-devouring heat;
750   In that absorbing sigh perchance more blest
Than vulgar minds may be with all they seek possest.

LXXX

His life was one long war with self-sought foes,
Or friends by him self-banish'd; for his mind
Had grown Suspicion's sanctuary, and chose,
755   For its own cruel sacrifice, the kind
'Gainst whom he raged with fury strange and blind.
But he was phrensied, – wherefore, who may know?
Since cause might be which skill could never find;
But he was phrensied by disease or woe,
760   To that worst pitch of all, which wears a reasoning show.

LXXXI

For then he was inspired, and from him came,
As from the Pythian's mystic cave of yore,
Those oracles which set the world in flame,
Nor ceased to burn till kingdoms were no more:
765   Did he not this for France? which lay before
Bow'd to the inborn tyranny of years?
Broken and trembling to the yoke she bore,
Till by the voice of him and his compeers
Roused up to too much wrath, which follows o'ergrown
          fears?

1. This refers to the account in his 'Confessions' of his passion for the
Comtesse d'Houdetot (the mistress of St Lambert), and his long walk every
morning, for the sake of the single kiss which was the common salutation of
French acquaintance. Rousseau's description of his feelings on this occasion
may be considered as the most passionate, yet not impure, description and
expression of love that ever kindled into words; which, after all, must be
felt, from their very force, to be inadequate to the delineation: a painting
can give no sufficient idea of the ocean.

LXXXII

770   They made themselves a fearful monument!
       The wreck of old opinions – things which grew,
       Breathed from the birth of time: the veil they rent,
       And what behind it lay all earth shall view.
       But good with ill they also overthrew,
775   Leaving but ruins, wherewith to rebuild
       Upon the same foundation, and renew
       Dungeons and thrones, which the same hour refill'd,
As heretofore, because ambition was self-will'd.

LXXXIII

       But this will not endure, nor be endured!
780   Mankind have felt their strength, and made it felt.
       They might have used it better, but, allured
       By their new vigour, sternly have they dealt
       On one another; pity ceased to melt
       With her once natural charities. But they,
785   Who in oppression's darkness caved had dwelt,
       They were not eagles, nourish'd with the day;
What marvel then, at times, if they mistook their prey?

LXXXIV

       What deep wounds ever closed without a scar?
       The heart's bleed longest, and but heal to wear
790   That which disfigures it; and they who war
       With their own hopes, and have been vanquished, bear
       Silence, but not submission: in his lair
       Fix'd Passion holds his breath, until the hour
       Which shall atone for years; none need despair:
795   It came, it cometh, and will come, – the power
To punish or forgive – in *one* we shall be slower.

LXXXV

       Clear, placid Leman! thy contrasted lake
       With the wild world I dwelt in, is a thing
       Which warns me, with its stillness, to forsake
800   Earth's troubled waters for a purer spring.

This quiet sail is as a noiseless wing
To waft me from distraction; once I loved
Torn ocean's roar, but thy soft murmuring
Sounds sweet as if a Sister's voice reproved,
805   That I with stern delights should e'er have been so moved.

LXXXVI

It is the hush of night, and all between
Thy margin and the mountains, dusk, yet clear,
Mellow'd and mingling, yet distinctly seen,
Save darken'd Jura, whose capt heights appear
810   Precipitously steep; and drawing near,
There breathes a living fragrance from the shore,
Of flowers yet fresh with childhood; on the ear
Drops the light drip of the suspended oar,
Or chirps the grasshopper one good-night carol more;

LXXXVII

815   He is an evening reveller, who makes
His life an infancy, and sings his fill;
At intervals, some bird from out the brakes
Starts into voice a moment, then is still.
There seems a floating whisper on the hill,
820   But that is fancy, for the starlight dews
All silently their tears of love instil,
Weeping themselves away, till they infuse
Deep into Nature's breast the spirit of her hues.

LXXXVIII

Ye stars! which are the poetry of heaven!
825   If in your bright leaves we would read the fate
Of men and empires, – 'tis to be forgiven,
That in our aspirations to be great,
Our destinies o'erleap their mortal state,
And claim a kindred with you; for ye are
830   A beauty and a mystery, and create
In us such love and reverence from afar,
That fortune, fame, power, life, have named themselves a
    star.

LXXXIX

All heaven and earth are still – though not in sleep,
But breathless, as we grow when feeling most;
835 And silent, as we stand in thoughts too deep: –
All heaven and earth are still: From the high host
Of stars, to the lull'd lake and mountain-coast,
All is concenter'd in a life intense,
Where not a beam, nor air, nor leaf is lost,
840 But hath a part of being, and a sense
Of that which is of all Creator and defence.

XC

Then stirs the feeling infinite, so felt
In solitude, where we are *least* alone;
A truth, which through our being then doth melt
845 And purifies from self: it is a tone,
The soul and source of music, which makes known
Eternal harmony, and sheds a charm,
Like to the fabled Cytherea's zone,
Binding all things with beauty; – 'twould disarm
850 The spectre Death, had he substantial power to harm.

XCI

Not vainly did the early Persian make
His altar the high places and the peak
Of earth-o'ergazing mountains,[1] and thus take
A fit and unwall'd temple, there to seek

---

1. It is to be recollected, that the most beautiful and impressive doctrines of
the divine Founder of Christianity were delivered, not in the *Temple*, but on
the *Mount*. To wave the question of devotion, and turn to human eloquence,
– the most effectual and splendid specimens were not pronounced within
walls. Demosthenes addressed the public and popular assemblies. Cicero
spoke in the forum. That this added to their effect on the mind of both
orator and hearers, may be conceived from the difference between what we
read of the emotions then and there produced, and those we ourselves
experience in the perusal in the closet. It is one thing to read the Iliad at
Sigæum and on the tumuli, or by the springs with Mount Ida above, and the
plain and rivers and Archipelago around you; and another to trim your
taper over it in a snug library – *this* I know. Were the early and rapid

855   The Spirit in whose honour shrines are weak,
            Uprear'd of human hands. Come, and compare
            Columns and idol-dwellings, Goth or Greek,
            With Nature's realms of worship, earth and air,
       Nor fix on fond abodes to circumscribe thy pray'r!

       XCII
860   Thy sky is changed! – and such a change! Oh night,
            And storm, and darkness, ye are wondrous strong,
            Yet lovely in your strength, as is the light
            Of a dark eye in woman! Far along,
            From peak to peak, the rattling crags among
865   Leaps the live thunder! Not from one lone cloud,
            But every mountain now hath found a tongue,
            And Jura answers, through her misty shroud,
       Back to the joyous Alps, who call to her aloud!

---

progress of what is called Methodism to be attributed to any cause beyond the enthusiasm excited by its vehement faith and doctrines (the truth or error of which I presume neither to canvass nor question), I should venture to ascribe it to the practice of preaching in the *fields*, and the unstudied and extemporaneous effusions of its teachers. – The Mussulmans, whose erroneous devotion (at least in the lower orders) is most sincere, and therefore impressive, are accustomed to repeat their prescribed orisons and prayers, wherever they may be, at the stated hours – of course, frequently in the open air, kneeling upon a light mat (which they carry for the purpose of a bed or cushion as required): the ceremony lasts some minutes, during which they are totally absorbed, and only living in their supplication: nothing can disturb them. On me the simple and entire sincerity of these men, and the spirit which appeared to be within and upon them, made a far greater impression than any general rite which was ever performed in places of worship, of which I have seen those of almost every persuasion under the sun; including most of our own sectaries, and the Greek, the Catholic, the Armenian, the Lutheran, the Jewish, and the Mahometan. Many of the negroes, of whom there are numbers in the Turkish empire, are idolaters, and have free exercise of their belief and its rites: some of these I had a distant view of at Patras; and, from what I could make out of them, they appeared to be of a truly Pagan description, and not very agreeable to a spectator.

XCIII

And this is in the night: — Most glorious night!
870   Thou wert not sent for slumber! let me be
A sharer in thy fierce and far delight, —
A portion of the tempest and of thee![1]
How the lit lake shines, a phosphoric sea,
And the big rain comes dancing to the earth!
875   And now again 'tis black, — and now, the glee
Of the loud hills shakes with its mountain-mirth,
As if they did rejoice o'er a young earthquake's birth.

XCIV

Now, where the swift Rhone cleaves his way between
Heights which appear as lovers who have parted
880   In hate, whose mining depths so intervene,
That they can meet no more, though brokenhearted!
Though in their souls, which thus each other thwarted,
Love was the very root of the fond rage
Which blighted their life's bloom, and then departed:
885   Itself expired, but leaving them an age
Of years all winters, — war within themselves to wage.

XCV

Now, where the quick Rhone thus hath cleft his way,
The mightiest of the storms hath ta'en his stand:
For here, not one, but many, make their play,
890   And fling their thunder-bolts from hand to hand,
Flashing and cast around: of all the band,
The brightest through these parted hills hath fork'd
His lightnings, — as if he did understand,
That in such gaps as desolation work'd,
895   There the hot shaft should blast whatever therein lurk'd.

1. The thunder-storm to which these lines refer occurred on the 13th of
June, 1816, at midnight. I have seen, among the Acrocerauniam mountains
of Chimari, several more terrible, but none more beautiful.

XCVI

Sky, mountains, river, winds, lake, lightnings! ye!
With night, and clouds, and thunder, and a soul
To make these felt and feeling, well may be
Things that have made me watchful; the far roll
900   Of your departing voices, is the knoll
Of what in me is sleepless, – if I rest.
But where of ye, oh tempests! is the goal?
Are ye like those within the human breast?
Or do ye find, at length, like eagles, some high nest?

XCVII

905   Could I embody and unbosom now
That which is most within me, – could I wreak
My thoughts upon expression, and thus throw
Soul, heart, mind, passions, feelings, strong or weak,
All that I would have sought, and all I seek,
910   Bear, know, feel, and yet breathe – into *one* word,
And that one word were Lightning, I would speak;
But as it is, I live and die unheard,
With a most voiceless thought, sheathing it as a sword.

XCVIII

The morn is up again, the dewy morn,
915   With breath all incense, and with cheek all bloom,
Laughing the clouds away with playful scorn,
And living as if earth contain'd no tomb, –
And glowing into day: we may resume
The march of our existence: and thus I,
920   Still on thy shores, fair Leman! may find room
And food for meditation, nor pass by
Much, that may give us pause, if ponder'd fittingly.

XCIX

Clarens! sweet Clarens, birthplace of deep Love!
Thine air is the young breath of passionate thought;
925   Thy trees take root in Love; the snows above
The very Glaciers have his colours caught,
And sunset into rose-hues sees them wrought

By rays which sleep there lovingly: the rocks,
The permanent crags, tell here of Love, who sought
930   In them a refuge from the worldly shocks,
Which stir and sting the soul with hope that woos, then
      mocks.

C

Clarens! by heavenly feet thy paths are trod, –
Undying Love's, who here ascends a throne
To which the steps are mountains; where the god
935   Is a pervading life and light, – so shown
Not on those summits solely, nor alone
In the still cave and forest; o'er the flower
His eye is sparkling, and his breath hath blown,
His soft and summer breath, whose tender power
940 Passes the strength of storms in their most desolate hour.[1]

1. Rousseau's Héloïse, Lettre 17, Part IV., note. 'Ces montagnes sont si hautes qu'une demi-heure après le soleil couche, leurs sommets sont éclairés de ses rayons; dont le rouge forme sur ces cimes blanches *une belle couleur de rose*, qu'on aperçoit de fort loin.' – This applies more particularly to the heights over Meillerie. – 'J'allai à Vevay loger à la Clef, et pendant deux jours que j'y restai sans voir personne, je pris pour cette ville un amour qui m'a suivi dans tous mes voyages, et qui m'y a fait établir enfin les héros de mon roman. Je dirois volontiers à ceux qui ont du goût et qui sont sensibles: Allez à Vevay – visitez le pays, examinez les sites, promenez-vous sur le lac, et dites si la Nature n'a pas fait ce beau pays pour une Julie, pour une Claire, et pour un St Preux; mais ne les y cherchez pas.' – *Les Confessions*, livre iv. p. 306, Lyon, ed. 1796. – In July, 1816, I made a voyage round the Lake of Geneva; and, as far as my own observations have led me in a not uninterested nor inattentive survey of all the scenes most celebrated by Rousseau in his 'Héloïse,' I can safely say, that in this there is no exaggeration. It would be difficult to see Clarens (with the scenes around it, Vevay, Chillon, Bôveret, St Gingo, Meillerie, Eivan, and the entrances of the Rhone) without being forcibly struck with its peculiar adaptation to the persons and events with which it has been peopled. But this is not all; the feeling with which all around Clarens, and the opposite rocks of Meillerie, is invested, is of a still higher and more comprehensive order than the mere sympathy with individual passion; it is a sense of the existence of love in its most extended and sublime capacity, and of our own participation of its good and of its glory: it is the great principle of the universe, which is there more condensed, but not less manifested; and of which, though knowing ourselves a part, we lose our individuality, and mingle in the beauty of the whole. – If Rousseau had never written, nor lived, the same associations would not less have belonged to such scenes. He has added to the interest of

CI

    All things are here of *him*; from the black pines,
    Which are his shade on high, and the loud roar
    Of torrents, where he listeneth, to the vines
    Which slope his green path downward to the shore,
945   Where the bow'd waters meet him, and adore,
    Kissing his feet with murmurs; and the wood,
    The covert of old trees, with trunks all hoar,
    But light leaves, young as joy, stands where it stood,
Offering to him, and his, a populous solitude.

CII

950   A populous solitude of bees and birds,
    And fairy-formed and many-colour'd things,
    Who worship him with notes more sweet than words,
    And innocently open their glad wings,

---

his works by their adoption; he has shown his sense of their beauty by the selection; but they have done that for him which no human being could do for them. – I had the fortune (good or evil as it might be) to sail from Meillerie (where we landed for some time) to St Gingo during a lake storm, which added to the magnificence of all around, although occasionally accompanied by danger to the boat, which was small and overloaded. It was over this very part of the lake that Rousseau has driven the boat of St Preux and Madame Wolmar to Meillerie for shelter during a tempest. On gaining the shore at St Gingo, I found that the wind had been sufficiently strong to blow down some fine old chestnut trees on the lower part of the mountains. On the opposite height of Clarens is a château. The hills are covered with vineyards, and interspersed with some small but beautiful woods; one of these was named the 'Bosquet de Julie;' and it is remarkable that, though long ago cut down by the brutal selfishness of the monks of St Bernard (to whom the land appertained), that the ground might be enclosed into a vineyard for the miserable drones of an execrable superstition, the inhabitants of Clarens still point out the spot where its trees stood, calling it by the name which consecrated and survived them. Rousseau has not been particularly fortunate in the preservation of the 'local habitations' he has given to 'airy nothings.' The Prior of Great St Bernard has cut down some of his woods for the sake of a few casks of wine, and Buonaparte has levelled part of the rocks of Meillerie in improving the road to the Simplon. The road is an excellent one; but I cannot quite agree with a remark which I heard made, that 'La route vaut mieux que les souvenirs.'

Fearless and full of life: the gush of springs,
955   And fall of lofty fountains, and the bend
Of stirring branches, and the bud which brings
The swiftest thought of beauty, here extend,
Mingling, and made by Love, unto one mighty end.

CIII

He who hath loved not, here would learn that lore,
960   And make his heart a spirit; he who knows
That tender mystery, will love the more,
For this is Love's recess, where vain men's woes,
And the world's waste, have driven him far from those,
For 'tis his nature to advance or die;
965   He stands not still, but or decays, or grows
Into a boundless blessing, which may vie
With the immortal lights, in its eternity!

CIV

'Twas not for fiction chose Rousseau this spot,
Peopling it with affections; but he found
970   It was the scene which passion must allot
To the mind's purified beings; 'twas the ground
Where early Love his Psyche's zone unbound,
And hallow'd it with loveliness: 'tis lone,
And wonderful, and deep, and hath a sound,
975   And sense, and sight of sweetness; here the Rhone
Hath spread himself a couch, the Alps have rear'd a throne.

CV

Lausanne! and Ferney! ye have been the abodes
Of names which unto you bequeath'd a name;[1]
Mortals, who sought and found, by dangerous roads,
980   A path to perpetuity of fame:
They were gigantic minds, and their steep aim
Was, Titan-like, on daring doubts to pile
Thoughts which should call down thunder, and the flame
Of Heaven, again assail'd, if Heaven the while
985   On man and man's research could deign do more than smile.

1. Voltaire and Gibbon.

CVI

The one was fire and fickleness, a child,
Most mutable in wishes, but in mind,
A wit as various, – gay, grave, sage, or wild, –
Historian, bard, philosopher, combined;
990   He multiplied himself among mankind,
The Proteus of their talents: But his own
Breathed most in ridicule, – which, as the wind,
Blew where it listed, laying all things prone, –
Now to o'erthrow a fool, and now to shake a throne.

CVII

995   The other, deep and slow, exhausting thought,
And hiving wisdom with each studious year,
In meditation dwelt, with learning wrought,
And shaped his weapon with an edge severe,
Sapping a solemn creed with solemn sneer;
1000   The lord of irony, – that master-spell,
Which stung his foes to wrath, which grew from fear,
And doom'd him to the zealot's ready Hell,
Which answers to all doubts so eloquently well.

CVIII

Yet, peace be with their ashes, – for by them,
1005   If merited, the penalty is paid;
If it is not ours to judge, – far less condemn;
The hour must come when such things shall be made
Known unto all, – or hope and dread allay'd
By slumber, on one pillow, – in the dust,
1010   Which, thus much we are sure, must lie decay'd;
And when it shall revive, as is our trust,
'Twill be to be forgiven, or suffer what is just.

CIX

But let me quit man's works, again to read
His Maker's, spread around me, and suspend
1015   This page, which from my reveries I feed,
Until it seems prolonging without end.
The clouds above me to the white Alps tend,

And I must pierce them, and survey whate'er
May be permitted, as my steps I bend
1020   To their most great and growing region, where
The earth to her embrace compels the powers of air.

CX

Italia! too, Italia! looking on thee,
Full flashes on the soul the light of ages,
Since the fierce Carthaginian almost won thee,
1025   To the last halo of the chiefs and sages
Who glorify thy consecrated pages;
Thou wert the throne and grave of empires; still,
The fount at which the panting mind assuages
Her thirst of knowledge, quaffing there her fill,
1030 Flows from the eternal source of Rome's imperial hill.

CXI

Thus far have I proceeded in a theme
Renew'd with no kind auspices: – to feel
We are not what we have been, and to deem
We are not what we should be, – and to steel
1035   The heart against itself; and to conceal,
With a proud caution, love, or hate, or aught, –
Passion or feeling, purpose, grief, or zeal, –
Which is the tyrant spirit of our thought,
Is a stern task of soul: – No matter, – it is taught.

CXII

1040   And for these words, thus woven into song,
It may be that they are a harmless wile, –
The colouring of the scenes which fleet along,
Which I would seize, in passing, to beguile
My breast, or that of others, for a while.
1045   Fame is the thirst of youth, – but I am not
So young as to regard men's frown or smile,
As loss or guerdon of a glorious lot;
I stood and stand alone, – remember'd or forgot.

CXIII

I have not loved the world, nor the world me;
1050   I have not flatter'd its rank breath, nor bow'd
To its idolatries a patient knee, –
Nor coin'd my cheek to smiles, – nor cried aloud
In worship of an echo; in the crowd
They could not deem me one of such; I stood
1055   Among them, but not of them; in a shroud
Of thoughts which were not their thoughts, and still
       could,
Had I not filed[1] my mind, which thus itself subdued.

CXIV

I have not loved the world, nor the world me, –
But let us part fair foes; I do believe,
1060   Though I have found them not, that there may be
Words which are things, – hopes which will not deceive,
And virtues which are merciful, nor weave
Snares for the failing: I would also deem
O'er others' griefs that some sincerely grieve;[2]
1065   That two, or one, are almost what they seem,
That goodness is no name, and happiness no dream.

CXV

My daughter! with thy name this song begun –
My daughter! with thy name thus much shall end –
I see thee not, – I hear thee not, – but none
1070   Can be so wrapt in thee; thou art the friend
To whom the shadows of far years extend:
Albeit my brow thou never should'st behold,
My voice shall with thy future visions blend,
And reach into thy heart, – when mine is cold, –
1075 A token and a tone, even from thy father's mould.

1.   ——'If it be thus,
     For Banquo's issue have I *filed* my mind.' – MACBETH
2. It is said by Rochefoucault, that 'there is always something in the misfortunes of men's best friends not displeasing to them.'

CXVI

To aid thy mind's developement, – to watch
Thy dawn of little joys, – to sit and see
Almost thy very growth, – to view thee catch
Knowledge of objects, – wonders yet to thee!
1080 To hold thee lightly on a gentle knee,
And print on thy soft cheek a parent's kiss, –
This, it should seem, was not reserved for me;
Yet this was in my nature: – as it is,
I know not what is there, yet something like to this.

CXVII

1085 Yet, though dull Hate as duty should be taught,
I know that thou wilt love me; though my name
Should be shut from thee, as a spell still fraught
With desolation, – and a broken claim:
Though the grave closed between us, – 'twere the same,
1090 I know that thou wilt love me; though to drain
My blood from out thy being were an aim,
And an attainment, – all would be in vain, –
Still thou would'st love me, still that more than life retain.

CXVIII

The child of love, – though born in bitterness
1095 And nurtured in convulsion. Of thy sire
These were the elements, – and thine no less.
As yet such are around thee, – but thy fire
Shall be more temper'd, and thy hope far higher.
Sweet be thy cradled slumbers! O'er the sea,
1100 And from the mountains where I now respire,
Fain would I waft such blessing upon thee,
As, with a sigh, I deem thou might'st have been to me!

Epistle to Augusta ('My sister! my sweet sister!'
&c.)

I

My sister! my sweet sister! if a name
Dearer and purer were, it should be thine.
Mountains and seas divide us, but I claim
No tears, but tenderness to answer mine:
Go where I will, to me thou art the same –
A loved regret which I would not resign.
There yet are two things in my destiny, –
A world to roam through, and a home with thee.

II

The first were nothing – had I still the last,
It were the haven of my happiness;
But other claims and other ties thou hast,
And mine is not the wish to make them less.
A strange doom is thy father's son's, and past
Recalling, as it lies beyond redress;
Reversed for him our grandsire's[1] fate of yore, –
He had no rest at sea, nor I on shore.

III

If my inheritance of storms hath been
In other elements, and on the rocks
Of perils, overlook'd or unforeseen,
I have sustain'd my share of worldly shocks,

1. Admiral Byron was remarkable for never making a voyage without a
tempest. He was known to the sailors by the facetious name of 'Foul-weather
Jack.'

> 'But, though it were tempest toss'd,
> Still his bark could not be lost.'

He returned safely from the wreck of the Wager (in Anson's voyage), and
subsequently circumnavigated the world, many years after, as commander
of a similar expedition.

The fault was mine; nor do I seek to screen
My errors with defensive paradox;
I have been cunning in mine overthrow,
The careful pilot of my proper woe.

IV

25   Mine were my faults, and mine be their reward.
My whole life was a contest, since the day
That gave me being, gave me that which marr'd
The gift, – a fate, or will, that walk'd astray;
And I at times have found the struggle hard,
30   And thought of shaking off my bonds of clay:
But now I fain would for a time survive,
If but to see what next can well arrive.

V

Kingdoms and empires in my little day
I have outlived, and yet I am not old;
35   And when I look on this, the petty spray
Of my own years of trouble, which have roll'd
Like a wild bay of breakers, melts away:
Something – I know not what – does still uphold
A spirit of slight patience; – not in vain,
40   Even for its own sake, do we purchase pain.

VI

Perhaps the workings of defiance stir
Within me, – or perhaps a cold despair,
Brought on when ills habitually recur, –
Perhaps a kinder clime, or purer air,
45   (For even to this may change of soul refer,
And with light armour we may learn to bear,)
Have taught me a strange quiet, which was not
The chief companion of a calmer lot.

VII

I feel almost at times as I have felt
50   In happy childhood; trees, and flowers, and brooks,
Which do remember me of where I dwelt
Ere my young mind was sacrificed to books,

Come as of yore upon me, and can melt
My heart with recognition of their looks;
55   And even at moments I could think I see
Some living thing to love – but none like thee.

VIII
Here are the Alpine landscapes which create
A fund for contemplation; – to admire
Is a brief feeling of a trivial date;
60   But something worthier do such scenes inspire:
Here to be lonely is not desolate,
For much I view which I could most desire,
And, above all, a lake I can behold
Lovelier, not dearer, than our own of old.

IX
65   Oh that thou wert but with me! – but I grow
The fool of my own wishes, and forget
The solitude which I have vaunted so
Has lost its praise in this but one regret;
There may be others which I less may show; –
70   I am not of the plaintive mood, and yet
I feel an ebb in my philosophy,
And the tide rising in my alter'd eye.

X
I did remind thee of our own dear Lake,
By the old Hall which may be mine no more.
75   Leman's is fair; but think not I forsake
The sweet remembrance of a dearer shore:
Sad havoc Time must with my memory make
Ere *that* or *thou* can fade these eyes before;
Though, like all things which I have loved, they are
80   Resign'd for ever, or divided far.

XI
The world is all before me; I but ask
Of Nature that with which she will comply –
It is but in her summer's sun to bask,
To mingle with the quiet of her sky,

85 To see her gentle face without a mask,
  And never gaze on it with apathy.
  She was my early friend, and now shall be
My sister – till I look again on thee.

XII
  I can reduce all feelings but this one;
90 And that I would not; – for at length I see
  Such scenes as those wherein my life begun.
  The earliest – even the only paths for me –
  Had I but sooner learnt the crowd to shun,
  I had been better than I now can be;
95 The passions which have torn me would have slept;
I had not suffer'd, and *thou* hadst not wept.

XIII
  With false Ambition what had I to do?
  Little with Love, and least of all with Fame;
  And yet they came unsought, and with me grew,
100 And made me all which they can make – a name.
  Yet this was not the end I did pursue;
  Surely I once beheld a nobler aim.
  But all is over – I am one the more
To baffled millions which have gone before.

XIV
105 And for the future, this world's future may
  From me demand but little of my care;
  I have outlived myself by many a day;
  Having survived so many things that were;
  My years have been no slumber, but the prey
110 Of ceaseless vigils; for I had the share
  Of life which might have fill'd a century,
Before its fourth in time had pass'd me by.

XV
  And for the remnant which may be to come
  I am content; and for the past I feel
115 Not thankless, – for within the crowded sum
  Of struggles, happiness at times would steal,

And for the present, I would not benumb
My feelings farther. – Nor shall I conceal
That with all this I still can look around
120   And worship Nature with a thought profound.

XVI

For thee, my own sweet sister, in thy heart
I know myself secure, as thou in mine;
We were and are – I am, even as thou art –
Beings who ne'er each other can resign;
125   It is the same, together or apart,
From life's commencement to its slow decline
We are entwined – let death come slow or fast,
The tie which bound the first endures the last!

Lines (On Hearing that Lady Byron was Ill)

And thou wert sad – yet I was not with thee;
And thou wert sick, and yet I was not near;
Methought that joy and health alone could be
Where I was not – and pain and sorrow here!
5   And is it thus? – it is as I foretold,
And shall be more so; for the mind recoils
Upon itself, and the wreck'd heart lies cold,
While heaviness collects the shatter'd spoils
It is not in the storm nor in the strife
10   We feel benumb'd, and wish to be no more,
But in the after-silence on the shore,
When all is lost, except a little life.

I am too well avenged! – but 'twas my right;
Whate'er my sins might be, *thou* wert not sent
15   To be the Nemesis who should requite –
Nor did Heaven choose so near an instrument.

Mercy is for the merciful! – if thou
Hast been of such, 'twill be accorded now.

Thy nights are banish'd from the realms of sleep! –
20   Yes! they may flatter thee, but thou shalt feel
      A hollow agony which will not heal,
For thou art pillow'd on a curse too deep;
Thou hast sown in my sorrow, and must reap
      The bitter harvest in a woe as real!
25 I have had many foes, but none like thee;
      For 'gainst the rest myself I could defend,
      And be avenged, or turn them into friend;
But thou in safe implacability
Hadst nought to dread – in thy own weakness shielded,
30 And in my love, which hath but too much yielded,
      And spared, for thy sake, some I should not spare –
And thus upon the world – trust in thy truth –
And the wild fame of my ungovern'd youth –
      On things that were not, and on things that are –
35 Even upon such a basis hast thou built
A monument, whose cement hath been guilt!
      The moral Clytemnestra of thy lord,
And hew'd down, with an unsuspected sword,
Fame, peace, and hope – and all the better life
40   Which, but for this cold treason of thy heart,
Might still have risen from out the grave of strife,
And found a nobler duty than to part.
But of thy virtues didst thou make a vice,
      Trafficking with them in a purpose cold,
45   For present anger, and for future gold –
And buying other's grief at any price.
And thus once enter'd into crooked ways,
The early truth, which was thy proper praise,
Did not still walk beside thee – but at times,
50 And with a breast unknowing its own crimes,
Deceit, averments incompatible,
Equivocations, and the thoughts which dwell
      In Janus-spirits – the significant eye
Which learns to lie with silence – the pretext
55 Of Prudence, with advantages annex'd –

The acquiescence in all things which tend,
No matter how, to the desired end –
  All found a place in thy philosophy.
The means were worthy, and the end is won –
60 I would not do by thee as thou hast done!

September, 1816.

MANFRED

A Dramatic Poem

'There are more things in heaven and earth, Horatio,
Than are dreamt of in your philosophy.'

Dramatis Personæ

MANFRED
CHAMOIS HUNTER
ABBOT OF ST MAURICE
MANUEL
HERMAN

WITCH OF THE ALPS
ARIMANES
NEMESIS
THE DESTINIES
SPIRITS, &C.

The Scene of the Drama is amongst the Higher Alps – partly in the Castle of Manfred, and partly in the Mountains.

Act I

SCENE I

MANFRED *alone. – Scene, a Gothic Gallery. – Time, Midnight.*

MANFRED: The lamp must be replenish'd, but even then
It will not burn so long as I must watch:
My slumbers – if I slumber – are not sleep,

But a continuance of enduring thought,
5   Which then I can resist not: in my heart
There is a vigil, and these eyes but close
To look within; and yet I live, and bear
The aspect and the form of breathing men.
(But grief should be the instructor of the wise;)
10   Sorrow is knowledge: they who know the most
Must mourn the deepest o'er the fatal truth,
The Tree of Knowledge is not that of Life.
Philosophy and science, and the springs
Of wonder, and the wisdom of the world,
15   I have essay'd, and in my mind there is
A power to make these subject to itself –
But they avail not: I have done men good,
And I have met with good even among men –
But this avail'd not: I have had my foes,
20   And none have baffled, many fallen before me –
But this avail'd not: – Good, or evil, life,
Powers, passions, all I see in other beings,
Have been to me as rain unto the sands,
Since that all-nameless hour. I have no dread,
25   And feel the curse to have no natural fear,
Nor fluttering throb, that beats with hopes or wishes,
Or lurking love of something on the earth. –
Now to my task. –
                 Mysterious Agency!
Ye spirits of the unbounded Universe!
30   Whom I have sought in darkness and in light –
Ye, who do compass earth about, and dwell
In subtler essence – ye, to whom the tops
Of mountains inaccessible are haunts,
And earth's and ocean's caves familiar things –
35   I call upon ye by the written charm
Which gives me power upon you — Rise! appear!
       [*A pause.*]
They come not yet. – Now by the voice of him
Who is the first among you – by this sign,
Which makes you tremble – by the claims of him

40   Who is undying, – Rise! appear! — Appear!
            [*A pause.*]
        If it be so. – Spirits of earth and air,
        Ye shall not thus elude me: by a power,
        Deeper than all yet urged, a tyrant-spell,
        Which had its birthplace in a star condemn'd,
45   The burning wreck of a demolish'd world,
        A wandering hell in the eternal space;
        By the strong curse which is upon my soul,
        The thought which is within me and around me,
        I do compel ye to my will. – Appear!
            [*A star is seen at the darker end of the gallery: it is
            stationary; and a voice is heard singing.*]

FIRST SPIRIT

50   Mortal! to thy bidding bow'd,
        From my mansion in the cloud,
        Which the breath of twilight builds,
        And the summer's sunset gilds
        With the azure and vermilion,
55   Which is mix'd for my pavilion;
        Though thy quest may be forbidden,
        On a star-beam I have ridden;
        To thine adjuration bow'd,
        Mortal – be thy wish avow'd!

Voice of the SECOND SPIRIT

60   Mont Blanc is the monarch of mountains;
            They crown'd him long ago
        On a throne of rocks, in a robe of clouds,
            With a diadem of snow.
        Around his waist are forests braced,
65   The Avalanche in his hand;
        But ere it fall, that thundering ball
            Must pause for my command.
        The Glacier's cold and restless mass
            Moves onward day by day;

70   But I am he who bids it pass,
            Or with its ice delay.
        I am the spirit of the place,
            Could make the mountain bow
        And quiver to his cavern'd base –
75   And what with me wouldst *Thou?*

    Voice of the THIRD SPIRIT
        In the blue depth of the waters,
            Where the wave hath no strife,
        Where the wind is a stranger,
            And the sea-snake hath life,
80   Where the Mermaid is decking
            Her green hair with shells;
        Like the storm on the surface
            Came the sound of thy spells;
        O'er my calm Hall of Coral
85   The deep echo roll'd –
        To the Spirit of Ocean
            Thy wishes unfold!

    FOURTH SPIRIT
        Where the slumbering earthquake
            Lies pillow'd on fire,
90   And the lakes of bitumen
            Rise boilingly higher;
        Where the roots of the Andes
            Strike deep in the earth,
        As their summits to heaven
95   Shoot soaringly forth;
        I have quitted my birthplace,
            Thy bidding to bide –
        Thy spell hath subdued me,
            Thy will be my guide!

FIFTH SPIRIT

100   I am the Rider of the wind,
            The Stirrer of the storm;
         The hurricane I left behind
            Is yet with lightning warm;
         To speed to thee, o'er shore and sea
105   I swept upon the blast:
         The fleet I met sail'd well, and yet
            'Twill sink ere night be past.

SIXTH SPIRIT

         My dwelling is the shadow of the night,
         Why doth thy magic torture me with light?

SEVENTH SPIRIT

110   The star which rules thy destiny
         Was ruled, ere earth began, by me:
         It was a world as fresh and fair
         As e'er revolved round sun in air;
         Its course was free and regular,
115   Space bosom'd not a lovelier star.
         The hour arrived – and it became
         A wandering mass of shapeless flame,
         A pathless comet, and a curse,
         The menace of the universe;
120   Still rolling on with innate force,
         Without a sphere, without a course,
         A bright deformity on high,
         The monster of the upper sky!
         And thou! beneath its influence born –
125   Thou worm! whom I obey and scorn –
         Forced by a power (which is not thine,
         And lent thee but to make thee mine)
         For this brief moment to descend,
         Where these weak spirits round thee bend
130   And parley with a thing like thee –
         What wouldst thou, Child of Clay! with me?

The SEVEN SPIRITS

Earth, ocean, air, night, mountains, winds, thy star,
　　Are at thy beck and bidding, Child of Clay!
Before thee at thy quest their spirits are –
135　　What wouldst thou with us, son of mortals – say?

MANFRED: Forgetfulness –
FIRST SPIRIT:　　　　　　　　Of what – of whom – and why?
MANFRED: Of that which is within me; read it there –
　　Ye know it, and I cannot utter it.
SPIRIT: We can but give thee that which we possess:
140　　Ask of us subjects, sovereignty, the power
　　O'er earth, the whole, or portion, or a sign
　　Which shall control the elements, whereof
　　We are the dominators, each and all,
　　These shall be thine.
MANFRED:　　　　　　　　Oblivion, self-oblivion –
145　　Can ye not wring from out the hidden realms
　　Ye offer so profusely what I ask?
SPIRIT: It is not in our essence, in our skill;
　　But – thou mayst die.
MANFRED:　　　　　　　　Will death bestow it on me?
SPIRIT: We are immortal, and do not forget;
150　　We are eternal; and to us the past
　　Is, as the future, present. Art thou answer'd?
MANFRED: Ye mock me – but the power which brought ye
　　　here
　　Hath made you mine. Slaves, scoff not at my will!
　　The mind, the spirit, the Promethean spark,
155　　The lightning of my being, is as bright,
　　Pervading, and far darting as your own,
　　And shall not yield to yours, though coop'd in clay!
　　Answer, or I will teach you what I am.
SPIRIT: We answer as we answer'd; our reply
160　　Is even in thine own words.
MANFRED:　　　　　　　　Why say ye so?
SPIRIT: If, as thou say'st, thine essence be as ours,
　　We have replied in telling thee, the thing
　　Mortals call death hath nought to do with us.

MANFRED: I then have call'd ye from your realms in vain;
165   Ye cannot, or ye will not, aid me.
SPIRIT: Say;
     What we possess we offer; it is thine:
     Bethink ere thou dismiss us, ask again –
     Kingdom, and sway, and strength, and length of days—
MANFRED: Accursed! what have I to do with days?
170   They are too long already. – Hence – begone!
SPIRIT: Yet pause: being here, our will would do thee
         service;
     Bethink thee, is there then no other gift
     Which we can make not worthless in thine eyes?
MANFRED: No, none: yet stay – one moment, ere we part –
175   I would behold ye face to face. I hear
     Your voices, sweet and melancholy sounds,
     As music on the waters; and I see
     The steady aspect of a clear large star;
     But nothing more. Approach me as ye are,
180   Or one, or all, in your accustom'd forms.
SPIRIT: We have no forms, beyond the elements
     Of which we are the mind and principle:
     But choose a form – in that we will appear.
MANFRED: I have no choice; there is no form on earth
185   Hideous or beautiful to me. Let him,
     Who is most powerful of ye, take such aspect
     As unto him may seem most fitting – Come!
SEVENTH SPIRIT [*Appearing in the shape of a beautiful female
     figure*]: Behold
MANFRED: Oh God! if it be thus, and *thou*
     Art not a madness and a mockery,
190   I yet might be most happy. I will clasp thee,
     And we again will be —
       [The figure vanishes.]
                 My heart is crush'd!
     [MANFRED *falls senseless.*]

[A Voice is heard in the Incantation which follows.]

    When the moon is on the wave,
      And the glow-worm in the grass,
    And the meteor on the grave,
195   And the wisp on the morass;
    When the falling stars are shooting,
    And the answer'd owls are hooting,
    And the silent leaves are still
    In the shadow of the hill,
200   Shall my soul be upon thine,
    With a power and with a sign.

    Though thy slumber may be deep,
    Yet thy spirit shall not sleep;
    There are shades which will not vanish,
205   There are thoughts thou canst not banish;
    By a power to thee unknown,
    Thou canst never be alone;
    Thou art wrapt as with a shroud,
    Thou art gather'd in a cloud;
210   And for ever shalt thou dwell
    In the spirit of this spell.

    Though thou seest me not pass by,
    Thou shalt feel me with thine eye
    As a thing that, though unseen,
215   Must be near thee, and hath been;
    And when in that secret dread
    Thou hast turn'd around thy head,
    Thou shalt marvel I am not
    As thy shadow on the spot,
220   And the power which thou dost feel
    Shall be what thou must conceal.

    And a magic voice and verse
    Hath baptized thee with a curse;
    And a spirit of the air
225   Hath begirt thee with a snare;

In the wind there is a voice
Shall forbid thee to rejoice;
And to thee shall Night deny
All the quiet of her sky;
230 And the day shall have a sun,
Which shall make thee wish it done.

From thy false tears I did distil
An essence which hath strength to kill;
From thy own heart I then did wring
235 The black blood in its blackest spring;
From thy own smile I snatch'd the snake,
For there it coil'd as in a brake;
From thy own lip I drew the charm
Which gave all these their chiefest harm;
240 In proving every poison known,
I found the strongest was thine own.

By thy cold breast and serpent smile,
By thy unfathom'd gulfs of guile,
By that most seeming virtuous eye,
245 By thy shut soul's hypocrisy;
By the perfection of thine art
Which pass'd for human thine own heart;
By thy delight in others' pain,
And by thy brotherhood of Cain,
250 I call upon thee! and compel
Thyself to be thy proper Hell!

And on thy head I pour the vial
Which doth devote thee to this trial;
Nor to slumber, nor to die,
255 Shall be in thy destiny;
Though thy death shall still seem near
To thy wish, but as a fear;
Lo! the spell now works around thee,
And the clankless chain hath bound thee;
260 O'er thy heart and brain together
Hath the word been pass'd – now wither!

SCENE II

The Mountain of the Jungfrau. – Time, Morning. – MANFRED
alone upon the Cliffs.

MANFRED: The spirits I have raised abandon me –
   The spells which I have studied baffle me –
   The remedy I reck'd of tortured me;
   I lean no more on super-human aid,
5   It hath no power upon the past, and for
   The future, till the past be gulf'd in darkness,
   It is not of my search. – My mother Earth!
   And thou fresh breaking Day, and you, ye Mountains,
   Why are ye beautiful? I cannot love ye.
10   And thou, the bright eye of the universe,
   That openest over all, and unto all
   Art a delight – thou shin'st not on my heart.
   And you, ye crags, upon whose extreme edge
   I stand, and on the torrent's brink beneath
15   Behold the tall pines dwindled as to shrubs
   In dizziness of distance; when a leap,
   A stir, a motion, even a breath, would bring
   My breast upon its rocky bosom's bed
   To rest for ever – wherefore do I pause?
20   I feel the impulse – yet I do not plunge;
   I see the peril – yet do not recede;
   And my brain reels – and yet my foot is firm:
   There is a power upon me which withholds,
   And makes it my fatality to live;
25   If it be life to wear within myself
   This barrenness of spirit, and to be
   My own soul's sepulchre, for I have ceased
   To justify my deeds unto myself –
   The last infirmity of evil. Ay,
30   Thou winged and cloud-cleaving minister,
    [An eagle passes.)
   Whose happy flight is highest into heaven,
   Well may'st thou swoop so near me – I should be
   Thy prey, and gorge thine eaglets; thou art gone

Where the eye cannot follow thee; but thine
35   Yet pierces downward, onward, or above,
With a pervading vision. – Beautiful!
How beautiful is all this visible world!
How glorious in its action and itself!
But we, who name ourselves its sovereigns, we,
40   Half dust, half deity, alike unfit
To sink or soar, with our mix'd essence make
A conflict of its elements, and breathe
The breath of degradation and of pride,
Contending with low wants and lofty will,
45   Till our mortality predominates,
And men are – what they name not to themselves,
And trust not to each other. Hark! the note,
        [*The Shepherd's pipe in the distance is heard.*]
The natural music of the mountain reed –
For here the patriarchal days are not
50   A pastoral fable – pipes in the liberal air,
Mix'd with the sweet bells of the sauntering herd;
My soul would drink those echoes. – Oh, that I were
The viewless spirit of a lovely sound,
A living voice, a breathing harmony,
55   A bodiless enjoyment – born and dying
With the blest tone which made me!
        [*Enter from below a* CHAMOIS HUNTER.]
CHAMOIS HUNTER: Even so
This way the chamois leapt: her nimble feet
Have baffled me; my gains to-day will scarce
Repay my break-neck travail. – What is here?
60   Who seems not of my trade, and yet hath reach'd
A height which none even of our mountaineers,
Save our best hunters, may attain: his garb
Is goodly, his mien manly, and his air
Proud as a free-born peasant's, at this distance –
65   I will approach him nearer.
MANFRED [*not perceiving the other*]: To be thus –
Grey-hair'd with anguish, like these blasted pines,
Wrecks of a single winter, barkless, branchless,
A blighted trunk upon a cursed root,

Which but supplies a feeling to decay –
70 And to be thus, eternally but thus,
Having been otherwise! Now furrow'd o'er
With wrinkles, plough'd by moments, not by years
And hours – all tortured into ages – hours
Which I outlive! – Ye toppling crags of ice!
75 Ye avalanches, whom a breath draws down
In mountainous o'erwhelming, come and crush me!
I hear ye momently above, beneath,
Crash with a frequent conflict; but ye pass,
And only fall on things that still would live;
80 On the young flourishing forest, or the hut
And hamlet of the harmless villager.
CHAMOIS HUNTER: The mists begin to rise from up the
    valley;
I'll warn him to descend, or he may chance
To lose at once his way and life together.
85 MANFRED: The mists boil up around the glaciers;
    clouds
Rise curling fast beneath me, white and sulphury,
Like foam from the roused ocean of deep Hell,
Whose every wave breaks on a living shore,
Heap'd with the damn'd like pebbles. – I am giddy.
90 CHAMOIS HUNTER: I must approach him cautiously; if near,
A sudden step will startle him, and he
Seems tottering already.
MANFRED: Mountains have fallen,
Leaving a gap in the clouds, and with the shock
Rocking their Alpine brethren; filling up
95 The ripe green valleys with destruction's splinters;
Damming the rivers with a sudden dash,
Which crush'd the waters into mist, and made
Their fountains find another channel – thus,
Thus, in its old age, did Mount Rosenberg –
100 Why stood I not beneath it?
CHAMOIS HUNTER: Friend! have a care,
Your next step may be fatal! – for the love
Of him who made you, stand not on that brink!

MANFRED [*not hearing him*]: Such would have been for me a
    fitting tomb;
My bones had then been quiet in their depth;
105   They had not then been strewn upon the rocks
For the wind's pastime – as thus – thus they shall be –
In this one plunge. – Farewell, ye opening heavens!
Look not upon me thus reproachfully –
Ye were not meant for me – Earth! take these atoms!
    [As MANFRED *is in act to spring from the cliff, the*
    CHAMOIS HUNTER *seizes and retains him with a sudden*
    grasp.]
110 CHAMOIS HUNTER: Hold, madman! – though aweary of thy
    life,
Stain not our pure vales with thy guilty blood –
Away with me — I will not quit my hold.
MANFRED: I am most sick at heart – nay, grasp me not –
I am all feebleness – the mountains whirl
115   Spinning around me — I grow blind — What art thou?
CHAMOIS HUNTER: I'll answer that anon. – Away with
    me —
The clouds grow thicker — there – now lean on me –
Place your foot here – here, take this staff, and cling
A moment to that shrub – now give me your hand,
120   And hold fast by my girdle – softly – well –
The Chalet will be gain'd within an hour –
Come on, we'll quickly find a surer footing,
And something like a pathway, which the torrent
Hath wash'd since winter. – Come, 'tis bravely done –
125   You should have been a hunter. – Follow me.
    [*As they descend the rocks with difficulty, the scene*
    closes.]

Act II

SCENE I

A Cottage amongst the Bernese Alps.

[MANFRED *and the* CHAMOIS HUNTER.]

CHAMOIS HUNTER: No, no – yet pause – thou must not yet
    go forth:
    Thy mind and body are alike unfit
    To trust each other; for some hours, at least;
    When thou art better, I will be thy guide –
5   But whither?
MANFRED: It imports not: I do know
    My route full well, and need no further guidance.
CHAMOIS HUNTER: Thy garb and gait bespeak thee of high
    lineage –
    One of the many chiefs, whose castled crags
    Look o'er the lower valleys – which of these
10   May call thee lord? I only know their portals;
    My way of life leads me but rarely down
    To bask by the huge hearths of those old halls,
    Carousing with the vassals; but the paths,
    Which step from out our mountains to their doors,
15   I know from childhood – which of these is thine?
MANFRED: No matter.
CHAMOIS HUNTER: Well, sir, pardon me the question,
    And be of better cheer. Come, taste my wine;
    'Tis of an ancient vintage; many a day
    'T has thawed my veins among our glaciers, now
20   Let it do thus for thine – Come, pledge me fairly.
MANFRED: Away, away! there's blood upon the brim!
    Will it then never – never sink in the earth?
CHAMOIS HUNTER: What dost thou mean? thy senses
    wander from thee.
MANFRED: I say 'tis blood – my blood! the pure warm
    stream
25   Which ran in the veins of my fathers, and in ours
    When we were in our youth, and had one heart,
    And loved each other as we should not love,

And this was shed: but still it rises up,
Colouring the clouds, that shut me out from heaven,
30   Where thou art not – and I shall never be.
CHAMOIS HUNTER: Man of strange words, and some half-
        maddening sin,
        Which makes thee people vacancy, whate'er
        Thy dread and sufferance be, there's comfort yet –
        The aid of holy men, and heavenly patience —
35   MANFRED: Patience and patience! Hence – that word was
        made
        For brutes of burthen, not for birds of prey;
        Preach it to mortals of a dust like thine, –
        I am not of thine order.
CHAMOIS HUNTER: Thanks to heaven!
        I would not be of thine for the free fame
40   Of William Tell; but whatsoe'er thine ill,
        It must be borne, and these wild starts are useless.
MANFRED: Do I not bear it? – Look on me – I live.
CHAMOIS HUNTER: This is convulsion, and no healthful
        life.
MANFRED: I tell thee, man! I have lived many years,
45   Many long years, but they are nothing now
        To those which I must number: ages – ages –
        Space and eternity – and consciousness,
        With the fierce thirst of death – and still unslaked!
CHAMOIS HUNTER: Why, on thy brow the seal of middle age
50   Hath scarce been set; I am thine elder far.
MANFRED: Think'st thou existence doth depend on time?
        It doth; but actions are our epochs: mine
        Have made my days and nights imperishable,
        Endless, and all alike, as sands on the shore,
55   Innumerable atoms; and one desert,
        Barren and cold, on which the wild waves break,
        But nothing rests, save carcasses and wrecks,
        Rocks, and the salt-surf weeds of bitterness.
        CHAMOIS HUNTER: Alas! he's mad – but yet I must not
        leave him.
60   MANFRED: I would I were – for then the things I see

Would be but a distemper'd dream.

CHAMOIS HUNTER: What is it
That thou dost see, or think thou look'st upon?

MANFRED: Myself, and thee – a peasant of the Alps –
Thy humble virtues, hospitable home,
65 And spirit patient, pious, proud, and free;
Thy self-respect, grafted on innocent thoughts;
Thy days of health, and nights of sleep; thy toils,
By danger dignified, yet guiltless; hopes
Of cheerful old age and a quiet grave,
70 With cross and garland over its green turf,
And thy grandchildren's love for epitaph;
This do I see – and then I look within –
It matters not – my soul was scorch'd already!

CHAMOIS HUNTER: And would'st thou then exchange thy lot
for mine?

75 MANFRED: No, friend! I would not wrong thee, nor exchange
My lot with living being: I can bear –
However wretchedly, 'tis still to bear –
In life what others could not brook to dream,
But perish in their slumber.

CHAMOIS HUNTER: And with this –
80 This cautious feeling for another's pain,
Canst thou be black with evil? – say not so.
Can one of gentle thoughts have wreak'd revenge
Upon his enemies?

MANFRED: Oh! no, no, no!
My injuries came down on those who loved me –
85 On those whom I best loved: I never quell'd
An enemy, save in my just defence –
My wrongs were all on those I should have cherished
But my embrace was fatal.

CHAMOIS HUNTER: Heaven give thee rest!
And penitence restore thee to thyself;
90 My prayers shall be for thee.

MANFRED: I need them not,
But can endure thy pity. I depart –
'Tis time – farewell! – Here's gold, and thanks for
thee –
No words – it is thy due. – Follow me not –

I know my path – the mountain peril's past:
95   And once again, I charge thee, follow not!
            [*Exit* MANFRED.]

SCENE II

A lower Valley in the Alps. – A Cataract.

        [*Enter* MANFRED.]
        It is not noon – the sunbow's rays[1] still arch
        The torrent with the many hues of heaven,
        And roll the sheeted silver's waving column
        O'er the crag's headlong perpendicular,
5   And fling its lines of foaming light along,
        And to and fro, like the pale courser's tail,
        The Giant steed, to be bestrode by Death,
        As told in the Apocalypse. No eyes
        But mine now drink this sight of loveliness;
10   I should be sole in this sweet solitude,
        And with the Spirit of the place divide
        The homage of these waters. – I will call her.
            [MANFRED *takes some of the water into the palm of his*
            hand, and flings it into the air, muttering the adjuration.
            After a pause, the WITCH OF THE ALPS *rises beneath the*
            arch of the sunbow of the torrent.]
        Beautiful Spirit! with thy hair of light,
        And dazzling eyes of glory, in whose form
15   The charms of earth's least mortal daughters grow
        To an unearthly stature, in an essence
        Of purer elements; while the hues of youth, –
        Carnation'd like a sleeping infant's cheek,
        Rock'd by the beating of her mother's heart,
20   Or the rose tints, which summer's twilight leaves
        Upon the lofty glacier's virgin snow,
        The blush of earth embracing with her heaven, –

1. This iris is formed by the rays of the sun over the lower part of the
Alpine torrents: it is exactly like a rainbow come down to pay a visit, and so
close that you may walk into it: this effect lasts till noon.

        Tinge thy celestial aspect, and make tame
        The beauties of the sunbow which bends o'er thee.
25   Beautiful Spirit! in thy calm clear brow,
        Wherein is glass'd serenity of soul,
        Which of itself shows immortality,
        I read that thou wilt pardon to a Son
        Of Earth, whom the abstruser powers permit
30   At times to commune with them – if that he
        Avail him of his spells – to call thee thus,
        And gaze on thee a moment.
      WITCH: Son of Earth!
        I know thee, and the powers which give thee power;
        I know thee for a man of many thoughts,
35   And deeds of good and ill, extreme in both,
        Fatal and fated in thy sufferings.
        I have expected this – what would'st thou with me?
      MANFRED: To look upon thy beauty – nothing further.
        The face of the earth hath madden'd me, and I
40   Take refuge in her mysteries, and pierce
        To the abodes of those who govern her –
        But they can nothing aid me. I have sought
        From them what they could not bestow, and now
        I search no further.
      WITCH: What could be the quest
45   Which is not in the power of the most powerful,
        The rulers of the invisible?
      MANFRED: A boon;
        But why should I repeat it? 'twere in vain.
      WITCH: I know not that; let thy lips utter it.
      MANFRED: Well, though it torture me, 'tis but the same;
50   My pang shall find a voice. From my youth upwards
        My spirit walk'd not with the souls of men,
        Nor look'd upon the earth with human eyes;
        The thirst of their ambition was not mine,
        The aim of their existence was not mine;
55   My joys, my griefs, my passions, and my powers,
        Made me a stranger; though I wore the form,
        I had no sympathy with breathing flesh,
        Nor midst the creatures of clay that girded me

Was there but one who — but of her anon.
60   I said with men, and with the thoughts of men,
I held but slight communion; but instead,
My joy was in the Wilderness, to breathe
The difficult air of the iced mountain's top,
Where the birds dare not build, nor insect's wing
65   Flit o'er the herbless granite; or to plunge
Into the torrent, and to roll along
On the swift whirl of the new breaking wave
Of river-stream, or ocean, in their flow.
In these my early strength exulted; or
70   To follow through the night the moving moon,
The stars and their development; or catch
The dazzling lightnings till my eyes grew dim;
Or to look, list'ning, on the scatter'd leaves,
While Autumn winds were at their evening song.
75   These were my pastimes, and to be alone;
For if the beings, of whom I was one, –
Hating to be so, – cross'd me in my path,
I felt myself degraded back to them,
And was all clay again. And then I dived,
80   In my lone wanderings, to the caves of death,
Searching its cause in its effect; and drew
From wither'd bones, and skulls, and heap'd up dust,
Conclusions most forbidden. Then I pass'd
The nights of years in sciences untaught,
85   Save in the old time; and with time and toil,
And terrible ordeal, and such penance
As in itself hath power upon the air,
And spirits that do compass air and earth,
Space, and the peopled infinite, I made
90   Mine eyes familiar with Eternity,
Such as, before me, did the Magi, and
He who from out their fountain dwellings raised
Eros and Anteros,[1] at Gadara,
As I do thee; – and with my knowledge grew

1. The philosopher Jamblicus. The story of the raising of Eros and Anteros may be found in his life by Eunapius. It is well told.

95   The thirst of knowledge, and the power and joy
        Of this most bright intelligence, until —
   WITCH: Proceed.
   MANFRED: Oh! I but thus prolong'd my words,
        Boasting these idle attributes, because
        As I approach the core of my heart's grief –
100   But to my task. I have not named to thee
        Father or mother, mistress, friend, or being,
        With whom I wore the chain of human ties;
        If I had such, they seem'd not such to me –
        Yet there was one —
   WITCH: Spare not thyself – proceed.
105 MANFRED: She was like me in lineaments – her eyes,
        Her hair, her features, all, to the very tone
        Even of her voice, they said were like to mine;
        But soften'd all, and temper'd into beauty;
        She had the same lone thoughts and wanderings,
110   The quest of hidden knowledge, and a mind
        To comprehend the universe: nor these
        Alone, but with them gentler powers than mine,
        Pity, and smiles, and tears – which I had not;
        And tenderness – but that I had for her;
115   Humility – and that I never had.
        Her faults were mine – her virtues were her own –
        I loved her, and destroy'd her!
   WITCH: With thy hand?
   MANFRED: Not with my hand, but heart – which broke her
           heart –
        It gazed on mine, and wither'd. I have shed
120   Blood, but not hers – and yet her blood was shed –
        I saw – and could not stanch it.
   WITCH: And for this –
        A being of the race thou dost despise,
        The order which thine own would rise above,
        Mingling with us and ours, thou dost forego
125   The gifts of our great knowledge, and shrink'st back
        To recreant mortality — Away!
   MANFRED: Daughter of Air! I tell thee, since that hour –
        But words are breath – look on me in my sleep,

Or watch my watchings – Come and sit by me!
130 My solitude is solitude no more,
But peopled with the Furies; – I have gnash'd
My teeth in darkness till returning morn,
Then cursed myself till sunset; – I have pray'd
For madness as a blessing – 'tis denied me.
135 I have affronted death – but in the war
Of elements the waters shrunk from me,
And fatal things pass'd harmless – the cold hand
Of an all-pitiless demon held me back,
Back by a single hair, which would not break.
140 In fantasy, imagination, all
The affluence of my soul – which one day was
A Crœsus in creation – I plunged deep,
But, like an ebbing wave, it dash'd me back
Into the gulf of my unfathom'd thought.
145 I plunged amidst mankind – Forgetfulness
I sought in all, save where 'tis to be found,
And that I have to learn – my sciences,
My long pursued and super-human art,
Is mortal here – I dwell in my despair –
150 And live – and live for ever.

WITCH: It may be
That I can aid thee.

MANFRED: To do this thy power
Must wake the dead, or lay me low with them.
Do so – in any shape – in any hour –
With any torture – so it be the last.

155 WITCH: That is not in my province; but if thou
Wilt swear obedience to my will, and do
My bidding, it may help thee to thy wishes.

MANFRED: I will not swear – Obey! and whom? the spirits
Whose presence I command, and be the slave
160 Of those who served me – Never!

WITCH: Is this all?
Hast thou no gentler answer? – Yet bethink thee,
And pause ere thou rejectest.

MANFRED: I have said it.

WITCH: Enough! – I may retire then – say!

MANFRED: Retire!
    [*The* WITCH *disappears.*]
MANFRED [*alone*]:
    We are the fools of time and terror: Days
165   Steal on us and steal from us; yet we live,
    Loathing our life, and dreading still to die.
    In all the days of this detested yoke –
    This heaving burthen, this accursed breath –
    This vital weight upon the struggling heart,
170   Which sinks with sorrow, or beats quick with pain,
    Or joy that ends in agony or faintness –
    In all the days of past and future, for
    In life there is no present, we can number
    How few – how less than few – wherein the soul
175   Forbears to pant for death, and yet draws back
    As from a stream in winter, though the chill
    Be but a moment's. I have one resource
    Still in my science – I can call the dead,
    And ask them what it is we dread to be:
180   The sternest answer can but be the Grave,
    And that is nothing – if they answer not –
    The buried Prophet answered to the Hag
    Of Endor; and the Spartan Monarch drew
    From the Byzantine maid's unsleeping spirit
185   An answer and his destiny – he slew
    That which he loved, unknowing what he slew,
    And died unpardon'd – though he call'd in aid
    The Phyxian Jove, and in Phigalia roused
    The Arcadian Evocators to compel
190   The indignant shadow to depose her wrath,
    Or fix her term of vengeance – she replied
    In words of dubious import, but fulfill'd.[1]
    If I had never lived, that which I love
    Had still been living; had I never loved,
195   That which I love would still be beautiful –
    Happy and giving happiness. What is she?

---

1. The story of Pausanias, king of Sparta (who commanded the Greeks at the battle of Platea, and afterwards perished for an attempt to betray the Lacedæmonians), and Cleonice, is told in Plutarch's life of Cimon; and in the Laconics of Pausanias the sophist, in his description of Greece.

What is she now? – a sufferer for my sins –
A thing I dare not think upon – or nothing.
Within few hours I shall not call in vain –
200   Yet in this hour I dread the thing I dare:
Until this hour I never shrunk to gaze
On spirit, good or evil – now I tremble,
And feel a strange cold thaw upon my heart.
But I can act even what I most abhor,
205   And champion human fears. – The night approaches.
[*Exit.*]

SCENE III

The Summit of the Jungfrau Mountain.

[*Enter* FIRST DESTINY.]
The moon is rising broad, and round, and bright;
And here on snows, where never human foot
Of common mortal trod, we nightly tread,
And leave no traces; o'er the savage sea,
5   The glassy ocean of the mountain ice,
We skim its rugged breakers, which put on
The aspect of a tumbling tempest's foam,
Frozen in a moment – a dead whirlpool's image:
And this most steep fantastic pinnacle,
10   The fretwork of some earthquake – where the clouds
Pause to repose themselves in passing by –
Is sacred to our revels, or our vigils;
Here do I wait my sisters, on our way
To the Hall of Arimanes, for to-night
15   Is our great festival – 'tis strange they come not.

A Voice without, singing.
The Captive Usurper,
Hurl'd down from the throne,
Lay buried in torpor,
Forgotten and lone;
20   I broke through his slumbers,
I shiver'd his chain,

I leagued him with numbers —
He's Tyrant again!
With the blood of a million he'll answer my care,
25   With a nation's destruction — his flight and despair.

Second Voice, without.
The ship sail'd on, the ship sail'd fast,
But I left not a sail, and I left not a mast;
There is not a plank of the hull or the deck,
30   And there is not a wretch to lament o'er his wreck;
Save one, whom I held, as he swam, by the hair,
And he was a subject well worthy my care;
A traitor on land, and a pirate at sea —
But I saved him to wreak further havoc for me!

FIRST DESTINY, *answering.*
The city lies sleeping;
35   The morn, to deplore it,
May dawn on it weeping:
Sullenly, slowly,
The black plague flew o'er it —
Thousands lie lowly;
40   Tens of thousands shall perish —
The living shall fly from
The sick they should cherish;
But nothing can vanquish
The touch that they die from.
45   Sorrow and anguish,
And evil and dread,
Envelope a nation —
The blest are the dead,
Who see not the sight
50   Of their own desolation —
This work of a night —
This wreck of a realm — this deed of my doing —
For ages I've done, and shall still be renewing!

[*Enter the* SECOND *and* THIRD DESTINIES.]

The Three.

> Our hands contain the hearts of men,
> 55   Our footsteps are their graves;
> We only give to take again
> The spirits of our slaves!

FIRST DESTINY: Welcome! – Where's Nemesis?

SECOND DESTINY: At some great work;
But what I know not, for my hands were full.

60 THIRD DESTINY: Behold she cometh.

               [*Enter* NEMESIS.]

FIRST DESTINY: Say, where hast thou been?
My sisters and thyself are slow to-night.

NEMESIS: I was detain'd repairing shatter'd thrones,
Marrying fools, restoring dynasties,
Avenging men upon their enemies,
65 And making them repent their own revenge;
Goading the wise to madness; from the dull
Shaping out oracles to rule the world
Afresh, for they were waxing out of date,
And mortals dared to ponder for themselves,
70 To weigh kings in the balance, and to speak
Of freedom, the forbidden fruit. – Away!
We have outstay'd the hour – mount we our clouds!

       [*Exeunt.*]

SCENE IV

The Hall of Arimanes – Arimanes on his Throne, a Globe of Fire, surrounded by the Spirits.

Hymn of the SPIRITS

> Hail to our Master! – Prince of Earth and Air!
>   Who walks the clouds and waters – in his hand
> The sceptre of the elements, which tear
>   Themselves to chaos at his high command!

5   He breatheth – and a tempest shakes the sea;
           He speaketh – and the clouds reply in thunder;
       He gazeth – from his glance the sunbeams flee;
           He moveth – earthquakes rend the world asunder.
       Beneath his footsteps the volcanoes rise;
10   His shadow is the Pestilence; his path
       The comets herald through the crackling skies;
           And planets turn to ashes at his wrath.
       To him War offers daily sacrifice;
           To him Death pays his tribute; Life is his,
15   With all its infinite of agonies –
           And his the spirit of whatever is!

       [*Enter the* DESTINIES *and* NEMESIS.]
       FIRST DESTINY: Glory to Arimanes! on the earth
       His power increaseth – both my sisters did
       His bidding, nor did I neglect my duty!
20   SECOND DESTINY: Glory to Arimanes! we who bow
       The necks of men, bow down before his throne!
       THIRD DESTINY: Glory to Arimanes! we await
       His nod!
       NEMESIS: Sovereign of Sovereigns! we are thine,
       And all that liveth, more or less, is ours,
25   And most things wholly so; still to increase
       Our power, increasing thine, demands our care,
       And we are vigilant – Thy late commands
       Have been fulfill'd to the utmost.
           [*Enter* MANFRED.]
       A SPIRIT: What is here?
       A mortal! – Thou most rash and fatal wretch,
30   Bow down and worship!
       SECOND SPIRIT: I do know the man –
       A Magian of great power, and fearful skill!
       THIRD SPIRIT: Bow down and worship, slave! –
                                        What, know'st thou not
       Thine and our Sovereign? – Tremble, and obey!
       ALL THE SPIRITS: Prostrate thyself, and thy condemned
           clay,

35   Child of the Earth! or dread the worst.
MANFRED: I know it;
    And yet ye see I kneel not.
FOURTH SPIRIT: 'Twill be taught thee.
MANFRED: 'Tis taught already; – many a night on the earth,
    On the bare ground, have I bow'd down my face,
    And strew'd my head with ashes; I have known
40   The fulness of humiliation, for
    I sunk before my vain despair, and knelt
    To my own desolation.
FIFTH SPIRIT: Dost thou dare
    Refuse to Arimanes on his throne
    What the whole earth accords, beholding not
45   The terror of his Glory? – Crouch! I say.
MANFRED: Bid *him* bow down to that which is above him,
    The overruling Infinite – the Maker
    Who made him not for worship – let him kneel,
    And we will kneel together.
THE SPIRITS: Crush the worm!
50   Tear him in pieces! –
FIRST DESTINY: Hence! Avaunt! – he's mine.
    Prince of the Powers invisible! This man
    Is of no common order, as his port
    And presence here denote; his sufferings
    Have been of an immortal nature, like
55   Our own; his knowledge, and his powers and will,
    As far as is compatible with clay,
    Which clogs the ethereal essence, have been such
    As clay hath seldom borne; his aspirations
    Have been beyond the dwellers of the earth,
60   And they have only taught him what we know –
    That knowledge is not happiness, and science
    But an exchange of ignorance for that
    Which is another kind of ignorance.
    This is not all – the passions, attributes
65   Of earth and heaven, from which no power, nor being,
    Nor breath from the worm upwards is exempt,
    Have pierced his heart; and in their consequence

Made him a thing, which I, who pity not,
Yet pardon those who pity. He is mine,
70   And thine, it may be – be it so, or not,
No other Spirit in this region hath
A soul like his – or power upon his soul.
NEMESIS: What doth he here then?
FIRST DESTINY: Let him answer that.
MANFRED: Ye know what I have known; and without
    power
75   I could not be amongst ye: but there are
Powers deeper still beyond – I come in quest
Of such, to answer unto what I seek.
NEMESIS: What would'st thou?
MANFRED: Thou canst not reply to me.
Call up the dead – my question is for them.
80   NEMESIS: Great Arimanes, doth thy will avouch
The wishes of this mortal?
ARIMANES: Yea.
NEMESIS: Whom would'st thou
    Uncharnel?
MANFRED: One without a tomb – call up
    Astarte.
NEMESIS
        Shadow! or Spirit!
85   Whatever thou art,
            Which still doth inherit
                The whole or a part
                Of the form of thy birth,
                Of the mould of thy clay,
90   Which return'd to the earth,
                Re-appear to the day!
            Bear what thou borest,
                The heart and the form,
            And the aspect thou worest
95   Redeem from the worm.
        Appear! – Appear! – Appear!
Who sent thee there requires thee here!

[*The Phantom of* ASTARTE *rises and stands in the midst.*]

MANFRED: Can this be death? there's bloom upon her cheek;

But now I see it is no living hue,

100 But a strange hectic – like the unnatural red
Which Autumn plants upon the perish'd leaf.
It is the same! Oh, God! that I should dread
To look upon the same – Astarte! – No,
I cannot speak to her – but bid her speak –

105 Forgive me or condemn me.

NEMESIS

By the power which hath broken
The grace which enthrall'd thee,
Speak to him who hath spoken,
Or those who have call'd thee!

110 MANFRED: She is silent,
And in that silence I am more than answer'd.
NEMESIS: My power extends no further. Prince of air!
It rests with thee alone – command her voice.
ARIMANES: Spirit – obey this sceptre!
NEMESIS: Silent still!

115 She is not of our order, but belongs
To the other powers. Mortal! thy quest is vain,
And we are baffled also.
MANFRED: Hear me, hear me –
Astarte! my beloved! speak to me:
I have so much endured – so much endure –

120 Look on me! the grave hath not changed thee more
Than I am changed for thee. Thou lovedst me
Too much, as I loved thee: we were not made
To torture thus each other, though it were
The deadliest sin to love as we have loved.

125 Say that thou loath'st me not – that I do bear
This punishment for both – that thou wilt be
One of the blessed – and that I shall die;
For hitherto all hateful things conspire
To bind me in existence – in a life

130   Which makes me shrink from immortality –
             A future like the past. I cannot rest.
             I know not what I ask, nor what I seek:
             I feel but what thou art – and what I am;
             And I would hear yet once before I perish
135   The voice which was my music – Speak to me!
             For I have call'd on thee in the still night,
             Startled the slumbering birds from the hush'd boughs,
             And woke the mountain wolves, and made the caves
             Acquainted with thy vainly echoed name,
140   Which answer'd me – many things answer'd me –
             Spirits and men – but thou wert silent all.
             Yet speak to me! I have outwatch'd the stars,
             And gazed o'er heaven in vain in search of thee.
             Speak to me! I have wander'd o'er the earth,
145   And never found thy likeness – Speak to me!
             Look on the fiends around – they feel for me!
             I fear them not, and feel for thee alone –
             Speak to me! though it be in wrath; – but say –
             I reck not what – but let me hear thee once –
150   This once – once more!
       PHANTOM OF ASTARTE: Manfred!
       MANFRED: Say on, say on –
             I live but in the sound – it is thy voice!
       PHANTOM: Manfred! To-morrow ends thine earthly ills.
             Farewell!
       MANFRED: Yet one word more – am I forgiven?
       PHANTOM: Farewell!
       MANFRED: Say, shall we meet again?
155   PHANTOM: Farewell!
       MANFRED: One word for mercy! Say, thou lovest me.
       PHANTOM: Manfred!
             [*The Spirit of* ASTARTE *disappears.*]
       NEMESIS: She's gone, and will not be recall'd;
             Her words will be fulfill'd. Return to the earth.
       A SPIRIT: He is convulsed – This is to be a mortal
160   And seek the things beyond mortality.
       ANOTHER SPIRIT: Yet, see, he mastereth himself, and
             makes

His torture tributary to his will.
Had he been one of us, he would have made
An awful spirit.

NEMESIS: Hast thou further question
165   Of our great sovereign, or his worshippers?
MANFRED: None.
NEMESIS: Then for a time farewell.
MANFRED: We meet then –
Where? On the earth?
NEMESIS: That will be seen hereafter.
MANFRED: Even as thou wilt: and for the grace accorded
I now depart a debtor. Fare ye well!

    [*Exit* MANFRED.]

                [*Scene closes*]

Act III

SCENE I

A Hall in the Castle of Manfred.

    [MANFRED *and* HERMAN.]
MANFRED: What is the hour?
HERMAN: It wants but one till sunset,
And promises a lovely twilight.
MANFRED: Say,
Are all things so disposed of in the tower
As I directed?
HERMAN: All, my lord, are ready:
5   Here is the key and casket.
MANFRED: It is well:
Thou may'st retire.
    [*Exit* HERMAN.]
                        There is a calm upon me –
Inexplicable stillness! which till now
Did not belong to what I knew of life.
If that I did not know philosophy
10   To be of all our vanities the motliest,

The merest word that ever fool'd the ear
From out the schoolman's jargon, I should deem
The golden secret, the sought 'Kalon,' found,
And seated in my soul. It will not last,

15   But it is well to have known it, though but once:
It hath enlarged my thoughts with a new sense,
And I within my tablets would note down
That there is such a feeling. Who is there?
     [*Re-enter* HERMAN.]

HERMAN: My lord, the abbot of St Maurice craves
20   To greet your presence.
     [*Enter the* ABBOT OF ST MAURICE.]

ABBOT: Peace be with Count Manfred!

MANFRED: Thanks, holy father! welcome to these walls;
     Thy presence honours them, and blesseth those
     Who dwell within them.

ABBOT: Would it were so, Count! –
     But I would fain confer with thee alone.

25   MANFRED: Herman, retire. – What would my reverend
         guest?

ABBOT: Thus, without prelude: – Age and zeal, my office,
     And good intent, must plead my privilege;
     Our near, though not acquainted neighbourhood,
     May also be my herald. Rumours strange,
30   And of unholy nature, are abroad,
     And busy with thy name; a noble name
     For centuries: may he who bears it now
     Transmit it unimpair'd!

MANFRED: Proceed, – I listen.

ABBOT: 'Tis said thou holdest converse with the things
35   Which are forbidden to the search of man;
     That with the dwellers of the dark abodes,
     The many evil and unheavenly spirits
     Which walk the valley of the shade of death,
     Thou communest. I know that with mankind,
40   Thy fellows in creation, thou dost rarely
     Exchange thy thoughts, and that thy solitude
     Is as an anchorite's, were it but holy.

MANFRED: And what are they who do avouch these things?

ABBOT: My pious brethren – the scared peasantry –
45   Even thy own vassals – who do look on thee
        With most unquiet eyes. Thy life's in peril.
MANFRED: Take it.
ABBOT: I come to save, and not destroy –
        I would not pry into thy secret soul;
        But if these things be sooth, there still is time
50   For penitence and pity: reconcile thee
        With the true church, and through the church to
            heaven.
MANFRED: I hear thee. This is my reply: whate'er
        I may have been, or am, doth rest between
        Heaven and myself. – I shall not choose a mortal
55   To be my mediator. Have I sinn'd
        Against your ordinances? prove and punish!
ABBOT: My son! I did not speak of punishment,
        But penitence and pardon; – with thyself
        The choice of such remains – and for the last,
60   Our institutions and our strong belief
        Have given me power to smooth the path from sin –
        To higher hope and better thoughts; the first
        I leave to heaven, – 'Vengeance is mine alone!'
        So saith the Lord, and with all humbleness
65   His servant echoes back the awful word.
MANFRED: Old man! there is no power in holy men,
        Nor charm in prayer – nor purifying form
        Of penitence – nor outward look – nor fast –
        Nor agony – nor, greater than all these,
70   The innate tortures of that deep despair,
        Which is remorse without the fear of hell,
        But all in all sufficient to itself
        Would make a hell of heaven – can exorcise
        From out the unbounded spirit the quick sense
75   Of its own sins, wrongs, sufferance, and revenge
        Upon itself; there is no future pang
        Can deal that justice on the self–condemn'd
        He deals on his own soul.
ABBOT: All this is well;
        For this will pass away, and be succeeded

80   By an auspicious hope, which shall look up
        With calm assurance to that blessed place,
        Which all who seek may win, whatever be
        Their earthly errors, so they be atoned:
        And the commencement of atonement is
85   The sense of its necessity. – Say on –
        And all our church can teach thee shall be taught;
        And all we can absolve thee shall be pardon'd.
MANFRED: When Rome's sixth emperor was near his last,
        The victim of a self-inflicted wound,
90   To shun the torments of a public death
        From senates once his slaves, a certain soldier,
        With show of loyal pity, would have stanch'd
        The gushing throat with his officious robe;
        The dying Roman thrust him back, and said –
95   Some empire still in his expiring glance,
        'It is too late – is this fidelity?'
ABBOT: And what of this?
MANFRED: I answer with the Roman –
        'It is too late!'
ABBOT: It never can be so,
        To reconcile thyself with thy own soul,
100   And thy own soul with heaven. Hast thou no hope?
        'Tis strange – even those who do despair above,
        Yet shape themselves some fantasy on earth,
        To which frail twig they cling, like drowning men.
MANFRED: Ay – father! I have had those earthly visions
105   And noble aspirations in my youth,
        To make my own the mind of other men;
        The enlightener of nations; and to rise
        I knew not whither – it might be to fall;
        But fall, even as the mountain-cataract,
110   Which having leapt from its more dazzling height,
        Even in the foaming strength of its abyss,
        (Which casts up misty columns that become
        Clouds raining from the re-ascended skies,)
        Lies low but mighty still. – But this is past,
115   My thoughts mistook themselves.
ABBOT: And wherefore so?
MANFRED: I could not tame my nature down; for he

Must serve who fain would sway – and soothe – and sue –
And watch all time – and pry into all place –
And be a living lie – who would become
120 A mighty thing amongst the mean, and such
The mass are; I disdain'd to mingle with
A herd, though to be leader – and of wolves.
The lion is alone, and so am I.

ABBOT: And why not live and act with other men?

125 MANFRED: Because my nature was averse from life;
And yet not cruel; for I would not make,
But find a desolation: – like the wind,
The red-hot breath of the most lone Simoom,
Which dwells but in the desert, and sweeps o'er
130 The barren sands which bear no shrubs to blast,
And revels o'er their wild and arid waves,
And seeketh not, so that it is not sought,
But being met is deadly; such hath been
The course of my existence; but there came
135 Things in my path which are no more.

ABBOT: Alas!
I 'gin to fear that thou art past all aid
From me and from my calling; yet so young,
I still would —

MANFRED: Look on me! there is an order
Of mortals on the earth, who do become
140 Old in their youth, and die ere middle age,
Without the violence of warlike death:
Some perishing of pleasure – some of study –
Some worn with toil – some of mere weariness –
Some of disease – and some insanity –
145 And some of wither'd, or of broken hearts;
For this last is a malady which slays
More than are number'd in the lists of Fate,
Taking all shapes, and bearing many names.
Look upon me! for even of all these things
150 Have I partaken; and of all these things,
One were enough; then wonder not that I
Am what I am, but that I ever was,
Or having been, that I am still on earth.

ABBOT: Yet, hear me still —

MANFRED: Old man! I do respect
155   Thine order, and revere thine years; I deem
Thy purpose pious, but it is in vain:
Think me not churlish; I would spare thyself,
Far more than me, in shunning at this time
All further colloquy – and so – farewell.
        [*Exit* MANFRED.]
160   ABBOT: This should have been a noble creature: he
Hath all the energy which would have made
A goodly frame of glorious elements,
Had they been wisely mingled; as it is,
It is an awful chaos – light and darkness –
165   And mind and dust – and passions and pure thoughts
Mix'd, and contending without end or order,
All dormant or destructive: he will perish,
And yet he must not; I will try once more,
For such are worth redemption; and my duty
170   Is to dare all things for a righteous end.
I'll follow him – but cautiously, though surely.
        [*Exit* ABBOT.]

SCENE II

Another Chamber.

[MANFRED *and* HERMAN.]
HERMAN: My lord, you bade me wait on you at sunset:
He sinks behind the mountain.
MANFRED: Doth he so?
I will look on him.
        [MANFRED *advances to the Window of the Hall.*]
                          Glorious Orb! the idol
Of early nature, and the vigorous race
5   Of undiseased mankind, the giant sons[1]

1. 'And it came to pass, that the *Sons of God* saw the daughters of men, that
they were fair,' &c. – 'There were giants in the earth in those days; and also
after that, when the *Sons of God* came in unto the daughters of men, and
they bare children to them, the same became mighty men which were of
old, men of renown.' – *Genesis*, ch. vi. verses 2 and 4.

Of the embrace of angels, with a sex
More beautiful than they, which did draw down
The erring spirits who can ne'er return. –
Most glorious orb! that wert a worship, ere
10   The mystery of thy making was reveal'd!
Thou earliest minister of the Almighty,
Which gladden'd, on their mountain tops, the hearts
Of the Chaldean shepherds, till they pour'd
Themselves in orisons! Thou material God!
15   And representative of the Unknown –
Who chose thee for his shadow! Thou chief star!
Centre of many stars! which mak'st our earth
Endurable, and temperest the hues
And hearts of all who walk within thy rays!
20   Sire of the seasons! Monarch of the climes,
And those who dwell in them! for near or far,
Our inborn spirits have a tint of thee
Even as our outward aspects; – thou dost rise,
And shine, and set in glory. Fare thee well!
25   I ne'er shall see thee more. As my first glance
Of love and wonder was for thee, then take
My latest look: thou wilt not beam on one
To whom the gifts of life and warmth have been
Of a more fatal nature. He is gone:
30   I follow.
        [*Exit* MANFRED.]

SCENE III

*The Mountains – The Castle of Manfred at some distance – A
Terrace before a Tower. – Time, Twilight.*

[HERMAN, MANUEL, *and other Dependants of*
MANFRED.]
HERMAN: 'Tis strange enough; night after night, for years,
He hath pursued long vigils in this tower,
Without a witness. I have been within it, –
So have we all been oft-times; but from it,
5   Or its contents, it were impossible

   To draw conclusions absolute, of aught
   His studies tend to. To be sure, there is
   One chamber where none enter: I would give
   The fee of what I have to come these three years,
10 To pore upon its mysteries.
 MANUEL: 'Twere dangerous;
  Content thyself with what thou know'st already.
 HERMAN: Ah! Manuel! thou art elderly and wise,
  And couldst say much; thou hast dwelt within the
   castle –
  How many years is't?
 MANUEL: Ere Count Manfred's birth,
15 I served his father, whom he nought resembles.
 HERMAN: There be more sons in like predicament.
  But wherein do they differ?
 MANUEL: I speak not
  Of features or of form, but mind and habits;
  Count Sigismund was proud, – but gay and free, –
20 A warrior and a reveller; he dwelt not
  With books and solitude, nor made the night
  A gloomy vigil, but a festal time,
  Merrier than day; he did not walk the rocks
  And forests like a wolf, nor turn aside
25 From men and their delights.
 HERMAN: Beshrew the hour,
  But those were jocund times! I would that such
  Would visit the old walls again; they look
  As if they had forgotten them.
 MANUEL: These walls
  Must change their chieftain first. Oh! I have seen
30 Some strange things in them, Herman.
 HERMAN: Come, be friendly;
  Relate me some to while away our watch:
  I've heard thee darkly speak of an event
  Which happen'd hereabouts, by this same tower.
 MANUEL: That was a night indeed! I do remember
35 'Twas twilight, as it may be now, and such
  Another evening; – yon red cloud, which rests
  On Eigher's pinnacle, so rested then, –

So like that it might be the same; the wind
Was faint and gusty, and the mountain snows
40   Began to glitter with the climbing moon;
Count Manfred was, as now, within his tower, –
How occupied, we knew not, but with him
The sole companion of his wanderings
And watchings – her, whom of all earthly things
45   That lived, the only thing he seem'd to love, –
As he, indeed, by blood was bound to do,
The lady Astarte, his —

                       Hush! who comes here?
    [*Enter the* ABBOT.]
ABBOT: Where is your master?
HERMAN: Yonder in the tower.
ABBOT: I must speak with him.
MANUEL: 'Tis impossible;
50   He is most private, and must not be thus
Intruded on.
ABBOT: Upon myself I take
The forfeit of my fault, if fault there be –
But I must see him.
HERMAN: Thou hast seen him once
This eve already.
ABBOT: Herman! I command thee,
55   Knock, and apprize the Count of my approach.
HERMAN: We dare not.
ABBOT: Then it seems I must be herald
Of my own purpose.
MANUEL: Reverend father, stop –
I pray you pause.
ABBOT: Why so?
MANUEL: But step this way,
And I will tell you further.
    [*Exeunt.*]

SCENE IV

Interior of the Tower.

[MANFRED *alone.*]

The stars are forth, the moon above the tops
Of the snow-shining mountains. – Beautiful!
I linger yet with Nature, for the night
Hath been to me a more familiar face
Than that of man; and in her starry shade
Of dim and solitary loveliness,
I learn'd the language of another world.
I do remember me, that in my youth,
When I was wandering, – upon such a night
I stood within the Coliseum's wall,
Midst the chief relics of almighty Rome;
The trees which grew along the broken arches
Waved dark in the blue midnight, and the stars
Shone through the rents of ruin; from afar
The watchdog bay'd beyond the Tiber; and
More near from out the Cæsars' palace came
The owl's long cry, and, interruptedly,
Of distant sentinels the fitful song
Begun and died upon the gentle wind.
Some cypresses beyond the time-worn breach
Appear'd to skirt the horizon, yet they stood
Within a bowshot – Where the Cæsars dwelt,
And dwell the tuneless birds of night, amidst
A grove which springs through levell'd battlements,
And twines its roots with the imperial hearths,
Ivy usurps the laurel's place of growth; –
But the gladiators' bloody Circus stands,
A noble wreck in ruinous perfection!
While Cæsar's chambers, and the Augustan halls,
Grovel on earth in indistinct decay. –
And thou didst shine, thou rolling moon, upon
All this, and cast a wide and tender light,
Which soften'd down the hoar austerity
Of rugged desolation, and fill'd up,
As 'twere anew, the gaps of centuries;

Leaving that beautiful which still was so,
And making that which was not, till the place
Became religion, and the heart ran o'er
With silent worship of the great of old! —

40 The dead, but sceptred sovereigns, who still rule
Our spirits from their urns. —
                                        'Twas such a night!
'Tis strange that I recall it at this time;
But I have found our thoughts take wildest flight
Even at the moment when they should array

45 Themselves in pensive order.
          [*Enter the* ABBOT.]

ABBOT: My good lord!
I crave a second grace for this approach;
But yet let not my humble zeal offend
By its abruptness — all it hath of ill
Recoils on me; its good in the effect

50 May light upon your head — could I say *heart* —
Could I touch *that*, with words or prayers, I should
Recall a noble spirit which hath wander'd;
But is not yet all lost.

MANFRED: Thou know'st me not;
My days are number'd, and my deeds recorded:

55 Retire, or 'twill be dangerous — Away!

ABBOT: Thou dost not mean to menace me?

MANFRED: Not I;
I simply tell thee peril is at hand,
And would preserve thee.

ABBOT: What dost thou mean?

MANFRED: Look there!
What dost thou see?

ABBOT: Nothing.

MANFRED: Look there, I say,

60 And steadfastly; — now tell me what thou seest?

ABBOT: That which should shake me, — but I fear it not —
I see a dusk and awful figure rise,
Like an infernal god, from out the earth;
His face wrapt in a mantle, and his form

65 Robed as with angry clouds: he stands between

Thyself and me – but I do fear him not.

MANFRED: Thou hast no cause – he shall not harm thee – but

His sight may shock thine old limbs into palsy.

I say to thee – Retire!

ABBOT: And I reply –

70   Never – till I have battled with this fiend: –

What doth he here?

MANFRED: Why – ay – what doth he here? –

I did not send for him, – he is unbidden.

ABBOT: Alas! lost mortal! what with guests like these

Hast thou to do? I tremble for thy sake:

75   Why doth he gaze on thee, and thou on him?

Ah! he unveils his aspect: on his brow

The thunder-scars are graven; from his eye

Glares forth the immortality of hell –

Avaunt! —

MANFRED: Pronounce – what is thy mission?

SPIRIT: Come!

80   ABBOT: What art thou, unknown being? answer! – speak!

SPIRIT: The genius of this mortal. – Come! 'tis time.

MANFRED: I am prepared for all things, but deny

The power which summons me. Who sent thee here?

SPIRIT: Thou'lt know anon – Come! come!

MANFRED: I have commanded

85   Things of an essence greater far than thine,

And striven with thy masters. Get thee hence!

SPIRIT: Mortal! thine hour is come – Away! I say.

MANFRED: I knew, and know my hour is come, but not

To render up my soul to such as thee:

90   Away! I'll die as I have lived – alone.

SPIRIT: Then I must summon up my brethren. – Rise!

[*Other Spirits rise up.*]

ABBOT: Avaunt! ye evil ones! – Avaunt! I say, –

Ye have no power where piety hath power,

And I do charge ye in the name —

SPIRIT: Old man!

95   We know ourselves, our mission, and thine order;

Waste not thy holy words on idle uses,

It were in vain: this man is forfeited.
Once more I summon him – Away! away!
MANFRED: I do defy ye, – though I feel my soul
100   Is ebbing from me, yet I do defy ye;
Nor will I hence, while I have earthly breath
To breathe my scorn upon ye – earthly strength
To wrestle, though with spirits; what ye take
Shall be ta'en limb by limb.
SPIRIT: Reluctant mortal!
105   Is this the Magian who would so pervade
The world invisible, and make himself
Almost our equal? – Can it be that thou
Art thus in love with life? the very life
Which made thee wretched!
MANFRED: Thou false fiend, thou liest!
110   My life is in its last hour, – *that* I know,
Nor would redeem a moment of that hour;
I do not combat against death, but thee
And thy surrounding angels; my past power
Was purchased by no compact with thy crew,
115   But by superior science – penance – daring –
And length of watching – strength of mind – and skill
In knowledge of our fathers – when the earth
Saw men and spirits walking side by side,
And gave ye no supremacy: I stand
120   Upon my strength – I do defy – deny –
Spurn back, and scorn ye! –
SPIRIT: But thy many crimes
Have made thee ——
MANFRED: What are they to such as thee?
Must crimes be punish'd but by other crimes,
And greater criminals? – Back to thy hell!
125   Thou hast no power upon me, *that* I feel;
Thou never shalt possess me, *that* I know:
What I have done is done; I bear within
A torture which could nothing gain from thine:
The mind which is immortal makes itself
130   Requital for its good or evil thoughts –
Is its own origin of ill and end –

And its own place and time – its innate sense,
When stripp'd of this mortality, derives
No colour from the fleeting things without;
135 But is absorb'd in sufferance or in joy,
Born from the knowledge of its own desert.
Thou didst not tempt me, and thou couldst not tempt me;
I have not been thy dupe, nor am thy prey –
But was my own destroyer, and will be
140 My own hereafter. – Back, ye baffled fiends!
The hand of death is on me – but not yours!
          [*The Demons disappear.*]
ABBOT: Alas! how pale thou art – thy lips are white –
And thy breast heaves – and in thy gasping throat
The accents rattle – Give thy prayers to Heaven –
145 Pray – albeit but in thought, – but die not thus.
MANFRED: 'Tis over – my dull eyes can fix thee not;
But all things swim around me, and the earth
Heaves as it were beneath me. Fare thee well –
Give me thy hand.
ABBOT: Cold – cold – even to the heart –
150 But yet one prayer – Alas! how fares it with thee?
MANFRED: Old man! 'tis not so difficult to die.
          [MANFRED *expires.*]
ABBOT: He's gone – his soul hath ta'en its earthless flight –
Whither? I dread to think – but he is gone.

So, we'll go no more a roving

I

So, we'll go no more a roving
    So late into the night,
Though the heart be still as loving,
    And the moon be still as bright.

II

5   For the sword outwears its sheath,
    And the soul wears out the breast,
And the heart must pause to breathe,
    And love itself have rest.

III

Though the night was made for loving,
10   And the day returns too soon,
Yet we'll go no more a roving
    By the light of the moon.

CHILDE HAROLD'S PILGRIMAGE

Canto the Fourth

Visto ho Toscana, Lombardia, Romagna,
   Quel Monte che divide, e quel che serra
Italia, e un mare e l' altro, che la bagna.

Ariosto, Satira iii.

Venice, January 2, 1818.

TO JOHN HOBHOUSE, ESQ. A.M. F.R.S. &c. &c. &c.

MY DEAR HOBHOUSE,

    After an interval of eight years between the composition of the first and last cantos of Childe Harold, the conclusion of the poem is about to be submitted to the public. In parting with so old a friend, it is not extraordinary that I should recur to one still older and better, – to one who has beheld the birth and death of the other, and to whom I am far more indebted for the social advantages of an enlightened friendship, than – though not ungrateful – I can, or could be, to Childe Harold, for any public favour reflected through the poem on the poet, – to one, whom I have known long, and accompanied far, whom I have found wakeful over my sickness and kind in my sorrow, glad in my prosperity and firm in my adversity, true in counsel and trusty in peril, – to a friend often tried and never found wanting; – to yourself.

    In so doing, I recur from fiction to truth; and in dedicating to you in its complete, or at least concluded state, a poetical work which is the longest, the most thoughtful and comprehensive of my compositions, I wish to do honour to myself by the record of many years' intimacy with a man of learning, of talent, of steadiness, and of honour. It is not for minds like ours to give or to receive flattery; yet the praises of sincerity have ever been permitted to the voices of friendship; and it is not for you, nor even for others, but to relieve a heart which has not elsewhere, or lately, been so much accustomed to the encounter of good-will as to withstand the shock firmly, that I thus attempt to commemorate your good qualities, or rather the advantages which I have derived from their exertion. Even the recurrence of the date of this letter, the anniversary of the most unfortunate day of my past existence, but which cannot poison my future while I retain the resource of your friendship, and of my own faculties, will henceforth have a more agreeable recollection for both, inasmuch as it will remind us of this my attempt to thank you for an indefatigable regard, such as few men have experienced, and no one could experience, without thinking better of his species and of himself.

It has been our fortune to traverse together, at various periods, the countries of chivalry, history, and fable – Spain, Greece, Asia Minor, and Italy; and what Athens and Constantinople were to us a few years ago, Venice and Rome have been more recently. The poem also, or the pilgrim, or both, have accompanied me from first to last; and perhaps it may be a pardonable vanity which induces me to reflect with complacency on a composition which in some degree connects me with the spot where it was produced, and the objects it would fain describe; and however unworthy it may be deemed of those magical and memorable abodes, however short it may fall of our distant conceptions and immediate impressions, yet as a mark of respect for what is venerable, and of feeling for what is glorious, it has been to me a source of pleasure in the production, and I part with it with a kind of regret, which I hardly suspected that events could have left me for imaginary objects.

With regard to the conduct of the last canto, there will be found less of the pilgrim than in any of the preceding, and that little slightly, if at all, separated from the author speaking in his own person. The fact is, that I had become weary of drawing a line which every one seemed determined not to perceive: like the Chinese in Goldsmith's 'Citizen of the World,' whom nobody would believe to be a Chinese, it was in vain that I asserted, and imagined that I had drawn, a distinction between the author and the pilgrim; and the very anxiety to preserve this difference, and disappointment at finding it unavailing, so far crushed my efforts in the composition, that I determined to abandon it altogether – and have done so. The opinions which have been, or may be, formed on that subject, are *now* a matter of indifference; the work is to depend on itself, and not on the writer; and the author, who has no resources in his own mind beyond the reputation, transient or permanent, which is to arise from his literary efforts, deserves the fate of authors.

In the course of the following canto it was my intention, either in the text or in the notes, to have touched upon the present state of Italian literature, and perhaps of manners. But the text, within these limits I proposed, I soon found hardly sufficient for the labyrinth of external objects, and the consequent reflections; and for the whole of the notes, excepting a few of the shortest, I am indebted to yourself, and these were necessarily limited to the elucidation of the text.

It is also a delicate, and no very grateful task, to dissert upon the literature and manners of a nation so dissimilar; and requires an attention and impartiality which would induce us – though perhaps no inattentive observers, nor ignorant of the language or customs of the people amongst whom we have recently abode – to distrust, or at least defer our judgment, and more narrowly examine our information. The state of literary, as well as political party, appears to run, or to *have* run, so high, that for a stranger to steer impartially between them is next to impossible. It may be enough, then, at least for my purpose, to quote from their own beautiful language – 'Mi pare che in un paese tutto poetico, che vante la lingua la più nobile ed insieme la più dolce, tutte tutte le vie diverse si possono tentare, e che sinche la patria di Alfieri e di Monti non ha perduto l'antico valore, in tutte essa dovrebbe essere la prima.' Italy has great names still – Canova, Monti, Ugo Foscalo, Pindemonte, Visconti, Morelli, Cicognara, Albrizzi, Mezzophanti, Mai, Mustoxidi, Aglietti, and Vacca, will secure to the present generation an honourable place in most of the departments of Art, Science, and Belles Lettres; and in some the very highest – Europe – the World – has but one Canova.

It has been somewhere said by Alfieri, that 'La pianta uomo nasce più robusta in Italia che in qualunque altra terra – e che gli stessi atroci delitti che vi si commettono ne sono una prova.' Without subscribing to the latter part of his proposition, a dangerous doctrine, the truth of which may be disputed on better grounds, namely, that the Italians are in no respect more ferocious than their neighbours, that man must be wilfully blind, or ignorantly heedless, who is not struck with the extraordinary capacity of this people, or, if such a word be admissible, their *capabilities*, the facility of their acquisitions, the rapidity of their conceptions, the fire of their genius, their sense of beauty, and, amidst all the disadvantages of repeated revolutions, the desolation of battles, and the despair of ages, their still unquenched 'longing after immortality,' – the immortality of independence. And when we ourselves, in riding round the walls of Rome, heard the simple lament of the labourers' chorus, 'Roma! Roma! Roma! Roma non è più come era prima,' it was difficult not to contrast this melancholy dirge with the bacchanal roar of the songs of exultation still yelled from the London taverns, over the carnage of Mont St Jean, and the betrayal of Genoa, of Italy, of France, and of the world, by men whose conduct you yourself have exposed in a work worthy of the better days of our history. For me, –

> 'Non movero mai corda
> Ove la turba di sue ciance assorda.'

What Italy has gained by the late transfer of nations, it were useless for Englishmen to enquire, till it becomes ascertained that England has acquired something more than a permanent army and a suspended Habeas Corpus; it is enough for them to look at home. For what they have done abroad, and especially in the South, 'Verily they *will have* their reward,' and at no very distant period.

Wishing you, my dear Hobhouse, a safe and agreeable return to that country whose real welfare can be dearer to

none than to yourself, I dedicate to you this poem in its
completed state; and repeat once more how truly I am ever,
Your obliged
And affectionate friend,
BYRON.

I

I stood in Venice, on the Bridge of Sighs;
A palace and a prison on each hand:
I saw from out the wave her structures rise
As from the stroke of the enchanter's wand:
5   A thousand years their cloudy wings expand
Around me, and a dying Glory smiles
O'er the far times, when many a subject land
Look'd to the winged Lion's marble piles,
Where Venice sate in state, throned on her hundred isles!

II

10   She looks a sea Cybele, fresh from ocean,[1]
Rising with her tiara of proud towers
At airy distance, with majestic motion,
A ruler of the waters and their powers:
And such she was; – her daughters had their dowers
15   From spoils of nations, and the exhaustless East
Pour'd in her lap all gems in sparkling showers.
In purple was she robed, and of her feast
Monarchs partook, and deem'd their dignity increased.

III

In Venice Tasso's echoes are no more,
20   And silent rows the songless gondolier;
Her palaces are crumbling to the shore,
And music meets not always now the ear:

1. Sabellicus, describing the appearance of Venice, has made use of the
above image, which would not be poetical were it not true. – 'Quo fit ut qui
superne urbem contempletur, turritan telluris imaginem medio Oceano
figuratam se putet inspicere.'

Those days are gone – but Beauty still is here.
States fall, arts fade – but Nature doth not die,
25   Nor yet forget how Venice once was dear,
The pleasant place of all festivity,
The revel of the earth, the masque of Italy!

IV

But unto us she hath a spell beyond
Her name in story, and her long array
30   Of mighty shadows, whose dim forms despond
Above the dogeless city's vanish'd sway;
Ours is a trophy which will not decay
With the Rialto; Shylock and the Moor,
And Pierre, can not be swept or worn away—
35   The keystones of the arch! though all were o'er,
For us repeopled were the solitary shore.

V

The beings of the mind are not of clay;
Essentially immortal, they create
And multiply in us a brighter ray
40   And more beloved existence: that which Fate
Prohibits to dull life, in this our state
Of mortal bondage, by these spirits supplied
First exiles, then replaces what we hate;
Watering the heart whose early flowers have died,
45   And with a fresher growth replenishing the void.

VI

Such is the refuge of our youth and age,
The first from Hope, the last from Vacancy;
And this worn feeling peoples many a page,
And, may be, that which grows beneath mine eye:
50   Yet there are things whose strong reality
Outshines our fairy-land; in shape and hues
More beautiful than our fantastic sky,
And the strange constellations which the Muse
O'er her wild universe is skilful to diffuse:

VII

55   I saw or dream'd of such, – but let them go, –
        They came like truth, and disappear'd like dreams;
        And whatsoe'er they were – are now but so:
        I could replace them if I would; still teems
        My mind with many a form which aptly seems
60   Such as I sought for, and at moments found;
        Let these too go – for waking Reason deems
        Such over-weening phantasies unsound,
And other voices speak, and other sights surround.

VIII

        I've taught me other tongues – and in strange eyes
65   Have made me not a stranger; to the mind
        Which is itself, no changes bring surprise;
        Nor is it harsh to make, nor hard to find
        A country with – ay, or without mankind;
        Yet was I born where men are proud to be,
70   Not without cause; and should I leave behind
        The inviolate island of the sage and free,
And seek me out a home by a remoter sea.

IX

        Perhaps I loved it well; and should I lay
        My ashes in a soil which is not mine,
75   My spirit shall resume it – if we may
        Unbodied choose a sanctuary. I twine
        My hopes of being remember'd in my line
        With my land's language: if too fond and far
        These aspirations in their scope incline, –
80   If my fame should be, as my fortunes are,
Of hasty growth and blight, and dull Oblivion bar

X

        My name from out the temple where the dead
        Are honour'd by the nations – let it be –
        And light the laurels on a loftier head!
85   And be the Spartan's epitaph on me –

'Sparta hath many a worthier son than he.'[1]
Meantime I seek no sympathies, nor need;
The thorns which I have reap'd are of the tree
I planted, – they have torn me, – and I bleed:
90   I should have known what fruit would spring from such a
   seed.

XI

The spouseless Adriatic mourns her lord;
And, annual marriage, now no more renew'd,
The Bucentaur lies rotting unrestored,
Neglected garment of her widowhood!
95   St Mark yet sees his lion where he stood,
Stand, but in mockery of his wither'd power,
Over the proud Place where an Emperor sued,
And monarchs gazed and envied in the hour
When Venice was a queen with an unequall'd dower.

XII

100   The Suabian sued, and now the Austrian reigns –
An Emperor tramples where an Emperor knelt;
Kingdoms are shrunk to provinces, and chains
Clank over sceptred cities; nations melt
From power's high pinnacle, when they have felt
105   The sunshine for a while, and downward go
Like lauwine loosen'd from the mountain's belt;
Oh for one hour of blind old Dandolo!
Th' octogenarian chief, Byzantium's conquering foe.

XIII

Before St Mark still glow his steeds of brass,
110   Their gilded collars glittering in the sun;
But is not Doria's menace come to pass?
Are they not *bridled?* – Venice, lost and won,

1. The answer of the mother of Brasidas, the Lacedæmonian general, to
the strangers who praised the memory of her son.

Her thirteen hundred years of freedom done,
Sinks, like a sea-weed, into whence she rose!
115   Better be whelm'd beneath the waves, and shun,
Even in destruction's depth, her foreign foes,
From whom submission wrings an infamous repose.

XIV

In youth she was all glory, – a new Tyre, –
Her very by-word sprung from victory,
120   The 'Planter of the Lion,'[1] which through fire
And blood she bore o'er subject earth and sea;
Though making many slaves, herself still free,
And Europe's bulwark 'gainst the Ottomite;
Witness Troy's rival, Candia! Vouch it, ye
125   Immortal waves that saw Lepanto's fight!
For ye are names no time nor tyranny can blight.

XV

Statues of glass – all shiver'd – the long file
Of her dead Doges are declined to dust;
But where they dwelt, the vast and sumptuous pile
130   Bespeaks the pageant of their splendid trust;
Their sceptre broken, and their sword in rust,
Have yielded to the stranger: empty halls,
Thin streets, and foreign aspects, such as must
Too oft remind her who and what enthrals,
135 Have flung a desolate cloud o'er Venice' lovely walls.

XVI

When Athens' armies fell at Syracuse,
And fetter'd thousands bore the yoke of war
Redemption rose up in the Attic Muse,[2]
Her voice their only ransom from afar:
140   See! as they chant the tragic hymn, the car
Of the o'ermaster'd victor stops, the reins
Fall from his hands – his idle scimitar

1. That is, the Lion of St Mark, the standard of the republic, which is the origin of the word Pantaloon – Piantaleone, Pantaleon, Pantaloon.
2. The story is told in Plutarch's Life of Nicias.

Starts from its belt – he rends his captive's chains,
And bids him thank the bard for freedom and his strains.

XVII

145   Thus, Venice, if no stronger claim were thine,
Were all thy proud historic deeds forgot,
Thy choral memory of the Bard divine,
Thy love of Tasso, should have cut the knot
Which ties thee to thy tyrants; and thy lot
150   Is shameful to the nations, – most of all,
Albion! to thee: the Ocean queen should not
Abandon Ocean's children; in the fall
Of Venice think of thine, despite thy watery wall.

XVIII

I loved her from my boyhood – she to me
155   Was as a fairy city of the heart,
Rising like water-columns from the sea,
Of joy the sojourn, and of wealth the mart;
And Otway, Radcliffe, Schiller, Shakspeare's art,[1]
Had stamp'd her image in me, and even so,
160   Although I found her thus, we did not part,
Perchance even dearer in her day of woe,
Than when she was a boast, a marvel, and a show.

XIX

I can repeople with the past – and of
The present there is still for eye and thought,
165   And meditation chasten'd down, enough;
And more, it may be, than I hoped or sought;
And of the happiest moments which were wrought
Within the web of my existence, some
From thee, fair Venice! have their colours caught:
170   There are some feelings Time cannot benumb,
Nor Torture shake, or mine would now be cold and dumb.

---

1. Venice Preserved; Mysteries of Udolpho; the Ghost-Seer, or Armenian;
the Merchant of Venice; Othello.

XX

But from their nature will the tannen grow[1]
Loftiest on loftiest and least shelter'd rocks,
Rooted in barrenness, where nought below
175   Of soil supports them 'gainst the Alpine shocks
Of eddying storms; yet springs the trunk, and mocks
The howling tempest, till its height and frame
Are worthy of the mountains from whose blocks
Of bleak, gray granite into life it came,
180   And grew a giant tree; – the mind may grow the same.

XXI

Existence may be borne, and the deep root
Of life and sufferance make its firm abode
In bare and desolated bosoms: mute
The camel labours with the heaviest load,
185   And the wolf dies in silence, – not bestow'd
In vain should such example be; if they,
Things of ignoble or of savage mood,
Endure and shrink not, we of nobler clay
May temper it to bear, – it is but for a day.

XXII

190   All suffering doth destroy, or is destroy'd,
Even by the sufferer; and, in each event,
Ends: – Some, with hope replenish'd and rebuoy'd,
Return to whence they came – with like intent,
And weave their web again; some, bow'd and bent,
195   Wax gray and ghastly, withering ere their time,
And perish with the reed on which they leant;
Some seek devotion, toil, war, good or crime,
According as their souls were form'd to sink or climb:

1. *Tannen* is the plural of *tanne*, a species of fir peculiar to the Alps, which only thrives in very rocky parts, where scarcely soil sufficient for its nourishment can be found. On these spots it grows to a greater height than any other mountain tree.

XXIII

But ever and anon of griefs subdued
200   There comes a token like a scorpion's sting,
Scarce seen, but with fresh bitterness imbued;
And slight withal may be the things which bring
Back on the heart the weight which it would fling
Aside for ever: it may be a sound –
205   A tone of music – summer's eve – or spring –
A flower – the wind – the ocean – which shall wound,
Striking the electric chain wherewith we are darkly bound;

XXIV

And how and why we know not, nor can trace
Home to its cloud this lightning of the mind,
210   But feel the shock renew'd, nor can efface
The blight and blackening which it leaves behind,
Which out of things familiar, undesign'd,
When least we deem of such, calls up to view
The spectres whom no exorcism can bind,
215   The cold – the changed – perchance the dead – anew,
The mourn'd, the loved, the lost – too many! – yet how
      few!

XXV

But my soul wanders; I demand it back
To meditate amongst decay, and stand
A ruin amidst ruins; there to track
220   Fall'n states and buried greatness, o'er a land
Which *was* the mightiest in its old command,
And *is* the loveliest, and must ever be
The master-mould of Nature's heavenly hand,
Wherein were cast the heroic and the free,
225   The beautiful, the brave – the lords of earth and sea,

XXVI

The commonwealth of kings, the men of Rome!
And even since, and now, fair Italy!
Thou art the garden of the world, the home
Of all Art yields, and Nature can decree;
230   Even in thy desert, what is like to thee?

Thy very weeds are beautiful, thy waste
More rich than other climes' fertility;
Thy wreck a glory, and thy ruin graced
With an immaculate charm which cannot be defaced.

XXVII

235   The moon is up, and yet it is not night –
Sunset divides the sky with her – a sea
Of glory streams along the Alpine height
Of blue Friuli's mountains; Heaven is free
From clouds, but of all colours seems to be
240   Melted to one vast Iris of the West,
Where the Day joins the past Eternity;
While, on the other hand, meek Dian's crest
Floats through the azure air – an island of the blest![1]

XXVIII

A single star is at her side, and reigns
245   With her o'er half the lovely heaven; but still
Yon sunny sea heaves brightly, and remains
Roll'd o'er the peak of the far Rhaetian hill,
As Day and Night contending were, until
Nature reclaim'd her order: – gently flows
250   The deep-dyed Brenta, where their hues instil
The odorous purple of a new-born rose,
Which streams upon her stream, and glass'd within it
        glows,

XXIX

Fill'd with the face of heaven, which, from afar,
Comes down upon the waters; all its hues,
255   From the rich sunset to the rising star,
Their magical variety diffuse:

---

1. The above description may seem fantastical or exaggerated to those who
have never seen an Oriental or an Italian sky, yet it is but a literal and hardly
sufficient delineation of an August evening (the eighteenth), as contemplated
in one of many rides along the banks of the Brenta, near La Mira.

And now they change; a paler shadow strews
Its mantle o'er the mountains; parting day
Dies like the dolphin, whom each pang imbues
260   With a new colour as it gasps away,
The last still loveliest, till – 'tis gone – and all is gray.

XXX

There is a tomb in Arqua; – rear'd in air,
Pillar'd in their sarcophagus, repose
The bones of Laura's lover: here repair
265   Many familiar with his well-sung woes,
The pilgrims of his genius. He arose
To raise a language, and his land reclaim
From the dull yoke of her barbaric foes:
Watering the tree which bears his lady's name
270 With his melodious tears, he gave himself to fame.

XXXI

They keep his dust in Arqua, where he died;
The mountain-village where his latter days
Went down the vale of years; and 'tis their pride –
An honest pride – and let it be their praise,
275   To offer to the passing stranger's gaze
His mansion and his sepulchre; both plain
And venerably simple, such as raise
A feeling more accordant with his strain
Than if a pyramid form'd his monumental fane.

XXXII

280   And the soft quiet hamlet where he dwelt
Is one of that complexion which seems made
For those who their mortality have felt,
And sought a refuge from their hopes decay'd
In the deep umbrage of a green hill's shade,
285   Which shows a distant prospect far away
Of busy cities, now in vain display'd,
For they can lure no further; and the ray
Of a bright sun can make sufficient holiday.

XXXIII

Developing the mountains, leaves, and flowers,
290 And shining in the brawling brook, where-by,
Clear as its current, glide the sauntering hours
With a calm languor, which, though to the eye
Idlesse it seem, hath its morality.
If from society we learn to live,
295 'Tis solitude should teach us how to die;
It hath no flatterers; vanity can give
No hollow aid; alone – man with his God must strive:

XXXIV

Or, it may be, with demons, who impair[1]
The strength of better thoughts, and seek their prey
300 In melancholy bosoms, such as were
Of moody texture from their earliest day,
And loved to dwell in darkness and dismay,
Deeming themselves predestined to a doom
Which is not of the pangs that pass away;
305 Making the sun like blood, the earth a tomb,
The tomb a hell, and hell itself a murkier gloom.

XXXV

Ferrara! in thy wide and grass-grown streets,
Whose symmetry was not for solitude,
There seems as 'twere a curse upon the seats
310 Of former sovereigns, and the antique brood
Of Este, which for many an age made good
Its strength within thy walls, and was of yore
Patron or tyrant, as the changing mood
Of petty power impell'd, of those who wore
315 The wreath which Dante's brow alone had worn before.

1. The struggle is to the full as likely to be with demons as with our better thoughts. Satan chose the wilderness for the temptation of our Saviour. And our own unsullied John Locke preferred the presence of a child to complete solitude.

XXXVI

And Tasso is their glory and their shame.
Hark to his strain! and then survey his cell!
And see how dearly earn'd Torquato's fame,
And where Alfonso bade his poet dwell:
320   The miserable despot could not quell
The insulted mind he sought to quench, and blend
With the surrounding maniacs, in the hell
Where he had plunged it. Glory without end
Scatter'd the clouds away – and on that name attend

XXXVII

325   The tears and praises of all time; while thine
Would rot in its oblivion – in the sink
Of worthless dust, which from thy boasted line
Is shaken into nothing; but the link
Thou formest in his fortunes bids us think
330   Of thy poor malice, naming thee with scorn –
Alfonso! how thy ducal pageants shrink
From thee! if in another station born,
Scarce fit to be the slave of him thou madest to mourn:

XXXVIII

Thou! form'd to eat, and be despised, and die,
335   Even as the beasts that perish, save that thou
Hadst a more splendid trough and wider sty:
He! with a glory round his furrow'd brow,
Which emanated then, and dazzles now,
In face of all his foes, the Cruscan quire,
340   And Boileau, whose rash envy could allow
No strain which shamed his country's creaking lyre,
That whetstone of the teeth – monotony in wire!

XXXIX

Peace to Torquato's injured shade! 'twas his
In life and death to be the mark where Wrong
345   Aim'd with her poison'd arrows, but to miss.
Oh, victor unsurpass'd in modern song!

Each year brings forth its millions; but how long
The tide of generations shall roll on,
And not the whole combined and countless throng
350   Compose a mind like thine? though all in one
Condensed their scatter'd rays, they would not form a sun.

XL

Great as thou art, yet parallel'd by those,
Thy countrymen, before thee born to shine,
The Bards of Hell and Chivalry: first rose
355   The Tuscan father's comedy divine;
Then, not unequal to the Florentine,
The southern Scott, the minstrel who call'd forth
A new creation with his magic line,
And, like the Ariosto of the North,
360   Sang ladye-love and war, romance and knightly worth.

XLI

The lightning rent from Ariosto's bust
The iron crown of laurel's mimic'd leaves;
Nor was the ominous element unjust,
For the true laurel-wreath which Glory weaves
365   Is of the tree no bolt of thunder cleaves,
And the false semblance but disgraced his brow;
Yet still, if fondly Superstition grieves,
Know, that the lightning sanctifies below
Whate'er it strikes; – yon head is doubly sacred now.

XLII

370   Italia! oh Italia! thou who hast
The fatal gift of beauty, which became
A funeral dower of present woes and past,
On thy sweet brow is sorrow plough'd by shame,
And annals graved in characters of flame.
375   Oh, God! that thou wert in thy nakedness
Less lovely or more powerful, and couldst claim
Thy right, and awe the robbers back, who press
To shed thy blood, and drink the tears of thy distress;

XLIII

Then might'st thou more appal; or, less desired,
Be homely and be peaceful, undeplored
For thy destructive charms; then, still untired,
Would not be seen the armed torrents pour'd
Down the deep Alps; nor would the hostile horde
Of many-nation'd spoilers from the Po
Quaff blood and water; nor the stranger's sword
Be thy sad weapon of defence, and so,
Victor or vanquish'd, thou the slave of friend or foe.[1]

XLIV

Wandering in youth, I traced the path of him,[2]
The Roman friend of Rome's least-mortal mind,
The friend of Tully: as my bark did skim
The bright blue waters with a fanning wind,
Came Megara before me, and behind
Ægina lay, Piræus on the right,
And Corinth on the left; I lay reclined
Along the prow, and saw all these unite
In ruin, even as he had seen the desolate sight;

1. The two stanzas XLII and XLIII are, with the exception of a line or two, a translation of the famous sonnet of Filicaja: – 'Italia, Italia, O tu cui feo la sorte!'

2. The celebrated letter of Servius Sulpicius to Cicero, on the death of his daughter, describes as it then was, and now is, a path which I often traced in Greece, both by sea and land, in different journeys and voyages. 'On my return from Asia, as I was sailing from Ægina towards Megara, I began to contemplate the prospect of the countries around me: Ægina was behind, Megara before me; Piræus on the right, Corinth on the left: all which towns, once famous and flourishing, now lie overturned and buried in their ruins. Upon this sight, I could not but think presently within myself, Alas! how do we poor mortals fret and vex ourselves if any of our friends happen to die or be killed, whose life is yet so short, when the carcasses of so many noble cities lie here exposed before me in one view.' – See Middleton's Cicero, vol. ii, p. 371.

XLV

For Time hath not rebuilt them, but uprear'd
Barbaric dwellings on their shatter'd site,
Which only make more mourn'd and more endear'd
400   The few last rays of their far-scatter'd light,
And the crush'd relics of their vanish'd might.
The Roman saw these tombs in his own age,
These sepulchres of cities, which excite
Sad wonder, and his yet surviving page
405   The moral lesson bears, drawn from such pilgrimage.

XLVI

That page is now before me, and on mine
His country's ruin added to the mass
Of perish'd states he mourn'd in their decline,
And I in desolation: all that *was*
410   Of then destruction *is*; and now, alas!
Rome – Rome imperial, bows her to the storm,
In the same dust and blackness, and we pass
The skeleton of her Titanic form,[1]
Wrecks of another world, whose ashes still are warm.

XLVII

415   Yet, Italy! through every other land
Thy wrongs should ring, and shall, from side to side;
Mother of Arts! as once of arms; thy hand
Was then our guardian, and is still our guide;
Parent of our Religion! whom the wide
420   Nations have knelt to for the keys of heaven!
Europe, repentant of her parricide,
Shall yet redeem thee, and, all backward driven,
Roll the barbarian tide, and sue to be forgiven.

1. It is Poggio, who, looking from the Capitoline hill upon ruined Rome,
breaks forth into the exclamation, 'Ut hunc omni: nudata, prostrata jacet,
instar gigantei cadaveris corrupti atque undique exesi.'

XLVIII

But Arno wins us to the fair white walls,
425   Where the Etrurian Athens claims and keeps
A softer feeling for her fairy halls.
Girt by her theatre of hills, she reaps
Her corn, and wine and oil, and Plenty leaps
To laughing life, with her redundant horn.
430   Along the banks where smiling Arno sweeps
Was modern Luxury of Commerce born,
And buried Learning rose, redeem'd to a new morn.

XLIX

There, too, the Goddess loves in stone, and fills
The air around with beauty; we inhale
435   The ambrosial aspect, which, beheld, instils
Part of its immortality; the veil
Of heaven is half undrawn; within the pale
We stand, and in that form and face behold
What mind can make, when Nature's self would fail;
440   And to the fond idolaters of old
Envy the innate flash which such a soul could mould:

L

We gaze and turn away, and know not where,
Dazzled and drunk with beauty, till the heart
Reels with its fulness; there – for ever there –
445   Chain'd to the chariot of triumphal Art,
We stand as captives, and would not depart.
Away! – there need no words, nor terms precise,
The paltry jargon of the marble mart,
Where Pedantry gulls Folly – we have eyes:
450   Blood – pulse – and breast, confirm the Dardan Shepherd's
        prize.

LI

Appear'dst thou not to Paris in this guise?
Or to more deeply blest Anchises? or,
In all thy perfect goddess-ship, when lies
Before thee thy own vanquish'd Lord of War?

455   And gazing in thy face as toward a star,
           Laid on thy lap, his eyes to thee upturn,
           Feeding on thy sweet cheek![1] while thy lips are
           With lava kisses melting while they burn,
     Shower'd on his eyelids, brow, and mouth, as from an urn!

LII

460   Glowing, and circumfused in speechless love,
           Their full divinity inadequate
           That feeling to express, or to improve,
           The gods become as mortals, and man's fate
           Has moments like their brightest; but the weight
465   Of earth recoils upon us; – let it go!
           We can recal such visions, and create,
           From what has been, or might be, things which grow
     Into thy statue's form, and look like gods below.

LIII

       I leave to learned fingers, and wise hands,
470   The artist and his ape, to teach and tell
           How well his connoisseurship understands
           The graceful bend, and the voluptuous swell:
           Let these describe the undescribable:
           I would not their vile breath should crisp the stream
475   Wherein that image shall for ever dwell;
           The unruffled mirror of the loveliest dream
     That ever left the sky on the deep soul to beam.

LIV

       In Santa Croce's holy precincts lie[2]
           Ashes which make it holier, dust which is
480   Even in itself an immortality,
           Though there were nothing save the past, and this,

---

1.   ' Ὀφθαλμοὺς ἑστιᾶν.
          'Atque oculos pascat uterque suos.' – OVID. *Amor.* lib. ii.
2. This name will recall the memory, not only of those whose tombs have raised the Santa Croce into the centre of pilgrimage, the Mecca of Italy, but of her whose eloquence was poured over the illustrious ashes, and whose voice is now as mute as those she sung. CORINNA is no more, and with her

The particle of those sublimities
Which have relapsed to chaos: – here repose
Angelo's, Alfieri's bones, and his,
485   The starry Galileo, with his woes;
Here Machiavelli's earth return'd to whence it rose.

---

should expire the fear, the flattery, and the envy, which threw too dazzling
or too dark a cloud round the march of genius, and forbad the steady gaze of
disinterested criticism. We have her picture embellished or distorted, as
friendship or detraction has held the pencil: the impartial portrait was
hardly to be expected from a contemporary. The immediate voice of her
survivors will, it is probable, be far from affording a just estimate of her
singular capacity. The gallantry, the love of wonder, and the hope of associ-
ated fame, which blunted the edge of censure, must cease to exist. – The
dead have no sex; they can surprise by no new miracles; they can confer no
privilege: Corinna has ceased to be a woman – she is only an author: and it
may be foreseen that many will repay themselves for former complaisance,
by a severity to which the extravagance of previous praises may perhaps
give the colour of truth. The latest posterity, for to the latest posterity they
will surely descend, will have to pronounce upon her various productions;
and the longer the vista through which they are seen, the more accurately
minute will be the object, the more certain the justice, of the decision. She
will enter into that existence in which the great writers of all ages and
nations are, as it were, associated in a world of their own, and, from that
superior sphere, shed their eternal influence for the control and consolation
of mankind. But the individual will gradually disappear as the author is
more distinctly seen: some one, therefore, of all those whom the charms of
involuntary wit, and of easy hospitality, attracted within the friendly circles
of Coppet, should rescue from oblivion those virtues which, although they
are said to love the shade, are, in fact, more frequently chilled than excited
by the domestic cares of private life. Some one should be found to portray
the unaffected graces with which she adorned those dearer relationships, the
performance of whose duties is rather discovered amongst the interior se-
crets, than seen in the outward management, of family intercourse; and
which, indeed, it requires the delicacy of genuine affection to qualify for the
eye of an indifferent spectator. Some one should be found, not to celebrate,
but to describe, the amiable mistress of an open mansion, the centre of a
society, ever varied, and always pleased, the creator of which, divested of
the ambition and the arts of public rivalry, shone forth only to give fresh
animation to those around her. The mother tenderly affectionate and ten-
derly beloved, the friend unboundedly generous, but still esteemed, the
charitable patroness of all distress, cannot be forgotten by those whom she
cherished and protected, and fed. Her loss will be mourned the most where
she was known the best; and, to the sorrows of very many friends, and more
dependants, may be offered the disinterested regret of a stranger, who,
amidst the sublimer scenes of the Leman lake, received his chief satisfaction
from contemplating the engaging qualities of the incomparable Corinna.

LV

These are four minds, which, like the elements,
Might furnish forth creation: – Italy!
Time, which hath wrong'd thee with ten thousand rents
490   Of thine imperial garment, shall deny,
And hath denied, to every other sky,
Spirits which soar from ruin: – thy decay
Is still impregnate with divinity,
Which gilds it with revivifying ray;
495 Such as the great of yore, Canova is to-day.

LVI

But where repose the all Etruscan three –
Dante, and Petrarch, and, scarce less than they,
The Bard of Prose, creative spirit! he
Of the Hundred Tales of love – where did they lay
500   Their bones, distinguish'd from our common clay
In death as life? Are they resolved to dust,
And have their country's marbles nought to say?
Could not her quarries furnish forth one bust?
Did they not to her breast their filial earth intrust?

LVII

505 Ungrateful Florence! Dante sleeps afar,
Like Scipio, buried by the upbraiding shore;
Thy factions, in their worse than civil war,
Proscribed the bard whose name for evermore
Their children's children would in vain adore
510   With the remorse of ages; and the crown
Which Petrarch's laureate brow supremely wore,
Upon a far and foreign soil had grown,
His life, his fame, his grave, though rifled – not thine own.

LVIII

Boccaccio to his parent earth bequeath'd
515 His dust, – and lies it not her Great among,
With many a sweet and solemn requiem breathed
O'er him who form'd the Tuscan's siren tongue?

That music in itself, whose sounds are song,
The poetry of speech? No; – even his tomb
520   Uptorn, must bear the hyæna bigot's wrong,
No more amidst the meaner dead find room,
Nor claim a passing sigh, because it told for *whom!*

LIX

And Santa Croce wants their mighty dust;
Yet for this want more noted, as of yore
525   The Cæsar's pageant, shorn of Brutus' bust,
Did but of Rome's best Son remind her more:
Happier Ravenna! on thy hoary shore,
Fortress of falling empire! honour'd sleeps
The immortal exile; – Arqua, too, her store
530   Of tuneful relics proudly claims and keeps,
While Florence vainly begs her banish'd dead and weeps.

LX

What is her pyramid of precious stones?
Of porphyry, jasper, agate, and all hues
Of gem and marble, to encrust the bones
535   Of merchant-dukes? the momentary dews
Which, sparkling to the twilight stars, infuse
Freshness in the green turf that wraps the dead,
Whose names are mausoleums of the Muse,
Are gently prest with far more reverent tread
540   Than ever paced the slab which paves the princely head.

LXI

There be more things to greet the heart and eyes
In Arno's dome of Art's most princely shrine,
Where Sculpture with her rainbow sister vies;
There be more marvels yet – but not for mine;
545   For I have been accustom'd to entwine
My thoughts with Nature rather in the fields,
Than Art in galleries: though a work divine
Calls for my spirit's homage, yet it yields
Less than it feels, because the weapon which it wields

LXII

550   Is of another temper, and I roam
       By Thrasimene's lake, in the defiles
       Fatal to Roman rashness, more at home;
       For there the Carthaginian's warlike wiles
       Come back before me, as his skill beguiles
555   The host between the mountains and the shore,
       Where Courage falls in her despairing files,
       And torrents, swoll'n to rivers with their gore,
Reek through the sultry plain, with legions scatter'd o'er,

LXIII

       Like to a forest fell'd by mountain winds;
560   And such the storm of battle on this day,
       And such the frenzy, whose convulsion blinds
       To all save carnage, that, beneath the fray,
       An earthquake reel'd unheededly away!
       None felt stern Nature rocking at his feet,
565   And yawning forth a grave for those who lay
       Upon their bucklers for a winding sheet;
Such is the absorbing hate when warring nations meet!

LXIV

       The Earth to them was as a rolling bark
       Which bore them to Eternity; they saw
570   The Ocean round, but had no time to mark
       The motions of their vessel; Nature's law,
       In them suspended, reck'd not of the awe
       Which reigns when mountains tremble, and the birds
       Plunge in the clouds for refuge and withdraw
575   From their down-toppling nests; and bellowing herds
Stumble o'er heaving plains, and man's dread hath no words.

LXV

       Far other scene is Thrasimene now;
       Her lake a sheet of silver, and her plain
       Rent by no ravage save the gentle plough;
580   Her aged trees rise thick as once the slain

Lay where their roots are; but a brook hath ta'en –
A little rill of scanty stream and bed –
A name of blood from that day's sanguine rain;
And Sanguinetto tells ye where the dead
585   Made the earth wet, and turn'd the unwilling waters red.

LXVI

But thou, Clitumnus! in thy sweetest wave
Of the most living crystal that was e'er
The haunt of river nymph, to gaze and lave
Her limbs where nothing hid them, thou dost rear
590   Thy grassy banks whereon the milk-white steer
Grazes; the purest god of gentle waters!
And most serene of aspect, and most clear;
Surely that stream was unprofaned by slaughters –
A mirror and a bath for Beauty's youngest daughters!

LXVII

595   And on thy happy shore a Temple still,
Of small and delicate proportion, keeps,
Upon a mild declivity of hill,
Its memory of thee; beneath it sweeps
Thy current's calmness; oft from out it leaps
600   The finny darter with the glittering scales,
Who dwells and revels in thy glassy deeps;
While, chance, some scatter'd water-lily sails
Down where the shallower wave still tells its bubbling tales.

LXVIII

Pass not unblest the Genius of the place!
605   If through the air a zephyr more serene
Win to the brow, 'tis his; and if ye trace
Along his margin a more eloquent green,
If on the heart the freshness of the scene
Sprinkle its coolness, and from the dry dust
610   Of weary life a moment lave it clean
With Nature's baptism, – 'tis to him ye must
Pay orisons for this suspension of disgust.

LXIX

The roar of waters! – from the headlong height
Velino cleaves the wave-worn precipice;
615   The fall of waters! rapid as the light
The flashing mass foams shaking the abyss;
The hell of waters! where they howl and hiss,
And boil in endless torture; while the sweat
Of their great agony, wrung out from this
620   Their Phlegethon, curls round the rocks of jet
That gird the gulf around, in pitiless horror set,

LXX

And mounts in spray the skies, and thence again
Returns in an unceasing shower, which round,
With its unemptied cloud of gentle rain,
625   Is an eternal April to the ground,
Making it all one emerald: – how profound
The gulf! and how the giant element
From rock to rock leaps with delirious bound,
Crushing the cliffs, which, downward worn and rent
630   With his fierce footsteps, yield in chasms a fearful vent!

LXXI

To the broad column which rolls on, and shows
More like the fountain of an infant sea
Torn from the womb of mountains by the throes
Of a new world, than only thus to be
635   Parent of rivers, which flow gushingly,
With many windings, through the vale: – Look back!
Lo! where it comes like an eternity,
As if to sweep down all things in its track,
Charming the eye with dread, – a matchless cataract,[1]

1. I saw the 'Cascata del marmore' of Terni twice, at different periods;
once from the summit of the precipice, and again from the valley below.
The lower view is far to be preferred, if the traveller has time for one only;
but in any point of view, either from above or below, it is worth all the
cascades and torrents of Switzerland put together: the Staubach, Reichen-
bach, Pisse Vache, fall of Arpenaz, &c. are rills in comparative appearance.
Of the fall of Schaffhaussen I cannot speak, not yet having seen it.

LXXII

640   Horribly beautiful! but on the verge,
      From side to side, beneath the glittering morn,
      An Iris sits, amidst the infernal surge,[1]
      Like Hope upon a death-bed, and, unworn
      Its steady dyes, while all around is torn
645   By the distracted waters, bears serene
      Its brilliant hues with all their beams unshorn:
      Resembling, 'mid the torture of the scene,
Love watching Madness with unalterable mien.

LXXIII

      Once more upon the woody Apennine,
650   The infant Alps, which – had I not before
      Gazed on their mightier parents, where the pine
      Sits on more shaggy summits, and where roar
      The thundering lauwine[2] – might be worshipp'd more;
      But I have seen the soaring Jungfrau rear
655   Her never-trodden snow, and seen the hoar
      Glaciers of bleak Mont Blanc both far and near,
And in Chimari heard the thunder-hills of fear,

LXXIV

      Th' Acroceraunian mountains of old name;
      And on Parnassus seen the eagles fly
660   Like spirits of the spot, as 'twere for fame,
      For still they soar'd unutterably high:

1. Of the time, place, and qualities of this kind of iris, the reader will see a short account in a note to *Manfred*. The fall looks so much like 'the hell of waters,' that Addison thought the descent alluded to by the gulf in which Alecto plunged into the infernal regions. It is singular enough, that two of the finest cascades in Europe should be artificial – this of the Velino, and the one at Tivoli. The traveller is strongly recommended to trace the Velino, at least as high as the little lake, called *Pie' di Lup*. The Reatine territory was the Italian Tempe (Cicer. Epist. ad Attic. xv. lib. iv.), and the ancient naturalist (Plin. Hist. Nat. lib. ii. cap. lxii), amongst other beautiful varieties, remarked the daily rainbows of the lake Velinus. A scholar of great name has devoted a treatise to this district alone. Ald. Manut de Reatina Urbe Agroque, ap. Sallengre, Thesaur. tom. i. p. 773.

2. In the greater part of Switzerland, the avalanches are known by the name of lauwine.

     I've look'd on Ida with a Trojan's eye;
     Athos, Olympus, Ætna, Atlas, made
     These hills seem things of lesser dignity,
665   All, save the lone Soracte's heights display'd
Not *now* in snow, which asks the lyric Roman's aid

LXXV

     For our remembrance, and from out the plain
     Heaves like a long-swept wave about to break,
     And on the curl hangs pausing: not in vain
670   May he, who will, his recollections rake
     And quote in classic raptures, and awake
     The hills with Latian echoes; I abhorr'd
     Too much, to conquer for the poet's sake,
     The drill'd dull lesson, forced down word by word[1]
675 In my repugnant youth, with pleasure to record

1. These stanzas may probably remind the reader of Ensign Northerton's remarks, 'D – n Homo,' &c.; but the reasons for our dislike are not exactly the same. I wish to express, that we become tired of the task before we can comprehend the beauty; that we learn by rote before we can get by heart; that the freshness is worn away, and the future pleasure and advantage deadened and destroyed, by the didactic anticipation, at an age when we can neither feel nor understand the power of compositions which it requires an acquaintance with life, as well as Latin and Greek, to relish, or to reason upon. For the same reason, we never can be aware of the fulness of some of the finest passages of Shakespeare ('To be, or not to be,' for instance), from the habit of having them hammered into us at eight years old, as an exercise, not of mind, but of memory: so that when we are old enough to enjoy them, the taste is gone, and the appetite palled. In some parts of the continent, young persons are taught from more common authors, and do not read the best classics till their maturity. I certainly do not speak on this point from any pique or aversion towards the place of my education. I was not a slow, though an idle boy; and I believe no one could, or can be, more attached to Harrow than I have always been, and with reason; – a part of the time passed there was the happiest of my life; and my preceptor, the Rev. Dr Joseph Drury, was the best and worthiest friend I ever possessed, whose warnings I have remembered but too well, though too late, when I have erred, – and whose counsels I have but followed when I have done well or wisely. If ever this imperfect record of my feelings towards him should reach his eyes, let it remind him of one who never thinks of him but with gratitude and veneration – of one who would more gladly boast of having been his pupil, if, by more closely following his injunctions, he could reflect any honour upon his instructor.

LXXVI
Aught that recals the daily drug which turn'd
My sickening memory; and, though Time hath taught
My mind to meditate what then it learn'd,
Yet such the fix'd inveteracy wrought
680   By the impatience of my early thought,
That, with the freshness wearing out before
My mind could relish what it might have sought,
If free to choose, I cannot now restore
Its health; but what it then detested, still abhor.

LXXVII
685   Then farewell, Horace; whom I hated so,
Not for thy faults, but mine; it is a curse
To understand, not feel thy lyric flow,
To comprehend, but never love thy verse,
Although no deeper Moralist rehearse
690   Our little life, nor Bard prescribe his art,
Nor livelier Satirist the conscience pierce,
Awakening without wounding the touch'd heart,
Yet fare thee well – upon Soracte's ridge we part.

LXXVIII
Oh Rome! my country! city of the soul!
695   The orphans of the heart must turn to thee,
Lone mother of dead empires! and control
In their shut breasts their petty misery.
What are our woes and sufferance? Come and see
The cypress, hear the owl, and plod your way
700   O'er steps of broken thrones and temples, Ye!
Whose agonies are evils of a day –
A world is at our feet as fragile as our clay.

LXXIX
The Niobe of nations! there she stands,
Childless and crownless, in her voiceless woe;
705   An empty urn within her wither'd hands,
Whose holy dust was scatter'd long ago;

The Scipios' tomb contains no ashes now;
The very sepulchres lie tenantless
Of their heroic dwellers: dost thou flow,
710   Old Tiber! through a marble wilderness?
Rise, with thy yellow waves, and mantle her distress.

LXXX

The Goth, the Christian, Time, War, Flood, and Fire,
Have dealt upon the seven-hill'd city's pride;
She saw her glories star by star expire,
715   And up the steep barbarian monarchs ride,
Where the car climb'd the capitol; far and wide
Temple and tower went down, nor left a site: —
Chaos of ruins! who shall trace the void,
O'er the dim fragments cast a lunar light,
720   And say, 'here was, or is,' where all is doubly night?

LXXXI

The double night of ages, and of her,
Night's daughter, Ignorance, hath wrapt and wrap
All round us; we but feel our way to err:
The ocean hath his chart, the stars their map,
725   And Knowledge spreads them on her ample lap;
But Rome is as the desert, where we steer
Stumbling o'er recollections; now we clap
Our hands, and cry 'Eureka!' it is clear —
When but some false mirage of ruin rises near.

LXXXII

730   Alas! the lofty city! and alas!
The trebly hundred triumphs![1] and the day
When Brutus made the dagger's edge surpass
The conqueror's sword in bearing fame away!
Alas, for Tully's voice, and Virgil's lay,
735   And Livy's pictured page! — but these shall be
Her resurrection; all beside — decay.
Alas, for Earth, for never shall we see
That brightness in her eye she bore when Rome was free!

1. Orosius gives 320 for the number of triumphs. He is followed by Panvinius; and Panvinius by Mr Gibbon and the modern writers.

LXXXIII

    Oh thou, whose chariot roll'd on Fortune's wheel,
740   Triumphant Sylla! Thou, who didst subdue
    Thy country's foes ere thou wouldst pause to feel
    The wrath of thy own wrongs, or reap the due
    Of hoarded vengeance till thine eagles flew
    O'er prostrate Asia; – thou, who with thy frown
745   Annihilated senates – Roman, too,
    With all thy vices, for thou didst lay down
With an atoning smile a more than earthly crown –

LXXXIV

    The dictatorial wreath – couldst thou divine
    To what would one day dwindle that which made
750   Thee more than mortal? and that so supine
    By aught than Romans Rome should thus be laid?
    She who was named Eternal, and array'd
    Her warriors but to conquer – she who veil'd
    Earth with her haughty shadow, and display'd,
755   Until the o'er-canopied horizon fail'd,
Her rushing wings – Oh! she who was Almighty hail'd!

LXXXV

    Sylla was first of victors; but our own
    The sagest of usurpers, Cromwell; he
    Too swept off senates while he hew'd the throne
760   Down to a block – immortal rebel! See
    What crimes it costs to be a moment free
    And famous through all ages! but beneath
    His fate the moral lurks of destiny;
    His day of double victory and death
765 Beheld him win two realms, and, happier, yield his
        breath.[1]

1. On the 3d of September Cromwell gained the victory of Dunbar: a year afterwards he obtained 'his crowning mercy' of Worcester; and a few years after, on the same day, which he had ever esteemed the most fortunate for him, died.

LXXXVI

The third of the same moon whose former course
Had all but crown'd him, on the selfsame day
Deposed him gently from his throne of force,
And laid him with the earth's preceding clay.
770   And show'd not Fortune thus how fame and sway,
And all we deem delightful, and consume
Our souls to compass through each arduous way,
Are in her eyes less happy than the tomb?
Were they but so in man's, how different were his doom!

LXXXVII

775   And thou, dread statue! yet existent in
The austerest form of naked majesty,
Thou who beheldest, 'mid the assassins' din,
At thy bathed base the bloody Cæsar lie,
Folding his robe in dying dignity,
780   An offering to thine altar from the queen
Of gods and men, great Nemesis! did he die,
And thou, too, perish, Pompey? have ye been
Victors of countless kings, or puppets of a scene?

LXXXVIII

And thou, the thunder-stricken nurse of Rome
785   She-wolf! whose brazen-imaged dugs impart
The milk of conquest yet within the dome
Where, as a monument of antique art,
Thou standest: — Mother of the mighty heart,
Which the great founder suck'd from thy wild teat,
790   Scorch'd by the Roman Jove's etherial dart,
And thy limbs black with lightning — dost thou yet
Guard thine immortal cubs, nor thy fond charge forget?

LXXXIX

Thou dost; — but all thy foster-babes are dead —
The men of iron; and the world hath rear'd
795   Cities from out their sepulchres: men bled
In imitation of the things they fear'd,

And fought and conquer'd, and the same course steer'd,
At apish distance; but as yet none have,
Nor could, the same supremacy have near'd,
800   Save one vain man, who is not in the grave,
But, vanquish'd by himself, to his own slaves a slave –

XC

The fool of false dominion – and a kind
Of bastard Cæsar, following him of old
With steps unequal; for the Roman's mind
805   Was modell'd in a less terrestrial mould,
With passions fiercer, yet a judgment cold,
And an immortal instinct which redeem'd
The frailties of a heart so soft, yet bold,
Alcides with the distaff now he seem'd
810   At Cleopatra's feet, – and now himself he beam'd.

XCI

And came – and saw – and conquer'd! But the man
Who would have tamed his eagles down to flee,
Like a train'd falcon, in the Gallic van,
Which he, in sooth, long led to victory,
815   With a deaf heart which never seem'd to be
A listener to itself, was strangely framed;
With but one weakest weakness – vanity,
Coquettish in ambition – still he aim'd –
At what? can he avouch – or answer what he claim'd?

XCII

820   And would be all or nothing – nor could wait
For the sure grave to level him; few years
Had fix'd him with the Cæsars in his fate,
On whom we tread: For *this* the conqueror rears
The arch of triumph! and for this the tears
825   And blood of earth flow on as they have flow'd,
An universal deluge, which appears
Without an ark for wretched man's abode,
And ebbs but to reflow! – Renew thy rainbow, God!

XCIII

What from this barren being do we reap?
Our senses narrow, and our reason frail,
Life short, and truth a gem which loves the deep,
And all things weigh'd in custom's falsest scale:
Opinion an omnipotence, – whose veil
Mantles the earth with darkness, until right
And wrong are accidents, and men grow pale
Lest their own judgments should become too bright,
And their free thoughts be crimes, and earth have too much
        light.

XCIV

And thus they plod in sluggish misery,
Rotting from sire to son, and age to age,
Proud of their trampled nature, and so die,
Bequeathing their hereditary rage
To the new race of inborn slaves, who wage
War for their chains, and rather than be free,
Bleed gladiator-like, and still engage
Within the same arena where they see
Their fellows fall before, like leaves of the same tree.

XCV

I speak not of men's creeds – they rest between
Man and his Maker – but of things allow'd,
Averr'd, and known, – and daily, hourly seen –
The yoke that is upon us doubly bow'd,
And the intent of tyranny avow'd,
The edict of Earth's rulers, who are grown
The apes of him who humbled once the proud,
And shook them from their slumbers on the throne;
Too glorious, were this all his mighty arm had done.

XCVI

Can tyrants but by tyrants conquer'd be,
And Freedom find no champion and no child
Such as Columbia saw arise when she
Sprung forth a Pallas, arm'd and undefiled?

860   Or must such minds be nourish'd in the wild,
         Deep in the unpruned forest, 'midst the roar
         Of cataracts, where nursing Nature smiled
         On infant Washington? Has Earth no more
     Such seeds within her breast, or Europe no such shore?

         XCVII
865   But France got drunk with blood to vomit crime,
         And fatal have her Saturnalia been
         To Freedom's cause, in every age and clime;
         Because the deadly days which we have seen,
         And vile Ambition, that built up between
870   Man and his hopes an adamantine wall,
         And the base pageant last upon the scene,
         Are grown the pretext for the eternal thrall
     Which nips life's tree, and dooms man's worst – his second
             fall.

         XCVIII
         Yet, Freedom! yet thy banner, torn, but flying
875   Streams like the thunder-storm *against* the wind;
         Thy trumpet voice, though broken now and dying,
         The loudest still the tempest leaves behind;
         Thy tree hath lost its blossoms, and the rind,
         Chopp'd by the axe, looks rough and little worth,
880   But the sap lasts, and still the seed we find
         Sown deep, even in the bosom of the North;
     So shall a better spring less bitter fruit bring forth.

         XCIX
         There is a stern round tower of other days,
         Firm as a fortress, with its fence of stone,
885   Such as an army's baffled strength delays,
         Standing with half its battlements alone,
         And with two thousand years of ivy grown,
         The garland of eternity, where wave
         The green leaves over all by time o'erthrown; –
890   What was this tower of strength? within its cave
     What treasure lay so lock'd, so hid? – A woman's grave.

C

But who was she, the lady of the dead,
Tomb'd in a palace? Was she chaste and fair?
Worthy a king's – or more – a Roman's bed?
895   What race of chiefs and heroes did she bear?
What daughter of her beauties was the heir?
How lived – how loved – how died she? Was she not
So honour'd – and conspicuously there,
Where meaner relics must not dare to rot,
900   Placed to commemorate a more than mortal lot?

CI

Was she as those who love their lords, or they
Who love the lords of others? such have been
Even in the olden time, Rome's annals say.
Was she a matron of Cornelia's mien,
905   Or the light air of Egypt's graceful queen,
Profuse of joy – or 'gainst it did she war,
Inveterate in virtue? Did she lean
To the soft side of the heart, or wisely bar
Love from amongst her griefs? – for such the affections are.

CII

910   Perchance she died in youth: it may be, bow'd
With woes far heavier than the ponderous tomb
That weigh'd upon her gentle dust, a cloud
Might gather o'er her beauty, and a gloom
In her dark eye, prophetic of the doom
915   Heaven gives its favourites – early death; yet shed
A sunset charm around her, and illume
With hectic light, the Hesperus of the dead,
Of her consuming cheek the autumnal leaf-like red.

CIII

Perchance she died in age – surviving all,
920   Charms, kindred, children – with the silver gray
On her long tresses, which might yet recal,
It may be, still a something of the day

When they were braided, and her proud array
And lovely form were envied, praised, and eyed
925   By Rome – but whither would Conjecture stray?
Thus much alone we know – Metella died,
The wealthiest Roman's wife: Behold his love or pride!

CIV

I know not why – but standing thus by thee
It seems as if I had thine inmate known,
930   Thou tomb! and other days come back on me
With recollected music, though the tone
Is changed and solemn, like the cloudy groan
Of dying thunder on the distant wind;
Yet could I seat me by this ivied stone
935   Till I had bodied forth the heated mind
Forms from the floating wreck which Ruin leaves behind;

CV

And from the planks, far shatter'd o'er the rocks,
Built me a little bark of hope, once more
To battle with the ocean and the shocks
940   Of the loud breakers, and the ceaseless roar
Which rushes on the solitary shore
Where all lies founder'd that was ever dear:
But could I gather from the wave-worn store
Enough for my rude boat, where should I steer?
945   There woos no home, nor hope, nor life, save what is here.

CVI

Then let the winds howl on! their harmony
Shall henceforth be my music, and the night
The sound shall temper with the owlets' cry,
As I now hear them, in the fading light
950   Dim o'er the bird of darkness' native site,
Answering each other on the Palatine,
With their large eyes, all glistening gray and bright,
And sailing pinions. – Upon such a shrine
What are our petty griefs? – let me not number mine.

CVII

955   Cypress and ivy, weed and wallflower grown
    Matted and mass'd together, hillocks heap'd
    On what were chambers, arch crush'd, column strown
    In fragments, choked up vaults, and frescos steep'd
    In subterranean damps, where the owl peep'd,
960 Deeming it midnight: – Temples, baths, or halls?
    Pronounce who can; for all that Learning reap'd
    From her research hath been, that these are walls—
Behold the Imperial Mount! 'tis thus the mighty falls.[1]

CVIII

    There is the moral of all human tales;
965 'Tis but the same rehearsal of the past,
    First Freedom and then Glory – when that fails,
    Wealth, vice, corruption, – barbarism at last.
    And History, with all her volumes vast,
    Hath but *one* page, – 'tis better written here,
970 Where gorgeous Tyranny hath thus amass'd
    All treasures, all delights, that eye or ear,
Heart, soul could seek, tongue ask – Away with words! draw
        near,

CIX

    Admire, exult – despise – laugh, weep, – for here
    There is such matter for all feeling: – Man!
975 Thou pendulum betwixt a smile and tear,
    Ages and realms are crowded in this span,
    This mountain, whose obliterated plan
    The pyramid of empires pinnacled,
    Of Glory's gewgaws shining in the van
980 Till the sun's rays with added flame were fill'd!
Where are its golden roofs! where those who dared to
        build?

1. The Palatine is one mass of ruins, particularly on the side towards the
Circus Maximus. The very soil is formed of crumbled brickwork. Nothing
has been told, nothing can be told, to satisfy the belief of any but a Roman
antiquary.

CX

    Tully was not so eloquent as thou,
    Thou nameless column with the buried base!
    What are the laurels of the Cæsar's brow?
985   Crown me with ivy from his dwelling-place.
    Whose arch or pillar meets me in the face,
    Titus or Trajan's? No – 'tis that of Time:
    Triumph, arch, pillar, all he doth displace
    Scoffing; and apostolic statues climb
990 To crush the imperial urn, whose ashes slept sublime,

CXI

    Buried in air, the deep blue sky of Rome,
    And looking to the stars: they had contain'd
    A spirit which with these would find a home,
    The last of those who o'er the whole earth reign'd,
995   The Roman globe, for after none sustain'd,
    But yielded back his conquests: – he was more
    Than a mere Alexander, and, unstain'd
    With household blood and wine, serenely wore
His sovereign virtues – still we Trajan's name adore.

CXII

1000   Where is the rock of Triumph, the high place
    Where Rome embraced her heroes? where the steep
    Tarpeian? fittest goal of Treason's race,
    The promontory whence the Traitor's Leap
    Cured all ambition. Did the conquerors heap
1005   Their spoils here? Yes; and in yon field below,
    A thousand years of silenced factions sleep –
    The Forum, where the immortal accents glow,
And still the eloquent air breathes – burns with Cicero!

CXIII

    The field of freedom, faction, fame, and blood:
1010   Here a proud people's passions were exhaled,
    From the first hour of empire in the bud
    To that when further worlds to conquer fail'd;

But long before had Freedom's face been veil'd,
And Anarchy assumed her attributes;
1015   Till every lawless soldier who assail'd
Trod on the trembling senate's slavish mutes,
Or raised the venal voice of baser prostitutes.

CXIV
Then turn we to her latest tribune's name,
From her ten thousand tyrants turn to thee,
1020   Redeemer of dark centuries of shame –
The friend of Petrarch – hope of Italy –
Rienzi! last of Romans! While the tree
Of freedom's wither'd trunk puts forth a leaf,
Even for thy tomb a garland let it be –
1025   The forum's champion, and the people's chief –
Her new-born Numa thou – with reign, alas! too brief.

CXV
Egeria! sweet creation of some heart
Which found no mortal resting-place so fair
As thine ideal breast; whate'er thou art
1030   Or wert, – a young Aurora of the air,
The nympholepsy of some fond despair;
Or, it might be, a beauty of the earth,
Who found a more than common votary there
Too much adoring; whatso'er thy birth,
1035   Thou wert a beautiful thought, and softly bodied forth.

CXVI
The mosses of thy fountain still are sprinkled
With thine Elysian water-drops; the face
Of thy cave-guarded spring, with years unwrinkled,
Reflects the meek-eyed genius of the place,
1040   Whose green, wild margin now no more erase
Art's works; nor must the delicate waters sleep,
Prison'd in marble, bubbling from the base
Of the cleft statue, with a gentle leap
The rill runs o'er, and round, fern, flowers, and ivy, creep

CXVII

1045
Fantastically tangled; the green hills
Are clothed with early blossoms, through the grass
The quick-eyed lizard rustles, and the bills
Of summer-birds sing welcome as ye pass;
Flowers fresh in hue, and many in their class,
1050
Implore the pausing step, and with their dyes
Dance in the soft breeze in a fairy mass;
The sweetness of the violet's deep blue eyes,
Kiss'd by the breath of heaven, seems colour'd by its skies.

CXVIII

Here didst thou dwell, in this enchanted cover,
1055
Egeria! thy all heavenly bosom beating
For the far footsteps of thy mortal lover;
The purple Midnight veiled that mystic meeting
With her most starry canopy, and seating
Thyself by thine adorer, what befel?
1060
This cave was surely shaped out for the greeting
Of an enamoured Goddess, and the cell
Haunted by holy Love – the earliest oracle!

CXIX

And didst thou not, thy breast to his replying,
Blend a celestial with a human heart;
1065
And Love, which dies as it was born, in sighing,
Share with immortal transports? could thine art
Make them indeed immortal, and impart
The purity of heaven to earthly joys,
Expel the venom and not blunt the dart –
1070
The dull satiety which all destroys –
And root from out the soul the deadly weed which
    cloys?

CXX

Alas! our young affections run to waste,
Or water but the desert; whence arise
But weeds of dark luxuriance, tares of haste,
1075
Rank at the core, though tempting to the eyes,

Flowers whose wild odours breathe but agonies,
And trees whose gums are poison; such the plants
Which spring beneath her steps as Passion flies
O'er the world's wilderness, and vainly pants
1080   For some celestial fruit forbidden to our wants.

CXXI

Oh Love! no habitant of earth thou art –
An unseen seraph, we believe in thee,
A faith whose martyrs are the broken heart,
But never yet hath seen, nor e'er shall see
1085   The naked eye, thy form, as it should be;
The mind hath made thee, as it peopled heaven,
Even with its own desiring phantasy,
And to a thought such shape and image given,
As haunts the unquench'd soul – parch'd – wearied – wrung
            – and riven.

CXXII

1090   Of its own beauty is the mind diseased,
And fevers into false creation: – where,
Where are the forms the sculptor's soul hath seized?
In him alone. Can Nature show so fair?
Where are the charms and virtues which we dare
1095   Conceive in boyhood and pursue as men,
The unreach'd Paradise of our despair,
Which o'er-informs the pencil and the pen,
And overpowers the page where it would bloom again?

CXXIII

Who loves, raves – 'tis youth's frenzy – but the cure
1100   Is bitterer still; as charm by charm unwinds
Which robed our idols, and we see too sure
Nor worth nor beauty dwells from out the mind's
Ideal shape of such; yet still it binds
The fatal spell, and still it draws us on,
1105   Reaping the whirlwind from the oft-sown winds;
The stubborn heart, its alchemy begun,
Seems ever near the prize – wealthiest when most undone.

CXXIV

We wither from our youth, we gasp away –
Sick – sick; unfound the boon – unslaked the thirst,
1110   Though to the last, in verge of our decay,
Some phantom lures, such as we sought at first –
But all too late, – so are we doubly curst.
Love, fame, ambition, avarice – 'tis the same,
Each idle – and all ill – and none the worst –
1115   For all are meteors with a different name,
And Death the sable smoke where vanishes the flame.

CXXV

Few – none – find what they love or could have loved,
Though accident, blind contact, and the strong
Necessity of loving, have removed
1120   Antipathies – but to recur, ere long,
Envenom'd with irrevocable wrong;
And Circumstance, that unspiritual god
And miscreator, makes and helps along
Our coming evils with a crutch-like rod,
1125   Whose touch turns Hope to dust, – the dust we all have
            trod.

CXXVI

Our life is a false nature – 'tis not in
The harmony of things, – this hard decree,
This uneradicable taint of sin,
This boundless upas, this all-blasting tree,
1130   Whose root is earth, whose leaves and branches be
The skies which rain their plagues on men like dew –
Disease, death, bondage – all the woes we see –
And worse, the woes we see not – which throb through
The immedicable soul, with heart-aches ever new.

CXXVII

1135   Yet let us ponder boldly – 'tis a base
Abandonment of reason to resign
Our right of thought – our last and only place
Of refuge; this, at least, shall still be mine:

Though from our birth the faculty divine
1140   Is chain'd and tortured – cabin'd, cribb'd, confined,
And bred in darkness, lest the truth should shine
Too brightly on the unprepared mind,
The beam pours in, for time and skill will couch the blind.

CXXVIII
Arches on arches! as it were that Rome,
1145   Collecting the chief trophies of her line,
Would build up all her triumphs in one dome,
Her Coliseum stands; the moonbeams shine
As 'twere its natural torches, for divine
Should be the light which streams here, to illume
1150   This long-explored but still exhaustless mine
Of contemplation; and the azure gloom
Of an Italian night, where the deep skies assume

CXXIX
Hues which have words, and speak to ye of heaven,
Floats o'er this vast and wondrous monument,
1155   And shadows forth its glory. There is given
Unto the things of earth, which Time hath bent,
A spirit's feeling, and where he hath leant
His hand, but broke his scythe, there is a power
And magic in the ruin'd battlement,
1160   For which the palace of the present hour
Must yield its pomp, and wait till ages are its dower.

CXXX
Oh Time! the beautifier of the dead,
Adorner of the ruin, comforter
And only healer when the heart hath bled –
1165   Time! the corrector where our judgments err,
The test of truth, love, – sole philosopher,
For all beside are sophists, from thy thrift,
Which never loses though it doth defer –
Time, the avenger! unto thee I lift
1170   My hands, and eyes, and heart, and crave of thee a gift:

CXXXI

Amidst this wreck, where thou hast made a shrine
And temple more divinely desolate,
Among thy mightier offerings here are mine,
Ruins of years – though few, yet full of fate: –
1175 If thou hast ever seen me too elate,
Hear me not; but if calmly I have borne
Good, and reserved my pride against the hate
Which shall not whelm me, let me not have worn
This iron in my soul in vain – shall *they* not mourn?

CXXXII

1180 And thou, who never yet of human wrong
Left the unbalanced scale, great Nemesis!
Here, where the ancient paid thee homage long –
Thou, who didst call the Furies from the abyss,
And round Orestes bade them howl and hiss
1185 For that unnatural retribution – just,
Had it but been from hands less near – in this
Thy former realm, I call thee from the dust!
Dost thou not hear my heart? – Awake! thou shalt, and
must.

CXXXIII

It is not that I may not have incurr'd
1190 For my ancestral faults or mine the wound
I bleed withal, and, had it been conferr'd
With a just weapon, it had flow'd unbound;
But now my blood shall not sink in the ground;
To thee I do devote it – *thou* shalt take
1195 The vengeance, which shall yet be sought and found,
Which if *I* have not taken for the sake —
But let that pass – I sleep, but thou shalt yet awake.

CXXXIV

And if my voice break forth, 'tis not that now
I shrink from what is suffer'd: let him speak
1200 Who hath beheld decline upon my brow,
Or seen my mind's convulsion leave it weak;

But in this page a record will I seek.
Not in the air shall these my words disperse,
Though I be ashes; a far hour shall wreak
1205   The deep prophetic fulness of this verse,
And pile on human heads the mountain of my curse!

CXXXV

That curse shall be Forgiveness. — Have I not —
Hear me, my mother Earth! behold it, Heaven! —
Have I not had to wrestle with my lot!
1210   Have I not suffer'd things to be forgiven?
Have I not had my brain sear'd, my heart riven,
Hopes sapp'd, name blighted, Life's life lied away?
And only not to desperation driven,
Because not altogether of such clay
1215   As rots into the souls of those whom I survey.

CXXXVI

From mighty wrongs to petty perfidy
Have I not seen what human things could do?
From the loud roar of foaming calumny
To the small whisper of the as paltry few,
1220   And subtler venom of the reptile crew,
The Janus glance of whose significant eye,
Learning to lie with silence, would *seem* true,
And without utterance, save the shrug or sigh,
Deal round to happy fools its speechless obloquy.

CXXXVII

1225   But I have lived, and have not lived in vain:
My mind may lose its force, my blood its fire,
And my frame perish even in conquering pain;
But there is that within me which shall tire
Torture and Time, and breathe when I expire;
1230   Something unearthly, which they deem not of,
Like the remember'd tone of a mute lyre,
Shall on their soften'd spirits sink, and move
In hearts all rocky now the late remorse of love.

CXXXVIII

The seal is set. – Now welcome, thou dread power!
Nameless, yet thus omnipotent, which here
Walk'st in the shadow of the midnight hour
With a deep awe, yet all distinct from fear;
Thy haunts are ever where the dead walls rear
Their ivy mantles, and the solemn scene
Derives from thee a sense so deep and clear
That we become a part of what has been,
And grow unto the spot, all-seeing but unseen.

CXXXIX

And here the buzz of eager nations ran,
In murmur'd pity, or loud-roar'd applause,
As man was slaughter'd by his fellow man.
And wherefore slaughter'd? wherefore, but because
Such were the bloody Circus' genial laws,
And the imperial pleasure. – Wherefore not?
What matters where we fall to fill the maws
Of worms – on battle-plains or listed spot?
Both are but theatres where the chief actors rot.

CXL

I see before me the Gladiator lie:
He leans upon his hand – his manly brow
Consents to death, but conquers agony,
And his droop'd head sinks gradually low –
And through his side the last drops, ebbing slow
From the red gash, fall heavy, one by one,
Like the first of a thunder-shower; and now
The arena swims around him – he is gone,
Ere ceased the inhuman shout which hail'd the wretch who
won.

CXLI

He heard it, but he heeded not – his eyes
Were with his heart, and that was far away:
He reck'd not of the life he lost nor prize,
But where his rude hut by the Danube lay,

1265   *There* were his young barbarians all at play,
          There was their Dacian mother – he, their sire,
          Butcher'd to make a Roman holiday[1] –
          All this rush'd with his blood – Shall he expire
          And unavenged? – Arise! ye Goths, and glut your ire!

CXLII

1270   But here, where Murder breathed her bloody steam;
          And here, where buzzing nations choked the ways,
          And roar'd or murmur'd like a mountain stream
          Dashing or winding as its torrent strays;

1. Gladiators were of two kinds, compelled and voluntary; and were supplied from several conditions; – from slaves sold for that purpose; from culprits; from barbarian captives either taken in war, and, after being led in triumph, set apart for the games, or those seized and condemned as rebels; also from free citizens, some fighting for hire (*auctorati*), others from a depraved ambition: at last even knights and senators were exhibited, – a disgrace of which the first tyrant was naturally the first inventor. In the end, dwarfs, and even women, fought; an enormity prohibited by Severus. Of these the most to be pitied undoubtedly were the barbarian captives; and to this species a Christian writer justly applies the epithet 'innocent' to distinguish them from the professional gladiators. Aurelian and Claudius supplied great numbers of these unfortunate victims; the one after his triumph, and the other on the pretext of a rebellion. No war, says Lipsius, was ever so destructive to the human race as these sports. In spite of the laws of Constantine and Constans, gladiatorial shows survived the old established religion more than seventy years; but they owed their final extinction to the courage of a Christian. In the year 404, on the kalends of January, they were exhibiting the shows in the Flavian amphitheatre before the usual immense concourse of people. Almachius, or Telemachus, an eastern monk, who had travelled to Rome intent on his holy purpose, rushed into the midst of the area, and endeavoured to separate the combatants. The Prætor Alypius, a person incredibly attached to these games, gave instant orders to the gladiators to slay him; and Telemachus gained the crown of martyrdom, and the title of saint, which surely has never either before or since been awarded for a more noble exploit. Honorius immediately abolished the shows, which were never afterwards revived. The story is told by Theodoret and Cassiodorus, and seems worthy of credit notwithstanding its place in the Roman martyrology. Besides the torrents of blood which flowed at the funerals, in the amphitheatres, the circus, the forums, and other public places, gladiators were introduced at feasts, and tore each other to pieces amidst the supper tables, to the great delight and applause of the guests. Yet Lipsius permits himself to suppose the loss of courage, and the evident degeneracy of mankind, to be nearly connected with the abolition of these bloody spectacles.

Here, where the Roman millions' blame or praise
1275   Was death or life, the playthings of a crowd,
My voice sounds much – and fall the stars' faint rays
On the arena void – seats crush'd – walls bow'd –
And galleries, where my steps seem echoes strangely loud.

CXLIII

A ruin – yet what ruin! from its mass
1280   Walls, palaces, half-cities, have been rear'd;
Yet oft the enormous skeleton ye pass,
And marvel where the spoil could have appear'd.
Hath it indeed been plunder'd, or but clear'd?
Alas! developed, opens the decay,
1285   When the colossal fabric's form is near'd:
It will not bear the brightness of the day,
Which streams too much on all years, man, have reft away.

CXLIV

But when the rising moon begins to climb
Its topmast arch, and gently pauses there;
1290   When the stars twinkle through the loops of time,
And the low night-breeze waves along the air
The garland forest, which the gray walls wear,
Like laurels on the bald first Cæsar's head;
When the light shines serene but doth not glare,
1295   Then in this magic circle raise the dead:
Heroes have trod this spot – 'tis on their dust ye tread.

CXLV

'While stands the Coliseum, Rome shall stand;
When falls the Coliseum, Rome shall fall;
And when Rome falls – the World.' From our own land
1300   Thus spake the pilgrims o'er this mighty wall
In Saxon times, which we are wont to call
Ancient; and these three mortal things are still
On their foundations, and unalter'd all;
Rome and her Ruin past Redemption's skill,
1305   The World, the same wide den – of thieves, or what ye
will.

CXLVI

Simple, erect, severe, austere, sublime –
Shrine of all saints and temple of all gods,
From Jove to Jesus – spared and blest by time;
Looking tranquillity, while falls or nods
1310   Arch, empire, each thing round thee, and man plods
His way through thorns to ashes – glorious dome!
Shalt thou not last? Time's scythe and tyrants' rods
Shiver upon thee – sanctuary and home
Of art and piety – Pantheon! – pride of Rome!

CXLVII

1315   Relic of nobler days, and noblest arts!
Despoil'd yet perfect, with thy circle spreads
A holiness appealing to all hearts –
To art a model; and to him who treads
Rome for the sake of ages, Glory sheds
1320   Her light through thy sole aperture; to those
Who worship, here are altars for their beads;
And they who feel for genius may repose
Their eyes on honour'd forms, whose busts around them close.

CXLVIII

There is a dungeon, in whose dim drear light
1325   What do I gaze on? Nothing: Look again!
Two forms are slowly shadow'd on my sight –
Two insulated phantoms of the brain:
It is not so; I see them full and plain –
An old man, and a female young and fair,
1330   Fresh as a nursing mother, in whose vein
The blood is nectar: – but what doth she there,
With her unmantled neck, and bosom white and bare?

CXLIX

Full swells the deep pure fountain of young life,
Where *on* the heart and *from* the heart we took
1335   Our first and sweetest nurture, when the wife,
Blest into mother, in the innocent look,

Or even the piping cry of lips that brook
No pain and small suspense, a joy perceives
Man knows not, when from out its cradled nook
1340 She sees her little bud put forth its leaves –
What may the fruit be yet? – I know not – Cain was Eve's.

CL

But here youth offers to old age the food,
The milk of his own gift: – it is her sire
To whom she renders back the debt of blood
1345 Born with her birth. No; he shall not expire
While in those warm and lovely veins the fire
Of health and holy feeling can provide
Great Nature's Nile, whose deep stream rises higher
Than Egypt's river: – from that gentle side
1350 Drink, drink and live, old man! Heaven's realm holds no
        such tide.

CLI

The starry fable of the milky way
Has not thy story's purity; it is
A constellation of a sweeter ray,
And sacred Nature triumphs more in this
1355 Reverse of her decree, than in the abyss
Where sparkle distant worlds: – Oh, holiest nurse!
No drop of that clear stream its way shall miss
To thy sire's heart, replenishing its source
With life, as our freed souls rejoin the universe.

CLII

1360 Turn to the Mole which Hadrian rear'd on high,
Imperial mimic of old Egypt's piles,
Colossal copyist of deformity,
Whose travell'd phantasy from the far Nile's
Enormous model, doom'd the artist's toils
1365 To build for giants, and for his vain earth,
His shrunken ashes, raise this dome: How smiles
The gazer's eye with philosophic mirth,
To view the huge design which sprung from such a birth!

CLIII

But lo! the dome – the vast and wondrous dome,
1370   To which Diana's marvel was a cell –
Christ's mighty shrine above his martyr's tomb!
I have beheld the Ephesian's miracle –
Its columns strew the wilderness, and dwell
The hyæna and the jackall in their shade;
1375   I have beheld Sophia's bright roofs swell
Their glittering mass i' the sun, and have survey'd
Its sanctuary the while the usurping Moslem pray'd;

CLIV

But thou, of temples old, or altars new,
Standest alone – with nothing like to thee –
1380   Worthiest of God, the holy and the true.
Since Zion's desolation, when that He
Forsook his former city, what could be,
Of earthly structures, in his honour piled,
Of a sublimer aspect? Majesty,
1385   Power, Glory, Strength, and Beauty, all are aisled
In this eternal ark of worship undefiled.

CLV

Enter: its grandeur overwhelms thee not;
And why? it is not lessen'd; but thy mind,
Expanded by the genius of the spot,
1390   Has grown colossal, and can only find
A fit abode wherein appear enshrined
Thy hopes of immortality; and thou
Shalt one day, if found worthy, so defined,
See thy God face to face, as thou dost now
1395   His Holy of Holies, nor be blasted by his brow.

CLVI

Thou movest – but increasing with the advance,
Like climbing some great Alp, which still doth rise,
Deceived by its gigantic elegance;
Vastness which grows – but grows to harmonise –

1400   All musical in its immensities;
    Rich marbles – richer painting – shrines where flame
    The lamps of gold – and haughty dome which vies
    In air with Earth's chief structures, though their frame
  Sits on the firm-set ground – and this the clouds must
     claim.

   CLVII

1405   Thou seest not all; but piecemeal thou must break,
    To separate contemplation, the great whole;
    And as the ocean many bays will make,
    That ask the eye – so here condense thy soul
    To more immediate objects, and control
1410   Thy thoughts until thy mind hath got by heart
    Its eloquent proportions, and unroll
    In mighty graduations, part by part,
  The glory which at once upon thee did not dart,

   CLVIII

    Not by its fault – but thine: Our outward sense
1415   Is but of gradual grasp – and as it is
    That what we have of feeling most intense
    Outstrips our faint expression; even so this
    Outshining and o'erwhelming edifice
    Fools our fond gaze, and greatest of the great
1420   Defies at first our Nature's littleness,
    Till, growing with its growth, we thus dilate
  Our spirits to the size of that they contemplate.

   CLIX

    Then pause, and be enlighten'd; there is more
    In such a survey than the sating gaze
1425   Of wonder pleased, or awe which would adore
    The worship of the place, or the mere praise
    Of art and its great masters, who could raise
    What former time, nor skill, nor thought could plan;
    The fountain of sublimity displays
1430   Its depth, and thence may draw the mind of man
  Its golden sands, and learn what great conceptions can.

CLX

 Or, turning to the Vatican, go see
 Laocoon's torture dignifying pain –
 A father's love and mortal's agony
1435 With an immortal's patience blending: – Vain
 The struggle; vain, against the coiling strain
 And gripe, and deepening of the dragon's grasp,
 The old man's clench; the long envenom'd chain
 Rivets the living links, – the enormous asp
1440 Enforces pang on pang, and stifles gasp on gasp.

CLXI

 Or view the Lord of the unerring bow,
 The God of life, and poesy, and light –
 The Sun in human limbs array'd, and brow
 All radiant from his triumph in the fight;
1445 The shaft hath just been shot – the arrow bright
 With an immortal's vengeance; in his eye
 And nostril beautiful disdain, and might
 And majesty, flash their full lightnings by,
Developing in that one glance the Deity.

CLXII

1450 But in his delicate form – a dream of Love,
 Shaped by some solitary nymph, whose breast
 Long'd for a deathless lover from above,
 And madden'd in that vision – are exprest
 All that ideal beauty ever bless'd
1455 The mind with in its most unearthly mood,
 When each conception was a heavenly guest –
 A ray of immortality – and stood,
Starlike, around, until they gather'd to a god!

CLXIII

 And if it be Prometheus stole from Heaven
1460 The fire which we endure, it was repaid
 By him to whom the energy was given
 Which this poetic marble hath array'd

With an eternal glory – which, if made
By human hands, is not of human thought;
1465   And Time himself hath hallow'd it, nor laid
One ringlet in the dust – nor hath it caught
A tinge of years, but breathes the flame with which 'twas
        wrought.

CLXIV

But where is he, the Pilgrim of my song,
The being who upheld it through the past?
1470   Methinks he cometh late and tarries long.
He is no more – these breathings are his last;
His wanderings done, his visions ebbing fast,
And he himself as nothing: – if he was
Aught but a phantasy, and could be class'd
1475   With forms which live and suffer – let that pass –
His shadow fades away into Destruction's mass,

CLXV

Which gathers shadow, substance, life, and all
That we inherit in its mortal shroud,
And spreads the dim and universal pall
1480   Through which all things grow phantoms; and the cloud
Between us sinks and all which ever glow'd,
Till Glory's self is twilight, and displays
A melancholy halo scarce allow'd
To hover on the verge of darkness; rays
1485   Sadder than saddest night, for they distract the gaze,

CLXVI

And send us prying into the abyss,
To gather what we shall be when the frame
Shall be resolved to something less than this
Its wretched essence; and to dream of fame,
1490   And wipe the dust from off the idle name
We never more shall hear, – but never more,
Oh, happier thought! can we be made the same:
It is enough in sooth that *once* we bore
These fardels of the heart – the heart whose sweat was gore.

CLXVII

1495   Hark! forth from the abyss a voice proceeds,
    A long low distant murmur of dread sound,
    Such as arises when a nation bleeds
    With some deep and immedicable wound;
    Through storm and darkness yawns the rending ground,
1500   The gulf is thick with phantoms, but the chief
    Seems royal still, though with her head discrown'd,
    And pale, but lovely, with maternal grief
She clasps a babe, to whom her breast yields no relief.

CLXVIII

    Scion of chiefs and monarchs, where art thou?
1505   Fond hope of many nations, art thou dead?
    Could not the grave forget thee, and lay low
    Some less majestic, less beloved head?
    In the sad midnight, while thy heart still bled,
    The mother of a moment, o'er thy boy,
1510   Death hush'd that pang for ever: with thee fled
    The present happiness and promised joy
Which fill'd the imperial isles so full it seem'd to cloy.

CLXIX

    Peasants bring forth in safety. – Can it be,
    Oh thou that wert so happy, so adored!
1515   Those who weep not for kings shall weep for thee,
    And Freedom's heart, grown heavy, cease to hoard
    Her many griefs for ONE; for she had pour'd
    Her orisons for thee, and o'er thy head
    Beheld her Iris. – Thou, too, lonely lord,
1520   And desolate consort – vainly wert thou wed!
The husband of a year! the father of the dead!

CLXX

    Of sackcloth was thy wedding garment made;
    Thy bridal's fruit is ashes: in the dust
    The fair-hair'd Daughter of the Isles is laid,
1525   The love of millions! How we did intrust
    Futurity to her! and, though it must

Darken above our bones, yet fondly deem'd
Our children should obey her child, and bless'd
Her and her hoped-for seed, whose promise seem'd
1530 Like stars to shepherds' eyes: — 'twas but a meteor beam'd.

CLXXI

Woe unto us, not her; for she sleeps well:
The fickle reek of popular breath, the tongue
Of hollow counsel, the false oracle,
Which from the birth of monarchy hath rung
1535 Its knell in princely ears, 'till the o'erstung
Nations have arm'd in madness, the strange fate[1]
Which tumbles mightiest sovereigns, and hath flung
Against their blind omnipotence a weight
Within the opposing scale, which crushes soon or late, —

CLXXII

1540 These might have been her destiny; but no,
Our hearts deny it: and so young, so fair,
Good without effort, great without a foe;
But now a bride and mother — and now *there!*
How many ties did that stern moment tear!
1545 From thy Sire's to his humblest subject's breast
Is link'd the electric chain of that despair,
Whose shock was as an earthquake's, and opprest
The land which loved thee so that none could love thee best.

CLXXIII

Lo, Nemi! navell'd in the woody hills
1550 So far, that the uprooting wind which tears
The oak from his foundation, and which spills
The ocean o'er its boundary, and bears
Its foam against the skies, reluctant spares
The oval mirror of thy glassy lake;

1. Mary died on the scaffold; Elizabeth of a broken heart; Charles V a hermit; Louis XIV a bankrupt in means and glory; Cromwell of anxiety; and, 'the greatest is behind,' Napoleon lives a prisoner. To these sovereigns a long but superfluous list might be added of names equally illustrious and unhappy.

1555   And, calm as cherish'd hate, its surface wears
        A deep cold settled aspect nought can shake,
All coil'd into itself and round, as sleeps the snake.

CLXXIV

        And near Albano's scarce divided waves
        Shine from a sister valley; – and afar
1560   The Tiber winds, and the broad ocean laves
        The Latian coast where sprang the Epic war,
        'Arms and the Man,' whose re-ascending star
        Rose o'er an empire: – but beneath thy right
        Tully reposed from Rome; – and where yon bar
1565   Of girdling mountains intercepts the sight
The Sabine farm was till'd, the weary bard's delight.

CLXXV

        But I forget. – My Pilgrim's shrine is won,
        And he and I must part, – so let it be, –
        His task and mine alike are nearly done;
1570   Yet once more let us look upon the sea;
        The midland ocean breaks on him and me,
        And from the Alban Mount we now behold
        Our friend of youth, that ocean, which when we
        Beheld it last by Calpe's rock unfold
1575   Those waves, we follow'd on till the dark Euxine roll'd

CLXXVI

        Upon the blue Symplegades: long years –
        Long, though not very many, since have done
        Their work on both; some suffering and some tears
        Have left us nearly where we had begun:
1580   Yet not in vain our mortal race hath run,
        We have had our reward – and it is here;
        That we can yet feel gladden'd by the sun,
        And reap from earth, sea, joy almost as dear
As if there were no man to trouble what is clear.

CLXXVII

1585   Oh! that the Desert were my dwelling-place,
        With one fair Spirit for my minister,

That I might all forget the human race,
And, hating no one, love but only her!
Ye Elements! – in whose ennobling stir
1590   I feel myself exalted – Can ye not
Accord me such a being? Do I err
In deeming such inhabit many a spot?
Though with them to converse can rarely be our lot.

CLXXVIII
There is a pleasure in the pathless woods,
1595   There is a rapture on the lonely shore,
There is society, where none intrudes,
By the deep Sea, and music in its roar:
I love not Man the less, but Nature more,
From these our interviews, in which I steal
1600   From all I may be, or have been before,
To mingle with the Universe, and feel
What I can ne'er express, yet can not all conceal.

CLXXIX
Roll on, thou deep and dark blue Ocean – roll!
Ten thousand fleets sweep over thee in vain;
1605   Man marks the earth with ruin – his control
Stops with the shore; – upon the watery plain
The wrecks are all thy deed, nor doth remain
A shadow of man's ravage, save his own,
When, for a moment, like a drop of rain,
1610   He sinks into thy depths with bubbling groan,
Without a grave, unknell'd, uncoffin'd, and unknown.

CLXXX
His steps are not upon thy paths, – thy fields
Are not a spoil for him, – thou dost arise
And shake him from thee; the vile strength he wields
1615   For earth's destruction thou dost all despise,
Spurning him from thy bosom to the skies,
And send'st him, shivering in thy playful spray
And howling, to his Gods, where haply lies
His petty hope in some near port or bay,
1620   And dashest him again to earth: – there let him lay.

CLXXXI

    The armaments which thunderstrike the walls
    Of rock-built cities, bidding nations quake,
    And monarchs tremble in their capitals,
    The oak leviathans, whose huge ribs make
1625   Their clay creator the vain title take
    Of lord of thee, and arbiter of war;
    These are thy toys, and, as the snowy flake,
    They melt into thy yeast of waves, which mar
Alike the Armada's pride, or spoils of Trafalgar.

CLXXXII

1630   Thy shores are empires, changed in all save thee –
    Assyria, Greece, Rome, Carthage, what are they?
    Thy waters wasted them while they were free,
    And many a tyrant since; their shores obey
    The stranger, slave, or savage; their decay
1635   Has dried up realms to deserts: – not so thou,
    Unchangeable save to thy wild waves' play –
    Time writes no wrinkle on thine azure brow –
Such as creation's dawn beheld, thou rollest now.

CLXXXIII

    Thou glorious mirror, where the Almighty's form
1640   Glasses itself in tempests; in all time,
    Calm or convulsed – in breeze, or gale, or storm,
    Icing the pole, or in the torrid clime
    Dark-heaving; – boundless, endless, and sublime –
    The image of Eternity – the throne
1645   Of the Invisible; even from out thy slime
    The monsters of the deep are made; each zone
Obeys thee; thou goest forth, dread, fathomless, alone.

CLXXXIV

    And I have loved thee, Ocean! and my joy
    Of youthful sports was on thy breast to be
1650   Borne, like thy bubbles, onward: from a boy
    I wanton'd with thy breakers – they to me

Were a delight; and if the freshening sea
Made them a terror – 'twas a pleasing fear,
For I was as it were a child of thee,
1655   And trusted to thy billows far and near,
And laid my hand upon thy mane – as I do here.

CLXXXV

My task is done – my song hath ceased – my theme
Has died into an echo; it is fit
The spell should break of this protracted dream.
1660   The torch shall be extinguish'd which hath lit
My midnight lamp – and what is writ, is writ, –
Would it were worthier! but I am not now
That which I have been – and my visions flit
Less palpably before me – and the glow
1665   Which in my spirit dwelt is fluttering, faint, and low.

CLXXXVI

Farewell! a word that must be, and hath been –
A sound which makes us linger; – yet – farewell!
Ye! who have traced the Pilgrim to the scene
Which is his last, if in your memories dwell
1670   A thought which once was his, if on ye swell
A single recollection, not in vain
He wore his sandal-shoon, and scallop-shell;
Farewell! with *him* alone may rest the pain,
If such there were – with *you*, the moral of his strain!

Epistle from Mr Murray to Dr Polidori

Dear Doctor, I have read your play,
Which is a good one in its way, –
Purges the eyes and moves the bowels,
And drenches handkerchiefs like towels
5   With tears, that, in a flux of grief,
Afford hysterical relief
To shatter'd nerves and quicken'd pulses,
Which your catastrophe convulses.

    I like your moral and machinery;
10 Your plot, too, has such scope for scenery;
Your dialogue is apt and smart;
The play's concoction full of art;
Your hero raves, your heroine cries,
All stab, and every body dies.
15 In short, your tragedy would be
The very thing to hear and see:
And for a piece of publication,
If I decline on this occasion,
It is not that I am not sensible
20 To merits in themselves ostensible,
But – and I grieve to speak it – plays
Are drugs – mere drugs, sir – now-a-days.
I had a heavy loss by 'Manuel,' –
Too lucky if it prove not annual, –
25 And Sotheby, with his 'Orestes,'
(Which, by the by, the author's best is,)
Has lain so very long on hand
That I despair of all demand.
I've advertised, but see my books,
30 Or only watch my shopman's looks; –
Still Ivan, Ina, and such lumber,
My back-shop glut, my shelves encumber.

There's Byron too, who once did better,
Has sent me, folded in a letter,
35 A sort of – it's no more a drama
Than Darnley, Ivan, or Kehama;
So alter'd since last year his pen is,
I think he's lost his wits at Venice,
Or drained his brains away as Stallion
40 To some dark-eyed and warm Italian;
In short, sir, what with one and t'other,
I dare not venture on another.
I write in haste; excuse each blunder;
The coaches through the street so thunder!
45 My room's so full – we've Gifford here
Reading MS., with Hookham Frere,
Pronouncing on the nouns and particles
Of some of our forthcoming Articles.

The Quarterly – Ah, sir, if you
50 Had but the genius to review! –
A smart critique upon St Helena,
Or if you only would but tell in a
Short compass what – but, to resume:
As I was saying, sir, the room –
55 The room's so full of wits and bards,
Crabbes, Campbells, Crokers, Freres, and Wards
And others, neither bards nor wits: –
My humble tenement admits
All persons in the dress of gent.,
60 From Mr Hammond to Dog Dent.

A party dines with me to-day,
All clever men, who make their way;
Crabbe, Malcolm, Hamilton, and Chantrey,
Are all partakers of my pantry.
65 They're at this moment in discussion
On poor De Staël's late dissolution.

Her book, they say, was in advance –
Pray Heaven, she tell the truth of France!
Thus run our time and tongues away. –

70 But, to return, sir, to your play:
Sorry, sir, but I can not deal,
Unless 'twere acted by O'Neill.
My hands so full, my head so busy,
I'm almost dead, and always dizzy;

75 And so, with endless truth and hurry,
Dear Doctor, I am yours,

JOHN MURRAY.

BEPPO

A Venetian Story

ROSALIND: Farewell, Monsieur Traveller: Look, you lisp, and wear strange suits: disable all the benefits of your own country; be out of love with your Nativity, and almost chide God for making you that countenance you are; or I will scarce think that you have swam in a *Gondola*.   *As You Like It*, Act IV. Sc. 1.

[*Annotation of the Commentators.*]
    That is, been at *Venice*, which was much visited by the young English gentlemen of those times, and was then what *Paris* is *now* – the seat of all dissoluteness. S.A.   [Samuel Ayscough]

I
'Tis known, at least it should be, that throughout
    All countries of the Catholic persuasion,
Some weeks before Shrove Tuesday comes about,
    The people take their fill of recreation,
5 And buy repentance, ere they grow devout,
    However high their rank, or low their station,
With fiddling, feasting, dancing, drinking, masquing,
And other things which may be had for asking.

II
The moment night with dusky mantle covers
10   The skies (and the more duskily the better),
The time less liked by husbands than by lovers
    Begins, and prudery flings aside her fetter;
And gaiety on restless tiptoe hovers,
    Giggling with all the gallants who beset her;
15 And there are songs and quavers, roaring, humming,
Guitars, and every other sort of strumming.

III

And there are dresses splendid, but fantastical,
    Masks of all times and nations, Turks and Jews,
And harlequins and clowns, with feats gymnastical,
20   Greeks, Romans, Yankee-doodles, and Hindoos;
All kinds of dress, except the ecclesiastical,
    All people, as their fancies hit, may choose,
But no one in these parts may quiz the clergy, –
Therefore take heed, ye Freethinkers! I charge ye.

IV

25 You'd better walk about begirt with briars,
    Instead of coat and smallclothes, than put on
A single stitch reflecting upon friars,
    Although you swore it only was in fun;
They'd haul you o'er the coals, and stir the fires
30   Of Phlegethon with every mother's son,
Nor say one mass to cool the caldron's bubble
That boil'd your bones, unless you paid them double.

V

But saving this, you may put on whate'er
    You like by way of doublet, cape, or cloak,
35 Such as in Monmouth-street, or in Rag Fair,
    Would rig you out in seriousness or joke;
And even in Italy such places are,
    With prettier name in softer accents spoke,
For, bating Covent Garden, I can hit on
40 No place that's call'd 'Piazza' in Great Britain.

VI

This feast is named the Carnival, which being
    Interpreted, implies 'farewell to flesh:'
So call'd, because the name and thing agreeing,
    Through Lent they live on fish both salt and fresh.
45 But why they usher Lent with so much glee in,
    Is more than I can tell, although I guess
'Tis as we take a glass with friends at parting,
In the stage-coach or packet, just at starting.

VII

And thus they bid farewell to carnal dishes,
50   And solid meats, and highly spiced ragouts,
To live for forty days on ill-dress'd fishes,
        Because they have no sauces to their stews,
A thing which causes many 'poohs' and 'pishes,'
        And several oaths (which would not suit the Muse),
55 From travellers accustom'd from a boy
To eat their salmon, at the least, with soy;

VIII

And therefore humbly I would recommend
        'The curious in fish-sauce,' before they cross
The sea, to bid their cook, or wife, or friend,
60   Walk or ride to the Strand, and buy in gross
(Or if set out beforehand, these may send
        By any means least liable to loss),
Ketchup, Soy, Chili-vinegar, and Harvey,
Or, by the Lord! a Lent will well nigh starve ye;

IX

65 That is to say, if your religion's Roman,
        And you at Rome would do as Romans do,
According to the proverb, – although no man,
        If foreign, is obliged to fast; and you,
If Protestant, or sickly, or a woman,
70   Would rather dine in sin on a ragout –
Dine and be d—d! I dont mean to be coarse,
But that's the penalty, to say no worse.

X

Of all the places where the Carnival
        Was most facetious in the days of yore,
75 For dance, and song, and serenade, and ball,
        And masque, and mime, and mystery and more,
Than I have time to tell now, or at all,
        Venice the bell from every city bore, –
And at the moment when I fix my story,
80   That sea-born city was in all her glory.

XI

They've pretty faces yet, those same Venetians,
 Black eyes, arch'd brows, and sweet expressions still;
Such as of old were copied from the Grecians,
 In ancient arts by moderns mimick'd ill;
85 And like so many Venuses of Titian's
 (The best's at Florence – see it, if ye will,)
They look when leaning over the balcony,
Or stepp'd from out a picture by Giorgione,

XII

Whose tints are truth and beauty at their best;
90 And when you to Manfrini's palace go,
That picture (howsoever fine the rest)
 Is loveliest to my mind of all the show;
It may perhaps be also to *your* zest,
 And that's the cause I rhyme upon it so:
95 'Tis but a portrait of his son, and wife,
And self; but *such* a woman! love in life!

XIII

Love in full life and length, not love ideal,
 No, nor ideal beauty, that fine name.
But something better still, so very real,
100 That the sweet model must have been the same;
A thing that you would purchase, beg, or steal,
 Wer't not impossible, besides a shame:
The face recalls some face, as 'twere with pain,
You once have seen, but ne'er will see again;

XIV

105 One of those forms which flit by us, when we
 Are young, and fix our eyes on every face;
And, oh! the loveliness at times we see
 In momentary gliding, the soft grace,
The youth, the bloom, the beauty which agree,
110 In many a nameless being we retrace,
Whose course and home we knew not, nor shall know,
Like the lost Pleiad[1] seen no more below.

---

1. 'Quæ septem dici sex tamen esse solent.' – OVID.

XV

I said that like a picture by Giorgione
    Venetian women were, and so they *are*,
115 Particularly seen from a balcony,
    (For beauty's sometimes best set off afar)
And there, just like a heroine of Goldoni,
    They peep from out the blind, or o'er the bar;
And truth to say, they're mostly very pretty,
120 And rather like to show it, more's the pity!

XVI

For glances beget ogles, ogles sighs,
    Sighs wishes, wishes words, and words a letter,
Which flies on wings of light-heel'd Mercuries,
    Who do such things because they know no better;
125 And then, God knows, what mischief may arise,
    When love links two young people in one fetter,
Vile assignations, and adulterous beds,
Elopements, broken vows, and hearts, and heads.

XVII

Shakspeare described the sex in Desdemona
130   As very fair, but yet suspect in fame,
And to this day from Venice to Verona
    Such matters may be probably the same,
Except that since those times was never known a
    Husband whom mere suspicion could inflame
135 To suffocate a wife no more than twenty,
Because she had a 'cavalier servente.'

XVIII

Their jealousy (if they are ever jealous)
    Is of a fair complexion altogether,
Not like that sooty devil of Othello's
140   Which smothers women in a bed of feather,
But worthier of these much more jolly fellows,
    When weary of the matrimonial tether
His head for such a wife no mortal bothers,
But takes at once another, or another's.

XIX

145 Didst ever see a Gondola? For fear
    You should not, I'll describe it you exactly:
'Tis a long cover'd boat that's common here,
    Carved at the prow, built lightly, but compactly,
Row'd by two rowers, each call'd 'Gondolier,'
150   It glides along the water looking blackly,
Just like a coffin clapt in a canoe,
Where none can make out what you say or do.

XX

And up and down the long canals they go,
    And under the Rialto shoot along,
155 By night and day, all paces, swift or slow,
    And round the theatres, a sable throng,
They wait in their dusk livery of woe, –
    But not to them do woful things belong,
For sometimes they contain a deal of fun,
160 Like mourning coaches when the funeral's done.

XXI

But to my story. – 'Twas some years ago,
    It may be thirty, forty, more or less,
The carnival was at its height, and so
    Were all kinds of buffoonery and dress;
165 A certain lady went to see the show,
    Her real name I know not, nor can guess,
And so we'll call her Laura, if you please,
Because it slips into my verse with ease.

XXII

She was not old, nor young, nor at the years
170   Which certain people call a '*certain age*,'
Which yet the most uncertain age appears,
    Because I never heard, nor could engage
A person yet by prayers, or bribes, or tears,
    To name, define by speech, or write on page,
175 The period meant precisely by that word, –
Which surely is exceedingly absurd.

XXIII

Laura was blooming still, had made the best
 Of time, and time return'd the compliment,
And treated her genteelly, so that, dress'd,
180 She look'd extremely well where'er she went;
A pretty woman is a welcome guest,
 And Laura's brow a frown had rarely bent,
Indeed she shone all smiles, and seem'd to flatter
Mankind with her black eyes for looking at her.

XXIV

185 She was a married woman; 'tis convenient,
 Because in Christian countries 'tis a rule
To view their little slips with eyes more lenient;
 Whereas if single ladies play the fool,
(Unless within the period intervenient
190 A well-timed wedding makes the scandal cool)
I don't know how they ever can get over it,
Except they manage never to discover it.

XXV

Her husband sail'd upon the Adriatic,
 And made some voyages, too, in other seas,
195 And when he lay in quarantine for pratique
 (A forty days' precaution 'gainst disease),
His wife would mount, at times, her highest attic,
 For thence she could discern the ship with ease:
He was a merchant trading to Aleppo,
200 His name Giuseppe, call'd more briefly, Beppo.

XXVI

He was a man as dusky as a Spaniard,
 Sunburnt with travel, yet a portly figure;
Though colour'd, as it were, within a tanyard,
 He was a person both of sense and vigour –
205 A better seaman never yet did man yard:
 And *she*, although her manners show'd no rigour,
Was deem'd a woman of the strictest principle,
So much as to be thought almost invincible.

XXVII

But several years elapsed since they had met;
210   Some people thought the ship was lost, and some
That he had somehow blunder'd into debt,
    And did not like the thought of steering home;
And there were several offer'd any bet,
    Or that he would, or that he would not come,
215 For most men (till by losing render'd sager)
Will back their own opinions with a wager.

XXVIII

'Tis said that their last parting was pathetic,
    As partings often are, or ought to be,
And their presentiment was quite prophetic
220   That they should never more each other see,
(A sort of morbid feeling, half poetic,
    Which I have known occur in two or three,)
When kneeling on the shore upon her sad knee,
He left this Adriatic Ariadne.

XXIX

225 And Laura waited long, and wept a little,
    And thought of wearing weeds, as well she might;
She almost lost all appetite for victual,
    And could not sleep with ease alone at night;
She deem'd the window-frames and shutters brittle
230   Against a daring housebreaker or sprite,
And so she thought it prudent to connect her
With a vice-husband, *chiefly* to *protect her*.

XXX

She chose, (and what is there they will not choose,
    If only you will but oppose their choice?)
235 Till Beppo should return from his long cruise,
    And bid once more her faithful heart rejoice,
A man some women like, and yet abuse –
    A coxcomb was he by the public voice;
A Count of wealth, they said, as well as quality,
240 And in his pleasures of great liberality.

XXXI

And then he was a Count, and then he knew
    Music, and dancing, fiddling, French and Tuscan;
The last not easy, be it known to you,
    For few Italians speak the right Etruscan.
245 He was a critic upon operas, too,
    And knew all niceties of the sock and buskin;
And no Venetian audience could endure a
Song, scene, or air, when he cried 'seccatura!'

XXXII

His 'bravo' was decisive, for that sound
250   Hush'd 'Academie' sigh'd in silent awe;
The fiddlers trembled as he look'd around,
    For fear of some false note's detected flaw.
The 'prima donna's' tuneful heart would bound,
    Dreading the deep damnation of his 'bah!'
255 Soprano, basso, even the contra-alto,
Wish'd him five fathom under the Rialto.

XXXIII

He patronised the Improvisatori,
    Nay, could himself extemporise some stanzas,
Wrote rhymes, sang songs, could also tell a story,
260   Sold pictures, and was skilful in the dance as
Italians can be, though in this their glory
    Must surely yield the palm to that which France has;
In short, he was a perfect cavaliero,
And to his very valet seem'd a hero.

XXXIV

265 Then he was faithful too, as well as amorous;
    So that no sort of female could complain,
Although they're now and then a little clamorous,
    He never put the pretty souls in pain;
His heart was one of those which most enamour us,
270   Wax to receive, and marble to retain.
He was a lover of the good old school,
Who still become more constant as they cool.

XXXV

No wonder such accomplishments should turn
    A female head, however sage and steady –
275 With scarce a hope that Beppo could return,
    In law he was almost as good as dead, he
Nor sent, nor wrote, nor show'd the least concern,
    And she had waited several years already;
And really if a man won't let us know
280 That he's alive, he's *dead*, or should be so.

XXXVI

Besides, within the Alps, to every woman,
    (Although, God knows, it is a grievous sin,)
'Tis, I may say, permitted to have *two* men;
    I can't tell who first brought the custom in,
285 But 'Cavalier Serventes' are quite common,
    And no one notices nor cares a pin;
And we may call this (not to say the worst)
A *second* marriage which corrupts the *first*.

XXXVII

The word was formerly a 'Cicisbeo,'
290   But *that* is now grown vulgar and indecent;
The Spaniards call the person a 'Cortejo,'[1]
    For the same mode subsists in Spain, though recent;
In short it reaches from the Po to Teio,
    And may perhaps at last be o'er the sea sent.
295 But Heaven preserve Old England from such courses!
Or what becomes of damage and divorces?

XXXVIII

However, I still think, with all due deference
    To the fair *single* part of the Creation,
That married ladies should preserve the preference
300   In *tête-à-tête* or general conversation –

1. Cortejo is pronounced Corteho, with an aspirate, according to the Arabesque guttural. It means what there is as yet no precise name for in England, though the practice is as common as in any tramontane country whatever.

And this I say without peculiar reference
   To England, France, or any other nation –
Because they know the world, and are at ease,
And being natural, naturally please.

XXXIX

305 'Tis true, your budding Miss is very charming,
   But shy and awkward at first coming out,
So much alarm'd, that she is quite alarming,
   All Giggle, Blush; half Pertness, and half Pout
And glancing at *Mamma*, for fear there's harm in
310   What you, she, it, or they, may be about,
The Nursery still lisps out in all they utter –
Besides, they always smell of bread and butter.

XL

But 'Cavalier Servente' is the phrase
   Used in politest circles to express
315 This supernumerary slave, who stays
   Close to the lady as a part of dress,
Her word the only law which he obeys.
   His is no sinecure, as you may guess;
Coach, servants, gondola, he goes to call,
320 And carries fan and tippet, gloves and shawl.

XLI

With all its sinful doings, I must say,
   That Italy's a pleasant place to me,
Who love to see the Sun shine every day,
   And vines (not nail'd to walls) from tree to tree
325 Festoon'd, much like the back scene of a play,
   Or melodrame, which people flock to see,
When the first act is ended by a dance
In vineyards copied from the south of France.

XLII

I like on Autumn evenings to ride out,
330   Without being forced to bid my groom be sure
My cloak is round his middle strapp'd about,
   Because the skies are not the most secure;

I know too that, if stopp'd upon my route,
   Where the green alleys windingly allure,
335 Reeling with *grapes* red waggons choke the way, –
In England 'twould be dung, dust, or a dray.

XLIII

I also like to dine on becaficas,
   To see the Sun set, sure he'll rise to-morrow,
Not through a misty morning twinkling weak as
340   A drunken man's dead eye in maudlin sorrow,
But with all Heaven t'himself; that day will break as
   Beauteous as cloudless, nor be forced to borrow
That sort of farthing candlelight which glimmers
Where reeking London's smoky caldron simmers.

XLIV

345 I love the language, that soft bastard Latin,
   Which melts like kisses from a female mouth,
And sounds as if it should be writ on satin,
   With syllables which breathe of the sweet South,
And gentle liquids gliding all so pat in,
350   That not a single accent seems uncouth,
Like our harsh northern whistling, grunting guttural,
Which we're obliged to hiss, and spit, and sputter all.

XLV

I like the women too (forgive my folly),
   From the rich peasant cheek of ruddy bronze,
355 And large black eyes that flash on you a volley
   Of rays that say a thousand things at once,
To the high dama's brow, more melancholy,
   But clear, and with a wild and liquid glance,
Heart on her lips, and soul within her eyes,
360 Soft as her clime, and sunny as her skies.

XLVI

Eve of the land which still is Paradise!
  Italian beauty! didst thou not inspire
Raphael,[1] who died in thy embrace, and vies
  With all we know of Heaven, or can desire,
365 In what he hath bequeath'd us? – in what guise,
  Though flashing from the fervour of the lyre,
Would *words* describe thy past and present glow,
While yet Canova can create below?[2]

XLVII

'England! with all thy faults I love thee still,'
370   I said at Calais, and have not forgot it;
I like to speak and lucubrate my fill;
  I like the government (but that is not it);
I like the freedom of the press and quill;
  I like the Habeas Corpus (when we've got it);
375 I like a parliamentary debate,
Particularly when 'tis not too late;

XLVIII

I like the taxes, when they're not too many;
  I like a seacoal fire, when not too dear;
I like a beef-steak, too, as well as any;
380   Have no objection to a pot of beer;
I like the weather, when it is not rainy,
  That is, I like two months of every year.
And so God save the Regent, Church, and King!
Which means that I like all and every thing.

1. For the received accounts of the cause of Raphael's death, see his lives.
2. (In talking thus, the writer, more especially
    Of women, would be understood to say,
  He speaks as a spectator, not officially,
    And always, reader, in a modest way;

  Perhaps, too, in no very great degree shall he
    Appear to have offended in this lay,
  Since, as all know, without the sex, our sonnets
  Would seem unfinish'd, like their untrimm'd bonnets.)

                                    (Signed)   PRINTER'S DEVIL.

XLIX

385 Our standing army, and disbanded seamen,
        Poor's rate, Reform, my own, the nation's debt,
    Our little riots just to show we are free men,
        Our trifling bankruptcies in the Gazette,
    Our cloudy climate, and our chilly women,
390   All these I can forgive, and those forget,
    And greatly venerate our recent glories,
    And wish they were not owing to the Tories.

L

    But to my tale of Laura, – for I find
        Digression is a sin, that by degrees
395 Becomes exceeding tedious to my mind,
        And, therefore, may the reader too displease –
    The gentle reader, who may wax unkind,
        And caring little for the author's ease,
    Insist on knowing what he means, a hard
400 And hapless situation for a bard.

LI

    Oh that I had the art of easy writing
        What should be easy reading! could I scale
    Parnassus, where the Muses sit inditing
        Those pretty poems never known to fail,
405 How quickly would I print (the world delighting)
        A Grecian, Syrian, or Assyrian tale;
    And sell you, mix'd with western sentimentalism,
    Some samples of the finest Orientalism.

LII

    But I am but a nameless sort of person,
410   (A broken Dandy lately on my travels)
    And take for rhyme, to hook my rambling verse on,
        The first that Walker's Lexicon unravels,
    And when I can't find that, I put a worse on,
        Not caring as I ought for critics' cavils;
415 I've half a mind to tumble down to prose,
    But verse is more in fashion – so here goes.

LIII

The Count and Laura made their new arrangement,
   Which lasted, as arrangements sometimes do,
For half a dozen years without estrangement;
420   They had their little differences, too;
Those jealous whiffs, which never any change meant:
   In such affairs there probably are few
Who have not had this pouting sort of squabble,
From sinners of high station to the rabble.

LIV

425 But, on the whole, they were a happy pair,
   As happy as unlawful love could make them;
The gentleman was fond, the lady fair,
   Their chains so slight, 'twas not worth while to break
         them:
The world beheld them with indulgent air;
430   The pious only wish'd 'the devil take them!'
He took them not; he very often waits,
And leaves old sinners to be young ones' baits.

LV

But they were young: Oh! what without our youth
   Would love be! What would youth be without love!
435 Youth lends it joy, and sweetness, vigour, truth,
   Heart, soul, and all that seems as from above;
But, languishing with years, it grows uncouth –
   One of few things experience don't improve,
Which is, perhaps, the reason why old fellows
440 Are always so preposterously jealous.

LVI

It was the Carnival, as I have said
   Some six and thirty stanzas back, and so
Laura the usual preparations made,
   Which you do when your mind's made up to go
445 To-night to Mrs. Boehm's masquerade,
   Spectator, or partaker in the show;
The only difference known between the cases
Is – here, we have six weeks of 'varnish'd faces.'

LVII

Laura, when dress'd, was (as I sang before)
450   A pretty woman as was ever seen,
Fresh as the Angel o'er a new inn door,
   Or frontispiece of a new Magazine,
With all the fashions which the last month wore,
   Colour'd, and silver paper leaved between
455 That and the title-page, for fear the press
Should soil with parts of speech the parts of dress.

LVIII

They went to the Ridotto; – 'tis a hall
   Where people dance, and sup, and dance again;
Its proper name, perhaps, were a masqued ball,
460   But that's of no importance to my strain;
'Tis (on a smaller scale) like our Vauxhall,
   Excepting that it can't be spoilt by rain:
The company is 'mix'd' (the phrase I quote is
As much as saying, they're below your notice);

LIX

465 For a 'mix'd company' implies that, save
   Yourself and friends, and half a hundred more,
Whom you may bow to without looking grave,
   The rest are but a vulgar set, the bore
Of public places, where they basely brave
470   The fashionable stare of twenty score
Of well-bred persons, call'd '*the World*;' but I,
Although I know them, really don't know why.

LX

This is the case in England; at least was
   During the dynasty of Dandies, now
475 Perchance succeeded by some other class
   Of imitated imitators: – how
Irreparably soon decline, alas!
   The demagogues of fashion: all below
Is frail; how easily the world is lost
480 By love, or war, and now and then by frost!

LXI

Crush'd was Napoleon by the northern Thor,
　　Who knock'd his army down with icy hammer,
Stopp'd by the *elements*, like a whaler, or
　　A blundering novice in his new French grammar;
485　Good cause had he to doubt the chance of war,
　　And as for Fortune – but I dare not d——n her,
Because, were I to ponder to infinity,
The more I should believe in her divinity.

LXII

She rules the present, past, and all to be yet,
490　She gives us luck in lotteries, love, and marriage;
I cannot say that she's done much for me yet;
　　Not that I mean her bounties to disparage,
We've not yet closed accounts, and we shall see yet
　　How much she'll make amends for past miscarriage;
495　Meantime the goddess I'll no more importune,
Unless to thank her when she's made my fortune.

LXIII

To turn, – and to return; – the devil take it!
　　This story slips for ever through my fingers,
Because, just as the stanza likes to make it,
500　It needs must be – and so it rather lingers;
This form of verse began, I can't well break it,
　　But must keep time and tune like public singers;
But if I once get through my present measure,
I'll take another when I'm next at leisure.

LXIV

505　They went to the Ridotto ('tis a place
　　To which I mean to go myself to-morrow,
Just to divert my thoughts a little space,
　　Because I'm rather hippish, and may borrow
Some spirits, guessing at what kind of face
510　May lurk beneath each mask; and as my sorrow
Slackens its pace sometimes, I'll make, or find,
Something shall leave it half an hour behind.)

LXV

Now Laura moves along the joyous crowd,
     Smiles in her eyes, and simpers on her lips:
515 To some she whispers, others speaks aloud;
     To some she curtsies, and to some she dips,
Complains of warmth, and this complaint avow'd,
     Her lover brings the lemonade, she sips;
She then surveys, condemns, but pities still
520 Her dearest friends for being dress'd so ill.

LXVI

One has false curls, another too much paint,
     A third – where did she buy that frightful turban?
A fourth's so pale she fears she's going to faint,
     A fifth's look's vulgar, dowdyish, and suburban,
525 A sixth's white silk has got a yellow taint,
     A seventh's thin muslin surely will be her bane,
And lo! an eighth appears, – 'I'll see no more!'
For fear, like Banquo's kings, they reach a score.

LXVII

Meantime, while she was thus at others gazing,
530   Others were levelling their looks at her;
She heard the men's half-whisper'd mode of praising,
     And, till 'twas done, determined not to stir;
The women only thought it quite amazing
     That, at her time of life, so many were
535 Admirers still, – but men are so debased,
Those brazen creatures always suit their taste.

LXVIII

For my part, now, I ne'er could understand
     Why naughty women – but I won't discuss
A thing which is a scandal to the land,
540   I only don't see why it should be thus;
And if I were but in a gown and band,
     Just to entitle me to make a fuss,
I'd preach on this till Wilberforce and Romilly
Should quote in their next speeches from my homily.

LXIX

545 While Laura thus was seen and seeing, smiling,
        Talking, she knew not why and cared not what,
    So that her female friends, with envy broiling,
        Beheld her airs and triumph, and all that;
    And well dress'd males still kept before her filing,
550   And passing bow'd and mingled with her chat;
    More than the rest one person seem'd to stare
    With pertinacity that's rather rare.

LXX

    He was a Turk, the colour of mahogany;
        And Laura saw him, and at first was glad,
555 Because the Turks so much admire philogyny,
        Although their usage of their wives is sad;
    'Tis said they use no better than a dog any
        Poor woman, whom they purchase like a pad:
    They have a number, though they ne'er exhibit 'em,
560 Four wives by law, and concubines 'ad libitum.'

LXXI

    They lock them up, and veil, and guard them daily,
        They scarcely can behold their male relations,
    So that their moments do not pass so gaily
        As is supposed the case with northern nations;
565 Confinement, too, must make them look quite palely:
        And as the Turks abhor long conversations,
    Their days are either pass'd in doing nothing,
    Or bathing, nursing, making love, and clothing.

LXXII

    They cannot read, and so don't lisp in criticism;
570   Nor write, and so they don't affect the muse;
    Were never caught in epigram or witticism,
        Have no romances, sermons, plays, reviews, –
    In harams learning soon would make a pretty schism!
        But luckily these beauties are no 'Blues,'
575 No bustling Botherbys have they to show 'em
    'That charming passage in the last new poem.'

LXXIII

No solemn, antique gentleman of rhyme,
   Who having angled all his life for fame,
And getting but a nibble at a time,
580   Still fussily keeps fishing on, the same
Small 'Triton of the minnows,' the sublime
   Of mediocrity, the furious tame,
The echo's echo, usher of the school
Of female wits, boy bards – in short, a fool!

LXXIV

585   A stalking oracle of awful phrase,
   The approving '*Good!*' (by no means GOOD in law)
Humming like flies around the newest blaze,
   The bluest of bluebottles you e'er saw,
Teasing with blame, excruciating with praise,
590   Gorging the little fame he gets all raw,
Translating tongues he knows not even by letter,
And sweating plays so middling, bad were better.

LXXV

One hates an author that's *all author*, fellows
   In foolscap uniforms turn'd up with ink,
595 So very anxious, clever, fine, and jealous,
   One don't know what to say to them, or think,
Unless to puff them with a pair of bellows;
   Of coxcombry's worst coxcombs e'en the pink
Are preferable to these shreds of paper,
600 These unquench'd snuffings of the midnight taper.

LXXVI

Of these same we see several, and of others,
   Men of the world, who know the world like men,
Scott, Rogers, Moore, and all the better brothers,
   Who think of something else besides the pen;
605 But for the children of the 'mighty mother's,'
   The would-be wits and can't-be gentlemen,
I leave them to their daily 'tea is ready,'
Smug coterie, and literary lady.

LXXVII

The poor dear Mussulwomen whom I mention
610   Have none of these instructive pleasant people,
And *one* would seem to them a new invention,
    Unknown as bells within a Turkish steeple;
I think 'twould almost be worth while to pension
    (Though best-sown projects very often reap ill)
615 A missionary author, just to preach
Our Christian usage of the parts of speech.

LXXVIII

No chemistry for them unfolds her gasses,
    No metaphysics are let loose in lectures,
No circulating library amasses
620   Religious novels, moral tales, and strictures
Upon the living manners, as they pass us;
    No exhibition glares with annual pictures;
They stare not on the stars from out their attics,
Nor deal (thank God for that!) in mathematics.

LXXIX

625 Why I thank God for that is no great matter,
    I have my reasons, you no doubt suppose,
And as, perhaps, they would not highly flatter,
    I'll keep them for my life (to come) in prose;
I fear I have a little turn for satire,
630   And yet methinks the older that one grows
Inclines us more to laugh than scold, though laughter
Leaves us so doubly serious shortly after.

LXXX

Oh, Mirth and Innocence! Oh, Milk and Water!
    Ye happy mixtures of more happy days!
635 In these sad centuries of sin and slaughter,
    Abominable Man no more allays
His thirst with such pure beverage. No matter,
    I love you both, and both shall have my praise:
Oh, for old Saturn's reign of sugar-candy! —
640 Meantime I drink to your return in brandy.

LXXXI

Our Laura's Turk still kept his eyes upon her,
　　Less in the Mussulman than Christian way,
Which seems to say, 'Madam, I do you honour,
　　And while I please to stare, you'll please to stay:'
645 Could staring win a woman, this had won her,
　　But Laura could not thus be led astray;
She had stood fire too long and well, to boggle
Even at this stranger's most outlandish ogle.

LXXXII

The morning now was on the point of breaking,
650 　　A turn of time at which I would advise
Ladies who have been dancing, or partaking
　　In any other kind of exercise,
To make their preparations for forsaking
　　The ball-room ere the sun begins to rise,
655 Because when once the lamps and candles fail,
His blushes make them look a little pale.

LXXXIII

I've seen some balls and revels in my time,
　　And stay'd them over for some silly reason,
And then I look'd (I hope it was no crime)
660 　　To see what lady best stood out the season;
And though I've seen some thousands in their prime,
　　Lovely and pleasing, and who still may please on,
I never saw but one (the stars withdrawn),
Whose bloom could after dancing dare the dawn.

LXXXIV

665 The name of this Aurora I'll not mention,
　　Although I might, for she was nought to me
More than that patent work of God's invention,
　　A charming woman, whom we like to see;
But writing names would merit reprehension,
670 　　Yet if you like to find out this fair *she*,
At the next London or Parisian ball
You still may mark her cheek, out-blooming all.

LXXXV

Laura, who knew it would not do at all
    To meet the daylight after seven hours sitting
675 Among three thousand people at a ball,
    To make her curtsy thought it right and fitting;
The Count was at her elbow with her shawl,
    And they the room were on the point of quitting,
When lo! those cursed gondoliers had got
680 Just in the very place where they *should not*.

LXXXVI

In this they're like our coachmen, and the cause
    Is much the same – the crowd, and pulling, hauling,
With blasphemies enough to break their jaws,
    They make a never intermitting bawling.
685 At home, our Bow-street gemmen keep the laws,
    And here a sentry stands within your calling;
But for all that, there is a deal of swearing,
And nauseous words past mentioning or bearing.

LXXXVII

The Count and Laura found their boat at last,
690   And homeward floated o'er the silent tide,
Discussing all the dances gone and past;
    The dancers and their dresses, too, beside;
Some little scandals eke: but all aghast
    (As to their palace stairs the rowers glide)
695 Sate Laura by the side of her Adorer,
When lo! the Mussulman was there before her.

LXXXVIII

'Sir,' said the Count, with brow exceeding grave,
    'Your unexpected presence here will make
It necessary for myself to crave
700   Its import? But perhaps 'tis a mistake;
I hope it is so; and at once to wave
    All compliment, I hope so for *your* sake;
You understand my meaning, or you *shall*.'
'Sir,' (quoth the Turk) ''tis no mistake at all.

LXXXIX

705 'That lady is *my wife!*' Much wonder paints
  The lady's changing cheek, as well it might;
But where an Englishwoman sometimes faints,
  Italian females don't do so outright;
They only call a little on their saints,
710   And then come to themselves, almost or quite;
Which saves much hartshorn, salts, and sprinkling faces,
And cutting stays, as usual in such cases.

XC

She said, — what could she say? Why, not a word:
  But the Count courteously invited in
715 The stranger, much appeased by what he heard:
  'Such things, perhaps, we'd best discuss within,'
Said he; 'don't let us make ourselves absurd
  In public, by a scene, nor raise a din,
For then the chief and only satisfaction
720 Will be much quizzing on the whole transaction.'

XCI

They enter'd, and for coffee call'd — it came,
  A beverage for Turks and Christians both,
Although the way they make it's not the same.
  Now Laura, much recover'd, or less loth
725 To speak, cries 'Beppo! what's your pagan name?
  Bless me! your beard is of amazing growth!
And how came you to keep away so long?
Are you not sensible 'twas very wrong?

XCII

And are you *really*, *truly*, now a Turk?
730   With any other women did you wive?
Is't true they use their fingers for a fork?
  Well, that's the prettiest shawl — as I'm alive!
You'll give it me? They say you eat no pork.
  And how so many years did you contrive
735 To — Bless me! did I ever? No, I never
Saw a man grown so yellow! How's your liver?

XCIII

Beppo! that beard of yours becomes you not;
  It shall be shaved before you're a day older:
Why do you wear it? Oh! I had forgot –
740   Pray don't you think the weather here is colder?
How do I look? You shan't stir from this spot
  In that queer dress, for fear that some beholder
Should find you out, and make the story known.
How short your hair is! Lord! how grey it's grown!'

XCIV

745   What answer Beppo made to these demands
  Is more than I know. He was cast away
About where Troy stood once, and nothing stands;
  Became a slave of course, and for his pay
Had bread and bastinadoes, till some bands
750   Of pirates landing in a neighbouring bay,
He join'd the rogues and prosper'd, and became
A renegado of indifferent fame.

XCV

But he grew rich, and with his riches grew so
  Keen the desire to see his home again,
755   He thought himself in duty bound to do so,
  And not be always thieving on the main;
Lonely he felt, at times, as Robin Crusoe,
  And so he hired a vessel come from Spain,
Bound for Corfu: she was a fine polacca,
760   Mann'd with twelve hands, and laden with tobacco.

XCVI

Himself, and much (heaven knows how gotten!) cash,
  He then embark'd with risk of life and limb,
And got clear off, although the attempt was rash;
  He said that *Providence* protected him –
765   For my part, I say nothing – lest we clash
  In our opinions: – well, the ship was trim,
Set sail, and kept her reckoning fairly on,
Except three days of calm when off Cape Bonn.

XCVII

They reach'd the island, he transferr'd his lading.
And self and live stock, to another bottom,
And pass'd for a true Turkey-merchant, trading
With goods of various names, but I've forgot 'em.
However, he got off by this evading,
Or else the people would perhaps have shot him;
And thus at Venice landed to reclaim
His wife, religion, house, and Christian name.

XCVIII

His wife received, the patriarch re-baptized him,
(He made the church a present, by the way);
He then threw off the garments which disguised him,
And borrow'd the Count's smallclothes for a day:
His friends the more for his long absence prized him,
Finding he'd wherewithal to make them gay,
With dinners, where he oft became the laugh of them,
For stories – but *I* don't believe the half of them.

XCIX

Whate'er his youth had suffer'd, his old age
With wealth and talking make him some amends;
Though Laura sometimes put him in a rage,
I've heard the Count and he were always friends.
My pen is at the bottom of a page,
Which being finish'd, here the story ends;
'Tis to be wish'd it had been sooner done,
But stories somehow lengthen when begun.

Epistle to Mr Murray

I

My dear Mr Murray,
You're in a damn'd hurry
    To set up this ultimate Canto;
But (if they don't rob us)
5   You'll see Mr Hobhouse
      Will bring it safe in his portmanteau.

II

For the Journal you hint of,
As ready to print off,
    No doubt you do right to commend it;
10   But as yet I have writ off
The devil a bit of
      Our 'Beppo:' – when copied, I'll send it.

III

In the mean time you've 'Gally'
Whose verses all tally,
15   Perhaps you may say he's a Ninny,
But if you abashed are
Because of 'Alashtar'
      He'll piddle another 'Phrosine.' –

IV

Then you've [Sotheby]'s Tour, –
20   No great things, to be sure, –
    You could hardly begin with a less work;
For the pompous rascallion,
Who don't speak Italian
      Nor French, must have scribbled by Guesswork.

V

25 No doubt he's a rare man
    Without knowing German
        Translating his way up Parnassus,
    And now still absurder
    He meditates Murder
30   As you'll see in the trash he calls *Tasso's*.

VI

    But you've others his betters
    The real men of letters –
        Your orators – critics – and wits –
    And I'll bet that your Journal
35 (Pray is it diurnal?)
        Will pay with your luckiest hits. –

VII

    You can make any loss up
    With 'Spence' and his gossip,
        A work which must surely succeed;
40 Then Queen Mary's Epistle-craft,
    With the new 'Fytte' of 'Whistlecraft,'
        Must make people purchase and read.

VIII

    Then you've General Gordon
    Who girded his sword on,
45   To serve with a Muscovite master,
    And help him to polish
    A nation so owlish,
        They thought shaving their beards a disaster.

IX

    For the man, 'poor and shrewd,'
50 With whom you'd conclude
        A compact without more delay,
    Perhaps some such pen is
    Still extant in Venice;
        But please, sir, to mention *your pay*.

X

55 Now tell me some news
Of your friends and the Muse
 Of the Bar, – or the Gown – or the House,
From Canning the tall wit
To Wilmot the small wit
60 Ward's creeping Companion and *Louse* –

XI

Who's so damnably bit
With fashion and Wit
 That he crawls on the surface like Vermin,
But an Insect in both, –
65 By his Intellect's growth
 Of what *size* you may quickly determine.

XII

Now, I'll put out my taper
(I've finished my paper
 For these stanzas you see on the *brink* stand),
70 There's a whore on my right,
For I rhyme best at night
 When a C—t is tied close to my *inkstand*.

XIII

It was Mahomet's notion
That comical motion
75 Increased his 'devotion in prayer' –
If that tenet holds good
In a Prophet, it should
 In a poet be equally fair. –

XIV

For in rhyme or in love
80 (Which both come from above)
 I'll stand with our '*Tommy*' or '*Sammy*'
But the Sopha and lady
Are both of them ready
 And so, here's 'Good night to you dammee!'

MAZEPPA

ADVERTISEMENT

'Celui qui remplissait alors cette place était un gentilhomme
Polonais, nommé Mazeppa, né dans le palatinat de Padolie:
il avait été élevé page de Jean Casimir, et avait pris à sa cour
quelque teinture des belles-lettres. Une intrigue qu'il eut
dans sa jeunesse avec la femme d'un gentilhomme Polonais
ayant été découverte, le mari le fit lier tout nu sur un cheval
farouche, et le laissa aller en cet état. Le cheval, qui était du
pays de l'Ukraine, y retourna, et y porta Mazeppa, demi-
mort de fatigue et de faim. Quelques paysans le secoururent:
il resta longtems parmi eux, et se signala dans plusieurs
courses contre les Tartares. La supériorité de ses lumières
lui donna une grande considération parmi les Cosaques: sa
réputation s'augmentait de jour en jour, obligea le Czar à le
faire Prince de l'Ukraine.' – VOLTAIRE, *Hist. de Charles
XII*. p. 196.

'Le roi fuyant, et poursuivi, eut son cheval tué sous lui; le
Colonel Gieta, blessé, et perdant tout son sang, lui donna le
sien. Ainsi on remit deux fois à cheval, dans la fuite, ce
conquérant qui n'avait pu y monter pendant la bataille.' –
p. 216.

'Le roi alla par un autre chemin avec quelques cavaliers.
Le carrosse, où il était, rompit dans la marche; on le remit à
cheval. Pour comble de disgrace, il s'égara pendant la nuit
dans un bois; là, son courage ne pouvant plus suppléer à ses
forces épuisées, les douleurs de sa blessure devenues plus
insupportables par la fatigue, son cheval étant tombé de
lassitude, il se coucha quelques heures au pied d'un arbre, en
danger d'être surpris à tout moment par les vainqueurs, qui
le cherchaient de tous côtés.' – p. 218.

I

'Twas after dread Pultowa's day,
    When fortune left the royal Swede,
Around a slaughter'd army lay,
    No more to combat and to bleed.
5 The power and glory of the war,
    Faithless as their vain votaries, men,
Had pass'd to the triumphant Czar,
    And Moscow's walls were safe again,
Until a day more dark and drear,
10 And a more memorable year,
Should give to slaughter and to shame
A mightier host and haughtier name;
A greater wreck, a deeper fall,
A shock to one – a thunderbolt to all.

II

15 Such was the hazard of the die;
The wounded Charles was taught to fly
By day and night through field and flood,
Stain'd with his own and subjects' blood;
For thousands fell that flight to aid:
20 And not a voice was heard t' upbraid
Ambition in his humbled hour,
When truth had nought to dread from power.
His horse was slain, and Gieta gave
His own – and died the Russians' slave.
25 This too sinks after many a league
Of well sustain'd, but vain fatigue;
And in the depth of forests, darkling
The watch-fires in the distance sparkling –
    The beacons of surrounding foes –
30 A king must lay his limbs at length.
    Are these the laurels and repose
For which the nations strain their strength?
They laid him by a savage tree,
In outworn nature's agony;
35 His wounds were stiff – his limbs were stark –
The heavy hour was chill and dark;

The fever in his blood forbade
A transient slumber's fitful aid:
And thus it was; but yet through all,
40   Kinglike the monarch bore his fall,
And made, in this extreme of ill,
His pangs the vassals of his will:
All silent and subdued were they,
As once the nations round him lay.

III

45   A band of chiefs! – alas! how few,
        Since but the fleeting of a day
Had thinn'd it; but this wreck was true
        And chivalrous: upon the clay
Each sate him down, all sad and mute,
50   Beside his monarch and his steed,
For danger levels man and brute,
        And all are fellows in their need.
Among the rest, Mazeppa made
His pillow in an old oak's shade –
55   Himself as rough, and scarce less old,
The Ukraine's hetman, calm and bold;
But first, outspent with this long course,
The Cossack prince rubb'd down his horse,
And made for him a leafy bed,
60   And smooth'd his fetlocks and his mane,
        And slack'd his girth, and stripp'd his rein,
And joy'd to see how well he fed;
For until now he had the dread
His wearied courser might refuse
65   To browse beneath the midnight dews:
But he was hardy as his lord,
And little cared for bed and board;
But spirited and docile too;
Whate'er was to be done, would do.
70   Shaggy and swift, and strong of limb,
All Tartar-like he carried him;
Obey'd his voice, and came to call,
And knew him in the midst of all:

Though thousands were around, – and Night,
75 Without a star, pursued her flight, –
That steed from sunset until dawn
His chief would follow like a fawn.

IV
This done, Mazeppa spread his cloak,
And laid his lance beneath his oak,
80 Felt if his arms in order good
The long day's march had well withstood –
If still the powder fill'd the pan,
And flints unloosen'd kept their lock –
His sabre's hilt and scabbard felt,
85 And whether they had chafed his belt –
And next the venerable man,
From out his havresack and can,
Prepared and spread his slender stock;
And to the monarch and his men
90 The whole or portion offer'd then
With far less of inquietude
Than courtiers at a banquet would.
And Charles of this his slender share
With smiles partook a moment there,
95 To force of cheer a greater show,
And seem above both wounds and woe; –
And then he said – 'Of all our band,
Though firm of heart and strong of hand,
In skirmish, march, or forage, none
100 Can less have said or more have done
Than thee, Mazeppa! On the earth
So fit a pair had never birth,
Since Alexander's days till now,
As thy Bucephalus and thou:
105 All Scythia's fame to thine should yield
For pricking on o'er flood and field.'
Mazeppa answer'd – 'Ill betide
The school wherein I learn'd to ride!'

Quoth Charles – 'Old Hetman, wherefore so,
110   Since thou hast learn'd the art so well?'
Mazeppa said – ''Twere long to tell;
And we have many a league to go,
With every now and then a blow,
And ten to one at least the foe,
115   Before our steeds may graze at ease,
Beyond the swift Borysthenes:
And, sire, your limbs have need of rest,
And I will be the sentinel
Of this your troop.' – 'But I request,'
120   Said Sweden's monarch, 'thou wilt tell
This tale of thine, and I may reap,
Perchance, from this the boon of sleep;
For at this moment from my eyes
The hope of present slumber flies.'

125   'Well, sire, with such a hope, I'll track
My seventy years of memory back:
I think 'twas in my twentieth spring, –
Ay, 'twas, – when Casimir was king –
John Casimir, – I was his page
130   Six summers, in my earlier age:
A learned monarch, faith! was he,
And most unlike your majesty:
He made no wars, and did not gain
New realms to lose them back again;
135   And (save debates in Warsaw's diet)
He reign'd in most unseemly quiet;
Not that he had no cares to vex,
He loved the muses and the sex;
And sometimes these so froward are,
140   They made him wish himself at war;
But soon his wrath being o'er, he took
Another mistress, or new book:
And then he gave prodigious fêtes –
All Warsaw gather'd round his gates
145   To gaze upon his splendid court,
And dames, and chiefs, of princely port:

He was the Polish Solomon,
So sung his poets, all but one,
Who, being unpension'd, made a satire,
150   And boasted that he could not flatter.
It was a court of jousts and mimes,
Where every courtier tried at rhymes;
Even I for once produced some verses,
And sign'd my odes 'Despairing Thyrsis.'
155   There was a certain Palatine,
       A count of far and high descent,
Rich as a salt or silver mine;[1]
And he was proud, ye may divine,
       As if from heaven he had been sent:
160   He had such wealth in blood and ore
       As few could match beneath the throne;
And he would gaze upon his store,
And o'er his pedigree would pore,
Until by some confusion led,
165   Which almost look'd like want of head,
       He thought their merits were his own.
His wife was not of his opinion –
       His junior she by thirty years –
Grew daily tired of his dominion;
170   And, after wishes, hopes, and fears,
       To virtue a few farewell tears,
A restless dream or two, some glances
At Warsaw's youth, some songs, and dances,
Awaited but the usual chances,
175   Those happy accidents which render
The coldest dames so very tender,
To deck her Count with titles given,
'Tis said, as passports into heaven;
But, strange to say, they rarely boast
180   Of these, who have deserved them most.

---

1. This comparison of a 'salt' mine' may, perhaps, be permitted to a Pole, as
the wealth of the country consists greatly in the salt mines.

V

'I was a goodly stripling then;
　　At seventy years I so may say,
That there were few, or boys or men,
　　Who, in my dawning time of day,
185　Of vassal or of knight's degree,
　　Could vie in vanities with me;
　　For I had strength, youth, gaiety,
　　A port, not like to this ye see,
　　But smooth, as all is rugged now;
190　　For time, and care, and war, have plough'd
　　My very soul from out my brow;
　　　And thus I should be disavow'd
　　By all my kind and kin, could they
　　Compare my day and yesterday;
195　This change was wrought, too, long ere age
　　Had ta'en my features for his page:
　　With years, ye know, have not declined
　　My strength, my courage, or my mind,
　　Or at this hour I should not be
200　Telling old tales beneath a tree,
　　With starless skies my canopy.
　　But let me on: Theresa's form –
　　Methinks it glides before me now,
　　Between me and yon chestnut's bough,
205　The memory is so quick and warm;
　　And yet I find no words to tell
　　The shape of her I loved so well:
　　She had the Asiatic eye,
　　　Such as our Turkish neighbourhood,
210　　Hath mingled with our Polish blood,
　　Dark as above us is the sky;
　　But through it stole a tender light,
　　Like the first moonrise of midnight;
　　Large, dark, and swimming in the stream,
215　Which seem'd to melt to its own beam;
　　All love, half languor, and half fire,
　　Like saints that at the stake expire,

And lift their raptured looks on high,
As though it were a joy to die.
220 A brow like a midsummer lake,
    Transparent with the sun therein,
When waves no murmur dare to make,
    And heaven beholds her face within.
A cheek and lip – but why proceed?
225   I loved her then – I love her still;
And such as I am, love indeed
    In fierce extremes – in good and ill.
But still we love even in our rage,
And haunted to our very age
230 With the vain shadow of the past,
As is Mazeppa to the last.

VI

'We met – we gazed – I saw, and sigh'd,
She did not speak, and yet replied;
There are ten thousand tones and signs
235 We hear and see, but none defines –
Involuntary sparks of thought,
Which strike from out the heart o'erwrought,
And form a strange intelligence,
Alike mysterious and intense,
240 Which link the burning chain that binds,
Without their will, young hearts and minds;
Conveying, as the electric wire,
We know not how, the absorbing fire. –
I saw, and sigh'd – in silence wept,
245 And still reluctant distance kept,
Until I was made known to her,
And we might then and there confer
Without suspicion – then, even then,
    I long'd, and was resolved to speak;
250 But on my lips they died again,
    The accents tremulous and weak,
Until one hour. – There is a game,
    A frivolous and foolish play,
    Wherewith we while away the day;
255 It is – I have forgot the name –

And we to this, it seems, were set,
By some strange chance, which I forget:
I reck'd not if I won or lost,
    It was enough for me to be
260   So near to hear, and oh! to see
The being whom I loved the most. —
I watch'd her as a sentinel,
(May ours this dark night watch as well!)
Until I saw, and thus it was,
265 That she was pensive, nor perceived
Her occupation, nor was grieved
Nor glad to lose or gain; but still
Play'd on for hours, as if her will
Yet bound her to the place, though not
270 That hers might be the winning lot.
Then through my brain the thought did pass
Even as a flash of lightning there,
That there was something in her air
Which would not doom me to despair;
275 And on the thought my words broke forth,
    All incoherent as they were —
Their eloquence was little worth,
But yet she listen'd — 'tis enough —
    Who listens once will listen twice;
280   Her heart, be sure, is not of ice,
And one refusal no rebuff.

VII

'I loved, and was beloved again —
    They tell me, Sire, you never knew
    Those gentle frailties; if 'tis true,
285 I shorten all my joy or pain;
To you 'twould seem absurd as vain;
But all men are not born to reign,
Or o'er their passions, or as you
Thus o'er themselves and nations too.
290 I am — or rather was — a prince,
    A chief of thousands, and could lead
    Them on where each would foremost bleed;

But could not o'er myself evince
The like control – But to resume:
295   I loved, and was beloved again;
In sooth, it is a happy doom,
    But yet where happiest ends in pain. –
We met in secret, and the hour
Which led me to that lady's bower
300 Was fiery Expectation's dower.
My days and nights were nothing – all
Except that hour which doth recall
In the long lapse from youth to age
    No other like itself – I'd give
305   The Ukraine back again to live
It o'er once more – and be a page,
The happy page, who was the lord
Of one soft heart, and his own sword,
And had no other gem nor wealth
310 Save nature's gift of youth and health. –
We met in secret – doubly sweet,
Some say, they find it so to meet;
I know not that – I would have given
    My life but to have call'd her mine
315 In the full view of earth and heaven;
    For I did oft and long repine
That we could only meet by stealth.

VIII
'For lovers there are many eyes,
    And such there were on us; – the devil
320   On such occasions should be civil –
The devil! – I'm loth to do him wrong,
    It might be some untoward saint,
Who would not be at rest too long,
    But to his pious bile gave vent –
325 But one fair night, some lurking spies
Surprised and seized us both.
The Count was something more than wroth –
I was unarm'd; but if in steel,
All cap-à-pie from head to heel,

330   What 'gainst their numbers could I do? –
    'Twas near his castle, far away
        From city or from succour near,
    And almost on the break of day;
    I did not think to see another,
335   My moments seem'd reduced to few;
    And with one prayer to Mary Mother,
        And, it may be, a saint or two,
    As I resigned me to my fate,
    They led me to the castle gate:
340   Theresa's doom I never knew,
    Our lot was henceforth separate. –
    An angry man, ye may opine,
    Was he, the proud Count Palatine;
    And he had reason good to be,
345   But he was most enraged lest such
        An accident should chance to touch
    Upon his future pedigree;
    Nor less amazed, that such a blot
    His noble 'scutcheon should have got,
350   While he was highest of his line;
        Because unto himself he seem'd
        The first of men, nor less he deem'd
    In others' eyes, and most in mine.
    'Sdeath! with a *page* – perchance a king
355   Had reconciled him to the thing;
    But with a stripling of a page –
    I felt – but cannot paint his rage.

IX

'"Bring forth the horse!" – the horse was brought;
        In truth, he was a noble steed,
360   A Tartar of the Ukraine breed,
    Who look'd as though the speed of thought
    Were in his limbs; but he was wild,
        Wild as the wild deer, and untaught,
    With spur and bridle undefiled –
365   'Twas but a day he had been caught
    And snorting, with erected mane,
    And struggling fiercely, but in vain,

In the full foam of wrath and dread
To me the desert-born was led:
370 They bound me on, that menial throng,
Upon his back with many a thong;
Then loosed him with a sudden lash –
Away! – away! – and on we dash! –
Torrents less rapid and less rash.

            x

375 'Away! – away! – My breath was gone –
I saw not where he hurried on:
'Twas scarcely yet the break of day,
And on he foam'd – away! – away! –
The last of human sounds which rose,
380 As I was darted from my foes,
Was the wild shout of savage laughter,
Which on the wind came roaring after
A moment from that rabble rout:
With sudden wrath I wrench'd my head,
385   And snapp'd the cord, which to the mane
    Had bound my neck in lieu of rein,
And, writhing half my form about,
Howl'd back my curse; but 'midst the tread,
The thunder of my courser's speed,
390 Perchance they did not hear nor heed:
It vexes me – for I would fain
Have paid their insult back again.
I paid it well in after days:
There is not of that castle gate,
395 Its drawbridge and portcullis' weight,
Stone, bar, moat, bridge, or barrier left;
Nor of its fields a blade of grass,
    Save what grows on a ridge of wall,
    Where stood the hearth-stone of the hall;
400 And many a time ye there might pass,
Nor dream that e'er that fortress was:
I saw its turrets in a blaze,
Their crackling battlements all cleft,
    And the hot lead pour down like rain

405 From off the scorch'd and blackening roof,
Whose thickness was not vengeance-proof.
    They little thought that day of pain,
When launch'd, as on the lightning's flash,
They bade me to destruction dash,
410   That one day I should come again,
With twice five thousand horse, to thank
    The Count for his uncourteous ride.
They play'd me then a bitter prank,
    When, with the wild horse for my guide,
415 They bound me to his foaming flank:
At length I play'd them one as frank —
For time at last sets all things even —
    And if we do but watch the hour,
    There never yet was human power
420 Which could evade, if unforgiven,
The patient search and vigil long
Of him who treasures up a wrong.

XI
'Away, away, my steed and I,
    Upon the pinions of the wind,
425   All human dwellings left behind;
We sped like meteors through the sky,
When with its crackling sound the night
Is chequer'd with the northern light:
Town — village — none were on our track,
430   But a wild plain of far extent,
And bounded by a forest black;
    And, save the scarce seen battlement
On distant heights of some strong hold,
Against the Tartars built of old,
435 No trace of man. The year before
A Turkish army had march'd o'er;
And where the Spahi's hoof hath trod,
The verdure flies the bloody sod: —
The sky was dull, and dim, and gray,
440   And a low breeze crept moaning by —
    I could have answer'd with a sigh —

But fast we fled, away, away –
And I could neither sigh nor pray;
And my cold sweat-drops fell like rain
445 Upon the courser's bristling mane;
But, snorting still with rage and fear,
He flew upon his far career:
At times I almost thought, indeed,
He must have slacken'd in his speed;
450 But no – my bound and slender frame
  Was nothing to his angry might,
And merely like a spur became:
Each motion which I made to free
My swoln limbs from their agony
455   Increased his fury and affright:
I tried my voice, – 'twas faint and low,
But yet he swerved as from a blow;
And, starting to each accent, sprang
As from a sudden trumpet's clang:
460 Meantime my cords were wet with gore,
Which, oozing through my limbs, ran o'er;
And in my tongue the thirst became
A something fierier far than flame.

XII
'We near'd the wild wood – 'twas so wide,
465 I saw no bounds on either side;
'Twas studded with old sturdy trees,
That bent not to the roughest breeze
Which howls down from Siberia's waste,
And strips the forest in its haste, –
470 But these were few, and far between
Set thick with shrubs more young and green,
Luxuriant with their annual leaves,
Ere strown by those autumnal eves
That nip the forest's foliage dead,
475 Discolour'd with a lifeless red,
Which stands thereon like stiffen'd gore
Upon the slain when battle's o'er,

And some long winter's night hath shed
Its frost o'er every tombless head,
480 So cold and stark the raven's beak
May peck unpierced each frozen cheek:
'Twas a wild waste of underwood,
And here and there a chestnut stood,
The strong oak, and the hardy pine;
485   But far apart — and well it were,
Or else a different lot were mine —
     The boughs gave way, and did not tear
My limbs; and I found strength to bear
My wounds, already scarr'd with cold —
490 My bonds forbade to loose my hold.
We rustled through the leaves like wind,
Left shrubs, and trees, and wolves behind;
By night I heard them on the track,
Their troop came hard upon our back,
495 With their long gallop, which can tire
The hound's deep hate, and hunter's fire:
Where'er we flew they follow'd on,
Nor left us with the morning sun;
Behind I saw them, scarce a rood,
500 At day-break winding through the wood,
And through the night had heard their feet
Their stealing, rustling step repeat.
Oh! how I wish'd for spear or sword,
At least to die amidst the horde,
505 And perish — if it must be so —
At bay, destroying many a foe.
When first my courser's race begun,
I wish'd the goal already won;
But now I doubted strength and speed.
510 Vain doubt! his swift and savage breed
Had nerved him like the mountain-roe;
Nor faster falls the blinding snow
Which whelms the peasant near the door
Whose threshold he shall cross no more,
515 Bewilder'd with the dazzling blast,
Than through the forest-paths he past —

Untired, untamed, and worse than wild;
All furious as a favour'd child
Balk'd of its wish; or fiercer still –
520 A woman piqued – who has her will.

XIII

'The wood was past; 'twas more than noon,
But chill the air, although in June;
Or it might be my veins ran cold –
Prolong'd endurance tames the bold;
525 And I was then not what I seem,
But headlong as a wintry stream,
And wore my feelings out before
.I well could count their causes o'er:
And what with fury, fear, and wrath,
530 The tortures which beset my path,
Cold, hunger, sorrow, shame, distress,
Thus bound in nature's nakedness;
Sprung from a race whose rising blood
When stirr'd beyond its calmer mood,
535 And trodden hard upon, is like
The rattle-snake's, in act to strike,
What marvel if this worn-out trunk
Beneath its woes a moment sunk?
The earth gave way, the skies roll'd round,
540 I seem'd to sink upon the ground;
But err'd, for I was fastly bound.
My heart turn'd sick, my brain grew sore,
And throbb'd awhile, then beat no more:
The skies spun like a mighty wheel;
545 I saw the trees like drunkards reel,
And a slight flash sprang o'er my eyes,
Which saw no farther: he who dies
Can die no more than then I died.
O'ertortured by that ghastly ride,
550 I felt the blackness come and go,
       And strove to wake; but could not make
My senses climb up from below:
I felt as on a plank at sea,
When all the waves that dash o'er thee,

555 At the same time upheave and whelm,
And hurl thee towards a desert realm.
My undulating life was as
The fancied lights that flitting pass
Our shut eyes in deep midnight, when
560 Fever begins upon the brain;
But soon it pass'd, with little pain,
But a confusion worse than such:
I own that I should deem it much,
Dying, to feel the same again;
565 And yet I do suppose we must
Feel far more ere we turn to dust:
No matter; I have bared my brow
Full in Death's face – before – and now.

    XIV
'My thoughts came back; where was I? Cold,
570 And numb, and giddy: pulse by pulse
Life reassumed its lingering hold,
And throb by throb: till grown a pang
Which for a moment would convulse,
My blood reflow'd, though thick and chill;
575 My ear with uncouth noises rang,
My heart began once more to thrill;
My sight return'd, though dim; alas!
And thicken'd, as it were, with glass.
Methought the dash of waves was nigh;
580 There was a gleam too of the sky,
Studded with stars; – it is no dream;
The wild horse swims the wilder stream!
The bright broad river's gushing tide
Sweeps, winding onward, far and wide,
585 And we are half-way, struggling o'er
To yon unknown and silent shore.
The waters broke my hollow trance,
And with a temporary strength
My stiffen'd limbs were rebaptized.
590 My courser's broad breast proudly braves,
And dashes off the ascending waves,
And onward we advance!

We reach the slippery shore at length,
    A haven I but little prized,
595 For all behind was dark and drear,
And all before was night and fear.
How many hours of night or day
In those suspended pangs I lay,
I could not tell; I scarcely knew
600 If this were human breath I drew.

XV

'With glossy skin, and dripping mane,
    And reeling limbs, and reeking flank,
The wild steed's sinewy nerves still strain
    Up the repelling bank.
605 We gain the top: a boundless plain
Spreads through the shadow of the night,
    And onward, onward, onward, seems,
    Like precipices in our dreams,
To stretch beyond the sight;
610 And here and there a speck of white,
    Or scatter'd spot of dusky green,
In masses broke into the light,
As rose the moon upon my right.
    But nought distinctly seen
615 In the dim waste would indicate
The omen of a cottage gate;
No twinkling taper from afar
Stood like a hospitable star;
Not even an ignis-fatuus rose
620 To make him merry with my woes:
    That very cheat had cheer'd me then!
Although detected, welcome still,
Reminding me, through every ill,
    Of the abodes of men.

XVI

625 'Onward we went – but slack and slow;
    His savage force at length o'erspent,
The drooping courser, faint and low,
    All feebly foaming went.

A sickly infant had had power
630 To guide him forward in that hour;
    But useless all to me.
His new-born tameness nought avail'd,
My limbs were bound; my force had fail'd,
    Perchance, had they been free.
635 With feeble effort still I tried
To rend the bonds so starkly tied –
    But still it was in vain;
My limbs were only wrung the more,
And soon the idle strife gave o'er,
640   Which but prolong'd their pain:
The dizzy race seem'd almost done,
Although no goal was nearly won:
Some streaks announced the coming sun –
    How slow, alas! he came!
645 Methought that mist of dawning gray
Would never dapple into day;
How heavily it roll'd away –
    Before the eastern flame
Rose crimson, and deposed the stars,
650 And call'd the radiance from their cars,
And fill'd the earth, from his deep throne,
With lonely lustre, all his own.

XVII

'Up rose the sun; the mists were curl'd
Back from the solitary world
655 Which lay around – behind – before;
What booted it to traverse o'er
Plain, forest, river? Man nor brute,
Nor dint of hoof, nor print of foot,
Lay in the wild luxuriant soil;
660 No sign of travel – none of toil;
The very air was mute;
And not an insect's shrill small horn,
Nor matin bird's new voice was borne
From herb nor thicket. Many a werst,
665 Panting as if his heart would burst,

The weary brute still stagger'd on;
And still we were – or seem'd – alone:
At length, while reeling on our way,
Methought I heard a courser neigh,
670   From out yon tuft of blackening firs.
Is it the wind those branches stirs?
No, no! from out the forest prance
    A trampling troop; I see them come!
In one vast squadron they advance!
675   I strove to cry – my lips were dumb.
The steeds rush on in plunging pride;
But where are they the reins to guide?
A thousand horse – and none to ride!
With flowing tail, and flying mane,
680   Wide nostrils – never stretch'd by pain,
Mouths bloodless to the bit or rein,
And feet that iron never shod,
And flanks unscarr'd by spur or rod,
A thousand horse, the wild, the free,
685   Like waves that follow o'er the sea,
    Came thickly thundering on,
As if our faint approach to meet;
The sight re-nerved my courser's feet,
A moment staggering, feebly fleet,
690   A moment, with a faint low neigh,
    He answer'd, and then fell;
With gasps and glazing eyes he lay,
    And reeking limbs immoveable,
    His first and last career is done!
695   On came the troop – they saw him stoop,
    They saw me strangely bound along
    His back with many a bloody thong:
They stop – they start – they snuff the air,
Gallop a moment here and there,
700   Approach, retire, wheel round and round,
Then, plunging back with sudden bound,
Headed by one black mighty steed,
Who seem'd the patriarch of his breed,
    Without a single speck or hair

705 Of white upon his shaggy hide;
They snort – they foam – neigh – swerve aside,
And backward to the forest fly,
By instinct, from a human eye. –
    They left me there to my despair,
710 Link'd to the dead and stiffening wretch,
Whose lifeless limbs beneath me stretch,
Relieved from that unwonted weight,
From whence I could not extricate
Nor him nor me – and there we lay
715   The dying on the dead!
I little deem'd another day
    Would see my houseless, helpless head.

'And there from morn till twilight bound,
I felt the heavy hours toil round,
720 With just enough of life to see
My last of suns go down on me,
In hopeless certainty of mind,
That makes us feel at length resign'd
To that which our foreboding years
725 Presents the worst and last of fears
Inevitable – even a boon,
Nor more unkind for coming soon;
Yet shunn'd and dreaded with such care,
As if it only were a snare
730   That prudence might escape:
At times both wish'd for and implored,
At times sought with self-pointed sword,
Yet still a dark and hideous close
To even intolerable woes,
735   And welcome in no shape.
And, strange to say, the sons of pleasure,
They who have revell'd beyond measure
In beauty, wassail, wine, and treasure,
Die calm, or calmer, oft than he
740 Whose heritage was misery:
For he who hath in turn run through
All that was beautiful and new,

Hath nought to hope, and nought to leave;
And, save the future, (which is view'd
745   Not quite as men are base or good,
But as their nerves may be endued,)
    With nought perhaps to grieve: –
The wretch still hopes his woes must end,
And Death, whom he should deem his friend,
750   Appears, to his distemper'd eyes,
Arrived to rob him of his prize,
The tree of his new Paradise.
To-morrow would have given him all,
Repaid his pangs, repair'd his fall;
755   To-morrow would have been the first
Of days no more deplored or curst,
But bright, and long, and beckoning years,
Seen dazzling through the mist of tears,
Guerdon of many a painful hour;
760   To-morrow would have given him power
To rule, to shine, to smite, to save –
And must it dawn upon his grave?

XVIII

'The sun was sinking – still I lay
    Chain'd to the chill and stiffening steed,
765   I thought to mingle there our clay;
    And my dim eyes of death had need,
    No hope arose of being freed:
I cast my last looks up the sky,
    And there between me and the sun
770   I saw the expecting raven fly,
Who scarce would wait till both should die,
    Ere his repast begun;
He flew, and perch'd, then flew once more,
And each time nearer than before;
775   I saw his wing through twilight flit,
And once so near me he alit
    I could have smote, but lack'd the strength;
But the slight motion of my hand,
And feeble scratching of the sand,

780   The exerted throat's faint struggling noise,
       Which scarcely could be call'd a voice,
           Together scared him off at length. –
       I know no more – my latest dream
           Is something of a lovely star
785   Which fix'd my dull eyes from afar,
       And went and came with wandering beam,
       And of the cold, dull, swimming, dense
       Sensation of recurring sense,
       And then subsiding back to death,
790   And then again a little breath,
       A little thrill, a short suspense,
           An icy sickness curdling o'er
       My heart, and sparks that cross'd my brain –
       A gasp, a throb, a start of pain,
795   A sigh, and nothing more.

                 XIX

       'I woke – Where was I? – Do I see
       A human face look down on me?
       And doth a roof above me close?
       Do these limbs on a couch repose?
800   Is this a chamber where I lie?
       And is it mortal yon bright eye,
       That watches me with gentle glance?
           I closed my own again once more,
       As doubtful that the former trance
805   Could not as yet be o'er.
       A slender girl, long-hair'd, and tall,
       Sate watching by the cottage wall;
       The sparkle of her eye I caught,
       Even with my first return of thought;
810   For ever and anon she threw
           A prying, pitying glance on me
           With her black eyes so wild and free:
       I gazed, and gazed, until I knew
           No vision it could be, –
815   But that I lived, and was released
       From adding to the vulture's feast:

And when the Cossack maid beheld
My heavy eyes at length unseal'd,
She smiled – and I essay'd to speak,
820   But fail'd – and she approach'd, and made
      With lip and finger signs that said,
I must not strive as yet to break
The silence, till my strength should be
Enough to leave my accents free;
825   And then her hand on mine she laid,
And smooth'd the pillow for my head,
And stole along on tiptoe tread,
      And gently oped the door, and spake
In whispers – ne'er was voice so sweet!
830   Even music follow'd her light feet; –
      But those she call'd were not awake,
And she went forth; but, ere she pass'd,
Another look on me she cast,
      Another sign she made, to say,
835   That I had nought to fear, that all
Were near, at my command or call,
      And she would not delay
Her due return: – while she was gone,
Methought I felt too much alone.

XX

840   'She came with mother and with sire –
What need of more? – I will not tire
With long recital of the rest,
Since I became the Cossack's guest.
They found me senseless on the plain –
845   They bore me to the nearest hut –
They brought me into life again –
Me – one day o'er their realm to reign!
      Thus the vain fool who strove to glut
His rage, refining on my pain,
850   Sent me forth to the wilderness,
Bound, naked, bleeding, and alone,
To pass the desert to a throne, –
      What mortal his own doom may guess? –
Let none despond, let none despair!

855 To-morrow the Borysthenes
   May see our coursers graze at ease
   Upon his Turkish bank, – and never
   Had I such welcome for a river
     As I shall yield when safely there.
860 Comrades, good night!' – The Hetman threw
     His length beneath the oak-tree shade,
     With leafy couch already made,
   A bed nor comfortless nor new
   To him, who took his rest whene'er
865 The hour arrived, no matter where:
     His eyes the hastening slumbers steep.
   And if ye marvel Charles forgot
   To thank his tale, *he* wonder'd not, –
     The king had been an hour asleep.

Stanzas to the Po

I

River, that rollest by the ancient walls,
    Where dwells the lady of my love, when she
Walks by thy brink, and there perchance recalls
    A faint and fleeting memory of me;

II

What if thy deep and ample stream should be
    A mirror of my heart, where she may read
The thousand thoughts I now betray to thee,
    Wild as thy wave, and headlong as thy speed!

III

What do I say – a mirror of my heart?
    Are not thy waters sweeping, dark, and strong?
Such as my feelings were and are, thou art;
    And such as thou art were my passions long.

IV

Time may have somewhat tamed them, – not for ever;
    Thou overflow'st thy banks, and not for aye
Thy bosom overboils, congenial river!
    Thy floods subside, and mine have sunk away.

V

But left long wrecks behind, and now again,
    Borne in our old unchanged career, we move;
Thou tendest wildly onwards to the main,
    And I – to loving *one* I should not love.

VI

The current I behold will sweep beneath
    Her native walls and murmur at her feet;
Her eyes will look on thee, when she shall breathe
    The twilight air, unharm'd by summer's heat.

VII

25 She will look on thee, – I have look'd on thee,
    Full of that thought; and, from that moment, ne'er
Thy waters could I dream of, name, or see,
    Without the inseparable sigh for her!

VIII

Her bright eyes will be imaged in thy stream, –
30   Yes! they will meet the wave I gaze on now:
Mine cannot witness, even in a dream,
    That happy wave repass me in its flow!

IX

The wave that bears my tears returns no more:
    Will she return by whom that wave shall sweep? –
35 Both tread thy banks, both wander on thy shore,
    I by thy source, she by the dark-blue deep.

X

But that which keepeth us apart is not
    Distance, nor depth of wave, nor space of earth,
But the distraction of a various lot,
40   As various as the climates of our birth.

XI

A stranger loves the lady of the land,
    Born far beyond the mountains, but his blood
Is all meridian, as if never fann'd
    By the black wind that chills the polar flood.

XII

45 My blood is all meridian; were it not,
    I had not left my clime, nor should I be,
In spite of tortures, ne'er to be forgot,
    A slave again of love, – at least of thee.

XIII

'Tis vain to struggle – let me perish young –
50   Live as I lived, and love as I have loved;
To dust if I return, from dust I sprung,
    And then, at least, my heart can ne'er be moved.

The Isles of Greece

1

The isles of Greece, the isles of Greece!
    Where burning Sappho loved and sung,
Where grew the arts of war and peace,
    Where Delos rose, and Phœbus sprung!
5   Eternal summer gilds them yet,
But all, except their sun, is set.

2

The Scian and the Teian muse,
    The hero's harp, the lover's lute,
Have found the fame your shores refuse:
10   Their place of birth alone is mute
To sounds which echo further west
Than your sires' 'Islands of the Blest.'

3

The mountains look on Marathon –
    And Marathon looks on the sea;
15   And musing there an hour alone,
    I dream'd that Greece might still be free;
For standing on the Persians' grave,
I could not deem myself a slave.

4

A king sate on the rocky brow
20   Which looks o'er sea-born Salamis;
And ships, by thousands, lay below,
    And men in nations; – all were his!
He counted them at break of day –
And when the sun set where were they?

5

25 And where are they? and where art thou,
        My country? On thy voiceless shore
    The heroic lay is tuneless now –
        The heroic bosom beats no more!
    And must thy lyre, so long divine,
30 Degenerate into hands like mine?

6

    'Tis something, in the dearth of fame,
        Though link'd among a fetter'd race,
    To feel at least a patriot's shame,
        Even as I sing, suffuse my face;
35 For what is left the poet here?
    For Greeks a blush – for Greece a tear.

7

    Must *we* but weep o'er days more blest?
        Must *we* but blush? – Our fathers bled.
    Earth! render back from out thy breast
40   A remnant of our Spartan dead!
    Of the three hundred grant but three,
    To make a new Thermopylæ!

8

    What, silent still? and silent all?
        Ah! no; – the voices of the dead
45 Sound like a distant torrent's fall,
        And answer, 'Let one living head,
    But one arise, – we come, we come!'
    'Tis but the living who are dumb.

9

    In vain – in vain: strike other chords;
50   Fill high the cup with Samian wine!
    Leave battles to the Turkish hordes,
        And shed the blood of Scio's vine!
    Hark! rising to the ignoble call –
    How answers each bold Bacchanal!

10

55   You have the Pyrrhic dance as yet;
            Where is the Pyrrhic phalanx gone?
        Of two such lessons, why forget
            The nobler and the manlier one?
        You have the letters Cadmus gave –
60   Think ye he meant them for a slave?

11

        Fill high the bowl with Samian wine!
            We will not think of themes like these!
        It made Anacreon's song divine:
            He served – but served Polycrates –
65   A tyrant; but our masters then
        Were still, at least, our countrymen.

12

        The tyrant of the Chersonese
            Was freedom's best and bravest friend;
        That tyrant was Miltiades!
70   Oh! that the present hour would lend
        Another despot of the kind!
        Such chains as his were sure to bind.

13

        Fill high the bowl with Samian wine!
            On Suli's rock, and Parga's shore,
75   Exists the remnant of a line
            Such as the Doric mothers bore;
        And there, perhaps, some seed is sown,
        The Heracleidan blood might own.

14

        Trust not for freedom to the Franks –
80   They have a king who buys and sells;
        In native swords, and native ranks,
            The only hope of courage dwells:
        But Turkish force, and Latin fraud,
        Would break your shield, however broad.

15

85   Fill high the bowl with Samian wine!
  Our virgins dance beneath the shade –
I see their glorious black eyes shine;
  But gazing on each glowing maid,
My own the burning tear-drop laves,
90   To think such breasts must suckle slaves.

16

Place me on Sunium's marbled steep,
  Where nothing, save the waves and I,
May hear our mutual murmurs sweep;
  There, swan-like, let me sing and die:
95   A land of slaves shall ne'er be mine –
Dash down yon cup of Samian wine!

Francesca of Rimini

From the Inferno *of Dante, Canto the Fifth*

'The land where I was born sits by the seas,[1]
  Upon that shore to which the Po descends,
  With all his followers, in search of peace.
Love, which the gentle heart soon apprehends,
5 Seized him for the fair person which was ta'en
  From me, and me even yet the mode offends.
Love, who to none beloved to love again
  Remits, seized me with wish to please, so strong,
  That, as thou seest, yet, yet it doth remain.
10 Love to one death conducted us along,
  But Cainà waits for him our life who ended:'
  These were the accents utter'd by her tongue. –
Since I first listen'd to these souls offended,
  I bow'd my visage, and so kept it till –
15 'What think'st thou?' said the bard; when I unbended,

1. Ravenna.

And recommenced: 'Alas! unto such ill
 How many sweet thoughts, what strong ecstasies
 Led these their evil fortune to fulfil!'
And then I turn'd unto their side my eyes,
20 And said, 'Francesca, thy sad destinies
 Have made me sorrow till the tears arise.
But tell me, in the season of sweet sighs,
 By what and how thy love to passion rose,
 So as his dim desires to recognise?'
25 Then she to me: 'The greatest of all woes
 Is to remind us of our happy days
 In misery, and that thy teacher knows.
But if to learn our passion's first root preys
 Upon thy spirit with such sympathy,
30 I will do even as he who weeps and says.
We read one day for pastime, seated nigh,
 Of Lancilot, how love enchain'd him too.
 We were alone, quite unsuspiciously.
But oft our eyes met, and our cheeks in hue
35 All o'er discoloured by that reading were;
 But one point only wholly us o'erthrew;
When we read the long-sigh'd-for smile of her,
 To be thus kiss'd by such devoted lover,
 He who from me can be divided ne'er
40 Kiss'd my mouth, trembling in the act all over.
 Accursed was the book and he who wrote!
 That day no further leaf we did uncover. —
While thus one spirit told us of their lot,
 The other wept, so that with pity's thralls
45 I swoon'd as if by death I had been smote,
And fell down even as a dead body falls.'

Stanzas ('*When a man hath no freedom*')

When a man hath no freedom to fight for at home,
　　Let him combat for that of his neighbours;
Let him think of the glories of Greece and of Rome,
　　And get knock'd on the head for his labours.

5　　To do good to mankind is the chivalrous plan,
　　　And is always as nobly requited;
　　Then battle for freedom wherever you can,
　　　And, if not shot or hang'd, you'll get knighted.

SARDANAPALUS

A Tragedy

TO THE ILLUSTRIOUS GOETHE

A STRANGER PRESUMES TO OFFER THE HOMAGE OF A LITERARY
VASSAL TO HIS LIEGE LORD, THE FIRST OF EXISTING WRITERS,
WHO HAS CREATED THE LITERATURE OF HIS OWN COUNTRY,
AND ILLUSTRATED THAT OF EUROPE. THE UNWORTHY
PRODUCTION WHICH THE AUTHOR VENTURES TO INSCRIBE TO
HIM IS ENTITLED SARDANAPALUS.

PREFACE

In publishing the following Tragedies I have only to repeat,
that they were not composed with the most remote view to
the stage. On the attempt made by the Managers in a former
instance, the public opinion has been already expressed. With
regard to my own private feelings, as it seems that they are to
stand for nothing, I shall say nothing.

For the historical foundation of the following compositions
the reader is referred to the Notes.

The Author has in one instance attempted to preserve,
and in the other to approach, the 'unities;' conceiving that
with any very distant departure from them, there may be
poetry, but can be no drama. He is aware of the unpopularity
of this notion in present English literature; but it is not a
system of his own, being merely an opinion, which, not very
long ago, was the law of literature throughout the world, and
is still so in the more civilised parts of it. But 'nous avons
changé tout cela,' and are reaping the advantages of the
change. The writer is far from conceiving that any thing he
can adduce by personal precept or example can at all ap-
proach his regular, or even irregular predecessors: he is
merely giving a reason why he preferred the more regular
formation of a structure, however feeble, to an entire abandon-
ment of all rules whatsoever. Where he has failed, the failure
is in the architect, – and not in the art.

DRAMATIS PERSONÆ

Men
SARDANAPALUS, *King of Nineveh and Assyria, &c.*
ARBACES, *the Mede who aspired to the Throne*
BELESES, *a Chaldean and Soothsayer*
SALEMENES, *the King's Brother-in-law*
ALTADA, *an Assyrian Officer of the Palace*
PANIA
ZAMES
SFERO
BALEA

Women
ZARINA, *the Queen*
MYRRHA, *an Ionian female Slave, and the Favourite of*
   SARDANAPALUS
Women composing the Harem of SARDANAPALUS, *Guards,*
Attendants, Chaldean Priests, Medes, &c. &c.

Scene — a Hall in the Royal Palace of Nineveh.

In this tragedy it has been my intention to follow the account
of Diodorus Siculus; reducing it, however, to such dramatic
regularity as I best could, and trying to approach the unities.
I therefore suppose the rebellion to explode and succeed in
one day by a sudden conspiracy, instead of the long war of
the history.

Act I

SCENE I

A Hall in the Palace.

SALEMENES [*solus*]: He hath wrong'd his queen, but still he
   is her lord;
   He hath wrong'd my sister, still he is my brother;
   He hath wrong'd his people, still he is their sovereign,

And I must be his friend as well as subject:
5   He must not perish thus. I will not see
The blood of Nimrod and Semiramis
Sink in the earth, and thirteen hundred years
Of empire ending like a shepherd's tale;
He must be roused. In his effeminate heart
10   There is a careless courage which corruption
Has not all quench'd, and latent energies,
Repress'd by circumstance, but not destroy'd –
Steep'd, but not drown'd, in deep voluptuousness.
If born a peasant, he had been a man
15   To have reach'd an empire: to an empire born,
He will bequeath none; nothing but a name,
Which his sons will not prize in heritage: –
Yet, not all lost, even yet he may redeem
His sloth and shame, by only being that
20   Which he should be, as easily as the thing
He should not be and is. Were it less toil
To sway his nations than consume his life?
To head an army than to rule a harem?
He sweats in palling pleasures, dulls his soul,
25   And saps his goodly strength, in toils which yield not
Health like the chase, nor glory like the war –
He must be roused. Alas! there is no sound
        [*Sound of soft music heard from within.*]
To rouse him short of thunder. Hark! the lute,
The lyre, the timbrel; the lascivious tinklings
30   Of lulling instruments, the softening voices
Of women, and of beings less than women,
Must chime in to the echo of his revel,
While the great king of all we know of earth
Lolls crown'd with roses, and his diadem
35   Lies negligently by to be caught up
By the first manly hand which dares to snatch it.
Lo, where they come! already I perceive
The reeking odours of the perfumed trains,
And see the bright gems of the glittering girls,
40   At once his chorus and his council, flash

Along the gallery, and amidst the damsels,
As femininely garb'd, and scarce less female,
The grandson of Semiramis, the man-queen. –
He comes! Shall I await him? yes, and front him,
45   And tell him what all good men tell each other,
Speaking of him and his. They come, the slaves.
Led by the monarch subject to his slaves.

SCENE II

[*Enter* SARDANAPALUS *effeminately dressed, his Head
crowned with Flowers, and his Robe negligently flowing,
attended by a Train of Women and young Slaves.*]

SARDANAPALUS [*speaking to some of his attendants*]: Let the
    pavilion over the Euphrates
Be garlanded, and lit, and furnish'd forth
For an especial banquet; at the hour
Of midnight we will sup there: see nought wanting,
5   And bid the galley be prepared. There is
A cooling breeze which crisps the broad clear river:
We will embark anon. Fair nymphs, who deign
To share the soft hours of Sardanapalus,
We'll meet again in that the sweetest hour,
10   When we shall gather like the stars above us,
And you will form a heaven as bright as theirs;
Till then, let each be mistress of her time,
And thou, my own Ionian Myrrha, choose,
Wilt thou along with them or me?
MYRRHA: My lord —
15   SARDANAPALUS: My lord, my life! why answerest, thou so
    coldly?
It is the curse of kings to be so answer'd.
Rule thy own hours, thou rulest mine – say, wouldst
    thou
Accompany our guests, or charm away
The moments from me?
MYRRHA: The king's choice is mine.
20   SARDANAPALUS: I pray thee say not so: my chiefest joy

Is to contribute to thine every wish.
I do not dare to breathe my own desire,
Lest it should clash with thine; for thou art still
Too prompt to sacrifice thy thoughts for others.

25 MYRRHA: I would remain: I have no happiness
Save in beholding thine; yet —
SARDANAPALUS: Yet! what YET?
Thy own sweet will shall be the only barrier
Which ever rises betwixt thee and me.
MYRRHA: I think the present is the wonted hour

30 Of council; it were better I retire.
SALEMENES [*comes forward and says*]: The Ionian slave says
    well: let her retire.
SARDANAPALUS: Who answers? How now, brother?
SALEMENES: The *queen*'s brother,
And your most faithful vassal, royal lord.
SARDANAPALUS [*addressing his train*]: As I have said, let all
    dispose their hours

35 Till midnight, when again we pray your presence.
    [*The court retiring.*]
    [*To* MYRRHA, *who is going:*]
Myrrha! I thought *thou* wouldst remain.
MYRRHA: Great king,
Thou didst not say so.
SARDANAPALUS: But *thou* lookedst it:
I know each glance of those Ionic eyes,
Which said thou wouldst not leave me.
MYRRHA: Sire! your brother —

40 SALEMENES: His *consort*'s brother, minion of Ionia!
How darest *thou* name *me* and not blush?
SARDANAPALUS: Not blush!
Thou hast no more eyes than heart to make her
    crimson
Like to the dying day on Caucasus,
Where sunset tints the snow with rosy shadows,

45 And then reproach her with thine own cold blindness,
Which will not see it. What, in tears, my Myrrha?
SALEMENES: Let them flow on; she weeps for more than one,
And is herself the cause of bitterer tears.

SARDANAPALUS: Cursed be he who caused those tears to
    flow!
50   SALEMENES: Curse not thyself – millions do that
    already.
SARDANAPALUS: Thou dost forget thee: make me not
    remember
    I am a monarch.
SALEMENES: Would thou couldst!
MYRRHA: My sovereign,
    I pray, and thou, too, prince, permit my absence.
SARDANAPALUS: Since it must be so, and this churl has
    check'd
55   Thy gentle spirit, go; but recollect
    That we must forthwith meet: I had rather lose
    An empire than thy presence.
      [*Exit* MYRRHA.]
SALEMENES: It may be,
    Thou wilt lose both, and both for ever!
SARDANAPALUS: Brother,
    I can at least command myself, who listen
60   To language such as this: yet urge me not
    Beyond my easy nature.
SALEMENES: 'Tis beyond
    That easy, far too easy, idle nature,
    Which I would urge thee. O that I could rouse thee!
    Though 'twere against myself.
SARDANAPALUS: By the god Baal!
65   The man would make me tyrant.
SALEMENES: So thou art.
    Think'st thou there is no tyranny but that
    Of blood and chains? The despotism of vice –
    The weakness and the wickedness of luxury –
    The negligence – the apathy – the evils
70   Of sensual sloth – produce ten thousand tyrants,
    Whose delegated cruelty surpasses
    The worst acts of one energetic master,
    However harsh and hard in his own bearing.
    The false and fond examples of thy lusts
75   Corrupt no less than they oppress, and sap

In the same moment all thy pageant power
And those who should sustain it; so that whether
A foreign foe invade, or civil broil
Distract within, both will alike prove fatal:
80 The first thy subjects have no heart to conquer;
The last they rather would assist than vanquish.
SARDANAPALUS: Why, what makes thee the mouth-piece of
the people?
SALEMENES: Forgiveness of the queen, my sister's
wrongs;
A natural love unto my infant nephews;
85 Faith to the king, a faith he may need shortly,
In more than words; respect for Nimrod's line;
Also, another thing thou knowest not.
SARDANAPALUS: What's that?
SALEMENES: To thee an unknown word.
                                        Yet speak it;
I love to learn.
SALEMENES: Virtue.
SARDANAPALUS: Not know the word!
90 Never was word yet rung so in my ears —
Worse than the rabble's shout, or splitting
trumpet:
I've heard thy sister talk of nothing else.
SALEMENES: To change the irksome theme, then, hear of
vice.
SARDANAPALUS: From whom?
SALEMENES: Even from the winds, if thou couldst listen
95 Unto the echoes of the nation's voice.
SARDANAPALUS: Come, I'm indulgent, as thou knowest,
patient,
As thou hast often proved — speak out, what moves
thee?
SALEMENES: Thy peril.
SARDANAPALUS: Say on.
SALEMENES: Thus, then: all the nations,
For they are many, whom thy father left
100 In heritage, are loud in wrath against thee.
SARDANAPALUS: 'Gainst *me!* What would the slaves?

SALEMENES: A king.
SARDANAPALUS: And what
   Am I then?
SALEMENES: In their eyes a nothing; but
   In mine a man who might be something still.
SARDANAPALUS: The railing drunkards! why, what would
   they have?
105   Have they not peace and plenty?
SALEMENES: Of the first
   More than is glorious; of the last, far less
   Than the king recks of.
SARDANAPALUS: Whose then is the crime,
   But the false satraps, who provide no better?
SALEMENES: And somewhat in the monarch who ne'er
   looks
110   Beyond his palace walls, or if he stirs
   Beyond them, 'tis but to some mountain palace,
   Till summer heats wear down. O glorious Baal!
   Who built up this vast empire, and wert made
   A god, or at the least shinest like a god
115   Through the long centuries of thy renown,
   This, thy presumed descendant, ne'er beheld
   As king the kingdoms thou didst leave as hero,
   Won with thy blood, and toil, and time, and peril!
   For what? to furnish imposts for a revel,
120   Or multiplied extortions for a minion.
SARDANAPALUS: I understand thee – thou wouldst have
   me go
   Forth as a conqueror. By all the stars
   Which the Chaldeans read – the restless slaves
   Deserve that I should curse them with their wishes,
125   And lead them forth to glory.
SALEMENES: Wherefore not?
   Semiramis – a woman only – led
   These our Assyrians to the solar shores
   Of Ganges.
SARDANAPALUS: 'Tis most true. And *how* return'd?
SALEMENES: Why, like a *man* – a hero; baffled, but
130   Not vanquish'd. With but twenty guards, she made

Good her retreat to Bactria.

SARDANAPALUS: And how many
Left she behind in India to the vultures?

SALEMENES: Our annals say not.

SARDANAPALUS: Then I will say for them –
That she had better woven within her palace
135   Some twenty garments, than with twenty guards
Have fled to Bactria, leaving to the ravens,
And wolves, and men – the fiercer of the three,
Her myriads of fond subjects. Is *this* glory?
Then let me live in ignominy ever.

140   SALEMENES: All warlike spirits have not the same fate.
Semiramis, the glorious parent of
A hundred kings, although she fail'd in India,
Brought Persia, Media, Bactria, to the realm
Which she once sway'd – and thou *might'st* sway.

SARDANAPALUS: I *sway* them –
145   She but subdued them.

SALEMENES: It may be ere long
That they will need her sword more than your sceptre.

SARDANAPALUS: There was a certain Bacchus, was there
    not?
I've heard my Greek girls speak of such – they say
He was a god, that is, a Grecian god,
150   An idol foreign to Assyria's worship,
Who conquer'd this same golden realm of Ind
Thou prat'st of, where Semiramis was vanquish'd.

SALEMENES: I have heard of such a man; and thou
    perceiv'st
That he is deem'd a god for what he did.

155   SARDANAPALUS: And in his godship I will honour him –
Not much as man. What, ho! my cupbearer!

SALEMENES: What means the king?

SARDANAPALUS: To worship your new god
And ancient conqueror. Some wine, I say.
    [*Enter Cupbearer.*]

SARDANAPALUS [*addressing the Cupbearer*]: Bring me the
    golden goblet thick with gems,
160   Which bears the name of Nimrod's chalice. Hence,

    Fill full, and bear it quickly.
    [Exit Cupbearer.]
SALEMENES: Is this moment
    A fitting one for the resumption of
    Thy yet unslept-off revels?
    [Re-enter Cupbearer, with wine.]
SARDANAPALUS *[taking the cup from him]*: Noble kinsman,
    If these barbarian Greeks of the far shores
165   And skirts of these our realms lie not, this Bacchus
    Conquer'd the whole of India, did he not?
SALEMENES: He did, and thence was deem'd a deity.
SARDANAPALUS: Not so: – of all his conquests a few
     columns,
    Which may be his, and might be mine, if I
170   Thought them worth purchase and conveyance, are
    The landmarks of the seas of gore he shed,
    The realms he wasted, and the hearts he broke.
    But here, here in this goblet is his title
    To immortality – the immortal grape
175   From which he first express'd the soul, and gave
    To gladden that of man, as some atonement
    For the victorious mischiefs he had done.
    Had it not been for this, he would have been
    A mortal still in name as in his grave;
180   And, like my ancestor Semiramis,
    A sort of semi-glorious human monster.
    Here's that which deified him – let it now
    Humanise thee; my surly, chiding brother,
    Pledge me to the Greek god!
SALEMENES: For all thy realms
185   I would not so blaspheme our country's creed.
SARDANAPALUS: That is to say, thou thinkest him a hero,
    That he shed blood by oceans; and no god,
    Because he turn'd a fruit to an enchantment,
    Which cheers the sad, revives the old, inspires
190   The young, makes weariness forget his toil,
    And fear her danger; opens a new world
    When this, the present, palls. Well, then *I* pledge thee
    And *him* as a true man, who did his utmost

In good or evil to surprise mankind.
    [*Drinks.*]
195   SALEMENES: Wilt thou resume a revel at this hour?
SARDANAPALUS: And if I did, 'twere better than a trophy,
    Being bought without a tear. But that is not
    My present purpose: since thou wilt not pledge me,
    Continue what thou pleasest.
       [*To the Cupbearer:*]
                       Boy, retire.
    [Exit Cupbearer.]
200   SALEMENES: I would but have recall'd thee from thy
      dream;
    Better by me awaken'd than rebellion.
SARDANAPALUS: Who should rebel? or why? what cause?
      pretext?
    I am the lawful king, descended from
    A race of kings who knew no predecessors.
205   What have I done to thee, or to the people,
    That thou shouldst rail, or they rise up against me?
SALEMENES: Of what thou hast done to me, I speak not.
SARDANAPALUS: But
    Thou think'st that I have wrong'd the queen: is't
      not so?
SALEMENES: *Think!* Thou hast wrong'd her!
SARDANAPALUS: Patience, prince, and hear me.
210   She has all power and splendour of her station,
    Respect, the tutelage of Assyria's heirs,
    The homage and the appanage of sovereignty.
    I married her as monarchs wed – for state,
    And loved her as most husbands love their wives.
215   If she or thou supposedst I could link me
    Like a Chaldean peasant to his mate,
    Ye knew nor me, nor monarchs, nor mankind.
SALEMENES: I pray thee, change the theme: my blood disdains
    Complaint, and Salemenes' sister seeks not
220   Reluctant love even from Assyria's lord!
    Nor would she deign to accept divided passion
    With foreign strumpets and Ionian slaves.
    The queen is silent.

SARDANAPALUS: And why not her brother?

SALEMENES: I only echo thee the voice of empires,

225   Which he who long neglects not long will govern.

SARDANAPALUS: The ungrateful and ungracious slaves! they
     murmur
     Because I have not shed their blood, nor led them
     To dry into the desert's dust by myriads,
     Or whiten with their bones the banks of Ganges;

230   Nor decimated them with savage laws,
     Nor sweated them to build up pyramids,
     Or Babylonian walls.

SALEMENES: Yet these are trophies
     More worthy of a people and their prince
     Than songs, and lutes, and feasts, and concubines,

235   And lavish'd treasures, and contemned virtues.

SARDANAPALUS: Or for my trophies I have founded cities:
     There's Tarsus and Anchialus, both built
     In one day – what could that blood-loving beldame,
     My martial grandam, chaste Semiramis,

240   Do more, except destroy them?

SALEMENES: 'Tis most true;
     I own thy merit in those founded cities,
     Built for a whim, recorded with a verse
     Which shames both them and thee to coming ages.

SARDANAPALUS: Shame me! By Baal, the cities, though well
     built,

245   Are not more goodly than the verse! Say what
     Thou wilt 'gainst me, my mode of life or rule,
     But nothing 'gainst the truth of that brief record.
     Why, those few lines contain the history
     Of all things human: hear – 'Sardanapalus,

250   The king, and son of Anacyndaraxes,
     In one day built Anchialus and Tarsus.
     Eat, drink, and love; the rest's not worth a fillip.'

SALEMENES: A worthy moral, and a wise inscription,
     For a king to put up before his subjects!

255 SARDANAPALUS: Oh, thou wouldst have me doubtless set
     up edicts –
     'Obey the king – contribute to his treasure –

   Recruit his phalanx – spill your blood at bidding –
   Fall down and worship, or get up and toil.'
   Or thus – 'Sardanapalus on this spot
260 Slew fifty thousand of his enemies.
   These are their sepulchres, and this his trophy.'
   I leave such things to conquerors; enough
   For me, if I can make my subjects feel
   The weight of human misery less, and glide
265 Ungroaning to the tomb: I take no license
   Which I deny to them. We all are men.
SALEMENES: Thy sires have been revered as gods –
SARDANAPALUS: In dust
   And death, where they are neither gods nor men.
   Talk not of such to me! the worms are gods;
270 At least they banqueted upon your gods,
   And died for lack of farther nutriment.
   Those gods were merely men; look to their issue –
   I feel a thousand mortal things about me,
   But nothing godlike, – unless it may be
275 The thing which you condemn, a disposition
   To love and to be merciful, to pardon
   The follies of my species, and (that's human)
   To be indulgent to my own.
SALEMENES: Alas!
   The doom of Nineveh is seal'd. – Woe – woe
280 To the unrivall'd city!
SARDANAPALUS: What dost dread?
SALEMENES: Thou art guarded by thy foes: in a few hours
   The tempest may break out which overwhelms thee,
   And thine and mine; and in another day
   What *is* shall be the past of Belus' race.
285 SARDANAPALUS: What must we dread?
SALEMENES: Ambitious treachery,
   Which has environ'd thee with snares; but yet
   There is resource: empower me with thy signet
   To quell the machinations, and I lay
   The heads of thy chief foes before thy feet.
290 SARDANAPALUS: The heads – how many?
SALEMENES: Must I stay to number

When even thine own's in peril? Let me go;
Give me thy signet – trust me with the rest.
SARDANAPALUS: I will trust no man with unlimited lives.
When we take those from others, we nor know
295   What we have taken, nor the thing we give.
SALEMENES: Wouldst thou not take their lives who seek for
        thine?
SARDANAPALUS: That's a hard question – But I answer,
        Yes.
Cannot the thing be done without? Who are they
Whom thou suspectest? – Let them be arrested.
300   SALEMENES: I would thou wouldst not ask me; the next
        moment
Will send my answer through thy babbling troop
Of paramours, and thence fly o'er the palace,
Even to the city, and so baffle all. –
Trust me.
SARDANAPALUS: Thou knowest I have done so ever:
305   Take thou the signet. [Gives the signet.]
SALEMENES: I have one more request. –
SARDANAPALUS: Name it.
SALEMENES: That thou this night forbear
        the banquet
In the pavilion over the Euphrates.
SARDANAPALUS: Forbear the banquet! Not for all the
        plotters
That ever shook a kingdom! Let them come,
310   And do their worst: I shall not blench for them;
Nor rise the sooner; nor forbear the goblet;
Nor crown me with a single rose the less;
Nor lose one joyous hour. – I fear them not.
SALEMENES: But thou wouldst arm thee, wouldst thou not,
        if needful?
315   SARDANAPALUS: Perhaps. I have the goodliest armour, and
A sword of such a temper; and a bow
And javelin, which might furnish Nimrod forth:
A little heavy, but yet not unwieldy.
And now I think on 't, 'tis long since I've used them,
320   Even in the chase. Hast ever seen them, brother?

SALEMENES: Is this a time for such fantastic trifling? –
   If need be, wilt thou wear them?
SARDANAPALUS: Will I not?
   Oh! if it must be so, and these rash slaves
   Will not be ruled with less, I'll use the sword
325   Till they shall wish it turn'd into a distaff.
SALEMENES: They say thy sceptre's turn'd to that already.
SARDANAPALUS: That's false! but let them say so: the old
      Greeks,
   Of whom our captives often sing, related
   The same of their chief hero, Hercules,
330   Because he loved a Lydian queen: thou seest
   The populace of all the nations seize
   Each calumny they can to sink their sovereigns.
SALEMENES: They did not speak thus of thy fathers.
SARDANAPALUS: No;
   They dared not. They were kept to toil and combat;
335   And never changed their chains but for their armour:
   Now they have peace and pastime, and the license
   To revel and to rail; it irks me not.
   I would not give the smile of one fair girl
   For all the popular breath that e'er divided
340   A name from nothing. What are the rank tongues
   Of this vile herd, grown insolent with feeding,
   That I should prize their noisy praise, or dread
   Their noisome clamour?
SALEMENES: You have said they are men;
   As such their hearts are something.
SARDANAPALUS: So my dogs' are;
345   And better, as more faithful: – but, proceed;
   Thou hast my signet: – since they are tumultuous,
   Let them be temper'd, yet not roughly, till
   Necessity enforce it. I hate all pain,
   Given or received; we have enough within us,
350   The meanest vassal as the loftiest monarch,
   Not to add to each other's natural burthen
   Of mortal misery, but rather lessen,
   By mild reciprocal alleviation,
   The fatal penalties imposed on life:

355   But this they know not, or they will not know.
         I have, by Baal! done all I could to soothe them:
         I made no wars, I added no new imposts,
         I interfered not with their civic lives,
         I let them pass their days as best might suit them,
360   Passing my own as suited me.
SALEMENES: Thou stopp'st
         Short of the duties of a king; and therefore
         They say thou art unfit to be a monarch.
SARDANAPALUS: They lie. – Unhappily, I am unfit
         To be aught save a monarch; else for me
365   The meanest Mede might be the king instead.
SALEMENES:
         There is one Mede, at least, who seeks to be so.
SARDANAPALUS:
         What mean'st thou? – 'tis thy secret; thou desirest
         Few questions, and I'm not of curious nature.
         Take the fit steps; and, since necessity
370   Requires, I sanction and support thee. Ne'er
         Was man who more desired to rule in peace
         The peaceful only: if they rouse me, better
         They had conjured up stern Nimrod from his ashes,
         'The mighty hunter.' I will turn these realms
375   To one wide desert chase of brutes, who *were*,
         But *would* no more, by their own choice, be human.
         What they have found me, they belie; *that which*
         They yet may find me – shall defy their wish
         To speak it worse; and let them thank themselves.
380 SALEMENES: Then thou at last canst feel?
SARDANAPALUS: Feel! who feels not
         Ingratitude?
SALEMENES: I will not pause to answer
         With words, but deeds. Keep thou awake that energy
         Which sleeps at times, but is not dead within thee,
385   And thou may'st yet be glorious in thy reign,
         As powerful in thy realm. Farewell!
              [*Exit* SALEMENES.]
SARDANAPALUS [*solus*]:   Farewell!
         He's gone; and on his finger bears my signet,

Which is to him a sceptre. He is stern
As I am heedless; and the slaves deserve
To feel a master. What may be the danger,
390   I know not: he hath found it, let him quell it.
Must I consume my life – this little life –
In guarding against all may make it less?
It is not worth so much! It were to die
Before my hour, to live in dread of death,
395   Tracing revolt; suspecting all about me,
Because they are near; and all who are remote,
Because they are far. But if it should be so –
If they should sweep me off from earth and empire,
Why, what is earth or empire of the earth?
400   I have loved, and lived, and multiplied my image;
To die is no less natural than those
Acts of this clay! 'Tis true I have not shed
Blood as I might have done, in oceans, till
My name became the synonyme of death –
405   A terror and a trophy. But for this
I feel no penitence; my life is love:
If I must shed blood, it shall be by force.
Till now, no drop from an Assyrian vein
Hath flow'd for me, nor hath the smallest coin
410   Of Nineveh's vast treasures e'er been lavish'd
On objects which could cost her sons a tear:
If then they hate me, 'tis because I hate not:
If they rebel, 'tis because I oppress not.
Oh, men! ye must be ruled with scythes, not sceptres,
415   And mow'd down like the grass, else all we reap
Is rank abundance, and a rotten harvest
Of discontents infecting the fair soil,
Making a desert of fertility. –
I'll think no more. — Within there, ho!
        [*Enter an* ATTENDANT.]
SARDANAPALUS: Slave, tell
420   The Ionian Myrrha we would crave her presence.
ATTENDANT: King, she is here.
        [MYRRHA *enters.*]

SARDANAPALUS [*apart to* ATTENDANT]: Away!
    [Addressing MYRRHA]   Beautiful being!
    Thou dost almost anticipate my heart;
    It throbb'd for thee, and here thou comest: let me
    Deem that some unknown influence, some sweet oracle,
425   Communicates between us, though unseen,
    In absence, and attracts us to each other.

MYRRHA: There doth.

SARDANAPALUS: I know there doth, but not its name:
    What is it?

MYRRHA: In my native land a God,
    And in my heart a feeling like a God's,
430   Exalted; yet I own 'tis only mortal;
    For what I feel is humble, and yet happy –
    That is, it would be happy; but —
        [MYRRHA *pauses.*]

SARDANAPALUS: There comes
    For ever something between us and what
    We deem our happiness: let me remove
435   The barrier which that hesitating accent
    Proclaims to thine, and mine is seal'd.

MYRRHA: My lord! –

SARDANAPALUS: My lord – my king – sire – sovereign;
    thus it is –
    For ever thus, address'd with awe. I ne'er
    Can see a smile, unless in some broad banquet's
440   Intoxicating glare, when the buffoons
    Have gorged themselves up to equality,
    Or I have quaff'd me down to their abasement.
    Myrrha, I can hear all these things, these names,
    Lord – king – sire – monarch – nay, time was I prized
    them;
445   That is, I suffer'd them – from slaves and nobles;
    But when they falter from the lips I love,
    The lips which have been press'd to mine, a chill
    Comes o'er my heart, a cold sense of the falsehood
    Of this my station, which represses feeling
450   In those for whom I have felt most, and makes me

Wish that I could lay down the dull tiara,
And share a cottage on the Caucasus
With thee, and wear no crowns but those of flowers.
MYRRHA: Would that we could!
SARDANAPALUS: And dost *thou* feel this? – Why?
455 MYRRHA: Then thou wouldst know what thou canst never
    know.
SARDANAPALUS: And that is ——
MYRRHA: The true value of a heart;
    At least, a woman's.
SARDANAPALUS: I have proved a thousand –
    A thousand, and a thousand.
MYRRHA: Hearts?
SARDANAPALUS: I think so.
MYRRHA: Not one! the time may come thou may'st.
SARDANAPALUS: It will.
460 Hear, Myrrha; Salemenes has declared –
    Or why or how he hath divined it, Belus,
    Who founded our great realm, knows more than I –
    But Salemenes hath declared my throne
    In peril.
MYRRHA: He did well.
SARDANAPALUS: And say'st *thou* so?
465 Thou whom he spurn'd so harshly, and now dared
    Drive from our presence with his savage jeers,
    And made thee weep and blush?
MYRRHA: I should do both
    More frequently, and he did well to call me
    Back to my duty. But thou spakest of peril –
470 Peril to thee ——
SARDANAPALUS: Ay, from dark plots and snares
    From Medes – and discontented troops and nations.
    I know not what – a labyrinth of things –
    A maze of mutter'd threats and mysteries:
    Thou know'st the man – it is his usual custom.
475 But he is honest. Come, we'll think no more on 't –
    But of the midnight festival.

MYRRHA: 'Tis time
   To think of aught save festivals. Thou hast not
   Spurn'd his sage cautions?
SARDANAPALUS: What? – and dost thou fear?
MYRRHA: Fear? – I'm a Greek, and how should I fear death?
480   A slave, and wherefore should I dread my freedom?
SARDANAPALUS: Then wherefore dost thou turn so pale?
MYRRHA: I love.
SARDANAPALUS: And do not I? I love thee far – far more
   Than either the brief life or the wide realm,
   Which, it may be, are menaced; – yet I blench not.
485 MYRRHA: That means thou lovest nor thyself nor me;
   For he who loves another loves himself,
   Even for that other's sake. This is too rash:
   Kingdoms and lives are not to be so lost.
SARDANAPALUS: Lost! – why, who is the aspiring chief who
   dared
490   Assume to win them?
MYRRHA: Who is he should dread
   To try so much? When he who is their ruler
   Forgets himself, will they remember him?
SARDANAPALUS: Myrrha!
MYRRHA: Frown not upon me: you have smiled
   Too often on me not to make those frowns
495   Bitterer to bear than any punishment
   Which they may augur. – King, I am your subject!
   Master, I am your slave! Man, I have loved you! –
   Loved you, I know not by what fatal weakness,
   Although a Greek, and born a foe to monarchs –
500   A slave, and hating fetters – an Ionian,
   And, therefore, when I love a stranger, more
   Degraded by that passion than by chains!
   Still I have loved you. If that love were strong
   Enough to overcome all former nature,
505   Shall it not claim the privilege to save you?
SARDANAPALUS: *Save* me, my beauty! Thou art very fair,
   And what I seek of thee is love – not safety.
MYRRHA: And without love where dwells security?

SARDANAPALUS: I speak of woman's love.

MYRRHA: The very first
510   Of human life must spring from woman's breast,
       Your first small words are taught you from her lips,
       Your first tears quench'd by her, and your last sighs
       Too often breathed out in a woman's hearing,
       When men have shrunk from the ignoble care
515   Of watching the last hour of him who led them.

SARDANAPALUS: My eloquent Ionian! thou speak'st music,
       The very chorus of the tragic song
       I have heard thee talk of as the favourite pastime
       Of thy far father-land. Nay, weep not — calm thee.

520   MYRRHA: I weep not. — But I pray thee, do not speak
       About my fathers or their land.

SARDANAPALUS: Yet oft
       Thou speakest of them.

MYRRHA: True — true: constant thought
       Will overflow in words unconsciously;
       But when another speaks of Greece, it wounds me.

525   SARDANAPALUS: Well, then, how wouldst thou _save_ me, as
           thou saidst?

MYRRHA: By teaching thee to save thyself, and not
       Thyself alone, but these vast realms, from all
       The rage of the worst war — the war of brethren.

SARDANAPALUS: Why, child, I loathe all war, and warriors;
530   I live in peace and pleasure: what can man
       Do more?

MYRRHA: Alas! my lord, with common men
       There needs too oft the show of war to keep
       The substance of sweet peace; and, for a king,
       'Tis sometimes better to be fear'd than loved.

535   SARDANAPALUS: And I have never sought but for the last.

MYRRHA: And now art neither.

SARDANAPALUS: Dost _thou_ say so, Myrrha?

MYRRHA: I speak of civic popular love, _self_-love,
       Which means that men are kept in awe and law,
       Yet not oppress'd — at least they must not think so;
540   Or if they think so, deem it necessary,

     To ward off worse oppression, their own passions.
     A king of feasts, and flowers, and wine, and revel,
     And love, and mirth, was never king of glory.
SARDANAPALUS: Glory! what's that?
MYRRHA: Ask of the gods thy fathers.
545   SARDANAPALUS: They cannot answer; when the priests
         speak for them,
     'Tis for some small addition to the temple.
MYRRHA: Look to the annals of thine empire's founders.
SARDANAPALUS: They are so blotted o'er with blood, I
        cannot.
     But what wouldst have? the empire *has been* founded.
550   I cannot go on multiplying empires.
MYRRHA: Preserve thine own.
SARDANAPALUS: At least, I will enjoy it.
     Come, Myrrha, let us go on to the Euphrates:
     The hour invites, the galley is prepared,
     And the pavilion, deck'd for our return,
555   In fit adornment for the evening banquet,
     Shall blaze with beauty and with light, until
     It seems unto the stars which are above us
     Itself an opposite star; and we will sit
     Crown'd with fresh flowers like —
MYRRHA: Victims.
SARDANAPALUS: No, like sovereigns,
560   The shepherd king of patriarchal times,
     Who knew no brighter gems than summer wreaths,
     And none but tearless triumphs. Let us on.
       [*Enter* PANIA.]
PANIA: May the king live for ever!
SARDANAPALUS: Not an hour
     Longer than he can love. How my soul hates
565   This language, which makes life itself a lie,
     Flattering dust with eternity. Well, Pania!
     Be brief.
PANIA: I am charged by Salemenes to
     Reiterate his prayer unto the king,
     That for this day, at least, he will not quit
570   The palace: when the general returns,

He will adduce such reasons as will warrant
His daring, and perhaps obtain the pardon
Of his presumption.
SARDANAPALUS: What! am I then coop'd?
Already captive? can I not even breathe
575   The breath of heaven? Tell prince Salemenes,
Were all Assyria raging round the walls
In mutinous myriads, I would still go forth.
PANIA: I must obey, and yet —
MYRRHA: Oh, monarch, listen. —
How many a day and moon thou hast reclined
580   Within these palace walls in silken dalliance,
And never shown thee to thy people's longing;
Leaving thy subjects' eyes ungratified,
The satraps uncontroll'd, the gods unworshipp'd,
And all things in the anarchy of sloth,
585   Till all, save evil, slumber'd through the realm!
And wilt thou not now tarry for a day, —
A day which may redeem thee? Wilt thou not
Yield to the few still faithful a few hours,
For them, for thee, for thy past father's race,
590   And for thy sons' inheritance?
PANIA: 'Tis true!
From the deep urgency with which the prince
Despatch'd me to your sacred presence, I
Must dare to add my feeble voice to that
Which now has spoken.
SARDANAPALUS: No, it must not be.
595   MYRRHA: For the sake of thy realm!
SARDANAPALUS: Away!
PANIA: For that
Of all thy faithful subjects, who will rally
Round thee and thine.
SARDANAPALUS: These are mere fantasies;
There is no peril: — 'tis a sullen scheme
Of Salemenes, to approve his zeal,
600   And show himself more necessary to us.
MYRRHA: By all that's good and glorious take this counsel.
SARDANAPALUS: Business to-morrow.

MYRRHA: Ay, or death to-night.
SARDANAPALUS: Why let it come then unexpectedly
    'Midst joy and gentleness, and mirth and love;
605   So let me fall like the pluck'd rose! – far better
    Thus than be wither'd.
MYRRHA: Then thou wilt not yield,
    Even for the sake of all that ever stirr'd
    A monarch into action, to forego
    A trifling revel.
SARDANAPALUS: No.
MYRRHA: Then yield for *mine*;
610   For my sake!
SARDANAPALUS: Thine, my Myrrha!
MYRRHA: 'Tis the first
    Boon which I ever ask'd Assyria's king.
SARDANAPALUS: That's true, and wer't my kingdom must
      be granted.
    Well, for thy sake, I yield me. Pania, hence!
    Thou hear'st me.
PANIA: And obey.
      [*Exit* PANIA.]
SARDANAPALUS: I marvel at thee.
615   What is thy motive, Myrrha, thus to urge me?
MYRRHA: Thy safety; and the certainty that nought
    Could urge the prince thy kinsman to require
    Thus much from thee, but some impending danger.
SARDANAPALUS: And if I do not dread it, why shouldst
      thou?
620 MYRRHA: Because *thou* dost not fear, I fear for *thee*.
SARDANAPALUS: To-morrow thou wilt smile at these vain
      fancies.
MYRRHA: If the worst come, I shall be where none weep,
    And that is better than the power to smile.
    And thou?
SARDANAPALUS: I shall be king, as heretofore.
625 MYRRHA: Where?
SARDANAPALUS: With Baal, Nimrod, and Semiramis,
    Sole in Assyria, or with them elsewhere.

Fate made me what I am – may make me nothing –
But either that or nothing must I be:
I will not live degraded.
MYRRHA: Hadst thou felt
630   Thus always, none would ever dare degrade thee.
SARDANAPALUS: And who will do so now?
MYRRHA: Dost thou suspect none?
SARDANAPALUS: Suspect! – that's a spy's office. Oh! we
    lose
Ten thousand precious moments in vain words,
And vainer fears. Within there! – ye slaves, deck
635   The hall of Nimrod for the evening revel:
If I must make a prison of our palace,
At least we'll wear our fetters jocundly;
If the Euphrates be forbid us, and
The summer dwelling on its beauteous border,
640   Here we are still unmenaced. Ho! within there!
        [Exit SARDANAPALUS.]
MYRRHA [sola]: Why do I love this man? My country's
    daughters
Love none but heroes. But I have no country!
The slave hath lost all save her bonds. I love him;
And that's the heaviest link of the long chain –
645   To love whom we esteem not. Be it so:
The hour is coming when he'll need all love,
And find none. To fall from him now were baser
Than to have stabb'd him on his throne when highest
Would have been noble in my country's creed:
650   I was not made for either. Could I save him,
I should not love him better, but myself;
And I have need of the last, for I have fallen
In my own thoughts, by loving this soft stranger:
And yet methinks I love him more, perceiving
655   That he is hated of his own barbarians,
The natural foes of all the blood of Greece.
Could I but wake a single thought like those
Which even the Phrygians felt when battling long
'Twixt Ilion and the sea, within his heart,

660   He would tread down the barbarous crowds, and
               triumph.
           He loves me, and I love him; the slave loves
           Her master, and would free him from his vices.
           If not, I have a means of freedom still,
           And if I cannot teach him how to reign,
665   May show him how alone a king can leave
           His throne. I must not lose him from my sight.
               [*Exit.*]

Act II

SCENE I

The Portal of the same Hall of the Palace.

BELESES [*solus*]: The sun goes down: methinks he sets more
               slowly,
           Taking his last look of Assyria's empire.
           How red he glares amongst those deepening clouds,
           Like the blood he predicts. If not in vain,
5   Thou sun that sinkest, and ye stars which rise,
           I have outwatch'd ye, reading ray by ray
           The edicts of your orbs, which make Time tremble
           For what he brings the nations, 'tis the furthest
           Hour of Assyria's years. And yet how calm!
10   An earthquake should announce so great a fall –
           A summer's sun discloses it. Yon disk,
           To the star-read Chaldean, bears upon
           Its everlasting page the end of what
           Seem'd everlasting; but oh! thou true sun!
15   The burning oracle of all that live,
           As fountain of all life, and symbol of
           Him who bestows it, wherefore dost thou limit
           Thy lore unto calamity? Why not
           Unfold the rise of days more worthy thine
20   All-glorious burst from ocean? why not dart
           A beam of hope athwart the future years,
           As of wrath to its days? Hear me! oh, hear me!
           I am thy worshipper, thy priest, thy servant –

I have gazed on thee at thy rise and fall,
25 And bow'd my head beneath thy mid-day beams,
When my eye dared not meet thee. I have watch'd
For thee, and after thee, and pray'd to thee,
And sacrificed to thee, and read, and fear'd thee,
And ask'd of thee, and thou hast answer'd – but
30 Only to thus much: while I speak, he sinks –
Is gone – and leaves his beauty, not his knowledge,
To the delighted west, which revels in
Its hues of dying glory. Yet what is
Death, so it be but glorious? 'Tis a sunset;
35 And mortals may be happy to resemble
The gods but in decay.

[*Enter* ARBACES, *by an inner door.*]

ARBACES: Beleses, why
So rapt in thy devotions? Dost thou stand
Gazing to trace thy disappearing god
Into some realm of undiscover'd day?
Our business is with night – 'tis come.

40 BELESES: But not
Gone.

ARBACES: Let it roll on – we are ready.

BELESES: Yes.
Would it were over!

ARBACES: Does the prophet doubt,
To whom the very stars shine victory?

BELESES: I do not doubt of victory – but the victor.

45 ARBACES: Well, let thy science settle that. Meantime
I have prepared as many glittering spears
As will out-sparkle our allies – your planets.
There is no more to thwart us. The she-king,
That less than woman, is even now upon
50 The waters with his female mates. The order
Is issued for the feast in the pavilion.
The first cup which he drains will be the last
Quaff'd by the line of Nimrod.

BELESES: 'Twas a brave one.

ARBACES: And is a weak one – 'tis worn out – we'll
mend it.

55   BELESES: Art sure of that?
    ARBACES: Its founder was a hunter –
      I am a soldier – what is there to fear?
    BELESES: The soldier.
    ARBACES: And the priest, it may be: but
      If you thought thus, or think, why not retain
      Your king of concubines? why stir me up?
60   Why spur me to this enterprise? your own
      No less than mine?
    BELESES: Look to the sky!
    ARBACES: I look.
    BELESES: What seest thou?
    ARBACES: A fair summer's twilight, and
      The gathering of the stars.
    BELESES: And midst them, mark
      Yon earliest, and the brightest, which so quivers,
65   As it would quit its place in the blue ether.
    ARBACES: Well?
    BELESES: 'Tis thy natal ruler – thy birth planet.
    ARBACES [*touching his scabbard*]: My star is in this scabbard:
        when it shines,
      It shall out-dazzle comets. Let us think
      Of what is to be done to justify
70   Thy planets and their portents. When we conquer,
      They shall have temples – ay, and priests – and thou
      Shalt be the pontiff of – what gods thou wilt;
      For I observe that they are ever just,
      And own the bravest for the most devout.
75   BELESES: Ay, and the most devout for brave – thou hast not
      Seen me turn back from battle.
    ARBACES: No; I own thee
      As firm in fight as Babylonia's captain,
      As skilful in Chaldea's worship: now,
      Will it but please thee to forget the priest,
80   And be the warrior?
    BELESES: Why not both?
    ARBACES: The better;
      And yet it almost shames me, we shall have
      So little to effect. This woman's warfare

Degrades the very conqueror. To have pluck'd
A bold and bloody despot from his throne,
85   And grappled with him, clashing steel with steel,
That were heroic or to win or fall;
But to upraise my sword against this silkworm,
And hear him whine, it may be —

BELESES: Do not deem it:
He has that in him which may make you strife yet;
90   And were he all you think, his guards are hardy,
And headed by the cool, stern Salemenes.

ARBACES: They'll not resist.

BELESES: Why not? they are soldiers.

ARBACES: True,
And therefore need a soldier to command them.

BELESES: That Salemenes is.

ARBACES: But not their king.
95   Besides, he hates the effeminate thing that governs,
For the queen's sake, his sister. Mark you not
He keeps aloof from all the revels?

BELESES: But
Not from the council – there he is ever constant.

ARBACES: And ever thwarted: what would you have more
100   To make a rebel out of? A fool reigning,
His blood dishonour'd, and himself disdain'd:
Why, it is *his* revenge we work for.

BELESES: Could
He but be brought to think so: this I doubt of.

ARBACES: What, if we sound him?

BELESES: Yes – if the time served.

    [*Enter* BALEA.]

105   BALEA: Satraps! The king commands your presence at
The feast to-night.

BELESES: To hear is to obey.
In the pavilion?

BALEA: No; here in the palace.

ARBACES: How! in the palace? it was not thus order'd.

BALEA: It is so order'd now.

ARBACES: And why?

BALEA: I know not.

110   May I retire?
   ARBACES: Stay.
   BELESES [*to* ARBACES *aside*]: Hush! let him go his way.
      [*Alternately to* BALEA:]
      Yes, Balea, thank the monarch, kiss the hem
      Of his imperial robe, and say, his slaves
      Will take the crums he deigns to scatter from
      His royal table at the hour – was't midnight?
115   BALEA: It was: the place, the hall of Nimrod. Lords,
      I humble me before you, and depart.
      [*Exit* BALEA.]
   ARBACES: I like not this same sudden change of place;
      There is some mystery: wherefore should he change it?
   BELESES: Doth he not change a thousand times a day?
120   Sloth is of all things the most fanciful –
      And moves more parasangs in its intents
      Than generals in their marches, when they seek
      To leave their foe at fault. – Why dost thou muse?
   ARBACES: He loved that gay pavilion, – it was ever
125   His summer dotage.
   BELESES: And he loved his queen –
      And thrice a thousand harlotry besides –
      And he has loved all things by turns, except
      Wisdom and glory.
   ARBACES: Still – I like it not.
      If he has changed – why, so must we: the attack
130   Were easy in the isolated bower,
      Beset with drowsy guards and drunken courtiers;
      But in the hall of Nimrod —
   BELESES: Is it so?
      Methought the haughty soldier fear'd to mount
      A throne too easily – does it disappoint thee
135   To find there is a slipperier step or two
      Than what was counted on?
   ARBACES: When the hour comes
      Thou shalt perceive how far I fear or no.
      Thou hast seen my life at stake – and gaily play'd for:
      But here is more upon the die – a kingdom.
140   BELESES: I have foretold already – thou wilt win it:

Then on, and prosper.

ARBACES: Now were I a soothsayer,
I would have boded so much to myself.
But be the stars obey'd – I cannot quarrel
With them, nor their interpreter. Who's here?
    [*Enter* SALEMENES.]

145 SALEMENES: Satraps!

BELESES: My prince!

SALEMENES: Well met – I sought ye both,
But elsewhere than the palace.

ARBACES: Wherefore so?

SALEMENES: 'Tis not the hour.

ARBACES: The hour! – what hour?

SALEMENES: Of midnight.

BELESES: Midnight, my lord!

SALEMENES: What, are you not invited?

BELESES: Oh! yes – we had forgotten.

SALEMENES: Is it usual
150 Thus to forget a sovereign's invitation?

ARBACES: Why – we but now received it.

SALEMENES: Then why here?

ARBACES: On duty.

SALEMENES: On what duty?

BELESES: On the state's.
We have the privilege to approach the presence;
But found the monarch absent.

SALEMENES: And I too
155 Am upon duty.

ARBACES: May we crave its purport?

SALEMENES: To arrest two traitors. Guards! Within there!
    [*Enter Guards.*]

SALEMENES [*continuing*]:   Satraps,
Your swords.

BELESES [*delivering his*]: My lord, behold my scimitar.

ARBACES [*drawing his sword*]: Take mine.

SALEMENES [*advancing*]:   I will.

ARBACES: But in your heart the blade –
The hilt quits not this hand.

SALEMENES [*drawing*]:   How! dost thou brave me?

160   'Tis well – this saves a trial, and false mercy.
       Soldiers, hew down the rebel!
ARBACES: Soldiers! Ay –
       Alone you dare not.
SALEMENES: Alone! foolish slave –
       What is there in thee that a prince should shrink from
       Of open force? We dread thy treason, not
165   Thy strength: thy tooth is nought without its venom –
       The serpent's, not the lion's. Cut him down
BELESES: [*interposing*]: Arbaces! Are you mad? Have I not
       render'd
       My sword? Then trust like me our sovereign's justice.
ARBACES: No – I will sooner trust the stars thou prat'st of,
170   And this slight arm, and die a king at least
       Of my own breath and body – so far that
       None else shall chain them.
SALEMENES [*to the Guards*]:   You hear *him* and *me.*
       Take him not, – kill.
           [*The Guards attack* ARBACES, *who defends himself
           valiantly and dexterously till they waver.*]
SALEMENES: Is it even so; and must
       I do the hangman's office? Recreants! see
175   How you should fell a traitor.
           [SALEMENES *attacks* ARBACES.]
           [*Enter* SARDANAPALUS *and Train.*]
SARDANAPALUS: Hold your hands –
       Upon your lives, I say. What, deaf or drunken?
       My sword! O fool, I wear no sword: here, fellow,
           [*To a Guard:*]
       Give me thy weapon.
           [SARDANAPALUS *snatches a sword from one of the
           soldiers, and rushes between the combatants – they
           separate.*]
SARDANAPALUS: In my very palace!
       What hinders me from cleaving you in twain,
180   Audacious brawlers?
BELESES: Sire, your justice.
SALEMENES: Or –
       Your weakness.

SARDANAPALUS [*raising the sword*]: How?

SALEMENES: Strike! so the blow's repeated
Upon yon traitor – whom you spare a moment,
I trust, for torture – I'm content.

SARDANAPALUS: What – him!
Who dares assail Arbaces?

SALEMENES: I!

SARDANAPALUS: Indeed!
185 Prince, you forget yourself. Upon what warrant?

SALEMENES [*showing the signet*]: Thine.

ARBACES [*confused*]:   The king's!

SALEMENES: Yes! and let the king confirm it.

SARDANAPALUS: I parted not from this for such a purpose.

SALEMENES: You parted with it for your safety – I
Employ'd it for the best. Pronounce in person.
190 Here I am but your slave – a moment past
I was your representative.

SARDANAPALUS: Then sheathe
Your swords.

          [ARBACES *and* SALEMENES *return their swords to the
          scabbards.*]

SALEMENES: Mine's sheathed: I pray you sheathe *not* yours:
'Tis the sole sceptre left you now with safety.

SARDANAPALUS: A heavy one; the hilt, too, hurts my hand.
          [*To a Guard:*]
195 Here, fellow, take thy weapon back. Well, sirs,
What doth this mean?

BELESES: The prince must answer that.

SALEMENES: Truth upon my part, treason upon theirs.

SARDANAPALUS: Treason – Arbaces! treachery and Beleses!
That were an union I will not believe.
200 BELESES: Where is the proof?

SALEMENES: I'll answer that, if once
The king demands your fellow-traitor's sword.

ARABACES [*to* SALEMENES]: A sword which hath been
          drawn as oft as thine
Against his foes.

SALEMENES: And now against his brother,

And in an hour or so against himself.

205 SARDANAPALUS: That is not possible: he dared not; no –
No – I'll not hear of such things. These vain bickerings
Are spawn'd in courts by base intrigues, and baser
Hirelings, who live by lies on good men's lives.
You must have been deceived, my brother.

SALEMENES: First
210 Let him deliver up his weapon, and
Proclaim himself your subject by that duty,
And I will answer all.

SARDANAPALUS: Why, if I thought so –
But no, it cannot be: the Mede Arbaces –
The trusty, rough, true soldier – the best captain
215 Of all who discipline our nations — No,
I'll not insult him thus, to bid him render
The scimitar to me he never yielded
Unto our enemies. Chief, keep your weapon.

SALEMENES [delivering back the signet]: Monarch, take back
your signet.

SARDANAPALUS: No, retain it;
220 But use it with more moderation.

SALEMENES: Sire,
I used it for your honour, and restore it
Because I cannot keep it with my own.
Bestow it on Arbaces.

SARDANAPALUS: So I should:
He never ask'd it.

SALEMENES: Doubt not, he will have it,
225 Without that hollow semblance of respect.

BELESES: I know not what hath prejudiced the prince
So strongly 'gainst two subjects, than whom none
Have been more zealous for Assyria's weal.

SALEMENES: Peace, factious priest, and faithless soldier!
thou
230 Unit'st in thy own person the worst vices
Of the most dangerous orders of mankind.
Keep thy smooth words and juggling homilies
For those who know thee not. Thy fellow's sin
Is, at the least, a bold one, and not temper'd

235   By the tricks taught thee in Chaldea.
     BELESES: Hear him,
       My liege – the son of Belus! he blasphemes
       The worship of the land, which bows the knee
       Before your fathers.
     SARDANAPALUS: Oh! for that I pray you
       Let him have absolution. I dispense with
240   The worship of dead men; feeling that I
       Am mortal, and believing that the race
       From whence I sprung are – what I see them – ashes.
     BELESES: King! Do not deem so: they are with the stars,
       And —
     SARDANAPALUS: You shall join them there ere they will
          rise,
245   If you preach farther – Why, *this* is rank treason.
     SALEMENES: My lord!
     SARDANAPALUS: To school me in the worship of
       Assyria's idols! Let him be released –
       Give him his sword.
     SALEMENES: My lord, and king, and brother,
       I pray ye pause.
     SARDANAPALUS: Yes, and be sermonised,
250   And dinn'd, and deafen'd with dead men and Baal,
       And all Chaldea's starry mysteries.
     BELESES: Monarch! respect them.
     SARDANAPALUS: Oh! for that – I love them:
       I love to watch them in the deep blue vault,
       And to compare them with my Myrrha's eyes;
255   I love to see their rays redoubled in
       The tremulous silver of Euphrates' wave,
       As the light breeze of midnight crisps the broad
       And rolling water, sighing through the sedges
       Which fringe his banks: but whether they may be
260   Gods, as some say, or the abodes of gods,
       As others hold, or simply lamps of night,
       Worlds, or the lights of worlds, I know nor care not.
       There's something sweet in my uncertainty
       I would not change for your Chaldean lore;
265   Besides, I know of these all clay can know

Of aught above it, or below it – nothing.
I see their brilliancy and feel their beauty –
When they shine on my grave I shall know neither.
BELESES: For *neither*, sire, say *better*.
SARDANAPALUS: I will wait,
270   If it so please you, pontiff, for that knowledge.
In the mean time receive your sword, and know
That I prefer your service militant
Unto your ministry – not loving either.
SALEMENES [*aside*]: His lusts have made him mad. Then
            must I save him,
275   Spite of himself.
SARDANAPALUS: Please you to hear me, Satraps!
And chiefly thou, my priest, because I doubt thee
More than the soldier; and would doubt thee all
Wert thou not half a warrior: let us part
In peace – I'll not say pardon – which must be
280   Earn'd by the guilty; this I'll not pronounce ye,
Although upon this breath of mine depends
Your own; and, deadlier for ye, on my fears.
But fear not – for that I am soft, not fearful –
And so live on. Were I the thing some think me,
285   Your heads would now be dripping the last drops
Of their attainted gore from the high gates
Of this our palace, into the dry dust,
Their only portion of the coveted kingdom
They would be crown'd to reign o'er – let that pass.
290   As I have said, I will not *deem* ye guilty,
Nor *doom* ye guiltless. Albeit better men
Than ye or I stand ready to arraign you;
And should I leave your fate to sterner judges,
And proofs of all kinds, I might sacrifice
295   Two men, who, whatsoe'er they now are, were
Once honest. Ye are free, sirs.
ARBACES: Sire, this clemency —
BELESES [*interrupting him*]: Is worthy of yourself and,
            although innocent,
       We thank—
SARDANAPALUS: Priest! keep your thanksgivings for Belus;

His offspring needs none.

BELESES: But being innocent —

300 SARDANAPALUS: Be silent – Guilt is loud. If ye are loyal,
Ye are injured men, and should be sad, not grateful.

BELESES: So we should be, were justice always done
By earthly power omnipotent; but innocence
Must oft receive her right as a mere favour.

305 SARDANAPALUS: That's a good sentence for a homily,
Though not for this occasion. Prithee keep it
To plead thy sovereign's cause before his people.

BELESES: I trust there is no cause.

SARDANAPALUS: No *cause*, perhaps;
But many causers: – if ye meet with such

310 In the exercise of your inquisitive function
On earth, or should you read of it in heaven
In some mysterious twinkle of the stars,
Which are your chronicles, I pray you note,
That there are worse things betwixt earth and heaven

315 Than him who ruleth many and slays none;
And, hating not himself, yet loves his fellows
Enough to spare even those who would not spare him
Were they once masters – but that's doubtful. Satraps!
Your swords and persons are at liberty

320 To use them as ye will – but from this hour
I have no call for either. Salemenes
Follow me.

[*Exeunt* SARDANAPALUS, SALEMENES, *and the Train,*
&c., leaving ARBACES *and* BELESES.]

ARBACES: Beleses!

BELESES: Now, what think you?

ARBACES: That we are lost.

BELESES: That we have won the kingdom.

ARBACES: What? thus suspected – with the sword slung o'er
us

325 But by a single hair, and that still wavering,
To be blown down by his imperious breath
Which spared us – why, I know not.

BELESES: Seek not why;
But let us profit by the interval.

The hour is still our own – our power the same –
330   The night the same we destined. He hath changed
Nothing except our ignorance of all
Suspicion into such a certainty
As must make madness of delay.

ARBACES: And yet —

BELESES: What, doubting still?

ARBACES: He spared our lives, nay, more,
335   Saved them from Salemenes.

BELESES: And how long
Will he so spare? till the first drunken minute.

ARBACES: Or sober, rather. Yet he did it nobly;
Gave royally what we had forfeited
Basely —

BELESES: Say bravely.

ARBACES: Somewhat of both, perhaps.
340   But it has touch'd me, and, whate'er betide,
I will no further on.

BELESES: And lose the world!

ARBACES: Lose any thing except my own esteem.

BELESES: I blush that we should owe our lives to such
A king of distaffs!

ARBACES: But no less we owe them;
345   And I should blush far more to take the grantor's!

BELESES: Thou may'st endure whate'er thou wilt – the
stars
Have written otherwise.

ARBACES: Though they came down,
And marshall'd me the way in all their brightness,
I would not follow.

BELESES: This is weakness – worse
350   Than a scared beldam's dreaming of the dead,
And waking in the dark. – Go to – go to.

ARBACES: Methought he look'd like Nimrod as he spoke,
Even as the proud imperial statue stands
Looking the monarch of the kings around it,
355   And sways, while they but ornament, the temple.

BELESES: I told you that you had too much despised him,

And that there was some royalty within him –
What then? he is the nobler foe.

ARBACES: But we

The meaner. – Would he had not spared us!

BELESES: So –

360   Wouldst thou be sacrificed thus readily?

ARBACES: No – but it had been better to have died
Than live ungrateful.

BELESES: Oh, the souls of some men!
Thou wouldst digest what some call treason, and
Fools treachery – and, behold, upon the sudden,

365   Because for something or for nothing, this
Rash reveller steps, ostentatiously,
'Twixt thee and Salemenes, thou art turn'd
Into – what shall I say? – Sardanapalus!
I know no name more ignominious.

ARBACES: But

370   An hour ago, who dared to term me such
Had held his life but lightly – as it is,
I must forgive you, even as he forgave us –
Semiramis herself would not have done it.

BELESES: No – the queen liked no sharers of the kingdom
Not even a husband.

375   ARBACES: I must serve him truly —

BELESES: And humbly?

ARBACES: No, sir, proudly – being honest.
I shall be nearer thrones than you to heaven;
And if not quite so haughty, yet more lofty.
You may do your own deeming – you have codes,

380   And mysteries, and corollaries of
Right and wrong, which I lack for my direction,
And must pursue but what a plain heart teaches.
And now you know me.

BELESES: Have you finish'd?

ARBACES: Yes –
With you.

BELESES: And would, perhaps, betray as well

385   As quit me?

ARBACES: That's a sacerdotal thought,

And not a soldier's.
BELESES: Be it what you will —
Truce with these wranglings, and but hear me.
ARBACES: No —
There is more peril in your subtle spirit
Than in a phalanx.
BELESES: If it must be so —
390   I'll on alone!
ARBACES: Alone!
BELESES: Thrones hold but one.
ARBASES: But this is fill'd.
BELESES: With worse than vacancy —
A despised monarch. Look to it, Arbaces:
I have still aided, cherish'd, loved, and urged you;
Was willing even to serve you, in the hope
395   To serve and save Assyria. Heaven itself
Seem'd to consent, and all events were friendly,
Even to the last, till that your spirit shrunk
Into a shallow softness; but now, rather
Than see my country languish, I will be
400   Her saviour or the victim of her tyrant,
Or one or both, for sometimes both are one;
And if I win, Arbaces is my servant.
ARBACES: *Your* servant!
BELESES: Why not? better than be slave,
The *pardon'd* slave of *she* Sardanapalus!
[*Enter* PANIA.]
405   PANIA: My lords, I bear an order from the king.
ARBACES: It is obey'd ere spoken.
BELESES: Notwithstanding,
Let's hear it.
PANIA: Forthwith, on this very night,
Repair to your respective satrapies
Of Babylon and Media.
BELESES: With our troops?
410   PANIA: My order is unto the satraps and
Their household train.
ARBACES: But—
BELESES: It must be obey'd:

Say, we depart.

PANIA: My order is to see you
Depart, and not to bear your answer.

BELESES [*aside*]:   Ay!
Well, sir, we will accompany you hence.

415   PANIA: I will retire to marshal forth the guard
Of honour which befits your rank, and wait
Your leisure, so that it the hour exceeds not.
        [*Exit* PANIA.]

BELESES: *Now* then obey!

ARBACES: Doubtless.

BELESES: Yes, to the gates
That grate the palace, which is now our prison —

420   No further.

ARBACES: Thou hast harp'd the truth indeed!
The realm itself, in all its wide extension,
Yawns dungeons at each step for thee and me.

BELESES: Graves!

ARBACES: If I thought so, this good sword should dig
One more than mine.

BELESES: It shall have work enough.

425   Let me hope better than thou augurest;
At present, let us hence as best we may.
Thou dost agree with me in understanding
This order as a sentence?

ARBACES: Why, what other
Interpretation should it bear? it is

430   The very policy of orient monarchs —
Pardon and poison — favours and a sword —
A distant voyage, and an eternal sleep.
How many satraps in his father's time —
For he I own is, or at least *was*, bloodless —

435   BELESES: But *will* not, *can* not be so now.

ARBACES: I doubt it.
How many satraps have I seen set out
In his sire's day for mighty vice-royalties,
Whose tombs are on their path! I know not how,
But they all sicken'd by the way, it was

440 So long and heavy.

BELESES: Let us but regain
The free air of the city, and we'll shorten
The journey.

ARBACES: 'Twill be shorten'd at the gates,
It may be.

BELESES: No; they hardly will risk that.
They mean us to die privately, but not
445 Within the palace or the city walls,
Where we are known, and may have partisans:
If they had meant to slay us here, we were
No longer with the living. Let us hence.

ARBACES: If I but thought he did not mean my life —

450 BELESES: Fool! hence — what else should despotism
    alarm'd
Mean? Let us but rejoin our troops, and march.

ARBACES: Towards our provinces?

BELESES: No; towards your kingdom.
There's time, there's heart, and hope, and power, and
    means,
Which their half measures leave us in full scope. —
455 Away!

ARBACES: And I even yet repenting must
Relapse to guilt!

BELESES: Self-defence is a virtue,
Sole bulwark of all right. Away, I say!
Let's leave this place, the air grows thick and choking,
And the walls have a scent of night-shade – hence!
460 Let us not leave them time for further council.
Our quick departure proves our civic zeal;
Our quick departure hinders our good escort,
The worthy Pania, from anticipating
The orders of some parasangs from hence:
465 Nay, there's no other choice, but – hence, I say.
    [*Exit with* ARBACES, *who follows reluctantly*.]
    [*Enter* SARDANAPALUS *and* SALEMENES.]

SARDANAPALUS: Well, all is remedied, and without
    bloodshed,
That worst of mockeries of a remedy;

We are now secure by these men's exile.
SALEMENES: Yes,
As he who treads on flowers is from the adder
470   Twined round their roots.
SARDANAPALUS: Why, what wouldst have me do?
SALEMENES: Undo what you have done.
SARDANAPALUS: Revoke my pardon?
SALEMENES: Replace the crown now tottering on your
      temples.
SARDANAPALUS: That were tyrannical.
SALEMENES: But sure.
SARDANAPALUS: We are so.
What danger can they work upon the frontier?
475   SALEMENES: They are not there yet – never should they be
      so,
Were I well listen'd to.
SARDANAPALUS: Nay, I *have* listen'd
Impartially to thee – why not to them?
SALEMENES: You may know that hereafter; as it is,
I take my leave to order forth the guard.
480   SARDANAPALUS: And you will join us at the banquet?
SALEMENES: Sire,
Dispense with me – I am no wassailer:
Command me in all service save the Bacchant's.
SARDANAPALUS: Nay, but 'tis fit to revel now and then.
SALEMENES: And fit that some should watch for those who
      revel
485   Too oft. Am I permitted to depart?
SARDANAPALUS: Yes — Stay a moment, my good
      Salemenes,
My brother, my best subject, better prince
Than I am king. You should have been the monarch,
And I – I know not what, and care not; but
490   Think not I am insensible to all
Thine honest wisdom, and thy rough yet kind,
Though oft reproving, sufferance of my follies.
If I have spared these men against thy counsel,
That is, their lives – it is not that I doubt
495   The advice was sound; but, let them live: we will not

Cavil about their lives – so let them mend them.
Their banishment will leave me still sound sleep,
Which their death had not left me.

SALEMENES: Thus you run
The risk to sleep for ever, to save traitors –

500   A moment's pang now changed for years of crime.
Still let them be made quiet.

SARDANAPALUS: Tempt me not:
My word is past.

SALEMENES: But it may be recall'd.

SARDANAPALUS: 'Tis royal.

SALEMENES: And should therefore be decisive.
This half indulgence of an exile serves

505   But to provoke – a pardon should be full,
Or it is none.

SARDANAPALUS: And who persuaded me
After I had repeal'd them, or at least
Only dismiss'd them from our presence, who
Urged me to send them to their satrapies?

510   SALEMENES: True; that I had forgotten; that is, sire,
If they e'er reach'd their satrapies – why, then,
Reprove me more for my advice.

SARDANAPALUS: And if
They do not reach them – look to it! – in safety,
In safety, mark me – and security –

515   Look to thine own.

SALEMENES: Permit me to depart;
Their *safety* shall be cared for.

SARDANAPALUS: Get thee hence, then;
And, prithee, think more gently of thy brother.

SALEMENES: Sire, I shall ever duly serve my sovereign.
    [*Exit* SALEMENES.]

SARDANAPALUS [*solus*]: That man is of a temper too
            severe;

520   Hard but as lofty as the rock, and free
From all the taints of common earth – while I
Am softer clay, impregnated with flowers:
But as our mould is, must the produce be.

If I have err'd this time, 'tis on the side
Where error sits most lightly on that sense
I know not what to call it; but it reckons
With me ofttimes for pain, and sometimes pleasure;
A spirit which seems placed about my heart
To count its throbs, not quicken them, and ask
Questions which mortal never dared to ask me,
Nor Baal, though an oracular deity —
Albeit his marble face majestical
Frowns as the shadows of the evening dim
His brows to changed expression, till at times
I think the statue looks in act to speak.
Away with these vain thoughts, I will be joyous —
And here comes Joy's true herald.

      [*Enter* MYRRHA.]

MYRRHA: King! the sky
Is overcast, and musters muttering thunder,
In clouds that seem approaching fast, and show
In forked flashes a commanding tempest.
Will you then quit the palace?

SARDANAPALUS: Tempest, say'st thou?

MYRRHA: Ay, my good lord.

SARDANAPALUS: For my own part, I should be
Not ill content to vary the smooth scene,
And watch the warring elements; but this
Would little suit the silken garments and
Smooth faces of our festive friends. Say, Myrrha,
Art thou of those who dread the roar of clouds?

MYRRHA: In my own country we respect their voices
As auguries of Jove.

SARDANAPALUS: Jove! — ay, your Baal —
Ours also has a property in thunder,
And ever and anon some falling bolt
Proves his divinity, — and yet sometimes
Strikes his own altars.

MYRRHA: That were a dread omen.

SARDANAPALUS: Yes — for the priests. Well, we will not go
    forth
Beyond the palace walls to-night, but make

    Our feast within.

MYRRHA: Now, Jove be praised! that he
    Hath heard the prayer thou wouldst not hear. The
       gods
    Are kinder to thee than thou to thyself,
    And flash this storm between thee and thy foes,

560   To shield thee from them.

SARDANAPALUS: Child, if there be peril,
    Methinks it is the same within these walls
    As on the river's brink.

MYRRHA: Not so; these walls
    Are high and strong, and guarded. Treason has
    To penetrate through many a winding way,

565   And massy portal; but in the pavilion
    There is no bulwark.

SARDANAPALUS: No, nor in the palace,
    Nor in the fortress, nor upon the top
    Of cloud-fenced Caucasus, where the eagle sits
    Nested in pathless clefts, if treachery be:

570   Even as the arrow finds the airy king,
    The steel will reach the earthly. But be calm:
    The men, or innocent or guilty, are
    Banish'd, and far upon their way.

MYRRHA: They live, then?

SARDANAPALUS: So sanguinary? *Thou!*

MYRRHA: I would not shrink

575   From just infliction of due punishment
    On those who seek your life: wer't otherwise,
    I should not merit mine. Besides, you heard
    The princely Salemenes.

SARDANAPALUS: This is strange;
    The gentle and the austere are both against me,

580   And urge me to revenge.

MYRRHA: 'Tis a Greek virtue.

SARDANAPALUS: But not a kingly one – I'll none on't; or
    If ever I indulge in't, it shall be
    With kings – my equals.

MYRRHA: These men sought to be so.

SARDANAPALUS: Myrrha, this is too feminine, and springs

585   From fear —
MYRRHA: For you.
SARDANAPALUS: No matter, still 'tis fear.
    I have observed your sex, once roused to wrath,
    Are timidly vindictive to a pitch
    Of perseverance, which I would not copy.
    I thought you were exempt from this, as from
590   The childish helplessness of Asian women.
MYRRHA: My lord, I am no boaster of my love,
    Nor of my attributes; I have shared your splendour
    And will partake your fortunes. You may live
    To find one slave more true than subject myriads:
595   But this the gods avert! I am content
    To be beloved on trust for what I feel,
    Rather than prove it to you in your griefs,
    Which might not yield to any cares of mine.
SARDANAPALUS: Grief cannot come where perfect love
        exists,
600   Except to heighten it, and vanish from
    That which it could not scare away. Let's in –
    The hour approaches, and we must prepare
    To meet the invited guests who grace our feast.
      [*Exeunt.*]

Act III

SCENE I

The Hall of the Palace illuminated – SARDANAPALUS *and his Guests at Table. – A Storm without, and Thunder occasionally heard during the Banquet.*

SARDANAPALUS: Fill full! why this is as it should be: here
    Is my true realm, amidst bright eyes and faces
    Happy as fair! Here sorrow cannot reach.
ZAMES: Nor elsewhere – where the king is, pleasure
      sparkles.
5   SARDANAPALUS: Is not this better now than Nimrod's
      huntings,

    Or my wild grandam's chase in search of kingdoms
    She could not keep when conquer'd?
ALTADA: Mighty though
    They were, as all thy royal line have been,
    Yet none of those who went before have reach'd
10   The acmé of Sardanapalus, who
    Has placed his joy in peace – the sole true glory.
SARDANAPALUS: And pleasure, good Altada, to which
       glory
    Is but the path. What is it that we seek?
    Enjoyment! We have cut the way short to it,
15   And not gone tracking it through human ashes,
    Making a grave with every footstep.
ZAMES: No;
    All hearts are happy, and all voices bless
    The king of peace, who holds a world in jubilee.
SARDANAPALUS: Art sure of that? I have heard otherwise;
20   Some say that there be traitors.
ZAMES: Traitors they
    Who dare to say so! – 'Tis impossible.
    What cause?
SARDANAPALUS: What cause? true, – fill the goblet up;
    We will not think of them: there are none such,
    Or if there be, they are gone.
ALTADA: Guests, to my pledge!
25   Down on your knees, and drink a measure to
    The safety of the king – the monarch, say I?
    The god Sardanapalus!
    [ZAMES *and the Guests kneel and exclaim –*]
                   Mightier than
    His father Baal, the god Sardanapalus!
    [*It thunders as they kneel; some start up in confusion.*]
ZAMES: Why do you rise, my friends? in that strong peal
30   His father gods consented.
MYRRHA: Menaced, rather.
    King, wilt thou bear this mad impiety?
SARDANAPALUS: Impiety! – nay, if the sires who reign'd
    Before me can be gods, I'll not disgrace
    Their lineage. But arise, my pious friends;

35   Hoard your devotion for the thunderer there:
        I seek but to be loved, not worshipp'd.
        ALTADA: Both –
        Both you must ever be by all true subjects.
        SARDANAPALUS: Methinks the thunders still increase:
            it is
        An awful night.
        MYRRHA: Oh yes, for those who have
40   No palace to protect their worshippers.
        SARDANAPALUS: That's true, my Myrrha; and could I
            convert
        My realm to one wide shelter for the wretched,
        I'd do it.
        MYRRHA: Thou'rt no god, then, not to be
        Able to work a will so good and general,
45   As thy wish would imply.
        SARDANAPALUS: And your gods, then,
        Who can, and do not?
        MYRRHA: Do not speak of that,
        Lest we provoke them.
        SARDANAPALUS: True, they love not censure
        Better than mortals. Friends, a thought has struck
            me:
        Were there no temples, would there, think ye, be
50   Air worshippers? that is, when it is angry,
        And pelting as even now.
        MYRRHA: The Persian prays
        Upon his mountain.
        SARDANAPALUS: Yes, when the sun shines.
        MYRRHA: And I would ask if this your palace were
        Unroof'd and desolate, how many flatterers
55   Would lick the dust in which the king lay low?
        ALTADA: The fair Ionian is too sarcastic
        Upon a nation whom she knows not well;
        The Assyrians know no pleasure but their king's,
        And homage is their pride.
        SARDANAPALUS: Nay, pardon, guests,
60   The fair Greek's readiness of speech.
        ALTADA: *Pardon!* sire:

We honour her of all things next to thee.
Hark! what was that?

ZAMES: That! nothing but the jar
Of distant portals shaken by the wind.

ALTADA: It sounded like the clash of — hark again!

65   ZAMES: The big rain pattering on the roof.

SARDANAPALUS: No more.
Myrrha, my love, hast thou thy shell in order?
Sing me a song of Sappho, her, thou know'st,
Who in thy country threw —

[*Enter* PANIA, *with his sword and garments bloody, and
disordered. The Guests rise in confusion.*]

PANIA [*to the Guards*]:   Look to the portals;
And with your best speed to the walls without.

70   Your arms! To arms! The king's in danger. Monarch!
Excuse this haste, — 'tis faith.

SARDANAPALUS: Speak on.

PANIA: It is
As Salemenes fear'd; the faithless satraps —

SARDANAPALUS: You are wounded — give some wine. Take
breath, good Pania.

PANIA: 'Tis nothing — a mere flesh wound. I am worn

75   More with my speed to warn my sovereign,
Than hurt in his defence.

MYRRHA: Well, sir, the rebels?

PANIA: Soon as Arbaces and Beleses reach'd
Their stations in the city, they refused
To march; and on my attempt to use the power

80   Which I was delegated with, they call'd
Upon their troops, who rose in fierce defiance.

MYRRHA: All?

PANIA: Too many.

SARDANAPALUS: Spare not of thy free speech,
To spare mine ears the truth.

PANIA: My own slight guard
Were faithful, and what's left of it is still so.

MYRRHA: And are these all the force still faithful?

85   PANIA: No —
The Bactrians, now led on by Salemenes,

Who even then was on his way, still urged
By strong suspicion of the Median chiefs,
Are numerous, and make strong head against
90   The rebels, fighting inch by inch, and forming
An orb around the palace, where they mean
To centre all their force, and save the king.
    [*He hesitates.*]
I am charged to—

MYRRHA: 'Tis no time for hesitation.

PANIA: Prince Salemenes doth implore the king
95   To arm himself, although but for a moment,
And show himself unto the soldiers: his
Sole presence in this instant might do more
Than hosts can do in his behalf.

SARDANAPALUS: What, ho!
My armour there.

MYRRHA: And wilt thou?

SARDANAPALUS: Will I not?
100   Ho, there! – but seek not for the buckler: 'tis
Too heavy: – a light cuirass and my sword.
Where are the rebels?

PANIA: Scarce a furlong's length
From the outward wall the fiercest conflict rages.

SARDANAPALUS: Then I may charge on horseback. Sfero,
    ho!
105   Order my horse out. – There is space enough
Even in our courts, and by the outer gate,
To marshal half the horsemen of Arabia.
    [*Exit* SFERO *for the armour.*]

MYRRHA: How I do love thee!

SARDANAPALUS: I ne'er doubted it.

MYRRHA: But now I know thee.

SARDANAPALUS [*to his Attendant*]: Bring down my spear
    too.—
110   Where's Salemenes?

PANIA: Where a soldier should be,
In the thick of the fight.

SARDANAPALUS: Then hasten to him — Is
The path still open, and communication

Left 'twixt the palace and the phalanx?

PANIA: 'Twas
When I late left him, and I have no fear:
Our troops were steady, and the phalanx form'd.

SARDANAPALUS: Tell him to spare his person for the present,
And that I will not spare my own – and say,
  I come.

PANIA: There's victory in the very word.

          [*Exit* PANIA.]

SARDANAPALUS:
          Altada – Zames – forth, and arm ye! There
Is all in readiness in the armoury.
See that the women are bestow'd in safety
In the remote apartments: let a guard
Be set before them, with strict charge to quit
The post but with their lives – command it, Zames.
Altada, arm yourself, and return here;
Your post is near our person.

          [*Exeunt* ZAMES, ALTADA, *and all save* MYRRHA.]
          [*Enter* SFERO *and others with the King's Arms*, &c.]

SFERO: King! your armour.

SARDANAPALUS [*arming himself*]: Give me the cuirass – so:
  my baldric; now
My sword: I had forgot the helm – where is it?
That's well – no, 'tis too heavy: you mistake, too –
It was not this I meant, but that which bears
A diadem around it.

SFERO: Sire, I deem'd
That too conspicuous from the precious stones
To risk your sacred brow beneath – and trust me,
This is of better metal, though less rich.

SARDANAPALUS: You deem'd! Are you too turn'd a rebel?
          Fellow!
Your part is to obey: return, and – no –
It is too late – I will go forth without it.

SFERO: At least, wear this.

SARDANAPALUS: Wear Caucasus! why, 'tis
A mountain on my temples.

SFERO: Sire, the meanest

140   Soldier goes not forth thus exposed to battle.
        All men will recognise you – for the storm
        Has ceased, and the moon breaks forth in her
           brightness.
        SARDANAPALUS: I go forth to be recognised, and thus
        Shall be so sooner. Now – my spear! I'm arm'd.
          [*In going stops short, and turns to* SFERO.]
145   Sfero – I had forgotten – bring the mirror.
        SFERO: The mirror, sire?
        SARDANAPALUS: Yes, sir, of polish'd brass,
        Brought from the spoils of India – but be speedy.
          [*Exit* SFERO.]
        SARDANAPALUS: Myrrha, retire unto a place of
          safety.
        Why went you not forth with the other damsels?
150   MYRRHA: Because my place is here.
        SARDANAPALUS: And when I am gone —
        MYRRHA: I follow.
        SARDANAPALUS: *You!* to battle?
        MYRRHA: If it were so,
        'Twere not the first Greek girl had trod the path.
        I will await here your *return*.
        SARDANAPALUS: The place
        Is spacious, and the first to be sought out,
155   If they prevail; and, if it be so,
        And I return not –
        MYRRHA: Still we meet again.
        SARDANAPALUS: How?
        MYRRHA: In the spot where all must meet at
          last –
        In Hades! if there be, as I believe,
        A shore beyond the Styx: and if there be not,
160   In ashes.
        SARDANAPALUS: Darest thou so much?
        MYRRHA: I dare all things
        Except survive what I have loved, to be
        A rebel's booty: forth, and do your bravest.
          [*Re-enter* SFERO *with the mirror.*]
        SARDANAPALUS [*looking at himself*]: This cuirass fits me
          well, the baldric better,

And the helm not at all. Methinks I seem
   [*Flings away the helmet after trying it again.*]
165   Passing well in these toys; and now to prove them.
Altada! Where's Altada?
SFERO: Waiting, sire,
Without: he has your shield in readiness.
SARDANAPALUS: True; I forgot he is my shield-bearer
By right of blood, derived from age to age.
170   Myrrha, embrace me; – yet once more – once more –
Love me, whate'er betide. My chiefest glory
Shall be to make me worthier of your love.
MYRRHA: Go forth, and conquer!
    [*Exeunt* SARDANAPALUS *and* SFERO.]
                      Now, I am alone,
All are gone forth, and of that all how few
175   Perhaps return. Let him but vanquish, and
Me perish! If he vanquish not, I perish;
For I will not outlive him. He has wound
About my heart, I know not how nor why.
Not for that he is king; for now his kingdom
180   Rocks underneath his throne, and the earth yawns
To yield him no more of it than a grave;
And yet I love him more. Oh, mighty Jove!
Forgive this monstrous love for a barbarian,
Who knows not of Olympus! yes, I love him
185   Now, now, far more than — Hark – to the war shout!
Methinks it nears me. If it should be so,
    [*She draws forth a small vial.*]
This cunning Colchian poison, which my father
Learn'd to compound on Euxine shores, and taught
    me
How to preserve, shall free me! It had freed me
190   Long ere this hour, but that I loved, until
I half forgot I was a slave: – where all
Are slaves save one, and proud of servitude,
So they are served in turn by something lower
In the degree of bondage, we forget
195   That shackles worn like ornaments no less
Are chains. Again that shout! and now the clash

Of arms – and now – and now —
    [*Enter* ALTADA.]

ALTADA: Ho, Sfero, ho!

MYRRHA: He is not here; what wouldst thou with him? How
    Goes on the conflict?

ALTADA: Dubiously and fiercely.

200 MYRRHA: And the king?

ALTADA: Like a king. I must find Sfero,
    And bring him a new spear and his own helmet.
    He fights till now bare-headed, and by far
    Too much exposed. The soldiers knew his face,
    And the foe too; and in the moon's broad light,
205   His silk tiara and his flowing hair
    Make him a mark too royal. Every arrow
    Is pointed at the fair hair and fair features,
    And the broad fillet which crowns both.

MYRRHA: Ye gods,
    Who fulminate o'er my father's land, protect him!
210   Were you sent by the king?

ALTADA: By Salemenes,
    Who sent me privily upon this charge,
    Without the knowledge of the careless sovereign.
    The king! the king fights as he revels! ho!
    What, Sfero! I will seek the armoury –
215   He must be there.
        [*Exit* ALTADA.]

MYRRHA: 'Tis no dishonour – no –
    'Tis no dishonour to have loved this man.
    I almost wish now, what I never wish'd
    Before, that he were Grecian. If Alcides
    Were shamed in wearing Lydian Omphale's
220   She-garb, and wielding her vile distaff; surely
    He, who springs up a Hercules at once,
    Nursed in effeminate arts from youth to manhood,
    And rushes from the banquet to the battle,
    As though it were a bed of love, deserves
225   That a Greek girl should be his paramour,
    And a Greek bard his minstrel, a Greek tomb

His monument. How goes the strife, sir?
[*Enter an* OFFICER.]
OFFICER: Lost,
Lost almost past recovery. Zames! Where
Is Zames?
MYRRHA: Posted with the guard appointed
230   To watch before the apartment of the women.
[*Exit* OFFICER.]
MYRRHA [*sola*]: He's gone; and told no more than that all's
            lost!
What need have I to know more? In those words,
Those little words, a kingdom and a king,
A line of thirteen ages, and the lives
235   Of thousands, and the fortune of all left
With life, are merged; and I, too, with the great,
Like a small bubble breaking with the wave
Which bore it, shall be nothing. At the least,
My fate is in my keeping: no proud victor
240   Shall count me with his spoils.
[*Enter* PANIA.]
PANIA: Away with me,
Myrrha, without delay; we must not lose
A moment – all that's left us now.
MYRRHA: The king?
PANIA: Sent me here to conduct you hence, beyond
The river, by a secret passage.
MYRRHA: Then
245   He lives –
PANIA: And charged me to secure your life,
And beg you to live on for his sake, till
He can rejoin you.
MYRRHA: Will he then give way?
PANIA: Not till the last. Still, still he does whate'er
Despair can do; and step by step disputes
250   The very palace.
MYRRHA: They are here, then: – ay,
Their shouts come ringing through the ancient halls,
Never profaned by rebel echoes till
This fatal night. Farewell, Assyria's line!

Farewell to all of Nimrod! Even the name
255   Is now no more.
PANIA: Away with me – away!
MYRRHA: No: I'll die here! – Away, and tell your king
I loved him to the last.
          [*Enter* SARDANAPALUS *and* SALEMENES *with Soldiers.*
          PANIA *quits* MYRRHA, *and ranges himself with them.*]
SARDANAPALUS: Since it is thus,
We'll die where we were born – in our own halls.
Serry your ranks – stand firm. I have despatch'd
260   A trusty satrap for the guard of Zames,
All fresh and faithful; they'll be here anon.
All is not over. – Pania, look to Myrrha.
          [PANIA *returns towards* MYRRHA.]
SALEMENES: We have breathing time; yet once more charge,
my friends –
One for Assyria!
SARDANAPALUS: Rather say for Bactria!
265   My faithful Bactrians, I will henceforth be
King of your nation, and we'll hold together
This realm as province.
SALEMENES: Hark! they come – they come.
          [*Enter* BELESES *and* ARBACES *with the Rebels.*]
ARBACES: Set on, we have them in the toil. Charge!
charge!
BELESES: On! on! – Heaven fights for us, and with us – On!
          [*They charge the King and* SALEMENES *with their
          Troops, who defend themselves till the arrival of*
          ZAMES, *with the Guard before mentioned. The Rebels
          are then driven off, and pursued by* SALEMENES, &c.
          As the King is going to join the pursuit,* BELESES
          crosses him.]
270   BELESES: Ho! tyrant – *I* will end this war.
SARDANAPALUS: Even so,
My warlike priest, and precious prophet, and
Grateful and trusty subject: – yield, I pray thee.
I would reserve thee for a fitter doom,
Rather than dip my hands in holy blood.
275   BELESES: Thine hour is come.
SARDANAPALUS: No, thine. – I've lately read,

Though but a young astrologer, the stars;
And ranging round the zodiac, found thy fate
In the sign of the Scorpion, which proclaims
That thou wilt now be crush'd.

BELESES: But not by thee.
  [*They fight;* BELESES *is wounded and disarmed.*]
SARDANAPALUS [*raising his sword to despatch him, exclaims*]:

280   Now call upon thy planets, will they shoot
From the sky to preserve their seer and credit?
  [*A party of Rebels enter and rescue* BELESES. *They
  assail the King, who, in turn, is rescued by a Party of
  his Soldiers, who drive the Rebels off.*]
The villain was a prophet after all.
Upon them – ho! there – victory is ours.
  [*Exit in pursuit.*]
MYRRHA [*to* PANIA]: Pursue! Why stand'st thou here, and
leavest the ranks

285   Of fellow soldiers conquering without thee?
PANIA: The king's command was not to quit thee.
MYRRHA: *Me!*
Think not of me – a single soldier's arm
Must not be wanting now. I ask no guard,
I need no guard: what, with a world at stake,

290   Keep watch upon a woman? Hence, I say,
Or thou art shamed! Nay, then, *I* will go forth,
A feeble female, 'midst their desperate strife,
And bid thee guard me *there* – where thou shouldst
shield
Thy sovereign.
  [*Exit* MYRRHA.]
PANIA: Yet stay, damsel! She's gone.

295   If aught of ill betide her, better I
Had lost my life. Sardanapalus holds her
Far dearer than his kingdom, yet he fights
For that too; and can I do less than he,
Who never flash'd a scimitar till now?

300   Myrrha, return, and I obey you, though
In disobedience to the monarch.
  [*Exit* PANIA.]

[*Enter* ALTADA *and* SFERO *by an opposite
door.*]

ALTADA: Myrrha!
What, gone? yet she was here when the fight
    raged
And Pania also. Can aught have befallen them?

SFERO: I saw both safe, when late the rebels fled:
305   They probably are but retired to make
Their way back to the harem.

ALTADA: If the king
Prove victor, as it seems even now he must,
And miss his own Ionian, we are doom'd
To worse than captive rebels.

SFERO: Let us trace them;
310   She cannot be fled far; and, found, she makes
A richer prize to our soft sovereign
Than his recover'd kingdom.

ALTADA: Baal himself
Ne'er fought more fiercely to win empire, than
His silken son to save it: he defies
315   All augury of foes or friends; and like
The close and sultry summer's day, which bodes
A twilight tempest, bursts forth in such thunder
As sweeps the air and deluges the earth.
The man's inscrutable.

SFERO: Not more than others.
320   All are the sons of circumstance: away —
Let's seek the slave out, or prepare to be
Tortured for his infatuation, and
Condemn'd without a crime.
    [*Exeunt.*]
    [*Enter* SALEMENES *and Soldiers, &c.*]

SALEMENES: The triumph is
Flattering: they are beaten backward from the
    palace,
325   And we have open'd regular access
To the troops station'd on the other side
Euphrates, who may still be true; nay, must be,
When they hear of our victory. But where

Is the chief victor? where's the king?
[*Enter* SARDANAPALUS, *cum suis,* &c. *and* MYRRHA.]
SARDANAPALUS: Here, brother.
330 SALEMENES: Unhurt, I hope.
SARDANAPALUS: Not quite; but let it pass.
We've clear'd the palace —
SALEMENES: And I trust the city.
Our numbers gather; and I've ordered onward
A cloud of Parthians, hitherto reserved,
All fresh and fiery, to be pour'd upon them
335 In their retreat, which soon will be a flight.
SARDANAPALUS: It is already, or at least they march'd
Faster than I could follow with my Bactrians,
Who spared no speed. I am spent: give me a seat.
SALEMENES: There stands the throne, sire.
SARDANAPALUS: 'Tis no place to rest on,
340 For mind nor body: let me have a couch,
[*They place a seat.*]
A peasant's stool, I care not what: so – now
I breathe more freely.
SALEMENES: This great hour has proved
The brightest and most glorious of your life.
SARDANAPALUS: And the most tiresome. Where's my
cupbearer?
345 Bring me some water.
SALEMENES [*smiling*]:   'Tis the first time he
Ever had such an order: even I,
Your most austere of counsellors, would now
Suggest a purpler beverage.
SARDANAPALUS: Blood – doubtless.
But there's enough of that shed; as for wine,
350 I have learn'd to-night the price of the pure element:
Thrice have I drank of it, and thrice renew'd,
With greater strength than the grape ever gave me,
My charge upon the rebels. Where's the soldier
Who gave me water in his helmet?
ONE OF THE GUARDS: Slain, sire!
355 An arrow pierced his brain, while, scattering

The last drops from his helm, he stood in act
To place it on his brows.
SARDANAPALUS: Slain! unrewarded!
And slain to serve my thirst: that's hard, poor
          slave!
Had he but lived, I would have gorged him with
360   Gold: all the gold of earth could ne'er repay
The pleasure of that draught; for I was parch'd
As I am now.
          [*They bring water – he drinks.*]
                    I live again – from henceforth
The goblet I reserve for hours of love,
But war on water.
SALEMENES: And that bandage, sire,
365   Which girds your arm?
SARDANAPALUS: A scratch from brave Beleses.
MYRRHA: Oh! he is wounded!
SARDANAPALUS: Not too much of that;
And yet it feels a little stiff and painful,
Now I am cooler.
MYRRHA: You have bound it with —
SARDANAPALUS: The fillet of my diadem: the first
          time
370   That ornament was ever aught to me,
Save an incumbrance.
MYRRHA [*to the Attendants*]: Summon speedily
A leech of the most skilful: pray, retire:
I will unbind your wound and tend it.
SARDANAPALUS: Do so,
For now it throbs sufficiently: but what
375   Know'st thou of wounds? yet wherefore do I ask?
Know'st thou, my brother, where I lighted on
This minion?
SALEMENES: Herding with the other females,
Like frighten'd antelopes.
SARDANAPALUS: No: like the dam
Of the young lion, femininely raging,
380   (And femininely meaneth furiously,
Because all passions in excess are female,)

Against the hunter flying with her cub,
She urged on with her voice and gesture, and
Her floating hair and flashing eyes, the soldiers,
385 In the pursuit.
SALEMENES: Indeed!
SARDANAPALUS: You see, this night
Made warriors of more than me. I paused
To look upon her, and her kindled cheek;
Her large black eyes, that flash'd through her long
  hair
As it stream'd o'er her; her blue veins that rose
390 Along her most transparent brow; her nostril
Dilated from its symmetry; her lips
Apart; her voice that clove through all the din,
As a lute's pierceth through the cymbal's clash,
Jarr'd but not drown'd by the loud brattling; her
395 Waved arms, more dazzling with their own born
   whiteness
Than the steel her hand held, which she caught
  up
From a dead soldier's grasp; – all these things made
Her seem unto the troops a prophetess
Of victory, or Victory herself,
400 Come down to hail us hers.
SALEMENES [*aside*]:   This is too much.
Again the love-fit's on him, and all's lost,
Unless we turn his thoughts.
  [*Aloud:*]   But pray thee, sire,
Think of your wound – you said even now 'twas
  painful.
SARDANAPALUS: That's true, too; but I must not think
  of it.
405 SALEMENES: I have look'd to all things needful, and will
   now
Receive reports of progress made in such
Orders as I had given, and then return
To hear your further pleasure.
SARDANAPALUS: Be it so.
SALEMENES [*in retiring*]: Myrrha!

MYRRHA: Prince!

SALEMENES: You have shown a soul to-night,

410   Which, were he not my sister's lord — But now
       I have no time: thou lovest the king?

MYRRHA: I love
       Sardanapalus.

SALEMENES: But wouldst have him king still?

MYRRHA: I would have him less than what he should
       be.

SALEMENES: Well then, to have him king, and yours,
       and all

415   He should, or should not be; to have him *live*,
       Let him not sink back into luxury.
       You have more power upon his spirit than
       Wisdom within these walls, or fierce rebellion
       Raging without: look well that he relapse not.

420   MYRRHA: There needed not the voice of Salemenes
       To urge me on to this: I will not fail.
       All that a woman's weakness can —

SALEMENES: Is power
       Omnipotent o'er such a heart as his:
       Exert it wisely.

       [*Exit* SALEMENES.]

SARDANAPALUS: Myrrha! what, at whispers

425   With my stern brother? I shall soon be jealous.

MYRRHA [*smiling*]: You have cause, sire; for on the earth
       there breathes not
       A man more worthy of a woman's love –
       A soldier's trust – a subject's reverence –
       A king's esteem – the whole woorld's admiration!

430   SARDANAPALUS: Praise him, but not so warmly. I must
       not
       Hear those sweet lips grow eloquent in aught
       That throws me into shade; yet you speak truth.

MYRRHA: And now retire, to have your wound look'd
       to.
       Pray, lean on me.

SARDANAPALUS: Yes, love! but not from pain.

       [*Exeunt omnes.*]

Act IV

SCENE I

SARDANAPALUS *discovered sleeping upon a Couch, and
    occasionally disturbed in his Slumbers, with* MYRRHA
    watching.

MYRRHA [*sola, gazing*]: I have stolen upon his rest, if rest it
        be,
    Which thus convulses slumber: shall I wake him?
    No, he seems calmer. Oh, thou God of Quiet!
    Whose reign is o'er seal'd eyelids and soft dreams,
5   Or deep, deep sleep, so as to be unfathom'd,
    Look like thy brother, Death, – so still – so stirless –
    For then we are happiest, as it may be, we
    Are happiest of all within the realm
    Of thy stern, silent, and unwakening twin.
10   Again he moves – again the play of pain
    Shoots o'er his features, as the sudden gust
    Crisps the reluctant lake that lay so calm
    Beneath the mountain shadow; or the blast
    Ruffles the autumn leaves, that drooping cling
15   Faintly and motionless to their loved boughs.
    I must awake him – yet not yet: who knows
    From what I rouse him? It seems pain; but if
    I quicken him to heavier pain? The fever
    Of this tumultuous night, the grief too of
20   His wound, though slight, may cause all this, and shake
    Me more to see than him to suffer. No:
    Let Nature use her own maternal means, –
    And I await to second, not disturb her.
SARDANAPALUS [*awakening*]: Not so – although ye
        multiplied the stars,
25   And gave them to me as a realm to share
    From you and with you! I would not so purchase
    The empire of eternity. Hence – hence –
    Old hunter of the earliest brutes! and ye,
    Who hunted fellow-creatures as if brutes!

30 Once bloody mortals – and now bloodier idols,
 If your priests lie not! And thou, ghastly beldame!
 Dripping with dusky gore, and trampling on
 The carcasses of Inde – away! away!
 Where am I? Where the spectres? Where – No – that
35 Is no false phantom: I should know it 'midst
 All that the dead dare gloomily raise up
 From their black gulf to daunt the living. Myrrha!
MYRRHA: Alas! thou art pale, and on thy brow the drops
 Gather like night dew. My beloved, hush –
40 Calm thee. Thy speech seems of another world,
 And thou art lord of this. Be of good cheer;
 All will go well.
SARDANAPALUS: Thy *hand* – so – 'tis thy hand;
 'Tis flesh; grasp – clasp – yet closer, till I feel
 Myself that which I was.
MYRRHA: At least know me
45 For what I am, and ever must be – thine.
SARDANAPALUS: I know it now. I know this life again.
 Ah, Myrrha! I have been where we shall be.
MYRRHA: My lord!
SARDANAPALUS: I've been i' the grave – where worms
  are lords,
 And kings are —— But I did not deem it so;
50 I thought 'twas nothing.
MYRRHA: So it is; except
 Unto the timid, who anticipate
 That which may never be.
SARDANAPALUS: Oh, Myrrha! if
 Sleep shows such things, what may not death disclose?
MYRRHA: I know no evil death can show, which life
55 Has not already shown to those who live
 Embodied longest. If there be indeed
 A shore where mind survives, 'twill be as mind,
 All unincorporate: or if there flits
 A shadow of this cumbrous clog of clay,
60 Which stalks, methinks, between our souls and heaven,
 And fetters us to earth – at least the phantom,
 Whate'er it have to fear, will not fear death.

SARDANAPALUS: I fear it not; but I have felt — have seen —
    A legion of the dead.
MYRRHA: And so have I.
65   The dust we tread upon was once alive,
    And wretched. But proceed: what hast thou seen?
    Speak it, 'twill lighten thy dimm'd mind.
SARDANAPALUS: Methought —
MYRRHA: Yet pause, thou art tired — in pain — exhausted;
    all
    Which can impair both strength and spirit: seek
70   Rather to sleep again.
SARDANAPALUS: Not now — I would not
    Dream; though I know it now to be a dream
    What I have dreamt: — and canst thou bear to hear it?
MYRRHA: I can bear all things, dreams of life or death,
    Which I participate with you in semblance
75   Or full reality.
SARDANAPALUS: And this look'd real,
    I tell you: after that these eyes were open,
    I saw them in their flight — for then they fled.
MYRRHA: Say on.
SARDANAPALUS: I saw, that is, I dream'd myself
    Here — here — even where we are, guests as we were,
80   Myself a host that deem'd himself but guest,
    Willing to equal all in social freedom;
    But, on my right hand and my left, instead
    Of thee and Zames, and our custom'd meeting,
    Was ranged on my left hand a haughty, dark,
85   And deadly face — I could not recognise it,
    Yet I had seen it, though I knew not where:
    The features were a giant's, and the eye
    Was still, yet lighted; his long locks curl'd down
    On his vast bust, whence a huge quiver rose
90   With shaft-heads feather'd from the eagle's wing,
    That peep'd up bristling through his serpent hair.
    I invited him to fill the cup which stood
    Between us, but he answer'd not — I fill'd it —
    He took it not, but stared upon me, till
95   I trembled at the fix'd glare of his eye:

I frown'd upon him as a king should frown –
He frown'd not in his turn, but look'd upon me
With the same aspect, which appall'd me more,
Because it changed not; and I turn'd for refuge
To milder guests, and sought them on the right,
Where thou wert wont to be. But —

    [*He pauses.*]

MYRRHA: What instead?

SARDANAPALUS: In thy own chair – thy own place in the
    banquet –
I sought thy sweet face in the circle – but
Instead – a grey-hair'd, wither'd, bloody-eyed,
And bloody-handed, ghastly, ghostly thing,
Female in garb, and crown'd upon the brow,
Furrow'd with years, yet sneering with the passion
Of vengeance, leering too with that of lust,
Sate: – my veins curdled.

MYRRHA: Is this all?

SARDANAPALUS: Upon
Her right hand – her lank, bird-like right hand – stood
A goblet, bubbling o'er with blood; and on
Her left, another, fill'd with – what I saw not,
But turn'd from it and her. But all along
The table sate a range of crowned wretches,
Of various aspects, but of one expression.

MYRRHA: And felt you not this a mere vision?

SARDANAPALUS: No:
It was so palpable, I could have touch'd them.
I turn'd from one face to another, in
The hope to find at last one which I knew
Ere I saw theirs: but no – all turn'd upon me,
And stared, but neither ate nor drank, but stared,
Till I grew stone, as they seem'd half to be,
Yet breathing stone, for I felt life in them,
And life in me: there was a horrid kind
Of sympathy between us, as if they
Had lost a part of death to come to me,
And I the half of life to sit by them.
We were in an existence all apart

From heaven or earth — And rather let me see

130   Death all than such a being!

MYRRHA: And the end?

SARDANAPALUS: At last I sate, marble, as they, when rose
The hunter and the crone; and smiling on me –
Yes, the enlarged but noble aspect of
The hunter smiled upon me – I should say,

135   His lips, for his eyes moved not – and the woman's
Thin lips relax'd to something like a smile.
Both rose, and the crown'd figures on each hand
Rose also, as if aping their chief shades –
Mere mimics even in death – but I sate still:

140   A desperate courage crept through every limb,
And at the last I fear'd them not, but laugh'd
Full in their phantom faces. But then – then
The hunter laid his hand on mine: I took it,
And grasp'd it – but it melted from my own;

145   While he too vanish'd, and left nothing but
The memory of a hero, for he look'd so.

MYRRHA: And was: the ancestor of heroes, too,
And thine no less.

SARDANAPALUS: Ay, Myrrha, but the woman,
The female who remain'd, she flew upon me,

150   And burnt my lips up with her noisome kisses;
And, flinging down the goblets on each hand,
Methought their poisons flow'd around us, till
Each form'd a hideous river. Still she clung;
The other phantoms, like a row of statues,

155   Stood dull as in our temples, but she still
Embraced me, while I shrunk from her, as if,
In lieu of her remote descendant, I
Had been the son who slew her for her incest.
Then – then – a chaos of all loathsome things

160   Throng'd thick and shapeless: I was dead, yet feeling –
Buried, and raised again – consumed by worms,
Purged by the flames, and wither'd in the air!
I can fix nothing further of my thoughts,
Save that I long'd for thee, and sought for thee,

165   In all these agonies, – and woke and found thee.

MYRRHA: So shalt thou find me ever at thy side,
    Here and hereafter, if the last may be.
    But think not of these things – the mere creations
    Of late events, acting upon a frame
170   Unused to toil, yet over-wrought by toil
    Such as might try the sternest.
SARDANAPALUS: I am better.
    Now that I see *thee once* more, *what was seen*
    Seems nothing.
        [*Enter* SALEMENES.]
SALEMENES: Is the king so soon awake?
SARDANAPALUS: Yes, brother, and I would I had not slept;
175   For all the predecessors of our line
    Rose up, methought, to drag me down to them.
    My father was amongst them, too; but he,
    I know not why, kept from me, leaving me
    Between the hunter-founder of our race,
180   And her, the homicide and husband-killer,
    Whom you call glorious.
SALEMENES: So I term you also,
    Now you have shown a spirit like to hers.
    By day-break I propose that we set forth,
    And charge once more the rebel crew, who still
185   Keep gathering head, repulsed, but not quite quell'd.
SARDANAPALUS: How wears the night?
SALEMENES: There yet remain some hours
    Of darkness: use them for your further rest.
SARDANAPALUS: No, not to-night, if 'tis not gone:
    methought
    I pass'd hours in that vision.
MYRRHA: Scarcely one;
190   I watch'd by you: it was a heavy hour,
    But an hour only.
SARDANAPALUS: Let us then hold council;
    To-morrow we set forth.
SALEMENES: But ere that time,
    I had a grace to seek.
SARDANAPALUS: 'Tis granted.
SALEMENES: Hear it

    Ere you reply too readily; and tis
195   For *your* ear only.

MYRRHA: Prince, I take my leave.

    [*Exit* MYRRHA.]

SALEMENES: That slave deserves her freedom.

SARDANAPALUS: Freedom
   only!
  That slave deserves to share a throne.

SALEMENES: Your patience –
  'Tis not yet vacant, and 'tis of its partner
  I come to speak with you.

SARDANAPALUS: How! of the queen?

200 SALEMENES: Even so. I judged it fitting for their safety,
  That, ere the dawn, she sets forth with her children
  For Paphlagonia, where our kinsman Cotta
  Governs; and there at all events secure
  My nephews and your sons their lives, and with them
205 Their just pretensions to the crown in case –

SARDANAPALUS: I perish – as is probable: well thought –
  Let them set forth with a sure escort.

SALEMENES: That
  Is all provided, and the galley ready
  To drop down the Euphrates; but ere they
210 Depart, will you not see —

SARDANAPALUS: My sons? It may
  Unman my heart, and the poor boys will weep;
  And what can I reply to comfort them,
  Save with some hollow hopes, and ill-worn smiles?
  You know I cannot feign.

SALEMENES: But you can feel
215 At least, I trust so: in a word, the queen
  Requests to see you ere you part – for ever.

SARDANAPALUS: Unto what end? what purpose? I will
   grant
  Aught – all that she can ask – but such a meeting.

SALEMENES: You know, or ought to know, enough of
   women,
220 Since you have studied them so steadily,
  That what they ask in aught that touches on
  The heart, is dearer to their feelings or

Their fancy, than the whole external world.
I think as you do of my sister's wish;
225   But 'twas her wish – she is my sister – you
Her husband – will you grant it?
SARDANAPALUS: 'Twill be useless:
But let her come.
SALEMENES: I go.
  [*Exit* SALEMENES.]
SARDANAPALUS: We have lived asunder
Too long to meet again – and *now* to meet!
Have I not cares enow, and pangs enow,
230   To bear alone, that we must mingle sorrows,
Who have ceased to mingle love?
  [*Re-enter* SALEMENES *and* ZARINA.]
SALEMENES: My sister! Courage:
Shame not our blood with trembling, but remember
From whence we sprung. The queen is present, sire.
ZARINA: I pray thee, brother, leave me.
SALEMENES: Since you ask it.
  [*Exit* SALEMENES.]
235   ZARINA: Alone with him! How many a year has pass'd,
Though we are still so young, since we have met,
Which I have worn in widowhood of heart.
He loved me not: yet he seems little changed –
Changed to me only – would the change were mutual!
240   He speaks not – scarce regards me – not a word –
Nor look – yet he *was* soft of voice and aspect,
Indifferent, not austere. My lord!
SARDANAPALUS: Zarina!
ZARINA: No, *not* Zarina – do not say Zarina.
That tone – that word – annihilate long years,
245   All things which make them longer.
SARDANAPALUS: 'Tis too late
To think of these past dreams. Let's not reproach –
That is, reproach me not – for the *last* time ——
ZARINA: And *first*. I ne'er reproach'd you.
SARDANAPALUS: 'Tis most true;
And that reproof comes heavier on my heart
250   Than —— But our hearts are not in our own power.

ZARINA: Nor hands; but I gave both.

SARDANAPALUS: Your brother said
    It was your will to see me, ere you went
    From Nineveh with —
      [*He hesitates*]

ZARINA: Our children: it is true.
    I wish'd to thank you that you have not divided

255   My heart from all that's left it now to love –
    Those who are yours and mine, who look like you,
    And look upon me as you look'd upon me
    Once — But they have not changed.

SARDANAPALUS: Nor ever will.
    I fain would have them dutiful.

ZARINA: I cherish

260   Those infants, not alone from the blind love
    Of a fond mother, but as a fond woman.
    They are now the only tie between us.

SARDANAPALUS: Deem not
    I have not done you justice: rather make them
    Resemble your own line than their own sire.

265   I trust them with you – to you: fit them for
    A throne, or, if that be denied — You have heard
    Of this night's tumults?

ZARINA: I had half forgotten,
    And could have welcomed any grief save yours,
    Which gave me to behold your face again.

270 SARDANAPALUS: The throne – I say it not in fear – but 'tis
    In peril; they perhaps may never mount it:
    But let them not for this lose sight of it.
    I will dare all things to bequeath it them,
    But if I fail, then they must win it back

275   Bravely – and, won, wear it wisely, not as I
    Have wasted down my royalty.

ZARINA: They ne'er
    Shall know from me of aught but what may honour
    Their father's memory.

SARDANAPALUS: Rather let them hear
    The truth from you than from a trampling world.

280   If they be in adversity, they'll learn

Too soon the scorn of crowds for crownless princes,
And find that all their father's sins are theirs.
My boys! – I could have borne it were I childless.
ZARINA: Oh! do not say so – do not poison all
285   My peace left, by unwishing that thou wert
A father. If thou conquerest, they shall reign,
And honour him who saved the realm for them,
So little cared for as his own; and if —
SARDANAPALUS: 'Tis lost, all earth will cry out thank your
          father!
290   And they will swell the echo with a curse.
ZARINA: That they shall never do; but rather honour
The name of him, who, dying like a king,
In his last hours did more for his own memory
Than many monarchs in a length of days,
295   Which date the flight of time, but make no annals.
SARDANAPALUS: Our annals draw perchance unto their
          close;
But at the least, whate'er the past, their end
Shall be like their beginning – memorable.
ZARINA: Yet, be not rash – be careful of your life,
300   Live but for those who love.
SARDANAPALUS: And who are they?
A slave, who loves from passion – I'll not say
Ambition – she has seen thrones shake, and loves;
A few friends who have revell'd till we are
As one, for they are nothing if I fall;
305   A brother I have injured – children whom
I have neglected, and a spouse —
ZARINA: Who loves.
SARDANAPALUS: And pardons?
ZARINA: I have never thought of this,
And cannot pardon till I have condemn'd.
SARDANAPALUS: My wife!
ZARINA: Now blessings on thee for that word!
310   I never thought to hear it more – from thee.
SARDANAPALUS: Oh! thou wilt hear it from my subjects.
          Yes –
These slaves whom I have nurtured, pamper'd, fed,

And swoln with peace, and gorged with plenty, till
They reign themselves – all monarchs in their
   mansions –
315 Now swarm forth in rebellion, and demand
His death, who made their lives a jubilee;
While the few upon whom I have no claim
Are faithful! This is true, yet monstrous.
ZARINA: 'Tis
Perhaps too natural; for benefits
320 Turn poison in bad minds.
SARDANAPALUS: And good ones make
Good out of evil. Happier than the bee,
Which hives not but from wholesome flowers.
ZARINA: Then reap
The honey, nor enquire whence 'tis derived.
Be satisfied – you are not all abandon'd.
325 SARDANAPALUS: My life insures me that. How long,
    bethink you,
Were not I yet a king, should I be mortal;
That is, where mortals *are*, not where they must be?
ZARINA: I know not. But yet live for my – that is,
Your children's sake!
SARDANAPALUS: My gentle, wrong'd Zarina!
330 I am the very slave of circumstance
And impulse – borne away with every breath!
Misplaced upon the throne – misplaced in life.
I know not what I could have been, but feel
I am not what I should be – let it end.
335 But take this with thee: if I was not form'd
To prize a love like thine, a mind like thine,
Nor dote even on thy beauty – as I've doted
On lesser charms, for no cause save that such
Devotion was a duty, and I hated
340 All that look'd like a chain for me or others
(This even rebellion must avouch); yet hear
These words, perhaps among my last – that none
E'er valued more thy virtues, though he knew not
To profit by them – as the miner lights
345 Upon a vein of virgin ore, discovering

That which avails him nothing: he hath found it,
But 'tis not his – but some superior's, who
Placed him to dig, but not divide the wealth
Which sparkles at his feet; nor dare he lift
350   Nor poise it, but must grovel on, upturning
The sullen earth.
ZARINA: Oh! if thou hast at length
Discover'd that my love is worth esteem,
I ask no more – but let us hence together,
And *I* – let me say *we* – shall yet be happy.
355   Assyria is not all the earth – we'll find
A world out of our own – and be more bless'd
Than I have ever been, or thou, with all
An empire to indulge thee.
    [*Enter* SALEMENES.]
SALEMENES: I must part ye –
The moments, which must not be lost, are passing.
360 ZARINA: Inhuman brother! wilt thou thus weigh out
Instants so high and blest?
SALEMENES: Blest!
ZARINA: He hath been
So gentle with me, that I cannot think
Of quitting.
SALEMENES: So – this feminine farewell
Ends as such partings end, in *no* departure.
365   I thought as much, and yielded against all
My better bodings. But it must not be.
ZARINA: Not be?
SALEMENES: Remain, and perish —
ZARINA: With my husband —
SALEMENES: And children.
ZARINA: Alas!
SALEMENES: Hear me, sister, like
My sister: – all's prepared to make your safety
370   Certain, and of the boys too, our last hopes;
'Tis not a single question of mere feeling,
Though that were much – but 'tis a point of state:
The rebels would do more to seize upon
The offspring of their sovereign, and so crush —

375   ZARINA: Ah! do not name it.
       SALEMENES: Well, then, mark me: when
           They are safe beyond the Median's grasp, the rebels
           Have miss'd their chief aim – the extinction of
           The line of Nimrod. Though the present king
           Fall, his sons live for victory and vengeance.
380   ZARINA: But could not I remain, alone?
       SALEMENES: What! leave
           Your children, with two parents and yet orphans –
           In a strange land – so young, so distant?
       ZARINA: No –
           My heart will break.
       SALEMENES: Now you know all – decide.
       SARDANAPALUS: Zarina, he hath spoken well, and we
385   Must yield awhile to this necessity.
           Remaining here, you may lose all; departing,
           You save the better part of what is left,
           To both of us, and to such loyal hearts
           As yet beat in these kingdoms.
       SALEMENES: The time presses.
390   SARDANAPALUS: Go, then. If e'er we meet again, perhaps
           I may be worthier of you – and, if not,
           Remember that my faults, though not atoned for,
           Are *ended*. Yet, I dread thy nature will
           Grieve more above the blighted name and ashes
395   Which once were mightiest in Assyria – than —
           But I grow womanish again, and must not;
           I must learn sternness now. My sins have all
           Been of the softer order — *hide* thy tears –
           I do not bid thee *not* to shed them – 'twere
400   Easier to stop Euphrates at its source
           Than one tear of a true and tender heart –
           But let me not behold them; they unman me
           Here when I had remann'd myself. My brother,
           Lead her away.
       ZARINA: Oh, God! I never shall
405   Behold him more!
       SARDANAPALUS [*striving to conduct her*]: Nay, sister, I *must*
           be obey'd.

ZARINA: I must remain – away! you shall not hold me.
　　What, shall he die alone? – *I* live alone?
SALEMENES: He shall *not die alone*; but lonely you
　　Have lived for years.
ZARINA:　　　　　　That's false! I knew *he* lived,
410　　And lived upon his image – let me go!
SALEMENES [*conducting her off the stage*]: Nay, then, I must
　　use some fraternal force,
　　Which you will pardon.
ZARINA:　　　　　　Never. Help me! Oh!
　　Sardanapalus, wilt thou thus behold me
　　Torn from thee?
SALEMENES:　　Nay – then all is lost again,
415　　If that this moment is not gain'd.
ZARINA:　　　　　　　　　　My brain turns –
　　My eyes fail – where is he?
　　　　[*She faints.*]
SARDANAPALUS [*advancing*]:　No – set her down –
　　She's dead – and you have slain her.
SALEMENES:　　　　　　　'Tis the mere
　　Faintness of o'erwrought passion: in the air
　　She will recover. Pray, keep back. – [*Aside.*] I must
420　　Avail myself of this sole moment to
　　Bear her to where her children are embark'd,
　　I' the royal galley on the river.
　　　　[SALEMENES *bears her off.*]
SARDANAPALUS [*solus*]:　　　　This, too –
　　And this too must I suffer – I, who never
　　Inflicted purposely on human hearts
425　　A voluntary pang! But that is false –
　　She loved me, and I loved her. – Fatal passion!
　　Why dost thou not expire *at once* in hearts
　　Which thou hast lighted up at once? Zarina!
　　I must pay dearly for the desolation
430　　Now brought upon thee. Had I never loved
　　But thee, I should have been an unopposed
　　Monarch of honouring nations. To what gulfs
　　A single deviation from the track
　　Of human duties leads even those who claim

435   The homage of mankind as their born due,
       And find it, till they forfeit it themselves!
         [*Enter* MYRRHA.]
    SARDANAPALUS: *You* here! Who call'd you?
    MYRRHA: No one – but I heard
       Far off a voice of wail and lamentation,
       And thought —
    SARDANAPALUS: It forms no portion of your duties
440   To enter here till sought for.
    MYRRHA: Though I might,
       Perhaps, recal some softer words of yours
       (Although they *too were chiding*), which reproved me,
       Because I ever dreaded to intrude;
       Resisting my own wish and your injunction
445   To heed no time nor presence, but approach you
       Uncall'd for: – I retire.
    SARDANAPALUS: Yet stay – being here.
       I pray you pardon me: events have sour'd me
       Till I wax peevish – heed it not: I shall
       Soon be myself again.
    MYRRHA: I wait with patience,
450   What I shall see with pleasure
    SARDANAPALUS: Scarce a moment
       Before your entrance in this hall, Zarina,
       Queen of Assyria, departed hence.
    MYRRHA: Ah!
    SARDANAPALUS: Wherefore do you start?
    MYRRHA: Did I do so?
    SARDANAPALUS: 'Twas well you enter'd by another portal,
455   Else you had met. That pang at least is spared her!
    MYRRHA: I know to feel for her.
    SARDANAPALUS: That is too much,
       And beyond nature – 'tis nor mutual
       Nor possible. You cannot pity her,
       Nor she aught but —
    MYRRHA: Despise the favourite slave?
460   Not more than I have ever scorn'd myself.
    SARDANAPALUS: Scorn'd! what, to be the envy of your
       sex,

And lord it o'er the heart of the world's lord?
MYRRHA: Were you the lord of twice ten thousand
worlds –
As you are like to lose the one you sway'd –
465   I did abase myself as much in being
Your paramour, as though you were a peasant –
Nay, more, if that the peasant were a Greek.
SARDANAPALUS: You talk it well —
MYRRHA: And truly.
SARDANAPALUS: In the hour
Of man's adversity all things grow daring
470   Against the falling; but as I am not
Quite fall'n, nor now disposed to bear reproaches,
Perhaps because I merit them too often,
Let us then part while peace is still between us.
MYRRHA: Part!
SARDANAPALUS: Have not all past human beings parted,
475   And must not all the present one day part?
MYRRHA: Why?
SARDANAPALUS: For your safety, which I will have look'd
to,
With a strong escort to your native land;
And such gifts, as, if you had not been all
A queen, shall make your dowry worth a kingdom.
480   MYRRHA: I pray you talk not thus.
SARDANAPALUS: The queen is gone:
You need not shame to follow. I would fall
Alone – I seek no partners but in pleasure.
MYRRHA: And I no pleasure but in parting not.
You shall not force me from you.
SARDANAPALUS: Think well of it –
485   It soon may be too late.
MYRRHA: So let it be;
For then you cannot separate me from you.
SARDANAPALUS: And will not; but I thought you wish'd it.
MYRRHA: I!
SARDANAPALUS: You spoke of your abasement.
MYRRHA: And I feel it
Deeply – more deeply than all things but love.

490   SARDANAPALUS: Then fly from it.
       MYRRHA: 'Twill not recal the past —
       'Twill not restore my honour, nor my heart.
       No — here I stand or fall. If that you conquer,
       I live to joy in your great triumph: should
       Your lot be different, I'll not weep, but share it.
495   You did not doubt me a few hours ago.
       SARDANAPALUS: Your courage never — nor your love till
               now;
       And none could make me doubt it save yourself.
       Those words —
       MYRRHA: Were words. I pray you, let the proofs
       Be in the past acts you were pleased to praise
500   This very night, and in my further bearing,
       Beside, wherever you are borne by fate.
       SARDANAPALUS: I am content: and, trusting in my cause,
       Think we may yet be victors and return
       To peace — the only victory I covet.
505   To me war is no glory — conquest no
       Renown. To be forced thus to uphold my right
       Sits heavier on my heart than all the wrongs
       These men would bow me down with. Never, never
       Can I forget this night, even should I live
510   To add it to the memory of others.
       I thought to have made mine inoffensive rule
       An era of sweet peace 'midst bloody annals,
       A green spot amidst desert centuries,
       On which the future would turn back and smile,
515   And cultivate, or sigh when it could not
       Recal Sardanapalus' golden reign.
       I thought to have made my realm a paradise,
       And every moon an epoch of new pleasures.
       I took the rabble's shouts for love — the breath
520   Of friends for truth — the lips of woman for
       My only guerdon — so they are, my Myrrha:
               [*He kisses her*.]
       Kiss me. Now let them take my realm and life!
       They shall have both, but never thee!
       MYRRHA: No, never!

Man may despoil his brother man of all
525   That's great or glittering – kingdoms fall – hosts yield –
Friends fail – slaves fly – and all betray – and, more
Than all, the most indebted – but a heart
That loves without self-love! 'Tis here – now prove it.
    [*Enter* SALEMENES.]
SALEMENES: I sought you – How! *she* here again?
SARDANAPALUS: Return not
530   *Now* to reproof: methinks your aspect speaks
Of higher matter than a woman's presence.
SALEMENES: The only woman whom it much imports me
At such a moment now is safe in absence —
The queen's embark'd.
SARDANAPALUS: And well? say that much.
SALEMENES: Yes.
535   Her transient weakness has pass'd o'er; at least,
It settled into tearless silence: her
Pale face and glittering eye, after a glance
Upon her sleeping children, were still fix'd
Upon the palace towers as the swift galley
540   Stole down the hurrying stream beneath the starlight;
But she said nothing.
SARDANAPALUS: Would I felt no more
Than she has said!
SALEMENES: 'Tis now too late to feel!
Your feelings cannot cancel a sole pang:
To change them, my advices bring sure tidings
545   That the rebellious Medes and Chaldees, marshall'd
By their two leaders, are already up
In arms again; and, serrying their ranks,
Prepare to attack: they have apparently
Been join'd by other satraps.
SARDANAPALUS: What! more rebels?
550   Let us be first, then.
SALEMENES: That were hardly prudent
Now, though it was our first intention. If
By noon to-morrow we are join'd by those
I've sent for by sure messengers, we shall be
In strength enough to venture an attack,

555   Ay, and pursuit too; but till then, my voice
         Is to await the onset.
   SARDANAPALUS: I detest
         That waiting; though it seems so safe to fight
         Behind high walls, and hurl down foes into
         Deep fosses, or behold them sprawl on spikes
560   Strew'd to receive them, still I like it not —
         My soul seems lukewarm; but when I set on them,
         Though they were piled on mountains, I would have
         A pluck at them, or perish in hot blood! —
         Let me then charge.
   SALEMENES: You talk like a young soldier.
565 SARDANAPALUS: I am no soldier, but a man: speak not
         Of soldiership, I loathe the word, and those
         Who pride themselves upon it; but direct me
         Where I may pour upon them.
   SALEMENES: You must spare
         To expose your life too hastily; 'tis not
570   Like mine or any other subject's breath:
         The whole war turns upon it – with it; this
         Alone creates it, kindles, and may quench it —
         Prolong it – end it.
   SARDANAPALUS: Then let us end both!
         'Twere better thus, perhaps, than prolong either;
575   I'm sick of one, perchance of both.
         [*A trumpet sounds without.*]
   SALEMENES: Hark!
   SARDANAPALUS: Let us
         Reply, not listen.
   SALEMENES: And your wound!
   SARDANAPALUS: 'Tis bound —
         'Tis heal'd – I had forgotten it. Away!
         A leech's lancet would have scratch'd me deeper;
         The slave that gave it might be well ashamed
580   To have struck so weakly.
   SALEMENES: Now, may none this hour
         Strike with a better aim!
   SARDANAPALUS: Ay, if we conquer;
         But if not, they will only leave to me

A task they might have spared their king. Upon them!
    [*Trumpet sounds again.*]
SALEMENES: I am with you.
SARDANAPALUS: Ho, my arms! again, my arms!
    [*Exeunt.*]

Act V

SCENE I

The same Hall in the Palace.

    [MYRRHA *and* BALEA.]
MYRRHA [*at a window*]:
    The day at last has broken. What a night
    Hath usher'd it! How beautiful in heaven!
    Though varied with a transitory storm,
    More beautiful in that variety!
5   How hideous upon earth! where peace and hope,
    And love and revel, in an hour were trampled
    By human passions to a human chaos,
    Not yet resolved to separate elements –
    'Tis warring still! And can the sun so rise,
10   So bright, so rolling back the clouds into
    Vapours more lovely than the unclouded sky,
    With golden pinnacles, and snowy mountains,
    And billows purpler than the ocean's, making
    In heaven a glorious mockery of the earth,
15   So like we almost deem it permanent;
    So fleeting, we can scarcely call it aught
    Beyond a vision, 'tis so transiently
    Scatter'd along the eternal vault: and yet
    It dwells upon the soul, and soothes the soul,
20   And blends itself into the soul, until
    Sunrise and sunset form the haunted epoch
    Of sorrow and of love; which they who mark not,
    Know not the realms where those twin genii
    (Who chasten and who purify our hearts,

25   So that we would not change their sweet rebukes
        For all the boisterous joys that ever shook
        The air with clamour) build the palaces
        Where their fond votaries repose and breathe
        Briefly; — but in that brief cool calm inhale
30   Enough of heaven to enable them to bear
        The rest of common, heavy, human hours,
        And dream them through in placid sufferance;
        Though seemingly employ'd like all the rest
        Of toiling breathers in allotted tasks
35   Of pain or pleasure, *two* names for *one* feeling,
        Which our internal, restless agony
        Would vary in the sound, although the sense
        Escapes our highest efforts to be happy.
    BALEA: You muse right calmly: and can you so, watch
40   The sunrise which may be our last?
    MYRRHA: It is
        Therefore that I so watch it, and reproach
        Those eyes, which never may behold it more,
        For having look'd upon it oft, too oft,
        Without reverence and the rapture due
45   To that which keeps all earth from being as fragile
        As I am in this form. Come, look upon it,
        The Chaldee's god, which, when I gaze upon,
        I grow almost a convert to your Baal.
    BALEA: As now he reigns in heaven, so once on earth
50   He sway'd.
    MYRRHA: He sways it now far more, then; never
        Had earthly monarch half the power and glory
        Which centres in a single ray of his.
    BALEA: Surely he is a god!
    MYRRHA: So we Greeks deem too;
        And yet I sometimes think that gorgeous orb
55   Must rather be the abode of gods than one
        Of the immortal sovereigns. Now he breaks
        Through all the clouds, and fills my eyes with light
        That shuts the world out. I can look no more.
    BALEA: Hark! heard you not a sound?
    MYRRHA: No, 'twas mere fancy;

60   They battle it beyond the wall, and not
        As in late midnight conflict in the very
        Chambers: the palace has become a fortress
        Since that insidious hour; and here, within
        The very centre, girded by vast courts
65   And regal halls of pyramid proportions,
        Which must be carried one by one before
        They penetrate to where they then arrived,
        We are as much shut in even from the sound
        Of peril as from glory.

BALEA: But they reach'd
70   Thus far before.

MYRRHA: Yes, by surprise, and were
        Beat back by valour: now at once we have
        Courage and vigilance to guard us.

BALEA: May they
        Prosper!

MYRRHA: That is the prayer of many, and
        The dread of more: it is an anxious hour;
75   I strive to keep it from my thoughts. Alas!
        How vainly!

BALEA: It is said the king's demeanour
        In the late action scarcely more appall'd
        The rebels than astonish'd his true subjects.

MYRRHA: 'Tis easy to astonish or appal
80   The vulgar mass which moulds a horde of slaves;
        But he did bravely.

BALEA: Slew he not Beleses?
        I heard the soldiers say he struck him down.

MYRRHA: The wretch was overthrown, but rescued to
        Triumph, perhaps, o'er one who vanquish'd him
85   In fight, as he had spared him in his peril;
        And by that heedless pity risk'd a crown.

BALEA: Hark!

MYRRHA: You are right: some steps approach but slowly.
        [*Enter Soldiers, bearing in* SALEMENES *wounded, with
        a broken Javelin in his Side: they seat him upon one of
        the Couches which furnish the Apartment.*]

MYRRHA: Oh, Jove!

BALEA: Then all is over.

SALEMENES: That is false.
    Hew down the slave who says so, if a soldier.

90   MYRRHA: Spare him – he's none: a mere court butterfly,
    That flutters in the pageant of a monarch.

SALEMENES: Let him live on, then.

MYRRHA: So wilt thou, I trust.

SALEMENES: I fain would live this hour out, and the event,
    But doubt it. Wherefore did ye bear me here?

95   SOLDIER: By the king's order. When the javelin struck you,
    You fell and fainted: 'twas his strict command
    To bear you to this hall.

SALEMENES: 'Twas not ill done:
    For seeming slain in that cold dizzy trance,
    The sight might shake our soldiers – but – 'tis vain,

100   I feel it ebbing!

MYRRHA: Let me see the wound;
    I am not quite skilless: in my native land
    'Tis part of our instruction. War being constant,
    We are nerved to look on such things.

SOLDIER: Best extract
    The javelin.

MYRRHA: Hold! no, no, it cannot be.

105   SALEMENES: I am sped, then!

MYRRHA: With the blood that fast must follow
    The extracted weapon, I do fear thy life.

SALEMENES: And I *not* death. Where was the king when
        you
    Convey'd me from the spot where I was stricken?

SOLDIER: Upon the same ground, and encouraging

110   With voice and gesture the dispirited troops
    Who had seen you fall, and falter'd back.

SALEMENES: Whom heard ye
    Named next to the command?

SOLDIER: I did not hear.

SALEMENES: Fly, then, and tell him, 'twas my last request
    That Zames take my post until the junction,

115   So hoped for, yet delay'd, of Ofratanes,

Satrap of Susa. Leave me here: our troops
Are not so numerous to spare your absence.

SOLDIER: But prince —

SALEMENES: Hence, I say! Here's a courtier and
A woman, the best chamber company.

120 As you would not permit me to expire
Upon the field, I'll have no idle soldiers
About my sick couch. Hence! and do my bidding!
    [*Exeunt the Soldiers.*]

MYRRHA: Gallant and glorious spirit! must the earth
So soon resign thee?

SALEMENES: Gentle Myrrha, 'tis

125 The end I would have chosen, had I saved
The monarch or the monarchy by this;
As 'tis, I have not outlived them.

MYRRHA: You wax paler.

SALEMENES: Your hand; this broken weapon but prolongs
My pangs, without sustaining life enough

130 To make me useful: I would draw it forth
And my life with it, could I but hear how
The fight goes.
    [*Enter* SARDANAPALUS *and Soldiers.*]

SARDANAPALUS: My best brother!

SALEMENES: And the battle
Is lost?

SARDANAPALUS [*despondingly*]: You see *me here.*

SALEMENES: I'd rather see you *thus!*
    [*He draws out the weapon from the wound, and dies.*]

SARDANAPALUS: And *thus* I will be seen; unless the
    succour,

135 The last frail reed of our beleaguer'd hopes,
Arrive with Ofratanes.

MYRRHA: Did you not
Receive a token from your dying brother,
Appointing Zames chief?

SARDANAPALUS: I did.

MYRRHA: Where's Zames?

SARDANAPALUS: Dead.

MYRRHA: And Altada?

SARDANAPALUS: Dying.
MYRRHA: Pania? Sfero?
140 SARDANAPALUS: Pania yet lives; but Sfero's fled or captive.
       I am alone.
     MYRRHA: And is all lost?
     SARDANAPALUS: Our walls,
       Though thinly mann'd, may still hold out against
       Their present force, or aught save treachery:
       But i' the field —
     MYRRHA: I thought 'twas the intent
145   Of Salemenes not to risk a sally
       Till ye were strenthen'd by the expected succours.
     SARDANAPALUS: *I* over-ruled him.
     MYRRHA: Well, the fault's a brave one.
     SARDANAPALUS: But fatal. Oh, my brother! I would give
       These realms, of which thou wert the ornament,
150   The sword and shield, the sole-redeeming honour,
       To call back — But I will not weep for thee;
       Thou shalt be mourn'd for as thou wouldst be mourn'd.
       It grieves me most that thou couldst quit this life
       Believing that I could survive what thou
155   Hast died for – our long royalty of race.
       If I redeem it, I will give thee blood
       Of thousands, tears of millions, for atonement
       (The tears of all the good are thine already).
       If not, we meet again soon, – if the spirit
160   Within us lives beyond: – thou readest mine,
       And dost me justice now. Let me once clasp
       That yet warm hand, and fold that throbless heart
             [*Embraces the body.*]
       To this which beats so bitterly. Now, bear
       The body hence.
     SOLDIER: Where?
     SARDANAPALUS: To my proper chamber.
165   Place it beneath my canopy, as though
       The king lay there: when this is done, we will
       Speak further of the rites due to such ashes.
             [*Exeunt Soldiers with the body of* SALEMENES.]
             [*Enter* PANIA.]

SARDANAPALUS: Well, Pania! have you placed the guards, and issued
    The orders fix'd on?

PANIA: Sire, I have obey'd.

170 SARDANAPALUS: And do the soldiers keep their hearts up?

PANIA: Sire?

SARDANAPALUS: I'm answer'd! When a king asks twice, and has
    A question as an answer to *his* question,
    It is a portent. What! they are dishearten'd?

PANIA: The death of Salemenes, and the shouts

175   Of the exulting rebels on his fall,
    Have made them —

SARDANAPALUS: *Rage* – not droop – it should have been.
    We'll find the means to rouse them.

PANIA: Such a loss
    Might sadden even a victory.

SARDANAPALUS: Alas!
    Who can so feel it as I feel? but yet,

180   Though coop'd within these walls, they are strong, and we
    Have those without will break their way through hosts,
    To make their sovereign's dwelling what it was –
    A palace; not a prison, nor a fortress.
        [*Enter an* OFFICER, *hastily.*]

SARDANAPALUS: Thy face seems ominous. Speak!

OFFICER: I dare not

SARDANAPALUS: Dare not?

185   While millions dare revolt with sword in hand!
    That's strange. I pray thee break that loyal silence
    Which loathes to shock its sovereign; we can hear
    Worse than thou hast to tell.

PANIA: Proceed, thou hearest.

OFFICER: The wall which skirted near the river's brink

190   Is thrown down by the sudden inundation
    Of the Euphrates, which now rolling, swoln
    From the enormous mountains where it rises,
    By the late rains of that tempestuous region,

O'erfloods its banks, and hath destroy'd the bulwark.

195 PANIA: That's a black augury! it has been said
For ages, 'That the city ne'er should yield
To man, until the river grew its foe.'

SARDANAPALUS: I can forgive the omen, not the ravage.
How much is swept down of the wall?

OFFICER: About

200 Some twenty stadii.

SARDANAPALUS: And all this is left
Pervious to the assailants?

OFFICER: For the present
The river's fury must impede the assault;
But when he shrinks into his wonted channel,
And may be cross'd by the accustom'd barks,

205 The palace is their own.

SARDANAPALUS: That shall be never.
Though men, and gods, and elements, and omens,
Have risen up 'gainst one who ne'er provoked them,
My father's house shall never be a cave
For wolves to horde and howl in.

PANIA: With your sanction,

210 I will proceed to the spot, and take such measures
For the assurance of the vacant space
As time and means permit,

SARDANAPALUS: About it straight,
And bring me back, as speedily as full
And fair investigation may permit,

215 Report of the true state of this irruption
Of waters.

        [*Exeunt* PANIA *and the* OFFICER.]

MYRRHA: Thus the very waves rise up
Against you.

SARDANAPALUS: They are not my subjects, girl,
And may be pardon'd, since they can't be punish'd.

MYRRHA: I joy to see this portent shakes you not.

220 SARDANAPALUS: I am past the fear of portents: they can tell
me
Nothing I have not told myself since midnight:
Despair anticipates such things.

MYRRHA: Despair!

SARDANAPALUS: No; not despair precisely. When we know
     All that can come, and how to meet it, our
225 Resolves, if firm, may merit a more noble
     Word than this is to give it utterances
     But what are words to us? we have well nigh done
     With them and all things.

MYRRHA: Save *one deed* – the last
     And greatest to all mortals; crowning act
230 Of all that was – or is – or is to be –
     The only thing common to all mankind,
     So different in their births, tongues, sexes, natures,
     Hues, features, climes, times, feelings, intellects,
     Without one point of union save in this,
235 . To which we tend, for which we're born, and thread
     The labyrinth of mystery, call'd life.

SARDANAPALUS: Our clew being well nigh wound out, let's
     be cheerful.
     They who have nothing more to fear may well
     Indulge a smile at that which once appall'd;
240 As children at discover'd bugbears.
          [*Re-enter* PANIA.]

PANIA: 'Tis
     As was reported: I have order'd there
     A double guard, withdrawing from the wall
     Where it was strongest the required addition
     To watch the breach occasion'd by the waters.

245 SARDANAPALUS: You have done your duty faithfully, and
          as
     My worthy Pania! further ties between us
     Draw near a close. I pray you take this key:
          [*Gives a key.*]
     It opens to a secret chamber, placed
     Behind the couch in my own chamber. (Now
250 Press'd by a nobler weight than e'er it bore –
     Though a long line of sovereigns have lain down
     Along its golden frame – as bearing for
     A time what late was Salenenes). Search
     The secret covert to which this will lead you;

255   'Tis full of treasure; take it for yourself
    And your companions: there's enough to load ye,
    Though ye be many. Let the slaves be freed, too;
    And all the inmates of the palace, of
    Whatever sex, now quit it in an hour.
260   Then launch the regal barks, once form'd for pleasure,
    And now to serve for safety, and embark.
    The river's broad and swoln, and uncommanded
    (More potent than a king) by these besiegers.
    Fly! and be happy!
PANIA: Under your protection!
265   So you accompany your faithful guard.
SARDANAPALUS: No, Pania! that must not be; get thee
        hence
    And leave me to my fate.
PANIA: 'Tis the first time
    I ever disobey'd: but now —
SARDANAPALUS: So all men
    Dare beard me now, and Insolence within
270   Apes Treason from without. Question no further;
    'Tis my command, my last command. Wilt *thou*
    Oppose it? *thou*!
PANIA: But yet – not yet.
SARDANAPALUS: Well, then,
    Swear that you will obey when I shall give
    The signal.
PANIA: With a heavy but true heart,
275   I promise.
SARDANAPALUS: 'Tis enough. Now order here
    Faggots, pine-nuts, and wither'd leaves, and such
    Things as catch fire and blaze with one sole spark;
    Bring cedar, too, and precious drugs, and spices,
    And mighty planks, to nourish a tall pile;
280   Bring frankincense and myrrh, too, for it is
    For a great sacrifice I build the pyre;
    And heap them round yon throne.
PANIA: My lord!
SARDANAPALUS: I have said it,
    And *you* have *sworn*.

PANIA: And could keep my faith
    Without a vow.
        [*Exit* PANIA.]
MYRRHA: What mean you?
SARDANAPALUS: You shall know
285   Anon – what the whole earth shall ne'er forget.
        [PANIA, *returning with a* HERALD.]
PANIA: My king, in going forth upon my duty,
    This herald has been brought before me, craving
    An audience.
SARDANAPALUS: Let him speak.
HERALD: The *King* Arbaces —
SARDANAPALUS: What, crown'd already? – But,
        proceed.
HERALD: Beleses,
290   The anointed high-priest —
SARDANAPALUS: Of what god or demon?
    With new kings rise new altars. But, proceed;
    You are sent to prate your master's will, and not
    Reply to mine.
HERALD: And Satrap Ofratanes —
SARDANAPALUS: Why, *he* is *ours*.
HERALD [*showing a ring*]:   Be sure that he is now
295   In the camp of the conquerors; behold
    His signet ring.
SARDANAPALUS: 'Tis his. A worthy triad!
    Poor Salemenes! thou hast died in time
    To see one treachery the less: this man
    Was thy true friend and my most trusted subject.
300   Proceed.
HERALD: They offer thee thy life, and freedom
    Of choice to single out a residence
    In any of the further provinces,
    Guarded and watch'd, but not confined in person,
    Where thou shalt pass thy days in peace; but on
305   Condition that the three young princes are
    Given up as hostages.
SARDANAPALUS [*ironically*]: The generous victors!

HERALD: I wait the answer.

SARDANAPALUS: Answer, slave! How long
    Have slaves decided on the doom of kings?

HERALD: Since they were free.

SARDANAPALUS: Mouthpiece of mutiny!
310   Thou at the least shalt learn the penalty
        Of treason, though its proxy only. Pania!
        Let his head be thrown from our walls within
        The rebels' lines, his carcass down the river.
        Away with him!

        [PANIA *and the Guards seizing him.*]

PANIA: I never yet obey'd
315   Your orders with more pleasure than the present.
        Hence with him, soldiers! do not soil this hall
        Of royalty with treasonable gore;
        Put him to rest without.

HERALD: A single word:
        My office, king, is sacred.

SARDANAPALUS: And what's *mine?*
320   That thou shouldst come and dare to ask of me
        To lay it down?

HERALD: I but obey'd my orders,
        At the same peril if refused, as now
        Incurr'd by my obedience.

SARDANAPALUS: So there are
        New monarchs of an hour's growth as despotic
325   As sovereigns swathed in purple, and enthroned
        From birth to manhood!

HERALD: My life waits your breath.
        Yours (I speak humbly) – but it may be – yours
        May also be in danger scarce less imminent:
        Would it then suit the last hours of a line
330   Such as is that of Nimrod, to destroy
        A peaceful herald, unarm'd, in his office;
        And violate not only all that man
        Holds sacred between man and man – but that
        More holy tie which links us with the gods?

335 SARDANAPALUS: He's right. – Let him go free. – My life's
        last act

Shall not be one of wrath. Here, fellow, take
    [*Gives him a golden cup from a table near.*]
This golden goblet, let it hold your wine,
And think of *me*; or melt it into ingots,
And think of nothing but their weight and value.

340 HERALD: I thank you doubly for my life, and this
    Most gorgeous gift, which renders it more precious.
    But must I bear no answer?

SARDANAPALUS: Yes, – I ask
    An hour's truce to consider.

HERALD: But an hour's?

SARDANAPALUS: An hour's: if at the expiration of
345   That time your masters hear no further from me,
    They are to deem that I reject their terms,
    And act befittingly.

HERALD: I shall not fail
    To be a faithful legate of your pleasure.

SARDANAPALUS: And hark! a word more.

HERALD: I shall not forget
    it,
350   Whate'er it be.

SARDANAPALUS: Commend me to Beleses;
    And tell him, ere a year expire, I summon
    Him hence to meet me.

HERALD: Where?

SARDANAPALUS: At Babylon.
    At least from thence he will depart to meet me.

HERALD: I shall obey you to the letter.
    [*Exit* HERALD.]

SARDANAPALUS: Pania! –
355   Now, my good Pania! – quick – with what I order'd.

PANIA: My lord, – the soldiers are already charged.
    And see! they enter.
    [*Soldiers enter, and form a Pile about the Throne, &c.*]

SARDANAPALUS: Higher, my good soldiers,
    And thicker yet; and see that the foundation
    Be such as will not speedily exhaust
340   Its own too subtle flame; nor yet be quench'd
    With aught officious aid would bring to quell it.
    Let the throne form the *core* of it; I would not

Leave that, save fraught with fire unquenchable,
To the new comers. Frame the whole as if

365   'Twere to enkindle the strong tower of our
Inveterate enemies. Now it bears an aspect!
How say you, Pania, will this pile suffice
For a king's obsequies?

PANIA: Ay, for a kingdom's.
I understand you, now.

SARDANAPALUS: And blame me?

PANIA: No –

370   Let me but fire the pile, and share it with you.

MYRRHA: That duty's mine.

PANIA: A woman's!

MYRRHA: 'Tis the soldier's
Part to die *for* his sovereign, and why not
The woman's with her lover?

PANIA: 'Tis most strange!

MYRRHA: But not so rare, my Pania, as thou think'st it.

375   In the mean time, live thou. – Farewell! the pile
Is ready.

PANIA: I should shame to leave my sovereign
With but a single female to partake
His death.

SARDANAPALUS: Too many far have heralded
Me to the dust, already. Get thee hence;

380   Enrich thee.

PANIA: And live wretched!

SARDANAPALUS: Think upon
Thy vow: – 'tis sacred and irrevocable.

PANIA: Since it is so, farewell.

SARDANAPALUS: Search well my chamber,
Feel no remorse at bearing off the gold;
Remember, what you leave you leave the slaves

385   Who slew me: and when you have borne away
All safe off to your boats, blow one long blast
Upon the trumpet as you quit the palace.
The river's brink is too remote, its stream
Too loud at present to permit the echo

390   To reach distinctly from its banks. Then fly, –

And as you sail, turn back; but still keep on
Your way along the Euphrates: if you reach
The land of Paphlagonia, where the queen
Is safe with my three sons in Cotta's court,
395 Say, what you *saw* at parting, and request
That she remember what I *said* at one
Parting more mournful still.
PANIA: That royal hand!
Let me then once more press it to my lips;
And these poor soldiers who throng round you, and
400 Would fain die with you!
          [*The Soldiers and* PANIA *throng round him, kissing his
          hand and the hem of his robe.*]
SARDANAPALUS: My best! my last friends!
Let's not unman each other: part at once:
All farewells should be sudden, when for ever,
Else they make an eternity of moments,
And clog the last sad sands of life with tears.
405 Hence, and be happy: trust me, I am not
Now to be pitied; or far more for what
Is past than present; – for the future, 'tis
In the hands of the deities, if such
There be: I shall know soon. Farewell – Farewell.
          [*Exeunt* PANIA *and Soldiers.*]
410 MYRRHA: These men were honest: it is comfort still
That our last looks should be on loving faces.
SARDANAPALUS: And *lovely* ones, my beautiful! – but hear
          me!
If at this moment, – for we now are on
The brink, – thou feel'st an inward shrinking from
415 This leap through flame into the future, say it:
I shall not love thee less; nay, perhaps more,
For yielding to thy nature: and there's time
Yet for thee to escape hence.
MYRRHA: Shall I light
One of the torches which lie heap'd beneath
420 The ever-burning lamp that burns without,
Before Baal's shrine, in the adjoining hall?
SARDANAPALUS: Do so. Is that thy answer?

MYRRHA: Thou shalt see.
        [*Exit* MYRRHA.]
SARDANAPALUS [*solus*]: She's firm. My fathers! whom I
        will rejoin,
It may be, purified by death from some
425   Of the gross stains of too material being,
        I would not leave your ancient first abode
        To the defilement of usurping bondmen;
        If I have not kept your inheritance
        As ye bequeath'd it, this bright part of it,
430   Your treasure, your abode, your sacred relics
        Of arms, and records, monuments, and spoils,
        In which *they* would have revell'd, I bear with me
        To you in that absorbing element,
        Which most personifies the soul as leaving
435   The least of matter unconsumed before
        Its fiery workings: – and the light of this
        Most royal of funereal pyres shall be
        Not a mere pillar form'd of cloud and flame,
        A beacon in the horizon for a day,
440   And then a mount of ashes, but a light
        To lesson ages, rebel nations, and
        Voluptuous princes. Time shall quench full many
        A people's records, and a hero's acts;
        Sweep empire after empire, like this first
445   Of empires, into nothing; but even then
        Shall spare this deed of mine, and hold it up
        A problem few dare imitate, and none
        Despise – but, it may be, avoid the life
        Which led to such a consummation.
                [MYRRHA *returns with a lighted Torch in one Hand,*
                and a Cup in the other.]
        MYRRHA: Lo!
450   I've lit the lamp which lights us to the stars.
SARDANAPALUS: And the cup?
MYRRHA: 'Tis my country's custom to
        Make a libation to the gods.
SARDANAPALUS: And mine
        To make libations amongst men. I've not

Forgot the custom; and although alone,
455   Will drain one draught in memory of many
A joyous banquet past.
   [SARDANAPALUS *takes the cup, and after drinking and*
   tinkling the reversed cup, as a drop falls, exclaims –]
                              And this libation
Is for the excellent Beleses.
MYRRHA: Why
   Dwells thy mind rather upon that man's name
   Than on his mate's in villany?
SARDANAPALUS: The one
460   Is a mere soldier, a mere tool, a kind
Of human sword in a friend's hand; the other
Is master-mover of his warlike puppet:
But I dismiss them from my mind. – Yet pause,
My Myrrha! dost thou truly follow me,
465   Freely and fearlessly?
MYRRHA: And dost thou think
   A Greek girl dare not do for love, that which
   An Indian widow braves for custom?
SARDANAPALUS: Then
   We but await the signal.
MYRRHA: It is long
   In sounding.
SARDANAPALUS: Now, farewell; one last embrace.
470   MYRRHA: Embrace, but *not* the last; there is one more.
SARDANAPALUS: True, the commingling fire will mix our
      ashes.
MYRRHA: And pure as is my love to thee, shall they,
      Purged from the dross of earth, and earthly passion,
      Mix pale with thine. A single thought yet irks me.
475   SARDANAPALUS: Say it.
MYRRHA: It is that no kind hand will gather
   The dust of both into one urn.
SARDANAPALUS: The better:
   Rather let them be borne abroad upon
   The winds of heaven, and scatter'd into air,
   Than be polluted more by human hands
480   Of slaves and traitors. In this blazing palace,

And its enormous walls of reeking ruin,
We leave a nobler monument than Egypt
Hath piled in her brick mountains, o'er dead kings,
Or *kine*, for none know whether those proud piles
485   Be for their monarch, or their ox-god Apis:
So much for monuments that have forgotten
Their very record!

MYRRHA: Then farewell, thou earth!
And loveliest spot of earth! farewell, Ionia!
Be thou still free and beautiful, and far
490   Aloof from desolation! My last prayer
Was for thee, my last thoughts, save *one*, were of thee!

SARDANAPALUS: And that?

MYRRHA: Is yours.

    [*The trumpet of* PANIA *sounds without.*]

SARDANAPALUS: Hark!

MYRRHA: *Now!*

SARDANAPALUS: Adieu, Assyria!
I loved thee well, my own, my fathers' land,
And better as my country than my kingdom.
495   I sated thee with peace and joys; and this
Is my reward! and now I owe thee nothing,
Not even a grave.

    [*He mounts the pile.*]

           Now, Myrrha!

MYRRHA: Art thou ready?

SARDANAPALUS: As the torch in thy grasp.

    [MYRRHA *fires the pile.*]

MYRRHA: 'Tis fired! I come.

    [*As* MYRRHA *springs forward to throw herself into the
    flames, the Curtain falls.*]

Who kill'd John Keats?

Are you aware that Shelley has written an Elegy on Keats, and accuses the Quarterly of killing him?

'Who kill'd John Keats?'
   'I,' says the Quarterly,
   'So savage and Tartarly;
'Twas one of my feats.'

5   'Who shot the arrow?'
   'The poet-priest Milman
   (So ready to kill man),
Or Southey or Barrow.'

THE BLUES
A Literary Eclogue

'Nimium ne crede colori.' – VIRGIL.

O trust not, ye beautiful creatures, to hue,
Though your *hair* were as *red*, as your *stockings* are *blue*.

Eclogue First

London – Before the Door of a Lecture Room.

[*Enter* TRACY, *meeting* INKEL.]

INKEL: You're too late.

TRACY: Is it over?

INKEL: Nor will be this hour.
  But the benches are cramm'd, like a garden in flower,
  With the pride of our belles, who have made it the
    fashion;
  So, instead of 'beaux arts,' we may say 'la *belle* passion'

5   For learning, which lately has taken the lead in
  The world, and set all the fine gentlemen reading.

TRACY: I know it too well, and have worn out my patience
  With studying to study your new publications.
  There's Vamp, Scamp, and Mouthy, and Wordswords
    and Co.

10   With their damnable –

INKEL: Hold, my good friend, do you know
  Whom you speak to?

TRACY: Right well, boy, and so does 'the Row:'
  You're an author – a poet –

INKEL: And think you that I

Can stand tamely in silence, to hear you decry
The Muses?
TRACY: Excuse me: I meant no offence
15   To the Nine; though the number who make some pretence
To their favours is such – but the subject to drop,
I am just piping hot from a publisher's shop,
(Next door to the pastry-cook's; so that when I
Cannot find the new volume I wanted to buy
20   On the bibliopole's shelves, it is only two paces,
As one finds every author in one of those places;)
Where I just had been skimming a charming critique,
So studded with wit, and so sprinkled with Greek!
Where your friend – you know who – has just got such
a threshing,
25   That it is, as the phrase goes, extremely *'refreshing.'*
What a beautiful word!
INKEL: Very true; 'tis so soft
And so cooling – they use it a little too oft;
And the papers have got it at last – but no matter.
So they've cut up our friend then?
TRACY: Not left him a tatter –
30   Not a rag of his present or past reputation,
Which they call a disgrace to the age and the nation.
INKEL: I'm sorry to hear this! for friendship, you know –
Our poor friend! – but I thought it would terminate so.
Our friendship is such, I'll read nothing to shock it.
35   You don't happen to have the Review in your pocket?
TRACY: No; I left a round dozen of authors and others
(Very sorry, no doubt, since the cause is a brother's)
All scrambling and jostling, like so many imps,
And on fire with impatience to get the next glimpse.
40   INKEL: Let us join them.
TRACY: What, won't you return to the lecture?
INKEL: Why, the place is so cramm'd, there's not room for
a spectre.
Besides, our friend Scamp is to-day so absurd –
TRACY: How can you know that till you hear him?
INKEL: I heard
Quite enough; and, to tell you the truth, my retreat

45   Was from his vile nonsense, no less than the heat.
TRACY: I have had no great loss then?
INKEL: Loss! – such a palaver!
        I'd inoculate sooner my wife with the slaver
        Of a dog when gone rabid, than listen two hours
        To the torrent of trash which around him he pours,
50   Pump'd up with such effort, disgorged with such
            labour,
        That — come – do not make me speak ill of one's
            neighbour.
TRACY: *I* make you!
INKEL: Yes, you! I said nothing until
        You compell'd me, by speaking the truth —
TRACY: *To speak ill?*
        Is that your deduction?
INKEL: When speaking of Scamp ill,
55   I certainly *follow, not set* an example.
        The fellow's a fool, an impostor, a zany.
TRACY: And the crowd of to-day shows that one fool makes
            many.
        But we two will be wise.
INKEL: Pray, then, let us retire.
TRACY: I would, but –
INKEL: There must be attraction much higher
60   Than Scamp, or the Jews' harp he nicknames his lyre,
        To call *you* to this hotbed.
TRACY: I own it – tis true –
        A fair lady –
INKEL: A spinster?
TRACY: Miss Lilac!
INKEL: The Blue!
        The heiress?
TRACY: The angel!
INKEL: The devil! why, man!
        Pray get out of this hobble as fast as you can.
65   *You* wed with Miss Lilac! 'twould be your perdition:
        She's a poet, a chymist, a mathematician.
TRACY: I say she's an angel.
INKEL: Say rather an *angle.*

If you and she marry, you'll certainly wrangle.
I say she's a Blue, man, as blue as the ether.

70 TRACY: And is that any cause for not coming together?
INKEL: Humph! I can't say I know any happy alliance
    Which has lately sprung up from a wedlock with
        science.
    She's so learned in all things, and fond of concerning
    Herself in all matters connected with learning,
75   That —
TRACY: What?
INKEL: I perhaps may as well hold my tongue;
    But there's five hundred people can tell you you're
        wrong.
TRACY: You forget Lady Lilac's as rich as a Jew.
INKEL: Is it miss or the cash of mamma you pursue?
TRACY: Why, Jack, I'll be frank with you — something of
        both.
80   The girl's a fine girl.
INKEL: And you feel nothing loth
    To her good lady-mother's reversion; and yet
    Her life is as good as your own, I will bet.
TRACY: Let her live, and as long as she likes; I demand
    Nothing more than the heart of her daughter and
        hand.
85 INKEL: Why, that heart's in the inkstand — that hand on the
        pen;
TRACY: A propos — Will you write me a song now and
        then?
INKEL: To what purpose?
TRACY: You know, my dear friend, that in prose
    My talent is decent, as far as it goes;
    But in rhyme —
INKEL: You're a terrible stick, to be sure.
90 TRACY: I own it; and yet, in these times, there's no lure
    For the heart of the fair like a stanza or two;
    And so, as I can't, will you furnish a few?
INKEL: In your name?
TRACY: In my name. I will copy them out,
    To slip into her hand at the very next rout.

95 INKEL: Are you so far advanced as to hazard this?
TRACY: Why,
    Do you think me subdued by a Blue-stocking's eye,
    So far as to tremble to tell her in rhyme
    What I've told her in prose, at the least, as sublime?
INKEL: *As sublime*! – If it be so, no need of my Muse.
100 TRACY: But consider, dear Inkel, she's one of the 'Blues.'
INKEL: As sublime! – Mr Tracy – I've nothing to say.
    Stick to prose – As sublime!! – but I wish you good day.
TRACY: Nay, stay, my dear fellow – consider – I'm wrong;
    I own it; but, prithee, compose me the song.
105 INKEL: *As* sublime!!
TRACY: I but used the expression in haste.
INKEL: That may be, Mr Tracy, but shows damn'd bad taste.
TRACY: I own it – I know it – acknowledge it – what
    Can I say to you more?
INKEL: I see what you'd be at:
    You disparage my parts with insidious abuse,
110   Till you think you can turn them best to your own use.
TRACY: And is that not a sign I respect them?
INKEL: Why that
    To be sure makes a difference.
TRACY: I know what is what:
    And you, who're a man of the gay world, no less
    Than a poet of t'other, may easily guess
115   That I never could mean, by a word, to offend
    A genius like you, and moreover my friend.
INKEL: No doubt; you by this time should know what is
        due.
    To a man of — but come – let us shake hands.
TRACY: You knew,
    And you *know*, my dear fellow, how heartily I,
120   Whatever you publish, am ready to buy.
INKEL: That's my bookseller's business; I care not for sale;
    Indeed the best poems at first rather fail.
    There were Renegade's epics, and Botherby's plays,
    And my own grand romance —

125 TRACY: Had its full share of praise.
    I myself saw it puff'd in the 'Old Girl's Review.'
    INKEL: What Review?
    TRACY: 'Tis the English 'Journal de Trevoux;'
    A clerical work of our jesuits at home.
    Have you never yet seen it?
    INKEL: That pleasure's to come.
    TRACY: Make haste then.
    INKEL: Why so?
    TRACY: I have heard people say
130   That it threaten'd to give up the *ghost* t'other day.
    INKEL: Well, that is a sign of some *spirit*.
    TRACY: No doubt.
    Shall you be at the Countess of Fiddlecome's rout?
    INKEL: I've a card, and shall go: but at present, as soon
    As friend Scamp shall be pleased to step down from the
       moon
135   (Where he seems to be soaring in search of his wits),
    And an interval grants from his lecturing fits,
    I'm engaged to the Lady Bluebottle's collation,
    To partake of a luncheon and learn'd conversation:
    'Tis a sort of re-union for Scamp, on the days
140   Of his lecture, to treat him with cold tongue and praise.
    And I own, for my own part, that 'tis not unpleasant.
    Will you go? There's Miss Lilac will also be present.
    TRACY: That 'metal's attractive.'
    INKEL: No doubt – to the pocket.
    TRACY: You should rather encourage my passion than shock
       it.
145   But let us proceed; for I think, by the hum —
    INKEL: Very true; let us go, then, before they can come,
    Or else we'll be kept here an hour at their levy,
    On the rack of cross questions, by all the blue bevy.
    Hark! Zounds, they'll be on us; I know by the drone
150   Of old Botherby's spouting ex-cathedrâ tone.
    Ay! there he is at it. Poor Scamp! better join
    Your friends, or he'll pay you back in your own coin.
    TRACY: All fair; 'tis but lecture for lecture.
    INKEL: That's clear.

But for God's sake let's go, or the Bore will be here.
155   Come, come: nay, I'm off.
      [*Exit* INKEL.]
TRACY: You are right, and I'll follow;
      'Tis high time for a '*Sic me servavit Apollo.*'
      And yet we shall have the whole crew on our kibes,
      Blues, dandies, and dowagers, and second-hand scribes,
      All flocking to moisten their exquisite throttles
160   With a glass of Madeira at Lady Bluebottle's.
      [*Exit* TRACY.]

Eclogue Second

An Apartment in the House of LADY BLUEBOTTLE.
A Table prepared.

[SIR RICHARD BLUEBOTTLE *solus.*]
      Was there ever a man who was married so sorry?
      Like a fool, I must needs do the thing in a hurry.
      My life is reversed, and my quiet destroy'd;
      My days, which once pass'd in so gentle a void,
5   Must now, every hour of the twelve, be employ'd:
      The twelve, do I say? – of the whole twenty-four,
      Is there one which I dare call my own any more?
      What with driving and visiting, dancing and dining,
      What with learning, and teaching, and scribbling, and
            shining,
10   In science and art, I'll be cursed if I know
      Myself from my wife; for although we are two,
      Yet she somehow contrives that all things shall be done
      In a style which proclaims us eternally one.
      But the thing of all things which distresses me more
15   Than the bills of the week (though they trouble me
            sore)
      Is the numerous, humorous, backbiting crew
      Of scribblers, wits, lecturers, white, black, and blue,
      Who are brought to my house as an inn, to my cost
      – For the bill here, it seems, is defray'd by the host –
20   No pleasure! no leisure! no thought for my pains,
      But to hear a vile jargon which addles my brains;

A smatter and chatter, glean'd out of reviews,
By the rag, tag, and bobtail, of those they call 'BLUES;'
A rabble who know not — But soft, here they come!

25 Would to God I were deaf! as I'm not, I'll be dumb.

[*Enter* LADY BLUEBOTTLE, MISS LILAC, LADY
BLUEMOUNT, MR BOTHERBY, INKEL, TRACY, MISS
MAZARINE, *and others, with* SCAMP *the Lecturer,* &c.
&c.]

LADY BLUEBOTTLE: Ah! Sir Richard, good morning; I've
brought you some friends.

SIR RICHARD [*bows, and afterwards aside*]: If friends, they're
the first.

LADY BLUEBOTTLE: But the luncheon attends.
I pray ye be seated, '*sans cérémonie*.'
Mr Scamp, you're fatigued; take your chair there, next
me.

[*They all sit.*]

30 SIR RICHARD [*aside*]: If he does, his fatigue is to come.

LADY BLUEBOTTLE: Mr Tracy —
Lady Bluemount — Miss Lilac — be pleased, pray, to
place ye;
And you, Mr Botherby —

BOTHERBY: Oh, my dear Lady,
I obey.

LADY BLUEBOTTLE: Mr Inkel, I ought to upbraid ye:
You were not at the lecture.

INKEL: Excuse me, I was;

35 But the heat forced me out in the best part – alas!
And when —

LADY BLUEBOTTLE: To be sure it was broiling; but then
You have lost such a lecture!

BOTHERBY: The best of the ten.

TRACY: How can you know that? there are two more.

BOTHERBY: Because
I defy him to beat this day's wondrous applause.

40 The very walls shook.

INKEL: Oh, if that be the test,
I allow our friend Scamp has this day done his best.

Miss Lilac, permit me to help you; – a wing?

MISS LILAC: No more, sir, I thank you. Who lectures next
     spring?

BOTHERBY: Dick Dunder.

INKEL: That is, if he lives.

MISS LILAC: And why not?

45   INKEL: No reason whatever, save that he's a sot.
     Lady Bluemount! a glass of Madeira?

LADY BLUEMOUNT: With pleasure.

INKEL: How does your friend Wordswords, that
          Windermere treasure?
     Does he stick to his lakes, like the leeches he sings,
     And their gatherers, as Homer sung warriors and
          kings?

50   LADY BLUEBOTTLE: He has just got a place.

INKEL: As a footman?

LADY BLUEMOUNT: For shame!
     Nor profane with your sneers so poetic a name.

INKEL: Nay, I meant him no evil, but pitied his
          master;
     For the poet of pedlers 'twere, sure, no disaster
     To wear a new livery; the more, as 'tis not

55   The first time he has turn'd both his creed and his coat.

LADY BLUEMOUNT: For shame! I repeat. If Sir George
          could but hear —

LADY BLUEBOTTLE: Never mind our friend Inkel; we all
          know, my dear,
     'Tis his way.

SIR RICHARD: But this place —

INKEL: Is perhaps like friend Scamp's,
     A lecturer's.

LADY BLUEBOTTLE: Excuse me – 'tis one in 'the Stamps:'

60   He is made a collector.

TRACY: Collector!

SIR RICHARD: How?

MISS LILAC: What?

INKEL: I shall think of him oft when I buy a new hat:
     There his works will appear—

LADY BLUEMOUNT: Sir, they reach to the Ganges.

INKEL: I sha'n't go so far – I can have them at Grange's.[1]

LADY BLUEBOTTLE: Oh fie!

MISS LILAC: And for shame!

LADY BLUEMOUNT: You're too bad.

BOTHERBY: Very good!

65   LADY BLUEMOUNT: How good?

LADY BLUEBOTTLE: He means nought – 'tis his phrase.

LADY BLUEMOUNT: He grows rude.

LADY BLUEBOTTLE: He means nothing; nay, ask him.

LADY BLUEMOUNT: Pray, sir! did you mean
    What you say?

INKEL: Never mind if he did; 'twill be seen
    That whatever he means won't alloy what he says.

BOTHERBY: Sir!

INKEL: Pray be content with your portion of praise;

70   'Twas in your defence.

BOTHERBY: If you please, with submission,
    I can make out my own.

INKEL: It would be your perdition.
    While you live, my dear Botherby, never defend
    Yourself or your works; but leave both to a friend.
    A propos – Is your play then accepted at last?

75   BOTHERBY: At last?

INKEL: Why I thought – that's to say – there had pass'd
    A few green-room whispers, which hinted – you know
    That the taste of the actors at best is so so.

BOTHERBY: Sir, the green-room's in rapture, and so's the
        committee.

INKEL: Ay – yours are the plays for exciting our 'pity

80   And fear,' as the Greek says: for 'purging the mind,'
    I doubt if you'll leave us an equal behind.

BOTHERBY: I have written the prologue, and meant to have
        pray'd
    For a spice of your wit in an epilogue's aid.

INKEL: Well, time enough yet, when the play's to be
        play'd.

85   Is it cast yet?

1. Grange is or was a famous pastry-cook and fruiterer in Piccadilly.

BOTHERBY: The actors are fighting for parts,
　　　As is usual in that most litigious of arts.
LADY BLUEBOTTLE: We'll all make a party, and go the *first*
　　　night.
TRACY: And you promised the epilogue, Inkel.
INKEL: Not quite.
　　　However, to save my friend Botherby trouble,
90　　I'll do what I can, though my pains must be double.
TRACY: Why so?
INKEL: To do justice to what goes before.
BOTHERBY: Sir, I'm happy to say, I have no fears on the
　　　score.
　　　Your parts, Mr Inkel, are —
INKEL: Never mind *mine*;
　　　Stick to those of your play, which is quite your own
　　　line.
95　　LADY BLUEMOUNT: Your're a fugitive writer, I think, sir,
　　　of rhymes?
INKEL: Yes, ma'am; and a fugitive reader sometimes.
　　　On Wordswords, for instance, I seldom alight,
　　　Or on Mouthey, his friend, without taking to
　　　flight.
LADY BLUEMOUNT: Sir, your taste is too common; but time
　　　and posterity
100　Will right these great men, and this age's severity
　　　Become its reproach.
INKEL: I've no sort of objection,
　　　So I'm not of the party to take the infection.
LADY BLUEBOTTLE: Perhaps you have doubts that they ever
　　　will *take*?
INKEL: Not at all; on the contrary, those of the lake
105　Have taken already, and still will continue
　　　To take – what they can, from a groat to a guinea,
　　　Of pension or place; – but the subject's a bore.
LADY BLUEMOUNT: Well, sir, the time's coming.
INKEL: Scamp! don't you feel sore?
　　　What say you to this?
SCAMP: They have merit, I own;
110　Though their system's absurdity keeps it unknown.

INKEL: Then why not unearth it in one of your lectures?

SCAMP: It is only time past which comes under my strictures.

LADY BLUEBOTTLE: Come, a truce with all tartness: – the joy of my heart

Is to see Nature's triumph o'er all that is art.

115   Wild Nature! – Grand Shakspeare!

BOTHERBY: And down Aristotle!

LADY BLUEMOUNT: Sir George thinks exactly with Lady Bluebottle;

And my Lord Seventy-four, who protects our dear Bard,

And who gave him his place, has the greatest regard

For the poet, who, singing of pedlers and asses,

120   Has found out the way to dispense with Parnassus.

TRACY: And you, Scamp! –

SCAMP: I needs must confess I'm embarrass'd.

INKEL: Don't call upon Scamp, who's already so harass'd

With old *schools*, and new *schools*, and no *schools*; and all *schools*.

TRACY: Well, one thing is certain, that *some* must be fools.

125   I should like to know who.

INKEL: And I should not be sorry

To know who are *not*: – it would save us some worry.

LADY BLUEBOTTLE: A truce with remark, and let nothing control

This 'feast of our reason, and flow of the soul.'

Oh! my dear Mr Botherby! sympathise! – I

130   Now feel such a rapture, I'm ready to fly,

I feel so elastic – '*so buoyant – so buoyant!*' – [1]

INKEL: Tracy! open the window.

TRACY: I wish her much joy on't.

BOTHERBY: For God's sake, my Lady Bluebottle, check not

This gentle emotion, so seldom our lot

135   Upon earth. Give it way; 'tis an impulse which lifts

Our spirits from earth; the sublimest of gifts;

For which poor Prometheus was chain'd to his mountain.

---

1. Fact from life, with the *words*.

'Tis the source of all sentiment – feeling's true fountain:
'Tis the Vision of Heaven upon Earth: 'tis the gas
140   Of the soul: 'tis the seizing of shades as they pass,
And making them substance: 'tis something divine: –
INKEL: Shall I help you, my friend, to a little more wine?
BOTHERBY: I thank you; not any more, sir, till I dine.
INKEL: A propos – Do you dine with Sir Humphry to-day?
145   TRACY: I should think with *Duke* Humphry was more in
your way.
INKEL: It might be of yore; but we authors now look
To the knight, as a landlord, much more than the Duke.
The truth is, each writer now quite at his ease is,
And (except with his publisher) dines where he pleases.
150   But 'tis now nearly five, and I must to the Park.
TRACY: And I'll take a turn with you there till 'tis dark.
And you, Scamp –
SCAMP: Excuse me; I must to my notes,
For my lecture next week.
INKEL: He must mind whom he quotes
Out of 'Elegant Extracts.'
LADY BLUEBOTTLE: Well, now we break up;
155   But remember Miss Diddle invites us to sup.
INKEL: Then at two hours past midnight we all meet again,
For the sciences, sandwiches, hock, and champaigne!
TRACY: And the sweet lobster salad!
BOTHERBY: I honour that meal;
For 'tis then that our feelings most genuinely – feel.
160   INKEL: True; feeling is truest *then*, far beyond question:
I wish to the gods 'twas the same with digestion!
LADY BLUEBOTTLE: Pshaw! – never mind that; for one
moment of feeling
Is worth – God knows what.
INKEL: 'Tis at least worth concealing
For itself, or what follows —— But here comes your carriage.
165   SIR RICHARD [*aside*]: I wish all these people were d——d with
my marriage!
[*Exeunt.*]

THE VISION OF JUDGMENT

By Quevedo Redivivus

SUGGESTED BY THE COMPOSITION SO ENTITLED BY THE
AUTHOR OF 'WAT TYLER.'

'A Daniel come to judgment! yea, a Daniel!
I thank thee, Jew, for teaching me that word.'

PREFACE

It hath been wisely said, that 'One fool makes many;' and it
hath been poetically observed,

'That fools rush in where angels fear to tread.' – *Pope*.

If Mr Southey had not rushed in where he had no business,
and where he never was before, and never will be again, the
following poem would not have been written. It is not impos-
sible that it may be as good as his own, seeing that it cannot,
by any species of stupidity, natural or acquired, be *worse*.
The gross flattery, the dull impudence, the renegado intoler-
ance and impious cant, of the poem by the author of 'Wat
Tyler,' are something so stupendous as to form the sublime
of himself – containing the quintessence of his own
attributes.

So much for his poem – a word on his preface. In this
preface it has pleased the magnanimous Laureate to draw
the picture of a supposed 'Satanic School,' the which he
doth recommend to the notice of the legislature; thereby
adding to his other laurels the ambition of those of an in-
former. If there exists any where, excepting in his imagina-
tion, such a School, is he not sufficiently armed against it by
his own intense vanity? The truth is, that there are certain
writers whom Mr S. imagines, like Scrub, to have 'talked of
him; for they laughed consumedly.'

I think I know enough of most of the writers to whom he is supposed to allude, to assert, that they, in their individual capacities, have done more good, in the charities of life, to their fellow-creatures in any one year, than Mr Southey has done harm to himself by his absurdities in his whole life; and this is saying a great deal. But I have a few questions to ask.

1stly, Is Mr Southey the author of 'Wat Tyler?'

2dly, Was he not refused a remedy at law by the highest judge of his beloved England, because it was a blasphemous and seditious publication?

3dly, Was he not entitled by William Smith, in full parliament, 'a rancorous renegado?'

4thly, Is he not poet laureate, with his own lines on Martin the regicide staring him in the face?

And, 5thly, Putting the four preceding items together, with what conscience dare *he* call the attention of the laws to the publications of others, be they what they may?

I say nothing of the cowardice of such a proceeding; its meanness speaks for itself; but I wish to touch upon the *motive*, which is neither more nor less than that Mr S. has been laughed at a little in some recent publications, as he was of yore in the 'Anti-jacobin' by his present patrons. Hence all this 'skimble scamble stuff' about 'Satanic,' and so forth. However, it is worthy of him – '*qualis ab incepto.*'

If there is any thing obnoxious to the political opinions of a portion of the public in the following poem, they may thank Mr Southey. He might have written hexameters, as he has written everything else, for aught that the writer cared – had they been upon another subject. But to attempt to canonise a monarch, who, whatever were his household virtues, was neither a successful nor a patriot king, – inasmuch as several years of his reign passed in war with America and Ireland, to say nothing of the aggression upon France, – like all other exaggeration, necessarily begets opposition. In whatever manner he may be spoken of in this new 'Vision,' his *public* career will not be more favourably transmitted by history. Of his private virtues (although a little expensive to the nation) there can be no doubt.

With regard to the supernatural personages treated of, I can only say that I know as much about them, and (as an honest man) have a better right to talk of them than Robert Southey. I have also treated them more tolerantly. The way in which that poor insane creature, the Laureate, deals about his judgments in the next world, is like his own judgment in this. If it was not completely ludicrous, it would be something worse. I don't think that there is much more to say at present.

QUEVEDO REDIVIVUS

P.S. – It is possible that some readers may object, in these objectionable times, to the freedom with which saints, angels, and spiritual persons discourse in this 'Vision.' But, for precedents upon such points, I must refer him to Fielding's 'Journey from this World to the next,' and to the Visions of myself, the said Quevedo, in Spanish or translated. The reader is also requested to observe, that no doctrinal tenets are insisted upon or discussed; that the person of the Deity is carefully withheld from sight, which is more than can be said for the Laureate, who hath thought proper to make him talk, not 'like a school divine,' but like the unscholarlike Mr Southey. The whole action passes on the outside of heaven; and Chaucer's Wife of Bath, Pulci's Morgante Maggiore, Swift's Tale of a Tub, and the other works above referred to, are cases in point of the freedom with which saints, &c. may be permitted to converse in works not intended to be serious.

Q.R.

₊ Mr Southey being, as he says, a good Christian and vindictive, threatens, I understand, a reply to this our answer. It is to be hoped that his visionary faculties will in the mean time have acquired a little more judgment, properly so called: otherwise he will get himself into new dilemmas. These apostate jacobins furnish rich rejoinders. Let him take a specimen. Mr Southey laudeth grievously 'one Mr Landor,' who cultivates much private renown in the shape of Latin

verses; and not long ago, the poet laureate dedicated to him, it appeareth, one of his fugitive lyrics, upon the strength of a poem called *Gebir*. Who could suppose, that in this same Gebir the aforesaid Savage Landor (for such is his grim cognomen) putteth into the infernal regions no less a person than the hero of his friend Mr Southey's heaven, – yea, even George the Third! See also how personal Savage becometh, when he hath a mind. The following is his portrait of our late gracious sovereign: –

(Prince Gebir having descended into the infernal regions, the shades of his royal ancestors are, at his request, called up to his view; and he exclaims to his ghostly guide) –

'Aroar, what wretch that nearest us? what wretch
Is that with eyebrows white and slanting brow?
Listen! him yonder, who, bound down supine,
Shrinks yelling from that sword there, engine-hung.
He too amongst my ancestors! I hate
The despot, but the dastard I despise.
Was he our countryman?'
      'Alas, O king!
Iberia bore him, but the breed accurst
Inclement winds blew blighting from north-east.'
'He was a warrior then, nor fear'd the gods?'
Gebir, he fear'd the demons, not the gods,
Though them indeed his daily face adored;
And was no warrior, yet the thousand lives
Squander'd, as stones to exercise a sling,
And the tame cruelty and cold caprice –
Oh madness of mankind! address'd, adored!' – *Gebir*, p. 28.

I omit noticing some edifying Ithyphallics of Savagius, wishing to keep the proper veil over them, if his grave but somewhat indiscreet worshipper will suffer it; but certainly these teachers of 'great moral lessons' are apt to be found in strange company.

I

Saint Peter sat by the celestial gate:
　　His keys were rusty, and the lock was dull,
So little trouble had been given of late;
　　Not that the place by any means was full,
But since the Gallic era 'eighty-eight'
　　The devils had ta'en a longer, stronger pull,
And 'a pull altogether,' as they say
At sea – which drew most souls another way.

II

The angels all were singing out of tune,
　　And hoarse with having little else to do,
Excepting to wind up the sun and moon,
　　Or curb a runaway young star or two,
Or wild colt of a comet, which too soon
　　Broke out of bounds o'er the ethereal blue,
Splitting some planet with its playful tail,
As boats are sometimes by a wanton whale.

III

The guardian seraphs had retired on high,
　　Finding their charges past all care below;
Terrestrial business fill'd nought in the sky
　　Save the recording angel's black bureau;
Who found, indeed, the facts to multiply
　　With such rapidity of vice and wo,
That he had stripp'd off both his wings in quills,
And yet was in arrear of human ills.

IV

His business so augmented of late years,
　　That he was forced, against his will, no doubt,
(Just like those cherubs, earthly ministers,)
　　For some resource to turn himself about
And claim the help of his celestial peers,
　　To aid him ere he should be quite worn out
By the increased demand for his remarks;
Six angels and twelve saints were named his clerks.

V

This was a handsome board – at least for heaven;
  And yet they had even then enough to do,
35 So many conquerors' cars were daily driven,
  So many kingdoms fitted up anew;
Each day too slew its thousands six or seven,
  Till at the crowning carnage, Waterloo,
They threw their pens down in divine disgust –
40 The page was so besmear'd with blood and dust.

VI

This by the way; 'tis not mine to record
  What angels shrink from: even the very devil
On this occasion his own work abhorr'd,
  So surfeited with the infernal revel:
45 Though he himself had sharpen'd every sword,
  It almost quench'd his innate thirst of evil.
(Here Satan's sole good work deserves insertion –
'Tis, that he has both generals in reversion.)

VII

Let's skip a few short years of hollow peace,
50   Which peopled earth no better, hell as wont,
And heaven none – they form the tyrant's lease,
  With nothing but new names subscribed upon't;
'Twill one day finish: meantime they increase,
  'With seven heads and ten horns,' and all in front,
55 Like Saint John's foretold beast; but ours are born
Less formidable in the head than horn.

VIII

In the first year of freedom's second dawn
  Died George the Third; although no tyrant, one
Who shielded tyrants, till each sense withdrawn
60   Left him nor mental nor external sun:
A better farmer ne'er brush'd dew from lawn,
  A worse king never left a realm undone!
He died – but left his subjects still behind,
One half as mad – and t'other no less blind.

IX

65 He died! – his death made no great stir on earth;
        His burial made some pomp; there was profusion
    Of velvet, gilding, brass, and no great dearth
        Of aught but tears – save those shed by collusion.
    For these things may be bought at their true worth;
70   Of elegy there was the due infusion –
    Bought also; and the torches, cloaks, and banners,
    Heralds, and relics of old Gothic manners,

X

    Form'd a sepulchral melodrame. Of all
        The fools who flock'd to swell or see the show,
75 Who cared about the corpse? The funeral
        Made the attraction, and the black the woe.
    There throbb'd not there a thought which pierced the pall;
        And when the gorgeous coffin was laid low,
    It seem'd the mockery of hell to fold
80 The rottenness of eighty years in gold.

XI

    So mix his body with the dust! It might
        Return to what it *must* far sooner, were
    The natural compound left alone to fight
        Its way back into earth, and fire, and air;
85 But the unnatural balsams merely blight
        What nature made him at his birth, as bare
    As the mere million's base unmummied clay –
    Yet all his spices but prolong decay.

XII

    He's dead – and upper earth with him has done;
90   He's buried; save the undertaker's bill,
    Or lapidary scrawl, the world is gone
        For him, unless he left a German will;
    But where's the proctor who will ask his son?
        In whom his qualities are reigning still,
95 Except that household virtue, most uncommon,
    Of constancy to a bad, ugly woman.

XIII

'God save the king!' It is a large economy
    In God to save the like; but if he will
Be saving, all the better; for not one am I
    Of those who think damnation better still:
I hardly know too if not quite alone am I
    In this small hope of bettering future ill
By circumscribing, with some slight restriction,
The eternity of hell's hot jurisdiction.

XIV

I know this is unpopular; I know
    'Tis blasphemous; I know one may be damn'd
For hoping no one else may e'er be so;
    I know my catechism; I know we are cramm'd
With the best doctrines till we quite o'erflow;
    I know that all save England's church have shamm'd,
And that the other twice two hundred churches
And synagogues have made a *damn'd* bad purchase.

XV

God help us all! God help me too! I am
    God knows, as helpless as the devil can wish,
And not a whit more difficult to damn
    Than is to bring to land a late-hook'd fish,
Or to the butcher to purvey the lamb;
    Nor that I'm fit for such a noble dish
As one day will be that immortal fry
Of almost every body born to die.

XVI

Saint Peter sat by the celestial gate,
    And nodded o'er his keys; when, lo! there came
A wondrous noise he had not heard of late –
    A rushing sound of wind, and stream, and flame;
In short, a roar of things extremely great,
    Which would have made aught save a saint exclaim;
But he, with first a start and then a wink,
Said, 'There's another star gone out, I think!'

XVII

But ere he could return to his repose,
130   A cherub flapp'd his right wing o'er his eyes –
At which Saint Peter yawn'd, and rubb'd his nose:
    'Saint porter,' said the angel, 'prithee rise!'
Waving a goodly wing, which glow'd, as glows
    An earthly peacock's tail, with heavenly dyes:
135 To which the saint replied, 'Well, what's the matter?
'Is Lucifer come back with all this clatter?'

XVIII

'No,' quoth the cherub; 'George the Third is dead.'
    'And who *is* George the Third?' replied the apostle:
'*What George? what Third?*' 'The king of England,' said
140   The angel. 'Well! he won't find kings to jostle
Him on his way; but does he wear his head?
    Because the last we saw here had a tustle,
And ne'er would have got into heaven's good graces,
Had he not flung his head in all our faces.

XIX

145 'He was, if I remember, king of France;
    That head of his, which could not keep a crown
On earth, yet ventured in my face to advance
    A claim to those of martyrs – like my own:
If I had had my sword, as I had once
150   When I cut ears off, I had cut him down;
But having but my *keys*, and not my brand,
I only knock'd his head from out his hand.

XX

'And then he set up such a headless howl,
    That all the saints came out and took him in;
155 And there he sits by St Paul, cheek by jowl;
    That fellow Paul – the parvenù! The skin
Of Saint Bartholomew, which makes his cowl
    In heaven, and upon earth redeem'd his sin
So as to make a martyr, never sped
160 Better than did this weak and wooden head.

XXI

'But had it come up here upon its shoulders,
    There would have been a different tale to tell:
The fellow-feeling in the saints beholders
    Seems to have acted on them like a spell;
165 And so this very foolish head heaven solders
    Back on its trunk: it may be very well,
And seems the custom here to overthrow
Whatever has been wisely done below.'

XXII

The angel answer'd, 'Peter! do not pout:
170   The king who comes has head and all entire,
And never knew much what it was about –
    He did as doth the puppet – by its wire,
And will be judged like all the rest, no doubt:
    My business and your own is not to enquire
175 Into such matters, but to mind our cue –
Which is to act as we are bid to do.'

XXIII

While thus they spake, the angelic caravan,
    Arriving like a rush of mighty wind,
Cleaving the fields of space, as doth the swan
180   Some silver stream (say Ganges, Nile, or Inde,
Or Thames, or Tweed), and 'midst them an old man
    With an old soul, and both extremely blind,
Halted before the gate, and in his shroud
Seated their fellow-traveller on a cloud.

XXIV

185 But bringing up the rear of this bright host
    A Spirit of a different aspect waved
His wings, like thunder-clouds above some coast
    Whose barren beach with frequent wrecks is paved;
His brow was like the deep when tempest-toss'd;
190   Fierce and unfathomable thoughts engraved
Eternal wrath on his immortal face,
And *where* he gazed a gloom pervaded space.

XXV

As he drew near, he gazed upon the gate
    Ne'er to be enter'd more by him or sin,
195   With such a glance of supernatural hate,
    As made Saint Peter wish himself within;
He patter'd with his keys at a great rate,
    And sweated through his apostolic skin:
Of course his perspiration was but ichor,
200   Or some such other spiritual liquor.

XXVI

The very cherubs huddled all together,
    Like birds when soars the falcon; and they felt
A tingling to the tip of every feather,
    And form'd a circle like Orion's belt
205   Around their poor old charge; who scarce knew whither
    His guards had led him, though they gently dealt
With royal manes (for by many stories,
And true, we learn the angels all are Tories).

XXVII

As things were in this posture, the gate flew
210   Asunder, and the flashing of its hinges
Flung over space an universal hue
    Of many-colour'd flame, until its tinges
Reach'd even our speck of earth, and made a new
    Aurora borealis spread its fringes
215   O'er the North Pole; the same seen, when ice-bound,
By Captain Parry's crew, in 'Melville's Sound.'

XXVIII

And from the gate thrown open issued beaming
    A beautiful and mighty Thing of Light,
Radiant with glory, like a banner streaming
220   Victorious from some world-o'erthrowing fight:
My poor comparisons must needs be teeming
    With earthly likenesses, for here the night
Of clay obscures our best conceptions, saving
Johanna Southcote, or Bob Southey raving.

XXIX

225 'Twas the archangel Michael: all men know
      The make of angels and archangels, since
    There's scarce a scribbler has not one to show,
      From the fiends' leader to the angels' prince.
    There also are some altar-pieces, though
230   I really can't say that they much evince
    One's inner notions of immortal spirits;
    But let the connoisseurs explain *their* merits.

XXX

    Michael flew forth in glory and in good;
      A goodly work of him from whom all glory
235 And good arise; the portal past – he stood;
      Before him the young cherubs and saints hoary –
      (I say *young*, begging to be understood
      By looks, not years; and should be very sorry
      To state, they were not older than St Peter,
240 But merely that they seem'd a little sweeter).

XXXI

    The cherubs and the saints bow'd down before
      That arch-angelic hierarch, the first
    Of essences angelical, who wore
      The aspect of a god; but this ne'er nursed
245 Pride in his heavenly bosom, in whose core
      No thought, save for his Maker's service, durst
    Intrude, however glorified and high;
    He knew him but the viceroy of the sky.

XXXII

    He and the sombre silent Spirit met –
250   They knew each other both for good and ill;
    Such was their power, that neither could forget
      His former friend and future foe; but still
    There was a high, immortal, proud regret
      In either's eye, as if 'twere less their will
255 Than destiny to make the eternal years
    Their date of war, and their 'champ clos' the spheres.

XXXIII
But here they were in neutral space: we know
    From Job, that Satan hath the power to pay
A heavenly visit thrice a year or so;
260   And that 'the sons of God,' like those of clay,
Must keep him company; and we might show
    From the same book, in how polite a way
The dialogue is held between the Powers
Of Good and Evil – but 'twould take up hours.

XXXIV
265 And this is not a theologic tract,
    To prove with Hebrew and with Arabic
If Job be allegory or a fact,
    But a true narrative; and thus I pick
From out the whole but such and such an act
270   As sets aside the slightest thought of trick.
'Tis every tittle true, beyond suspicion,
And accurate as any other vision.

XXXV
The spirits were in neutral space, before
    The gate of heaven; like eastern thresholds is
275 The place where Death's grand cause is argued o'er,
    And souls despatch'd to that world or to this;
And therefore Michael and the other wore
    A civil aspect: though they did not kiss,
Yet still between his Darkness and his Brightness
280 There pass'd a mutual glance of great politeness.

XXXVI
The Archangel bow'd, not like a modern beau,
    But with a graceful oriental bend,
Pressing one radiant arm just where below
    The heart in good men is supposed to tend.
285 He turn'd as to an equal, not too low,
    But kindly; Satan met his ancient friend
With more hauteur, as might an old Castilian
Poor noble meet a mushroom rich civilian.

XXXVII

He merely bent his diabolic brow
290   An instant; and then raising it, he stood
In act to assert his right or wrong, and show
       Cause why King George by no means could or should
Make out a case to be exempt from woe
       Eternal, more than other kings, endued
295   With better sense and hearts, whom history mentions,
Who long have 'paved hell with their good intentions.'

XXXVIII

Michael began: 'What wouldst thou with this man,
       Now dead, and brought before the Lord? What ill
Hath he wrought since his mortal race began,
300   That thou canst claim him? Speak! and do thy will,
If it be just: if in this earthly span
       He hath been greatly failing to fulfil
His duties as a king and mortal, say,
And he is thine; if not, let him have way.'

XXXIX

305   'Michael!' replied the Prince of Air, 'even here,
       Before the Gate of him thou servest, must
I claim my subject: and will make appear
       That as he was my worshipper in dust,
So shall he be in spirit, although dear
310   To thee and thine, because nor wine nor lust
Were of his weaknesses; yet on the throne
He reign'd o'er millions to serve me alone.

XL

'Look to *our* earth, or rather *mine*; it was,
       Once, *more* thy master's: but I triumph not
315   In this poor planet's conquest; nor, alas!
       Need he thou servest envy me my lot:
With all the myriads of bright worlds which pass
       In worship round him, he may have forgot
Yon weak creation of such paltry things:
320   I think few worth damnation save their kings, –

XLI

'And these but as a kind of quit-rent, to
   Assert my right as lord; and even had
I such an inclination, 'twere (as you
   Well know) superfluous: they are grown so bad,
325 That hell has nothing better left to do
   Than leave them to themselves: so much more mad
And evil by their own internal curse,
Heaven cannot make them better, nor I worse.

XLII

'Look to the earth, I said, and say again:
330   When this old, blind, mad, helpless, weak, poor worm
Began in youth's first bloom and flush to reign,
   The world and he both wore a different form,
And much of earth and all the watery plain
   Of ocean call'd him king: through many a storm
335 His isles had floated on the abyss of time;
For the rough virtues chose them for their clime.

XLIII

'He came to his sceptre young; he leaves it old:
   Look to the state in which he found his realm,
And left it; and his annals too behold,
340   How to a minion first he gave the helm;
How grew upon his heart a thirst for gold,
   The beggar's vice, which can but overwhelm
The meanest hearts; and for the rest, but glance
Thine eye along America and France.

XLIV

345 ''Tis true, he was a tool from first to last
   (I have the workmen safe); but as a tool
So let him be consumed. From out the past
   Of ages, since mankind have known the rule
Of monarchs – from the bloody rolls amass'd
350   Of sin and slaughter – from the Cæsars' school,
Take the worst pupil; and produce a reign
More drench'd with gore, more cumber'd with the slain.

XLV

'He ever warr'd with freedom and the free:
    Nations as men, home subjects, foreign foes,
355 So that they utter'd the word "Liberty!"
    Found George the Third their first opponent. Whose
History was ever stain'd as his will be
    With national and individual woes?
I grant his household abstinence; I grant
360 His neutral virtues, which most monarchs want;

XLVI

'I know he was a constant consort; own
    He was a decent sire, and middling lord.
All this is much, and most upon a throne;
    As temperance, if at Apicius' board,
365 Is more than at an anchorite's supper shown.
    I grant him all the kindest can accord;
And this was well for him, but not for those
Millions who found him what oppression chose.

XLVII

'The New World shook him off; the Old yet groans
370   Beneath what he and his prepared, if not
Completed: he leaves heirs on many thrones
    To all his vices, without what begot
Compassion for him – his tame virtues; drones
    Who sleep, or despots who have now forgot
375 A lesson which shall be re-taught them, wake
Upon the thrones of earth; but let them quake!

XLVIII

'Five millions of the primitive, who hold
    The faith which makes ye great on earth, implored
A *part* of that vast *all* they held of old, –
380   Freedom to worship – not alone your Lord,
Michael, but you, and you, Saint Peter! Cold
    Must be your souls, if you have not abhorr'd
The foe to catholic participation
In all the license of a Christian nation.

XLIX

385 'True! he allow'd them to pray God; but as
        A consequence of prayer, refused the law
    Which would have placed them upon the same base
        With those who did not hold the saints in awe.'
    But here Saint Peter started from his place,
390   And cried, 'You may the prisoner withdraw:
    Ere heaven shall ope her portals to this Guelph,
    While I am guard, may I be damn'd myself!

L

    'Sooner will I with Cerberus exchange
        My office (and *his* is no sinecure)
395 Than see this royal Bedlam bigot range
        The azure fields of heaven, of that be sure!'
    'Saint!' replied Satan, 'you do well to avenge
        The wrongs he made your satellites endure
    And if to this exchange you should be given,
400 I'll try to coax *our* Cerberus up to heaven.'

LI

    Here Michael interposed: 'Good saint! and devil!
        Pray, not so fast; you both outrun discretion.
    Saint Peter! you were wont to be more civil:
        Satan! excuse this warmth of his expression,
405 And condescension to the vulgar's level:
        Even saints sometimes forget themselves in session.
    Have you got more to say?' – 'No.' – 'If you please,
    I'll trouble you to call your witnesses.'

LII

    Then Satan turn'd and waved his swarthy hand,
410   Which stirr'd with its electric qualities
    Clouds farther off than we can understand,
        Although we find him sometimes in our skies;
    Infernal thunder shook both sea and land
        In all the planets, and hell's batteries
415 Let off the artillery, which Milton mentions
    As one of Satan's most sublime inventions.

LIII

This was a signal unto such damn'd souls
   As have the privilege of their damnation
Extended far beyond the mere controls
420   Of worlds past, present, or to come; no station
Is theirs particularly in the rolls
   Of hell assign'd; but where their inclination
Or business carries them in search of game,
They may range freely – being damn'd the same.

LIV

425 They are proud of this – as very well they may,
   It being a sort of knighthood, or gilt key
Stuck in their loins; or like to an 'entré'
   Up the back stairs, or such free-masonry.
I borrow my comparisons from clay,
430   Being clay myself. Let not those spirits be
Offended with such base low likenesses;
We know their posts are nobler far than these.

LV

When the great signal ran from heaven to hell –
   About ten million times the distance reckon'd
435 From our sun to its earth, as we can tell
   How much time it takes up, even to a second,
For every ray that travels to dispel
   The fogs of London, through which, dimly beacon'd,
The weathercocks are gilt some thrice a year,
440 If that the *summer* is not too severe: –

LVI

I say that I can tell – 'twas half a minute:
   I know the solar beams take up more time
Ere, pack'd up for their journey, they begin it;
   But then their telegraph is less sublime,
445 And if they ran a race, they would not win it
   'Gainst Satan's couriers bound for their own clime.
The sun takes up some years for every ray
To reach its goal – the devil not half a day.

LVII

Upon the verge of space, about the size
450   Of half-a-crown, a little speck appear'd
(I've seen a something like it in the skies
      In the Ægean, ere a squall); it near'd,
And, growing bigger, took another guise;
      Like an aërial ship it tack'd, and steer'd,
455 Or *was* steer'd (I am doubtful of the grammar
Of the last phrase, which makes the stanza stammer; —

LVIII

But take your choice); and then it grew a cloud;
      And so it was — a cloud of witnesses.
But such a cloud! No land e'er saw a crowd
460   Of locusts numerous as the heavens saw these;
They shadow'd with their myriads space; their loud
      And varied cries were like those of wild geese
(If nations may be liken'd to a goose),
And realised the phrase of 'hell broke loose.'

LIX

465 Here crash'd a sturdy oath of stout John Bull,
      Who damn'd away his eyes as heretofore:
There Paddy brogued 'By Jasus!' — 'What's your wull?'
      The temperate Scot exclaim'd: the French ghost swore
In certain terms I shan't translate in full,
470   As the first coachman will; and 'midst the roar
The voice of Jonathan was heard to express,
'*Our* president is going to war, I guess.'

LX

Besides there were the Spaniard, Dutch, and Dane;
      In short, an universal shoal of shades,
475 From Otaheite's isle to Salisbury Plain,
      Of all climes and professions, years and trades,
Ready to swear against the good king's reign,
      Bitter as clubs in cards are against spades:
All summon'd by this grand 'subpœna,' to
480 Try if kings mayn't be damn'd like me or you.

LXI

When Michael saw this host, he first grew pale,
    As angels can; next, like Italian twilight,
He turn'd all colours – as a peacock's tail,
    Or sunset streaming through a Gothic skylight
485 In some old abbey, or a trout not stale,
    Or distant lightning on the horizon *by* night,
Or a fresh rainbow, or a grand review
Of thirty regiments in red, green, and blue.

LXII

Then he address'd himself to Satan: 'Why –
490   My good old friend, for such I deem you, though
Our different parties make us fight so shy,
    I ne'er mistake you for a *personal* foe;
Our difference is *political*, and I
    Trust that, whatever may occur below,
495 You know my great respect for you: and this
Makes me regret whate'er you do amiss –

LXIII

'Why, my dear Lucifer, would you abuse
    My call for witnesses? I did not mean
That you should half of earth and hell produce;
500   'Tis even superfluous, since two honest, clean,
True testimonies are enough: we lose
    Our time, nay, our eternity, between
The accusation and defence: if we
Hear both, 'twill stretch our immortality.'

LXIV

505 Satan replied, 'To me the matter is
    Indifferent, in a personal point of view:
I can have fifty better souls than this
    With far less trouble than we have gone through
Already; and I merely argued his
510   Late majesty of Britain's case with you
Upon a point of form: you may dispose
Of him; I've kings enough below, God knows!'

LXV

Thus spoke the Demon (late call'd 'multifaced'
    By multo-scribbling Southey). 'Then we'll call
515 One or two persons of the myriads placed
    Around our congress, and dispense with all
The rest,' quoth Michael: 'Who may be so graced
    As to speak first? there's choice enough – who shall
It be?' Then Satan answer'd, 'There are many;
520 But you may choose Jack Wilkes as well as any.'

LXVI

A merry, cock-eyed, curious-looking sprite
    Upon the instant started from the throng,
Dress'd in a fashion now forgotten quite;
    For all the fashions of the flesh stick long
525 By people in the next world; where unite
    All the costumes since Adam's, right or wrong,
From Eve's fig-leaf down to the petticoat,
Almost as scanty, of days less remote.

LXVII

The spirit look'd around upon the crowds
530   Assembled, and exclaim'd, 'My friends of all
The spheres, we shall catch cold amongst these clouds;
    So let's to business: why this general call?
If those are freeholders I see in shrouds,
    And 'tis for an election that they bawl,
535 Behold a candidate with unturn'd coat!
Saint Peter, may I count upon your vote?'

LXVIII

'Sir,' replied Michael, 'you mistake; these things
    Are of a former life, and what we do
Above is more august; to judge of kings
540   Is the tribunal met: so now you know.'
'Then I presume those gentlemen with wings,'
    Said Wilkes, 'are cherubs; and that soul below
Looks much like George the Third, but to my mind
A good deal older – Bless me! is he blind?'

LXIX

545   'He is what you behold him, and his doom
            Depends upon his deeds,' the Angel said.
        'If you have aught to arraign in him, the tomb
            Gives license to the humblest beggar's head
        To lift itself against the loftiest.' – 'Some,'
550   Said Wilkes, 'don't wait to see them laid in lead,
        For such a liberty – and I, for one,
        Have told them what I thought beneath the sun.'

LXX

        '*Above* the sun repeat, then, what thou hast
            To urge against him,' said the Archangel. 'Why,'
555   Replied the spirit, 'since old scores are past,
            Must I turn evidence? In faith, not I.
        Besides, I beat him hollow at the last,
            With all his Lords and Commons: in the sky
        I don't like ripping up old stories, since
560   His conduct was but natural in a prince.

LXXI

        'Foolish, no doubt, and wicked, to oppress
            A poor unlucky devil without a shilling;
        But then I blame the man himself much less
            Than Bute and Grafton, and shall be unwilling
565   To see him punish'd here for their excess,
            Since they were both damn'd long ago, and still in
        Their place below: for me, I have forgiven,
        And vote his "habeas corpus" into heaven.'

LXXII

        'Wilkes,' said the Devil, 'I understand all this;
570   You turn'd to half a courtier ere you died,
        And seem to think it would not be amiss
            To grow a whole one on the other side
        Of Charon's ferry; you forget that *his*
            Reign is concluded; whatsoe'er betide,
575   He won't be sovereign more: you've lost your labour,
        For at the best he will but be your neighbour.

LXXIII

'However, I knew what to think of it,
    When I beheld you in your jesting way
Flitting and whispering round about the spit
580   Where Belial, upon duty for the day,
With Fox's lard was basting William Pitt,
    His pupil; I knew what to think, I say:
That fellow even in hell breeds farther ills;
I'll have him *gagg'd* – 'twas one of his own bills.

LXXIV

585 'Call Junius!' From the crowd a shadow stalk'd,
    And at the name there was a general squeeze,
So that the very ghosts no longer walk'd
    In comfort, at their own aërial ease,
But were all ramm'd, and jamm'd (but to be balk'd,
590   As we shall see), and jostled hands and knees,
Like wind compress'd and pent within a bladder,
Or like a human colic, which is sadder.

LXXV

The shadow came – a tall, thin, grey-hair'd figure,
    That look'd as it had been a shade on earth;
595 Quick in its motions, with an air of vigour,
    But nought to mark its breeding or its birth:
Now it wax'd little, then again grew bigger,
    With now an air of gloom, or savage mirth;
But as you gazed upon its features, they
600 Changed every instant – to *what*, none could say.

LXXVI

The more intently the ghosts gazed, the less
    Could they distinguish whose the features were;
The Devil himself seem'd puzzled even to guess;
    They varied like a dream – now here, now there;
605 And several people swore from out the press,
    They knew him perfectly; and one could swear
He was his father: upon which another
Was sure he was his mother's cousin's brother:

LXXVII

Another, that he was a duke, or knight,
610   An orator, a lawyer, or a priest,
A nabob, a man-midwife; but the wight
      Mysterious changed his countenance at least
As oft as they their minds: though in full sight
      He stood, the puzzle only was increased;
615 The man was a phantasmagoria in
Himself – he was so volatile and thin.

LXXVIII

The moment that you had pronounced him *one*,
      Presto! his face changed, and he was another,
And when that change was hardly well put on,
620   It varied, till I don't think his own mother
(If that he had a mother) would her son
      Have known, he shifted so from one to t'other;
Till guessing from a pleasure grew a task,
At this epistolary 'Iron Mask.'

LXXIX

625 For sometimes he like Cerberus would seem –
      'Three gentlemen at once' (as sagely says
Good Mrs Malaprop); then you might deem
      That he was not even *one*; now many rays
Were flashing round him; and now a thick steam
630   Hid him from sight – like fogs on London days:
Now Burke, now Tooke, he grew to people's fancies,
And certes often like Sir Philip Francis.

LXXX

I've an hypothesis – 'tis quite my own;
      I never let it out till now, for fear
635 Of doing people harm about the throne,
      And injuring some minister or peer,
On whom the stigma might perhaps be blown:
      It is – my gentle public, lend thine ear!
'Tis, that what Junius we are wont to call
640 Was *really, truly*, nobody at all.

LXXXI

I don't see wherefore letters should not be
 Written without hands, since we daily view
Them written without heads; and books, we see,
 Are fill'd as well without the latter too:
645 And really till we fix on somebody
 For certain sure to claim them as his due,
Their author, like the Niger's mouth, will bother
The world to say if *there* be mouth or author.

LXXXII

'And who and what art thou?' the Archangel said.
650 'For *that* you may consult my title-page,'
Replied this mighty shadow of a shade:
 'If I have kept my secret half an age,
I scarce shall tell it now.' – 'Canst thou upbraid,'
 Continued Michael, 'George Rex, or allege
655 Aught further?' Junius answer'd, 'You had better
First ask him for *his* answer to my letter:

LXXXIII

'My charges upon record will outlast
 The brass of both his epitaph and tomb.'
'Repent'st thou not,' said Michael, 'of some past
660 Exaggeration? something which may doom
Thyself if false, as him if true? Thou wast
 Too bitter – is it not so? – in thy gloom
Of passion?' – 'Passion!' cried the phantom dim,
'I loved my country, and I hated him.

LXXXIV

665 'What I have written, I have written: let
 The rest be on his head or mine!' So spoke
Old 'Nominis Umbra;' and while speaking yet,
 Away he melted in celestial smoke.
Then Satan said to Michael, 'Don't forget
670 To call George Washington, and John Horne Tooke,
And Franklin;' – but at this time there was heard
A cry for room, though not a phantom stirr'd.

LXXXV

At length with jostling, elbowing, and the aid
    Of cherubim appointed to that post,
675 The devil Asmodeus to the circle made
    His way, and look'd as if his journey cost
Some trouble. When his burden down he laid,
    'What's this?' cried Michael; 'why, 'tis not a ghost?'
'I know it,' quoth the incubus; 'but he
680 Shall be one, if you leave the affair to me.

LXXXVI

'Confound the renegado! I have sprain'd
    My left wing, he's so heavy; one would think
Some of his works about his neck were chain'd.
    But to the point; while hovering o'er the brink
685 Of Skiddaw (where as usual it still rain'd),
    I saw a taper, far below me, wink,
And stooping, caught this fellow at a libel –
No less on history than the Holy Bible.

LXXXVII

'The former is the devil's scripture, and
690   The latter yours, good Michael; so the affair
Belongs to all of us, you understand.
    I snatch'd him up just as you see him there,
And brought him off for sentence out of hand:
    I've scarcely been ten minutes in the air –
695 At least a quarter it can hardly be:
I dare say that his wife is still at tea.'

LXXXVIII

Here Satan said, 'I know this man of old,
    And have expected him for some time here;
A sillier fellow you will scarce behold,
700   Or more conceited in his petty sphere:
But surely it was not worth while to fold
    Such trash below your wing, Asmodeus dear:
We had the poor wretch safe (without being bored
With carriage) coming of his own accord.

LXXXIX

705 'But since he's here, let's see what he has done.'
　　　 'Done!' cried Asmodeus, 'he anticipates
The very business you're now upon,
　　　 And scribbles as if head clerk to the Fates.
Who knows to what his ribaldry may run,
710　　 When such an ass as this, like Balaam's, prates?'
'Let's hear,' quoth Michael, 'what he has to say;
You know we're bound to that in every way.'

XC

Now the bard, glad to get an audience, which
　　　 By no means often was his case below,
715 Began to cough, and hawk, and hem, and pitch
　　　 His voice into that awful note of woe
To all unhappy hearers within reach
　　　 Of poets when the tide of rhyme's in flow;
But stuck fast with his first hexameter,
720 Not one of all whose gouty feet would stir.

XCI

But ere the spavin'd dactyls could be spurr'd
　　　 Into recitative, in great dismay
Both cherubim and seraphim were heard
　　　 To murmur loudly through their long array;
725 And Michael rose ere he could get a word
　　　 Of all his founder'd verses under way,
And cried, 'For God's sake stop, my friend! 'twere best –
Non Di, non homines – you know the rest.'

XCII

A general bustle spread throughout the throng,
730　　 Which seem'd to hold all verse in detestation;
The angels had of course enough of song
　　　 When upon service; and the generation
Of ghosts had heard too much in life, not long
　　　 Before, to profit by a new occasion;
735 The monarch, mute till then, exclaim'd, 'What! what!
Pye come again? No more – no more of that!'

XCIII

The tumult grew; an universal cough
   Convulsed the skies, as during a debate,
When Castlereagh has been up long enough
740   (Before he was first minister of state,
I mean – the *slaves hear now*); some cried 'Off, off!'
   As at a farce; till, grown quite desperate,
The bard Saint Peter pray'd to interpose
(Himself an author) only for his prose.

XCIV

745   The varlet was not an ill-favour'd knave;
   A good deal like a vulture in the face,
With a hook nose and a hawk's eye, which gave
   A smart and sharper-looking sort of grace
To his whole aspect, which, though rather grave,
750   Was by no means so ugly as his case;
But that indeed was hopeless as can be,
Quite a poetic felony '*de se*.'

XCV

Then Michael blew his trump, and still'd the noise
   With one still greater, as is yet the mode
755 On earth besides; except some grumbling voice,
   Which now and then will make a slight inroad
Upon decorous silence, few will twice
   Lift up their lungs when fairly overcrow'd;
And now the bard could plead his own bad cause,
760 With all the attitudes of self-applause.

XCVI

He said – (I only give the heads) – he said,
   He meant no harm in scribbling; 'twas his way
Upon all topics; 'twas, besides, his bread,
   Of which he butter'd both sides; 'twould delay
765 Too long the assembly (he was pleased to dread),
   And take up rather more time than a day,
To name his works – he would but cite a few –
'Wat Tyler' – 'Rhymes on Blenheim' – 'Waterloo.'

XCVII

He had written praises of a regicide;
770   He had written praises of all kings whatever;
He had written for republics far and wide,
         And then against them bitterer than ever:
For pantisocracy he once had cried
         Aloud, a scheme less moral than 'twas clever;
775 Then grew a hearty anti-jacobin –
Had turn'd his coat – and would have turn'd his skin.

XCVIII

He had sung against all battles, and again
         In their high praise and glory; he had call'd
Reviewing[1] 'the ungentle craft,' and then
780   Become as base a critic as e'er crawl'd –
Fed, paid, and pamper'd by the very men
         By whom his muse and morals has been maul'd:
He had written much blank verse, and blanker prose,
And more of both than any body knows.

XCIX

785 He had written Wesley's life: – here turning round
         To Satan, 'Sir, I'm ready to write yours,
In two octavo volumes, nicely bound,
         With notes and preface, all that most allures
The pious purchaser; and there's no ground
790   For fear, for I can choose my own reviewers:
So let me have the proper documents,
That I may add you to my other saints.'

C

Satan bow'd, and was silent. 'Well, if you,
         With amiable modesty, decline
795 My offer, what says Michael? There are few
         Whose memoirs could be render'd more divine.

1. See 'Life of Henry Kirke White.'

Mine is a pen of all work; not so new
    As it was once, but I would make you shine
Like your own trumpet. By the way, my own
800   Has more of brass in it, and is as well blown.

CI

'But talking about trumpets, here's my Vision!
    Now you shall judge, all people; yes, you shall
Judge with my judgment, and by my decision
    Be guided who shall enter heaven or fall.
805   I settle all these things by intuition,
    Times present, past, to come, heaven, hell, and all,
Like King Alfonso.[1] When I thus see double,
I save the Deity some worlds of trouble.'

CII

He ceased, and drew forth an MS.; and no
810   Persuasion on the part of devils, or saints,
Or angels, now could stop the torrent; so
    He read the first three lines of the contents;
But at the fourth, the whole spiritual show
    Had vanish'd, with variety of scents,
815   Ambrosial and sulphureous, as they sprang,
Like lightning, off from his 'melodious twang.'[2]

CIII

Those grand heroics acted as a spell;
    The angels stopp'd their ears and plied their pinions;
The devils ran howling, deafen'd, down to hell;
820   The ghosts fled, gibbering, for their own dominions –
(For 'tis not yet decided where they dwell,
    And I leave every man to his opinions);
Michael took refuge in his trump – but, lo!
His teeth were set on edge, he could not blow!

1. Alfonso, speaking of the Ptolomean system, said, that 'had he been consulted at the creation of the world, he would have spared the Maker some absurdities.'
2. See Aubrey's account of the apparition which disappeared 'with a curious perfume and a *most melodious twang*;' or see the '*Antiquary*,' vol. i. p. 225.

CIV

825 Saint Peter, who has hitherto been known
  For an impetuous saint, upraised his keys,
And at the fifth line knock'd the poet down;
  Who fell like Phaeton, but more at ease,
Into his lake, for there he did not drown;
830   A different web being by the Destinies
Woven for the Laureate's final wreath, whene'er
Reform shall happen either here or there.

CV

He first sank to the bottom – like his works,
  But soon rose to the surface – like himself;
835 For all corrupted things are buoy'd like corks,[1]
  By their own rottenness, light as an elf,
Or wisp that flits o'er a morass: he lurks,
  It may be, still, like dull books on a shelf,
In his own den, to scrawl some 'Life' or 'Vision,'
840 As Welborn says – 'the devil turn'd precisian.'

CVI

As for the rest, to come to the conclusion
  Of this true dream, the telescope is gone
Which kept my optics free from all delusion,
  And show'd me what I in my turn have shown;
845 All I saw farther, in the last confusion,
  Was, that King George slipp'd into heaven for one;
And when the tumult dwindled to a calm,
I left him practising the hundredth psalm.

1. A drowned body lies at the bottom till rotten; it then floats, as most people know.

On This Day I Complete My Thirty-Sixth Year

Missolonghi, Jan. 22, 1824.

I

'Tis time this heart should be unmoved,
    Since others it hath ceased to move:
Yet, though I cannot be beloved,
        Still let me love!

II

5   My days are in the yellow leaf;
    The flowers and fruits of love are gone;
The worm, the canker, and the grief
        Are mine alone!

III

The fire that on my bosom preys
10   Is lone as some volcanic isle;
No torch is kindled at its blaze –
        A funeral pile!

IV

The hope, the fear, the jealous care,
    The exalted portion of the pain
15   And power of love, I cannot share,
        But wear the chain.

V

But 'tis not *thus* – and 'tis not *here* –
    Such thoughts should shake my soul, nor *now*,
Where glory decks the hero's bier,
20   Or binds his brow.

VI

The sword, the banner, and the field,
    Glory and Greece, around me see!
The Spartan, borne upon his shield,
        Was not more free.

VII

25   Awake! (not Greece – she *is* awake!)
    Awake, my spirit! Think through *whom*
Thy life-blood tracks its parent lake,
        And then strike home!

VIII

Tread those reviving passions down,
30   Unworthy manhood! – unto thee
Indifferent should the smile or frown
        Of beauty be.

IX

If thou regret'st thy youth, *why live?*
    The land of honourable death
35   Is here: – up to the field, and give
        Away thy breath!

X

Seek out – less often sought than found –
    A soldier's grave, for thee the best;
Then look around, and choose thy ground,
40   And take thy rest.

NOTES

A Fragment ('When, to their airy hall, my fathers' voice')

Written 1803; printed in *Fugitive Pieces* (1806); retained in *Hours of Idleness* (1807).

In this Ossianic 'fragment', as Byron called it, he invokes his noble ancestors as ground for a heroic destiny.

Criticism: Jerome J. McGann, *Fiery Dust* ('Feeling as He Writes: The Genesis of the Myth').

To Woman

Written 1805(?); printed in *Fugitive Pieces* (1806); retained in *Hours of Idleness* (1807).

In 1820 Byron wrote Thomas Moore that he 'knew by heart in 1803' Moore's *Poetical Works of the Late Thomas Little* (1801): 'I believe all the mischief I have ever done, or sung, has been owing to that confounded book of yours' (*BLJ*, Vol. 7, p. 117). Moore's erotic manner leaves traces throughout Byron's early verse.

The Cornelian

Written 1805 or 1806; printed in *Fugitive Pieces* (1806); not republished in *Hours of Idleness*.

The cornelian was a gift from John Edleston, a Cambridge chorister about whom Byron wrote: 'he has been my *almost constant* associate since October 1805, when I entered Trinity College . . . I certainly *love* him more than any human being' (*BLJ*, Vol. 1, p. 124). Edward Noel Long and others knew that Edleston was the subject, but by late February 1807 Byron was urging Long keep this reference 'a *Secret*', adding that although '*you* & all the Girls, I know not why think [it] my best', he omitted the work and 'most of the amatory poems' from *Hours of Idleness* (*BLJ*, Vol. 1, pp. 110, 118).

Criticism: Louis Crompton, *Byron and Greek Love*.

To Caroline ('*You say you love, and yet your eye*')

Written 1806(?); printed in *Fugitive Pieces* (1806); not republished in *Hours of Idleness*.

Objections among his Southwell circle to his amorous verses led Byron to drop this and other instances from his first public volume. See note to 'To Woman'.

ENGLISH BARDS AND SCOTCH
REVIEWERS: A Satire

Begun 1807; enlarged and recast 1808–9; published anonymously March 1809.

In 1807 Byron wrote a satire on 'the poetry of the present Day' titled *British Bards*; the condescending notice of *Hours of Idleness* in the *Edinburgh Review* (January 1808) goaded him to include the newly powerful critics, and deepened its tone from Horatian to Juvenalian, as the imitation announced in the note to the opening line indicates ('What! while with one eternal mouthing hoarse,/Codrus persists on my vex'd ear to force/His *Theseid*, must I, to my fate resign'd,/Hear, ONLY hear, and never pay in kind?'; translated by William Gifford, ll. 1–4). A Whig and half-Scot himself, Byron had not expected scorn from the Whig *Edinburgh Review*; his title shows Byron positioning himself to draw on accumulated English prejudice against the Scots, a tactic also signalled by echoes of Charles Churchill, whose satire *The Prophecy of Famine* (1763) contributed to the campaign of his friend John Wilkes against the ministry of the Scots Lord Bute: for example, 'Time was' (l. 103), a recurrent marker in Churchill's *The Times* (1764), and the echo of the repeated '*Health* to great Gloster' of Churchill's *Dedication to the Sermons* (1765) in Byron's 'Health to great Jeffrey!' (l. 460; cf. l. 438). Censure of the debased state of contemporary literature was conventional; *The Baeviad* (1794) and *The Maeviad* (1795), by William Gifford, attacking the English Della Cruscans, led by Robert Merry, were recent precursors (ll. 94, 702–3, 741–64). Byron's praise of Dryden, Pope and formally conservative contemporaries such as Thomas Campbell and Samuel Rogers (ll. 799–818), and his reiterated disdain for 'sons of song [who] descend to trade' (l. 175) are attitudes that his later styles and commercial success complicated. Some targets remained life-long: Byron savaged Robert Southey in the Dedication to *Don Juan*, which also mocks William Wordsworth and Samuel Taylor Coleridge, and he parodied Southey's *A Vision of Judgement* (1821) in *The Vision of Judgment* (1822) (ll. 202–34, 235–54, 255–64); William Lisle Bowles, whose sonnets of 'sympathy' (ll. 327–62) and 1806 edition of Pope Byron excoriates (ll. 363–84), further denigrated Pope in his *Invariable Principles of Poetry* (1819), sparking Byron to answer in two long essays (see *CMP*, pp. 120–83). The vigorous defence of traditional taste, carried in verse and notes, against 'romantic' tendencies ensured the poem's popularity: the first edition of 1,000 copies sold out; a second edition, augmented, with a Preface and bearing Byron's name, appeared in May 1809 and also sold out; by 1811 the poem had reached a fourth edition. Other dismissals were altered by experience: the satire, Byron later told Coleridge, 'was written when I was very young and very angry, and has been a thorn in my side ever since; more particularly as almost all the persons animadverted upon became subsequently my acquaintances, and some of them my friends' (*BLJ*, Vol. 4, p. 286): Lord and Lady Holland and Holland House formed the centre of the Whig society Byron joined after his début in Parliament (ll. 519, 540–59); M.G. Lewis, author of *The Monk* (1796) and *Tales of Terror* (1801) (ll. 148, 265–82, 919) became a friend, as did Walter Scott (ll. 153–84) and Thomas Moore ('Thomas Little'; see note to 'To Woman') (ll. 128, 283–94). Byron's assault on the editor of the *Edinburgh Review*, Francis Jeffrey, whose 1806 duel with Moore he burlesques (ll. 464 ff.) and whom he compares to the notorious judge of the 'Bloody Assizes' of 1685, George Jefferies (ll. 438–59), was motivated by the belief that the notice of *Hours of Idleness* was his; it was rather written by Henry Brougham (l. 524), and Jeffrey later welcomed Byron's Eastern Tales in the *Edinburgh Review*. Largely at Holland's request, Byron suppressed the printed but not published fifth edition in 1812; 'it is not in print for sale – nor ever will be – (if I can help it) – again' (*BLJ*, Vol. 4, p. 318), he declared in 1815, but pirated versions continued to appear.

Epigraphs: *1 Henry IV*, III.1.128–9; *Essay on Criticism* (ll. 610–11).

Criticism: on the provocation of the *Edinburgh Review* by Byron's self-presentation in *Hours of Idleness* as 'Lord Byron, A Minor', see Kurt Heinzelman, 'Byron's Poetry of Politics'.

Lines to Mr Hodgson (*Written on Board the Lisbon Packet*)

Written 30 June 1809; published in Moore's *Life* (1830).

Byron sailed for Lisbon on 2 July; this *jeu d'esprit*, sent to Francis Hodgson two days earlier, shows that Byron's *Childe Harold* mood was not his only one.

Maid of Athens, ere we part

Written 9 February 1810; published with *Childe Harold's Pilgrimage I–II* (1812).

Addressed to the twelve-year-old daughter of Byron's landlady at Athens. Byron described himself as 'dying for love' of the three Macri sisters, 'divinities all of them under 15', but their mother viewed the attentions of the English lord more interestedly (*BLJ*, Vol. 1, p. 240). She was 'mad enough to imagine I was going to marry the girl', he reported; 'I was near bringing away Theresa but the mother asked *30,000* piastres!' (*BLJ*, Vol. 2, pp. 13, 46). Byron wrote of the Greek refrain (*Zoë mou, sas agapo*),

a Romaic expression of tenderness: if I translate it, I shall affront the gentlemen, as it may seem I supposed they could not; and if I do not I may affront the ladies. For fear of any misconstruction on the part of the latter I shall do so, begging pardon of the learned. It means, 'My Life, I love you!'

Written after Swimming from Sestos to Abydos

Written 9 May 1810; published with *Childe Harold's Pilgrimage I–II* (1812).

The poem records Byron's re-enactment of the exploit, made famous by Ovid (Books XVIII and XIX of the *Heroides*); Musaeus, an Alexandrian poet of the fifth century AD, whose epyllion was translated by George Chapman in 1616; and the *Hero and Leander* of Christopher Marlowe and Chapman (1598). See Leslie A. Marchand, *Byron: A Biography*, Vol. 1, pp. 236–9).

To Thyrza ('Without a stone to mark the spot')

Dated 11 October 1811; published with *Childe Harold's Pilgrimage I–II* (1812).

The first of a series of elegies for John Edleston, of whose death in May Byron had just heard. Moore maintained in his biography of Byron that Thyrza was 'imaginary'; others assumed from the feminine name that the subject was a woman, an impression in which Byron colluded. Compare *Childe Harold* II.73–81, 891–9. See note to 'The Cornelian'.

Criticism: Louis Crompton, *Byron and Greek Love*.

CHILDE HAROLD'S PILGRIMAGE:

A Romaunt, Cantos I–II

Written from 31 October 1809 to 28 March 1810; published 10 March 1812.

Byron's travels in 1809–11 provided the materials for this poem, one largely written, as the Preface declares, 'amidst the scenes which it attempts to describe'. Byron left England for Portugal and Spain on 2 July 1809, accompanied by his friend from Cambridge, John Cam Hobhouse, his valet William Fletcher (I.158), the young son of one of his Newstead tenants, Robert Rushton (I.134) and an old servant, Joe Murray. The itinerary was partly determined by the wartime closing of the Continent, though the Iberian Peninsula too had been invaded by Napoleon in 1807, where local resistance was augmented by a British expeditionary force. On 4 July the party reached Gibraltar, whence Murray and Rushton returned to England; the others proceeded on 19 August to Malta, where Byron had a brief affair with Constance Spencer Smith (II.264–97). They arrived in Albania on 28 September, journeying to Janina and Tepelini, where they met Ali Pasha (II.554), the fierce local overlord, and Byron began the poem. From Christmas until March their centre was Athens. In spring 1810 they sailed to Smyrna, and visited Ephesus and the plains of Troy; on 13 May they arrived in Constantinople, returning to Greece on 17 July. Hobhouse then departed for England, and Byron settled in Athens until 21 April, when he returned to England by way of a month's stay in Malta, landing at Portsmouth on 11 July 1811.

Childe Harold derives from the eighteenth-century topographical poem, but so transformed that Scott could greet it as 'certainly the most original poem which we have had this many a day' (quoted in Samuel Smiles, *A Publisher and His Friends*, Vol. 1, p. 214). The Spenserian form, as the Preface observes, citing James Beattie, author of *The Minstrel* (1771–4), licensed flexibility of tone and a structure with 'no pretension to regularity'. In praising Byron in the *Quarterly Review* (March 1812) for conveying 'a good deal of curious information' about Greece, George Ellis pointed to the topical appeal of the work. English interest in the unfamiliar eastern Mediterranean was high, fed by books of travels and the strategic importance of the region. The contrast Byron draws in the second canto between Greece's heroic past and its condition under Turkish rule, including his attack on Thomas Bruce, seventh Earl of Elgin who, while serving as envoy to the Porte (the Ottoman Empire), removed from Athens the sculptures of the Parthenon (II.91–135), spurred the philhellenic movement that led to the Greek War of Independence (1821–9) in which Byron died, becoming a Greek national hero.

The mock-Spenserianisms of the opening stanzas imply a distance between Byron and his 'fictitious personage', as the Preface describes Harold; but Harold was 'Childe Burun' in the manuscripts and to contemporaries the effect of the poem was daringly personal: Scott ascribed its success to 'the novelty of an author speaking in his own person' (*Quarterly Review*, April 1818). In the context formed by Burke's invocation of the language of chivalry to defend the *ancien régime* in his *Reflections on the Revolution in France* (1790), the satiric and melancholic reduction of the chivalric 'romaunt' in the first canto – reiterated in the Addition to the Preface (for the fourth edition) – shocked; the *Antijacobin Review* (1812) denounced as 'the rant of democracy in its wildest form' Byron's treatment of the victories of Talavera (July 1809; I.405–58) and Albuera (May 1811; I.459–67), and his mockery of the Convention of Cintra (30 August 1808; I.288–314), by which the French defeated at Vimiero were convoyed home with their booty. Byron's anti-war sentiments vividly expressed the Whig position and simultaneously outraged the Tories. The balance of tones in *Childe Harold* was altered as Byron revised the poem on his return to England: satirical passages were excised in response to the objections of friends and of his publisher, John Murray, and additions reflected the deaths enumerated in his note to I.927, those of his Harrow friend John Wingfield (14 May 1811), of his mother (31 July 1811), of his Cambridge friend Charles Skinner Matthews (3 August 1811) and (not named) of John Edleston (May 1811, although Byron did not learn of it until October): see II.73–81, 891–908, and the notes to 'The Cornelian' and 'To Thyrza'. 'To Ianthe', addressed to Lady Charlotte Harley, the thirteen-year-old daughter of Lady Oxford (Byron enjoyed a liaison with the latter in 1812–14), was added to the seventh edition of the poem, in 1814. The counterpoint provided by the notes – worldly, scholarly, elegiac, indignant – forms an integral part of the work's effect. *Childe Harold* was published 10 March 1812 in an expensive edition of 500 quarto copies and sold out in three days, making the author, as he later commented, famous overnight. It went through four editions by the end of the year, and reached a tenth in 1815.

Epigraph: Louis Charles Fougeret de Monbron, *Le Cosmopolite, ou le Citoyen du Monde* (1753):

The universe is a kind of book of which one has read only the first page when one has seen only one's own country. I have leafed through a large enough number, which I have found equally bad. This examination was not at all fruitless for me. I hated my country. All the impertinences of the different peoples among whom I have lived have reconciled me to her. If I had not drawn any other benefit from my travels than that, I would regret neither the expense nor the fatigue.

Criticism: on Byron's travels, see William A. Borst, *Lord Byron's First Pilgrimage* and Gordon Kent Thomas, *Lord Byron's Iberian Pilgrimage*; on the Greek materials, see William St Clair, *Lord Elgin and the Marbles* and *That Greece Might Still be Free* (on the War of Independence); *English Romantic Hellenism 1700–1824*, edited by Timothy Webb, provides a useful collection of primary documents. Cecil Y. Lang speculates on the role of Ali Pacha in the inception of the poem ('Narcissus Jilted'), and William St Clair studies its reception ('The Impact of Byron's Writings'). Stuart Curran (*Poetic Form*, Chapter 6) and Marlon Ross ('Scott's Chivalric Pose') illuminate Byron's employment of the genre of romance. For general criticism: M.K. Joseph, *Byron the Poet*, Robert F. Gleckner, *Byron and the Ruins of Paradise*, and Jerome J. McGann, *Fiery Dust*.

An Ode to the Framers of the Frame Bill

Published anonymously in the *Morning Chronicle*, 2 March 1812; collected by E.H. Coleridge in *Works* (1898–1904).

On 27 February 1812 Byron made his maiden speech in the House of Lords, attacking the Tory ministry who had responded to the Luddite Riots in Nottingham with a bill imposing the death penalty for destruction of the weaving frames recently installed in the local mills. The proximity of Newstead Abbey to Nottingham gave Byron the standing of a personally concerned magnate.

Lines to a Lady Weeping

Written, and published anonymously in the *Morning Chronicle*, in March 1812; republished under Byron's name with *The Corsair* (1814).

When increased authority was granted to the Prince Regent in early 1812 the Whigs assumed that as a reward for their support he would bring them into power. Instead he proposed a coalition with their Tory enemies; when the outraged Whigs refused, the Prince denounced them at a banquet at Carlton House in a speech that provoked his daughter, Princess Charlotte, to tears. By acknowledging the verses as his in 1814 Byron generated a furor in the Tory press – 'the 8 lines . . . have I believe given birth to as many volumes' (*BLJ*, Vol. 4, p. 82) – that contributed to the unprecedented sales of *The Corsair* volume: see note to that poem.

Criticism: Peter J. Manning, 'Tales and Politics', in *Reading Romantics*.

THE WALTZ: An Apostrophic Hymn

Written October 1812; printed privately and anonymously in 1813, and in a pirated edition in 1821.

The epigraph is from the *Aeneid* I.498–9, describing Dido's arrival at the temple. When the waltz was introduced in England from Germany in the eighteenth century, it was controversial, deemed voluptuous and indecorous. The enthusiasm of the Prince Regent (of the German House of Hanover) made it a vogue, but to English chauvinism, as well as by some Continental standards, it symptomized everything wanton and vulgar 'imported from the Rhine' (l.29). Byron's disapproval was aggravated by his lameness, which kept him from dancing. Contemplating marriage to Annabella Milbanke, he inquired of her aunt, Lady Melbourne, 'Does Annabella *waltz*?' adding, 'it is . . . a very essential point with me' (*BLJ*, Vol. 2, p. 218). Because Byron's criticism of waltzing was fuelled by its association with the Regent and extended into a general satire on the royal family and their influence, he decided on anonymous publication. Even with this precaution, his publisher, John Murray, declined the option, and the poem came out under a different imprint. When it was criticized, Byron was concerned to maintain his anonymity and urged Murray's silence (*BLJ*, Vol. 3, p. 41).

Remember Thee! Remember Thee!

Written 1813(?); published in Thomas Medwin's *Conversations of Lord Byron* (1824).

After Byron broke off his affair with Lady Caroline Lamb, she called one day at his apartment when he was out, and, 'finding *Vathek* [William Beckford's popular Arabian novel of 1786] on the table, she wrote in the first page, "Remember me!"' Byron took up the echo of the ghost in *Hamlet* (I.v.91–111): 'Yes! I had cause to remember her; and in the irritability of the moment, wrote under the two words these two stanzas' (Thomas Medwin, p. 218).

THE GIAOUR: A Fragment of a Turkish Tale

Written September 1812–March 1813; published June 1813 as a poem of 684 lines, and subsequently in longer versions.

'*Giaour*' (with a soft G and rhymed with 'power' (ll. 457–8)) is Arabic for 'Infidel', a non-Muslim – in this tale, an aristocratic Venetian. This is the first in a wildly successful series in a genre that Byron called the 'Eastern tale' (*BLJ*, Vol. 3, p. 157), and its title character is one of the first delineations, after Childe Harold, of the 'Byronic hero'. The *Satirist* gave the poem a nasty review (1 July 1813), but Jeffrey praised it in the *Edinburgh Review* (July 1813), and sales nearly matched those of *Childe Harold I–II* in the previous year. By the end of summer 1813, *The Giaour* was in its fifth edition and went through nine more by 1815. While the 'Fragment' form indicated in its subtitle is a deliberate narrative device, the illusion of the poem's basis in 'disjointed fragments' of reports (Advertisement) was sustained as Byron added increments to each edition, implying a fuller recovery of the matter. By the seventh edition (December 1813), he had nearly doubled the length of the original text. Lines 1131–257 first appeared in the fifth edition, the proofs of which Byron returned to Murray, commenting, 'I have but with some difficulty *not* added any more to this snake of a poem – which has been lengthening its rattles every month – it is now fearfully long – being more than a Canto & a half of C[hilde] H[arold]' (*BLJ*, Vol. 3, p. 100).

The Dedication honours a friendship with Samuel Rogers and the influence of his *Voyage of Columbus* (1810), also a fragment form. The Advertisement sets the poem 'at the time the Seven Islands were possessed by the Republic of Venice' – shortly after 1779 (*CPW*, Vol. 3, p. 415); Greece's subjection then is meant to evoke its subjection by the Ottomans in 1813, a relevance underscored in the opening lament (ll. 1–167) on the 'lust and rapine [that] wildly reign/To darken o'er the fair domain' (ll. 60–61). Byron presents the story of 'the Turk' Hassan, his favourite haremite Leila, and her lover the Giaour, as an assemblage of several voices possessed of different knowledges and interests, incorporated with the poet's own meditations. Here is a rough scheme: ll. 1–167, the poet meditating on the lost past; ll. 168–79, the immediate scene; ll. 180–287, the Giaour's murder of Hassan; ll. 288–351, the subsequent history; ll. 352–86, a boatman's encounter with Hassan and Leila's corpse; ll. 387–438, the poet's meditations; ll. 439–71, an account of Leila's escape, told by one of Hassan's countrymen; ll. 472–518, a rapture about Leila from the male Turkish perspective; ll. 519–674, an anonymous Turkish report of the Giaour's revenge on Hassan; ll. 675–88, the Giaour's voice (for the first time); ll. 689–785, a Turkish narrator's tale of the Giaour's brutal murder of Hassan and his account of Hassan's mother's grief; ll. 786–97, a fisherman's encounter with the Giaour, some years later, now a Caloyer (a monk); ll. 798–830, the voice of a fellow monk; ll. 832–82, a general narrative; ll. 883–915, a monk's voice; ll. 916–70, the general narrator. Lines 971–1328 are the Giaour's confession, with a final six lines of general narration.

The core tale derived some of its sensation from its reputed basis in Byron's affair with a young Turkish woman in Athens, which he recounted, much later, to Thomas Medwin (*Conversations of Lord Byron*, pp. 86–7). Even so, a footnote in the 1832–4 *Works* (Vol. 9, p. 145) laboured to dispel the rumour that Byron had been 'the lover of this female slave': she was 'not . . . an object of his Lordship's attachment, but of that of his Turkish servant', it insisted, and Byron's part was only to prevent her execution – the sentence by the Turkish Governor for adultery, to be carried out (as the Advertisement puts it) 'in the Mussulman manner', by her being sewn into a sack and 'thrown . . . into the sea'. 'To describe the *feelings* of *that situation* were impossible – it is *icy* even to recollect them,' Byron wrote in his journal (5 December 1813; *BLJ*, Vol. 3, p. 230). Yet his tale is more divided: while it stresses tyranny by making Leila a harem slave and leaving her unrescued from the death sentence, it also forges a psychological sympathy between the male antagonists. Byron told Murray that he had 'thrown . . . in' the last lines 'to soften the ferocity of our infidel – & for a dying man have given him a good deal to say for himself' (*BLJ*, Vol. 3, p. 100). As in *Childe Harold* and subsequent Eastern tales, Byron's notes are part of his authorial performance, giving a patina of authenticity and cultural familiarity as well as conveying a modern, detached, anthropological reading of the East of recent history.

Criticism: Jerome J. McGann, *Fiery Dust*, on poetic form and narrative performance; Robert F. Gleckner, *Byron and the Ruins of Paradise*, on narrative form; Marjorie Levinson, *The Romantic Fragment Poem*, on the fragment form; Peter J. Manning, *Byron and His Fictions*, on the doubling of the male characters; Marilyn Butler, 'John Bull's Other Kingdom', on Orientalism; Caroline Franklin, *Byron's Heroines*, on patriarchal tyranny; and Daniel P. Watkins, *Social Relations in Byron's Eastern Tales*, on ideological contradictions in a social system of politicized violence.

THE BRIDE OF ABYDOS: A Turkish Tale

Written November 1813, in less than two weeks; dedicated to Byron's mentor in the House of Lords, the Whig liberal Lord Holland, and published 2 December, selling even more briskly than *The Giaour*: 6,000 copies the first month, 125,000 by early 1814, five editions in 1813, five more in 1814, and an eleventh by the end of 1815.

Byron described this Eastern tale as 'something of the *Giaour* cast – but not so *sombre* though rather more villainous' (*BLJ*, Vol. 3, p. 157). Writing his first tale with a heroine and even thinking of naming the poem for her ('Zuleika'; *BLJ*, Vol. 3, p. 205), he said that he wanted to 'preserve her purity without impairing the ardour of her attachment' (*BLJ*, Vol. 3, p. 199). A more private motive, he tells Lady Melbourne, was 'to dispel reflection during *inaction*' (*BLJ*, Vol. 3, p. 157) – or to find an outlet for erotic impasse, for Zuleika is created in the context of two inhibited passions, Byron's infatuation with the married Lady Frances Webster and his passion for his half-sister, Augusta (he first made Selim and Zuleika brother and sister, but social taboo 'induced [him] to alter their consanguinity & confine them to cousinship'; Vol. 3, p. 199). It is the incestuous passion to which Byron was most likely referring when he wrote in his journal that he was 'indebted to the tale' because 'it wrung my thoughts from reality to imagination – from selfish regrets to vivid recollections' (*BLJ*, Vol. 3, p. 230). Even without public knowledge of this frisson, Zuleika proved controversial in the reviews, especially in her erotic effusion to Selim in I. XIII. The *British Critic* (January 1814) found her language 'foreign' to any notion of a 'poetical heroine'; the *Antijacobin Review* (March 1814) thought it 'indecent even in the mouth of a lover' and her forthrightness 'not very decorous nor yet very natural' (it also included *The Corsair*'s Medora and Gulnare in the complaint). This passion was a sticking-point even in otherwise favourable reviews in liberal journals. Zuleika 'by no means conveys the most elevated notions of delicacy', wrote *Drakard's Paper* (later the *Champion*), accusing Byron of using 'fine writing' to 'obtain mastery over a story which is in itself positively objectionable. So far from sharing *Zuleika's* passion . . . our feelings revolt from its contemplation' (December 1813); the *Monthly Museum* (February 1814) felt compelled to remark that some of her expressions were 'indelicate . . . conveying a sense of emotions not wholly compatible with the purity of the virgin character'.

Criticism: Edgar Allan Poe on metrics (reprinted in *BCH*); Peter J. Manning, *Byron and His Fictions*, on oedipal configurations; Daniel P. Watkins, *Social Relations in Byron's Eastern Tales*, on social structure; and Caroline Franklin, *Byron's Heroines*, on the character of Zuleika.

THE CORSAIR: A Tale

Written late 1813; published 1 February 1814, bound with a few other poems, including the already notorious 'Lines to a Lady Weeping'. On 3 February, Murray reported to Byron that the 'sensation' in sales was 'unprecedented' (Samuel Smiles, *A Publisher and His Friends*, Vol. 1 pp. 223–4). On the day of publication, it sold 10,000 copies, went through five editions in the same month, six more (25,000 copies) by the end of the next, and sold out an eighth edition by the end of the year; a ninth appeared in 1815 and a tenth in 1818.

The epigraphs appeared in Italian. The general one, from Tasso, may be translated as 'His thoughts cannot sleep within him.' The Cantos' epigraphs are all from the episode of Dante's encounter with Francesca of Rimini, in *Inferno*, Canto V. For Byron's own later translations of these lines, see 'Francesca of Rimini': his epigraph for Canto I (*Inferno* V.121–3) corresponds to ll. 25–7; for Canto II (*Inferno* V.120) to l. 24; for Canto III (*Inferno* V.105) to l. 9. The description of Conrad, the Corsair, in Canto I, stanzas VIII–XII (ll. 171–308) emerged as a canonical portrait of the Byronic hero: a dark, mysterious, brooding outlaw, whose 'one virtue' midst his 'thousand crimes' is his devotion to his wife and, in general, an ethic of chivalry with regard to women. As in other Eastern tales, the projection of tyranny, especially sexual tyranny over enslaved women, as a feature of an 'Eastern' society and the corresponding narrative of liberation by an enemy of this system reflect early nineteenth-century 'Orientalism' (that is, the implied cultural superiority of West to East). Yet this ideological structure is complicated by the other sensational figure in the poem, the Pacha's harem favourite, Gulnare, whose rebellion unsettles Western as well as Eastern orthodoxies of gender. She is first a damsel-in-distress rescued by Conrad; but when he is defeated and imprisoned for execution by the Pacha, she emerges as a determined murderer of this oppressor and liberator of the Corsair. Byron's ambivalence about female violence (however this violence might be politically justified) is reflected in the tale's structural pairing of Gulnare in antithesis to Conrad's passive, patient, devoted wife, Medora.

The poem's popular sales were matched by controversial reviews, the chief issue being the elevation of the Corsair, a criminal and outlaw, to heroic status; Gulnare also proved disturbing. Related to the redefinition of the hero, another point of discussion was Byron's heroic couplet (a verse form advertised in the Dedication); *The Corsair* is his first use of the measure for an extended romance tale. Jeffrey's praise in the *Edinburgh Review* (April 1814) included admiration for Byron's verse technique, but other reviewers protested both the impropriety of the heroic measure for this narrative and, more particularly, Byron's indulgence of non-Augustan effects such as racy enjambment, unorthodox caesurae, and feminine and slant rhymes.

Criticism: Peter J. Manning, *Byron and His Fictions*, on psychological configurations, and 'Hone-ing' and 'Tales and Politics' (both in *Reading Romantics*) on political and social contexts; Jerome Christensen, *Lord Byron's Strength*, on political power; Daniel P. Watkins, *Social Relations in Byron's Eastern Tales*, on social structure; and Caroline Franklin, *Byron's Heroines*, and Cheryl Fallon Giuliano, 'Gulnare/Kaled's "Untold" Feminization', on gender trouble; Susan Wolfson, *Formal Charges*, on the location of many of these issues in verse form.

Ode to Napoleon Buonaparte

Written, and published anonymously, in April 1814; Byron's name appeared in the tenth edition (also 1814).

The allies entered Paris at the end of March 1814 and forced Napoleon's abdication. The decision of the heroic figure, in whom he saw himself and with whom he was paired in the popular imagination, to capitulate rather than nobly to commit suicide left Byron 'utterly bewildered and confounded' (*BLJ*, Vol. 3, p. 256); he could not know that on 12 April, two days after he composed his first draft, Napoleon did attempt to poison himself. Byron's disappointment issues in the flood of comparisons: the Greek athlete Milo (l. 46); Sulla, who resigned in 79 BC after a cruel dictatorship (l. 55); Charles V, who abdicated in 1556 (l. 64); Dionysius, who fell from tyrant of Syracuse to schoolteacher at Corinth (l. 125); Tamerlane, who confined the captive King Bajazet in a cage (l. 127); Nebuchadnezzar (l. 131); Prometheus (l. 136); Othello, echoed in l. 142 (*Othello* IV.i.70); Cincinnatus, the Roman general who returned from triumph to his farm (l. 168). The first motto, from Juvenal's Satire X, underscores the decay of glory: 'Produce the urn that Hannibal contains,/And weigh the mighty dust which yet remains:/AND IS THIS ALL!' (ll. 147–8; translated by William Gifford). Stanza V first appeared in the third edition; stanzas XVII–XIX were written in response to Murray's plea to lengthen the poem to avoid the tax on pamphlets of less than a sheet; Byron did not like these stanzas '*at all* – and they had better be left out' (*BLJ*, Vol. 4, p. 107). They did not appear in any of the lifetime editions; despite the violation of Byron's intentions, their inclusion in the 1832 *Works*, our base text, governed all subsequent versions of the poem until *CPW* (see Vol. 3, p. 456).

Stanzas for Music

Written May(?) 1814; published in *Fugitive Pieces and Reminiscences of Lord Byron*, by Isaac Nathan, containing a new edition of *Hebrew Melodies* (1829).

'Thou hast asked me for a song,' Byron wrote to Thomas Moore on 4 May 1814, 'and I enclose you an experiment, which has cost me something more than trouble' (*BLJ*, Vol. 4, p. 114). Annabella reported in 1817 that Augusta acknowledged herself the subject; Byron gave Nathan permission to publish on the condition that the poem be dated 'more than two years previously to his marriage', which Nathan did, adding a protest against 'calumniators' who 'distorted' Byron's 'amatory' pieces by applying them 'to the lamented circumstances of his later life' (*Fugitive Pieces*, p. 65).

She walks in beauty

Written June 1814; published in *Hebrew Melodies* (1815).

The subject is Anne Wilmot, the wife of Byron's first cousin, whom he had seen at a party wearing 'mourning, with dark spangles on her dress'. *Hebrew Melodies* was initiated by the Jewish composer Isaac Nathan, and brought out by him in April 1815, in a large folio, with music, priced at a guinea. The volume responded to the vogue for national songs, such as Thomas Moore's *Irish Melodies* (1807; many successive editions), and sold 10,000 copies; Murray brought out an edition without music in June. As this poem, placed first, suggests, the collection does not consist solely of biblical lyrics.

Criticism: On the date of composition and Byron's relations with his cousin, see Noel McLachlan, '*She Walks in Beauty*: Some Byron Mysteries'; on the *Hebrew Melodies* generally, see T.L. Ashton's monograph, *Byron's Hebrew Melodies*, and Frederick Burwick and Paul Douglass's edition (with music), *A Selection of Hebrew Melodies, Ancient and Modern*.

LARA: A Tale

Written quickly, May–June 1814; published anonymously August, with Samuel Rogers's *Jacqueline*.

The Advertisement prefixed to the first three editions invited a regard of this tale 'as a sequel' to *The Corsair*, proposing affinities in 'the hero's character, the turn of his adventures, and the general outline and colouring of the story' (*CPW*, Vol. 3, p. 453). The coyness notwithstanding, every-one took the poem to be Byron's. Not only were there obvious parallels of verse form (heroic couplets) and character – Conrad seemed legible in Lara (returned after a long, mysterious absence) and Gulnare in his dis-guised page, Kaled – but the extensive set-piece description of Lara in Canto I (stanzas II–VIII; XVI–XIX) even more elaborately delineated the Byronic hero, a portrait that became one of the poem's most popular passages. Though not matching *The Corsair*'s, sales were impressive: three editions in 1814 of about 7,000 copies, and a fourth, now under Byron's name, of about 3,000. Even so, Byron and Murray were disappointed by the relative falling-off. In spring 1815, Byron told Leigh Hunt, 'I fear you stand almost single in your liking of "Lara" – it is . . . my last & most unpopular effervescence'; he surmised that the tale had 'too little narrative – and [was] too metaphysical to please the greater number of readers' (*BLJ*, Vol. 4, p. 295).

Criticism: Peter J. Manning, *Byron and His Fictions*, on psychological configurations; Jerome Christensen, *Lord Byron's Strength*, on political power; Daniel P. Watkins, *Social Relations in Byron's Eastern Tales*, on social structure; and Caroline Franklin, *Byron's Heroines*, and Cheryl Fallon Giuliano, 'Gulnare/Kaled's "Untold" Feminization', on gender.

The Destruction of Sennacherib

Written February 1815; published in *Hebrew Melodies* (1815).

The biblical sources are 2 Kings 19 and Isaiah 37. Sennacherib may by analogy figure Napoleon, but without topical reference the poem's captivat-ing anapestic rhythms have secured its place in anthologies. For criticism see note to 'She walks in beauty'.

Napoleon's Farewell (From the French)

Written, and published anonymously in the *Examiner*, July 1815; reprinted in *Poems* (1816).

Not the translation that the subtitle feigns, the poem obtained wide circulation when William Hone included it in his pirated edition of Byron, *Poems on His Domestic Circumstances* (1816), for which see note to 'Fare thee well!'.

From the French ('Must thou go, my glorious Chief')

Written 1815; first published in *Poems* (1816). Not a translation.

The two notes are taken from letters to Byron from John Cam Hobhouse, then in Paris.

THE SIEGE OF CORINTH

Composed, with difficulty, at various points between autumn 1813 and autumn 1815; published with *Parisina* 13 February 1816. Lines 1–45, here separately numbered, were written in 1813 but first published in Moore's *Life* (1830) and first included in the poem in the 1832 *Works*.

The first edition of 6,000 was followed by two others in 1816, but the poem was severely reviewed for the nihilism of the last stanza and for some ghoulish passages, especially the canine 'carnival' (ll. 409–33). Byron's Advertisement sets out the historical co-ordinates: the end of a long competition between the Venetian and Ottoman Empires for the control of Peloponnesus. Byron alters the history to make the explosion of the magazine a sabotage by the Venetian Governor, Minotti, that destroys everyone. The oedipal contest at the centre of the tale – the love of Alp, a Venetian turned renegade to the Muslims, for Francesca, the daughter of Minotti, who had opposed the match – is also his invention. The nervous note about *Christabel* in reference to the last twelve lines of stanza XIX recognizes a debt to I.43–8 of Coleridge's poem, which had been circulating in manuscript for over a decade. When Byron realized the influence, he wrote to Coleridge, attached a note of excuse to the 1816 edition, and subsequently helped Coleridge get *Christabel* published by Murray in 1816 (*BLJ*, Vol. 4, p. 321).

Criticism: Peter J. Manning, *Byron and His Fictions*, on psychological configurations; and Caroline Franklin, *Byron's Heroines*, on Francesca and gender ideology.

When we two parted

Written and published as a song-sheet in 1815; republished in *Poems* (1816).

In *Poems* Byron dated the poem 1808, thus screening its subject, Lady Frances Wedderburn Webster, with whom he had a brief 'platonic' affair in 1813, and whose current affair with the Duke of Wellington raised London gossip in 1815. A cancelled stanza –

> Then – fare thee well – Fanny –
>   Now doubly undone –
> To prove false unto many –
>   As faithless to *One* –
> Thou art past all recalling
>   Even *would* I recall
> For the woman once *falling*
>   Forever must *fall*.

– drew on lines Byron had written in 1812 about Lady Caroline Lamb, casting the two women together in his self-mythologizing erotic drama (*BLJ* Vol. 10, p. 198; see *CPW*, Vol. 3, pp. 475–6).

Criticism: Jerome J. McGann, 'The Significance of Biographical Context'.

Fare thee well!

Written March 1816; printed in an edition of fifty copies for private circulation; published without authorization in the *Champion*, 14 April 1816, and widely pirated thereafter. The poem was included in *Poems* (1816), for which Byron added the epigraph from Coleridge's *Christabel* (ll. 408–13, 419–26).

The preliminary separation agreement between Byron and his wife was signed on 17 March; Byron drafted the poem the next day and sent a copy to her in the next few weeks with a mollifying letter (*BLJ*, Vol. 5, pp. 51–2). The reprinting of the poem in the *Champion* marked a reprisal against Byron, as a prominent Whig critic of the Regent's morality now himself tainted with scandal. The coupling of Byron's poems on Napoleon with those on his domestic circumstances in the pirated editions emphasizes the inseparability of the personal and the political, but the dissemination of the poems also served Byron's attempts to shape public opinion in the scandal of the separation.

Criticism: David Erdman, '"Fare thee well!" – Byron's Last Days in England', on the political context; and Paul W. Elledge, 'Talented Equivocation', on Byron's treatment of separation.

Prometheus

Written in Switzerland July or August 1816; published with *The Prisoner of Chillon* (1816).

'Of the Prometheus of Æschylus I was passionately fond as a boy,'

Byron wrote; '[it] has always been so much in my head – that I can easily conceive its influence over all or anything that I have written' (*BLJ*, Vol. 5, p. 268); he included in *Hours of Idleness* a translation of some lines done at Harrow.

Criticism: John Clubbe, 'The New Prometheus of New Men', on the biographical background of the Swiss poems and the evolution of Byron's treatment of this cardinal Romantic figure.

THE PRISONER OF CHILLON: *A Fable*

and *Sonnet on Chillon*

Written 1816 and published 5 December by Murray in a slender volume, *The Prisoner of Chillon and Other Poems*, which Murray advertised in advance to capitalize on the success of *Childe Harold III*, published 18 November. He sold out the first edition of 6,000 at a booksellers' dinner at which he also marketed *Childe Harold III*. Scott reviewed both volumes favourably in the February 1817 issue of the *Quarterly Review* (also published by Murray).

In June 1816, Byron and Shelley visited the Castle of Chillon on Lake Geneva, in whose dungeons had been chained political prisoners for years on end, often for life sentences. 'These prisons are excavated below the lake ... Close to the very walls, the lake is 800 feet deep,' Shelley wrote to Peacock (12 July 1816). The verse tale, composed within the week, is cast as the dramatic monologue of François Bonnivard, who was imprisoned for six years (1530–36). The sonnet was written later and prefixed, so Byron's last note indicates, to 'dignify' the account of wretched suffering with a celebration of the 'courage and virtues' of the political prisoner. With this signal, the pair of poems became widely admired for their expression of defiant spiritual resistance to the tyranny described by Shelley's letter:

At the commencement of the Reformation, and indeed long after that period, this dungeon was the receptacle of those who shook, or who denied the system of idolatry, from the effects of which mankind is even now slowly emerging ... I never saw a monument more terrible of that cold and inhuman tyranny, which it has been the delight of man to exercise over man.

Even so, the sonnet's stirring anthem remains at odds with the tale's concentration on the prisoner's suffering and despair: his last sentence, 'I/ Regain'd my freedom with a sigh' is in an entirely different key from the sonnet's famous first line, 'Eternal Spirit of the chainless Mind!'

Criticism: Jerome J. McGann, *Fiery Dust*, on the thematic relations to *Childe Harold III*; and Andrew Rutherford, *Byron: A Critical Study*, on dramatic power.

Darkness

Written in Switzerland in July or August 1816; published with *The Prisoner of Chillon* (1816).

Criticism: Scott, reviewing *The Prisoner of Chillon* volume in the *Quarterly Review*, complained that in 'Darkness' Byron 'contented himself with presenting a mass of powerful ideas unarranged, and the meaning of which it is not easy to attain' (October 1816). On the despair of the poem see Robert F. Gleckner, *Byron and the Ruins of Paradise*; on the popularity in Byron's day of such apocalyptic visions and on Byron's sources, see R.J. Dingley, ' "I had a dream . . .": Byron's "Darkness" '.

CHILDE HAROLD'S PILGRIMAGE:

A Romaunt, Canto III

Written 25 April–4 July 1816; published 18 November 1816.

Byron departed from England on 25 April 1816, and the opening stanzas were written while he was still 'at Sea', on the crossing from Dover to Ostend. The melancholy that Harold, the 'wandering outlaw of his own dark mind' (l. 20), had embodied in 1809 was repeated in the scandal of the separation. Byron's daughter Augusta Ada had been born 10 December 1815; Annabella took the unweaned infant with her when she left Byron on 15 January 1816, and he never saw her again (ll. 1–4; 1067–102). For the biographical details of the period of composition see note to *Manfred*; the sublime mode of the poem excluded the range of Byron's actual moods. His physician, John Polidori, reported that at Ostend 'Byron fell like a thunderbolt upon the chambermaid' (Leslie A. Marchand, *Byron: A Biography*, Vol. 2, p. 610), and he replied to Thomas Moore's praise of the 'magnificence' of the canto by commenting:

I am glad you like it; it is a fine indistinct piece of poetical desolation, and my favourite. I was half mad during the time of its composition, between metaphysics, mountains, lakes, love unextinguishable, thoughts unutterable, and the nightmare of my own delinquencies. I should, many a good day, have blown my brains out, but for the recollection that it would have given pleasure to my mother-in-law; and, even *then*, if I could have been certain to haunt her – but I won't dwell upon these trifling family matters. (*BLJ*, Vol. 5, p. 165)

In *Stanzas from the Grand Chartreuse* (1855) Matthew Arnold asked,

What helps it now, that Byron bore,
With haughty scorn which mock'd the smart,
Through Europe to the Aetolian shore
The pageant of his bleeding heart?
That thousands quoted every groan,
And Europe made his *wee* their own? (ll. 133–8)

but in *Childe Harold* personal experience becomes the register of an era. Byron folded self-reflection into the meditation on Napoleon (ll. 316–78); he was travelling in a replica of Napoleon's carriage and, having taken the additional surname 'Noel' on his marriage, was 'delighted', as Leigh Hunt observed, 'to sign himself N.B.; "because," said he, "Bonaparte and I are the only public persons whose initials are the same"' (quoted in *BLJ*, Vol. 9, note to p. 171). Byron visited Waterloo, the site of Napoleon's final defeat (18 June 1815) on 4 May 1816, and his stanzas on the battle and the ball given by the Duchess of Richmond the night before, from the dramatic command – 'Stop! – for thy tread is on an Empire's dust!' – to the elegy for the slain 'thousands' represented by 'young, gallant Howard' (Byron's cousin Frederick Howard, son of the Earl of Carlisle, his guardian, satirized in *English Bards and Scotch Reviewers* (ll. 681–96)) memorialized the events for a generation (ll. 145–405).

Self-analysis and social commentary merge also in the figures of Jean-Jacques Rousseau, who appears as the author of the *Confessions* (posthumously published 1782–9) and of the novel *Julie, ou la Nouvelle Héloïse* (1761) (ll. 725–69), set at Clarens on Lake Geneva (ll. 923–76), as well as a critical thinker whose work, like that of Voltaire, paired with Gibbon, author of *The Decline and Fall of the Roman Empire* (1776–88), hastened the French Revolution (ll. 977–1003). Against the costs of ambition and conquest Byron sets the examples of François Marceau, who died defending the French Republic against the Austrians (ll. 536–53), of Morat, where in 1476 the Swiss repulsed the invading Burgundian army (ll. 601–16), and of Julia Alpinula, who, according to a first-century AD legend, died after a futile effort to save her father from execution by the Romans (ll. 626–34). Her role parallels that of Ada, and epitomizes the idealized function of the feminine in the canto.

Byron recurrently opposes to masculine will and warfare ('rotting from sire to son') the world of nature; he told Medwin that 'Shelley, when I was in Switzerland, used to dose me with Wordsworth physic even to nausea' (Thomas Medwin, *Conversations of Lord Byron*, p. 194), and *Childe Harold III* may be seen as testing both Shelleyan ideal love and Wordsworthian nature. Wordsworth enviously insisted that 'the whole third canto of Childe Harold's founded on his style and sentiments – the feeling of natural objects, which is there expressed not caught by B. from Nature herself but from him, Wordsworth, and spoiled in the transmission – *Tintern Abbey* the source of it all' (Thomas Moore, *Letters and Journals of Lord Byron*, Vol. 1, p. 355). Byron's Titanism, as in the echoes of Coriolanus at ll. 1049–55 (*Coriolanus* III.i. 66–7), plays against the prescribed cure. Jeffrey noted that the poem displayed 'the same stern and lofty disdain of mankind' as Byron's previous works, 'but mixed ... with deeper and more matured reflections, and a more intense sensibility to all that is grand and lovely in the external world' (*Edinburgh Review*, December 1816). Murray paid £2,000 for *Childe Harold III* and *The Prisoner of Chillon*; he published the former on 18 November 1817, and on 13 December told Byron that he had sold 7,000 copies of each to the booksellers (Samuel Smiles, *A Publisher and His Friends*, Vol. 1, p. 369).

Epigraph: Frederick the Great to Jean D'Alembert: 'So that this application force you to think of something else. In truth there is no remedy other than that and time.'

Criticism: Ernest J. Lovell, Jr., *Byron: The Record of a Quest*, on the treatment of nature; Jerome Christensen, *Lord Byron's Strength*, particularly on the significance of 'NB'; John A. Hodgson on 'The Structures of *Childe Harold III*'; Peter J. Manning, *Byron and His Fictions*, on the psychological patterns; Sheila Emerson, 'Byron's "One Word"', on Byron's reflexive language; and the works of general criticism listed in note to *Childe Harold I–II*.

Epistle to Augusta (*'My sister! my sweet sister!'* &c.)

In forwarding a manuscript of this poem to Murray from Switzerland on 28 August 1816 Byron indicated that it was not to be published without the consent of his sister. Augusta objected, and the poem was not published until Thomas Moore's *Life* (1830) and then collected in the 1831 *Works*.

The 'grandsire' of l. 15 is Admiral John Byron (1723–86). Byron draws echoes of *Hamlet* (III.i.67) in l. 30, of *Macbeth* (V.v.ff.) in l. 107, of *Paradise Lost* (XII.646) in l. 81, of his own contemporaneous *Manfred* (I.i.3–7) in ll. 109–11 and of *Childe Harold III*, throughout, into an account of his life so rhetorically crafty that he must have wished it published. The poem is Byron's first extended employment of *ottava rima*.

Criticism: on the Wordsworthian parallels, see Robert Harson, 'Byron's *Tintern Abbey*'.

Lines (*On Hearing that Lady Byron was Ill*)

Written September 1816; published in Lady Blessington's *Conversations of Lord Byron* (serial form 1832–3; 1834), and collected in the 1832 *Works*.

MANFRED: A Dramatic Poem

Written August 1816–May 1817; published 16 June 1817.

Byron quit England on 25 April 1816, arriving a month later in Geneva, where he re-met Claire Clairmont, who was bearing his child (Allegra, born 1817); Claire, travelling with Percy and Mary Shelley (her stepsister), introduced the two poets. By early June they had taken neighbouring houses, Byron Villa Diodati and the Shelley party Montalègre. English tourists gazed at and gossiped about the group; rumours circulated that they were living in 'a League of Incest' (*BLJ*, Vol. 6, p. 76). In mid August M.G. Lewis, author of *The Monk* (1796) and other Gothic works, visited and 'translated most of' Goethe's *Faust* (Part I, 1808) '*viva voce*' to Byron, who in 1813 had read a 'sorry French translation' of excerpts in de Staël's *De l'Allemagne* (Thomas Medwin, *Conversations of Lord Byron*, p. 141). 'I was naturally much struck with it,' Byron told Murray, 'but it was the *Staubach* & the *Jungfrau* – and something else – much more than Faustus that made me write Manfred,' though he acknowledged that the 'first Scene . . . & that of Faustus are very similar' (*BLJ* Vol. 7, p. 113). Of the incantation that concludes I.i Byron noted that it 'was a Chorus in an unfinished Witch drama, which was begun some years ago', a period coinciding with his first exposure to *Faust* (see *CPW*, Vol. 4, pp. 463–4). The concurrent success of Coleridge's *Remorse* (1813) showed what could be done with the popular form of Gothic melodrama; while serving on the Drury Lane Theatre Management Committee in 1815 Byron encouraged Coleridge to write more plays, and though he disavowed all wishes for representation, the experience may have strengthened his desire to try himself. Behind *Manfred* stand the Gothic dramas he encountered at Drury Lane and the Gothic tradition generally: William Beckford's Oriental tale *Vathek* (1786) furnished the details of Manfred's underworld visit in II.iv, and Horace Walpole's *The Castle of Otranto* (1764) is the probable source of the protagonist's name. The many verbal similarities between the play and the journal that Byron kept for Augusta of his Alpine tour with Hobhouse in September (17–29) underscore the impact of the spectacular scenery on the drama (*BLJ*, Vol. 5, pp. 96–105).

The most significant impulse underlying the play – the 'something else' to which he alluded to Murray – was Byron's bitterness over the separation from Annabella; he added stanzas IV and V to the incantation, and, as a note from Moore in the 1832 edition observed: 'it is needless to say who was in the poet's thoughts'. (Byron also published the incantation separately with *The Prisoner of Chillon* (1816).) Inseparable from this complex of feelings was Augusta; by naming Manfred's beloved Astarte after an incestuous pagan goddess, as M. J. Quinlan points out, Byron revived the scandal surrounding his departure from England. In breaking off the colloquy between Manuel and Herman as the former is about to declare 'The lady Astarte, his —' Byron seems to tease his audience to find the line between biographical revelation and dramatic fiction (III.iii.47).

If *Manfred* exhibits the obsession with remorse of Byron's earlier Eastern tales – he admitted to Murray that it was 'too much in my old style' (*BLJ*, Vol. 5, p. 185) – it also transforms confession into myth (see Manfred's invocation of Prometheus at I.i.154 and the note to 'Prometheus' above), speculation (see the parallel to *Hamlet* suggested by the epigraph (I.v.166–7)), and the romantic, particularly Shelleyan, concern with the epipsyche. Byron sent Murray a fair copy of the 'very wild – metaphysical – and inexplicable' play (*BLJ*, Vol. 5, p. 170) from Venice in March 1817; when Gifford criticized the third act, he conceded that it was 'certainly d—d bad' and agreed to 'reform it – or re-write it altogether' (*BLJ*, Vol. 5, p. 211). In the original third act (printed in *CPW*, Vol. 4, pp. 467–71), a demon carries off the Abbot, who has crudely threatened Manfred; in the revised text, sent from Rome on 5 May, the 'Abbot is become a good man' (*BLJ*, Vol. 5, p. 219). The new calm Byron strove for, countering the Titanism of the earlier acts, was weakened when Murray omitted Manfred's final speech: 'Old man! 'tis not so difficult to die' (III.iv.151). 'You have destroyed the whole effect & moral of the poem by omitting the last line of Manfred's speaking,' Byron protested (*BLJ*, Vol. 5, p. 257), and the line was restored in 1818. Goethe declared the play a 'wonderful phenomenon' in which Byron had taken the principles of *Faust* 'in his own way for his own purposes, so that none of them remains the same', and fashioned them into 'the quintessence of the most astonishing talent born to be its own tormentor'. Jeffrey, in the *Edinburgh Review*, disapproved of the 'painful and offensive' theme of incest, but saw the drama's 'obscurity' as 'part of its grandeur': 'the darkness that rests upon it, and the smoky distance in which it is lost, are all devices to increase its majesty, to stimulate our curiosity, and to impress us with deeper awe' (August 1817). Despite Byron's insistence that he had rendered his 'dramatic poem' '*quite impossible* for the stage' (*BLJ*, Vol. 5, p. 170), *Manfred* was produced at Covent Garden in 1834 with a travesty ending in which Astarte saves Manfred from the demons, at Sadler's

Wells in 1863 by Samuel Phelps, with a melodramatic conclusion in which Manfred is crushed by an avalanche, and in 1873 at the Princess's Theatre, with an interpolated ballet of female chamois-hunters.

Criticism: Peter L. Thorslev, *The Byronic Hero*, on Manfred 'as the Byronic hero in the process of maturing'; Robert F. Gleckner, *Byron and the Ruins of Paradise*, on Manfred as the embodiment of the human condition; Michael G. Cooke, *The Blind Man Traces the Circle*, on the play as testing the limits of the will; Peter J. Manning, *Byron and His Fictions*, on the psychological issues; Paul W. Elledge, *Byron and the Dynamics of Metaphor* on 'the vacuum of Manfred's selfhood'; and Stuart Sperry, 'Byron and the Meaning of *Manfred*', on the play as 'Byron's confrontation with his own persona'. Studies by Samuel Chew, Jr., *The Dramas of Lord Byron*, and Martyn Corbett, *Byron and Tragedy*, elucidate the play's dramatic form. E. M. Butler narrates the relationship of the two poets in *Byron and Goethe*.

So, we'll go no more a roving

Published in Moore's *Life* (1830), and collected in the 1831 *Works*.

The poem appears as part of a letter Byron wrote from Venice to Thomas Moore on 28 February 1817:

The Carnival – that is, the latter part of it – and sitting up late o'nights, had knocked me up a little. But it is over, – and it is now Lent . . . though I did not dissipate much upon the whole, yet I find 'the sword wearing out the scabbard,' though I have but just turned the corner of twenty-nine. (*BLJ*, Vol. 5, p. 176)

CHILDE HAROLD'S PILGRIMAGE:

A Romaunt, Canto IV

Written 26 June–19 July 1817; expanded 3 September–7 January 1818; published 28 April 1818.

The final canto continues the parallel between Byron's experience and the course of European civilization: I 'stand/A ruin amidst ruins', declares the poet (ll. 218–19), dating the poem in the Dedication to Hobhouse on the third anniversary of his marriage, 'the most unfortunate day of my past existence'. He had left Switzerland with Hobhouse for Italy in October 1817, settling in Venice on 10 November. There he remained until a month-long visit to Rome, by way of Ferrara, Bologna and Florence (17 April–28 May 1817), followed by removal for the summer to La Mira (14 June–13 November), where he began Canto IV. Venice, which fell to Napoleon in 1797 and passed between France and Austria before being assigned to Austria in 1814 (l. 100), and Rome, where one cannot avoid 'Stumbling o'er recollections' (l. 727), exemplify the destiny of 'the fatal gift of beauty' (l. 371). Abandoning the 'unavailing' 'distinction between the author and the pilgrim', Byron projects his history into the 'Spirits which soar from ruin' (l. 492): Michelangelo, the dramatist Vittorio Alfieri, Galileo and Machiavelli. The instances of unhappy genius include Dante and Boccaccio, mistreated by 'ungrateful Florence' (ll. 496–522), and culminate in Tasso, author of *Jerusalem Delivered* (1581) and according to legend imprisoned for madness for seven years by his patron, Alfonso II of Ferrara (ll. 316–51). With Petrarch, who 'arose/To raise a language, and his land reclaim/From the dull yoke of her barbaric foes' (ll. 266–8), these writers established Italian literature. 'I twine/My hopes of being remember'd in my line/With my land's language', declared (self-)exiled Byron (ll. 76–8), and he found in the Italians a nationalist model. His interest overflowed into *The Lament of Tasso* (1817) and *The Prophecy of Dante* (1821). The cycles of oppression that make up the 'one page' of history (l. 969) from Hannibal's defeat of the Romans near Lake Trasimene in 217 BC (ll. 550–85) to Napoleon's career, and illustrated as well by the Roman dictator Sulla and Oliver Cromwell (ll. 739–74), are epitomized in the evocation of the Dying Gladiator (ll. 1252–69). Against them Byron sets figures of heroic virtue such as Cola di Rienzi, who in the fourteenth century attempted to restore Roman greatness (ll. 1018–26), and apostrophes to 'Freedom!' ('yet thy banner, torn, but flying/Streams like the thunder-storm *against* the wind' (ll. 874–5), but the possibilities of redemption are carried chiefly by literature and art.

Ekphrastic passages, from that on the Venus de Medici (ll. 433–77), recently restored to Florence after Napoleon's transfer of it to Paris, through St Peter's (ll. 1369–431), the Gladiator (now thought to be a dying Gaul) in the Capitoline Museum, and those on statues in the Vatican, the Laocoon and the Apollo Belvedere (ll. 1432–67), play a significant role in the canto. Hobhouse and Byron had been reading *Geschichte der Kunst des Alterthums* (1764; translated into Italian 1779) and *Monumenti Antichi Inediti* (1767), by Johann Joachim Winckelmann, and other sources, and Hobhouse suggested sites for Byron to comment upon. Nature is less prominent than in Canto III, but the set pieces on the Clitumnus (l. 586) and the Falls of Terni (ll. 613–48) made these famous spots more famous. The theme of feminine nurture, evident in the commentary on the tomb of Cecilia Metella (ll. 883–945) and the Grotto of Egeria, the nymph who according to legend counselled Numa Pompilius, successor to Romulus as King of Rome (ll. 1027–66), culminates in the story of the 'Caritas Romana' (ll. 1324–59); the fantasy is offset by the six-stanza elegy on the death in childbirth of Princess Charlotte (6 November 1817), addressee of Byron's 'Lines to a Lady Weeping', and whose loss inspired national mourning (ll. 1495–548). The concluding apostrophe to the ocean (ll. 1603–56) marks a turn from the stability of sculpture and architecture to fluidity, and points towards *Don Juan*.

Childe Harold's Pilgrimage IV was published on 28 April 1818 in an edition of 10,000. The politics of the poem were underlined by extensive 'historical notes' – fifty-six pages of reduced type in the 1832 edition – but because of their length and because they were written by Hobhouse they are omitted here; Hobhouse amplified them further in his *Historical Illustrations of the Fourth Canto of Childe Harold*, also published by Murray in 1818. In the *Quarterly Review* (April 1818) Scott greeted Canto IV as Byron's 'gravest and most serious performance'; in the *Edinburgh Review* (June 1818) John Wilson astutely remarked upon the 'singular illusion' that the poem produces,

by which these disclosures, when read with that high and tender interest which attaches to poetry, seem to have something of the nature of private and confidential communications. They are not felt, while we read, as declarations published to the world, – but almost as secrets whispered to chosen ears . . . There is an unobserved beauty that smiles on us alone; and the more beautiful to us, because we feel as if chosen out from a crowd of lovers.

Epigraph: Ariosto, Satire IV (incorrectly cited as III): 'I have seen Tuscany, Lombardy, Romagna,/The mountain that divides [the Apennines], and that which encloses [the Alps]/Italy, and the one sea [the Adriatic] and the other [the Tyrrhenian], that bathes it.'

Criticism: In addition to the works cited in notes to previous cantos, see Bernard Blackstone, *Byron: A Survey*, on Byron's historical 'ideograms'; and Peter J. Manning, 'Childe Harold in the Marketplace', on production and reception.

Epistle from Mr Murray to Dr Polidori (*'Dear Doctor, I have read your play'*)

Published in Moore's *Life* (1830), and collected thereafter (but without ll. 39–40).

On 5 August 1817 Murray asked Byron to furnish 'a *delicate* declension' of *Ximenes*, a tragedy submitted to him by J. W. Polidori (Samuel Smiles, *A Publisher and His Friends*, Vol. 1, p. 386), whose tenure as Byron's physician in 1816 had ended unhappily. Byron volunteered this *jeu d'esprit*, part of a letter of 21 August (*BLJ*, Vol. 5, pp. 258–61). The literal interpretation of catharsis in the opening lines was particularly appropriate to its intended recipient, but there is no evidence that Murray, despite his intention 'faithfully to copy' Byron's reply, sent Polidori the poem. *Ximenes* was published by Longman in 1819. Among the works Byron dismisses are Maturin's drama *Manuel* (1817) (l. 23), Sotheby's tragedies *Ivan* and *The Death of Darnley* (1814) and Southey's 1810 epic *The Curse of Kehama* (l. 36).

On Polidori and his tangled relationship with Byron, see D. L. Macdonald, *Poor Polidori*.

BEPPO: A Venetian Story

Written October 1817; published anonymously February 1818.

On 29 August 1817 Byron heard from the husband of his mistress Marianna Segati an anecdote of a 'buxom lady of 40' surprised by the return of her husband, presumed lost at sea many years before. She does not suspect the identity of a Turkish stranger until

said the Turk pulling down his robe – I am your husband – I have been to Turkey – I have made a large fortune and I make you three offers – either to quit your amoroso and come with me – or to stay with your amoroso or to accept a pension and live alone. The lady has not yet given an answer, but Mᶜ Zagati [*sic*] said I'm sure I would not leave my amoroso for any husband – looking at B. this is too gross even for me. (quoted in Leslie A. Marchand, *Byron: A Biography*, Vol. 2, p. 708)

This layered instance of Venetian *mores* shocked Hobhouse, who recorded it, but suited the request Murray had made of Byron in January: 'Give me a poem – a good Venetian tale describing manners formerly from the story itself, and now from your own observations, and call it "Marianna"' (Samuel Smiles, *A Publisher and His Friends*, Vol. 1 p. 372). Byron acknowledged that he had written 'in imitation of' John Hookham Frere's recently published pseudonymous *Prospectus and Specimen of an Intended National Work, The Monks and the Giants* (*BLJ*, Vol. 5, p. 269), but if Frere showed Byron how the Italian medley style might be adopted to English *ottava rima*, Byron already knew the Italian originals of Francesco Berni, Luigi Pulci, whose *Morgante Maggiore* he translated in 1819–20, and

Giambattista Casti, whose *Gli Animali parlanti* he read in 1816 (translated by his friend W. S. Rose in 1819 as *Court and Parliament of Beasts*).

Notwithstanding Jeffrey's judgement of *Beppo* as 'absolutely a thing of nothing' (*Edinburgh Review*, February 1818), it was a significant turn from the style of *Childe Harold's Pilgrimage* and the Eastern tales on which Byron's popularity rested; 'it will at any rate shew', he wrote, 'that I can write cheerfully, & repel the charge of monotony & mannerism' (*BLJ*, Vol. 6, p. 25). Byron dissolves the heroic style visible in the allusions to Othello (ll. 139–40) and Napoleon (ll. 481–5) into colloquial ease, and through the Carnival setting diffuses the violent rivalries of his tales and the pains of his separation (see the barb at Annabella's mathematics in l. 624). The contrast between Venice and England reveals how thoroughly he kept track of the world he had left, claiming still to know it better than 'bustling Botherbys' (l. 575), based on William Sotheby (1757–1833), who, he thought, had sent him an anonymous criticism of *The Prisoner of Chillon*. Byron's satire on authors that are '*all author*' (l. 593) and on 'female wits' (ll. 569–624) stems from unease about his own commercial success and the dependence of his reputation on women; compare *The Blues*. The portrait of the Count, arbiter of taste and 'cavalier servente' (l. 285), mirrors these anxieties within the parallel Venetian locale. Byron sets in motion images of himself – professional writer, 'broken Dandy' (l. 410), one of the 'Men of the world, who know the world like men . . . all the better brothers' (ll. 602–3) – that play complexly against each other. His cosmopolitanism does not preclude 'politics & ferocity' (*BLJ*, Vol. 6, p. 9); the manner itself was read politically: the *British Review* (May 1818) thought it symptomatic of a 'denationalizing spirit' and the 'decay of that masculine decency, and sobriety, and soundness of sentiment, which, about half a century ago, made us dread the contagion of French or Italian manners'. The poem reached a fifth edition by April 1818; the success of the new mode assured, Murray affixed Byron's name to the title-page.

Criticism: T.G. Steffan, 'The Devil a Bit of Our *Beppo*', on the composition of the poem, also the starting-point for Jerome J. McGann's thorough Introduction to the Manuscript P text in *Shelley and His Circle*, Vol. 7; Frederick L. Beaty, *Byron the Satirist*, on the role of Sotheby; Peter Vassallo, *Byron: The Italian Literary Influence*, on the Italian models and William Keach, 'Political Inflection', on their English mediations; Paul W. Elledge, *Byron and the Dynamics of Metaphor* especially on the function of digression ('Divorce Italian Style'); Peter J. Manning, *Reading Romantics*; and Cheryl Fallon Giuliano, 'Marginal Discourse', on authorship, gender and gossip.

Epistle to Mr Murray ('My dear Mr Murray')

Dated Venice, 8 January 1818; published in part in Moore's *Life* (1830), and collected thereafter; stanzas XII–XIV first published in Leslie A. Marchand's *Byron: A Biography* (Vol. 2, p. 722).

Hobhouse left Venice for London on 8 January (the date of this epistle) with the manuscript of *Childe Harold IV* (l. 5). Byron refers to Murray's intended founding of a literary journal (l. 7), and to Murray's publication of the tales of Henry Gally Knight, *Alashtar* and *Phrosyne*, in 1817 (ll. 13–18). Sotheby, also lampooned in *Beppo* (see note to *Beppo*), was the author of *Farewell to Italy* (1818) and translator of Tasso and Wieland's *Oberon* (1798) (ll. 20–30). Edward Malone's edition of Joseph Spence's *Observations* appeared in 1820, George Chalmers's *Life* of Mary Queen of Scots in 1819, *The Monks and the Giants*, by William and Robert 'Whistlecraft' (John Hookham Frere) in 1817 (ll. 37–41). George Canning was a prominent Tory, later Prime Minister, contributor to the *Antijacobin Review* and famous for his wit (l. 58). Byron's cousin John Wilmot (see note to 'She walks in beauty') travelled on the Continent in 1816 with Byron's acquaintance John William Ward, as Byron had planned to do in 1813 (ll. 55–66). 'Tommy' and 'Sammy' (l. 81) are Thomas Moore and Samuel Rogers.

MAZEPPA

Written April 1817–September 1818; published June 1819, with two other poems, in an edition of 8,000.

This is a frame tale, based, as Byron's untranslated headnotes indicate, on an incident in Voltaire's *Histoire de Charles XII* (1772). Its teller, Mazeppa, is a Polish gentleman who had been a Hetman (Prince) of the Ukraine under Peter the Great, before defecting to Charles XII of Sweden, under whom he served in the Battle of Poltáva ('Pultowa's day', 8 July 1709), and to whom he tells this story in order to ease him to sleep in their retreat after a devastating defeat by Peter. The immediate historical frame of the opening stanza situates Charles's warmongering in relation to Napoleon's disastrous Moscow campaign of 1812. Thomas Moore suspected a still more immediate frame in 'the circumstances of [Byron's] own personal history', his liaison with Teresa Guiccioli under the ambiguous approval of her much older husband; as Peter J. Manning remarks, this is yet another story in which a young man becomes the lover of the young wife of an old man, is discovered by the latter, and punished (*Byron and His*

Fictions, p. 101) – in this case, tied naked to the back of a wild Arabian horse and driven off to die (the means by which Mazeppa arrived in the Ukraine).

The unexpectedly comic closing of the narrative frame signals Byron's departure from the idiom of his previous successes in tale-telling and may be compared to the narrative manner being tested in *Don Juan I*, written during the same months. The central, sensationally elaborated episode of the horse-ride became the most famous passage, a set piece in itself; in an adaptation, it provided international celebrity for Adah Isaacs Menken, a nineteenth-century actress who, in flesh-coloured tights and lightly cross-dressed, played the title-role with a real horse. For this Byronic coda, see Wolf Mankowitz's *Mazeppa*.

Stanzas to the Po

Written 1 or 2 June 1819; published in Thomas Medwin's *Conversations of Lord Byron* (1824), collected in the 1831 *Works*.

Byron and Teresa Guiccioli began their liaison in April 1819, but it was interrupted almost immediately by her removal from Venice by her husband; the poem reflects the uncertainties of the period before the lovers met again in mid June in Ravenna. Byron sent the stanzas to England in 1820, admonishing Murray that they 'must *not* be published . . . as they are mere verses of Society – & written upon private feelings and passions' (*BLJ*, Vol. 7, p. 97).

Criticism: on the biographical and textual cruxes of the poem, see Jerome J. McGann's note in *CPW*, Vol. 4, pp. 496–9.

The Isles of Greece

Written September–November 1819; published in Canto III of *Don Juan* (1821).

By placing this passionate, patriotic song in the mouth of the trimmer poet at the court of Haidée and Juan, Byron initiated a dynamic series of perspectives on his own erotic and heroic investments; we include it because it has become, in its repeated anthologizing out of dramatic context, Byron's most celebrated lyric.

Criticism: Jerome J. McGann, 'The Book of Byron and the Book of a World'.

Francesca of Rimini. From the Inferno of Dante, Canto the Fifth

In June 1819, Byron read the famous passage about Paolo and Francesca in *The Inferno* with Teresa Guiccioli, his lover, who was still living with Count Guiccioli, her much older husband, in his palace in Ravenna, the city where Francesca was born and where Dante wrote *The Inferno*. When Teresa asked Byron if this episode had been translated into English he replied, '*Non tradotto, ma tradito*' – 'Not translated, but betrayed' (Leslie A. Marchand, *Byron: A Biography*, Vol. 2, pp. 794–5). He rendered his own translation of *Inferno*, V: 97–142 in March 1820, and sent 'Fanny of Rimini' to Murray the same month, asking him to publish this '*cramp* English' attempt at *terza rima* ('line for line & rhyme for rhyme') '*with the original* – and *together* with the *Pulci* translation – *or the Dante Imitation*' (*BLJ*, Vol. 7, p. 58) – that is, his *terza-rima Prophecy of Dante* and his *ottava-rima* translation of Pulci's *Morgante Maggiore*, already in Murray's possession. *Prophecy* was published by Murray in April 1821 with *Marino Faliero*, and 'the *Pulci*' was eventually ceded to John Hunt, who put it in the fourth issue of the *Liberal*, July 1823; but 'Francesca of Rimini' languished amid Byron's deteriorating relations with Murray and did not appear until 1830, posthumously, in Moore.

The famous and historically true story, from the late thirteenth century, of the adulterous lovers, Paolo and Francesca, and their fatal punishment by her enraged husband, bears parallels to Byron's situation with the Count and Countess, as well as recalls the oedipal triangles in a number of his poems (see Peter J. Manning, *Byron and His Fictions*). In Dante's scheme, the lovers are condemned to the second circle of hell, that of voluptuaries (also inhabited by Helen of Troy and Cleopatra). The circumstances of their 'crime' evoked sympathy in literary renderings and cultural transmissions. Dante's own sympathy was influenced by the fact that Francesca's father, Count of Ravenna, was his friend, protector and patron in the exile of his later days (when he wrote the *Divina Commedia*); he had probably known Francesca as a girl. Francesca's father, to make peace with his enemy, the Count of Rimini, engaged her to Rimini's eldest son who was (in Boccaccio's commentary on this episode) courageous but also 'hideously deformed in countenance and figure'. This son thought it best, in fact, to approach Francesca by the proxy of his younger, handsome brother, Paolo. When these two fell passionately in love, friends of Ravenna pleaded with him not to force Francesca into an untenable political marriage, but he was eager to end his war with Rimini. The marriage took place in 1275; the lovers were discovered and murdered some time between 1283 and 1286.

Byron admired Dante's interview with Francesca for its 'gentle feelings';
'there is a gentleness in Dante beyond all gentleness, when he is tender. It
is true that, treating of the Christian Hades, or Hell, there is not much
scope or site for gentleness – but who *but* Dante could have introduced any
"gentleness" at all into *Hell*? Is there any in Milton's? – No' (*BLJ*, Vol. 8,
pp. 39–40). The episode interested many of Byron's contemporaries, es-
pecially after Cary's translation of *The Divine Comedy* in 1814. It was also a
politicized subject, by virtue of Leigh Hunt's *Story of Rimini* (1816),
which he dedicated to Byron, and which the Tory press, severely critical
of Hunt's liberal, anti-royalist politics, subjected to abuse and ridicule,
usually coded as contempt of 'vulgar' poetics (see the first paper 'On the
Cockney School of Poetry' in *Blackwood's*, October 1817, by 'Z' (thought
to be John Gibson Lockhart)). In June 1820, Keats, well versed in both
Cary's translation and Hunt's *Rimini* (and similarly abused by 'Z' for his
association with Hunt), published a sonnet in Hunt's journal the *Indicator*,
over the signature 'Caviare', on a poet's dream of Paolo and Francesca.

Criticism: Frederick L. Beaty, 'Byron and Francesca da Rimini'.

Stanzas ('When a man hath no freedom')

Sent to Thomas Moore in a letter, 5 November 1820; printed in Moore's
Life (1830), collected in the 1831 *Works*.

Byron's involvement with the Italian revolutionaries displays his usual
mixture of commitment and irony; he introduced the poem to Moore by
echoing Falstaff (1 *Henry IV*, V.iii.60–61): 'If "honour should come un-
looked for" to any of your acquaintance, make a Melody of it, that his
ghost, like poor Yorick's, may have the satisfaction of being plaintively
pitied . . . In case you should not think him worth it, here is a Chant for
you instead' (*BLJ*, Vol. 7, pp. 218–19).

SARDANAPALUS: A Tragedy

Written mid January to late May 1821 in Ravenna, amid Byron's restless
shifting between romance, social diversions and political intrigue with the
revolutionary Carbonari (see his journal; *BLJ*, Vol. 8, pp. 15–50). Murray
paid Byron £1,100 for this play, *Cain* and *The Two Foscari*, all published
together on Byron's insistence; an edition of 6,099 copies was issued in
December.

In Byron's blank-verse metres, the eponym is pronounced Sar-*day*-
nah-*pay*-lus. Byron did not intend the play for the stage (*BLJ*, Vol. 8, p.

129), and it was not performed until the 1830s. *Cain* focused the most reviewers' commentary, bristling with charges of blasphemy (enhanced by Leigh Hunt's defence in the *Examiner*, 2 June 1822) and contributing to Murray's growing nervousness in 1822 over publishing Byron, culminating in Byron's switch to John Hunt. The most influential reactions to *Sardanapalus* were mixed at best, and some were purely negative: although Heber, writing for Murray's *Quarterly Review* (1822), offered measured praise for the volume as a whole and a strong defence of Byron's characterization of Sardanapalus, Jeffrey (*Edinburgh Review*, February/April 1822) found the play, indeed all the poetry in the volume, 'heavy, verbose, inelegant'; Lockhart, writing for *Blackwood's* (January 1822) also thought the two plays 'dullish' and *Cain* 'wicked and blasphemous'. Although *Cain* was the lightning rod, *Sardanapalus* too must have embarrassed Murray's Tory allegiances, for notwithstanding Byron's claim that he did not intend it as 'a *political* play' (*BLJ*, Vol. 8, p. 152), Act I insinuates some deprecatory parallels to George IV's spendthrift luxury and wronging of his Queen – the divorce scandal was a notorious rallying-point for opposition to the Crown. Jerome J. McGann ('Hero with a Thousand Faces') has also proposed that Sardanapalus's meeting in Act IV with his neglected but still adoring Queen Zarina is Byron's fantasy of reconciliation with an unforgiving Lady Byron, their separation another highly public scandal. Relevant to this, Jerome J. McGann's *CPW* adds a line from a manuscript to IV.i. at l. 428 (italics indicate the addition): '. . . at once? *but leavest/ One to grieve o'er the other's change?* – Zarina!'

Byron was distressed that Murray omitted the dedication to Goethe from the first edition, and Murray included it in a much smaller, separate edition of the play in 1823; Goethe was deeply touched by the gesture. In the 1832–4 *Works* the dedication appears on a full page, along with Goethe's response (Vol. 13, p. 57). Byron also asked Murray to print the relevant chapters from one of his sources: Book II of *Bibliothecae Historicae*, by Diodorus Siculus, a Greek historian (born in Sicily) of the first century BC (*BLJ*, Vol. 8, pp. 128–9). Murray did not honour the request in the early editions, but *Works* supplies an ample note (Vol. 13, p. 64).

Along with Diodorus Siculus, Byron cites his reading of William Mitford's *History of Greece* (1818) and his admiration for its sympathetic portrait of Sardanapalus (*BLJ*, Vol. 8, p. 26). Mitford gives the translation of the epitaph that Sardanapalus ordered for his tomb (which Aristotle reported in Greek, and judged 'fit for a hog'): 'Sardanapalus, son of Anacyndaraxes, in one day founded Anchialus and Tarsus./Eat, drink, play: all other human joys are not worth a fillip.' Byron consciously refigured the negative precedents for his hero – in, for instance, Lydgate's *Fall of Princes*, Surrey's sonnet, 'Th'Assyrians king', and their touchstone in Diodorus's characterization of the 'effeminate' king as a degenerate: a companion of courtesans and eunuchs, a transvestite, bisexual, coward, reprobate, gross indulger of appetites, and an utterly selfish and cruel tyrant in defeat. Byron makes Sardanapalus emphatically heterosexual and converts his love of luxury and cynicism about the exercise of civic and imperial power into a rhetoric of enlightened pacifism and human sympathy. He cast his hero as '*brave*' and '*amiable*' as well as 'voluptuous' (*BLJ*, Vol. 8, p. 127), and he radically altered the accounts of his self-immolation to have him release all his slaves and send his soldiers off with his wealth, instead of forcing them all to die with him. The scene in Act III in which Sardanapalus calls for a mirror to view himself in military garb Byron referred to Juvenal's Satire II on Otho, describing this self-regard as 'natural in an effeminate character' (*BLJ*, Vol. 8, p. 128); Murray printed Byron's comment as well as the passage from Juvenal and Gifford's English translation in *Works*, 1834 (Vol. 13, p. 132). In addition to these historical sources and references, there are several literary influences, most obviously Shakespeare's tragedies (*Hamlet, Macbeth*), histories (*Richard II, Richard III*), and, patently, *Antony and Cleopatra*, as well as Dryden's *All for Love*; on the last, see Michael G. Cooke's essay, 'The Restoration Ethos of Byron's Classical Plays'.

As for other of Byron's additions and interpolations to the source material: the spectre of Sardanapalus's ancestor, Semiramis, derives from popular accounts of her monstrosity. In contrast, Voltaire's *Sémiramis* (1748), a play that Byron may have known, gives a sympathetic representation of this incestuous queen, casting her as a kind of tormented Byronic hero. The other female characters are Byron's invention. Zarina's name was taken from another account in Diodorus, of a female ruler of a central Asian tribe, a warrior, a beauty, and ultimately a humanitarian civilizer. The character of Myrrha was inspired by Teresa Guiccioli's request for a heroic play involving love. Her name is also that of the incestuously passionate heroine in Book X of Ovid's *Metamorphoses*, on which Alfieri based *Mirra* (1788), a play that greatly agitated Byron when he saw it performed in 1819 (*BLJ*, Vol. 6, p. 206), perhaps because its theme of consummated illicit desire was too close to his affair with his half-sister Augusta. Myrrha's incest inverts that of Semiramis, the incestuous mother: donning a disguise, she has sex with her father. Her story is hinted at very tangentially in Byron's play in the 'myrrh' that Sardanapalus orders for the funeral pyre to which he and his Myrrha commit themselves: in Ovid, Myrrha is changed into the myrrh tree when she begs the gods to relieve her of her agonies as she gives birth to her child by her father.

Criticism has traditionally described Sardanapalus as a mixture of voluptuary and doomed idealist (a pacifist and pleasure-lover in a culture that values military imperialism), or yet another version of Byron and the latest serial variation on the Byronic hero. For these themes, see, in Byron's day, Reginald Heber, 'Lord Byron's Dramas', in the *Quarterly Review*, and Francis Jeffrey, 'Lord Byron's Tragedies', in the *Edinburgh Review*, and the modern elaborations in Jerome J. McGann's *Fiery Dust*, Leslie A. Marchand's *Byron's Poetry*, and G. Wilson Knight's 'The Two Eternities'. More recent studies have focused on social performance (Jerome J. McGann, 'Hero with a Thousand Faces'); political ideologies (Daniel P. Watkins, 'Violence in Byron's History Plays'; Jerome Christensen, *Lord Byron's Strength*; Marilyn Butler, 'John Bull's Other Kingdom') and gender (Peter J. Manning, *Byron and his Fictions*; Gordon Spence, 'Moral and Sexual Ambivalence'; Susan Wolfson, 'A Problem Few Dare Imitate'; Diane Long Hoeveler, *Romantic Androgyny*; Caroline Franklin, *Byron's Heroines*). For representations of *Sardanapalus* in pictorial art and on the nineteenth-century stage, see Barry Weller's essay in *CPW* (Vol. 6, pp. 584–5) and Margaret Howell, *Byron Tonight*. The fall 1992 issue of *Studies in Romanticism* (31, Part 3) is devoted to the play, including an account of a performance at Yale University in 1990.

Who kill'd John Keats?

A squib in a letter of July 1821; first published in Moore, 1830. Byron had used the key rhyme in *Don Juan I* in his mock complaint about the way Scotch reviews and the 'Quarterly/Treat a dissenting author very martyrly' (stanza CCXI).

In April 1821, a dismayed Shelley reported to Byron, 'Young Keats . . . died lately at Rome from the consequences of breaking a blood-vessel, in paroxysms of despair at the contemptuous attack on his book [*Endymion*, 1818] in the *Quarterly Review*.' He was misinformed: Keats was stung, but not fatally, by the reviews; it was tuberculosis that killed him in February 1821. Byron was frankly incredulous: 'is it *actually* true? I did not think criticism had been so killing . . . Poor fellow! . . . in this world of bustle and broil, and especially in the career of writing, a man should calculate upon his powers of *resistance* before he goes into the arena' (26 April 1821; *BLJ*, Vol. 8, p. 103). More snidely, he wrote to Murray in the letter containing these verses that 'he who would die of an article in a review – would probably have died of something else equally trivial' (*BLJ*, Vol. 8, pp. 162–3). The other writers mentioned in these verses are Henry Milman, a poet, ecclesiastical scholar and vicar ('Jew Milman' Byron called him elsewhere; *BLJ*, Vol. 8, p. 228); John Barrow, a travel writer who published frequently in the *Quarterly Review*; and the poet laureate Robert Southey, whom Shelley (wrongly) suspected as the *Quarterly*'s executioner. An elegy on Keats that Byron did publish, in Canto XI of *Don Juan* (1823), proved so quotable that it gained an immediate and lasting influence, at least equal to that of Shelley's *Adonais*: 'John Keats . . . was killed off by one critique,/Just as he really promised something great,/ . . . /Poor fellow! His was an untoward fate: – /'Tis strange the mind, that very fiery particle,/Should let itself be snuffed out by an Article' (stanza LX).

THE BLUES: *A Literary Eclogue*

Written August 1821. The piece was too short for Murray to publish separately, and he frustrated Byron by holding on to it for two years, after which Byron gave it to the Hunts, who published it in April 1823 as the front piece in the third issue of the *Liberal*. Its reception was affected by reviewers' political abuse of the *Liberal*, and it was not reprinted until 1831, in the first edition of the collected *Works*.

The title refers to the 'Bluestockings', a derisive term for women, primarily from the professional and upper-middle classes, who, instead of confining themselves to the routine female gatherings for card-playing, frivolous 'accomplishments' and gossip, attended intellectual and literary salons (the name derived from one of the literary lions often invited to read works or lecture to these salons, Benjamin Stillingfleet, who wore blue rather than the customary white stockings of male dress). Such salons developed in the mid eighteenth century; Lady Mary Wortley Montagu, the 'Queen of the Blues', founded the first; others in attendance included Elizabeth Robinson Montagu, Elizabeth Carter, Elizabeth Vesey, Hester Chapone and Frances Boscawen. Because women were typically denied higher education and never admitted to universities, these clubs were a vital resource for their intellectual life, and helped to bring a number of women writers into the literary culture. In Byron's day, the two women writers most associated with this culture were Hannah More and Anna Laetitia Barbauld. Byron despised both.

Jerome J. McGann gives a plausible key to Byron's characters (*CPW*, Vol. 6, pp. 665–6): Inkel is Byron himself; Tracy is Moore; Miss Lilac is Byron's estranged wife, the mathematical Annabella Milbanke; Scamp is Coleridge (the scene is Coleridge's London lectures of 1811–12, some of which Byron attended; Hazlitt's 1818 lectures may also figure in the representation); Botherby is William Sotheby, a minor poet and man of letters; the Bluebottles are Byron's friends and political mentors, Lord and Lady Holland; Lady Bluemount is Lady Beaumont, a friend of

Wordsworth ('Wordswords'), whose poetry Byron ridicules along with that of other Lake poets, in particular Southey ('Mouthey'). The epigraph is from Virgil's Eclogue II: 'Do not believe too much in colouring,' the shepherd Corydon moans in solitude to the beautiful boy Alexis, whom he adores, but who has rejected him for his own master, who also adores him.

Don Juan and *Beppo* include other parodies and lampoons of the Blues (see Jerome J. McGann's list, *CPW*, Vol. 6, p. 666). Byron told Murray that he 'scratched off' this eclogue as 'a mere buffoonery – to quiz [ridicule] "the Blues"', and he sarcastically urged him to publish it '*anonymously* . . . don't let *my* name out – for the present – or I shall have all the old women in London about my ears – since it sneers at the solace of their antient Spinsterstry' (7 August; *BLJ*, Vol. 8, p. 172). The contempt, as well as the linking of female intelligence to sexual frustration, was a common tone; the general commentary and the parodies and satires in which it sounds are impressive for crossing the class lines that mark other social antipathies. Dr Johnson called the Bluestockings 'Amazons of the pen' (*The Adventurer*, December 1753); Moore wrote a comic operetta titled *M.P. or The Blue-Stocking* (1811), which lampooned the pretensions and clumsy arts of scientific women; Keats 'detest[ed]' these women for their lack of 'real feminine Modesty', despised the thought of his being read by them (letter, 21 September 1817), and longed to upset the 'drawling bluestocking world' (letter, 14 August 1819); Hazlitt expressed his 'utter aversion' to them (*Table-Talk* XXIII, 'On Great and Little Things'). There were a few late revisions of this discourse: in 1827, William P. Scargill's *Blue-Stocking Hall* praised literary women; a decade later, as a complement to his all-male *Feast of the Poets*, Leigh Hunt celebrated them in *Blue-Stocking Revels; or, The Feast of the Violets*, suggesting that the colour be redeemed as 'violet' for women, and that 'blue' henceforth be 'confined to the masculine, vain, and absurd'.

THE VISION OF JUDGMENT

Written 20 September–4 October 1821; Byron sent Murray *The Vision of Judgment* on 4 October, but Murray, alarmed by the outcry over the blasphemy of *Don Juan* (1819) and *Cain*, published in December 1821, hesitated, and in July 1822 Byron withdrew it. The poem was printed anonymously in the first number of the *Liberal* (15 October 1822), the journal on which Byron collaborated with Leigh Hunt and Percy Shelley. The reviews were hostile, and John Hunt, the publisher, was found guilty of *lèse-majesté* in 1824 (Byron's estate paid the £100 damages).

George III died on 29 January 1820; on 11 April 1821 Robert Southey, the poet laureate, published *A Vision of Judgement*, recounting in un-rhymed hexameters the poet's vision of the dead king's ascent to Heaven, where he confounds his former antagonists, John Wilkes and 'Junius' (today thought to be Philip Francis), pseudonymous author of letters (1769–71) attacking the government, is welcomed by former monarchs of England and great figures of English history, and reunited with his family. To Byron, Southey's *Vision* exemplified the worst of the Lake School: bad verse defended upon 'system', and turncoat politics, further displayed in the fulsome dedication to George IV. The pirated publication in 1817 of Southey's radical drama of 1794, *Wat Tyler*, made clear the reversal of the laureate's revolutionary youth. Byron determined to 'put the said George's Apotheosis in a Whig point of view, not forgetting the Poet Laureate for his preface and his other demerits' (*BLJ*, Vol. 8, p. 229). In his Preface Southey declared that the 'publication of a lascivious book is one of the worst offences which can be committed against the well-being of society', and denounced the men 'of diseased hearts and depraved imaginations' who made up what he termed 'the Satanic school', conclud-ing: 'Let rulers of the state look to this, in time!' Byron, already angry in his conviction that Southey had spread rumours about his conduct in Switzerland (see note to *Manfred*), could not miss the allusion. He began a rejoinder on 7 May, but laid it aside, instead condemning Southey's 'cowardly ferocity' and 'impious impudence' in a note to *The Two Foscari*, published 19 December 1821. To this Southey replied in a letter to the *Courier* on 5 January, not knowing that his counsel, 'when he attacks me again let it be in rhyme', had been anticipated by Byron's return to his poem in late September. In signing himself 'Quevedo Redivivus' Byron invoked as precedent Francisco Gomez de Quevedo y Villegas, the Spanish satirist whose *Sueños* attacked the court corruption of his day. The influence of *Paradise Lost*, by way of parody as well as allusion, is apparent through-out. Byron's *Vision* follows Southey's in citing some of the king's chief opponents, John Wilkes (ll. 521–68), 'Junius' (ll. 593–668), and two writers Byron's contemporaries thought might be hiding behind the pseudonym (l. 631), Edmund Burke and John Horne Tooke, a radical philologist.

Southey's appearance in his own poem invited Byron to follow suit, having Southey expose himself as 'a pen of all work' (l. 797), the indiscrimi-nate author of the radical *Wat Tyler*, the conservative *Battle of Blenheim* (1800) and *The Poet's Pilgrimage to Waterloo* (1816) (l. 768), and a *Life* (1820) of the Methodist John Wesley (l. 785). The scorn is the aristocrat's for the professional author (see note to *Beppo*). At the same time, Byron avoids the presumption for which he berates Southey in the Preface, of 'deal[ing] about his judgments in the next world'. In contrast to Southey's apotheosis, in his *Vision* George III 'slipp'd' into heaven: the hundredth psalm that he is 'practising' at the conclusion praises the Lord's everlasting mercy (ll. 846–8).

Epigraph: *The Merchant of Venice* (IV.i.222, 340).

Criticism: Malcolm Kelsall, *Byron's Politics*, on the Whig heritage of the poem, and Stuart Peterfreund, 'The Politics of "Neutral Space"', on the contemporary context; William H. Marshall on the *Liberal*; Emrys Jones, 'Byron's Visions of Judgement', on the literary traditions; Peter T. Murphy, 'Visions of Success', on metre, poetry and politics in the two *Visions* and Byron's *Cain*; and Andrew Rutherford, *Byron: A Critical Study*, who acclaims the *Vision* as 'Byron's masterpiece'.

On This Day I Complete My Thirty-Sixth Year

Written 22 January 1824; published in the *Morning Chronicle* 29 October 1824, collected in the 1831 *Works*.

On the day it was written Byron gave a copy of this poem, the last entry in his Missolonghi journal, to Pietro Gamba; widely published in the newspapers after Byron's death on 19 April, it significantly influenced the image of his last days.

Criticism: Jerome J. McGann, 'Shall These Bones Live?'; on the poem as Byron's confession of love for his page, Loukas Chalandritsanos, see Louis Crompton, *Byron and Greek Love*, pp. 318–28.

WORKS CITED IN THE NOTES

Byron

BLJ. *Byron's Letters and Journals*, ed. Leslie A. Marchand, 12 vols., Cambridge, MA: Harvard University Press/London: John Murray, 1973–82.

CMP. *Lord Byron: The Complete Miscellaneous Prose*, ed. Andrew Nicholson, Oxford: Clarendon Press, 1991.

CPW. *Lord Byron: The Complete Poetical Works*, ed. Jerome J. McGann, 7 vols.; Vol. 6 coedited with Barry Weller, Oxford: Clarendon Press, 1980–93.

Works. *The Works of Lord Byron: With His Letters and Journals, and His Life, by Thomas Moore, Esq.*, 17 vols., London: John Murray, 1832–4.

Contemporary Reviews and Documents

Most of the reviews cited may be found in the collections listed Further Reading. Other works cited are:

BCH. *Byron: The Critical Heritage*, ed. Andrew Rutherford, New York: Barnes and Noble/London: Routledge & Kegan Paul, 1970.

Thomas Moore, *Letters and Journals of Lord Byron: With Notices of His Life*, London: John Murray, 1830.

Critical Works

Short titles are given for works already listed in Further Reading.

T.L. Ashton, *Byron's Hebrew Melodies*, Austin: University of Texas Press/London: Routledge & Kegan Paul, 1972.

Frederick L. Beaty, 'Byron and Francesca da Rimini', *Publications of the Modern Language Association of America* 75 (1960), pp. 395–401.

— *Byron the Satirist*, DeKalb: Northern Illinois University Press, 1985.

Bernard Blackstone, *Byron: A Survey*, London: Longman, 1975.

William A. Borst, *Lord Byron's First Pilgrimage*, New Haven: Yale University Press, 1948.

Frederick Burwick and Paul Douglass, eds., *A Selection of Hebrew Melodies, Ancient and Modern, by Isaac Nathan and Lord Byron*, Tuscaloosa: University of Alabama Press, 1988.

E.M. Butler, *Byron and Goethe*, London: Bowes & Bowes, 1956.

Marilyn Butler, 'John Bull's Other Kingdom: Byron's Intellectual Comedy', *Studies in Romanticism* 31 (1992), pp. 281–95.

— 'The Orientalism of Byron's *Giaour*', in *Byron and the Limits of Fiction*, ed. Bernard Beatty and Vincent Newey, Totowa, NJ: Barnes and Noble, 1988.

Samuel C. Chew, Jr., *The Dramas of Lord Byron: A Critical Study* (1915), New York: Russell & Russell, 1964.

Jerome Christensen, *Lord Byron's Strength*, Baltimore: Johns Hopkins University Press, 1993.

John Clubbe, ' "The New Prometheus of New Men": Byron's 1816 *Poems* and *Manfred*', in *Nineteenth-Century Literary Perspectives*, ed. Clyde de L. Ryals et al., Durham, NC: Duke University Press, 1974, pp. 17–47.

Michael G. Cooke, *The Blind Man Traces the Circle*, Princeton: Princeton University Press, 1969.

— 'The Restoration Ethos of Byron's Classical Plays', *PMLA* 79 (1964), pp. 569–78.

Martyn Corbett, *Byron and Tragedy*, New York: St Martin's Press, 1988.

Louis Crompton, *Byron and Greek Love*, Berkeley: University of California Press, 1985.

Stuart Curran, *Poetic Form and British Romanticism*, New York: Oxford University Press, 1986.

R.J. Dingley, ' "I had a dream . . .": Byron's "Darkness" ', *Byron Journal* 9 (1981), pp. 20–33.

Wilfred S. Dowden, ed., *The Journal of Thomas Moore*, 6 vols., Newark: University of Delaware Press, 1983.

Paul W. Elledge, *Byron and the Dynamics of Metaphor*, Nashville, TN: Vanderbilt University Press, 1968.

— 'Divorce Italian Style: Byron's *Beppo*', *Modern Language Quarterly* 46 (1985), pp. 29–47.

— 'Talented Equivocation: Byron's "Fare thee well!" ', *Keats–Shelley Journal* 35 (1986), pp. 42–61.

Sheila Emerson, 'Byron's "one word": The Language of Self-Expression in *Childe Harold III*', *Studies in Romanticism* 20 (1981), pp. 363–82.

David Erdman, ' "Fare thee well!" – Byron's Last Days in England', in *Shelley and His Circle, 1773–1822*, ed. Kenneth Neill Cameron, Vol. 4, pp. 638–53.

Caroline Franklin, *Byron's Heroines*, Oxford: Clarendon Press, 1992.

Cheryl Fallon Giuliano, 'Gulnare/Kaled's "Untold" Feminization of Byron's Oriental Tales', *Studies in English Literature* 23 (1993), pp. 785–807.

— 'Marginal Discourse: The Authority of Gossip in *Beppo*', in *Rereading Byron*, ed. Alice Levine and Robert N. Keane, New York and London: Garland, 1993, pp. 151–63.

Robert F. Gleckner, *Byron and the Ruins of Paradise*, Baltimore: Johns Hopkins University Press, 1967.

Robert R. Harson, 'Byron's *Tintern Abbey*', *Keats–Shelley Journal* 20 (1971), pp. 113–21.

[Reginald Heber], 'Lord Byron's Dramas', *Quarterly Review* 27 (1822), pp. 476–524; attribution by Andrew Rutherford, *BCH*, 1970, p. 236.

Kurt Heinzelman, 'Byron's Poetry of Politics: The Economic Basis of the "Poetical Character"', *Texas Studies in Literature and Language* 23 (1981), pp. 361–88.

John A. Hodgson, 'The Structures of *Childe Harold III*', *Studies in Romanticism* 18 (1979), pp. 363–82.

Diane Long Hoeveler, *Romantic Androgyny: The Women Within*, University Park: Pennsylvania State University Press, 1990.

Margaret J. Howell, *Byron Tonight: A Poet's Plays on the Nineteenth-Century Stage*, Surrey: Springwood Books, 1982.

[Francis Jeffrey], Review of *Childe Harold's Pilgrimage* and *The Prisoner of Chillon, and Other Poems*, *Edinburgh Review* 27 (12 December 1816), pp. 277–310; attribution by Donald H. Reiman, *Romantics Reviewed*, 1972, Part B, Vol. 2, p. 864.

—'Lord Byron's Tragedies', *Edinburgh Review* 36 (1822), pp. 413–52; attribution by Donald H. Reiman, *Romantics Reviewed*, 1972, Part B, Vol. 2, p. 918.

Emrys Jones, 'Byron's Visions of Judgment', *Modern Language Review* 76 (1981), pp. 1–19.

M.K. Joseph, *Byron the Poet*, London: Gollancz, 1964.

William Keach, 'Political Inflection in Byron's *Ottava Rima*'. *Studies in Romanticism* 27 (1988), pp. 551–62.

Malcolm Kelsall, *Byron's Politics*, Sussex: Harvester Press, 1987.

G. Wilson Knight, 'The Two Eternities: An Essay on Byron', in *The Burning Oracle*, Oxford: Oxford University Press, 1939, pp. 199–288.

Cecil Y. Lang, 'Narcissus Jilted: Byron, *Don Juan* and the Biographical Imperative', in *Historical Studies and Literary Criticism*, ed. Jerome J. McGann, Madison: University of Wisconsin Press, 1985, pp. 143–79.

Marjorie Levinson, *The Romantic Fragment Poem: A Critique of a Form*, Chapel Hill: University of North Carolina Press, 1986.

Ernest J. Lovell, Jr., *Byron: The Record of a Quest*, (1949), Connecticut: Archon Books, 1966.

— ed, see Thomas Medwin.

D.L. Macdonald, *Poor Polidori*, Toronto: University of Toronto Press, 1991.

Wolf Mankowitz, *Mazeppa: The Lives and Loves of Adah Isaacs Menken*, London: Blond & Briggs, 1982.

Peter J. Manning, *Byron and His Fictions*, Detroit: Wayne State University Press, 1978.

— 'Childe Harold in the Marketplace: From Romaunt to Handbook', *Modern Language Quarterly* 52 (1991), pp. 170–90.

— *Reading Romantics: Texts and Contexts*, New York and London: Oxford University Press, 1990.

Leslie A. Marchand, *Byron: A Biography*, 3 vols., New York: Knopf, 1957/London: John Murray, 1958.

— *Byron's Poetry*, Cambridge, MA: Harvard University Press, 1968.

William H. Marshall, *Byron, Shelley, Hunt and THE LIBERAL*, Philadelphia: University of Pennsylvania Press, 1960.

Jerome J. McGann, 'The Book of Byron and the Book of a World', in *The Beauty of Inflections*, Oxford: Clarendon Press, 1988, pp. 255–93.

— *Fiery Dust*, Chicago: University of Chicago Press, 1968.

— 'Hero with a Thousand Faces: The Rhetoric of Byronism', *Studies in Romanticism* 31 (1992), pp. 295–314.

— '"Mixed Company": Byron's *Beppo* and the Italian Medley', in *Shelley and His Circle, 1773–1822*, Vol. 7, ed. Donald H. Reiman, Cambridge, MA: Harvard University Press, 1986, pp. 234–97.

— 'Shall These Bones Live?' in *The Beauty of Inflections*, Oxford: Clarendon Press, 1988, pp. 90–110.

— 'The Significance of Biographical Context: Two Poems by Lord Byron', in *The Author in His Work*, ed. Louis L. Martz and Aubrey Williams, New Haven: Yale University Press, 1978, pp. 347–64.

Noel McLachlan, '"She walks in beauty": Some Byron Mysteries', *London Magazine* 30 (August–September 1990), pp. 20–33.

Thomas Medwin, *Medwin's CONVERSATIONS OF LORD BYRON* (1824), ed. Ernest J. Lovell, Jr., Princeton: Princeton University Press, 1966.

Peter T. Murphy, 'Visions of Success: Byron and Southey', *Studies in Romanticism* 24 (1985), pp. 355–73.

Isaac Nathan, ed., *Fugitive Pieces and Reminiscences of Lord Byron*, London: Whittaker, Treacher, 1829.

Stuart Peterfreund, 'The Politics of 'Neutral Space' in Byron's *Vision of Judgment*', *Modern Language Quarterly* 40 (1979), pp. 275–91.

Marlon Ross, 'Scott's Chivalric Pose: The Function of Metrical Romance in the Romantic Period', *Genre* 18 (1986), pp. 267–97.

Andrew Rutherford, *Byron: A Critical Study*, Stanford: Stanford University Press/Edinburgh, Oliver & Boyd, 1961.

Sir Walter Scott, Reviews of *Childe Harold's Pilgrimage, Canto III*, *Quarterly Review* 16 (October 1816/February 1817), pp. 172–208; and *Canto IV, Quarterly Review* 19 (April/September 1816), pp. 215–32.

Samuel Smiles, *A Publisher and His Friends: Memoir and Correspondence of the Late John Murray with an Account of the Origin and Progress of the House, 1768–1843*, 2 vols., London: John Murray, 1891.

Gordon Spence, 'Moral and Sexual Ambivalence in *Sardanapalus*', *Byron Journal* 12 (1984), pp. 59–69.

Stuart Sperry, 'Byron and the Meaning of *Manfred*', *Criticism* 16 (1974), pp. 189–202.

William St Clair, 'The Impact of Byron's Writings: An Evaluative Approach', in *Byron: Augustan and Romantic*, ed. Andrew Rutherford, London: Macmillan, 1990, pp. 1–25.

— *Lord Elgin and the Marbles*, London: Oxford University Press, 1967.

— *That Greece Might Still be Free*, London: Oxford University Press, 1972.

T.G. Steffan, 'The Devil a Bit of Our Beppo', *Philological Quarterly* 32 (1953), pp. 154–71.

Studies in Romanticism 31 no. 3 (Fall 1992); special issue on *Sardanapalus*.

Gordon Kent Thomas, *Lord Byron's Iberian Pilgrimage*, Provo, UT: Brigham Young University Press, 1983.

Peter L. Thorslev, *The Byronic Hero*, Minneapolis: University of Minnesota Press, 1962.

Peter Vassallo, *Byron: The Italian Literary Influence*, New York: St Martin's Press, 1984.

Daniel P. Watkins, *Social Relations in Byron's Eastern Tales*, Rutherford, NJ: Fairleigh Dickinson University Press, 1987.

— 'Violence, Class Consciousness and Ideology in Byron's History Plays', *ELH* 48 (1981), pp. 799–816.

Timothy Webb, ed., *English Romantic Hellenism, 1700–1824*, Manchester: Manchester University Press, 1982.

Susan J. Wolfson, 'Couplets, Self and *The Corsair*', 'Heroic Form: Couplets, "Self," and Byron's *Corsair*'; *Formal Charges: The Shaping of Poetry in British Romanticism* (Stanford: Stanford University Press, 1997).

— "'A Problem Few Dare Imitate": *Sardanapalus* and "Effeminate Character"', *ELH* 58 (1991), pp. 867–902.

INDEX OF TITLES

INDEX OF FIRST LINES

PENGUIN (●) CLASSICS

www.penguinclassics.com

- *Details about every Penguin Classic*

- *Advanced information about forthcoming titles*

- *Hundreds of author biographies*

- *FREE resources including critical essays on the books and their historical background, reader's and teacher's guides.*

- *Links to other web resources for the Classics*

- *Discussion area*

- *Online review copy ordering for academics*

- *Competitions with prizes, and challenging Classics trivia quizzes*

PENGUIN CLASSICS ONLINE

READ MORE IN PENGUIN

In every corner of the world, on every subject under the sun, Penguin represents quality and variety – the very best in publishing today.

For complete information about books available from Penguin – including Puffins, Penguin Classics and Arkana – and how to order them, write to us at the appropriate address below. Please note that for copyright reasons the selection of books varies from country to country.

In the United Kingdom: Please write to *Dept. EP, Penguin Books Ltd, Bath Road, Harmondsworth, West Drayton, Middlesex UB7 0DA*

In the United States: Please write to *Consumer Services, Penguin Putnam Inc., 405 Murray Hill Parkway, East Rutherford, New Jersey 07073-2136.* VISA and MasterCard holders call 1-800-631-8571 to order Penguin titles

In Canada: Please write to *Penguin Books Canada Ltd, 10 Alcorn Avenue, Suite 300, Toronto, Ontario M4V 3B2*

In Australia: Please write to *Penguin Books Australia Ltd, 487 Maroondah Highway, Ringwood, Victoria 3134*

In New Zealand: Please write to *Penguin Books (NZ) Ltd, Private Bag 102902, North Shore Mail Centre, Auckland 10*

In India: Please write to *Penguin Books India Pvt Ltd, 11 Community Centre, Panchsheel Park, New Delhi 110017*

In the Netherlands: Please write to *Penguin Books Netherlands bv, Postbus 3507, NL-1001 AH Amsterdam*

In Germany: Please write to *Penguin Books Deutschland GmbH, Metzlerstrasse 26, 60594 Frankfurt am Main*

In Spain: Please write to *Penguin Books S. A., Bravo Murillo 19, 1°B, 28015 Madrid*

In Italy: Please write to *Penguin Italia s.r.l., Via Vittorio Emanuele 45/a, 20094 Corsico, Milano*

In France: Please write to *Penguin France, 12, Rue Prosper Ferradou, 31700 Blagnac*

In Japan: Please write to *Penguin Books Japan Ltd, Iidabashi KM-Bldg, 2-23-9 Koraku, Bunkyo-Ku, Tokyo 112-0004*

In South Africa: Please write to *Penguin Books South Africa (Pty) Ltd, P.O. Box 751093, Gardenview, 2047 Johannesburg*

PENGUIN CLASSICS

SELECTED ESSAYS, POEMS AND OTHER WRITINGS
GEORGE ELIOT

'We can often detect a man's deficiencies in what he admires more clearly than in what he condemns'

The works collected in this volume provide an illuminating introduction to George Eliot's incisive views on religion, art and science, and the nature and purpose of fiction. Essays such as 'Evangelical Teaching' show her rejecting her earlier religious beliefs, while 'Woman in France' questions conventional ideas about female virtues and marriage, and 'Notes on Form in Art' sets out theories of idealism and realism that she developed further in *Middlemarch* and *Daniel Deronda*. It also includes selections from Eliot's translations of works by Strauss and Feuerbach that challenged many ideas about Christianity; excerpts from her poems; and reviews of writers such as Wollstonecraft, Goethe and Browning. Wonderfully rich in imagery and observations, these pieces reveal the intellectual development of this most challenging and rewarding of writers.

This volume, the first paperback collection of George Eliot's non-fiction, makes available many works never before published in book form. In her introduction, A. S. Byatt discusses Eliot's place in the literary world of Victorian London and the views expounded in these works.

Edited by A. S. Byatt and Nicholas Warren

With an introduction by A. S. Byatt

PENGUIN CLASSICS

THE NEW PENGUIN BOOK OF ROMANTIC POETRY

'And what if all of animated Nature
Be but organic harps, diversely framed'

The Romanticism that emerged after the American and French revolutions of 1776 and 1789 represented a new flowering of the imagination and the spirit, and a celebration of the soul of humanity with its capacity for love. This extraordinary collection sets the acknowledged genius of poems such as Blake's 'Tyger', Coleridge's 'Khubla Khan' and Shelley's 'Ozymandias' alongside verse from less familiar figures and women poets such as Charlotte Smith and Mary Robinson. We also see familiar poets in an unaccustomed light, as Blake, Wordsworth and Shelley demonstrate their comic skills, while Coleridge, Keats and Clare explore the Gothic and surreal.

This volume is arranged by theme and genre, revealing unexpected connections between the poets. In their introduction Jonathan and Jessica Wordsworth explore Romanticism as a way of responding to the world, and they begin each section with a helpful preface, notes and bibliography.

'An absolutely fascinating selection – notable for its women poets, its intriguing thematic categories and its helpful mini biographies' Richard Holmes

Edited with an introduction by Jonathan and Jessica Wordsworth

PENGUIN CLASSICS

DON JUAN
LORD BYRON

'Let us have wine and women's mirth and laughter,
Sermons and soda water the day after'

Byron's exuberant parody involves the adventures of a youth named Don Juan.
His exploits include an adulterous liaison in Spain, an affair on a Greek island
with a pirate's daughter, a stay in a Sultan's harem, a bloody battle in Turkey and
a sojourn in Russia as the lover of Catherine the Great – all described by a
narrator who frequently digresses from his hero in order to converse with his
readers about war, society and convention. A revolutionary experiment in epic,
Don Juan blends high drama with earthy humour, outrageous satire of Byron's
contemporaries (in particular Wordsworth and Southey) and mockery of Western
culture, with England under particular attack.

This edition represents a significant contribution to Byron scholarship and the
editors have drawn on their authoritative edition of the poem published by the
University of Texas Press. Their extensive annotation covers points of interest,
selected variant readings and historical allusions Byron wove into his poem.
This edition also includes an illuminating new introduction by Susan J. Wolfson
and Peter J. Manning, and updated further reading.

Edited by T. G. Steffan, E. Steffan and W. W. Pratt

With a new introduction by Susan J. Wolfson and Peter J. Manning

PENGUIN CLASSICS

THE COMPLETE POEMS
ANDREW MARVELL

'Thus, though we cannot make our sun
Stand still, yet we will make him run'

Member of Parliament, tutor to Oliver Cromwell's ward, satirist and friend of
John Milton, Andrew Marvell was one of the most significant poets of the
seventeenth century. *The Complete Poems* demonstrates his unique skill and
immense diversity, and includes lyrical love-poetry, religious works and biting
satire. From the passionately erotic 'To his Coy Mistress', to the astutely political
Cromwellian poems and the prescient 'Garden' and 'Mower' poems, which
consider humankind's relationship with the environment, these works are
masterpieces of clarity and metaphysical imagery. Eloquent and compelling, they
remain among the most vital and profound works of the era – works by a figure
who, in the words of T. S. Eliot, 'speaks clearly and unequivocally with the voice
of his literary age'.

This edition of Marvell's complete poems is based on a detailed study of the extant
manuscripts, with modern translations provided for Marvell's Greek and Latin
poems. This edition also includes a chronology, further reading, appendices, notes
and indexes of titles and first lines, with a new introduction by Jonathan Bate.

Edited by Elizabeth Story Donno

With an introduction by Jonathan Bate
